THE
COUNTRY HOUSE
DESCRIBED

HAVELL (R.) *the Elder and* (R.) *the Younger*. A series of picturesque views of noblemen's and gentlemen's seats [etc.], 1823. (Title-page.).

THE
COUNTRY HOUSE
DESCRIBED

An index to the Country Houses

of Great Britain and Ireland

MICHAEL HOLMES
Victoria and Albert Museum

ST PAUL'S BIBLIOGRAPHIES
in association with
VICTORIA & ALBERT MUSEUM

First published in 1986 by
St Paul's Bibliographies, 1 Step Terrace, Winchester SO22 5BW, UK

British Library Cataloguing in Publication Data

Holmes, Michael
The country house described: an index to
the country houses of Great Britain and
Ireland. – (St Paul's Bibliographies)
1. Country homes – Great Britain –
Bibliography
I. Title II. Victoria and Albert Museum
016 941   Z2021.H49

ISBN 0-906795-39-7

Printed in England by St Edmundsbury Press, Blenheim Road, Bury St Edmunds, Suffolk

CONTENTS

LIST OF
ILLUSTRATIONS

All illustrations Crown Copyright

INTRODUCTION

The aim of this index is to provide a quick reference to the literature on individual country houses in England, Wales, Scotland and Ireland, held in the National Art Library at the Victoria and Albert Museum.

Over 4,000 country houses are included. The contents of 135 general books on architecture, architectural details and county histories have been indexed, as well as guides to individual country houses, catalogues of collections and sales catalogues. Only a few periodicals, apart from *Country Life* up to 1982, have been included.

The index was started as an aid to people seeking illustrations of country houses and was later expanded to include unillustrated material. Naturally the books indexed vary a great deal in scope and detail, many having a single page or less of text. Some have no text at all, but simply show architectural details or illustrations and in these cases only the plate number is given.

For the purpose of this index some royal residences such as Windsor Castle and Hampton Court (Middlesex), as well as town houses and ruined castles, have been excluded. Buildings described as country houses in the works indexed have been included, as well as inhabited castles and buildings now demolished, or houses now in ruins but built originally as country houses.

How to use the index

The alphabetical arrangement is in three sequences under the name of the house:
(1) England and Wales; (2) Ireland; (3) Scotland. The arrangement is:

1 Any book completely devoted to the house.
2 Extracts from books indexed in alphabetical order.
3 Sales catalogues in chronological order.

If there is a book completely devoted to a single country house it is listed with a full catalogue entry in the alphabetical sequence. In some cases it may be a house of the same name rebuilt on the same site. When a house is known under two names the alternative is given in square brackets, e.g. ATTINGHAM HALL [PARK], DENTON PARK [HALL].

When the description or illustration of the house is part of a larger work, an abbreviated entry is given in the alphabetical sequence. This gives volume, page or plate number (where applicable) and date. By referring to the list of indexed books given at the beginning of the work, it may be easily identified.

A word in square brackets after the page or plate number indicates that the entry is devoted to a particular subject, e.g. [Paintings], as also at the end of sales entries [Contents].

In some cases if there is a plan of the house it is indicated in the entry.

The size of books is given in centimetres.

An asterisk* at the end of an entry indicates that the house is not illustrated.

Pre-1974 county boundaries are used throughout this work.

The illustrations are not always contemporary with the book in which they appear, e.g. Atkyns (R.) *Gloucestershire*, 2 ed. 1768, still uses the engravings of Kip, 1714–15. The engravings in Neale (J.P.). *Views of seats of noblemen and gentlemen*, 1818–29, are in almost every case the same as those in Jones & Co., *Great Britain Illustrated,* 1828–30.

Sales catalogues are listed last in the entries under each house. The word *sales* is placed in square brackets at the beginning of the entry to indicate that there is a separate catalogue for sales catalogues in the Library. It is not noted in the index whether a sale catalogue is illustrated or not. The initials (K., F. & R.) which appear after some sales catalogue entries stand for Knight, Frank and Rutley; the sales catalogues of this firm are only on loan to the library and are not included in its catalogue, but are available on request.

Entries for all the books indexed will be found under the heading given in the author catalogue of the National Art Library at the Victoria and Albert Museum. The exception is Kip (J.). *Nouveau théâtre de la Grande Bretagne,* 1714–15, which is kept in the Department of Prints, Drawings & Photographs and Paintings.

A short bibliography of works not indexed is included because although they do not readily lend themselves to indexing they will be of help to anyone studying country houses and their contents.

Acknowledgments

I should like to express my gratitude to R.W. Lightbown for his encouragement, to Michael Wilson and also to Peter Castle for his invaluable help in reading through the proofs with me; to Arline Pickard who helped with the proofs, Nicky Bird, Publications Officer, Lesley Burton and Philip Spruyt de Bay who took the photographs.

LIST OF BOOKS
INDEXED

ADAM, Robert and James
— The works in architecture of Robert and James Adam. [Also in French. Bibliogr. notes.] Engr. plates (some folding) incl. sections, elevations and plans. 11 pts. in 3 vols. Fol. 65x50 London: for the authors (1773) [-1779]; for Priestly and Weale, 1822.
Vols. I and II issued with 19th century title-pages.

ADAM, William.
— Vitruvius scoticus; being a collection of plans, elevations and sections ... principally from the designs of the late W.A. Engr. plates (1 folding). 50x38 Edinburgh: A. Black [1810].

ANGUS, William.
— The seats of the nobility and gentry in Great Britain and Wales, in a collection of select views engraved by W.A. from pictures and drawings by the most eminent artists with descriptions of each view. Engr. plates. 21x27 (London) W, Angus, 1787 (-1815).

ANGUS-BUTTERWORTH, Lionel Milner.
— Old Cheshire families & their seats. [Bibliogr.] 10 plates and genealog. tables. 21x14 Manchester: Sherratt & Hughes, 1932.

ATKYNS, *Sir* Robert.
— The ancient and present state of Glocestershire. 2 ed. Engr. plates (many folding) incl. map, most by J. Kip. Fol. 42x26 London: by T. Spilsbury for W. Herbert, 1768.

BADESLADE, Thomas.
— Thirty six different views of noblemen and gentlemen's seats in the county of Kent, all designed upon the spot by ... T.B., and engraved by the best hands [mainly by J. Kip and J. Harris]. [No text.] 2ff. Engr. plates. Fol. 44x30 London: H. Chapelle [*c.* 1750].

BAKER, James.
— Home beauties as communicated to the author of the Royal Atlas and Imperial Guide, by some of the royal family, the nobility, gentry &c. for an illuminated appendix to these works. Engr. plates incl. maps and title-page. 21x13 [London, 1804].

Bound with: BRIDGMAN, (J.). An historical and topographical sketch of Knole, 1817.

BARTLETT, John.
— Selections from views of the residences and country seats of the nobility and gentry, which illustrate the ... work entitled *The mansions of England and Wales.* 15ff. Lithogr. plates. 28x37 London: Bartlett & Wood, 1851.

BARTLETT, John.
— The mansions of England and Wales, illustrated in a series of views of the principle [sic.] seats. Lithogr. plates. vols. 36x26 London: Bartlett & Co., 1853.
[I.] The county palatine of Lancaster. [No text.] Plates after I. Shaw, and others. 2 vols. in I. 1853.

BIRKBECK, Geoffrey.
— Old Norfolk houses. Illustrated ... in colour by G.B. [Bibliogr.] 36 col. plates. 27x22 London: Norwich: Jarrold & Sons [1908].

BOLTON, Arthur Thomas.
— The architecture of Robert & James Adam, 1758-1794. (Topographical index to the Adam drawings in the Soane Museum included). [Bibliogr.] Illus. (1 col.) incl. sections, elevations, plans and map. 2 vols. 38x27 London: Country Life, 1922.
One of: COUNTRY LIFE library.

BRAYLEY, Edward Wedlake.
— A topographical history of Surrey. By E.W.B., assisted by J. Britton and E.W. Brayley, jun.; the geological section by G. Mantell. (The illustrative department under the superintendence of T. Allom.) [Bibliogr. notes.] Illus. incl. hand-col. title-pages, plates, plans, maps and genealog. tables. 5 vols. 27x22 Dorking: R.B. Ede; London: Tilt & Bogue, 1841 (—48?)

BRIDGES, John.
— The history and antiquities of Northamptonshire. Compiled from the manuscript collections of ... J.B. by the Rev. P. Whalley. [Bibliogr. notes.] Engr. plates, and genealog. tables. 2 vols. Fol. 43x27 Oxford: D. Prince and J. Cooke, 1791.

BRITTON, John.
— The beauties of Wiltshire, displayed in statistical, historical, and descriptive sketches: interspersed with anecdotes of the arts. [Bibliogr.] Illus. (some engr.) incl. plates (1 folding) map and title-pages and woodcuts. 3 vols. 8vo. 21x13; 23x14 London: Vernor & Hood; J. Wheble; the author, 1801-25.

BRITTON, John.
— Devonshire & Cornwall illustrated, from original drawings by Thomas Allom, W.H. Bartlett, &c. With historical and topographical descriptions by J.B., & E.W. Brayley. [Bibliogr. notes.] Engr. plates, title-pages and maps. 2 parts in 1 vol. 2 vol. 27x21 London: H. Fisher, R. Fisher, & P. Jackson, 1832 (1829, 1831).

BUCK, Samuel and Nathaniel.
— Buck's antiquities; or, venerable remains of ... castles, monasteries, palaces, &c, &c. in England and Wales, with ... views of cities and chief towns. Engr. incl. plates (some folding), map and tables. 3 vols. Fol. 45x27; 45x45 London: by D. Bond for R. Sayer, 1774.

BURKE, *Sir* John Bernard, *Ulster King of Arms.*
— A visitation of the seats and arms of the noblemen and gentlemen of Great Britain. Illus. incl. tinted lithogr. and engr. plates, and cuts. 2 vols. 25x15 London: Colburn & Co. (London: Hurst & Blackett), 1852–1853.
Second series. 2 vols. London: Hurst & Blackett, 1854-1855.

CAMPBELL, Colin.
— Vitruvius Britannicus; or, the British architect [etc.]. Facsimile edition. Illus. 9 vols. in 4. 33x26 etc. New York: B. Blom, 1967-72.
[I.] Vols. I-III, 1715-25. Introduction by J. Harris. Illus. incl. sections, elevations, plans and maps (on end-papers). 3 vols. in I. 1967.
[II.] Volume the fourth ... Design'd by J. Badeslade and J. Rocque, 1739 ... Vols. IV, V. By Woolfe and Gandon, 1767-71. Illus. incl. sections, elevations, plans and maps (on end-papers). 3 vols. in 1. 1967.

CAMPBELL, Colin.
— Vitruvius Britannicus [etc.]. [Contd.]
The new Vitruvius Britannicus ... By G. Richardson. [Title-page, introduction and explanation of the plates also in French.] Engr. plates (some folding) incl. elevations and plans. 2 vols. Fol. 54x36 London: for the author and J. Taylor, 1802-08.
See also facsimile ed. 1970.

CHAUNCY, *Sir* Henry.
— The historical antiquities of Hertfordshire [etc.]. [Reprint of 1700 ed. Bibliogr. notes.] Illus. incl. plates (1 folding) map and genealog. tables. 2 vols. 25x15 Bishops Stortford: J.M. Mullinger, 1826.

CLARKE, Thomas Hutchings.
— The domestic architecture of the reigns of Queen Elizabeth and James the First illustrated by a series of views of English mansions, with brief historical and descriptive accounts of each subject. xvi, 24pp. 20 lithogr. plates and 2 woodcuts (1 on title-page). 25x17 London: Priestley & Weale, 1833.

COLLINSON, *Rev.* John.
— The history and antiquities of the county of Somerset, collected from authentick records [etc.]. [Bibliogr. notes.] Engr. plates (1 folding) incl. plans and map, and cuts: head- and tail pieces. 3 vols. 4to. 30x24 Bath: by R. Crutwell, 1791.

COOKE, Robert.
— West country houses: an illustrated account of some country houses and their owners, in the counties of Bristol, Gloucester, Somerset and Wiltshire; being also a guide to domestic architecture from the reign of Henry II to Victoria. [Bibliogr.] Illus. incl. elevations and plans. 31x23 Bristol: by the author, 1957.

COPPER PLATE MAGAZINE.
— The copper plate magazine: or, the monthly treasure for the admirers of the imitative arts. Engr.: title-page and plates. 26x21 London: Kearsly, 1778.

COPPER PLATE MAGAZINE.
— The Copper Plate Magazine; or monthly cabinet of picturesque prints, consisting of ... views in Great Britain and Ireland [etc.]. Engr. plates. 5 vols. Fol. 20x25 London: Harrison & Co. (1792-1802).

COUNTRY LIFE.
— English country houses. Published by (Country Life). Illus. incl. sections, elevations and plans. vols. 31x23 London, 1955–
Early Georgian, 1715-1760. [By] C. Hussey. 1955.
Mid Georgian, 1760-1800. [By] C. Hussey. 1956.
Late Georgian, 1800-1840. [By] C. Hussey. 1958.
Caroline, 1625-1685. [By] O. Hill and J. Cornforth. 1966.
Baroque, 1685-1715. [By] J. Lees-Milne. 1970.

COUNTRY LIFE.
— Country Life illustrated: the journal for all interested in country life and country pursuits. Illus. vols. 36x24 London, 1897–

CROMWELL, *Rev.* Thomas Kitson.
—[Excursions through England and Wales, Scotland and Ireland.][Contd.]
STOCKDALE, F.W.L. Excursions in the county of Cornwall, comprising a concise historical and topographical delineation of the principal towns and villages [etc.]. Engr. incl. title-page and folding map. 25x16 London: Simpkin & Marshall, 1824.

CROMWELL, *Rev.* Thomas Kitson.
—[Excursions through England and Wales, Scotland and Ireland.][Contd.]
History of Essex; or, excursions in the county: comprising a

brief historical and topographical delineation of every town and village [etc.]. Engr. plates incl. title-pages and folding maps. 2 vols. 16x10 Witham & Maldon: by and for B. Youngman, 1825.

CROMWELL, *Rev*. Thomas Kitson.

—[Excursions through England and Wales, Scotland and Ireland.] [Contd.]
Excursions in the County of Kent: comprising brief historical and topographical delineations; together with descriptions of the residences of the nobility and gentry [etc.]. Engr. plates incl. title-page and folding maps. 22x14 London: Longman, Hurst, Rees, Orme and Brown, 1822.

CROMWELL, *Rev*. Thomas Kitson.

—[Excursions through England and Wales, Scotland and Ireland.] [Contd.]
Excursions in the County of Norfolk: comprising a brief historical and topographical delineation of every town and village [etc.]. Engr. plates incl. title-page and folding maps. 2 vols. London: Longman, Hurst, Rees, Orme and Brown,1818-19.

CROMWELL, *Rev*. Thomas Kitson.

—[Excursions through England and Wales, Scotland and Ireland.] [Contd.]
Excursions in the County of Suffolk: comprising a brief historical and topographical delineation of every town and village [etc.]. Engr. plates incl. title-page and folding map. 2 vols. 22x14 London: Longman, Hurst, Rees, Orme and Brown, 1818-19.

CUMBERLAND: Cumberland and Westmorland Antiquarian and Archaeological Society.

— Extra Series.
VIII. TAYLOR, M.W. The old manorial halls of Westmorland & Cumberland. [Bibliogr. notes.] Illus. incl. plates, plans and folding genealog. table. 1892.

CUMMING, Gershom.

— Forfarshire illustrated: being views of gentlemen's seats, antiquities, and scenery in Forfarshire [Angus], with descriptive and historical notices. Engr. plates by G.C. 27x21 Dundee: by the author, 1843.

DAVY, Henry.

— Views of the seats of the noblemen and gentlemen in Suffolk. From drawings by H.D. ... Part first. 42pp. 20 engr. plates. 43x29 Southwold: by the author, 1827.
No more published?

DELDERFIELD, Eric. R.

— West Country historic houses and their families. (Biographical notes on artists and craftsmen.) Illus. (some col.) vols. 23x18 Newton Abbot: David & Charles, 1968-.
I. [Cornwall, Devon and West Somerset.] 160pp. 1968.
II. Dorset, Wiltshire and North Somerset. 128pp. 1970.
III. The Cotswold area. 124pp. 1973.

ELWES, Dudley George Cary.

— A history of the castles, mansions and manors of Western Sussex. By D.G.C.E., assisted by the Rev. C.J. Robinson [etc.]. [Bibliogr. notes.] vi, 330pp. Illus. incl. plates (some folding) and genealog. tables. 28x21 London: Longmans & Co.; Lewes: G.P. Bacon,1876 [1879].

ELYARD, S. John.

— Some old Wiltshire homes. Illustrated by S.J.E., with short notices on their architecture, history and associations. Illus. incl. plates. 36x27 London: Clark, 1894.

ENGLAND.

— A new display of the beauties of England; or, a description of ... noblemen's and gentlemen's seats ... in the different parts of the kingdom. New ed. Engr. plates. 2 vols. 8vo. 21x12 London: R. Goadby, 1787.

ENGLAND.

— Picturesque views of the principal seats of the nobility and gentry in England and Wales ... With a description of each seat. Engr. plates incl. title-page. 4to. 19x26 London: Harrison & Co. (1786-88).

ENGLISH CONNOISSEUR.

— The English connoisseur: containing an account of whatever is curious in painting, sculpture, &c. In the palaces and seats of the nobility and principal gentry of England, both in town and country. [By T. Martyn.] 2 vols. 8vo. 15x9 London: L. Davis and C. Reymers, 1766.

ESSEX.

— A new and complete history of Essex ... By a gentleman [i.e. P. Muilman]. [Bibliogr. notes.] Engr. plates (some folding) incl. title-pages, plans and map. 6 vols. 8vo. 20x12 Chelmsford: L. Hassall, 1769-72.

GARNER, Thomas.

— The domestic architecture of England during the Tudor period. Illustrated in a series of photographs & measured drawings of country mansions, manor houses and smaller buildings, with historical and descriptive text. By T.G., and A. Stratton. Illus. incl. plates, sections, elevations and plans. 2 vols. 48x37 London: Batsford, [1908-] 1911.

GARRATT, Thomas.

— Some of the old halls and manor-houses in the county of Norfolk, by the late E.P. Willins. ... Edited by T.G. Illus. incl. 50 plates, plans and map (on title-page). 36x28 London: Jarrold & Sons, 1890.

GLASGOW.

— The old country houses of the old Glasgow gentry. One hundred photographs by Annan, of well known places in the neighbourhood of Glasgow, with descriptive notices of the houses and families. [Some of the papers contributed by J. Buchanan.] Plates: photographs. 32x25 Glasgow: Maclehose, 1870.

GOTCH, John Alfred.
— Architecture of the Renaissance in England: Illustrated by a series of views and details from buildings erected between the years 1560-1630, with historical and critical text; by J.A.G., assisted by W.T. Brown. [Bibliogr. notes.] Illus. incl. plates, sections, elevations and plans. 2 vols. 48x35 London: Batsford, 1894.

GOTCH, John Alfred.
— The old halls & manor-houses of Northamptonshire: an illustrated review. Illus. incl. plates, elevations, plans and folding map. 28x20 London: Batsford, 1936.

GOTCH, John Alfred.
— Squires' homes and other old buildings of Northamptonshire. Illus. incl. plates. 28x20 London: Batsford, 1939.

GRAY, Henry.
— Views of the old halls of Lancashire and Cheshire; ... Drawn and mostly etched by N.G. Philips, 1822-24. With descriptive letterpress by twenty four local contributors. Also a brief memoir of the artist-engraver, and pedigree of his family. [Bibliogr. notes.] Illus. incl. engr. plates, cuts and folding genealog. table. 37x28 London: by the author, 1893.

GREENWOOD, C.
— An epitome of county history, wherein the most remarkable objects, persons, and events are briefly treated of; the seats, residences, etc. of the nobility, clergy, and gentry ... With notices of the principal churches and the monuments and memorials of distinguished families ... Vol. I. County of Kent. xx480pp. Illus. incl. lithogr. plates and col. map. 32x25 London: by the author, 1838.

GROVE, Richard Andrew.
— Views of the principal seats and marine & landscape scenery, in the neighbourhood of Lymington: drawn on stone by L. Haghe, from original pictures taken on the spot by J.M. Gilbert ... Accompanied by historical and topographical descriptions. 44pp. Lithogr. incl. plates and title-page. 30x23 Lymington: By the author, 1832.

GUINNESS, Desmond.
— Irish houses and castles. [By] (D.G., W. Ryan.) [Bibliogr.] Illus. (some col., 1 on title-page) incl. elevations, plans, maps and end-papers. 32x23 London: Thames & Hudson, 1971.

HALL, Samuel Carter.
— The baronial halls and picturesque edifices of England. From drawings by J.D. Harding, G. Cattermole, S. Prout, W. Müller, J. Holland and other eminent artists. Executed in lithotint under the superintendence of Mr. Harding. The text by S.C.H. Illus. incl. lithogr. plates and cuts. 2 vols. 41x28 London: Chapman & Hall, 1848.
2 ed. 33x27 [c. 1855?].

HAMPSHIRE.
— Architectural and picturesque views of noble mansions in Hampshire. Taken and drawn on stone by J. Hewetson [etc.]. 25ff. Lithogr. plates. 42x32 London: J. Carpenter & Son [1830?].
Second copies of plates bound in: India paper proofs pasted down.

HANNAN, Thomas.
— Famous Scottish houses: the Lowlands. [Bibliogr.] viii, 206pp. Plates. 23x18 London: A. & C. Black, 1928.

HARRIS, *Rev.* John.
— The history of Kent, in five parts ... Vol. I. [Bibliogr. notes.] Engr. plates (some folding), most by J. Kip after T. Badeslade, incl. map. 2 pts. in 1 vol. Fol. 39x24 London: by D. Midwinter, 1719.
No more published.

HASTED, Edward.
— The history and topographical survey of the county of Kent [etc.]. [Bibliogr. notes.] Engr. (1 on title-page) incl. plates (some folding), plans and maps. 4 vols. Fol. 40x24 Canterbury: by Simmons & Kirkby for the author, 1778-99.

HAVELL, Robert *the Elder* and Robert *the Younger*.
— A series of picturesque views of noblemen's & gentlemen's seats: with historical and descriptive accounts of each subject. Engraved in aquatinta by R. Havell & Son [after designs by W. Havell and others]. 42pp. 20 hand-col. aquatint plates incl. title-page. 48x34 London: R. Havell, 1823.
Wanting two plates.

HEARNE, Thomas.
— Antiquities of Great Britain, illustrated in views of monasteries, castles and churches now existing. Engraved by W. Byrne from drawings made by T.H. With descriptions in English and French. Plates. 2 vols. 30x42 London: for T. Cadell and W. Davies, 1807.

HEATH, Sidney.
— Some Dorset manor houses; with their literary and historical associations. By S.H., and W. de C. Prideaux [etc.]. [Bibliogr. notes.] xlii, 280pp. Illus. incl. plates (some tinted). 31x25 London: Bemrose and Sons, 1907.

HOARE, *Sir* Richard Colt, *Bart.*
— A collection of ... views of noblemen's and gentlemen's seats ... and romantic places in north and south Wales, principally from drawings by Sir R.C.H. [etc.] Engr. plates. 4to. 21x26 London: J. & J. Boydell (1792).

HODGES, Elizabeth.
— Some ancient English homes and their associations, personal, archaeological & historic ... Illustrated by S.J. Loxton. 280pp. Illus. 21x17 London: T. Fisher Unwin, 1895.

HUTCHINS, *Rev.* John.

— Vitruvius Dorsettiensis; or, thirty-six views of some of the more principal seats of the nobility and gentry of the county of Dorset. Beautifully engraved by the most eminent artists. Selected from the new edition of Hutchins's History [of Dorset]. 2pp. 36 hand-col. engr. plates. 46x28 London: Nichols, Son & Bentley, 1816.

HUTCHINS, *Rev.* John.

— The history and antiquities of the county of Dorset. ... with a copy of Domesday Book, and the Inquisitio Gheldi for the county, ... views of antiquities, seats of the nobility and gentry &c. ... The third edition corrected, augmented and improved by W. Shipp and J.W. Hodson. [Bibliogr. notes.] Illus. incl. engr. plates, sections, elevations, plans, maps and genealog. tables. 4 vols. 41x25 London: J.B. Nichols & Sons, 1861-70.

JEWITT, Llewellynn.

— The stately homes of England. By L.J., and S.C. Hall. Illustrated with ... engravings on wood. xii, 400pp. 22x16 London: Virtue & Co., 1874.

JONES & CO.

— Great Britain illustrated. Views of the seats, mansions, castles &c. of the noblemen and gentlemen in England, Wales, Scotland and Ireland [etc.]. Engr. plates and title-pages. 5 vols. in 3. 27x21 London: 1829– [1830].
I. England. 1829.
II. England: Western counties. 1829.
III. Wanting.
IV. Scotland. [1829?] Bound with vol. II.
V, VI. Wales. 2 vols. in 1? [1830]
No more published?

KIP, John.

— Nouveau théâtre de la Grande Bretagne. Engr. (1 on title-pages) incl. plates by J.K. and others after L. Knyff and others. 3 vols. Fol. 51x32 Londres: D. Mortier, 1714-15.
I. Description exacte des palais du roy et des maisons les plus considerables des seigneurs & gentilshommes de la Grande Bretagne. [etc.]. 1715.
II, III. Description exacte des villes, eglises, cathedrales, hôpitaux, ports de mer [etc.] 2 vols. 1714-15.
Wanting some plates.

KROLL, Alexander.

— Historic houses: conversations in stately homes. (Editor: A.K.) [Bibliogr. notes.] Illus. (some col.) 31x23 London: Condé Nast, 1969.

LATHAM, Charles.

— In English homes: the internal character, furniture and adornment of some of the most notable houses of England historically depicted from photographs specially taken by C.L. Illus. 3 vols. 39x28 London: Country Life, 1904-09.

LEACH, Francis.

— The county seats of Shropshire; a series of descriptive sketches, with historical and antiquarian notes, of the principal family mansions. Edited by F.L. [Bibliogr.] Illus. incl. plates and col. cover. 33x25 Shrewsbury: Eddowes Shrewsbury Journal, 1891.

LEIGHTON, Stanley.

— Shropshire houses past & present. Illustrated from drawings by S.L. ... With descriptive letterpress by the artist. xii, 100pp. Plates. 28x22 London: G. Bell & Sons, 1901.

LINCOLNSHIRE.

— A selection of views of the county of Lincoln; comprising the principal towns and churches, the remains of castles and religious houses, and seats of the nobility and gentry; with topographical and historical accounts of each view. 80pp. Illus. (on title-pages) incl. engr. plates. 33x27 London: W. Miller, 1805.

LONDON: Committee for the Survey of the Memorials of Greater London.

— Monographs. Illus. incl. plates. 16 vols. 29x23 London, 1896–1963.

LUGAR, Robert.

— Plans and views of buildings, executed in England and Scotland, in the castellated and other styles. New ed. 28pp. Engr. plates incl. plans. 31x24 London: J. Taylor, 1823.

MALAN, *Rev.* Alfred Henry.

— Famous homes of Great Britain and their stories. Edited by A.H.M. Illus. incl. plate and cover. 29x19. New York; London: G.P. Putman's Sons, 1902.
Second series. More famous homes of Great Britain [etc.]. 1902.
Third series. Other famous homes of Great Britain [etc.]. 1902.

MANNING, *Rev.* Owen.

— The history and antiquities of the county of Surrey; compiled from the best and most authentic historians, valuable records, and manuscripts in the public offices and libraries and in private hands. With a fac-simile copy of Domesday. ... By the late Rev. O.M. Continued to the present time by W. Bray. Illus. incl. engr. plates (some folding), maps, facsimiles and tables (some genealog.), vols. Fol. 45x27 London: J. White, 1804-14.

MILLAR, Alexander Hastie.

— The castles and mansions of Ayrshire: illustrated in seventy views with historical and descriptive accounts. Plates: photographs. 37x29 Edinburgh: Paterson, 1885.

MILLAR, Alexander Hastie.

— The historical castles and mansions of Scotland: Perthshire and Forfarshire [Angus]. Illus. (1 on title-page) incl. plate. 22x16 Paisley; London: A. Gardner, 1890.

MILTON, Thomas.
— The seats and demesnes of the nobility and gentry of Ireland, in a collection of the most interesting and picturesque views, engraved by T.M., from drawings by the most eminent artists, with descriptions of each view. [Facsimile reprint.] [Bibliogr.] 142pp. Illus. 21x27 Dublin: by the author, 1783-1794. (Kilkenny: Boethius Press) [1982?] Vol. 2 of: SERIES FOUR.

MITCHELL, Robert.
— Plans, and views in perspective, with descriptions of buildings erected in England and Scotland: also an essay, to elucidate the Grecian, Roman and Gothic architecture accompanied with designs. (Text also in French.) 36 pp. Plates (some hand col.) incl. elevations and plans. Fol. 53x36 London: by the author, 1801.
Wanting one plate.

MORANT, *Rev.* Philip.
— The history and antiquities of the county of Essex. Compiled ... by P.M. [Bibliogr. notes.] Engr. plates (some folding) incl. plans and maps. 3 vols. in 2. Fol. 36x22 London: T. Osborne, 1768.
With additional plates and MS notes, inserted.

MORRIS, *Rev.* Francis Orpen.
— A series of picturesque views of seats of the noblemen and gentlemen of Great Britain and Ireland. With descriptive letterpress. Illus. incl. col. plates and col. title-pages. 6 vols. 27x21 London: Mackenzie [1880].
Fac-simile of autographs of subscribers to the picturesque views of seats [etc.]. Col. Illus. on title-page. London: Clarke, 1880.

MOSS, Fletcher.
— Pilgrimages to old homes. [Books 2-6.] Illus. 5 vols. 25x16 Didsbury: by the author, 1903-1913.

NASH, Joseph.
— The mansions of England in the olden time. No text. Tinted lithogr. plates. 4 vols. 52x37 London: M'Lean, 1839-49.
Descriptions of the plates of the mansions of England [etc.]. 68pp. 22x14 1849.

NASH, *Rev.* Treadway Russell.
— Collections for the history of Worcestershire. [Bibliogr. notes.] Engr. (2 on title-pages) incl. plates (some folding), plans, map, facsimiles and genealog. tables. 2 vols. Fol. 42x27 [London] by J. Nichols for T. Payne and Son [etc.], 1781-82.
Supplement. 43x27 [London] for J. White, 1799.
For index see WORCESTER: Worcestershire Historical Society. AMPHLETT (J.) 1894-5.

NEALE, John Preston.
— Views of seats of noblemen and gentlemen in England, Wales, Scotland and Ireland. From drawings by J.P.N. Engr. plates incl. title-pages. 6 vols. 29x23 London: Reid, (Sherwood Neely & Jones, T. Moule), (Sherwood Jones & Co., T. Moule). 1818-1823.

Second series. 5 vols. London: Sherwood Jones & Co. T. Moule (Sherwood Jones & Co.), (Sherwood Gilbert & Piper), 1824-1829.

NEALE, John Preston.
— [Views of noblemen's and gentlemen's seats in Scotland, with descriptions.] 86pp. Engr. plates. 28x22 [London: Jones & Co. ? *c.* 1830.]

NICHOLAS, Thomas.
— Annals and antiquities of the counties and county families of Wales; containing a record of all ranks of the gentry ... accompanied by brief notices of the history ... of each county [etc.]. Illus. incl. plates and decorated covers. 2 vols. 25x17 London: Longmans, Green, Reader, & Co., 1872.

NICHOLS, John.
— The history and antiquities of the county of Leicester ... including also Mr. Burton's description of the county, published in 1622 [etc.]. [Bibliogr. notes.] Engr. (some on title-pages) incl. plates (some folding), elevations, plans, maps and facsimiles, and cuts incl. tables (some genealog.). 4 vols. in 8. Fol. 43x26 London: by and for the author, 1795-1811.

NICOLSON, Nigel.
— Great houses of Britain. Illus. (40 col.) incl. sections, elevations, plans, facsimiles and end-papers. 31x24 London: Weidenfeld & Nicolson, 1965.

NIVEN, William.
— Illustrations of old Staffordshire houses. 40pp. Plates: etchings. 32x25 London: For the author, 1882.

NIVEN, William.
— Illustrations of old Warwickshire houses. 48pp. Etchings incl. plates and title-page. 31x25 London: For the author, 1878.

NIVEN, William.
— Illustrations of old Worcestershire houses. Drawn and etched on copper by W.N., with notes historical and descriptive. 60pp. Engr. plates 31x25 London: for the author, 1873.

NOBLE, Thomas.
— The counties of Chester, Derby, Nottingham, Leicester, Rutland, & Lincoln. Illustrated from original drawings by T. Allom. (With historical and topographical descriptions by T.N., and T. Rose.) 78pp. Engr. plates and title-page. 29x22 London: Fisher, Son & Co., 1836 [1837].

NORFOLK.
— The Norfolk tour: or, traveller's pocket companion. Being a concise description of all the noblemens and gentlemens seats, as well as of the principal towns, and other remarkable places in the county of Norfolk [etc.]. [Edited by R. Beatniffe.] 3 ed. 12mo. 17x11 Norwich: by R. Beatniffe, 1777.

ORMEROD, George.

— The history of the County Palatine and City of Chester ... incorporated with a republication of King's *Vale Royal* and Leycester's *Cheshire Antiquities*. [Bibliogr. notes.] Illus. incl. plates, plans, map and genealog. tables. 3 vols. 38x24 London: Lackington, Hughes, Harding, Mavor, and Jones, 1819.
2 ed. Revised and enlarged by T. Helsby. 38x25 London: G. Routledge & Sons, 1882.

OSWALD, Arthur.

— Country houses of Kent. [Bibliogr.] xvi, 76 pp. Illus. incl. plates, plans and folding map. 25x18 London: Country Life, 1933.

OSWALD, Arthur.

— Country houses of Dorset. [Bibliogr.] Illus. incl. plates (1 folding), section, elevations, plans and map. 25x18 London: Country Life, 1935.
2 ed. 1959.

PAINE, James.

— Plans, elevations and sections of noblemen and gentlemen's houses, and also of stabling, bridges, public and private, temples, and other garden buildings, executed in the counties of Derby, Durham, Middlesex, Northumberland, Nottingham, and York. Part I. 36pp. Engr. plates incl. sections, elevations and plans. Fol. 55x38 London: by the author, 1767.

PAINE, James.

— Plans, elevations, and sections of noblemen and gentlemen's houses [etc.]. [Contd.]
Plans elevations and sections of ... buildings executed in the counties of Nottingham, Essex, Wilts, Derby, Hertford, Suffolk, Salop, Middlesex, and Surrey. Part II. 38pp. 59x38 1783.

PLOT, Robert.

— The natural history of Staffordshire. [Bibliogr. notes.] Engr. (1 on title-page) incl. plates (some folding) and map. Fol. 31x19 Oxford: printed at the Theater, 1686.

PROSSER, George Frederick.

— Select illustrations of the county of Surrey comprising, picturesque views of the seats of the nobility and gentry, interesting remains &c with descriptions. Illus. incl. lithogr. plates. 29x23 London: C. & J. Rivington, 1828.

PYNE, William Henry.

— Lancashire illustrated, from original drawings by S. Austin, J. Harwood, and G & C. Pyne. With descriptions (by W.H.P., D. Wylie &c.). 108pp. Illus. (some engr. incl. title-page) and plates. 27x21 London: H. Fisher, Son, and Jackson, 1831 (1829).

REPTON, Humphry.

— Observations on the theory and practice of landscape gardening. Including some remarks on Grecian and gothic architecture, collected from various manuscripts, in the possession of the different noblemen and gentlemen, for whose use they were originally written; the whole tending to establish fixed principles in the respective arts. Illus. incl. 27 plates (engr. and aquatints: 11 hand-col., 2 folding, 14 moveables), cuts, sections, elevations, plans, diagr., maps and head- and tail-pieces. 4to. 35x29 London: J. Taylor, 1803.

REPTON, Humphry.

— Fragments on the theory and practice of landscape gardening. Including some remarks on Grecian and gothic architecture [etc.]. By H.R., assisted by his son, J.A. Repton. Illus. incl. 42 plates (engr. and aquatints: 22 hand-col., 3 folding, 10 moveables), cuts, sections, elevations, plans, diagr., and maps. 4to. 34x28 London: J. Taylor, 1816.

REPTON, Humphry.

— The Red Books of Humphry Repton. [Facsimile reprints.] Illus. incl. plates (some col., some folding) sections, elevations, plans, maps and moveables. 4 vols. 48x34 London: Basilisk Press, 1976.

RICHARDSON, Charles James.

— Studies from old English mansions, their furniture, gold and silver plate &c. By an architect [i.e. C.J.R.]. Tinted lithogr. plates (1 hand-col.) incl. title-pages. 4 vols. 49x33 London: T. McLean, 1841-48.
Another copy. 4 vols. in 2. 37x27.

ROBERTSON, Archibald.

— A topographical survey of the great road from London to Bath and Bristol, with historical and descriptive accounts of the country, towns, villages and gentlemen's seats on and adjacent to it [etc.]. [Large paper copy.] Plates: aquatints and engr. maps. 2 vols. 8vo. 29x33 London: for the author, 1792.
Another copy. 2 vols. in 1. 23x14.

ROBINSON, *Rev.* Charles John.

— A history of the mansions and manors of Herefordshire. Plates and genealog. tables. 28x22 London: Longmans & Co.; Hereford: Hull, 1873.

RUDDER, Samuel.

— A new history of Gloucestershire [etc.]. [Bibliogr. notes.] Engr. plates (some folding) incl. sections and maps. Fol. 42x26 Cirencester: by the author, 1779.

RUSH, Joseph Arthur.

— Seats in Essex; comprising picturesque views of the seats of the noblemen and gentry, with historical and architectural descriptions. Plates. 21x14 London: King, Sell & Railton [1897].

SADLEIR, Thomas Ulick.

— Georgian mansions in Ireland, with some account of the evolution of Georgian architecture and decoration. By T.U.S., and P.L. Dickinson. [Bibliogr.] Illus. (1 on Title-page) incl. 81 plates, elevations and plans. 30x24 Dublin: privately printed, 1915.

SANDBY, Paul.

— A collection of ... select views in England, Wales, Scotland and Ireland. Drawn by P.S. [Title-pages and descriptions of the plates also in French.] Engr. (2 on title-pages) incl. plates. 2 vols. Fol. 43x28 London: J. Boydell, 1782-83.

SANDON, Eric.

— Suffolk houses: a study of domestic architecture. By E.S., with contributions by S. West, & E. Owles [etc.]. [Bibliogr.] Illus. (some col.) incl. sections, plans, diagr., map and endpapers. 30x20 Woodbridge: Baron Publishing, 1977.

SHAW, Henry.

— Details of Elizabethan architecture. (Elizabethan architecture and its ornamental details. By T. Moule.) 56pp. Engr. plates (3 hand-col.) incl. title-page. 37x27 London: W. Pickering, 1839. Another copy. 28x14.

SHAW, *Rev.* Stebbing.

— The history and antiquities of Staffordshire [etc.]. [Bibliogr. notes.] Engr. incl. plates (some folding), plans and map and genealog. tables. 2 vols. 42x26 London: by and for J. Nichols, 1798-1801.
Reprint. Introduction by M.W. Greenslade and C.C. Baugh. (Additions I. Unpublished proof-sheets for the continuation of Shaw's History ... Additions II. Unpublished plates from a series of engravings from Shaw's History [etc.].) East Ardsley, Wakefield: E.P. Publishing Ltd., 1976.
One of: CLASSICAL COUNTY HISTORIES.

SHROPSHIRE.

— The castles & old mansions of Shropshire. [By Mrs. F.S. Acton.] 80pp. Plates. incl. plan. 28x22 Shrewsbury: Leake & Evans, 1868.

SMITH, William.

— A new & compendious history of the county of Warwick, from the earliest period to the present time, comprising views of the principal towns, buildings, modern improvements, seats of the nobility and gentry, ecclesiastical edifices, &c. &c. vi, 384pp. Engr. plates incl. map and title-page. 27x22 Birmingham: W. Emans, 1830.

SOANE, *Sir* John, *R.A.*

— Plans, elevations and sections of buildings executed in ... Norfolk, Suffolk, Yorkshire, Staffordshire, Warwickshire, Hertfordshire, et caetera. 20pp. Engr. plates. Fol. 54x37 London: Messrs. Taylor, 1788.

SPROULE, Anna.

— Lost houses of Britain. [Bibliogr.] 288pp. Illus. incl. title-page. 24x15 Newton Abbot: David & Charles, 1982.

SUMMERSON, *Sir* John.

— The country seat: studies in the history of the British country house, presented to Sir John Summerson on his sixty-fifth birthday, together with a select bibliography of his published writings. Edited by H. Colvin and J. Harris. [Bibliogr.] Illus.

incl. sections, elevations and plans. 27x18 London: Allen Lane, 1970.

THAMES, River.

— An history of the river Thames. [By W. Combes.] Plates (many hand-col. aquatint by J.C. Stalder after J. Farington) incl. folding engr. map. 2 vols. Fol. 41x31 London: by W. Bulmer for J. and J. Boydell, 1794-96.

THOMPSON, Stephen.

— Old English homes, a summer's sketch-book. ... The illustrations by the author. x, 216pp. Plates: photographs. 28x21 London: printed at the Chiswick Press for Sampson Low, Marston, Low and Searle, 1876 [1875].

THOROTON, Robert.

— Thoroton's history of Nottinghamshire (1677): republished with large additions by J. Throsby [etc.]. [Bibliogr. notes.] Engr. plates (some folding) incl. title-pages, plans and map, and genealog. tables. 3 vols. 4to. 27x21 London: B. & J. White, 1797.

THROSBY, John.

— Select views in Leicestershire ... accompanied with descriptive and historical relations by J.T. Engr. (1 on title-page) incl. plates and facsimiles, and folding genealog. table. 4to. 25x20 Leicester: by the author, 1789.

TILLEY, Joseph.

— The old halls, manors, and families of Derbyshire by J.T. [i.e. Joseph Tilley. Bibliogr. notes.] Illus. 4 vols. 28x22 London: Simpkin, Marshall, Hamilton, Kent & Co. Ltd., 1892-1902.
I. The High Peak hundred. 1892.
II. The Appletree hundred and wapentake of Wirksworth, 1893.
III. The Scarsdale hundred. 1899.
IV. The hundred of Repton and Gresley; and the hundred of Morleston and Litchurch. 1902.

TIPPING, Henry Avray.

— English homes. Illus. incl. plans. 10 vols. 39x27 London: Country Life, 1912-1937.
Period I, Vol. I. Norman and Plantagenet, 1066-1485. 1921.
Period II, Vol. I. Early Tudor, 1485-1558. 1924.
Periods I & II, Vol. II. Mediaeval and early Tudor, 1066-1558. 1937.
Early Renaissance: Elizabethan and Jacobean. 1912.
Period III, Late Tudor and early Stuart, 1558-1649. 2 vols. 1922, 1927.
Period IV, Late Stuart, 1649-1714. 2 vols. 1920, 1928.
Period V, Early Georgian, 1714-1760. 1921.
Period VI, Late Georgian, 1760-1820. 1926.

TWYCROSS, Edward.

— The mansions of England and Wales. Illustrated in a series of views of the principal seats with historical and topographical descriptions [etc.]. Lithogr. plates. 5 vols. 36x27 London: Ackermann & Co. (Stovin & Bartlett), 1847-50.
The county palatine of Lancaster. 3 vols. 1847.

I. Northern division. The hundreds of Blackburn and Leyland.
II. Northern division. The hundreds of Lonsdale and Amounderness.
III. Southern division. The hundreds of West Derby and Salford.
The county palatine of Chester. 2 vols. 1850.
I. The hundreds of Broxton, Wirrall, Eddisbury and Northwich.
II. The hundreds of Nantwich, Bucklow and Macclesfield.

UNITED KINGDOM.
— Historic houses of the United Kingdom: descriptive, historical, pictorial. viii, 328pp. Illus. incl. plates and plans. 28x21 London: Cassell, 1892.

WATTS, William.
— The seats of the nobility and gentry, in a collection of the most interesting & picturesque views. Engraved by W.W. from drawings by the most eminent artists. With descriptions of each view. Engr. plates incl. title-page. 4to. 20x26 London: by the author, 1779 (-1786).
Plates bound out of order.

WEST, William.
— Picturesque views and descriptions of cities, towns, castles, mansions, and other objects of interesting features in Shropshire, from original drawings, taken expressly for this work, by F. Calvert, engraved on steel by T. Radclyffe. With historical and topographical illustrations, by W.W. Engr. (1 on title-page) incl. plates. 27x22 Birmingham: W. Emans, 1831.

WHEATER, William.
— Some historic mansions of Yorkshire and their associations. By W.W., with ... etched illustrations, drawn on the spot by A. Buckle, S. Medway, and J.A. Symington. Illus.: plates and title-page. 28x20 Leeds: R. Jackson, 1888.

WHITEMAN, George Wallaby.
— Some famous English country homes from the time of Henry VIII to the Regency. Illus. 31x25 London: Antique Collector, 1951.

WOOD, G. Bernard.
— Historic homes of Yorkshire. [Bibliogr.] viii, 152pp. 48 plates incl. facsimiles and map (on end-papers). 25x18 Edinburgh; London: Oliver & Boyd, 1957.

YORKSHIRE.
— A series of picturesque views of castles and country houses in Yorkshire, principally in the northern division of the West Riding ... Reprinted from the Bradford Illustrated Weekly Telegraph. 132pp. Plates. 31x24 Bradford: T. Shields, 1885.

COUNTRY HOUSES OF
ENGLAND AND WALES

ABBERLEY HALL (Worcestershire).
MOILLIET, *Rev.* John Lewis.
— Abberley Manor, Worcestershire: notes on its history, Augustines Oak, churches and families connected with the parish to the present day. [Bibliogr. notes.] x, 118pp. Illus. incl. plates and genealog. tables. 22x14 London: Elliot Stock, 1905.

ABBERLEY LODGE (Worcestershire).
NASH, T.R. Worcestershire. I, 5. 1781.

ABBERTON HALL (Worcestershire).
BURKE, J.B. Visitation of Seats. Vol. II, p.175. 1853.*

ABBEY CWMHIR HALL (Radnorshire).
BURKE, J.B. Visitation of Seats. Vol. I, p.46. 1852.*

ABBEYFIELD (Cheshire).
TWYCROSS, E. Mansions of England and Wales. Vol. I, p.142. 1850.*

ABBEY HOUSE, Waltham Abbey (Essex).
ESSEX: A new and complete history. IV, 157. 1771.

ABBEY HOUSE, Barrow-in-Furness (Lancashire).
COUNTRY LIFE. XLIX, 398 plan. 1921.

ABBOTSBURY CASTLE (Dorsetshire).
ILCHESTER, Henry Edward Fox-Strangways, *Earl of.*
— Catalogue of pictures belonging to the Earl of Ilchester. (At Melbury House, Redlynch House, Abbotsbury Castle and 42, Belgrave Square; index of portraits.) 24x18 (London) privately printed at the Chiswick Press, 1883.

ABBOT'S GRANGE, Broadway (Worcestershire).
COUNTRY LIFE. XXIX, 54. 1911.
NIVEN, W. Old Worcestershire Houses. p.36, pl.14. 1873.
[Sales] BROADWAY, 1912, November 6, 7 [Studio properties, furniture etc.].

ABBOTSWOOD, Nether Swell (Gloucestershire).
COUNTRY LIFE. XXXIII, 272 plan. 1913.

ABBOT'S WOOTON HOUSE (Dorsetshire).
HUTCHINS, J. Vitruvius Dorsettiensis. pl. 1. 1816.

ABERAMAN (Glamorganshire).
BURKE, J.B. Visitation of Seats. 2.S. Vol.I, p.203. 1854.*

ABERCAMLAIS (Brecknockshire).
COUNTRY LIFE. CLXX. 930. 1981.

ABERGLASNEY (Carmarthenshire).
BURKE, J.B. Visitation of Seats. Vol.I, p.119. 1852.*

ABERPERGWM (Glamorganshire).
NICHOLAS, T. Counties of Wales. II, p.475. 1872.

ABINGER HALL (Surrey).
BRAYLEY, E.W. History of Surrey. V, 7. 1841.

ABINGTON ABBEY [Hall.] (Northamptonshire).
GOTCH, J.A. Squires' Homes. 34. 1939.
NEALE, J.P. Views of Seats. Vol. III. 1820.

ABLINGTON MANOR (Gloucestershire).
BURKE, J.B. Visitation of Seats. Vol.I, p.268. 1852.*

ABNEY HALL (Cheshire).
COUNTRY LIFE. CXXXIII, 846, 910. 1963.
MOSS, F. Pilgrimages. [II] 389. 1903.
[SALES] ABNEY HALL, 1958, March 17-21, 24-28 [Contents].

ACKLAM HALL (Yorkshire).
BURKE, J.B. Visitation of Seats. Vol.II, p.106. 1853.*
COUNTRY LIFE. XXXV, 342 plan. 1914.
KIP, J. Nouveau théâtre de la Grande Bretagne. I, pl. 64. 1715.

ACRESFIELD (Lancashire).
BARTLETT, J. Mansions of England and Wales. pl.148. 1853.
TWYCROSS, E. Mansions of England and Wales. Vol.III, p.85, 1847.

ACRISE PLACE (Kent).
BURKE, J.B. Visitation of Seats. 2.S. Vol.I, p.114. 1854.*
COUNTRY LIFE, CXXII, 258, 300 plan. 1957.

ACTON BURNELL PARK (Shropshire).
BURKE, J.B. Visitation of Seats. Vol.II, p.90. 1853.*
JONES. Views of Seats. I. 1829.
LEACH, F. Seats of Shropshire. p.219. 1891.
LEIGHTON, S. Shropshire houses. 3. 1901.
NEALE, J.P. Views of Seats. 2.S. Vol.II. 1825.

ACTON PARK (Denbighshire).
BURKE, J.B. Visitation of Seats. Vol.II, p.213. 1853.*
ENGLAND: Picturesque Views. p.87. 1786-88.
NEALE, J.P. Views of Seats. 2.S. Vol.V. 1829.

ACTON ROUND (Shropshire).
COUNTRY LIFE. CLXIII, 522, 614, 1978.

ACTON REYNALD (Shropshire).

BURKE, J.B. Visitation of Seats. Vol.II, p.174. 1853.*
JONES. Views of Seats. I. 1829.
LEACH, F. Seats of Shropshire. p.71. 1891.
MORRIS, F.O. Views of Seats. Vol.VI, p.47. 1880.
NEALE, J.P. Views of Seats. 2.S. Vol.III. 1826.
SHROPSHIRE. Castles & Old Mansions. 54. 1868.

ACTON SCOTT HALL (Shropshire).

SHROPSHIRE. Castles & Old Mansions. 40. 1868.

ADCOTE (Shropshire).

COUNTRY LIFE. XXVI, 912 plan. 1909.
COUNTRY LIFE. CXLVIII, 1056 plan. 1970.
LEIGHTON, S. Shropshire houses. 17. 1901.

ADDERBURY HOUSE (Oxfordshire).

COUNTRY LIFE. CV, 30. 1941.

ADDINGTON PARK (Kent).

[Sales] MAIDSTONE, Concert Hall, 1923 June 14 [Estate].

ADDINGTON PARK (Surrey).

CAMPBELL, C. New Vitruvius Britannicus. I, pls.32, 33. 1802.
PROSSER, G.F. Surrey Seats. p.87. 1828.

ADDISCOMBE PLACE (Surrey).

ANGUS, W. Seats of the Nobility. pl.58. 1787.

ADLESTROP PARK (Gloucestershire).

BURKE, J.B. Visitation of Seats. 2.S. Vol.II, p.134. 1855.*
JONES. Views of Seats. II. 1829.
NEALE, J.P. Views of Seats. Vol. II. 1819.

ADLINGTON HALL (Cheshire).

ANGUS-BUTTERWORTH, L.M. Old Cheshire families. p.105. 1932.
BURKE, J.B. Visitation of Seats. Vol. I, p.23. 1852.*
COUNTRY LIFE. XVIII, 126, 1905.
COUNTRY LIFE. CXII, 1734, 1828, 1960, 1952.
LATHAM, C. In English Homes. Vol.II, p.71. 1907.
NASH, J. Mansions of England. IV, pl. 19. 1849.
TWYCROSS, E. Mansions of England and Wales. Vol.II, p.100. 1850.*

ADLINGTON HALL (Lancashire).

BARTLETT, J. Mansions of England and Wales. pls. 4, 30, 31. 1853.
BURKE, J.B. Visitation of Seats. 2.S. Vol.I, p.105. 1854.*
TWYCROSS, E. Mansions of England and Wales. Vol.I, p.55, 1847.

AFTON HOUSE (Hampshire, Isle of Wight).

BURKE, J.B. Visitation of Seats. Vol.I, p.177. 1852.*

AGDEN HALL (Cheshire).

TWYCROSS, E. Mansions of England and Wales. Vol. II, p.57. 1850.*

AGECROFT HALL (Lancashire).

COUNTRY LIFE. XII, 432. 1902.
COUNTRY LIFE. XIII, 434. 1903.
COUNTRY LIFE. LXVI, 452 plan. 1929.
LATHAM, C. In English Homes. Vol.I, p.11. 1904.
TIPPING, H.A. English Homes. Period I & II, Vol. II, p.218. 1937.

AKELEY WOOD (Buckinghamshire).

[Sales] AKELEY WOOD, 1911, January 3-6 [Furniture etc.].

A-LA-RONDE, Exmouth. (Devonshire).

COUNTRY LIFE. LXXXIII, 448. 1938.

ALBOURNE PLACE (Sussex).

COUNTRY LIFE. LVI, 398. 1924.

ALBRIGHT HUSSEY (Shropshire).

LEACH, F. Seats of Shropshire. p.360.* 1891.
LEIGHTON, S. Shropshire houses. 12. 1901
SHROPSHIRE. Castles & Old Mansions. 32. 1868.

ALBRIGHTON HALL (Shropshire).

LEACH, F. Seats of Shropshire. p.147. 1891.
SHROPSHIRE. Castles & Old Mansions. 66. 1868.

ALBURY PARK (Surrey).

ALBURY PARK.
—Albury Park: a brief history and guide. 4pp. 1 illus. 20x13 n.p. [c. 1950.]
NORTHUMBERLAND, Helen Magdalen Percy, *Duchess of.*
— Albury Park. By H. Northumberland. 4 ed. 36pp. Illus. (1 on title-page.) 22x16 Albury: Park Estate, 1959.
BURKE, J.B. Visitation of Seats. Vol.II, p. 85. 1853.*
COUNTRY LIFE. CVIII, 598,674. 1950.
MANNING, O. Surrey. II, 125. 1804.
NEALE, J.P. Views of Seats. 2.S. Vol. III. 1826.
PROSSER, G.F. Surrey Seats. p.17. 1828.

ALBYNS (Essex).

ESSEX: A new and complete history. IV, 33. 1771.
RUSH, J.A. Seats in Essex. p.17. 1897.
[Sales] ALBYNS, Stapleford Abbots, 1926, December 9 [Contents].

ALCASTON MANOR (Shropshire).
SHROPSHIRE. Castles & Old Mansions. 40. 1868.

ALDBOROUGH MANOR (Yorkshire).
BURKE, J.B. Visitation of Seats. VolI, p.128. 1852.*

ALDBY PARK (Yorkshire).
BURKE, J.B. Visitation of Seats. Vol.I, p.59. 1852.*
COUNTRY LIFE. LXXVIII, 486. 1935.
COUNTRY LIFE. LXXVIII, 491 [Pictures]. 1935.
MORRIS, F.O. Views of Seats. Vol.V, p.47. 1880.

ALDCLIFFE HALL (Lancashire).
BARTLETT, J. Mansions of England and Wales. pl.62. 1853.
TWYCROSS, E. Mansions of England and Wales. Vol.II, p.19. 1847.

ALDENHAM ABBEY (Hertfordshire).
BURKE, J.B. Visitation of Seats. Vol.I, p.264. 1852.*

ALDENHAM HOUSE (Hertfordshire).
ALDENHAM, Henry Hucks Gibbs, *Baron.*
— A catalogue of some printed books and manuscripts at St. Dunstan's, Regent's Park, and Aldenham House, Herts., collected by H.H.G. [Lord Aldenham]. 28x19 London: privately printed, 1888.
RUDD, Helen.
— Catalogue of the Aldenham Library mainly collected by Henry Hucks Gibbs, first Lord Aldenham; revised and brought up to date by H.R. 28x20 Letchworth: privately printed at the Arden Press, 1914.
COUNTRY LIFE. LV, 282. 1924.

ALDENHAM PARK (Shropshire).
COUNTRY LIFE. CLXI, 1734, 1802. 1977.
COUNTRY LIFE. CLXII, 18. 1977.
LEACH, F. Seats of Shropshire. p.183. 1891.
LEIGHTON, S. Shropshire houses. 37. 1901.
WEST, W. Picturesque views of Shropshire. p.126. 1831.

ALDERLEY GRANGE (Gloucestershire)
ATKYNS, R. Glocestershire. p.107. 1768.

ALDERLEY PARK (Cheshire).
ANGUS-BUTTERWORTH, L.M. Old Cheshire families. p.209. 1932.
TWYCROSS, E. Mansions of England and Wales. Vol.II, p.87. 1850.*

ALDERMASTON COURT (Berkshire).
BURKE, J.B. Visitation of Seats. Vol.I, p.46. 1852.*
COUNTRY LIFE. XXII, 54. 1907.
JONES. Views of Seats. I. 1829.
NASH, J. Mansions of England. III, pl.7. 1841.
NEALE, J.P. Views of Seats. 2.S. Vol.IV. 1828.

ALDERSEY HALL (Cheshire).
BURKE, J.B. Visitation of Seats. Vol.I, p.120. 1852.*
TWYCROSS, E. Mansions of England and Wales. Vol.I, p.39. 1850.

ALDERWASLEY HALL (Derbyshire).
BURKE, J.B. Visitation of Seats. 2.S. Vol.II, p.99. 1855. *

ALDINGTON COURT (Kent).
BADESLADE, T. Seats in Kent. pl. 1. 1750.
HARRIS, J. History of Kent. p.98. 1719.

ALFOXTON PARK (Somerset).
BURKE, J.B. Visitation of Seats. Vol.II, p.186.1853.*

ALFRETON HALL (Derbyshire).
BURKE, J.B. Visitation of Seats. 2.S. Vol.II, p.94 & 111. 1855.*

ALKRINGTON HALL (Lancashire).
SUMMERSON, J. The Country Seat. 139 plan. 1970.

ALLANGATE, Halifax (Yorkshire).
YORKSHIRE. Picturesque views. 1885.

ALLERTON HALL (Lancashire).
BARTLETT, J. Mansions of England and Wales. pls.109, 110. 1853.
JONES. Views of Seats. I. 1829.
NEALE, J.P. Views of Seats. 2.S. Vol.I. 1824.
TWYCROSS, E. Mansions of England and Wales. Vol.III, p.47. 1847.

ALLERTON PARK (Yorkshire).
[Sales] ALLERTON PARK, 1965, November 25, 26 [Large portion of contents].

ALLERTON PRIORY (Lancashire).
BARTLETT, J. Mansions of England and Wales. Pls.114, 115. 1853.
TWYCROSS, E. Mansions of England and Wales. Vol.III, p.53. 1847.

ALLESLEY HALL [PARK] (Warwickshire).
BURKE, J.B. Visitation of Seats. 2.S. Vol.I, p.153. 1854.*
SMITH, W. History of the County of Warwick. 169. 1830.

ALLESTREE HALL (Derbyshire).
TILLEY, J. Halls of Derbyshire. IV, p.123. 1902.*

[Sales] ALLESTREE HALL, 1916, September 18-20 [Remaining contents]. (K., F. & R.)

ALLINGTON CASTLE (Kent).
MAC GREAL, Wilfrid, *O. Carm.*
— An introduction to Allington Castle. 20pp. Illus. (some col., some on covers) incl. plan and map. 20x15 (Faversham) [c. 1975.]

BUCK, S. & N. Antiquities. I, pl.121. 1774.

COUNTRY LIFE. XLIII, 386, 404, 424. 1918.

COUNTRY LIFE. LXIII, 438. 1928.

CROMWELL, T.K. Excursions in Kent. p.160. 1822.

HEARNE, T. Antiquities. I, pl.44. 1807.

OSWALD, A. Country houses of Kent. 7. 1933.

TIPPING, H.A. English Homes. Period I, Vol. I, p.189. 1921.

ALLT-Y-FERIN (Carmarthenshire).
NICHOLAS, T. Counties of Wales. I, p.219. 1872.

ALNWICK CASTLE (Northumberland).
ALNWICK CASTLE.
— A description of Alnwick Castle. For the use of visitors. 38pp. Cuts. 18x11 Alnwick: privately printed, 1851.

ALNWICK CASTLE.
— Alnwick Castle: a seat of the Duke of Northumberland. 32pp. Illus. (some col., 1 on title-page, some on cover.) 23x18 (Derby: English Life Publications, 1971.)
Folding plan, inserted. 22x27

BIRCH, Samuel.
— Catalogue of the collection of Egyptian antiquities at Alnwick Castle. Illus. incl. plates (1 col.) 31x25 London: privately printed, 1880.

BRUCE, John Collingwood.
— A descriptive catalogue of antiquities, chiefly British, at Alnwick Castle. [Edited by J.C.B.; largely from materials by A. Way.] Illus. incl. plates (some col. lithogr.) and cuts, 1 on title-page. 32x25 Newcastle-upon-Tyne, 1880.

DAVISON, William.
— The history of Alnwick, the county town of Northumberland. Cut. 17x10 Alnwick: by the author, 1813. 2 ed. A descriptive and historical view of Alnwick ... and of Alnwick Castle [etc.]. [Bibliogr. notes.] Engr. plates (some folding) incl. plans. 22x13 1822.

FOSTER, Joshua James.
— A catalogue of miniatures, the property of His Grace the Duke of Northumberland [The Alnwick collection]. 72pp. Plates. 25x19 London: privately printed at the Chiswick Press, 1921.

HARTSHORNE, *Rev.* Charles Henry.
— A guide to Alnwick Castle. Plates and genealog. tables. 22x14 London: Longmans, Green, Reader, & Dyer; Alnwick: M. Smith, 1865.

NORTHUMBERLAND, Helen Magdalen Percy, *Duchess of.*
— Alnwick Castle [and its contents]. 30pp. Plates: photographs. Fol. 58x44 n.p. privately printed [1930?] With MS. captions to photographs, and some typewritten descriptions inserted.

BUCK, S. & N. Antiquities. I, pl.213. 1774.

BURKE, J.B. Visitation of Seats. Vol.I, p.78. 1852.*

COUNTRY LIFE. LXV, 890, 952 plan. 1929.

COUNTRY LIFE. LXVI, 16 plan, 52 plan. 1929.

COUNTRY LIFE. LXV, 617 [Furniture]. 1929.

JEWITT, L. Stately homes of England. 78. 1874.

JONES. Views of Seats. I. 1829.

MALAN, A.H. Famous homes. p.367. 1902.

MORRIS, F.O. Views of Seats. Vol.II, p.1. 1880.

NEALE, J.P. Views of Seats. Vol.III. 1820.

SANDBY, P. Select Views. I, pl.40. 1783.

UNITED KINGDOM. Historic houses. 65. 1892.

ALRESFORD HALL (Essex).
BURKE, J.B. Visitation of Seats. 2.S. Vol.I, p.205. 1854.*

ALRESFORD HOUSE (Hampshire).
COUNTRY LIFE. CLXIII, 18. 1978

HAMPSHIRE: Architectural views. 1830.

[Sales] LONDON, 1939, May 22, 23 [Books].

[Sales] LONDON, 1939, June 19-21 [Books].

[Sales] LONDON, 1939, June 27 [Books].

[Sales] LONDON, 1939, July 10, 11 [Books].

[Sales] LONDON, 1946, March 11, 12 [Books].

[Sales] LONDON, 1946, July 15, 16 [Books, Mss.].

ALSCOT PARK (Warwickshire).
BURKE, J.B. Visitation of Seats. Vol.II, p.20. 1853.*

COUNTRY LIFE. CXXIII, 1064 plan, 1124, 1184. 1958.

JONES. Views of Seats. II. 1829.

NEALE, J.P. Views of Seats. Vol.II. 1819.

[Sales] ALSCOT PARK, 1772, October 19 [Live and dead stock etc.] [Photocopy].

[Sales] LONDON, 1773, January 19 and following days [Prints & Drawings] [Photocopy].

[Sales] LONDON, 1773, February 27 and following days [Curiosities] [Photocopy].

[Sales] LONDON. 1773, March 29 and following days [Library.] [Photocopy].

[Sales] LONDON, 1773, March 31, April 1-3 [Pictures, prints etc.] [Photocopy].

ALSOP HALL (Derbyshire).
TILLEY, J. Halls of Derbyshire. II, p.191. 1893.

ALSPRINGS (Lancashire).
BARTLETT, J. Mansions of England and Wales. pl.35. 1853.

TWYCROSS, E. Mansions of England and Wales.Vol.I, p.33. 1847.

ALSTON COURT (Suffolk)
COUNTRY LIFE. LVI, 100 plan.1924.

SANDON, E. Suffolk houses. 322. 1977.

TIPPING, H.A. English homes. Period I & II, Vol.II, p.197. 1937.

ALTHORP (Northamptonshire).
ALTHORP.

— Catalogue of the pictures at Althorp House, in the county of Northampton. 40pp. 22x14 n.p. privately printed, 1831. With MS. additions.

ALTHORP.

— Catalogue of the pictures at Althorp House, in the county of Northampton, with occasional notices, biographical or historical. [By D. Morton.] 22x14 [London: privately printed] 1851.

ARMSTRONG, *Sir* Walter.

— Sir Joshua Reynolds at Althorp House. Reproductions ... of some of the finest pictures by Sir J. Reynolds, P.R.A., in the possession of ... the Earl Spencer. With an introduction by Sir W.A. 10pp. 11 col. plates. 74x55 London (1904.)

BOYLE, Mary Louisa.

— An imperfect narrative of the gay doings and marvellous festivities holden at Althorp in the county of Northants. On the occasion of my lord, John Poyntz, Viscount Althorp, completing his twenty-first year on the 27th day of October in the year of Grace 1856. 34pp. Plate. 30x24 London: privately printed (at the Chiswick Press) 1857. MS. dedication by Viscount Althorp.

DIBDIN, *Rev.* Thomas Frognall.

— Bibliotheca Spenceriana; or, a descriptive catalogue of the books printed in the fifteenth century, and of many valuable first editions in the library of George John, Earl Spencer, K.G. &c. Illus. incl. plates (some folding.) 4 vols. 27x18 London: Longman, Hurst, Rees, & Co.; Payne; White & Cochrane; J. Murray; and J. & A. Arch, 1814-15. For supplement see: DIBDIN, *Rev.* (T.F.) Aedes Althorpianae, vol.II. 1822.

DIBDIN, *Rev.* Thomas Frognall.

— Aedes Althorpianae; or, an account of the mansion, books, and pictures, at Althorp; the residence of George John, Earl Spencer, K.G. To which is added a supplement to the Bibliotheca Spenceriana. [Bibliogr. notes.] Illus. incl. plates and folding plan. 2 vols. 27x17 London: privately printed, 1822.

DIBDIN, *Rev.* Thomas Frognall.

— A descriptive catalogue of the books printed in the fifteenth century, lately forming part of the library of the Duke di Cassano Serra, and now the property of George John, Earl Spencer, K.G. With a general index of authors and editions contained in the present volume, and in the Bibliotheca Spenceriana and Aedes Althorpianae. 27x17 London: privately printed, 1823.

GARLICK, Kenneth J.

— A catalogue of pictures at Althorp. Compiled by K.J.G. [Bibliogr.] XVI. 128pp. Plates. In LONDON: Walpole Society. Annual volume XLV. 1974-6 (1976).

SPENCER, Family.

— A short history of Althorp and the Spencer family. (The pictures by E.K. Waterhouse.) 32pp. Illus. incl. genealog. table. 22x14 Northampton: privately printed [c. 1960].

STEINMAN, George Steinman.

— Althorp memoirs, or biographical notices of Lady Denham, the Countess of Shrewsbury, the Countess of Falmouth, Mrs. Jenyns, the Duchess of Tyrconnel, and Lucy Walter. Six ladies whose portraits are to be found in the picture galley of his excellency Earl Spencer. (Addenda to Althorp memoirs, including corrections.) [Bibliogr. notes.] iv, 128pp. Plate. 23x14 Oxford: privately printed, 1869-80.

Copy signed by the author and presented to G.J. Armytage, also a MS. letter to him from the author, 18x11, inserted.

BRIDGES, J. Northamptonshire. I, 480. 1791.

CAMPBELL, C. Vitruvius Britannicus. II, pls. 95-97. 1717.

CAMPBELL, C. Vitruvius Britannicus. Vol. III, pls. 83, 84. 1725.

COUNTRY LIFE. English Country Houses: Mid Georgian. p.203. 1956.

COUNTRY LIFE. XLIX, 714 furniture, 764 furniture, 792. 1921.

COUNTRY LIFE. L. 14. 1921.

COUNTRY LIFE, LXXVIII, 204 [Furniture]. 1935.

COUNTRY LIFE. LXXXIII, 293 [Pictures]. 1938.

COUNTRY LIFE. CXXVII, 1122, 1186. 1960.

COUNTRY LIFE. CLXX, 375. 1981.

GOTCH, J.A. Halls of Northants. p.68. 1936.

JONES. Views of Seats. I. 1829.

KIP, J. Nouveau théâtre de la Grande Bretagne. I, pl. 27. 1715.

NEALE, J.P. Views of Seats. Vol. III. 1820.

NICOLSON, N. Great Houses of Britain. p.262. 1965.

TIPPING, H.A. English Homes. Period VI, Vol.I, p.299. 1926.

WHITEMAN, G.W. English country homes. p.139. 1951.

ALTON CASTLE (Staffordshire).
COUNTRY LIFE. CXXVIII, 1226. 1960.

ALTON MANOR (Derbyshire).
BURKE, J.B. Visitation of Seats. 2.S. Vol.I, p. 196. 1854.*

ALTON TOWERS (Staffordshire).
PORTER, Lindsey

— The Chumet Valley and Alton Towers. By L.P., & L. Landon. 48pp. Illus. (1 col. on cover) incl. maps. 21x15 Hartington: Moorland Publishing Company, 1977.

BURKE, J.B. Visitation of Seats. 2.S. Vol.II, p.127. 1855.*
COUNTRY LIFE. CXXVII, 1304. 1960.
JEWITT, L. Stately homes of England. 1. 1874.
JONES. Views of Seats. I. 1829.
MORRIS, F.O. Views of Seats. Vol.I, p.67. 1880.
NEALE, J.P. Views of Seats. Vol. IV. 1821.
[Sales] LONDON, 1857, June 22 and following days [Library ... removed from A.T.].
[Sales] ALTON TOWERS, 1857, July 6 and following days [Contents].
[Sales] ALTON TOWERS, 1924, January 15 [Contents].

ALVESTON (Gloucestershire).
ATKYNS, R. Glocestershire. p.111. 1768.

ALVESTON HOUSE (Warwickshire).
COUNTRY LIFE. XCVII, 904, 948. 1945.

AMBERLEY CASTLE (Sussex).
BUCK, S. & N. Antiquities. II. pl.285. 1774.

AMESBURY ABBEY (Wiltshire).
CAMPBELL, C. Vitruvius Britannicus. III, pl.7. 1725.
ENGLAND: Picturesque Views. p.51. 1786-88.

AMMERDOWN PARK (Somerset).
AMMERDOWN.
— Description of the mansion, marbles, and pictures, at Ammerdown in Somersetshire. 24pp. 2 lithogr. plates. 26x20 London: Saunders and Otley, 1857.
BURKE, J.B. Visitation of Seats. 2.S. Vol.II, p.112. 1855.*
COOKE, R. West Country Houses. p.144. 1957.
COUNTRY LIFE. LXV, 216. 1929.

AMPNEY PARK (Gloucestershire).
ATKYNS, R. Glocestershire. p.113. 1768.

AMPORT HOUSE (Hampshire).
JONES. Views of Seats. II. 1829.
NEALE, J.P. Views of Seats. Vol.II. 1819.
[Sales] AMPORT HOUSE, Amport St. Mary's, Hants., 1919 July 14-18, 21 [Contents].

AMPTHILL LODGE Bedfordshire).
SUMMERSON, J. The Country Seat. 13 [Designs for Lodge.] 1970.

AMPTHILL PARK (Bedfordshire).
COUNTRY LIFE. CL, 1085. 1971.
NEALE. J.P. Views of Seats. Vol.I. 1818.

AMPTON HALL (Suffolk).
CROMWELL, T.K. Excursions in Suffolk. I, p.79. 1818.

ANDERSON MANOR (Dorsetshire).
COUNTRY LIFE. XXXVII, 446. 1915.
GARNER, T. Domestic architecture. II, p.167. 1911.
HEATH, S. Dorset Manor Houses. 197. 1907.
OSWALD, A. Country Houses of Dorset. p.102. 1959.

ANGLESEY ABBEY (Cambridgeshire).
BUNT, Cyril George Edward.
— Windsor Castle through three centuries: a description and catalogue of the Windsor collection formed by the Lord Fairhaven, F.S.A., Anglesey Abbey, Cambridgeshire. 112pp. 48 (9 col.) plates. 25x20 Leigh-on-Sea: F. Lewis, 1949.
LONDON: National Trust for Places of Historic Interest or Natural Beauty.
— FEDDEN, R. Anglesey Abbey: a guide. [Bibliogr. note.] 40pp. Illus. incl. folding plate: map. 23x18 Oxford, 1968. Rev. ed. [Bibliogr. notes.] 36pp. Illus. (1 col.) incl. Plates, plan and folding map on cover. 24x18 [London] 1982.
COUNTRY LIFE. LXVIII, 832 plan. 1930.
COUNTRY LIFE. LXIX, 110 [Pictures], 376 [Pictures]. 1931.
COUNTRY LIFE. CXV, 860. 1954.

ANKERWYKE HOUSE (Buckinghamshire).
BURKE, J.B. Visitation of Seats. Vol.I, p.32. 1852.*

ANMER HALL (Norfolk).
BURKE, J.B. Visitation of Seats. Vol.I, p.90. 1852.*

ANNINGSLEY PARK (Surrey).
COUNTRY LIFE. LVIII, 449 plan. 1925.

ANSLEY HALL (Warwickshire).
BURKE, J.B. Visitation of Seats. 2.S. Vol.II, p.132. 1855.*
NICHOLS, J. History of Leicestershire. IV, ii, 1017. 1811.

ANSTY HALL (Warwickshire).
BURKE, J.B. Visitation of Seats. Vol.I, p.244. 1852.

ANTONY HOUSE (Cornwall).
LONDON: National Trust for Places of Historic Interest or Natural Beauty.
— Antony House, Cornwall. 30pp. Illus. (1 on cover.) 18x12 London, 1963.
New ed. 32pp. Illus. (1 col. on cover) 21x15 [London] 1981.
BURKE, J.B. Visitation of Seats. 2.S, Vol.I, p.96. 1854.*
COUNTRY LIFE.LXXIV, 172, 202. 1933.
NICOLSON, N. Great Houses of Britain. p.190. 1965.
REPTON, H. Red Books. II. 1976.

ALTHORP, Northamptonshire. From: KIP (J.). *Nouveau théâtre de la Grande Bretagne*, vol. I, London, 1715.

APETHORPE HALL (Northamptonshire).
BURKE, J.B. Visitation of Seats. 2.S. Vol.II, p.96. 1855.*
COUNTRY LIFE. XXV. 414, 450. 1909.
GOTCH, J.A. Architecture of the Renaissance. I, p.9 plan. 1894.
GOTCH, J.A. Halls of Northants. p.29. 1936.
JONES. Views of Seats. I. 1829.
LATHAM, C. In English Homes. Vol. III, p.57. 1909.
NEALE, J.P. Views of Seats. 2.S. Vol.III. 1826.
TIPPING, H.A. English Homes. Period III, Vol. II, p.1. 1927.

APLEY (Hampshire, Isle of Wight).
BURKE, J.B. Visitation of Seats. Vol.I, p.197. 1852.*

APLEY CASTLE (Shropshire).
BURKE, J.B. Visitation of Seats. Vol. II, p.135. 1853.*
LEACH, F. Seats of Shropshire. p.55. 1891.
LEIGHTON, S. Shropshire houses. 11. 1901.
SHROPSHIRE. Castles & Old Mansions. 45. 1868.

APLEY PARK (Shropshire).
BURKE, J.B. Visitation of Seats. Vol.II, p.77. 1853.*
JONES. Views of Seats. I. 1829.
LEACH, F. Seats of Shropshire. p.109. 1891.
LEIGHTON, S. Shropshire houses. 34. 1901.
MORRIS, F.O. Views of Seats. Vol.VI, p.53. 1880.
NEALE, J.P. Views of Seats. 2.S. Vol. III. 1826.

APPLEBY CASTLE (Westmorland).
FERGUSON INDUSTRIAL HOLDINGS, Ltd.
— HOLMES, M. Appleby Castle. 66pp. Illus. (some col.) incl. sections and plans (on inside cover). 24x18 Appleby, 1974.
BUCK, S. & N. Antiquities. II, pl.307. 1774.
BURKE, J.B. Visitation of Seats. Vol.I, p.163. 1852.*
COUNTRY LIFE. LXXXVII, 382 plan, 408. 1940.
CUMBERLAND: C. & W. A. & A.S. Extra Series, VIII, 27. 1892.
MORRIS, F.O. Views of Seats. Vol. IV, p.41. 1880.

APPLEBY PARVA HALL (Leicestershire).
NICHOLS, J. History of Leicestershire. IV, ii, 439. 1811.
TILLEY, J. Halls of Derbyshire. IV, p.83. 1902.*

APPLETON HALL (Cheshire).
BURKE, J.B. Visitation of Seats. Vol.II, p.127. 1853.*
TWYCROSS, E. Mansions of England and Wales. Vol.II, p.81. 1850.

APPLETON MANOR (Berkshire).
COUNTRY LIFE. XLV, 372. 1919.
COUNTRY LIFE. LXV, 670. 1929.

APPULDURCOMBE (Hampshire, Isle of Wight).
GREAT BRITAIN: Ministry of Public Buildings and Works [Ancient Monuments and Historic Buildings].
— BOYNTON, L.O.J. Appledurcombe House, Isle of Wight. [Bibliogr. notes.] 24pp. Plates (2 folding) incl. plans and table. 21x14 London, 1967.
GREAT BRITAIN: Department of the Environment [Ancient Monuments and Historic Buildings].
— BOYNTON, L.O.J. Appledurcombe House, Isle of Wight. 38pp. Illus. incl. 2 folding plates, plans, map and table. 1976.
WORSLEY, *Sir* Richard, *Bart.*
— A catalogue raisonné of the principal paintings, sculptures, drawings, &c. at Appuldurcombe House, the seat of the Rt. Hon. Sir Richard Worsley, Bart. Taken June 1, 1804. 60pp. Engr. plate. 36x26 London: privately printed, 1804.
CAMPBELL, C. Vitruvius Britannicus. III, pl.61. 1725.
COUNTRY LIFE. LXXII, 568 plan. 1932.
WATTS, W. Seats of the Nobility. pl.14. 1779.

APSLEY WOOD COTTAGE (Bedfordshire).
REPTON, H. Fragments on landscape gardening. p.14. 1816.

AQUALATE HOUSE (Staffordshire).
PLOT, R. Staffordshire. 246. 1686.

ARAMSTONE HOUSE (Herefordshire).
ANGUS, W. Seats of the Nobility. pl.12. 1787.

ARBORFIELD HALL (Berkshire).
BURKE, J.B. Visitation of Seats. Vol.I, p.186. 1852. (Plate 2.S. Vol.II. p.228).

ARBURY HALL (Warwickshire).
NARES, Gordon.
— Arbury Hall, Warwickshire. 32pp. Illus. (1 on cover) incl. genealog. table. 22x14 [London] Country Life, 1969.
BURKE, J.B. Visitation of Seats. Vol.II, p.13. 1853.*
COUNTRY LIFE. English Country Houses: Mid Georgian, p.41. 1956.
COUNTRY LIFE. XXXIV, 356. 1913.
COUNTRY LIFE. CXIV, 1126, 1210, 1414. 1953.
MORRIS. F.O. Views of Seats. Vol.III, p.41. 1880.

ARDEN (Lancashire).
BURKE, J.B. Visitation of Seats.Vol. II, p.250. 1853.

ARDENRUN PLACE (Surrey)
COUNTRY LIFE. XXIX, 90 plan. 1911.

ARDERN HALL (Cheshire).
ORMEROD, G. Cheshire. III, 822. 1882.

ARDINGTON HOUSE (Berkshire).

TEMPLE, Alfred George.
— Catalogue of pictures forming the collection of Lord and Lady Wantage at 2, Carlton Gardens, London, Lockinge House, Berks., and Overstone Park and Ardington House. [By A.G.T., R.H. Benson and Lady Wantage; introduction by S.A. Strong.] Plates. 34x26 London: Wetherman & Co., 1902.

COUNTRY LIFE. CLXX, 1282. 1981.

ARELEY HALL (Worcestershire).

NASH, T.R. Worcestershire. I, 38. 1781.

ARLEBURY (Hampshire).

[SALES] ARLEBURY, 1935, May 28-30 [Contents]. (K.F. & R.)

ARLESCOTE (Warwickshire).

COUNTRY LIFE. CII, 478. 1947.

ARLEY CASTLE (Worcestershire).

BARTLETT, J. Selections from views of mansions. 1851.
[Sales] ARLEY CASTLE, 1852, December 6-18 [Contents].

ARLEY HALL (Cheshire).

MOSS, F. Pilgrimages. [II] 287. 1903.
TWYCROSS, E. Mansions of England and Wales. Vol. II. p.61, 1850.

ARLEY HALL (Lancashire).

BARTLETT, J. Mansions of England and Wales. pl.147. 1853.
TWYCROSS, E. Mansions of England and Wales. Vol.III, p.85, 1847.

ARLINGTON COURT (Devonshire).

LONDON: National Trust for Places of Historic Interest or Natural Beauty.
— Arlington Court, Devonshire. 4pp. 1 illus. 18x12 [London, *c*. 1955.]

LONDON: National Trust for Places of Historic Interest or Natural Beauty.
— TRINICK, M. Arlington Court. 28pp. Col. illus. (1 on cover) incl. map. 25x16 [London] (1977.)

LONDON: National Trust for Places of Historic Interest or Natural Beauty.
— Arlington Court, Devon: collection of 19th. century vehicles. 8pp, 1 illus. 19x13 [London, *c*. 1970.]

LONDON: National Trust for Places of Historic Interest or Natural Beauty.
— Model ships at Arlington Court. 8pp. 1 illus. 21x16 (London) [1970.]

COUNTRY LIFE. CLXIX, 1178. 1981.
COUNTRY LIFE. CLXX, 1327 [Carriage Collection] 1981.

ARMADA HOUSE, Weston (Northamptonshire).

GOTCH, J.A. Halls of Northants. p.87. 1936.

ARMINGHALL OLD HALL (Norfolk).

CROMWELL, T.K. Excursions in Norfolk. I, p.42, 1818.
GARRATT, T. Halls of Norfolk. pls. 1-3. 1890.

ARMITAGE BRIDGE HOUSE (Yorkshire).

ELLIS, G.I.
— A catalogue of the manuscripts and printed books collected by Thomas Brooke, F.S.A., and preserved at Armitage Bridge House, near Huddersfield. [Compiled by] (G.I.E.) Illus. (2 on title-pages) incl. plates and plan. 2 vols. 25x16 London: The Chiswick Press for Ellis and Elvey, 1891.

ARMITAGE PARK (Staffordshire).

RYAN, Columba, *O.P.*
— A guide and history of Hawkesyard Priory and Spode House (Armitage Park) Rugeley, Staffordshire. [Bibliogr. notes.] 28pp. 6 illus. (1 on cover.) 18x12 Gloucester: B.P.C., 1970.
BURKE, J.B. Visitation of Seats. Vol. I, p.211. 1852.
JONES. Views of Seats. I. 1829.
NEALE, J.P. Views of Seats. Vol. IV. 1821.

ARMLEY HOUSE (Yorkshire).

JONES. Views of Seats. I. 1829.
NEALE, J.P. Views of Seats. Vol.V. 1822.

ARMSCOTE MANOR (Warwickshire).

COUNTRY LIFE. LIII, 63 plan. 1923.

ARMSTON (Herefordshire).

See ARAMSTONE HOUSE.

ARNCLIFFE HALL (Yorkshire).

COUNTRY LIFE. XLVIII, 846. 1920.

ARNOS CASTLE (Gloucestershire).

COUNTRY LIFE. CIX, 1880. 1951.

ARNOS COURT (Gloucestershire).

COOKE, R. West Country Houses. p.138. 1957.
COUNTRY LIFE. CIX, 1880. 1951.

ARNOS GROVE (Middlesex).

WATTS, W. Seats of the Nobility. pl.63. 1779.

ARRETON MANOR (Hampshire, Isle of Wight).

— Arreton Manor, Isle of Wight. The home of Mr. & Mrs. L.H. Slade. 12pp. Illus. (some on covers.) 20x13 n.p. [c.1950.]

GARNER, T. Domestic architecture. II, p.160 plan. 1911.

ARROWE PARK (Cheshire).

TWYCROSS, E. Mansions of England and Wales. Vol.I, p.82. 1850.

ARUNDEL CASTLE (Sussex).

BACKLER, J.
— Catalogue of pictures painted on glass, containing principally, the great Norfolk window, for the Barons' Hall of Arundel Castle; &c. Now exhibiting at Mr. Backler's stained glass works. 12pp. Engr. plate. 25x17 London: privately printed, 1817.

EUSTACE, George Wallace.
— Arundel: borough and castle. [Bibliogr. notes.] Illus. incl. plates and plan. 21x14 London: R. Scott, 1922.

MUSGRAVE, Clifford.
— The history and treasures of Arundel Castle [etc.]. (A brief history of Arundel Castle and the Fitzalan-Howard family. By P.W. Montague-Smith.) 32pp. Illus. (1 col., some on covers, 1 on title-page) incl. plan, map and genealog. table. 23x18 (London: Pitkin, 1963.)
One of the series: PRIDE OF BRITAIN.
Another ed. 24pp. Illus. (many col., some on covers, 1 on title-page) incl. plan, map, and genealog. table. (1973.)

NORFOLK, Gwendolen Mary Fitzalan Howard, *Duchess of.*
— Arundel Castle. 36pp. Plates (some col.) 23x16 London: Heinemann, 1913.

TIERNEY, *Rev.* Mark Aloysius.
— The history and antiquities of the castle and town of Arundel; including the biography of its Earls, from the Conquest to the present time. [Bibliogr. notes.] Illus. incl. plates (1 folding) and genealog. tables. 2 vols. 24x15 London: G. & W. Nicol, 1834.

WRIGHT, Charles.
— The history and description of Arundel Castle, Sussex; the seat of his Grace the Duke of Norfolk, with an abstract of the lives of the Earls of Arundel, from the Conquest to the present time: to which is annexed, topographical delineations of the Roman pavement at Bignor, Littlehampton and Bognor Rocks. 2 ed. 2 folding engr. plates. 18x11 London: privately printed, 1818.

BUCK, S. & N. Antiquities. II, pl. 286. 1774.

BURKE, J.B. Visitation of Seats. Vol.I, p.87. 1852.*

COUNTRY LIFE. XXXVI, 746, 782 plan, 814, 853 [Furniture]. 1914.

COUNTRY LIFE. CLXXIII, 196 [Collection], 280 [Collection], 332 [Collection]. 1983.

ELWES, D.G.C. Mansions of Western Sussex. 15. 1876.

ENGLAND: Beauties of England. II, p.319. 1787.

JEWITT, L. Stately homes of England. 153. 1874.

MORRIS, F.O. Views of Seats. Vol.IV, p.1. 1880.

MOSS, F. Pilgrimages. IV, 267, 1908.

NEALE, J.P. Views of Seats. 2.S. Vol.IV. 1828.

TIPPING, H.A. English Homes. Period I, Vol.I, p.21. 1921.

ASCOTT, Wing (Buckinghamshire).

LONDON: National Trust for Places of Historic Interest or Natural Beauty.
— The Ascott collection, Ascott, Buckinghamshire. 30pp. 4 plates. 18x12 London (1951).
New ed. The Ascott collection, Ascott, Buckinghamshire. [Guide and catalogue of paintings. Bibliogr. notes.] 40pp. Illus. (1 col. on cover) incl. 8 plates and map. 25x18 [London] 1963.

COUNTRY LIFE. II, 210. 1897.

COUNTRY LIFE. CVIII, 826 [Collection]. 1950.

ASGILL HOUSE, Richmond (Surrey).

BURKE, J.B. Visitation of Seats. Vol.I, p.154. 1852.*

CAMPBELL, C. Vitruvius Britannicus. IV, pl.74. 1767.

COUNTRY LIFE. XCV, 992 plan. 1944.

ENGLAND: Picturesque Views. p.55. 1786-88.

ASHBOURNE HALL (Derbyshire).

TILLEY, J. Halls of Derbyshire. II, p.189. 1893.

ASHBURNHAM PLACE (Sussex).

BURKE, J.B. Visitation of Seats. 2.S. Vol.I, p.161. 1854.*

COUNTRY LIFE. XXXIX, 112, 144. 1916.

COUNTRY LIFE. CXIII, 1158, 1246, 1334. 1953.

NEALE, J.P. Views of Seats. 2.S. Vol.IV. 1828.

WATTS, W. Seats of the Nobility. pl.61. 1779.

[SALES] LONDON, 1850, July 20 [Paintings].

[SALES] LONDON, 1897, June 25, 26, 28-30, July 1-3 [Library, pt.I].

[Sales] LONDON, 1897, December 6-11 [Library, pt.II].

[Sales] LONDON, 1898, May 9-14 [Library, pt.III].

[Sales] LONDON, 1953, June 24 [Ashburnham Collection, pt.I. paintings etc.].

[Sales] LONDON, 1953, June 26 [Ashburnham Collection, pt.II. furniture etc.].

[Sales] ASHBURNHAM PLACE, 1953, July 7-9 [Contents].

[Sales] LONDON, 1953, July 15 [Ashburnham Collection, pt.III. portraits etc.].

ASHBURY MANOR (Berkshire).

COUNTRY LIFE. CXL, 974, 1084 plan. 1966.

ASHBY ST. LEDGERS (Northamptonshire).

COUNTRY LIFE. CX, 274, 348 plan, 420 plan. 1951.

GOTCH, J.A. Halls of Northants. p.65. 1936.

ASHCOMBE PARK (Staffordshire).
MORRIS, F.O. Views of Seats.Vol.IV, p.75. 1880.

ASHDOWN HOUSE (Berkshire).
LONDON: National Trust for Places of Historic Interest or Natural Beauty.
— Ashdown House, Berkshire. 8pp. 1 illus. 22x14 [London] 1969.
COUNTRY LIFE. English Country Houses: Caroline, p.137. 1966.
COUNTRY LIFE. XXXIII, 454. 1913.
KIP. J. Nouveau théâtre de la Grande Bretagne. I, pl.46. 1715.

ASHFIELD HALL (Cheshire).
TWYCROSS, E. Mansions of England and Wales. Vol.I, p.61. 1850.

ASHFORD ROOKERY (Derbyshire).
TILLEY, J. Halls of Derbyshire. I, p.35. 1892.

ASHGATE COTTAGE (Derbyshire).
TILLEY, J. Halls of Derbyshire. III, p.39. 1899.

ASH HALL (Glamorganshire).
BURKE, J.B. Visitation of Seats. Vol.I, p.6. 1852.*

ASHLEY MANOR (Gloucestershire).
COOKE, R. West Country Houses. p.88. 1957.

ASHLEY PARK (Surrey).
BRAYLEY, E.W. History of Surrey. II, 350. 1841.
BURKE, J.B. Visitation of Seats. 2.S. Vol.II, p.14. 1855.*
NEALE, J.P. Views of Seats. Vol.IV. 1821.

ASHMANS (Suffolk).
NEALE, J.P. Views of Seats. 2.S. Vol.II. 1825.

ASHRIDGE PARK (Hertfordshire).
BRYANT, *Sir* Arthur.
— The story of Ashridge. The Bonar Law Memorial College. 24pp. 7 illus. 22x14 Westminster (1920).
Reprint from: The Nineteenth Century and After.
COULT, Douglas.
— Ashridge: a short guide to the history and principal features of Ashridge in the county of Hertfordshire. [Bibliogr.] 20pp. Col. illus. 18x14 Ashridge: Management College, 1971.
JAMES, Montague Rhodes.
— Notes of glass in Ashridge Chapel. 16pp. 28x21 Grantham? privately printed? 1906.
TODD, Henry John.
— The history of the College of Bonhommes, at Ashridge, in the County of Buckingham, founded in the year 1276, by

Edmund, Earl of Cornwall. Compiled from original records and other authentic sources. To which is added, a description of the present mansion, erected on the site of the ancient college. [Bibliogr. notes] viii, 94pp. Engr. plates incl. plan and genealog. table. 55x38 London: privately printed, 1823.
BURKE, J.B. Visitation of Seats. Vol.I, p.145. 1852.*
COUNTRY LIFE. L, 160, 192. 1921.
NEALE, J.P. Views of Seats. 2.S. Vol.V. 1829.
TIPPING, H.A. English Homes. Period VI, Vol. I, p. 339. 1926.
[Sales] LONDON, 1923, May 4, 7 [Pictures from A.P.].
[Sales] ASHRIDGE, 1924, October 13-15, 20-22 [Antique and modern furniture etc.].

ASHTEAD PARK (Surrey).
NEALE, J.P. Views of Seats. Vol. IV. 1821.

ASHTON COURT (Somerset).
BURKE, J.B. Visitation of Seats. 2.S. Vol.I, p.206. 1854.*
COLLINSON, J. History of Somerset. II, 294. 1791.
COOKE, R. West Country Houses. p.73. 1957.
COUNTRY LIFE. CLI, 1318 plan. 1972.
REPTON, H. Observations on landscape gardening. 200. 1803.

ASHTON HALL (Lancashire).
BARTLETT, J. Mansions of England and Wales. pl. 45. 1853.
BURKE, J.B. Visitation of Seats. 2.S. Vol.I, p.208. 1854.*
PYNE, W.H. Lancashire illustrated. 95. 1831.
TWYCROSS, E. Mansions of England and Wales. Vol.II, p.1. 1847.

ASHTON HAYES (Cheshire).
TWYCROSS, E. Mansions of England and Wales. Vol.I, p.125. 1850.

ASHTON HOUSE (Wiltshire).
COUNTRY LIFE. XCII, 842. 1942.

ASHTON LODGE (Lancashire).
BARTLETT, J. Mansions of England and Wales. pl.94. 1853.
TWYCROSS, E. Mansions of England and Wales. Vol.II, p.58. 1847.

ASHURST (Surrey).
BRAYLEY, E.W. History of Surrey. IV, 457. 1841.

ASHURST LODGE [PLACE] (Kent).
GREENWOOD, C. Kent. 118. 1838.

ASHWELL BURY (Hertfordshire).
COUNTRY LIFE. CI, 810. 1947.

ASHWELL END (Hertfordshire).
COUNTRY LIFE. CV, 101. 1949.

ASHWELLTHORPE HALL (Norfolk)
BURKE, J.B. Visitation of Seats. 2.S. Vol.I, p.83. 1854.*

ASKE HALL (Yorkshire).
MORRIS, F.O. Views of Seats. Vol.V, p.25. 1880.

ASKHAM HALL (Westmorland).
CUMBERLAND: C. & W. A. & A.S. Extra Series, VIII, 88 plan. 1892.

ASPALL HALL (Suffolk).
COUNTRY LIFE. IV, 599. 1898.
SANDON, E. Suffolk houses. 160. 1977.

ASPENDEN HALL (Hertfordshire).
CHAUNCY, H. Hertfordshire. I, 240. 1826.

ASTHALL MANOR (Oxfordshire).
COUNTRY LIFE. XCVII, 1124. 1945.

ASTLE HALL (Cheshire).
TWYCROSS, E. Mansions of England and Wales. Vol.II, p.113. 1850.

ASTLEY CASTLE (Warwickshire).
BURKE, J.B. Visitation of Seats. Vol.II, p.85. 1853.*
NIVEN, W. Old Warwickshire houses. p.16, pl.16. 1878.
SMITH, W. History of the county of Warwick. 148. 1830.

ASTLEY HALL (Lancashire).
CHORLEY: Astley Hall Art Gallery and Museum.
— Astley Hall, Chorley. 12pp. Illus. 16x12 (Chorley) [c. 1925.]
Another ed. 16pp. 18x12 (1951.)
Another ed. 1973.
Titles on covers.
BURKE, J.B. Visitation of Seats. Vol.I, p.54. 1852.*
COUNTRY LIFE. LI, 284 [Furniture]. 1922.
COUNTRY LIFE. LII, 14 plan, 50. 1922.
COUNTRY LIFE, CXVIII, 1214. 1955.
MORRIS, F.O. Views of Seats. Vol.V, p.5. 1880.
TWYCROSS, E. Mansions of England and Wales. Vol.I, p.41. 1847.*

ASTONBURY (Hertfordshire).
COUNTRY LIFE. XXVII, 450 plan. 1910.
GARNER, T. Domestic architecture. I, p.77 plan. 1911.

ASTON CLINTON PARK (Buckinghamshire).
SPROULE, A. Lost houses of Britain. 38. 1982.
[Sales] ASTON CLINTON PARK, 1923, July 23-26 [Remaining contents].

ASTON HALL (Cheshire).
TWYCROSS, E. Mansions of England and Wales. Vol.II, p.47. 1850.*

ASTON HALL (Derbyshire).
TILLEY, J. Halls of Derbyshire. I, p.209. 1892.

ASTON HALL, near Oswestry (Shropshire).
BURKE, J.B. Visitation of Seats. Vol.II, p.248. 1853.*
LEIGHTON, S. Shropshire houses. 24. 1901.
[Sales] ASTON HALL, 1923, July 2 and following days [Contents].

ASTON HALL (Warwickshire).
ASTON HALL.
— Aston Hall: an illustrated survey [etc.]. 32pp. Illus. (some col., some on covers) incl. maps (on inside covers) and genealog. table. 14x22 Derby: E.L.P. [1953?].

BIRMINGHAM: Museum & Art Gallery [Aston Hall].
— WALLIS, W. Handbook to Aston Hall, with historical and descriptive notes, and a catalogue of pictures, &c. 46pp. Illus. incl. plans. 21x16 Birmingham, 1892.
2 ed. 48pp. 1902.
Another ed. 1907.
Another ed. 1909.
Another ed. 1919.
DAVIDSON, Alfred.
— A history of the Holtes of Aston, Baronets; with a description of the family mansion, Aston Hall, Warwickshire ... with illustrations from drawings by A.E. Everitt. [Bibliogr. notes.] 76pp. Tinted lithogr. plates and genealog. table. 37x27 Birmingham: Everitt, 1854.
NIVEN, William.
— Monograph of Aston Hall, Warwickshire, geometrical drawings and views ... with a brief sketch and description. 8pp. Plates incl. sections, elevations and plan. 37x28 London: J. Rimell & Son; Birmingham: W. Downing [1881].
BUCK, S. & N. Antiquities. II, pl.297. 1774.
CLARKE, T.H. Domestic architecture. 5. 1833.
COUNTRY LIFE. XVIII, 306. 1905.
COUNTRY LIFE. CXIV, 552 plan, 620, 694. 1953.
GOTCH, J.A. Architecture of the Renaissance. II, p.22 plan. 1894.
HALL, S.C. Baronial Halls. Vol.II. 1848.
JONES. Views of Seats. I. 1829.
LATHAM, C. In English Homes. Vol.II, p.271. 1907.
NASH, J. Mansions of England. IV, pls. 22-24. 1849.
NEALE, J.P. Views of Seats. Vol.IV. 1821.

NIVEN, W. Old Warwickshire houses. p.1, front. pls. 1 [Plan], 2-6. 1878.

RICHARDSON, C.J. Old English mansions. IV. 1848.

SHAW, H. Elizabethan architecture. pl.XLVIII. [Stone frieze] 1839.

SMITH, W. History of the County of Warwick. 305. 1830.

ASTON HALL (Yorkshire).

COUNTRY LIFE. CXIX, 752 plan. 1956.

[Sales] ASTON HALL, 1946, July 25-27 [Remaining contents.]

ASTON LODGE, Aston-on-Trent (Derbyshire).

[Sales] ASTON LODGE, 1924 September 22-25 [Furniture, carpets etc.]

ASTON ROWANT HOUSE (Oxfordshire).

[Sales] ASTON ROWANT HOUSE, 1917. November 5-7 [Contents]. (K., F. & R.).

[Sales] LONDON, 1917, November 30 [Portraits, drawings, library from A.R. House]. (K., F. & R.).

ASTWELL CASTLE (Northamptonshire).

GOTCH, J.A. Halls of Northants. p.93. 1936.

ATHELHAMPTON (Dorsetshire).

COOKE, Robert.
— Athelhampton. 11 ed. 8pp. illus. incl. plates (2 col.). 24x18 n.p. privately printed (1974).

COUNTRY LIFE. XIX, 834. 1906.

DELDERFIELD, E.R. West Country houses. II, 9. 1970.

GARNER, T. Domestic architecture. I, p.121. 1911.

HEATH, S. Dorset Manor Houses. 3. 1907.

LATHAM. C. In English Homes. Vol. II, p.33. 1907.

NASH, J. Mansions of England. III, pls. 9, 10. 1841.

OSWALD, A. Country houses of Dorset. p.65. 1959.

ATHERSTONE HALL (Warwickshire).

BURKE, J.B. Visitation of Seats. 2.S. Vol.II, p.129. 1855.*

ATHERTON HALL (Lancashire).

CAMPBELL, C. Vitruvius Britannicus. III, pl.89. 1725.

ATTINGHAM HALL [PARK] (Shropshire).

LONDON: National Trust for Places of Historic Interest or Natural Beauty.
— BROCKLEHURST, C. Attingham Park, Shropshire. 20pp. 4 plates. 18x12 London: Country Life (1949).
Rev. ed. [Bibliogr.] 36pp. Illus. (1 col. on cover) incl. plan and genealog. table. 24x18 [London] 1981.

LONDON: National Trust for Places of Historic Interest or Natural Beauty.
— Catalogue of pictures at Attingham Park. 8pp. 25x18 [London, c.1975.]

ANGUS, W. Seats of the Nobility. pl.52. 1787.

CAMPBELL, C. New Vitruvius Britannicus. II, pls. 25-30. 1808.

COUNTRY LIFE. English Country Houses: Mid Georgian, p.195. 1956.

COUNTRY LIFE. XLIX, 158 plan, 186. 1921.

COUNTRY LIFE. CXVI, 1350. 1954.

JONES. Views of Seats. I. 1829.

LEACH, F. Seats of Shropshire. p.25. 1891.

LEIGHTON, S. Shropshire houses. 10. 1901.

NEALE, J.P. Views of Seats. 2.S. Vol.III. 1826.

REPTON, H. Red Books. III. 1976.

TIPPING, H.A. English Homes. Period VI, Vol.I, p.283. 1926.

WEST, W. Picturesque views of Shropshire. p.127. 1831.

AUBERIES (Essex).

ENGLAND: Beauties of England. I, p.256. 1787.

ESSEX: A new and complete history. II, 139. 1769.

RUSH, J.A. Seats in Essex. p.19. 1897.*

AUBOURN HALL (Lincolnshire).

COUNTRY LIFE. CXXI, 286. 1957.

AUCKLAND CASTLE (Durham).

RAINE, *Rev.* James.
— A brief historical account of the episcopal castle, or, palace of Auckland. Compiled from records in the auditors office at Durham and other authorities. [Bibliogr. notes.] Illus. incl. engr. plates. 32x15 Durham: G. Andrews, 1852.

BUCK, S. & N. Antiquities. I, pl.80. 1774.

COUNTRY LIFE. CLI, 198, 266, 334 [Photocopy]. 1972.

AUDLEY END (Essex).

ADDISON, William.
— Audley End ... Foreword by Lord Braybrooke. [Bibliogr. notes.] 17 (1 col.) plates and genealog. tables (on end-papers). 22x15 London: Dent & Sons, 1953.

BRAYBROOKE, Richard Griffin, *Baron.*
— The history of Audley End. To which are appended notices of the town and parish of Saffron Walden [etc.]. Illus. (cuts), engr. plates incl. title-page and plans, lithogr. maps and genealog. tables. 30x24 London: S. Bentley, 1836.

ESSEX: County Council [Essex Record Office].
— Publications.
XLV. WILLIAMS, J.D. Audley End: the restoration of 1762-1797. [Bibliogr.] 84pp. 17 plates incl. elevations, plan, maps facsimiles and genealog. table. 25x15 1966.

GREAT BRITAIN: Ministry of Works [Ancient Monuments and Historic Buildings].
— O'NEIL, B.H.St. J. Audley End, Essex. 20pp. Illus. incl. plates and plans. 21x14 London, 1950.
Another ed. O'NEIL, B.H. St. J., WALKER, R.J.B. and WATSON, F.J.B. 24pp. 1955.
Another ed. 36pp. Illus. (Some on covers) incl. plans. 1958.

GREAT BRITAIN: Ministry of Works [Ancient Monuments and Historic Buildings].
— WALKER, R.J.B. Audley End, Essex; catalogue of the pictures in the state rooms. [Bibliogr. notes.] 48pp. Folding genealog. table. 21x14 London, 1954.
3 ed. 60pp. Illus. (on cover) and plates incl. folding genealog. table. 1964.
6 ed. 66pp. 1974.

GREAT BRITAIN: Ministry of Public Building and Works [Ancient Monuments and Historic Buildings].
— Audley End Essex. 40pp. Illus. (Some col., some on covers) incl. plans. London, 1965.

GREAT BRITAIN: Department of the Environment [Ancient Monuments and Historic Buildings].
— Audley End, Essex. 40pp. Illus. (Some col., some on covers) incl. plans. London, 1974.

BURKE, J.B. Visitation of Seats. Vol.II, p.86. 1853.*
COUNTRY LIFE. LIX, 872, 916 plan. 1926.
COUNTRY LIFE. LX, 94, 128 plan. 1926.
COUNTRY LIFE. CLX. 104 [Victorian views.] 1976.
CROMWELL, T.K. Excursions in Essex. II, p.133. 1825.
GOTCH, J.A. Architecture of the Renaissance. I, p.46 plan. 1894.
HALL, S.C. Baronial Halls. Vol.I. 1848.
LATHAM, C. In English Homes. Vol.I, p.149. 1904.
MALAN, A.H. Other famous homes. p.173. 1902.
MORRIS, F.O. Views of Seats. Vol.II, p.55. 1880.
MORANT, P. Essex. II, 550 (Insert) 1768.
NASH, J. Mansions of England. II, pls. 1, 2. 1840.
NEALE, J.P. Views of Seats. Vol.I. 1818.
RICHARDSON, C.J. Old English mansions. III. 1845.
RUSH, J.A. Seats in Essex. p.21. 1897.
SHAW, H. Elizabethan architecture. pl.XLVII. [Plaster ceiling] 1839.
TIPPING, H.A. English Homes. Period III, Vol.II, p.239. 1927.
UNITED KINGDOM. Historic houses. 80. 1892.
WATTS, W. Seats of the Nobility. pl.26. 1779.
WHITEMAN, G.W. English country homes. p.71. 1951.

AUDLEY HOUSE, Salisbury (Wiltshire).
ELYARD, S.J. Old Wiltshire homes. p.27. 1894.

AUSTERFIELD MANOR (Yorkshire).
WOOD, G.B. Historic homes of Yorkshire. I. 1957.

AUSTY MANOR (Warwickshire)
[Sales] AUSTY MANOR, 1929, April 30, May 1-3, [Furniture etc.].

AVEBURY MANOR (Wiltshire).
KNOWLES, *Sir* Francis, *Bart.*
— Avebury Manor; the residence of Sir F. and Lady Knowles. 16pp. 4 illus. (on covers) and map. 14x20 (Derby) English Life Publications [*c.* 1955.]
Another ed. Avebury Manor. 20pp. Illus. (some on covers.) 16x19 [*c.* 1973.]
COOKE, R. West Country Houses. p.82. 1957.
COUNTRY LIFE. XLIX, 522, 552, 559 [Furniture]. 1921.
TIPPING, H.A. English Homes. Period III, Vol.I, p.269. 1922.

AVENUE HOUSE, Ampthill (Bedfordshire).
COUNTRY LIFE. LII, 744 plan. 1922.
COUNTRY LIFE. LXXVI, 614. 1934.

AVERHAM PARK (Nottinghamshire).
CAMPBELL, C. Vitruvius Britannicus. IVth. pls. 51, 52. 1739.

AVINGTON PARK (Hampshire).
BURKE, J.B. Visitation of Seats. Vol.II, p.54. 1853.*
HAMPSHIRE: Architectural views. 1830.

AVON TYRRELL (Hampshire).
COUNTRY LIFE. XXVII, 846 plan. 1910.

AXWELL PARK (Durham).
PAINE, J. Plans, elevations. Pt. I, pls. 53-60 plans. 1767.
WATTS, W. Seats of the Nobility. pl. 77. 1779.

AYDON CASTLE (Northumberland).
COUNTRY LIFE. XXXVI, 518 plan. 1914.
TIPPING, H.A. English Homes. Period I, Vol.I, p.101. 1921.

AYNHOE PARK (Northamptonshire).
AYNHOE PARK.
— Aynhoe Park: an illustrated survey of the Northamptonshire home of the Cartwright family. 32pp. Illus. (some col., some on covers) incl. maps (on inside covers). 14x22 Derby: E.L.P. [1953?].
COUNTRY LIFE. CXIV, 42, 122, 202, 1953.
GOTCH, J.A. Halls of Northants. p.93. 1936.
NEALE, J.P. Views of Seats. Vol. III. 1820.

AYNSOME (Lancashire).
BARTLETT, J. Mansions of England and Wales. pl.75. 1853.
TWYCROSS, E. Mansions of England and Wales. Vol.II, p.31. 1847.

BABBINGTON (Somerset).
COUNTRY LIFE. XCIII, 704. 1943.

BACHEGRAIG (Denbighshire).
SPROULE, A. Lost houses of Britain. 42. 1982.
SUMMERSON, J. The Country Seat. 30. 1970.

BACHE HALL (Cheshire).
TWYCROSS, E. Mansions of England and Wales. Vol.I, p.48. 1850.*

BACKFORD HALL (Cheshire).
TWYCROSS, E. Mansions of England and Wales. Vol.I, p.74. 1850.*

BACTON MANOR HOUSE (Suffolk).
SANDON, E. Suffolk houses. 226. 1977.

BADBY HOUSE (Northamptonshire).
BURKE, J.B. Visitation of Seats. 2.S. Vol.II, p.19. 1855.

BADDESLEY CLINTON (Warwickshire).
LONDON: National Trust for Places of Historic Interest or Natural Beauty.
— HAWORTH, J.P. Baddesley Clinton, Warwickshire. [Bibliogr.] 56pp. Illus. (1 col. on cover) incl. plan and genealog. table. 21x14 [London] 1983.
NORRIS, *Rev.* Henry.
— Baddesley Clinton: its manor, church and hall. With some account of the family of Ferrers [etc.]. Plates & genealog. tables. 25x18 London: Art & Book Co., 1897.
BURKE, J.B. Visitation of Seats. Vol.I, p.13. 1852.*
COUNTRY LIFE. XVIII, 942. 1905.
COUNTRY LIFE. LXX, 435 [Furniture]. 1931.
COUNTRY LIFE. LXXI, 408, 434. 1932.
COUNTRY LIFE. CLXIII, 1802, 1866. 1978.
COUNTRY LIFE. CLXVII, 1005. 1980.
GARNER, T. Domestic architecture. I, p.65. 1911.
LATHAM, C. In English Homes. Vol. II, p. 151. 1907.
MOSS, F. Pilgrimages. [III] 236. 1906.
NIVEN, W. Old Warwickshire houses. p.7, pls. 10, 11. 1878.
SMITH, W. History of the County of Warwick. 375. 1830.

BADGEMORE (Oxfordshire).
BURKE, J.B. Visitation of Seats. Vol.I, p.234. 1852.*

BADGER HALL (Shropshire).
BURKE, J.B. Visitation of Seats. Vol.I, p.49. 1852.*

BADGEWORTH MANOR (Gloucestershire).
[Sales] BADGEWORTH MANOR, 1965, July 13 [Furniture and effects].

BADLEY HALL (Suffolk).
SANDON, E. Suffolk houses. 246. 1977.

BADMINTON HOUSE (Gloucestershire).
MANUSCRIPTS (Typewritten). English.
— A catalogue of the paintings in the collection of His Grace the Duke of Beaufort at Badminton. (Copied ... from MS. [*c.*1800] recently purchased by the National Gallery.) 5ff. 37x20 1942.
ATKYNS, R. Glocestershire. p.125. 1768.
BURKE, J.B. Visitation of Seats. 2.S. Vol.I, p.44. 1854.*
COUNTRY LIFE. English Country Houses: Early Georgian. p.161. 1961.
COUNTRY LIFE. XXII, 378. 1907.
COUNTRY LIFE. LXXXVI, 550, 574, 600, 630 [Furniture]. 1939.
COUNTRY LIFE. CXLIII, 800 plan. 1968.
JONES. Views of Seats. II. 1829.
KIP, J. Nouveau théâtre de la Grande Bretagne. I, pls. 9-11. 1715.
LATHAM, C. In English Homes. Vol.III, p.225. 1909.
MORRIS, F.O. Views of Seats. Vol.II, p.75. 1880.
NEALE, J.P. Views of Seats. 2.S. Vol.II. 1825.

BADMONDISFIELD HALL (Suffolk).
SANDON, E. Suffolk houses. 216. 1977.

BADWELL ASH HALL (Suffolk).
SANDON, E. Suffolk houses. 161. 1977.

BAGBOROUGH HOUSE (Somerset).
BURKE, J.B. Visitation of Seats. Vol.II, p.236. 1853.*

BAGGRAVE HALL (Leicestershire).
BURKE, J.B. Visitation of Seats. 2.S. Vol.II, p.134. 1855.*
COUNTRY LIFE. CXI, 1908. 1952.
JONES. Views of Seats. I. 1829.
NICHOLS, J. History of Leicestershire. III, i, 289. 1800.

BAGINGTON HALL (Warwickshire).
BURKE, J.B. Visitation of Seats. 2.S. Vol.II, p.130. 1855.*
SMITH, W. History of the County of Warwick. 139. 1830.

BAGLAN HALL (Glamorganshire).
BURKE, J.B. Visitation of Seats. Vol.II, p.102. 1853.*

BAGNOR MANOR (Berkshire).
COUNTRY LIFE. CLII, 274. 1972.

BAGSHOT PARK (Surrey).
COPPER PLATE MAGAZINE. pl.96. 1778.
MORRIS, F.O. Views of Seats. Vol.VI, p.1. 1880.
PROSSER, G.F. Surrey Seats. p.33. 1828.
SANDBY, P. Select Views. I, pl.66. 1783.

BAGULEY HALL (Cheshire).
ORMEROD, G. Cheshire. I, 552. 1882.

BAILBROOK LODGE (Somerset).
COLLINSON, J. History of Somerset. I, 102. 1791.

BAILY PARK (Sussex).
See HEATHFIELD PARK.

BAKEWELL HALL (Derbyshire).
TILLEY, J. Halls of Derbyshire. I, p.9. 1892.

BALDERSBY PARK (Yorkshire).
CAMPBELL, C. Vitruvius Britannicus. III, pl.46. 1725.
JONES. Views of Seats. I. 1829.
NEALE, J.P. Views of Seats. Vol.V. 1822.
SUMMERSON, J. The Country Seat. 97. 1970.
[Sales] BALDERSBY PARK, 1927, July 4 and following days [Furniture, porcelain etc.]

BALIFFSCOURT (Sussex).
COUNTRY LIFE. CLXVII, 1394. 1980.

BALLS PARK (Hertfordshire).
CHAUNCY, H. Hertfordshire. I. 520. 1826.
COUNTRY LIFE. XXXI, 578 plan. 1912.

BAMBURGH CASTLE (Northumberland).
BAMBURGH CASTLE.
— Guide-book to Bamburgh Castle. 48pp. Illus. (1 on cover) incl. plans. 21x14 (Alnwick, 1974).
Archaeologia Aeliana, XIV, p.223. 1891.
Archaeological Journal, XLVI, p.93. 1889.
BUCK, S. & N. Antiquities. I, pl.214. 1774.
COPPER PLATE MAGAZINE. III, pl.136, 1792-1802.
COUNTRY LIFE. XXIV, 160. 1908.
TIPPING, H.A. English Homes. Period I, Vol.I, p.41. 1921.

BANKFIELD, Bingley (Yorkshire).
YORKSHIRE. Picturesque views. 1885.

BANK HALL (Lancashire).
Bretherton family.
BARTLETT, J. Mansions of England and Wales. pl.2. 1853.
TWYCROSS, E. Mansions of England and Wales. Vol.I, p.66. 1847.

BANK HALL, Near Warrington (Lancashire).
TWYCROSS, E. Mansions of England and Wales. Vol.III, p.35. 1847.*

BANK HOUSE, Wisbech (Cambridgeshire).
COUNTRY LIFE. CI, 1060. 1947.

BANKS HALL (Yorkshire).
[Sales] BANKS HALL, 1965, September 16, 17 [Contents].

BARASET HOUSE (Warwickshire).
BURKE, J.B. Visitation of Seats. Vol.I, p.106. 1852.*

BARDON HALL (Leicestershire).
NICHOLS, J. History of Leicestershire. III, i, 126. 1800.
NICHOLS, J. History of Leicestershire. IV, ii, 804. 1811.
THROSBY, J. Views in Leicestershire. p.221. 1789.

BARFORD HOUSE (Somerset).
COUNTRY LIFE. CLVI. 1354. 1974.

BARHAM COURT, Barham (Kent).
COUNTRY LIFE. XLV, 142 plan. 1919.
COUNTRY LIFE. CL, 816 plan. 1971.
OSWALD, A. Country houses of Kent. 61. 1933.

BARHAM COURT, Teston (Kent).
Formerly Teston House.
CROMWELL, T.K. Excursions in Kent. p.160. 1822.
HASTED, E. Kent. II, 292. 1782.
NEALE, J.P. Views of Seats 2.S. Vol.V. 1829.

BARKBY HALL (Leicestershire).
BURKE, J.B. Visitation of Seats. Vol. I, p.209. 1852.*
NICHOLS, J. History of Leicestershire. III, i, 47. 1800.

BARLASTON HALL (Staffordshire).
COUNTRY LIFE. CXLIII, 975. 1968.

BARLBOROUGH HALL (Derbyshire).
BURKE, J.B. Visitation of Seats. Vol.II, p.216. 1853.*
GOTCH, J.A. Architecture of the Renaissance. I, p.30 plan. 1894.
JONES. Views of Seats. I. 1829.
NEALE, J.P. Views of Seats. Vol.I. 1818.
TILLEY, J. Halls of Derbyshire. III, p.41. 1899.

BARLOW HALL (Lancashire).
MOSS, F. Pilgrimages. [II] 378. 1903.

BARLOW WOODSEATS HALL
(Derbyshire).
See WOODSEATS HALL.

BARNHAM BROOM HALL (Norfolk).
COUNTRY LIFE. CXLI, 402. 1967.
GARRATT, T. Halls of Norfolk. pls. 5-7. 1890.

BARNHAM HOUSE (Sussex).
ELWES, D.G.C. Mansions of Western Sussex. 24. 1876.

BARNINGHAM HALL (Norfolk).
BIRBECK, G. Old Norfolk houses. 13. 1908.
COUNTRY LIFE. XXVII, 198. 1910.
GARRATT, T. Halls of Norfolk. pl.9. 1890.
REPTON, H. Fragments on landscape gardening. p.30 plan.
1816.

BARNSLEY PARK (Gloucestershire).
COOKE, R. West Country Houses. p.127. 1957.
COUNTRY LIFE. English Country Houses: Early Georgian.
p.48. 1955.
COUNTRY LIFE. XXIII, 630. 1908.
COUNTRY LIFE. CXVI, 720, 806 plan. 1954.
DELDERFIELD, E.R. West Country houses. III, 11. 1973.
LATHAM, C. In English Homes. Vol. III, p.345. 1909.
TIPPING, H.A. English Homes. Period V, Vol.I, p.229. 1921.

BARNSTON MANOR (Dorsetshire).
OSWALD, A. Country houses of Dorset. p.48. 1959.

BARNWELL MANOR (Northamptonshire).
COUNTRY LIFE. CXXVI, 238, 298. 1959.

BARON HILL (Anglesey).
BURKE, J.B. Visitation of Seats. Vol.I, p.243. 1852.*
NICHOLAS, T. Counties of Wales. I, p.6. 1872.
WATTS, W. Seats of the Nobility. pl.11. 1779.

BARONS, The. Reigate (Surrey).
COUNTRY LIFE. LXXV, 473. 1934.

BARRINGTON COURT (Somerset).
LONDON: National Trust for Places of Historic Interest or
Natural Beauty.
— Barrington Court. 14pp. 4 plates and plan. 18x12 London
[c.1945].
Rev. ed. Barrington Court, Somerset.[Bibliogr.] 20pp. Illus. (1
on cover) incl. plates and plan. 22x14 [London] 1982.
COOKE, R. West Country Houses. p.52. 1957.
COUNTRY LIFE. XVI, 414. 1904.
COUNTRY LIFE. LXIII, 370 plan, 404 plan. 1928.

DELDERFIELD, E.R. West Country houses. II, 15. 1970.
GARNER, T. Domestic architecture. I, p.118 plan. 1911.
RICHARDSON, C.J. Old English mansions. I, pl.12. 1841.
TIPPING, H.A. English Homes. Period I & II, Vol.II, p.113.
1937.

BARRINGTON HALL (Cambridgeshire).
COUNTRY LIFE. LVII, 839 plan. 1925.

BARRINGTON HALL (Essex).
CROMWELL, T.K. Excursions in Essex. II, p.87. 1825.
ENGLAND: Beauties of England. I, p.248. 1787.
ESSEX: A new and complete history. IV, 113. 1771.
RUSH, J.A. Seats in Essex. p.30. 1897.*

BARRINGTON MANOR (Gloucestershire).
ATKYNS, R. Glostershire. p.131. 1768.

BARRINGTON PARK (Gloucestershire).
COPPER PLATE MAGAZINE. pl.57. 1778.
RUDDER, S. Gloucestershire. 262. 1779.
SANDBY, P. Select Views. I, pl.15. 1783.

BARROCK PARK (Cumberland).
BURKE, J.B. Visitation of Seats. Vol.I, p.85. 1852.*

BARROW COURT (Somerset).
COLLINSON, J. History of Somerset. II, 308. 1791.
COOKE, R. West Country Houses. p.62. 1957.

BARROW GREEN HOUSE, Oxted
(Surrey).
BURKE, J.B. Visitation of Seats. Vol.I, p.106. 1852.*

BARROW HALL (Lincolnshire).
BURKE, J.B. Visitation of Seats. Vol.II, p.219. 1853.*

BARSHAM HALL (Suffolk).
CROMWELL, T.K. Excursions in Suffolk. II, p.106. 1819.

BARTON (Lancashire).
BURKE, J.B. Visitation of Seats. Vol.I, p.120. 1852.*
TWYCROSS, E. Mansions of England and Wales. Vol.II, p.49.
1847.*

BARTON BLOUNT (Derbyshire).
TILLEY, J. Halls of Derbyshire. II, p.3. 1893.

BARTON HALL (Suffolk).
BURKE, J.B. Visitation of Seats. 2.S. Vol.I, p.105. 1854.*
CROMWELL, T.K. Excursions in Suffolk. I, p.100. 1818.

BARTON KIRKE HALL (Westmorland).
CUMBERLAND: C. & W. A. & A.S. Extra Series, VIII, 69. 1892.

BARTON SEAGRAVE HALL (Northamptonshire).
BRIDGES, J. Northamptonshire. II, 218. 1791.
GOTCH, J.A. Squires' Homes. 15. 1939.

BASILDON PARK (Berkshire).
LONDON: National Trust for Places of Historic Interest or Natural Beauty.
— JACKSON-STOPS, G. Basildon Park, Berkshire. [Bibliogr.] 48pp. Illus. (1 col. on cover) incl. plan. 25x18 [London] 1982.
ANGUS, W. Seats of the Nobility. pl.49. 1787.
CAMPBELL, C. New Vitruvius Britannicus. I, pls. 12-14. 1802.
COPPER PLATE MAGAZINE. II, pl.60. 1792-1802.
COUNTRY LIFE. CLXI. 1158, 1227, 1298. 1977.
ENGLAND: Picturesque Views. p.73. 1786-88.
JONES. Views of Seats. I. 1829.
NEALE, J.P. Views of Seats. 2.S. Vol.II. 1825.
[Exhibitions]
LONDON: Grosvenor Gallery. Pictures from Basildon Park [etc.]. 1914-15.
[Sales] BASILDON PARK, 1920 October 26 and following days [Furniture, pictures etc.].
[Sales] READING, 1929, December 13 [Estate].

BASSET DOWN HOUSE (Wiltshire).
ARNOLD-FORSTER, Mary.
— Basset Down: an old country house ... Foreword by C. Morgan. Illus. incl. folding genealog. table. 25x18 London: Country Life, [1949].
COUNTRY LIFE. LXIV, 531 [Furniture]. 1928.

BASSETSBURY, High Wycombe (Buckinghamshire).
COUNTRY LIFE. LXXIV, 338, 362. 1933.

BAST'S, (Grundisburgh (Suffolk).
COUNTRY LIFE. LII, 453 plan. 1922.
SANDON, E. Suffolk houses. 320. 1977.

BATCHACRE HALL (Staffordshire).
SHAW, S. Staffordshire. II, pl.23. Reprint 1976.

BATEMAN'S (Sussex).
DENNY, *Rev. Sir* Henry Lyttelton Lyster, *Bart.*
— A Kipling shrine. 8pp. 2 illus. 22x14 Burwash, 1947. Reprinted in part from: Journal of the Kipling Society.
LONDON: National Trust for Places of Historic Interest or Natural Beauty.
— Bateman's, Sussex. 12pp. 2 illus. 18x12 London: Country Life, 1956.

New ed. Bateman's, Burwash, Sussex. 16pp. Illus. (some on covers) incl. map. 18x12 London, 1965.
COUNTRY LIFE. XXIV, 224. 1908.
COUNTRY LIFE. LXXIX, 90. 1936.
TIPPING, H.A. English Homes. Early Renaissance, p.285. 1912.
TIPPING, H.A. English Homes. Period III, Vol.II, p.203. 1927.

BATSFORD PARK (Gloucestershire).
ATKYNS, R. Glocestershire. p.133. 1768.
NEALE, J.P. Views of Seats. 2.S. Vol.I. 1824.
RUDDER, S. Gloucestershire. 266. 1779.
[Sales] BATSFORD PARK, 1919, April 30, May 1, 2 [Portion of contents].

BATTLE ABBEY (Sussex).
BATTLE ABBEY.
— The hand-book to Battle Abbey: to which is added a description of Battle Church, its monuments &c. By the author of Gleanings respecting Battle and its Abbey [i.e. — Vidler]. (Description of pictures). 4 ed. 70pp. Illus. incl. plates (1 folding). 17x11 Battle: Ticehurst [1850?]
Another ed. the hand-book to Battle and its Abbey [etc.]. 84pp. Illus. incl. plates 18x11 [1860].
C., L.W.C.
— A guide to Battle Abbey. 86pp. 3 plates and folding plan. 18x12 Battle: Ticehurst Brothers [c.1890].
WALCOTT, *Rev.* Mackenzie Edward Charles.
— Battle Abbey; with notices of the parish church and town. vi, 90pp. Illus. incl. plates (some photographs) and folding plan. 18x12 Battle: Ticehurst, 1866.
With MS. note on fly leaf and extra plates pasted on to endpapers.
BUCK, S. & N. Antiquities. II, pl.287. 1774.
BURKE, J.B. Visitation of Seats. 2.S. Vol.I., p.180. 1854.*
COUNTRY LIFE. II, 496. 1897.
MALAN, A.H. Famous homes. p.197. 1902.
NEALE, J.P. Views of Seats. 2.S. Vol.IV. 1828.

BATTLESDEN PARK (Bedfordshire).
NEALE, J.P. Views of Seats. Vol.I. 1818.

BAWDSEY MANOR (Suffolk).
SANDON, E. Suffolk houses. 228. 1977.

BAYFORDBURY (Hertfordshire).
BURKE, J.B. Visitation of Seats. 2.S. Vol.I, p.49. 1854.*
COUNTRY LIFE. LVII, 92, 124. 1925.
TIPPING, H.A. English Homes. Period VI, Vol.I, p.375. 1926.

BAYHAM ABBEY (Kent).
MANUSCRIPTS. English.
— HOLYOKE, M. Condition of pictures at Bayham Abbey. 8ff. (1 blank.) 20.5x16.5 London. November 1873.
REPTON, H. Observations on landscape gardening. 208. 1803.

BAYLHAM HALL (Suffolk).
SANDON, E. Suffolk houses. 163. 1977.

BAYONS MANOR (Lincolnshire).
BURKE, J.B. Visitation of Seats. Vol.I, p.236. 1852.
COUNTRY LIFE. CXXVII, 430. 1960.

BEACHBOROUGH (Kent).
BADESLADE, T. Seats in Kent. pl.2. 1750.
GREENWOOD, C. Kent. 305. 1838.
HARRIS, J. History of Kent. p.216. 1719.
HASTED, E. Kent. III, 394. 1790.

BEACH HOUSE, Worthing (Sussex).
COUNTRY LIFE. XLIX, 126 plan. 1921.

BEAMHURST HALL (Staffordshire).
BURKE, J.B. Visitation of Seats. Vol.I, p.202. 1852.*

BEARD HALL (Derbyshire).
TILLEY, J. Halls of Derbyshire. I, p.163. 1892.

BEAR PLACE (Berkshire).
COPPER PLATE MAGAZINE. III, pl.110. 1792-1802.
ENGLAND: Picturesque Views. p.68. 1786-88.

BEARWOOD (Berkshire).
COUNTRY LIFE. CXLIV, 964, 1060 plan. 1968.
MORRIS, F.O. Views of Seats. Vol.VI, p.29. 1880.

BEAUCHIEF ABBEY HALL (Derbyshire).
BURKE, J.B. Visitation of Seats. 2.S. Vol.II, p.122. 1855.*
TILLEY, J. Halls of Derbyshire. III, p.47. 1899.

BEAUDESERT (Staffordshire).
BURKE, J.B. Visitation of Seats. 2.S. Vol.II, p.97. 1855.*
COUNTRY LIFE. XLVI, 658, 688. 1919.
JONES. Views of Seats. I. 1829.
MORRIS, F.O. Views of Seats. Vol.II, p.3. 1880.
NEALE, J.P. Views of Seats. Vol.IV. 1821.
NIVEN, W. Old Staffordshire houses. p.12, pls. 9, 10. 1882.
PLOT, R. Staffordshire. 126. 1686.
REPTON, H. Fragments on landscape gardening. p.40. 1816.
SHAW, S. Staffordshire. I, 221, 222. 1798.
TIPPING, H.A. English Homes, Period III, Vol.I, p.92. 1922.

BEAUFORT (Sussex).
BURKE, J.B. Visitation of Seats. Vol.II, p.93. 1853.*

BEAUFRONT CASTLE (Northumberland).
COUNTRY LIFE. CLIX, 286, 342. 1976.

BEAULIEU PALACE HOUSE (Hampshire).
WIDNELL, H.E.R.
— Beaulieu: the Abbey, Palace House and Buckler's Hard. [Bibliogr.] 40pp. Illus. (1 col. on cover.) incl. plan, maps (on endpaper) and genealog. table. 18x12 [Beaulieu] by Lord Montagu, 1952.
GROVE, R.A. Seats in the neighbourhood of Lymington. 1832.

BEAUMANOR PARK (Leicestershire).
BROOKMAN, Margot.
— The Woodhouse echo: a short history and account of the village of Old Woodhouse, Leicestershire; and of the Hall of Beaumanor, seat of the Herricks. [Bibliogr.] 38pp. Illus. (2 on cover) incl. map and genealog. table. 21x15 Loughborough: Brook House, 1979.
BURKE, J.B. Visitation of Seats. Vol.I, p.4. 1852.
NICHOLS, J. History of Leicestershire. III, i, 136. 1800.
NICHOLS, J. History of Leicestershire. III, ii, pl. CLVII, 1131. 1804.
THROSBY, J. Views in Leicestershire. p.227. 1789.

BEAUMONT LODGE (Berkshire).
JONES. Views of Seats. I. 1829.
NEALE, J.P. Views of Seats. Vol.I. 1818.
SUMMERSON, J. The Country Seat. 181. 1970.

BEAUPRÉ CASTLE (Glamorganshire).
BURKE, J.B. Visitation of Seats. 2.S. Vol.I, p.102. 1854.*

BEAUPRÉ HALL (Norfolk).
COUNTRY LIFE. LIV, 754. 1923.

BEAUVALE (Nottinghamshire).
SUMMERSON, J. The Country Seat. 262 plan. 1970.

BECCA HALL (Yorkshire).
BURKE, J.B. Visitation of Seats. Vol. II, p.249. 1853.*

BECKENHAM PLACE (Kent).
BURKE, J.B. Visitation of Seats. 2.S. Vol.II, p.110. 1855.*
HASTED, E. Kent. I, 83. 1778.
NEALE, J.P. Views of Seats. Vol.II. 1819.

BECKFORD HALL (Worcestershire).
JONES. Views of Seats. II. 1829.
NEALE, J.P. Views of Seats. Vol.II. 1819.

BECKLEY PARK (Oxfordshire).
COUNTRY LIFE. LXV, 400 plan. 1929.

BEDALE HALL (Yorkshire).
COUNTRY LIFE. CXLIX, 592. 1971.

BEDDINGTON HOUSE (Surrey).
BRAYLEY, E.W. History of Surrey. IV, 68*. 1841.

BEDDINGTON PLACE [PARK] (Surrey).
BRAYLEY, E.W. History of Surrey. IV, 66*. 1841.
BURKE, J.B. Visitation of Seats. 2.S. Vol.I, p.37. 1854.*
CAMPBELL, C. Vitruvius Britannicus. II, pls. 43-45. 1717.
NASH, J. Mansions of England. I, pl.13. 1839.
PROSSER, G.F. Surrey Seats. p.51. 1828.
[Sales] BEDDINGTON PARK, 1852, June 26-29 [Furniture and effects].

BEDFORDS (Essex).
NEALE, J.P. Views of Seats. Vol.I. 1818.

BEDGEBURY (Kent).
[Sales] BEDGEBURY, 1919, May 12 and following days [Contents].

BEDSTONE COURT (Shropshire).
LEIGHTON, S. Shropshire houses. 46. 1901.

BEDSTONE COURT (Yorkshire).
YORKSHIRE. Picturesque views. 1885.

BEDWELL PARK (Hertfordshire)
CHAUNCY, H. Hertfordshire.I, 544. 1826.

BEDWORTH HOSPITAL (Warwickshire).
BURKE, J.B. Visitation of Seats. Vol.II, p.215. 1853.*

BEECHLAND (Sussex).
BURKE, J.B. Visitation of Seats. Vol.II, p.38. 1853.*

BEECHWOOD, Lavington (Sussex).
COUNTRY LIFE. CVI, 538. 1949.

BEECHWOOD PARK (Hertfordshire).
NEALE, J.P. Views of Seats. Vol.II. 1819.

BEELEIGH ABBEY (Essex).
COUNTRY LIFE. LII, 406 plan. 1922.

BEELEY HALL (Derbyshire).
TILLEY, J. Halls of Derbyshire. I, p.59. 1892.

BEESTHORPE HALL (Nottinghamshire).
THOROTON, R. Nottinghamshire. III, 142. 1797.

BEESTON CASTLE (Cheshire).
TWYCROSS, E. Mansions of England and Wales. Vol.I, p.91. 1850.

BEESTON HALL, Beeston St. Lawrence (Norfolk).
BURKE, J.B. Visitation of Seats. 2.S. Vol.II, p.115. 1855.*
COUNTRY LIFE. CLXXIII, 270. 1983.
NEALE, J.P. Views of Seats. Vol.III. 1820.
WATTS, W. Seats of the Nobility. pl.36. 1779.

BEETHAM HALL (Westmorland).
CUMBERLAND: C.&W. A.&A. S. Extra Series VIII, 211. 1892.

BEILBY GRANGE (Yorkshire).
See WETHERBY GRANGE.

BELCHAMP HALL (Essex).
COUNTRY LIFE. CXXVI, 1206, 1258. 1959.
RUSH, J.R. Seats in Essex. p.32. 1897.

BELCOMBE COURT (Wiltshire).
COUNTRY LIFE. CVIII, 2146. 1950.
[Sales] BELCOMBE COURT, 1964, October 7, 8 [Furniture, silver etc.].

BELFIELD (Dorsetshire).
OSWALD, A. Country houses of Dorset. p.170. 1959.

BELFORD HALL (Northumberland).
PAINE, J. Plans, elevations. Pt.I, pls.33, 34 [Plan], 35, 36. 1767.

BELHUS (Essex.)
COUNTRY LIFE. XLVII, 656, 690. 1921.
COUNTRY LIFE. LIII, 600 [Heraldic Glass]. 1923.
CROMWELL, T.K. Excursions in Essex. I, p.183. 1825.
MORANT, P. Essex. I, 78. 1768.
NEALE, J.P. Views of seats. Vol.I. 1818.
RUSH, J.A. Seats in Essex. p.34. 1897.*
[Sales] BELHUS, 1923, May 8-11, 14-17 [Contents].

BELLAMOUR HALL (Staffordshire).
BURKE, J.B. Visitation of Seats. Vol.I, p.266. 1852.*

BELLAPORT (Shropshire).
SHROPSHIRE. Castles & Old Mansions. 38. 1868.

BELLE ISLE (Westmorland).
COUNTRY LIFE. LXXXVIII, 98, 120 plan. 1940.

BELLEVUE, Lympne (Kent).
COUNTRY LIFE. LIII, 783. 1923.

BELLE VUE, Halifax (Yorkshire).
YORKSHIRE. Picturesque views. 1885.

BELL HALL (Yorkshire).
COUNTRY LIFE. LI. 820. 1922.

BELMONT HALL (Cheshire).
NEALE, J.P. Views of Seats. 2.S. Vol.V. 1829.

TWYCROSS, E. Mansions of England and Wales. Vol.II, p.69. 1850.

BELMONT PARK (Kent).
COUNTRY LIFE. CXVII, 246 plan, 318. 1955.

WHITEMAN, G.W. English country homes. p.149. 1951.

BELSAY CASTLE (Northumberland).
COUNTRY LIFE. English Country Houses: Late Georgian. p.83. 1958.

COUNTRY LIFE. LXXXVIII, 300. 1940.

JONES. Views of Seats. I. 1829.

NEALE, J.P. Views of Seats. Vol. III. 1820.

BELSAY HOUSE (Northumberland).
COUNTRY LIFE. CXXV, 724 plan. 1959.

BELSTEAD HALL (Essex).
ESSEX: A new and complete history. I, 133. 1769.

BELSWARDINE HALL (Shropshire).
LEACH, F. Seats of Shropshire. p.377. 1891.

BELTON HOUSE (Lincolnshire).
BROWNLOW, Peregrine Francis Adelbert Cust, *Baron.*
— The history and treasures of Belton House, Grantham, Lincolnshire. 24pp. Illus. (few col., some on covers.) incl. map. 23x18 (London: Pitkin Pictorials) [c.1960].
   One of the series: PRIDE of Britain.
   With Additional notes for the use of visitors to Belton House. 4pp. inserted.

ANGUS, W. Seats of the Nobility. pl.39. 1787.

CAMPBELL, C. Vitruvius Britannicus. II, pls.37, 38. 1717.

CAMPBELL, C. Vitruvius Britannicus. III, pls. 69, 70. 1725.

CAMPBELL, C. Vitruvius Britannicus. IVth. pls.86-89. 1739.

COUNTRY LIFE. English Country Houses: Caroline. p.193. 1966.

COUNTRY LIFE. XIV, 614. 1903.

COUNTRY LIFE. XXX, 308 plan, 316 [Furniture], 382 [Furniture]. 1911.

COUNTRY LIFE. LXV, 311 [Furniture]. 1929.

COUNTRY LIFE. CXXXVI, 562, 620, 700. 1964.

JONES. Views of Seats. I. 1829.

LATHAM, C. In English Homes. Vol.I, p.1. 1904.

LINCOLNSHIRE. A selection of views. 55. 1805.

NEALE, J.P. Views of Seats. Vol.II. 1819.

NICOLSON, N. Great Houses of Britain. p.146. 1965.

TIPPING, H.A. English Homes. Period IV, Vol.I, p.205. 1920.

BELVEDERE (Kent).
BURKE, J.B. Visitation of Seats. 2.S. Vol.II, p.137. 1855.*

COPPER PLATE MAGAZINE. II, pl.56. 1792-1802.

ENGLAND: Beauties of England. I, p.390. 1787.

ENGLAND: Picturesque Views. p.12. 1786-88.

ENGLISH CONNOISSEUR. I, 12.1766.*

HASTED, E. Kent. I, 198. 1778.

BELVOIR CASTLE (Leicestershire).
ELLER, *Rev.* Irvin.
— The history of Belvoir Castle, from the Norman Conquest to the nineteenth century: accompanied by a description ... and notices of the paintings, tapestry, statuary, &c., with which it is enriched. Plates incl. title-page, plans and folding genealog. table. 22x14 London: R. Tyas; Grantham: S.Ridge, 1841.

MANNERS, *Lady* Victoria Alexandra Elizabeth Dorothy.
— Collection of miniatures at Belvoir Castle. 18pp. 31x24 Grantham: privately printed, 1913.
Title on cover.

RUTLAND, Charles John Robert Manners, *Duke of.*
— Belvoir Castle; an illustrated survey of the historic Leicestershire home of the Manners family. History and description of contents by the Duke of R. 32pp. Illus. (some col., some on covers) incl. maps. 14x21 Derby: E.L.P. [c.1955.].

RUTLAND, Charles John Robert Manners, *Duke of.*
— Belvoir Castle; the Leicestershire home of the Dukes of Rutland. 32pp. Illus. (some col., some on covers) incl. genealog. table. 23x18 (Derby: E.L.P., 1969).
Another ed. (1974).

BUCK, S.&N. Antiquities. I, pls. 158, 159. 1774.

BURKE, J.B. Visitation of Seats. Vol.II, p.61. 1853.*

CAMPBELL, C. Vitruvius Britannicus. IVth. pls.47-50. 1739.

COUNTRY LIFE. English Country Houses: Late Georgian. p.122. 1958.

COUNTRY LIFE. XCI. 851 [Plate], 1036 [Plate], 1130 [Plate]. 1942.

COUNTRY LIFE. CXX, 1284, 1402 plan, 1456, 1500. 1956.

ENGLAND: Beauties of England. I, p.445. 1787.

JONES. Views of Seats. I. 1829.

LINCOLNSHIRE. A selection of views. 53. 1805.

MALAN, A.H. Famous homes. p.1. 1902.

MORRIS, F.O. Views of Seats. Vol.II, p.5. 1880.

NEALE, J.P. Views of Seats. Vol.II. 1819.

NICHOLS, J. History of Leicestershire. II, i, 22 [List of pictures]. 1795.

NOBLE, T. Counties of Chester ... Lincoln. p.45. 1836.

THROSBY, J. Views in Leicestershire, p.104. 1789.

UNITED KINGDOM. Historic houses. 226. 1892.

BENACRE HALL (Suffolk).

CROMWELL, T.K. Excursions in Suffolk. II, p.130. 1819.

DAVY, H. Seats in Suffolk. pl.19. 1827.

BENACRE MANOR (Wiltshire).

COUNTRY LIFE. LXXXII, 578. 1937.

BENHALL LODGE (Suffolk).

DAVY, H. Seats in Suffolk. pl.10. 1827.

BENHAM PARK (Berkshire).

COPPER PLATE MAGAZINE. V, pl.218. 1792-1802.

ROBERTSON, A. Great Road. I, p.152. 1792.

BENINGBROUGH HALL (Yorkshire).

LONDON: National Trust for Places of Historic Interest or Natural Beauty.
— LEES-MILNE, J. Beningbrough Hall, Yorkshire. 16pp. Illus. (1 on cover) incl. plate and plan. 18x12 London: Country Life, 1961.
Another ed. 18pp. 1966.

BURKE, J.B. Visitation of Seats. Vol.I, p.3. 1852.*

COUNTRY LIFE. English Country Houses: Baroque. p.243. 1970.

COUNTRY LIFE. XX, 342. 1906.

COUNTRY LIFE. LXII, 772, 820. 1927.

COUNTRY LIFE. CLXX, 1950, 2098, 2170 plan. 1981.

LATHAM, C. In English Homes. Vol.II, p.377. 1907.

MORRIS, F.O. Views of Seats. Vol.V, p.7. 1880.

TIPPING, H.A. English Homes. Period IV, Vol.II, p.221. 1928.

[Sales] BENINGBROUGH HALL, 1958, June 10-13 [Contents].

BENTCLIFFE HOUSE (Lancashire).

BARTLETT, J. Mansions of England and Wales. pl.159. 1853.

TWYCROSS, E. Mansions of England and Wales. Vol.III, p.99. 1847.

BENTHALL HALL (Shropshire).

LONDON: National Trust for Places of Historic Interest or Natural Beauty.
— Benthall Hall, Shropshire. 20pp. Illus. (on cover) and 4 plates. 18x12 London: Country Life, 1965.
New ed. BENTHALL, *Sir* P. [Bibliogr.] 28pp. Illus. (1 col. on cover) incl. plates. 21x14 [London] 1983.

COUNTRY LIFE. XLI, 664. 1917.

HALL, S.C. Baronial Halls. Vol.II. 1848.

LEACH, F. Seats of Shropshire. p.376. 1891.

LEIGHTON, S. Shropshire houses. 48. 1901.

SHROPSHIRE. Castles & Old Mansions. 32. 1868.

TIPPING, H.A. English Homes. Period III, Vol.I, p.147. 1922.

BENTLEY HALL, Fenny Bentley (Derbyshire).

TILLEY, J. Halls of Derbyshire. II, p.219. 1893.

BENTLEY HALL (Staffordshire).

PLOT, R. Staffordshire. 308. 1686.

SHAW, S. Staffordshire. I, 81. 1798.

BENTLEY HALL (Suffolk).

SANDON E. Suffolk houses. 231. 1977.

BENTWORTH HALL (Hampshire).

BURKE, J.B. Visitation of Seats. 2.S. Vol.II, p.28. 1855.*

BENWELL TOWER (Northumberland).

KNOWLES, William Henry.
— Benwell Tower, Newcastle. [A paper] Read on the 27th April, 1922. [Bibliogr. notes.] 10pp. Illus. incl. plate. 22x17 [Newcastle-upon-Tyne] 1922.
Also in: NEWCASTLE-UPON-TYNE: Society of Antiquaries. Archaeologia Aeliana [etc.] 3.S. XIX. 89.

BERECHURCH HALL (Essex).

RUSH, J.A. Seats in Essex. p.37. 1897.

BERKELEY CASTLE (Gloucestershire).

COOKE, James Herbert.
— A hand-book for visitors to Berkeley, its castle and church, with a short account of the Berkeley family. 3 ed. 36pp. Illus. incl. plan. 18x12 Berkeley: Sinderby [1881].

PETER, Francis.
— Berkeley Castle: an illustrated survey [etc.]. 32pp. Illus. (some col., some on covers) incl. maps (on inside covers). 14x22 Derby: E.L.P. [1956?].

SACKVILLE-WEST, V.
— Berkeley Castle: an illustrated survey [etc.]. 36pp. Illus. (some col., some on covers) incl. maps (on inside covers). 14x22 Derby: E.L.P. [c.1960].

ATKYNS, R. Glocestershire. p.136. 1768.

BUCK, S.&N. Antiquities. I, pl.97. 1774.

COOKE, R. West Country Houses. p.15. 1957.

COUNTRY LIFE. XL. 126 plan, 154. 1916.

COUNTRY LIFE. LXXI. 626 plan, 668, 694. 1932.

COUNTRY LIFE. LXXIII. 126 [Furniture]. 1933.

COUNTRY LIFE. CXVIII. 1430. 1955.

DELDERFIELD, E.R. West Country houses. III, 19. 1973.

ENGLAND: Beauties of England. I, p.288. 1787.

HALL, S.C. Baronial Halls. Vol.I. 1848.

JONES. Views of Seats. II. 1829.

MORRIS, F.O. Views of Seats. Vol.VI, p.79. 1880.

NEALE, J.P. Views of Seats. Vol.II. 1819.

RUDDER, S. Gloucestershire. 270. 1779.

UNITED KINGDOM. Historic houses. 157. 1892.

BERKHAMSTED PLACE (Hertfordshire).
CHAUNCY, H. Hertfordshire. II, 530. 1826.

BERMERSIDE (Yorkshire).
YORKSHIRE. Picturesque views. 1885.

BERRINGTON HALL (Herefordshire).
LONDON: National Trust for Places of Historic Interest or Natural Beauty.
— Berrington Hall, Herefordshire. 20pp. Illus. (1 on cover) incl. 8 plates and plan. 22x14 [London, *c.* 1973.]

COUNTRY LIFE. English Country Houses: Mid Georgian. p.184. 1956.

COUNTRY LIFE. CXVI. 1952 plan, 2102, 2182 plan. 1954.

BERRY HALL (Norfolk).
COUNTRY LIFE. LXIX. 733. 1931.

BERRY HILL (Nottinghamshire).
BURKE, J.B. Visitation of Seats. 2.S. Vol.I, p.245. 1854.

BERTIE PLACE (Kent).
ENGLAND: Picturesque Views. p.30. 1786-88.

BERWICK HALL (Shropshire).
LEACH, F. Seats of Shropshire. p.1. 1891.

LEIGHTON, S. Shropshire houses. 15. 1901.

BERWICK MAVISON (Shropshire)
SHROPSHIRE. Castles & Old Mansions. 41. 1868.

BERWICK PLACE (Essex.).
BURKE, J.B. Visitation of Seats. 2.S. Vol.I, p.68. 1854.*

BESFORD COURT (Worcestershire).
NEWSOME, Thomas Aldhelm.
— The story of Besford Court. 36pp. 7 plates. 18x13 Birmingham: Herald Press, 1927.

BESSBOROUGH HOUSE, Roehampton (Surrey).
See MANRESA HOUSE.

BESSELSLEIGH (Berkshire).
BURKE, J.B. Visitation of Seats. Vol.I, p.117. 1852.*

BESTWOOD LODGE (Nottinghamshire).
COUNTRY LIFE. CXLVIII. 1282. 1970.

MORRIS, F.O. Views of Seats. Vol.III, p.61. 1880.

BESWICK HALL (Yorkshire).
WHEATER, W. Mansions of Yorkshire. p.40. 1888.

BETCHWORTH CASTLE (Surrey).
BUCK, S.&N. Antiquities. II, pl.277. 1774.

NEALE, J.P. Views of Seats. Vol.IV. 1821.

PROSSER, G.F. Surrey Seats. p.19. 1828.

BETCHWORTH HOUSE (Surrey).
PROSSER, G.F. Surrey Seats. p.93. 1828.

BETTISCOMBE (Dorsetshire).
OSWALD, A. Country houses of Dorset. p.170. 1959.

BETTISFIELD (Flintshire).
BURKE, J.B. Visitation of Seats. Vol.II, p.67. 1853.*

BEVERE HOUSE (Worcestershire).
NASH, T.R. Worcestershire. I, Title-page. 1781.

BEVERSTON CASTLE (Gloucestershire).
COUNTRY LIFE. XCV. 288, 332. 1944.

HEARNE, T. Antiquities. I, pl.4. 1807.

HODGES, E. Ancient English homes. 46. 1895.

BEWLEY CASTLE (Westmorland).
CUMBERLAND: C.&W. A.&A.S. Extra Series, VIII, 119. 1892.

BEWSEY HALL (Lancashire).
BURKE, J.B. Visitation of Seats. Vol.II, p.75. 1853.*

TWYCROSS, E. Mansions of England and Wales. Vol.III, p.21. 1847.*

BIBURY COURT (Gloucestershire).
COUNTRY LIFE, XXXII. 324. 1912.
RUDDER, S. Gloucestershire. 284. 1779.

BICKLEIGH CASTLE (Devonshire).
BICKLEIGH CASTLE.
—Bickleigh Castle. 12pp. Illus. incl. cover. 21x15 (Stafford) privately printed [*c.* 1975.]
Title on cover.
COUNTRY LIFE. LXXXV, 416, 442. 1939.

BICKLEY HALL (Kent).
NEALE, J.P. Views of Seats. Vol.II. 1819.

BICTON HOUSE (Devonshire).
BRITTON, J. Devonshire illustrated. 100. 1832.
BURKE, J.B. Visitation of Seats. 2.S. Vol.II, p.168. 1855.*
COPPER PLATE MAGAZINE. V, pl.210. 1792-1802.
DELDERFIELD, E.R. West Country houses. I, 11. 1968.
[Sales] LONDON, 1950, July 19 [Paintings from B.H.].

BIDDESDEN HOUSE (Wiltshire).
COUNTRY LIFE. English Country Houses: Baroque. p.213. 1970.
COUNTRY LIFE. XLV, 782. 1919.
COUNTRY LIFE. LXXXIII, 352, 376. 1938.

BIDDESTONE MANOR (Wiltshire).
COUNTRY LIFE. XVII, 666. 1905.

BIDDICK HALL (Durham).
COUNTRY LIFE. CXXXIX, 1016, 1082. 1966.

BIDDLESDEN HOUSE (Buckinghamshire).
BURKE, J.B. Visitation of Seats. Vol.I, p.30. 1852.*

BIDDULPH HALL (Staffordshire).
NIVEN, W. Old Staffordshire houses. p.6, pl.5. 1882.

BIDFORD GRANGE (Warwickshire).
HODGES, E. Ancient English homes. 244. 1895.

BIGGIN HALL (Northamptonshire).
COUNTRY LIFE. CXVI, 1758, 1852. 1954.
GOTCH, J.A. Squires' Homes. 9. 1939.

BIGLAND HALL (Lancashire).
BARTLETT, J. Mansions of England and Wales. pl.63. 1853.
TWYCROSS, E. Mansions of England and Wales. Vol.II, p.20. 1847.

BIGNOR PARK (Sussex).
COUNTRY LIFE. CXIX, 860, 924. 1956.

BILLESLEY MANOR [HALL] (Warwickshire).
BILLESLEY MANOR.
— (A genuine Tudor residence: Billesley Manor, Alcester, Warwickshire.) An interesting historical estate of exceptional architectural merit [etc.]. 20pp. 12 illus. (1 on cover). 31x24
London: Collins & Collins [1923].
COUNTRY LIFE. LXII, 56. 1927.
[Sales] BILLESLEY HALL, 1962, December 10-13 [Contents].

BILLINGBEAR (Berkshire).
HAVELL, R. Views of Noblemen's Seats. 1823.

BILLING HALL (Northamptonshire).
BURKE, J.B. Visitation of Seats. Vol.II, p.229. 1853.*

BILTON GRANGE (Warwickshire).
BURKE, J.B. Visitation of Seats. Vol.II, p.157. 1853.

BILTON HALL (Warwickshire).
KINGSBURY, Dorothy Grace.
— Bilton Hall: its history and literary association. Being a short collection of notes and quotations connected with this one-time home of Joseph Addison; his wife Charlotte, Countess of Warwick and Holland; and their daughter Charlotte Addison. 196pp. Plates and genealog. table. 21x13
London: Mitre press [1957].
BURKE, J.B. Visitation of Seats. 2.S. Vol.II, p.133. 1855.*
NIVEN, W. Old Warwickshire houses. p.20, pl.19. 1878.

BINFIELD PARK (Berkshire).
[Sales] BINFIELD PARK, 1935, January 30 [Remaining furnishings].

BINGHAM'S MELCOMBE (Dorsetshire).
COUNTRY LIFE. XXXV, 666 plan. 1914.
COUNTRY LIFE. CII, 778 plan, 826. 1947.
GARNER, T. Domestic architecture. I, p.58. 1911.
HEATH, S. Dorset Manor Houses. 23. 1907.
NASH, J. Mansions of England. IV, pl.12. 1849.
OSWALD, A. Country houses of Dorset. p.69. 1959.
[Sales] LONDON, 1978, November 3 [Furniture].

BINGLEY HOUSE (Warwickshire).
SMITH, W. History of the County of Warwick. 306. 1830.

BIRBURY HALL (Warwickshire).
BURKE, J.B. Visitation of Seats. Vol.II, p.78. 1853.*

BERKELEY CASTLE, Gloucestershire. From: RUDDER (S.). *A new history of Gloucestershire* [etc.] Cirencester, 1779.

BIRCHER HALL (Herefordshire).
BURKE, J.B. Visitation of Seats. 2.S. Vol.I, p.42. 1854.*

BIRCH HALL (Essex).
See also LITTLE BIRCH HALL.
RUSH, J.A. Seats in Essex. p.40. 1897.

BIRCH HALL (Surrey).
COUNTRY LIFE. CXXVIII, 986. 1960.

BIRCH HOUSE (Lancashire).
BURKE, J.B. Visitation of Seats. Vol.II, p.45. 1853.*
PYNE, W.H. Lancashire illustrated. 95. 1831.
TWYCROSS, E. Mansions of England and Wales. Vol.III, p.93. 1847.

BIRCHINGTON PLACE (Kent).
GREENWOOD, C. Kent. 327. 1838.

BIRKENHEAD PARK (Cheshire).
TWYCROSS, E. Mansions of England and Wales. Vol.I, p.86. 1850.

BIRTLES HALL (Cheshire).
TWYCROSS, E. Mansions of England and Wales. Vol.II, p.117. 1850.*

BIRTSMORTON COURT (Worcestershire).
NIVEN, W. Old Worcestershire houses. p.34, pls.12, 13. 1873.

BISHAM ABBEY (Berkshire).
COPPER PLATE MAGAZINE. I, pl.10. 1792-1802.
COUNTRY LIFE. XVII. 906. 1907.
COUNTRY LIFE. LXXXIX. 320 plan, 342, 364. 1941.
ENGLAND: Picturesque Views. p.38. 1786-88.
THAMES, River. An history. I, pl.33. 1794.

BISHOP AUCKLAND PALACE (Durham).
See AUCKLAND CASTLE.

BISHOP'S COURT (Derbyshire).
TILLEY, J. Halls of Derbyshire. III, p.159. 1899.

BISHOP'S HALL (Essex).
RUSH, J.A. Seats in Essex. p.42. 1897.

BISHOPSTONE HOUSE (Wiltshire).
COUNTRY LIFE. CXXVI, 838. 1959.

BISHOPTHORPE PALACE (Yorkshire).
KEBLE, John Robert, *Canon* of York.
— History of the parish and manor-house of Bishopthorpe, together with an account of the pre-reformation residences of the archbishops of York. Edited with a preface by the Very Rev. A.P. Purey-Cust. [Bibliogr. notes.] Illus. 25x19 Leeds: R. Jackson, 1905.
YORK: Borthwick Institute of Historical Research.
— INGAMELLS, J. Catalogue of portraits at Bishopthorpe palace. [Bibliogr. notes.] 94pp. 14 plates. 25x21 York, 1972.
COUNTRY LIFE. LXV, 50. 1929.
COUNTRY LIFE. CXXX. 566. 1961.
JONES. Views of Seats. I. 1829.
NEALE, J.P. Views of Seats. Vol.V. 1822.

BISHTON HALL (Staffordshire).
JONES. Views of Seats. I. 1829.
NEALE, J.P. Views of Seats. Vol.IV. 1821.

BISTERNE (Hampshire).
COUNTRY LIFE. CXVIII, 240, 286 plan. 1955.

BITTERLEY COURT (Shropshire).
LEACH, F. Seats of Shropshire. p.167. 1891.

BLACKDEN HALL (Cheshire).
BURKE, J.B. Visitation of Seats. Vol.II, p.154. 1853.

BLACKDOWN HOUSE (Sussex).
ELWES, D.G.C. Mansions of Western Sussex. 141. 1876.

BLACK HALL (Devonshire).
BURKE, J.B. Visitation of Seats. Vol.I, p.230. 1852.*

BLACK HALL, Oxford (Oxfordshire).
[SALES] OXFORD, Black Hall, 1925, April 28—May 1 [Contents]. (K.F.& R.).

BLACKHEATH, *Sir* Gregory Page Turner, *Bart.*
See WRICKLEMARSH (Kent).

BLACKHURST (Kent).
GREENWOOD, C. Kent. 124. 1838.

BLACKLADIES, Brewood (Staffordshire).
NIVEN, W. Old Staffordshire houses. p.13, pl.11. 1882.
SHAW, S. Staffordshire. II, pl.8. Reprint 1976.

BLACKMOOR HOUSE (Hampshire).
COUNTRY LIFE. CLVI, 554, 614 plan. 1974.

BLACKMORE PARK (Worcestershire).
NASH, T.R. Worcestershire. I, 559. 1781.

BLACKWELL GRANGE (Durham).
BURKE, J.B. Visitation of Seats. Vol.I, p.40. 1852.*

BLACKWELL HALL (Durham).
BURKE, J.B. Visitation of Seats. Vol.I, p.39. 1852.*

BLAGDON (Northumberland).
COUNTRY LIFE. CXII, 188, 260, 396. 1952.

BLAISE CASTLE (Gloucestershire).
BURKE, J.B. Visitation of Seats. Vol.I, p.121. 1852.*
COOKE, R. West Country houses. p.147. 1957.
JONES. Views of Seats. II. 1829.
NEALE, J.P. Views of Seats. Vol.II. 1819.

BLAKE HALL (Essex).
RUSH, J.A. Seats in Essex. p.44. 1897.

BLAKESLEY HALL (Northamptonshire).
[Sales] NORTHAMPTON, 1923, March 21, 22 [Works of art].

BLATHERWYCKE PARK (Northamptonshire).
BURKE, J.B. Visitation of Seats. Vol.II, p.43. 1853.*
GOTCH, J.A. Squires' Homes. 4. 1939.

BLEASBY HALL (Nottinghamshire).
BURKE, J.B. Visitation of Seats. Vol.I, p.202. 1852.*

BLEASDALE TOWER (Lancashire).
BARTLETT, J. Mansions of England and Wales. pl.54. 1853.
TWYCROSS, E. Mansions of England and Wales. Vol.II, p.13. 1847.

BLEASE HALL (Westmorland).
CUMBERLAND: C.&W. A.& A.S. Extra Series VIII, 229. 1892.

BLENCOW HALL (Cumberland).
CUMBERLAND: C.& W. A.& A.S. Extra Series VIII, 288 plan. 1892.

BLENDON HALL (Kent).
REPTON, H. Fragments on landscape gardening. p.23. 1816.
[SALES] BLENDON HALL, 1929, July 3-5 [Contents]. (K.F.& R.).

BLENHEIM PALACE (Oxfordshire).
BLENHEIM.
— New description of Blenheim ... containing a full account of the paintings, tapestry, and furniture; with a ... essay on landscape gardening. 6 ed. Engr. plates (1 folding) incl. map. 23x13 London: Cadell & Davis, 1803.
7 ed. viii, 152pp. Engr. plates (1 folding), woodcut and map. 22x14 1806.
BLENHEIM.
— A new guide to Blenheim, ... containing an accurate account of the paintings, tapestry and furniture, according to the present arrangement ... To which is added an account of the borough of Woodstock. 8 ed. 88pp. Plates: cuts. 16x10 Woodstock: W. Eccles, 1860. 14 ed. 90pp. [c. 1870]
EMMOTT, J.T.
— Guide to Blenheim and Woodstock. 72pp. Plates. 15x12 Oxford: J. Vincent; London: Simpkin, Marshall, Hamilton, Kent & Co. [1904?]
GREEN, David.
— Blenheim Palace, Oxfordshire. (By D.G.) 36pp. Illus. (1 col.) incl. covers and map (on inside cover). 16x21 Oxford (printed), 1950.
Rev. ed. 40pp. Illus. (some col., some on covers) incl. plan, maps and genealog. tables. (1967).
GREEN, David.
— Blenheim Palace. [Bibliogr.] Illus. incl. sections, elevations, plans and facsimiles. 30x23 London: Country Life, 1951.
LIGERTWOOD, John.
— Blenheim Palace and the Thames at Oxford. 32pp. Illus. (1 col. on cover) incl. plan and maps (1 folding) 18x12 Oxford: Thames Valley Art Productions (1967).
NEALE, John Preston.
— Six views of Blenheim, Oxfordshire; the seat of ... the Duke of Marlborough ... With an historical description of that magnificent edifice, a complete list of pictures according to the present arrangement, including those lately removed from Marlborough House, London, &c. 24pp. Engr. plates. 30x24 London: Sherwood, Jones, & Co.; Longman, Hurst, Rees, Orme, and Brown; T. Moule, 1823.
Also in: NEALE (J.P.). Views of the Seats of noblemen and gentlemen [etc.], III, 1820.
OXFORD.
— The new Oxford guide: or, companion through the University ... To which is added a tour to Blenheim, Ditchley, and Stow ... By a gentleman of Oxford. 5 ed. 4 engr. plates and cuts: head- and tail-pieces. 12mo. 16x9 Oxford: for J. Fletcher & S. Parker [1768?].
Wanting plan.
6 ed. The new Oxford guide ... To which is added a tour to Blenheim, Ditchley, Heythorp and Stow [etc.]. 5 (1 folding) engr. plates incl. plan, and cuts: head- and tail-pieces. [1769?]
OXFORD.
— A new pocket companion for Oxford: or, guide through the University ... To which are added, descriptions of the buildings, the tapestry, paintings, sculptures, temples, gardens, &c. at Blenheim, Ditchley, and Stow ... A new edition, corrected and much enlarged. 156pp. Engr. plates (1 folding) incl. map. 12mo. 16x10 Oxford: printed for Daniel Prince [1775].

BLENHEIM PALACE (Oxfordshire). [Contd.]

OXFORD.
— A new pocket companion for Oxford: or, guide through the university ... To which are added, descriptions of the buildings, tapestry, paintings, sculptures, temples, gardens, &c. at Blenheim and Nuneham, the seats of His Grace the Duke of Marlborough and Earl Harcourt. A new edition [etc.]. iv, 162pp. Engr. plates (1 folding) incl. map. 17x10 Oxford: J. Cooke, 1815.

OXFORD.
— The stranger's guide and historical & biographical handbook to Oxford ... Containing a description of the colleges, halls, public buildings, with an account of the dresses, degrees ... of the members of the University; to which is added a description of Blenheim, the Roman Villa, and Shotover House. xxx, 254pp. Illus. incl. plates (some engr., some folding) and map. 18x11 Oxford: F. Trash [c.1850].

OXFORD.
— Around Oxford: descriptive jaunts to Blenheim Palace and Park, Abingdon, Banbury, Bicester [etc.]. iv, 138pp. Folding map. 18x12 Oxford: T. Shrimpton, 1872.
One of: SHRIMPTON (T.), and Son. Shrimpton's popular handbooks.

SCHARF, *Sir* George.
— Catalogue raisonné; or, a list of the pictures in Blenheim Palace, with ... remarks and illustrative notes. [Bibliogr. notes.] Illus. incl. plates, plan and facsimiles of artists' signatures. 30x24 London: Dorrell & Son, 1862.

WACE, Alan John Bayard.
— The Marlborough tapestries at Blenheim Palace (Blenheim Palace "Art of War", ... Blenheim Palace "Victories") and their relation to other military tapestries of the War of the Spanish Succession. [Edited by] (H. Wace) [Bibliogr.] Illus. (1 col., 1 on cover) incl. tables. 30x22 London: Phaidon' 1968.

ANGUS, W. Seats of the Nobility. pl.5. 1787.

BURKE, J.B. Visitation of Seats. Vol.II, p.113. 1853.*

CAMPBELL, C. Vitruvius Britannicus. I, pls.55-62. 1715.

CAMPBELL, C. Vitruvius Britannicus. III, pls.71, 72. 1725.

COUNTRY LIFE. English Country Houses: Baroque. p.166. 1970.

COUNTRY LIFE. XXV. 786, 834. 1909.

COUNTRY LIFE. CV. 1182, 1246. 1949.

COUNTRY LIFE. CIX, 1184 [Furniture]. 1951.

COUNTRY LIFE. CLVII, 198 [State rooms] 262 [State rooms] 1975.

DELDERFIELD, E.R. West Country houses. III, 26. 1973.

ENGLAND: Beauties of England. II, p.186. 1787.

ENGLAND: Picturesque Views. p.45-48. 1786-88.

ENGLISH CONNOISSEUR. I, 14. 1766.*

HAVELL. R. Views of Noblemen's Seats. 1823.

JONES. Views of seats. I. 1829.

KIP, J. Nouveau théâtre de la Grande Bretagne. III, pls. 22-27. 1715.

KROLL, A. Historic houses. 112. 1969.

LATHAM, C. In English Homes. Vol.III, p.281. 1909.

MALAN, A.H. Famous homes. p.33. 1902.

MORRIS, F.O. Views of Seats. Vol.I, p.79. 1880.

NEALE, J.P. Views of Seats. Vol.III. 1820.

NICOLSON, J. Great Houses of Britain. p.210. 1965.

THAMES, River. An history. I, pls.10-12. 1794.

TIPPING, H.A. English Homes. Period IV, Vol.II, p.63. 1928.

[Sales] LONDON, 1875, June 28-July 1 [Marlborough gems].

[Sales] LONDON, 1881, December 1-3, 5-10, 12 [Bibliotheca Sunderlandiana, pt. I]

[Sales] LONDON, 1882, April 17-22, 24-27 [Bibliotheca Sunderlandiana, pt. II].

[Sales] LONDON, 1882, July 17-22, 24-27 [Bibliotheca Sunderlandiana, pt.III].

[Sales] LONDON, 1882, November 6-11, 13-16 [Bibliotheca Sunderlandiana, pt. IV].

[Sales] LONDON, 1883, March 10, 12-17, 19-21 [Bibliotheca Sunderlandiana, pt.V].

[Sales] LONDON, 1883, June 14 [Limoges enamels from Blenheim].

[Sales] LONDON, 1886, July 24, 26 [Pictures from Blenheim.].

[Sales] LONDON, 1899, June 26-29 [Marlborough gems].

BLENKINSOPP HALL (Northumberland).
BURKE, J.B. Visitation of Seats. Vol.I, p.44. 1852.*

BLICKLING HALL (Norfolk).
LONDON: National Trust for Places of Historic Interest or Natural Beauty.
—LEES-MILNE, J. Blickling Hall, Norfolk. 24pp. 4 plates and plan. 18x12 London: Country Life (1947).
Abridged ed. 8pp. 2 illus. incl. plan. 1949.
3 ed. 1955.
  Rev. ed. [Bibliogr.] 64pp. Illus. (1 col. on cover) incl. plans, map and genealog. table. 25x18 [London] 1982.

LONDON: National Trust for Places of Historic Interest or Natural Beauty.
— JACKSON-STOPS, G. An illustrated souvenir: Blickling Hall, Norfolk. 32pp. Col. illus. (1 on title-page, 1 on cover) 21x21 [London] (1982.)

ANGUS, W. Seats of the Nobility. pl.54. 1787.

BIRKBECK, G. Old Norfolk houses. 15. 1908.

BURKE, J.B. Visitation of Seats. 2.S. Vol.II, p.131. 1855.*

COUNTRY LIFE. XVIII, 822. 1905.

COUNTRY LIFE. LXVII. 814, 902, 936. 1930.

COUNTRY LIFE. LXXXIX. 160. 1941.

CROMWELL, T.K. Excursions in Norfolk. I, p.152. 1818.

GARRATT, T. Halls of Norfolk. pl.13. 1890.

GOTCH, J.A. Architecture of the Renaissance. I, p.44 plan. 1894.

HALL, S.C. Baronial Halls. Vol.II. 1848.

LATHAM, C. In English Homes. Vol. II, p.259. 1907.

MALAN, A.H. More famous homes. p.1. 1902.

NEALE, J.B. Views of Seats. Vol.III. 1820.

NICOLSON, N. Great Houses of Britain. p.116. 1965.

SHAW, H. Elizabethan architecture. pls.XLIX-LIX. [Elevation, staircase etc.] 1839.

[Exhibitions] LONDON: National Book League. Books from Blickling Hall. 1958.

BLITHFIELD (Staffordshire).

BAGOT, Nancy Constance, *Baroness.*

— Blithfield Hall: an illustrated survey of the Staffordshire home of the Bagot family. 32pp. Illus. (some col., some on covers). 14x21 Derby: E.L.P. [1956?].

BURKE, J.B. Visitation of Seats. 2.S. Vol.II, p.126. 1855.*

COUNTRY LIFE. CXVI, 1488, 1576 plan, 1664. 1954.

JONES. Views of Seats. I. 1829.

NEALE, J.P. Views of Seats. Vol.IV. 1821.

NEALE, J.P. Views of seats. 2.S. Vol.V. 1829.

PLOT, R. Staffordshire. 225. 1686.

SHAW, S. Staffordshire. II, pl.21. Reprint 1976.

[Sales] LONDON, 1978, June 8 [Toys, games and dolls].

BLOXWORTH HOUSE (Dorsetshire).

HEATH, S. Dorset Manor Houses. 37. 1907.

OSWALD, A. Country houses of Dorset. p.101. 1959.

BLUNDESTON HOUSE (Suffolk).

SANDON, E. Suffolk houses. 314. 1977.

BLYTH HALL (Nottinghamshire).

SPROULE, A. Lost houses of Britain. 54. 1982.

BLYTH HALL (Warwickshire).

NIVEN, W. Old Warwickshire houses. p.8, title-page. 1878.

BLYTHWOOD (Essex.)

RUSH, J.A. Seats in Essex. p.46. 1897.

BOCONNOC (Cornwall).

BURKE, J.B. Visitation of Seats. Vol.II, p.11. 1853.*

CROMWELL, T.K. Excursions in Cornwall. p.45. 1824.

DELDERFIELD, E.R. West Country houses. I, 14. 1968.

BODELWYDDAN (Flintshire).

BURKE, J.B. Visitation of Seats. Vol.I, p.47. 1852.*

BODIOR HOUSE, Rhoscolyn (Anglesey).

BURKE, J.B. Visitation of Seats. Vol.I, p.157. 1852.*

BODNANT (Denbighshire).

COUNTRY LIFE. CIX, 1628. 1951.

BODRHYDDAN HALL (Flintshire).

LANGFORD, Geofrey Alexander Rowley-Conwy, *Baron.*

— Bodrhyddan Hall. 3 ed. 30pp. Illus. incl. 18x11 (Denbigh) privately printed, 1971.

Title on cover.

COUNTRY LIFE. CLXIV. 158, 226. 1978.

BODYSGALLEN (Caernarvonshire).

COUNTRY LIFE. CLXIV. 2066. 1978.

BOLD HALL (Lancashire).

BARTLETT, J. Mansions of England and Wales. pl.102. 1853.

BURKE, J.B. Visitation of Seats. 2.S. Vol.I, p.48. 1854.*

TWYCROSS, E. Mansions of England and Wales. Vol.III, p.27. 1847.

BOLD OLD HALL (Lancashire).

BURKE, J.B. Visitation of Seats. 2.S. Vol.I, p.48. 1854.*

GRAY, H. Old halls of Lancashire. p.111. 1893.

BOLEHYDE MANOR (Wiltshire).

COUNTRY LIFE. CIV, 528, 578. 1948.

DELDERFIELD, E.R. West Country houses. II, 20. 1970.

BOLESWORTH CASTLE (Cheshire).

ENGLAND: Picturesque Views. p.79. 1786-88.

TWYCROSS, E. Mansions of England and Wales. Vol.I, p.45. 1850.

BOLEYN CASTLE (Essex).

SPROULE, A. Lost houses of Britain. 58. 1982.

BOLLING HALL (Yorkshire).

BRADFORD: Bolling Hall Museum.

— Official handbook ... Compiled by B. Wood. 4 ed. [Bibliogr.] 94 pp. Illus. incl. plans. 18x13 Bradford, 1923.

5 ed. Compiled by W.E. Preston. 1928.

7 ed. Compiled by W. Robertshaw. 1947.

Bolling Hall museum: official handbook. 28pp. Illus. (some on covers) incl. plans, diagr. and map. 15x20 Bradford, 1965.

JONES. Views of Seats. I. 1829.

NEALE, J.P. Views of seats. Vol.V. 1822.

WOOD, G.B. Historic homes of Yorkshire. 26. 1957.

YORKSHIRE. Picturesque views. 1885.

BOLSOVER CASTLE (Derbyshire).

CHESTERFIELD.
—The history of Chesterfield; with particulars of the hamlets contiguous to the town, and descriptive accounts of Chatsworth, Hardwick, and Bolsover Castle. [By Rev. G. Hall, enlarged and edited by T. Ford. Bibliogr. notes.] Illus. incl. plates (many engr., most by W. Radclyffe after C. Radclyffe), and tables. 22x14 London: Whittaker & Co.; Chesterfield: Ford, 1839.

GOULDING, Richard William.
— Bolsover Castle. [Bibliogr. notes.] 3 ed. 20pp. Illus. incl. plan. 23x18 n.p., by the author? 1917.

GREAT BRITAIN: Department of the Environment. [Ancient Monuments and Historic Buildings].
— FAULKNER, P.A. Bolsover Castle, Derbyshire. 68pp. Illus. 3 folding plates and plans. 21x14 London, 1972.
Another impression. 1975.

BUCK, S.&N. Antiquities. I, pls. 53, 54. 1774.

BURKE, J.B. Visitation of Seats. Vol.I, p.204. 1852.*

BURKE, J.B. Visitation of Seats. 2.S. Vol.II, p.199. 1855.*

COUNTRY LIFE. XVI, 198. 1904.

GOTCH, J.A. Architecture of the Renaissance. I, p.26 plan. 1894.

KIP, J. Nouveau théâtre de la Grande Bretagne. I, pl. 15. 1715.

LATHAM, C. In English Homes. Vol.II, p.235. 1907.

NASH, J. Mansions of England. II, pl.6. 1840.

TILLEY, J. Halls of Derbyshire. III, p.33. 1899.

TIPPING, H.A. English Homes. Period III. Vol.I, p.348. 1922.

BOLTON ABBEY (Yorkshire).

See BOLTON PRIORY HALL

BOLTON HALL, Bolton-by-Bowland. (Yorkshire).

BURKE, J.B. Visitation of Seats. Vol.II, p.137. 1853.*

BOLTON HALL, Leyburn (Yorkshire).

COPPER PLATE MAGAZINE. pl.33. 1778.

SANDBY, P. Select Views. I, pl.71. 1783.

WHEATER, W. Mansions of Yorkshire. p.13. 1888.

BOLTON PRIORY HALL (Yorkshire).

BURKE, J.B. Visitation of Seats. Vol.I, p.41. 1852.*

BOLTON ROYD, Bradford (Yorkshire).

YORKSHIRE. Picturesque views. 1885.

BONCHURCH (Hampshire, Isle of Wight).

ENGLAND: Picturesque Views. p.96. 1786-88.

BONVILSTON (Glamorganshire).

BURKE, J.B. Visitation of Seats. 2.S. Vol.II, p.4. 1855.*

BOOKHAM GROVE (Surrey).

BURKE, J.B. Visitation of Seats. 2.S. Vol.I, p.179. 1854.*

BOONS PARK, Four Elms (Kent)

[Sales] BOONS PARK, 1964, April 20-24 [Contents].

BOREATTON (Shropshire).

SHROPSHIRE. Castles & Old Mansions. 56. 1868.

BOREHAM HOUSE (Essex).

COUNTRY LIFE. XXXVI, 54 plan. 1914.

CROMWELL, T.K. Excursions in Essex. I, p.23. 1825.

ENGLAND: Beauties of England. I, p.246. 1787.

RUSH, J.A. Seats in Essex. p.51. 1897.

BORINGDON (Devonshire).

COUNTRY LIFE. XXXV, 914. 1914.

BOROUGHBRIDGE HALL (Yorkshire).

BURKE, J.B. Visitation of Seats. Vol.I, p.128. 1852.*

BORWICK HALL (Lancashire).

FORD, J. Rawlinson.
— Borwick Hall. [A paper] read at Borwick Hall, September 11th, 1924. 12pp. 2 plates. 22x14 (Kendal, 1925).
Also in: CUMBERLAND: Cumberland and Westmorland Antiquarian and Archaeological Society. Transactions. N.S., XXV, 275.

BURKE, J.B. Visitation of Seats. 2.S. Vol.I, p.44. 1854.*

COUNTRY LIFE. XXIX, 710 plan. 1911.

COUNTRY LIFE. LXXVIII, 142 plan. 1935.

GARNER, T. Domestic architecture. II, p.151 plan. 1911.

NASH, J. Mansions of England. IV, pl.21. 1849.

TIPPING, H.A. English Homes. Early Renaissance, p.163. 1912.

TIPPING, H.A. English Homes. Period III, Vol.II, p.61. 1927.

BOSBURY HOUSE (Herefordshire).

BURKE, J.B. Visitation of Seats. Vol.II, p.175. 1853.*

BOSCOBEL HOUSE (Shropshire).

GREAT BRITAIN: Ministry of Public Building and Works [Ancient Monuments and Historic Buildings].
— Boscobel House and White Ladies Priory, Shropshire. 56 pp. Illus. incl. plans and map. 19x13 London, 1970.

GREAT BRITAIN: Department of the Environment [Ancient Monuments and Historic Buildings].
— WEST J.J. Boscobel House. 8pp. Illus. incl. plan. 21x15 [London] (1981.).

COPPER PLATE MAGAZINE. V, pl.112. 1792-1802.

COUNTRY LIFE. XCVIII, 1048. 1945.

LEACH, F. Seats of Shropshire. p.361. 1891.

SHAW, S. Staffordshire. I, 79. 1798.

SHROPSHIRE. Castles & Old Mansions. 52. 1868.

BLICKLING HALL, NORFOLK.

PROOF

Published by Chapman & Hall, London, Dec 2nd 1848

BLICKLING HALL, Norfolk. From: HALL (S.C.). *The baronial halls and picturesque edifices of England* [etc.], vol. II, London, 1848.

BOSKENNA (Cornwall).
BURKE, J.B. Visitation of Seats. 2.S. Vol.I, p.196. 1854.*

BOSTOCK HALL (Cheshire).
BURKE, J.B. Visitation of Seats. Vol.I, p.62. 1852.*
TWYCROSS, E. Mansions of England and Wales.Vol.I, p.138. 1850.*

BOSTON MANOR (Middlesex).
BRENTFORD AND CHISWICK: Borough Council.
— Boston Manor house, ... Brentford. [Compiled by] (G. Mitchell.) 4pp. Illus. (on cover.) 20x13 (Chiswick) [1963?]
COUNTRY LIFE. CXXXVII. 603. 1965.
[Sales] BOSTON MANOR (HOUSE), 1922, July 4-7 [Contents]. (K.F.& R.).

BOSWORTH PARK (Leicestershire).
See MARKET BOSWORTH HALL.

BOTLEYS (Surrey).
BRAYLEY, E.W. History of Surrey. II, 221. 1841.
BURKE, J.B. Visitation of Seats. 2.S. Vol.I, p.115. 1854.*
CAMPBELL, C. Vitruvius Britannicus. V, pls. 56, 57. 1771.
PROSSER, G.F. Surrey Seats. p.37. 1828.

BOTTISHAM HALL (Cambridgeshire).
BURKE, J.B. Visitation of Seats. Vol.I, p.121. 1852.*

BOUGHTON COURT (Kent).
See BOUGHTON MONCHELSEA PLACE.

BOUGHTON HOUSE (Northamptonshire).
LONDON: Victoria and Albert Museum [Textiles].
— Guide to an exhibition of tapestries, carpets and furniture, lent by the Earl of Dalkeith, March to May, 1914. [From Boughton House] 28pp. 16 plates. 24x15 London, 1914. 2 ed. 20 plates.
LONDON: Victoria and Albert Museum [Woodwork].
— State bedstead from Boughton House, given by the Duke of Buccleuch, K.T., 4pp. 1 illus. 24x15 (London) 1917.
SCOTT, Charles Henry.
— Catalogue of the pictures at Boughton House, in the parish of Weekley, Northamptonshire. [The property of the Duke of Buccleuch and Queensberry.] 28x22 Edinburgh: Douglas, 1911.
WISE, Charles.
— The Montagus of Boughton and their Northamptonshire homes. Plates incl. folding map. 19x13 Kettering: Goss, 1888.
MANUSCRIPTS (Typewritten). English.
— An inventory of the goods of His Grace The Duke of Mountague at His Seat at Boughton in Northamptonshire, taken Novr. the 27, 1718 [From the original in the possession of the Duke of Buccleuch at Boughton House.] 22ff. 33x20 (1917).

BURKE, J.B. Visitation of Seats. 2.S. Vol.II, p.91. 1855.*
CAMPBELL, C. Vitruvius Britannicus. III, pls. 73, 74. 1725.
CAMPBELL, C. Vitruvius Britannicus. IVth. pls. 36, 37, 1739.
COUNTRY LIFE. English Country Houses: Baroque, p.35. 1970.
COUNTRY LIFE. XXV, 162, 198. 1909.
COUNTRY LIFE. LXXI, 322 [Furniture]. 1932.
COUNTRY LIFE. LXXII, 596, 626 plan, 649 [Furniture]. 1932.
COUNTRY LIFE. LXXVII, 278 [Furniture]. 1935.
COUNTRY LIFE. CXLVIII, 564, 624, 684. 1970.
COUNTRY LIFE. CXLIX, 420, 476. 1971.
GOTCH, J.A. Halls of Northants. p.47. 1936.
JONES. Views of Seats. I. 1829.
LATHAM. C. In English Homes. Vol.III, p.183. 1909.
NEALE, J.P. Views of Seats. 2.S. Vol.I. 1824.
WHITEMAN, G.W. English country homes. p.80. 1951.

BOUGHTON MALHERBE (Kent).
CHARLES of London.
— The gothic oak room from Boughton Malherbe, Kent. 16pp. 6 plates, and plan. 20x25 London [1923.]
WOTTON, Thomas.
— Thomas Wotton's letter-book, 1574-1586. Edited by G. Eland. [Bibliogr.] 6 plates incl. facsimiles, and genealog. table. 24x15 London: Oxford University Press, 1960.
COUNTRY LIFE. LI, 536, 570. 1922.
NASH, J. Mansions of England. I, pl.14. 1839.
OSWALD, A. Country houses of Kent. 17. 1933.
SHAW, H. Elizabethan architecture. pls.VIII, IX. [Drawing room & details] 1839.
TIPPING, H.A. English Homes. Period II, Vol.I, p.213. 1924.

BOUGHTON MONCHELSEA PLACE (Kent).
BOUGHTON MONCHELSEA PLACE.
— Guide to Boughton Monchelsea Place, near Maidstone, Kent. 8pp. 1 illus. 12x18 n.p. [1965?].
BADESLADE, T. Seats in Kent. pl.3. 1750.
COUNTRY LIFE. CXXXIII, 1489, 1552. 1963.
HARRIS, J. History of Kent. p.48. 1719.

BOULTIBROOKE (Radnorshire).
BURKE, J.B. Visitation of Seats. Vol.I, p.263. 1852.*

BOURNE PARK [PLACE] (Kent).
COUNTRY LIFE. LI, 602, 636 plan. 1922.
COUNTRY LIFE. XCVI, 816, 860 plan. 1944.
GREENWOOD, C. Kent. 399. 1838.
OSWALD, A. Country houses of Kent. 60. 1933.

BOURN HOUSE (Cambridgeshire).
NEALE, J.P. Views of Seats. Vol.I. 1818.

BOURTON HOUSE (Gloucestershire).
COUNTRY LIFE. LXXXVII, 302, 330. 1940.

BOURTON MANOR [Cottage] (Shropshire).
LEIGHTON, S. Shropshire houses. 49. 1901.

BOVERIDGE (Dorsetshire).
BURKE, J.B. Visitation of Seats. 2.S. Vol.II, p.228. 1855.*

BOVEY HOUSE (Devonshire).
COUNTRY LIFE. XXXII, 674. 1912.
TIPPING, H.A. English Homes. Period III, Vol.II, p.115. 1927.

BOWDEN PARK (Wiltshire).
CAMPBELL, C. New Vitruvius Britannicus. I. pls. 1, 2. 1802.

BOWER HALL (Essex.)
ESSEX: A new and complete history. II, 258. 1769.

BOWER HOUSE, The. Havering (Essex).
COUNTRY LIFE. XCV, 464, 508. 1944.

BOWERS, The. (Derbyshire).
TILLEY, J. Halls of Derbyshire. I, p.241. 1892.

BOWLING HALL (Yorkshire).
See BOLLING HALL

BOWLING PARK (Yorkshire).
YORKSHIRE. Picturesque views. 1885.

BOWOOD (Wiltshire).
AMBROSE, George E.
— Catalogue of the collection of pictures belonging to the Marquess of Lansdowne, K.G., at Lansdowne House, London and Bowood, Wilts. 28x17 London: privately printed, 1896.
ADAM, R. & J. Works in Architecture. Vol.II. no.3. pl.VII [Bridge] 1779.
BOLTON, A.T. Architecture of R. & J. Adam. I, 192 plan. 1922.
BRITTON, J. Beauties of Wiltshire. II, 213. 1801.
BURKE, J.B. Visitation of Seats. 2.S. Vol.I, p.92. 1854.*
COOKE, R. West Country Houses. p.140. 1957.
COUNTRY LIFE. XV, 738. 1904.
COUNTRY LIFE. XXXIV, 324 plan. 1913.
JONES. Views of Seats. II. 1829.
LATHAM, C. In English Homes. Vol.I, p.389. 1904.
MORRIS, F.O. Views of Seats. Vol.V, p.3. 1880.
NEALE, J.P. Views of Seats. 2.S. Vol.II. 1825.
ROBERTSON, A. Great Road. II, p.48. 1792.
[Sales] BOWOOD, 1955, June 30 [Fixtures, fittings etc.].

BOWRINGSLEIGH (Devonshire).
COUNTRY LIFE. XXXVII, 304. 1915.
TIPPING, H.A. English Homes. Period III, Vol.II, p.127. 1927.

BOYLAND HALL (Norfolk).
BURKE, J.B. Visitation of Seats. Vol.II, p.183. 1853.*

BOYNTON HALL (Yorkshire).
COUNTRY LIFE. CXVI, 280 plan, 356. 1954.
WOOD, G.B. Historic homes of Yorkshire. 118. 1957.
[Sales] BOYNTON HALL, 1950, November 21-23 [Major portion of contents].

BOYTON HOUSE (Wiltshire).
COUNTRY LIFE. XXVIII, 262. 1910.
TIPPING, H.A. English Homes. Early Renaissance, p.299. 1912.

BRABOEUF MANOR (Surrey).
BURKE, J.B. Visitation of Seats. 2.S. Vol.II, p.161. 1855.*

BRACONDALE (Norfolk).
CROMWELL, T.K. Excursions in Norfolk. I, p.138. 1818.

BRADBOURNE HALL (Derbyshire).
TILLEY, J. Halls of Derbyshire. II, p.227. 1893.

BRADBOURNE HALL, Sevenoaks (Kent).
GREENWOOD, C. Kent. 94. 1838.
HASTED, E. Kent. I, 350. 1778.
[Sales] BRADBOURNE HALL, 1926, December 8, 9 [Antique and modern furniture].

BRADBOURNE HOUSE, Larkfield (Kent).
ANGUS, W. Seats of the Nobility. pl.46, 1787.
COUNTRY LIFE. XLIV, 152. 1952.
COUNTRY LIFE. CXLI, 774, 858, 922 plan. 1967.
HASTED, E. Kent. II, 214. 1778.
OSWALD, A. Country houses of Kent. 62. 1933.

BRADDEN HOUSE (Northamptonshire).
BURKE, J.B. Visitation of Seats. Vol.I, p.89. 1852.*

BRADENHAM MANOR (Buckinghamshire).
BRADENHAM, Buckinghamshire.
— Bradenham manor past and present. [Bibliogr. note.] 40pp. Illus. incl. plan, maps and genealog. table. 14x21 Bradenham Manor: Management and Systems Training Establishment (1965).

BRADFIELD, Cullumpton (Devonshire).
COUNTRY LIFE. XIV, 926. 1903.
GOTCH, J.A. Architecture of the Renaissance. I, p.13. 1894.
LATHAM, C. In English Homes. Vol.I, p.69. 1904.

BRADFIELD (Wiltshire).
ELYARD, S.J. Old Wiltshire homes. p.20. 1894.

BRADGATE HOUSE (Leicestershire).
KIP, J. Nouveau théâtre de la Grande Bretagne. I, pl.12. 1715.
NICHOLS, J. History of Leicestershire. III, ii, 661. 1804.
THROSBY, J. Views in Leicestershire. p.118. 1789.

BRADLEY COURT (Gloucestershire).
ATKYNS, R. Glocestershire. p.449. 1768.
HODGES, E. Ancient English homes. 42. 1895.

BRADLEY MANOR (Devonshire).
LONDON: National Trust for Places of Historic Interest or
Natural Beauty.
— Bradley Manor. 12pp. 4 plates and plan. 18x12
London(1940).
   New ed. WOOLNER, D. Bradley Manor, Devon. 14pp. Illus.
incl. plates and plans. London: Country Life, 1955.
COUNTRY LIFE. XCVI. 377. 1944.

BRADNINCH MANOR (Devonshire).
TIPPING, H.A. English Homes. Period III, Vol.II, p.121. 1927.

BRADSHAW HALL, Chapel-en-le-Frith
(Derbyshire).
TILLEY, J. Halls of Derbyshire. I, p.85. 1892.

BRADSHAW HALL, Eyam (Derbyshire).
TILLEY, J. Halls of Derbyshire. I, p.135. 1892.

BRADSTON BROOK HOUSE (Surrey).
BRAYLEY, E.W. History of Surrey. V, 145. 1841.
BURKE, J.B. Visitation of Seats. 2.S. Vol.II, p.15. 1855.*

BRADWALL HALL (Cheshire).
BURKE, J.B. Visitation of Seats. Vol.II, p.127. 1853.*
TWYCROSS, E. Mansions of England and Wales. Vol.I, p.131.
1850.

BRADWELL LODGE (Essex).
ANGUS, W. Seats of the Nobility. pl.35. 1787.
COUNTRY LIFE. CXL, 15. 1966.

BRAGBURY HOUSE (Hertfordshire).
NEALE, J.P. Views of Seats. Vol.II. 1819.

BRAILES HOUSE (Warwickshire).
BURKE, J.B. Visitation of Seats. Vol.II, p.171. 1853.*

BRAMALL HALL (Cheshire).
STOCKPORT: Metropolitan Borough [Recreation & Culture
Division].
— Dean, E.B. Bramall Hall: the story of an Elizabethan
manor house. [Bibliogr.] x, 124pp. Illus. incl. plates, plan and
map. 21x15 Stockport, 1977.
ANGUS-BUTTERWORTH, L.M. Old Cheshire families. p.60.
1932.
BURKE, J.B. Visitation of Seats. Vol.I, p.103. 1852.*
COUNTRY LIFE. XIII, 790. 1903.
LATHAM, C. In English Homes. Vol.I, p.249. 1904.
MORRIS, F.O. Views of Seats. Vol.V, p.19. 1880.
MOSS, F. Pilgrimages. VI. 39. 1913.
NASH, J. Mansions of England. III. pls.23-25, 1841 & IV, pl.8.
1849.
ORMEROD, G. Cheshire. III, 822, 826. 1882.
TWYCROSS, E. Mansions of England and Wales. Vol.II, p.89.
1850.
[Sales] BRAMHALL, 1923, July 9-14 [Furniture, tapestry etc.].

BRAMFIELD HALL (Suffolk).
SANDON, E. Suffolk houses. 231. 1977.

BRAMFORD HOUSE (Suffolk).
SANDON, E. Suffolk houses. 316. 1977.

BRAMHAM PARK (Yorkshire).
— Bramham Park. 22pp. Illus. incl. map. 22x14 n.p. [1952?].
CAMPBELL, C. Vitruvius Britannicus. II, pls.81, 82, 1717.
COUNTRY LIFE. English Country Houses: Baroque, p.201.
1970.
COUNTRY LIFE. L, 416, 448, 1921.
COUNTRY LIFE. CXXIII, 350, 400. 1958.
JONES. Views of Seats. I. 1829.
NEALE, J.P. Views of Seats. Vol.V. 1822.
PAINE, J. Plans, elevations. Pt.I, pl.73 [Temple.]. 1767.
WHEATER, W. Mansions of Yorkshire. p.25. 1888.
WOOD, G.B. Historic homes of Yorkshire. 31. 1957.

BRAMHOPE MANOR (Yorkshire).
[Sales] LONDON, 1865, February 6-8 [Antiquities, objects of
art and vertu etc.].
[Sales] LONDON, 1865, February 9-11 [Pictures].

BRAMLEY PARK [MANOR] (Surrey).
BRAYLEY, E.W. History of Surrey. V, 148. 1841.

BRAMPTON HALL (Derbyshire).
TILLEY, J. Halls of Derbyshire. III. p.35. 1899.

BRAMPTON HALL (Suffolk).
BURKE, J.B. Visitation of Seats. Vol.II, p.221. 1853.*
DAVY, H. Seats in Suffolk. pl.15. 1827.

BRAMSHILL (Hampshire).
COPE, *Sir* William Henry, *Bart.*
— Bramshill: its history & architecture. (List of the pictures.) Illus. incl. plates and plans. 25x18 London: Infield [1883].
BURKE, J.B. Visitation of Seats. Vol.II, p.46. 1853.*
BURKE, J.B. Visitation of Seats. 2.S. Vol.II, p.164. 1855.
CLARKE, T.H. Domestic architecture. 9. 1833.
COUNTRY LIFE. XIV, 54. 1903.
COUNTRY LIFE. LIII, 758, 818, 852 plan, 886. 1923.
COUNTRY LIFE. LXXVIII, 168. 1935.
GOTCH, J.A. Architecture of the Renaissance. II, p.54 plan. 1894.
HALL, S.C. Baronial Halls. Vol.I. 1848.
JONES. Views of Seats. II. 1829.
LATHAM, C. In English Homes. Vol.I, p.17. 1904.
NASH, J. Mansions of England. I, pls.8, 9, 1839. & II, pl.24. 1840.
NEALE, J.P. Views of Seats. Vol.II. 1819.
SHAW, H. Elizabethan architecture. pls.XXIX-XXXIX. [Elevations, arcade etc.] 1839.
TIPPING, H.A. English Homes. Period III, Vol.II, p.277. 1927.
[Sales] LONDON, 1952, July 16 [Historical portraits from B.].

BRANCASTER HALL (Norfolk).
[Sales] KING'S LYNN, 1922, October 3 [Estate].

BRANCEPETH CASTLE (Durham).
SURTEES, *Sir* Herbert Conyers, *Brigadier-Gen.*
— The history of the castle of Brancepeth at Brancepeth, Co. Durham. [Bibliogr. notes.] 48pp. Illus. incl. plates (some folding), plans and genealog. tables. 21x14 (London: D. Allen & Sons) 1920.
BUCK, S.&N. Antiquities. I, pl.81. 1774.
HEARNE, T. Antiquities. I, pl.34. 1807.
JONES. Views of Seats. I. 1829.
MORRIS, F.O. Views of Seats. Vol.VI, p.3. 1880.
NEALE, J.P. Views of Seats. Vol.I. 1818.
[Sales] BRANCEPETH CASTLE, 1922, October 9-14 [Furnishings and appointments].

BRANDON LODGE [COTTAGE] (Warwickshire).
BURKE, J.B. Visitation of Seats. Vol.II, p.244. 1853.*
LUGAR, R. Plans and views of buildings. 20, pls.XIV-XVI. 1823.

BRANDSBY HALL (Yorkshire).
BURKE, J.B. Visitation of Seats. Vol.II, p.125. 1853.*
COUNTRY LIFE. CXLV, 18, 66. 1969.

BRANKSOME TOWER (Dorsetshire).
HUTCHINS, J. History of Dorset. III, 303. 1868.

BRANTINGHAM THORPE (Yorkshire).
MORRIS, F.O. Views of Seats. Vol.III, p.19. 1880.

BRASTED PLACE (Kent).
BOLTON, A.T. Architecture of R.& J. Adam. II, 167 plan. 1922.
OSWALD, A. Country houses of Kent. 65. 1933.

BRATTON HOUSE (Wiltshire).
COUNTRY LIFE. CL, 326. 1971.

BRAUNSTONE HALL (Leicestershire).
NICHOLS, J. History of Leicestershire. IV, ii. 620. 1811.
THROSBY, J. Views in Leicestershire. p.257. 1789.

BRAXTED PARK (Essex).
BURKE, J.B. Visitation of Seats. 2.S. Vol.II, p.153. 1855.*
CROMWELL, T.K. Excursions in Essex. I, p.44. 1825.
RUSH, J.A. Seats in Essex. p.49. 1897.*

BREADSALL HALL (Derbyshire).
TILLEY, J. Halls of Derbyshire. II, p.17. 1893.

BREADSALL PRIORY (Derbyshire).
TILLEY, J. Halls of Derbyshire. II, p.15. 1893.

BREAMORE HOUSE (Hampshire).
BREAMORE.
— A short history of Breamore and the Hulse family. 24pp. Illus. incl. genealog. table. 14x18 (Bournemouth) privately printed [c.1975.]
COUNTRY LIFE. CXXI, 1198, 1268, 1320. 1957.

BRECCLES HALL (Norfolk).
BIRKBECK, G. Old Norfolk houses. 23. 1908.
COUNTRY LIFE. XXVI, 670, 706 plan. 1909.
GARRATT, T. Halls of Norfolk. pls.14, 15. 1890.
TIPPING, H.A. English Homes. Early Renaissance, p.35. 1912.
TIPPING, H.A. English Homes. Period III, Vol.I, p.22. 1922.

BREDE PLACE (Sussex).
COUNTRY LIFE. XX, 630. 1906.
GARNER, T. Domestic architecture. I, p.47 plan. 1911.

BRENCHLEY MANOR (Kent).
COUNTRY LIFE. XCIX, 1040. 1946.

BRENT PELHAM HALL (Hertfordshire).
CHAUNCY, H. Hertfordshire. I, 280. 1826.

BRERETON HALL (Cheshire).
ANGUS-BUTTERWORTH, L.M. Old Cheshire families. p.3. 1932.
CLARKE, T.H. Domestic architecture. 14. 1833.
COUNTRY LIFE. XXVI, 388. 1909.
GOTCH, J.A. Architecture of the Renaissance. II, p.24. 1894.
HALL, S.C. Baronial Halls. Vol.I. 1848.
NASH, J. Mansions of England. IV, pl.7. 1849.
ORMEROD, G. Cheshire. III, 84. 1882.
TIPPING, H.A. English Homes. Early Renaissance, p.199. 1912.
TWYCROSS, E. Mansions of England and Wales. Vol.I, p.141. 1850.*

BRETBY PARK (Derbyshire).
BURKE, J.B. Visitation of Seats. 2.S. Vol.II, p.103. 1855.*
KIP, J. Nouveau théâtre de la Grande Bretagne. I. pl.26. 1715.
TILLEY, J. Halls of Derbyshire. IV, p.75. 1902.*

BRETTON PARK (Yorkshire).
COUNTRY LIFE. LXXXIII, 530, 554. 1938.
JONES. Views of Seats. I. 1829.
NEALE, J.P. Views of Seats. Vol.V. 1822.

BRICKLEHAMPTON HALL [House] (Worcestershire).
BURKE, J.B. Visitation of Seats. 2.S. Vol.I, p.55. 1854.*

BRIDE HALL, Sandridge (Hertfordshire).
ANDREWS, Herbert Caleb.
— Bride Hall, Sandridge. 8pp. 2 plates. 25x16 St. Albans, 1932. Also in SAINT ALBANS: Architectural and Archaeological Society. Transactions. 1932.

BRIDGE HOUSE, Chilton Foliat (Wiltshire).
COUNTRY LIFE. CXXXV, 1048. 1964.

BRIDWELL (Devonshire).
COUNTRY LIFE. CLXIX, 710. 1981.

BRIGHTWELL HALL (Suffolk).
KIP, J. Nouveau théâtre de la Grande Bretagne. I, pl.52. 1715.

BRIGHTWELL PARK (Oxfordshire).
BURKE, J.B. Visitation of Seats. Vol.II, p.196. 1853.*

BRIGSTOCK MANOR (Northamptonshire).
GOTCH, J.A. Squires' Homes. 9. 1939.

BRIMINGTON HALL (Derbyshire).
TILLEY, J. Halls of Derbyshire. III, p.49. 1899.

BRINDLE LODGE (Lancashire).
BARTLETT, J. Mansions of England and Wales. pl.15. 1853.
TWYCROSS, E. Mansions of England and Wales. Vol.I, p.65. 1847.

BRINKBURN PRIORY (Northumberland).
BURKE, J.B. Visitation of Seats. 2.S. Vol.II, p.109. 1855.*

BRINSOP COURT (Herefordshire).
ASTLEY, Constance.
— Catalogue of the library of Constance Astley at Brinsop Court, Herefordshire [by C.A., revised by A.F. Johnson and designed by G.W. Jones]. Decorated borders incl. title-page. 33x23 (London: privately printed at The Sign of the Dolphin, 1928).
COUNTRY LIFE. XXV, 738. 1909.
COUNTRY LIFE. XXXVI, 614, 646 plan. 1914.
ROBINSON, C.J. Mansions of Herefordshire. pl.5. 1873.
TIPPING, H.A. English Homes. Period I, Vol.I, p.133. 1921.

BRISTOL: John Langley's House (Gloucestershire).
LATHAM, C. In English Homes. Vol.II, p.303.1907.

BRISTOL, The Royal Fort (Gloucestershire).
See ROYAL FORT.

BRITWELL COURT (Buckinghamshire).
BRITWELL COURT.
— The Britwell handlist; or, short-title catalogue of the principal volumes from the time of Caxton to the year 1800, formerly in the library of Britwell Court, Buckinghamshire. [Compiled by H. Collmann and G.A.P. Brown; the property of S.R. Christie-Miller.] Plates. 2 vols. 25x19 London: Quaritch, 1933.
[Sales] LONDON, 1916, August 15-17 [Library; Americana].
[Sales] LONDON, 1919, June 30, July 1-3 [Library; voyages, travel and foreign history].

[Sales] LONDON, 1919, December 15 [airs, ballads, songs and other music].

[Sales] LONDON, 1919, December 16 [Library].

[Sales] LONDON, 1920, May 3, 4 [Library; Jacques Auguste de Thou, bindings etc.].

[Sales] LONDON, 1920, May 5-7 [Library; English and Scottish works on theology].

[Sales] LONDON, 1920, June 14, 15 [Library; novels, romances etc.].

[Sales] LONDON, 1921, January 31-February 2 [Library; works on theology]. Pt. II.

[Sales] LONDON, 1921, March 10, 11 [Early English poetry and other literature].

[Sales] LONDON, 1922, February 6-10 [Library; early English poetry etc.].

[Sales] LONDON, 1923, March 12-16 [Library; early English poetry etc.].

[Sales] LONDON, 1924, March 31-April 4 [Library; early English poetry, literature].

[Sales] LONDON, 1924, April 7-9 [Library; all branches of literature].

[Sales] LONDON, 1927, July 11 [Library; books unsold or returned as imperfect].

[Sales] LONDON, 1971, March 29, 30 [Books].

BRITWELL SALOME HOUSE (Oxfordshire).
COUNTRY LIFE. CLII, 810, 883. 1972.

[Sales] BRITWELL HOUSE, 1979, March 20-22 [Contents].

BRIXWORTH HALL (Northamptonshire).
NEALE, J.P. Views of Seats. Vol.III. 1820.

BROADFIELD HALL (Hertfordshire).
CHAUNCY, H. Hertfordshire. I, 144. 1826.

BROADGATE (Leicestershire).
See BRADGATE HOUSE.

BROADHEMBURY, The Grange (Devonshire).
See GRANGE, The.

BROADLANDS, Ascot (Berkshire).
COUNTRY LIFE. LXXVI, 496 plan. 1934.

BROADLANDS (Hampshire).
ANGUS, W. Seats of the Nobility. pl.1. 1787.
BURKE, J.B. Visitation of Seats. Vol.I, p.216. 1852.*
COUNTRY LIFE. LIII, 434, 466. 1923.
COUNTRY LIFE. CLXVIII, 2099, 2246, 2334. 1980.
COUNTRY LIFE. CLXIX, 288 [Furniture.], 346 [Furniture.] 1981.
COUNTRY LIFE. CLXXI, 224 [Paintings.], 296 [Paintings.] 1982.
HAMPSHIRE: Architectural views. 1830.
JONES. Views of Seats. II, 1829.
MORRIS, F.O. Views of Seats. Vol.I, p.69. 1880.
NEALE, J.P. Views of Seats.Vol.II. 1819.
TIPPING, H.A. English Homes. Period VI, Vol.I, p.239. 1926.

BROADOAKS (Essex).
SQUIERS, Granville.
— Broadoaks. The story of an Essex manor house. 24pp. 6 illus. and section. 22x14 London: Dryden Press, 1933.

BROADWATER (Surrey).
BURKE, J.B. Visitation of Seats. Vol.I, p.144. 1852.

BROADWELL (Gloucestershire).
ATKYNS, R. Glocestershire. p.157. 1768.

BROCKENHURST (Hampshire).
COUNTRY LIFE. CXLII, 464 plan. 1967.
COPPER PLATE MAGAZINE. pl.120. 1778.
SANDBY, P. Select Views. I. pl.20. 1783.

BROCKET HALL (Hertfordshire).
ANGUS, W. Seats of the Nobility. pl.2. 1787.
COPPER PLATE MAGAZINE. II, pl.76. 1792-1802.
COUNTRY LIFE. English Country Houses: Mid Georgian. p.105. 1956.
COUNTRY LIFE. LVIII, 16 plan, 60 plan, 96. 1925.
ENGLAND: Picturesque Views. p.1. 1786-88.
NEALE, J.P. Views of Seats. 2.S. Vol.V.1829.
PAINE, J. Plans, elevations. Pt.II, pls.53-59 plans, 84, 85 [Bridge.], 90-92. [Ceilings.] 1783.
TIPPING, H.A. English Homes. Period VI, Vol.I, p.1 [Paine's ground plan]. 1926.
[Sales] BROCKET HALL, 1923, March 7 [Contents].

BROCKHALL (Northamptonshire).
BURKE, J.B. Visitation of Seats. 2.S. Vol.I, p.242. 1854.*
COUNTRY LIFE. CXXXVI, 1428. 1964.
GOTCH, J.A. Squires' Homes. 32. 1939.

BROCKHAMPTON PARK (Gloucestershire).
ATKYNS, R. Glocestershire. p.451. 1768.
[Sales] ANDOVERSFORD, 1934, July 23, 24 [Contents].

BROCKHURST, The (Cheshire).
TWYCROSS, E. Mansions of England and Wales. Vol.I, p.141. 1850.

BROCKLESBY PARK (Lincolnshire).
TATHAM, Charles Heathcote.
— The gallery at Brocklesby, in Lincolnshire; the seat of the Right Honourable Lord Yarborough, &c. 3ff. 6 Engr. plates incl. sections and plan. 49x30 London: T. Gardiner; Longman, Hurst, Rees, Orme, and Brown, 1811.
BURKE, J.B. Visitation of Seats. 2.S. Vol.I, p.71. 1854.*
COUNTRY LIFE. LXXV, 192, 218, 254 [Pictures]. 1934.
LINCOLNSHIRE. A selection of views. 17 [Mausoleum] 1805.

BROCKLEY HALL (Somerset).
MANUSCRIPTS (Typewritten). English.
— RUTTER, J. Extract from *the Westonian guide: intended as a visitor's companion to that favourite watering place* [etc.]. By J.R. 1829, pages 34-38. [A description of Brockley Hall, with a catalogue of the more important paintings.] 3ff. 33x20 1942.
MORRIS, F.O. Views of Seats. Vol.VI, p.75. 1880.

BRODSWORTH HALL (Yorkshire).
COUNTRY LIFE. CXXXIV, 804, 876 plan. 1963.

BROGYNTYN (Shropshire).
BURKE, J.B. Visitation of Seats. Vol.I, p.83. 1852.*
JONES. Views of Seats. I. 1829.
LEACH, F. Seats of Shropshire. p.129. 1891.
LEIGHTON, S. Shropshire houses. 21. 1901.
NEALE, J.P. Views of Seats. Vol.III. 1820.
WEST, W. Picturesque views of Shropshire. p.123. 1831.
[Sales] BROGYNTYN HALL, 1955, November 28, 29, December 1 [Remaining contents].

BROKE HALL (Suffolk).
NEALE, J.P. Views of Seats. Vol.IV. 1821.

BROMBOROUGH HALL (Cheshire).
TWYCROSS, E. Mansions of England and Wales. Vol.I, p.61. 1850.*

BROME HALL (Suffolk).
KIP, J. Nouveau théâtre de la Grande Bretagne. I, pl.44. 1715.

BRONDANW (Merionethshire).
See PLAS BRONDANW.

BRONWYDD (Cardiganshire).
BURKE, J.B. Visitation of Seats. Vol.II, p.70. 1853.*

BROOKE HALL (Norfolk).
BURKE, J.B. Visitation of Seats. Vol.II, p.185. 1853.*

BROOKFIELD HALL (Derbyshire).
[Sales] BROOKFIELD HALL, 1868, March 16-19 [Contents].

BROOK MANOR (Hampshire, Isle of Wight).
BURKE, J.B. Visitation of Seats. Vol.I, p.193. 1852.*

BROOKWOOD PARK (Hampshire).
JONES. Views of Sets. II. 1829.
NEALE, J.P. Views of Seats. 2.S. Vol.I. 1824.

BROOME PARK (Kent).
ANGUS, W. Seats of the Nobility. pl.18. 1787.
BADESLADE, T. Seats in Kent. pl.5. 1750.
COUNTRY LIFE. XXII, 18. 1907.
COUNTRY LIFE. LXXXVI, 494. 1939.
GREENWOOD, C. Kent. 402. 1838.
HARRIS, J. History of Kent. p.34. 1719.
LATHAM, C. In English Homes. Vol.I, p.99. 1904.
OSWALD, A. Country houses of Kent. 46. 1933.

BROOMFIELD LODGE, Clapham (Surrey).
CAMPBELL, C. New Vitruvius Britannicus. I, pls.17, 18. 1802.

BROUGHAM HALL (Westmorland).
BURKE, J.B. Visitation of Seats. Vol.I, p.159. 1852.*
HALL, S.C. Baronial Halls. Vol.II. 1848.

BROUGH HALL (Yorkshire).
ANGUS, W. Seats of the Nobility. pl.22. 1787.
COUNTRY LIFE. CXLII, 894, 948. 1967.
WOOD, G.B. Historic homes of Yorkshire. 72. 1957.

BROUGHTON CASTLE (Oxfordshire).
BROUGHTON CASTLE.
— Broughton Castle. 16pp. Illus. (some col., some on covers.) 19x13 [Broughton?: privately printed] (1972.)

BUCK, S.&N. Antiquities. II. pl.234. 1774.
BURKE, J.B. Visitation of Seats. Vol.I, p.136. 1852.
COUNTRY LIFE. IX, 112. 1901.
COUNTRY LIFE. LXVII, 50 plan, 84, 126. 1930.
COUNTRY LIFE. CLX. 1636, 1758 plan, 1834. 1976.
DELDERFIELD, E.R. West Country houses. III, 33. 1973.
GOTCH, J.A. Architecture of the Renaissance. I, p.6. 1894.
MORRIS, F.O. Views of Seats. Vol.III, p.25. 1880.
NASH, J. Mansions of England. II, pl.7. 1840.
SUMMERSON, J. The Country Seat. 9 [Chimney piece.] 1970.
[Sales] BROUGHTON CASTLE, 1837, July 4-8, 11-15, 17 [Pictures & contents.].

BROUGHTON HALL (Staffordshire).
COUNTRY LIFE. XXVIII, 126. 1910.
COUNTRY LIFE. LXXXVII, 349. 1940.
NIVEN, W. Old Staffordshire houses. p.1, pl.1. 1882.
PLOT, R. Staffordshire. 255. 1686.
TIPPING, H.A. English Homes. Early Renaissance, p.321.1912.

BROUGHTON HALL (Yorkshire).
BURKE, J.B. Visitation of Seats. 2.S. Vol.II, p.218. 1855.*
COUNTRY LIFE. English Country Houses: Late Georgian. p.91. 1958.
COUNTRY LIFE. CVII, 954, 1034. 1950.

BROUGHTON HOUSE (Kent).
GREENWOOD, C. Kent. 91. 1838.

BROUGHTON TOWER (Lancashire).
WATTS, W. Seats of the Nobility. pl.80. 1779.
[Sales] BROUGHTON TOWER, 1920, May 31-June 4 [Contents.]

BROWNSEA CASTLE (Dorsetshire).
COUNTRY LIFE. XLIX, 430. 1921.
HUTCHINS, J. History of Dorset. I, 646. 1861.
JONES. Views of Seats. II. 1829.
NEALE, J.P. Views of Seats. Vol.I. 1818.
OSWALD, A. Country houses of Dorset. p.174. 1959.
[Sales] BROWNSEA ISLAND, 1927, June 13-17, 20-23 [Contents; incl. musical instruments].

BROWSHOLME HALL (Yorkshire).
BROWSHOLME HALL.
— Catalogue of the paintings in the gallery at Brownsholme, the seat of T.L. Parker, Esq. [Typescript copy.] 6ff. 24x19 Lancaster, 1809.
BROWSHOLME HALL.
— Browsholme Hall, Near Clitheroe, Lancashire; the historic home of the Parker family. 16pp. Illus. (some on covers, 1 on title-page) incl. map 14x20 [Derby: E.L.P., c.1957.]

Another ed. Illus. (1 col., some on covers, 1 on title-page) incl. map. (Derby, 1973.)
Another ed. (Text by S. Jervis.) 24pp. Illus. (1 col., some on covers, 1 on title-page, Derby, 1980.)
PARKER, Thomas Lister.
— Description of Browsholme Hall in the ... county of York, and of the parish of Waddington in the same county: also a collection of letters from the original manuscripts in the reigns of Charles I and II and James II, in the possession of T.L.P. [Compiled and edited by T.L.P., and T.D. Whitaker.] Plates (1 folding) incl. plan, facsimiles and genealog. table. 30x23 London: S. Gosnell, 1815.
BURKE, J.B. Visitation of Seats. 2.S. Vol.I, p.232. 1854.*
COUNTRY LIFE. LXXVIII, 38. 1935.

BROWSTON HALL (Suffolk).
SANDON, E. Suffolk houses. 169. 1977.

BROXBOURNBURY (Hertfordshire).
BURKE, J.B. Visitation of Seats. Vol.II, p.215. 1853.*

BROXTON OLD HALL (Cheshire).
ORMEROD, G. Cheshire. II, 671. 1882.

BRUCE CASTLE, Tottenham (Middlesex).
COPPER PLATE MAGAZINE. II, pl.82. 1792-1802.
ENGLAND: Beauties of England. II, p.74. 1787.
ENGLAND: Picturesque Views. p.52. 1786-88.

BRUNDISH MANOR (Suffolk).
SANDON, E. Suffolk houses. 253. 1977.

BRYANSTON HOUSE (Dorsetshire).
HUTCHINS, J. History of Dorset. I, 263. 1861.
HUTCHINS, J. Vitruvius Dorsettiensis. pl.2. 1816.
JONES. Views of Seats. II. 1829.
KIP, J. Nouveau théâtre de la Grande Bretagne. I, pl.77. 1715.
NEALE, J.P. Views of Seats. Vol.I. 1818.
OSWALD, A. Country houses of Dorset. p.175. 1959.
[Sales] BRYANSTON, 1925, November 24 and following days [Contents].

BRYERSWOOD, Far Sawrey (Lancashire).
[Sales] BRYERSWOOD, Far Sawrey, 1935, April 23-27 [Contents] (K.F.& R.).

BRYMPTON D'EVERCY (Somerset).
CLIVE-PONSONBY-FANE, Charles.

— Brympton d'Evercy, Yeovil, Somerset. The historic seat of the d'Evercy and Sydenham families and since 1731, the home of the Clive-Ponsonby-Fane family. 20pp. Illus. (some on covers, 1 on title-page) incl. plan, map and genealog. table. 14x20 (Derby: E.L.P., 1974).

COUNTRY LIFE. XXII, 774. 1907.

COUNTRY LIFE. LXI, 718, 762, 775 [Furniture & Pictures]. 1927.

GARNER, T. Domestic architecture. I, 70. 1911.

KIP, J. Nouveau théâtre de la Grande Bretagne. I, pl.66. 1715.

RICHARDSON, C.J. Old English mansions. III. 1845.

TIPPING, H.A. English Homes. Periods I & II, Vol.II, p.31. 1937.

BRYN BRAS CASTLE (Caernarvonshire).
BRYN BRAS CASTLE.
— Bryn Bras Castle, Llanrug, North Wales ... Official guide. 16pp. Illus. (some on covers) incl. map. 14x20 [Derby: E.L.P., 1960.]

BURKE, J.B. Visitation of Seats. 2.S. Vol.I, p.68. 1854.*

BRYNLLYWARCH HOUSE (Montgomeryshire).
[Sales] NEWTOWN, Montgomeryshire. 1835. October 6 [Estate].

BRYN Y PYS (Flintshire).
BURKE, J.B. Visitation of Seats. Vol.I, p.155. 1852.*

ENGLAND: Picturesque Views. p.78. 1786-88.

BUBNELL HALL (Derbyshire).
TILLEY, J. Halls of Derbyshire. I, p.47. 1892.

BUCKDEN PALACE (Huntingdonshire).
EDLESTON, Robert Holmes.
— Buckden Palace and its owners. 8pp. 5 plates. 25x16 Peterborough (1921).
Reprint from: Transactions of the Peterborough Natural History and Museum Society. 1921.

BUCK, S.& N. Antiquities. I, pl.118. 1774.

COUNTRY LIFE. XXVI, 162. 1909.

ENGLAND: Beauties of England. I, p.358. 1787.

TIPPING, H.A. English Homes. Period II, Vol.I, p.305. 1924.

BUCKFASTLEIGH ABBEY (Devonshire).
BRITTON, J. Devonshire illustrated. 85. 1832.

BUCKHOLD (Berkshire).
[Sales] BUCKHOLD, 1932, October 5-7 [Contents]. (K.F.& R.).

BUCKHURST PARK (Sussex).
BURKE, J.B. Visitation of Seats. Vol.II, p.162. 1853.*

COUNTRY LIFE. XXXI, 686 plan, 722. 1912.

BUCKLAND (Berkshire).
BURKE, J.B. Visitation of Seats. Vol.II, p.176. 1853.*

CAMPBELL, C. Vitruvius Britannicus. IV, pls.90-93. 1767.

COUNTRY LIFE. English Country Houses: Early Georgian. p.204. 1955.

COUNTRY LIFE. XXXVII, 662, 698 plan. 1915.

JONES. Views of Seats. I. 1829.

NEALE, J.P. Views of Seats. Vol.I. 1818.

BUCKLAND ABBEY (Devonshire).
LONDON: National Trust for Places of Historic Interest or Natural Beauty.

— GILL, C. Buckland Abbey. 72pp. Illus. (1 on title-page) incl. map. 18x12 Plymouth: City Council, 1951.
Rev. ed. 76pp. 1956.
3 rev.ed. Illus. (1 on cover, 1 on title-page) incl. map. 1968.

LONDON: National Trust for Places of Historic Interest or Natural Beauty.
— GILL, C. How to look at Buckland Abbey. 8pp. Illus. 21x13 [London, c.1955.]

LONDON: National Trust for Places of Historic Interest or Natural Beauty.
— CUMMING, A.A. Buckland Abbey. 28pp. Illus. (some col.) 25x15 (Norwich, 1981.)

BRITTON, J. Devonshire illustrated. 105. 1832.

BUCK, S.&N. Antiquities. I, pl.60. 1774.

COUNTRY LIFE. XXIX, 338 plan. 1916.

TIPPING, H.A. English Homes. Period III, Vol.II, p.97. 1927.

BUCKLAND FILLEIGH (Devonshire).
JONES. Views of Seats. II. 1829.

NEALE, J.P. Views of Seats. 2.S. Vol.I. 1824.

SUMMERSON, J. The Country Seat. 229. 1970.

BUCKMINSTER PARK (Leicestershire).
CAMPBELL, C. New Vitruvius Britannicus. I, pls.69-72. 1802.

BUCKTON HALL (Yorkshire).
COUNTRY LIFE. CIV, 628. 1948.

BUGLAWTON HALL (Cheshire).
TWYCROSS, E. Mansions of England and Wales. Vol.I, p.143. 1850.

BUILDWAS ABBEY (Shropshire).
LEACH, F. Seats of Shropshire. p.369. 1891.

BUILE HILL (Lancashire).
BARTLETT, J. Mansions of England and Wales. pl.155. 1853.
TWYCROSS, E. Mansions of England and Wales. Vol.III, p.98. 1847.

BULBRIDGE HOUSE (Wiltshire).
COUNTRY LIFE. CXXXIII, 420 plan, 472. 1963.

BULEDGE, Chippenham. (Wiltshire).
ELYARD, S.J. Old Wiltshire homes. p.41. 1894.

BULSTRODE PARK (Buckinghamshire).
CAMPBELL, C. Vitruvius Britannicus. IVth. pls.40-44. 1739.
COPPER PLATE MAGAZINE. II, pl.54. 1792-1802.
ENGLAND: Picturesque Views. p.29. 1786-88.
REPTON, H. Observations on landscape gardening. 67 [Map of estate]. 1803.
[Sales] LONDON, 1932, May 27, 30 [Pictures from Bulstrode].
[Sales] LONDON, 1932, May 30, 31 [Books].
[Sales] LONDON, 1932, June 1 [Silver plate from Bulstrode].

BULWELL HALL (Nottinghamshire).
MORRIS, F.O. Views of Seats. Vol.IV, p.17. 1880.

BULWICK HALL (Northamptonshire).
GOTCH, J.A. Squires' Homes. 6. 1939.

BUNGALOW, THE (Lancashire).
See RIVINGTON, The Bungalow.

BUNNY HALL (Nottinghamshire).
THOROTON, R. Nottinghamshire. I, 94. 1797.
[Sales] BUNNY HALL, 1910, February 22-25 [Contents].

BUNTINGSDALE (Shropshire).
COUNTRY LIFE. XLII, 420. 1917.
LEIGHTON, S. Shropshire houses. 30. 1901.
TIPPING, H.A. English Homes. Period V, Vol.I, p.193. 1921.

BURBAGE HOUSE (Leicestershire).
NICHOLS, J. History of Leicestershire. IV, ii, 460. 1811.

BURE HOMAGE (Hampshire).
SPROULE, A. Lost houses of Britain. 82. 1982.

BURFORD HOUSE (Shropshire).
COUNTRY LIFE. CII, 1310. 1947.

BURFORD LODGE (Surrey).
BRAYLEY, E.W. History of Surrey. IV, 459. 1841.

BURFORD PRIORY (Oxfordshire).
COUNTRY LIFE. XXIX, 306 plan. 1911.
COUNTRY LIFE. LXXXV, 586 plan, 616. 1939.
GOTCH, J.A. Architecture of the Renaissance. I, p.22. 1894.
TIPPING, H.A. English Homes. Early Renaissance, p.217. 1912.
[Sales] BURFORD PRIORY, 1935, May 14-16 [Contents].

BURGH HALL (Norfolk).
BURKE, J.B. Visitation of Seats. Vol.II, p.217. 1853.*

BURGHLEY HOUSE (Northamptonshire).
BURGHLEY HOUSE.
— A history or, description, general and circumstantial, of Burghley House, the seat of the Right Honorable the Earl of Exeter. [By J. Horn] 21x13 Shrewsbury: J. & W. Eddowes, 1797.
BURGHLEY HOUSE.
— A guide to Burghley House, Northamptonshire, the seat of the Marquis of Exeter; containing a catalogue of all the paintings, antiquities, &c. with biographical notices of the artists. [By T. Blore.] Plates incl. folding genealog. table. 21x13 Stamford: J. Drakard, 1815.
BURGHLEY HOUSE.
— Burghley House, Stamford. 20pp. Illus. (some col., some on covers) incl. map and genealog. table. 23x18 (Stamford) privately printed [c.1965.]
EXETER, Myra Rowena Sibell Cecil, *Marchioness of.*
— Catalogue of pictures at Burghley House, Northampton-shire, 1954. By the Marchioness of Exeter, from her Ms. including many original notes. [Facsimile of Ms.] 22x14 [n.p.] for the author, 1954.
SHARP, Samuel.
— A handbook of Burghley, Northamptonshire; comprising an account of the house and its interesting contents, a list of the pictures, a genealogical and biographical history of the noble family of Cecil, and biographical notices of several hundreds of painters [etc.]. 148pp. Illus. incl. plates (1 engr.) 22x13 Stamford: by the author, 1851.
BRIDGES, J. Northamptonshire. II. 588. 1791.
COUNTRY LIFE. English Country Houses: Baroque. p.60. 1970.
COUNTRY LIFE. CXIV, 1828 plan, 1962, 2038, 2104 plan, 2164, 1953.
COUNTRY LIFE. CLIII, 1604 [Furniture]. 1973.
COUNTRY LIFE. CLVIII, 982 [Capability Brown at B.] 1975.
ENGLAND: Beauties of England. II, p.138. 1787.
GOTCH, J.A. Architecture of the Renaissance. I, p.1. 1894.
GOTCH, J.A. Halls of Northants. p.4. 1936.
HALL, S.C. Baronial Halls. Vol.II. 1848.
HAVELL, R. Views of Noblemen's Seats. 1823.
JONES. Views of Seats. I. 1829.

KIP, J. Nouveau théâtre de la Grande Bretagne. III, 34. 1715.
MORRIS, F.O. Views of Seats. Vol.I, p.65. 1880.
NASH, J. Mansions of England. III, pls.1, 2. 1841.
NEALE, J.P. View of Seats. Vol.III. 1820.
RICHARDSON, C.J. Old English mansions. II. 1842.
SANDBY, P. Select Views. I, pl.29. 1783.
WATTS, W. Seats of the Nobility. pls.21, 41. 1779.

BURLEIGH HOUSE [HALL] (Leicestershire).
NICHOLS, J. History of Leicestershire. III, i, 135. 1800.

BURLEY HALL (Leicestershire).
See BURLEIGH HOUSE [HALL].

BURLEY-ON-THE-HILL (Rutland).
BURLEY ON THE HILL.
— Burley on the Hill: an illustrated survey [etc.]. 32pp. Illus. (some col., some on covers) incl. maps (on inside covers). 14x22 Derby: E.L.P. [1960].
FINCH, Pearl.
— History of Burley-on-the-Hill, Rutland, with a short account of the owners ... and catalogue of the contents of the house. Plates incl. plans, maps and facsimiles of signatures. 2. vols. 25x19 London: Bale, Sons & Danielsson, 1901.
ANGUS, W. Seats of the Nobility. pl.63. 1787.
COUNTRY LIFE. English Country Houses: Baroque. p.112. 1970.
COUNTRY LIFE. LIII, 178, 210, 254 [Furniture]. 1923.
NEALE, J.P. Views of Seats. Vol.III. 1820.
NOBLE, T. Counties of Chester, ... Lincoln. p.61. 1836.
REPTON, H. Observations on landscape gardening. 133. 1803.

BURLINGHAM ST. EDMUND HALL (Norfolk).
BIRKBECK, G. Old Norfolk houses. 27. 1908.
GARRATT, T. Halls of Norfolk. pl.16. 1890.

BURLTON HALL (Shropshire).
BURKE, J.B. Visitation of Seats. Vol.I, p.158. 1852.*

BURNASTON HALL (Derbyshire).
TILLEY, J. Halls of Derbyshire. II, p.75. 1893.

BURNESIDE HALL (Westmorland).
CUMBERLAND: C.& W.A. & A.S. Extra Series VIII. 176 plan. 1892.

BURN HALL (Durham)
SOANE, J. Plans, elevations and sections. pls. XXIV-XXXVI [Proposed design.] 1788.

BURROW HALL (Lancashire).
COUNTRY LIFE. CXXVII, 806 plan, 864. 1960.

BURTON AGNES HALL (Yorkshire).
BURTON AGNES HALL.
— Burton Agnes Hall. 24pp. Illus. (some col., some on covers.) 25x15 [Burton Agnes? privately printed?] (1969).
MUSGRAVE, Ernest I.
— Burton Agnes Hall: an illustrated survey of the Yorkshire residence of Mr. Marcus Wickham-Boynton. For over 350 years the home of the Boynton family. 32pp. Illus. (some col., some on covers) incl. plan and map. 14x21 Derby: E.L.P., [c.1957].
COUNTRY LIFE. XIV, 208. 1903.
COUNTRY LIFE. XXXIII, 880, 916 plan. 1913.
COUNTRY LIFE. CXIII, 1804, 1886, 1972.1953.
GOTCH, J.A. Architecture of the Renaissance. II, p.30 plan. 1894.
LATHAM, C. In English Homes. Vol.I, p.131. 1904.
MORRIS, F.O. Views of Seats. Vol.I, p.89. 1880.
RICHARDSON, C.J. Old English mansions. II. 1842.
WOOD, G.B. Historic homes of Yorkshire. 128. 1957.
[Sales] LONDON, 1947, July 28, 29 [Burton Agnes papers].

BURTON AGNES OLD MANOR HOUSE (Yorkshire).
GREAT BRITAIN: Ministry of Works [Ancient Monuments and Historic Buildings].
— WOOD, M. 10pp. Plans. 21x14 [London] (1956).
2 ed [D.o.E.] 12pp. Plans. [London] (1981).

BURTON CONSTABLE (Yorkshire).
BURKE, J.B. Visitation of Seats. 2.S. Vol.I, p.89. 1854.*
COUNTRY LIFE. English Country Houses: Early Georgian. p.222. 1955.
COUNTRY LIFE. XXI, 126. 1907.
COUNTRY LIFE. LXXII, 238, 266 plan. 1932.
COUNTRY LIFE. CLIX, 1476 [Furniture.] 1622 [Furniture.] 1976.
COUNTRY LIFE. CLXXI, 1114, 1198, 1278, 1358. 1982.
LATHAM, C. In English Homes. Vol.II, p.143. 1907.
MORRIS, F.O. Views of Seats. Vol.I, p.45. 1880.
WATTS, W. Seats of the Nobility. pl.12. 1779.

BURTON HALL (Cheshire).
COUNTRY LIFE. XXXII, 490 plan. 1912.
TWYCROSS, E. Mansions of England and Wales. Vol.I, p.72. 1850.*

BURTON HALL (Leicestershire).
BURKE, J.B. Visitation of Seats. Vol.I, p.43. 1852.*

BURTON HALL (Lincolnshire).
BURKE, J.B. Visitation of Seats. Vol.II, p.226. 1853.*

BURTON LATIMER HALL (Northamptonshire).
GOTCH, J.A. Squires' Homes. 16. 1939.

BURTON PARK (Sussex).
COUNTRY LIFE. LXXX, 38. 1936.
NEALE, J.P. Views of Seats. 2.S. Vol.I. 1824.
[Sales] BURTON PARK, 1919, September 25, 26 [Contents].

BURTON PYNSENT (Somerset).
COLLINSON, J. History of Somerset. I, 24. 1791.

BURWARTON HALL [House] (Shropshire).
COUNTRY LIFE. CXXVII, 582 plan. 1960.
LEACH, F. Seats of Shropshire. p.225. 1891.
LEIGHTON, S. Shropshire houses. 41. 1901.
[Sales] BURWARTON HOUSE, 1956, July 17-20[Contents].

BURWELL PARK (Lincolnshire).
LINCOLNSHIRE. A selection of views. 35. 1805.

BURWOOD PARK (Surrey).
BURKE, J.B. Visitation of Seats. 2.S. Vol.II, p.13. 1855.*
[Sales] BURWOOD PARK, 1926, September 20-24 [Contents].

BURY HILL (Surrey).
BRAYLEY E.W. History of Surrey. V, 107. 1841.
MANNING, O. Surrey. I. 578. 1804.
NEALE, J.P. Views of Seats. 2.S. Vol.I. 1824.
PROSSER, G.F. Surrey Seats. p.15. 1828.

BUSBRIDGE (Surrey).
ANGUS, W. Seats of the Nobility. pl.6. 1787.
BRAYLEY, E.W. History of Surrey. V, 217. 1841.
NEALE, J.P. Views of Seats. 2.S. Vol.I. 1824.
PROSSER, G.F. Surrey Seats. p.69. 1828.

BUSCOT PARK (Berkshire).
LONDON: National Trust for Places of Historic Interest or Natural Beauty.
— The Faringdon collection, Buscot Park. [Guide and catalogue of paintings] 36pp. Illus. (on cover) and 9 plates. 25x18 (London) Faringdon collection, 1964.
Another ed. 40pp. Col. illus. (on cover) and 12 plates. 1975.
COUNTRY LIFE. LXXXVII, 502 plan, 524. 1940.
THAMES, River. An history. I, pl.7. 1794.

BUSHEY HALL (Hertfordshire).
CHAUNCY, H. Hertfordshire. II, 454. 1826.
[Sales] BUSHEY HALL, 1878, April 3 and following days [Furniture and contents].

BUSHEY PARK (Middlesex.)
GREAT BRITAIN AND IRELAND: Department of Scientific and Industrial Research [National Physical Laboratory].
— Museum and Archives. Publications. Illus. vols. 30x21 Teddington, 1976-
1. Bushy House. [By] P. Foster and E. Pyatt. [Bibliogr. notes.] 32pp. Illus. (some on cover) incl. elevation, plans and maps. 1976.
NEALE, J.P. Views of Seats. Vol.II. 1819.

BUSH HILL PARK (Middlesex).
COPPER PLATE MAGAZINE. II, pl.58. 1792-1802.
ENGLAND: Picturesque Views. p.60. 1786-88.

BUSHMEAD PRIORY (Bedfordshire).
BURKE, J.B. Visitation of Seats. Vol.I, p.82. 1852.*

BUTLER'S COURT (Buckinghamshire).
See GREGORIES.

BUTLEY PRIORY (Suffolk).
COUNTRY LIFE. LXXIII, 308. 1932.
SANDON, E. Suffolk houses. 301. 1977.

BUTTERTON HALL (Staffordshire).
SHAW, S. Staffordshire. II, pl.30. Reprint 1976.

BUXTED PARK (Sussex.)
LIVERPOOL, Cecil George Savile Foljambe, *Earl of.*
— Catalogues of portraits at Compton Place and at Buxted Park, in Sussex [and] (miniatures at Devonshire House). 28pp. Folding genealog. table. 21x14 n.p. privately printed, 1903. Also in SUSSEX: Archaeological Society, Collections. XLVII, 82, 1904.
Bound in vol. lettered: Portraits by Lord Hawkesbury, 1905.
COUNTRY LIFE. LXXV,404, 432.1934.
COUNTRY LIFE. LXXXVII, 191. 1940.
COUNTRY LIFE. CVIII, 374, 442, 518. 1950.
[Sales] BUXTED PARK, 1929, November 25 and following days [Contents].

BUXTON HALL (Derbyshire).
TILLEY, J. Halls of Derbyshire. I, p.63. 1892.

BYANNA (Staffordshire).
SHAW, S. Staffordshire. II, pl.24. Reprint 1976.

BYFORD COURT (Herefordshire).
ROBINSON, C.J. Mansions of Herefordshire. pl.5. 1873.

BYRAM HALL (Yorkshire).
[Sales] BYRAM, 1922, June 28—July 1, 3-5 [Contents].

BYRKLEY LODGE (Staffordshire).
[Sales] BYRKLEY LODGE, 1913, June 23 and following days [Contents]. (K.F. & R.).

BYWELL HALL (Northumberland).
PAINE, J. Plans, elevations. Pt. I, pls.53 [Plan.] 54, 55, 1767.

CADBURY HOUSE (Somerset).
BURKE, J.B. Visitation of Seats. Vol.II, p.152. 1853. *

CADENHAM HOUSE Foxham (Wiltshire).
ELYARD, S.J. Old Wiltshire Homes. p.57. 1894.

CADHAY (Devonshire).
CADHAY.
— Cadhay, Devon. 24pp. Illus. incl. plan. 22x14 (Exeter) privately printed [c.1970].
COUNTRY LIFE. XXXIII, 90 plan. 1913.
DELDERFIELD, E.R. West Country Houses. I, 18. 1968.
GARNER, T. Domestic architecture. I, p.114 plan. 1911.

CADLAND (Hampshire).
BURKE, J.B. Visitation of Seats. 2.S. Vol.II. p.56. 1854.
WATTS, W. Seats of the Nobility. pl.24. 1779.

CAE BAILEY (Glamorganshire).
NICHOLAS, T. Counties of Wales. II, p.477. 1872.

CAEN WOOD (Middlesex).
See KENWOOD HOUSE.

CAERHAYS CASTLE (Cornwall).
CROMWELL, T.K. Excursions in Cornwall. p.51. 1824.
JONES. Views of Seats. II. 1829.
NEALE, J.P. Views of Seats. Vol.I. 1818.

CAISTER CASTLE (Norfolk).
TIPPING, H.A. English Homes. Periods I & II, Vol.II, p.307. 1937.

CAISTER OLD HALL (Norfolk).
BIRKBECK, G. Old Norfolk Houses. 28. 1908.

CALDECOTE HALL (Warwickshire).
BURKE, J.B. Visitation of Seats. Vol.II, p.122. 1853.*

CALDERSTONE (Lancashire).
BARTLETT, J. Mansions of England and Wales. pls.125, 126. 1853.
TWYCROSS, E. Mansions of England and Wales. Vol.III, p. 57. 1847.

CALDMORE, Walsall. (Staffordshire).
NIVEN, W. Old Staffordshire Houses. p.17, pl.14. 1882.

CALGARTH PARK (Westmorland).
BURKE, J.B. Visitation of Seats. Vol.II, p.109. 1853. *

CALKE ABBEY (Derbyshire).
BURKE, J.B. Visitation of Seats. Vol.I, p.107. 1852.
TILLEY, J. Halls of Derbyshire. IV, p.5. 1902.

CALLALY CASTLE (Northumberland).
BURKE, J.B. Visitation of Seats. 2.S. Vol.I, p.12. 1854.*
COUNTRY LIFE. CXXV, 304 plan, 358. 1959.

CALLOW HALL (Derbyshire).
TILLEY, J. Halls of Derbyshire. II, p.267. 1893.

CALTHORPE HOUSE (Oxfordshire).
DRAPER, Eleanor.
— Notes on Calthorpe Manor House, Banbury, and its inhabitants. 40pp. Plates. 25x19 Banbury: privately printed, 1915.

CALVELEY HALL (Cheshire).
TWYCROSS, E. Mansions of England and Wales. Vol.I, p.117. 1850.*

CALVERLEY HOUSE (Yorkshire).
YORKSHIRE. Picturesque views. 1885.

CALWICH ABBEY (Staffordshire).
FORTESCUE, Mary Teresa.
— The History of Calwich Abbey. [Bibliogr.] Plates. incl. folding map and genealog. tables. 22x14 London: Simpkin & Co., Winchester: Warren & Son [1915].
BURKE, J.B. Visitation of Seats. Vol.I, p.269. 1852.*

CAMBRIDGE HOUSE, Twickenham (Middlesex)
See TWICKENHAM MEADOWS.

CAMDEN PLACE (Kent).
COPPER PLATE MAGAZINE. II, pl.62. 1792-1802.
ENGLAND: Picturesque Views. p.41. 1786-88.

CAME HOUSE (Dorsetshire).

COUNTRY LIFE. CXIII, 490, 572. 1953.
DELDERFIELD, E.R. West Country Houses. II, 24. 1970.
HUTCHINS, J. History of Dorset. II, 289. 1863.
HUTCHINS, J. Viturvius Dorsettiensis. pl.3. 1816.
OSWALD, A. Country Houses of Dorset. p.158. 1959.

CAMER (Kent).

GREENWOOD, C.Kent. 224. 1838.

CAMFIELD PLACE (Hertfordshire).

BURKE, J.B. Visitation of Seats. Vol.II, p.212. 1853.*
CHAUNCY, H. Hertfordshire. I. 544. 1826.

CAMILLA LACEY (Surrey).

[Sales] CAMILLA LACEY, 1922, November 28-30 [Contents].

CAMP, The. Windlesham (Surrey).

[Sales] CAMP, The. Windlesham, 1929, December 3-7
[Contents]. (K.F.& R.)

CAMPSEA ASH HIGH HOUSE (Suffolk).

CROMWELL, T.K. Excursions in Suffolk. II, p.64. 1819.

CAMS HALL (Hampshire).

HAMPSHIRE: Architectural views. 1830.
JONES. Views of Seats. II. 1829.
NEALE, J.P. Views of Seats. Vol.II. 1819.

CAN COURT (Wiltshire).

ELYARD, S.J. Old Wiltshire Homes. p.50. 1894.

CANFORD MANOR (Dorsetshire).

HEATH, S. Dorset Manor Houses. 45. 1907.
OSWALD, A. Country Houses of Dorset. p.174. 1959.

CANNON HALL (Yorkshire).

JONES. Views of Seats. I. 1829.
NEALE, J.P. Views of Seats. Vol.V. 1822.

CANNONS, Edgware (Middlesex).

CAMPBELL, C. Vitruvius Britannicus. IVth. pls.24-27. 1739.
COUNTRY LIFE. XXXV, 708 [Relics]. 1914.
COUNTRY LIFE. CVI, 1950. 1950.
SPROULE, A. Lost houses of Britain. 86. 1982.
WATTS, W. Seats of the Nobility. pl.40. 1779.
[Sales] CANNONS, 1747, June 16 and following days
[Materials of the dwelling house].

CANONBURY HOUSE (Middlesex).

COUNTRY LIFE. LIX, 630. 1926.
TIPPING, H.A. English Homes, Period III, Vol.II, p.179. 1927.

CANONS ASHBY (Northamptonshire).

COUNTRY LIFE. XVI, 978.1904.
COUNTRY LIFE. XLIX, 246, 278 plan, 306.1921.
COUNTRY LIFE. CLXIX, 930, 1026. 1981.
GOTCH, J.A. Architecture of the Renaissance. II, p.16 plan.
1894.
GOTCH, J.A. Halls of Northants. p.84. 1936.
LATHAM, C. In English Homes. Vol.II, p.281. 1907.

CANONS PARK (Middlesex).

See also CANNONS, Edgware.
COUNTRY LIFE. XL, 518. 1916.

CANONTEIGN (Devonshire).

BRITTON, J. Devonshire illustrated. 103. 1832.

CANWELL HALL (Staffordshire).

SHAW, S. Staffordshire. II, 22. 1801.

CAPERNWRAY HALL (Lancashire).

BARTLETT, J. Mansions of England and Wales. pl.50. 1853.
BURKE, J.B. Visitation of Seats. Vol.I, p.89. 1852.*
MORRIS, F.O. Views of Seats. Vol.IV, p.15. 1880.
TWYCROSS, E. Mansions of England and Wales. Vol.II.
p.10. 1847.

CAPESTHORNE (Cheshire).

BROMLEY-DAVENPORT, Lenette F.
— Capesthorne: an illustrated survey [etc] 32pp. Illus. (some
col., some on covers) incl. maps (on inside covers). 14x22 Derby:
E.L.P. [1959].
ANGUS-BUTTERWORTH, L.M. Old Cheshire families. p.49.
1932.
BURKE, J.B. Visitation of Seats. Vol.I, p.244. 1852.*
COUNTRY LIFE. CLXII. 535, 607. 1977.
MORRIS, F.O. Views of Seats. Vol.III, p.29. 1880.
TWYCROSS, E. Mansions of England and Wales. Vol.II.
p.103. 1850.
[Sales] LONDON, 1907, May 10, 11 [Portion of the library].

CAPHEATON HALL (Northumberland).

COUNTRY LIFE. CXXXVIII, 390. 1965.
JONES. Views of Seats. I. 1829.
NEALE, J.P. Views of Seats. Vol.III. 1820.

CARADOC COURT (Herefordshire).

ROBINSON, C.J. Mansions of Herefordshire. pl.18. 1873.

CARCLEW (Cornwall).
COUNTRY LIFE. XXXIX, 590. 1916.
COUNTRY LIFE. LXXV, 378. 1934.
CROMWELL, T.K. Excursions in Cornwall. p.60. 1824.

CARDEN HALL (Cheshire).
BURKE, J.B. Visitation of Seats. Vol.II, p.121. 1853.*
MOSS, F. Pilgrimages. [II] 372. 1903.
ORMEROD, G. Cheshire. II, 702.1882.
TWYCROSS, E. Mansions of England and Wales. Vol.I, p.27. 1850.

CARDIFF CASTLE (Glamorganshire).
CARDIFF CASTLE.
— A handy list of paintings at Cardiff Castle, the property of John Patrick Crichton Stuart, Marquess of Bute, K.T. 40pp. 22x17 (London) privately printed at the Chiswick Press, 1890.
CARDIFF: Castle.
— Cardiff Castle: an illustrated handbook. (By W. Rees.) 16pp. Illus. (some col., 3 on covers) incl. plan. 21x15 [Cardiff, 1978?].
CARDIFF: Corporation.
— Cardiff Castle: illustrated handbook. 8pp. 9 illus. (1 on cover) incl. 8 plates. 22x14 Cardiff [c.1950?].
BUCK, S.&N. Antiquities.II, pl.396. 1774.
BURKE, J.B. Visitation of Seats. 2.S. Vol.II, p.84, 1855.*
JONES. Views of Seats. VI. 1831.
NICHOLAS, T. Counties of Wales. II, p.462. 1872.
SANDBY, P. Select Views. II, pl.11 (Wales). 1782.
UNITED KINGDOM. Historic houses. 212. 1892.

CARHAM HALL (Northumberland).
NEALE, J.P. Views of Seats. Vol.III. 1820.

CARLTON CURLIEU HALL (Leicestershire).
JONES. Views of Seats. I. 1829.
NEALE, J.P. Views of Seats. 2.S. Vol.III. 1826.
NICHOLS, J. History of Leicestershire. II, ii, 538. 1798.
NICHOLS, J. History of Leicestershire. III, ii, pl. CLIII, 1127. 1804.
THROSBY, J. Views in Leicestershire. p.192. 1789.

CARLTON HALL (Northamptonshire).
BRIDGES, J. Northamptonshire. II, 292. 1791.
NEALE, J.P. Views of Seats. Vol.III. 1820.

CARLTON TOWERS (Yorkshire).
ROBINSON, John Martin.
— Carlton Towers: the Yorkshire home of the Duke of Norfolk [etc.]. 32pp. Illus. (some col., incl. 1 on cover.) map and genealog. table. 23x18 (London: Garden House Press) [c.1980.]
    The priests' hiding hole at Carlton Towers. 8pp. Illus. 21x15 London [c.1980]. Inserted.
COUNTRY LIFE. CXLI, 176, 230 plan, 280. 1967.

CARNANTON (Cornwall).
DELDERFIELD, E.R. West Country houses. I, 21. 1968.
MORRIS, F.O. Views of Seats. Vol.IV, p.25. 1880.

CARNFIELD HALL (Derbyshire).
TILLEY, J. Halls of Derbyshire. III, p.151. 1899.

CARR HALL (Lancashire).
BARTLETT, J. Mansions of England and Wales. pl.8. 1853.
TWYCROSS, E. Mansions of England and Wales. Vol.I, p.36. 1847.

CARROW PRIORY (Norfolk).
CARROW PRIORY.
— Notes on Carrow Priory, commonly called Carrow Abbey. [By F.R. Beecheno.] 2 ed. 18pp. 3 plates by C.J. Watson 24x20 (Norwich, privately printed) 1888.

CARSHALTON HOUSE (Surrey).
COUNTRY LIFE. CV, 480. 1949.
COUNTRY LIFE. CV, 1254 [Pavilion]. 1949.
WATTS, W. Seats of the Nobility. pl.60. 1779.

CARTER'S CORNER PLACE (Sussex).
CLARKE, T.H. Domestic architecture. 22. 1833.

CARTLEDGE HALL (Derbyshire).
TILLEY, J. Halls of Derbyshire. III, p.107. 1899.

CASEWICK (Lincolnshire).
COUNTRY LIFE. CXXXVI, 1762 plan,1808 plan. 1964.

CASHIOBURY (Hertfordshire).
See CASSIOBURY PARK.

CASSIOBURY PARK (Hertfordshire).
BRITTON, John.
— The history and description, with graphic illustrations of Cassiobury Park, Hertfordshire; the seat of the Earl of Essex. [Bibliogr. notes] 32pp. Illus. incl. plates, elevations and plans. 49x31 London: by the author, 1837.
BURKE, J.B. Visitation of Seats. 2.S. Vol.I, p.135. 1854.*
COUNTRY LIFE. XXVIII, 392. 1910.
ENGLAND: Beauties of England. I, p.349. 1787.
HAVELL, R. Views of Noblemen's Seats. 1823.
JEWITT, L. Stately homes of England. 308.1874.
JONES, Views of Seats. I. 1829.
KIP, J. Nouveau théâtre de la Grande Bretagne. I, pl.28. 1715.
LATHAM, C. In English Homes. Vol.I, p.405. 1904.
MORRIS, F.O. Views of Seats. Vol.II, p.73. 1880.
NEALE, J.P. Views of Seats. Vol.II. 1819.

[Sales] LONDON, 1922, May 24 [Library].
[Sales] CASSIOBURY PARK, 1922, June 12 and following days [Contents]. (K.F.& R.).
[Sales] LONDON, 1922, November 22-24 [Library].
[Sales] LONDON, 1922, November 30 [Library].

CASTELL COCH (Glamorganshire).
GREAT BRITAIN: Ministry of Works [Ancient Monuments and Historic Buildings].
— FLOUD, P. Castell Coch, Glamorgan. 20pp. Plates incl. sections and folding plan. 21x14 London, 1954.
GREAT BRITAIN: Ministry of Public Building and Works. [Ancient Monuments and Historic Buildings.]
— FLOUD. P. Castell Coch, Glamorgan. 20pp. Plates incl. sections and folding plan. 21x14 London, 1966.
GREAT BRITAIN: Department of the Environment [Ancient Monuments and Historic Buildings].
— FLOUD, P. Castell Coch, South Glamorgan, 28pp. Illus. incl. folding plate, sections and plan. London, 1975.

CASTELL PIGYN (Carmarthenshire).
See CASTLE PIGGIN.

CASTERN HALL (Staffordshire).
COUNTRY LIFE. CLXV. 274. 1979.

CASTLE ASHBY (Northamptonshire).
CASTLE ASHBY.
— A short history of Castle Ashby [etc.]. 32pp. Illus. (some on covers) incl. map. 15x22 n.p. privately printed, [c.1970]. Another ed. [c.1975].
ROBINSON, Peter Frederick.
— History of Castle Ashby. [Bibliogr. notes.] 26pp. Lithogr. plates incl. elevations and plan. 55x42 London: for the proprietor and J. Weale, 1841.
One of the series: VITRUVIUS BRITANNICUS.
BURKE, J.B. Visitation of Seats. 2.S. Vol.I, p.25. 1854.*
CAMPBELL, C. Vitruvius Britannicus. III, pl.8. 1725.
COUNTRY LIFE. XIV, 470. 1903.
COUNTRY LIFE. LX, 422 plan, 462, 901 [Furniture]. 1926.
COUNTRY LIFE. LXI, 925 [Pictures]. 1927.
GOTCH, J.A. Halls of Northants. p.74. 1936.
HALL, S.C. Baronial Halls. Vol.II. 1848.
JONES. Views of Seats. I. 1829.
LATHAM, C. In English Homes. Vol.I, p.139. 1904.
NEALE, J.P. Views of Seats. Vol.III. 1820.
TIPPING, H.A. English Homes. Period III, Vol.II, p.153. 1927.
WHITEMAN, G.W. English Country Homes. p.62. 1951.
[Sales] LONDON, 1980, July 2 [Vases].

CASTLE BROMWICH HALL (Warwickshire).
COUNTRY LIFE. XXXII, 228. 1912.
COUNTRY LIFE, CXI, 1408. 1952.
MALAN, A.H. Other famous homes. p.65. 1902.
NIVEN, W. Old Warwickshire Houses. p.5, pl.7. 1878.
SMITH, W. History of the County of Warwick. 363. 1830.
TIPPING, H.A. English Homes. Early Renaissance, p.337. 1912.

CASTLE COMBE (Wiltshire).
BURKE, J.B. Visitation of Seats. 2.S. Vol.I, p.245. 1854.*

CASTLE DROGO (Devonshire).
LONDON: National Trust for Places of Historic Interest or Natural Beauty.
— TRINICK, M. Castle Drogo, Devon, 24pp. Illus. (some on covers) incl. plates and plans. 21x15 [London] 1975. Leaflet, inserted. 4pp.
COUNTRY LIFE. XCVIII, 200 plan, 244 plan. 1945.

CASTLE EDEN (Durham).
BURKE, J.B. Visitation of Seats. 2.S. Vol.I, p.215. 1854.*

CASTLE GREEN (Cardiganshire).
NICHOLAS, T. Counties of Wales. I, p.139. 1872.

CASTLE HILL (Devonshire).
BRITTON, J. Devonshire illustrated. 80. 1832.
COUNTRY LIFE. LXXV, 272, 300. 1934.
DELDERFIELD, E.R. West Country houses. I, 24. 1968.
MORRIS, F.O. Views of Seats. Vol.VI, p.35. 1880.
WATTS, W. Seats of the Nobility. pl.74. 1779.

CASTLE HILL (Dorsetshire).
See DUNTISH COURT.

CASTLE HILL HOUSE Ealing (Middlesex).
COUNTRY LIFE. CXLVI, 949.1962.

CASTLE HOUSE, Aberystwyth (Cardiganshire).
COUNTRY LIFE. CXII, 33. 1952.

CASTLE HOUSE, Dedham (Essex).
CASTLE HOUSE.
— Castle House, Dedham, Essex: an illustrated survey of the home of the late Sir Alfred Munnings [etc.]. 16pp. Illus. (some on covers) incl. map. 14x20 [Derby] E.L.P. [c. 1962].

CASTLE HOUSE, Deddington (Oxfordshire).
COUNTRY LIFE. XXIII, 906. 1908.
LATHAM, C. In English homes. Vol. III, p.39. 1909.

CASTLE HOWARD (Yorkshire).
CASTLE HOWARD.
— A descriptive catalogue of the pictures at Castle Howard. 14pp. 16x10 Malton: privately printed, 1805. Imperfect?.
CASTLE HOWARD.
— A catalogue of the pictures at Castle-Howard. 22pp. 18x11 Malton: Smithson, 1845.
CASTLE HOWARD.
— The illustrated hand-book to Castle Howard, the Yorkshire seat of the Right Hon. The Earl of Carlisle. (Catalogue of the pictures ... statues, busts [etc].) 146pp. Plates. Malton: H. Smithson, 1857.
CLOUET.
— Three hundred French portraits representing personages of the courts of Francis I, Henry II, and Francis II, by Clouet. Auto-lithographed from the originals at Castle Howard, Yorkshire, by Lord R. Gower. [Preface also in French] 10pp. Lithogr. plates 2 vols. 43x34 London: Sampson, Low, Marston, Low & Searle; Paris: Hachette, 1875.
HOWARD, George.
— Castle Howard. 28pp. Illus. (some col., some on covers) incl. plan and maps. 23x18 (Castle Howard, 1958)
New ed.32pp. Illus. (some col. some on covers) incl. sections, plan and facsimiles. 19x24 (1972).
LIVERPOOL, Cecil George Savile Foljambe, *Earl of*.
— Catalogue of the portraits, miniatures, &c, at Castle Howard [and] (at Naworth Castle, Cumberland) in the possession of the Earl of Carlisle. 90pp. Plates. 21x14 n.p. privately printed [1904?].
With MS. notes by the Rev. E. Farrer.
Also in HULL: East Riding Antiquarian Society, Transactions, XI, 35, 1904.
Bound in vol. lettered: Portraits by Lord Hawkesbury, 1905.
TATHAM, Charles Heathcote.
— The gallery at Castle Howard, in Yorkshire, the seat of the Earl of Carlisle, K.G. &c. 3ff. 5 plates incl. elevations and plan. 48x30 London: T. Gardiner, Longman, Hurst, Rees, Orme, and Brown. 1811.
WHISTLER, Laurence.
— Some unpublished drawings of Sir John Vanbrugh ... in the Victoria and Albert Museum (and the British Museum). Excerpts. Illus. incl. elevations and plans. 3 pts. in 1 vol. 25x18 [London, 1948-9].
III. Unpublished drawings for Castle Howard. 7pp. 1949.
From: New English review magazine. III, no.1.
ANGUS, W. Seats of the Nobility. pl.3. 1787.
BURKE, J.B. Visitation of Seats. Vol.I, p.142. 1852.*
CAMPBELL, C. Vitruvius Britannicus. I, pls. 63-71. 1715.
CAMPBELL, C. Vitruvius Britannicus. III, pls.5, 6. 1725.
COPPER PLATE MAGAZINE. V. pl.235. 1792-1802.
COUNTRY LIFE. English Country Houses: Baroque, p.148. 1970.
COUNTRY LIFE. XV, 234. 1904.
COUNTRY LIFE. LXI, 884 plan, 948, 1005 [Pictures], 1022, 1043 [Pictures]. 1927.
COUNTRY LIFE. LXII, 200 [Outworks], 230 [Outworks]. 1927.
COUNTRY LIFE. CXIII, 276 plan. 1953.
ENGLAND: Beauties of England. II, p.421.1787.
JONES. Views of Seats. I. 1829.
KROLL, A. Historic Houses. 100. 1969.
LATHAM, C. In English Homes. Vol.I, p.233. 1904.
MALAN, A.H. Other famous Homes. p.95. 1902.
MORRIS, F.O. Views of Seats. Vol.I, p.11. 1880.
NEALE, J.P. Views of Seats. Vol.V. 1822.
NICOLSON, N. Great Houses of Britain. p. 180. 1965.
TIPPING, H.A. English Homes. Period IV, Vol.II, p.1. 1928.
UNITED KINGDOM. Historic houses. 198. 1892.
WHEATER, W. Mansions of Yorkshire. p.52. 1888.
[Sales] MALTON, 1924, 16 April [Furniture from C.H. etc.].

CASTLE PIGGIN (Carmarthenshire).
BURKE, J.B. Visitation of Seats. Vol.II, p.26. 1853.*
NICHOLAS, T. Counties of Wales. I, p.220. 1872.

CASTOR HOUSE (Northamptonshire).
GOTCH, J.A. Squires' Homes. 1. 1939.

CATTERLEN HALL (Cumberland).
CUMBERLAND: C.& W. A.& A.S. Extra Series VIII, 271. 1892.

CATTON HALL (Derbyshire).
COUNTRY LIFE. CXXVII, 566, 624. 1960.
SUMMERSON, J. The Country Seat. 157. 1970.
TILLEY, J. Halls of Derbyshire. IV, p.14. 1902.

CATTON HALL (Norfolk).
GARRATT, T. Halls of Norfolk. pl.19. 1890.

CAVE CASTLE (Yorkshire).
BURKE, J.B. Visitation of Seats. 2.S. Vol.II. p.135. 1855.*

CAVERSFIELD HOUSE (Oxfordshire).
BURKE, J.B. Visitation of Seats. Vol.I, p.69. 1852.*

Castle Howard in Yorkshire, the Seat of the Earl of Carlisle.

Published as the Act directs, Feb.1, 1787, by W. Angus W.4, Gwynnes Buildings, Islington.

Malone pinxt.

W. Angus sculp.

Pl. III.

CASTLE HOWARD, Yorkshire. From: ANGUS (W.). *The seats of the nobility and gentry in Great Britain and Wales* [etc.], (London) 1787(-1815).

CAVERSHAM PARK (Oxfordshire).
BURKE, J.B. Visitation of Seats. 2.S. Vol.II, p.160. 1855.*
CAMPBELL, C. Vitruvius Britannicus. III, pls.96, 97. 1725.
COPPER PLATE MAGAZINE. I, pl.29. 1792-1802.
ENGLAND: Picturesque Views. p.58. 1786-88.
NEALE, J.P. Views of Seats. 2.S. Vol.I. 1824.
[Sales] CAVERSHAM PARK, 1826, October 23-28 [effects].

CAVERSWALL CASTLE (Staffordshire).
COUNTRY LIFE . XXIX, 886, plan. 1911.
HALL, S.C. Baronial Halls. Vol.II. 1848.
NIVEN, W. Old Staffordshire houses. p.7, pl.6. 1882.
PLOT, R. Staffordshire. 448. 1686.
SHAW, S. Staffordshire. II, pl.28. Reprint 1976.
TIPPING, H.A. English Homes. Early Renaissance. p.329. 1912.

CAVICK HOUSE (Norfolk).
COUNTRY LIFE. CXVI, 1070. 1954.

CAYNHAM COURT (Shropshire).
LEACH, F. Seats of Shropshire. p.93. 1891.
WEST, W. Picturesque views of Shropshire. p.134. 1831.

CEDAR COURT, Alderton (Suffolk).
SANDON, E. Suffolk houses. 225. 1977.

CEFN MABLY (Glamorganshire).
COUNTRY LIFE. XXIV, 738. 1908.
LATHAM. C. In English Homes. Vol.III, p.267. 1909.

CHACOMBE PRIORY (Northamptonshire).
GOTCH, J.A. Halls of Northants. p.92. 1936.

CHADACRE HALL (Suffolk).
BURKE, J.B. Visitation of Seats. 2.S. Vol.I, p.207. 1854.*

CHADDESDEN HALL (Derbyshire).
TILLEY, J. Halls of Derbyshire. II, p.161. 1893.

CHALCOT HOUSE, Westbury (Wiltshire).
MANUSCRIPTS (Typewritten). English.
— SMITH, H.C. Inventory and valuation of the household furniture and effects at Chalcot House, Westbury, Wilts, the property of C.B.H. Phipps and the Lady Sybil Phipps. ... Prepared for the purposes of insurance by H.C.S. 20x25 (London) 1940.

CHALFONT PARK (Buckinghamshire).
ANGUS, W. Seats of the Nobility. pl.34. 1787.
BURKE, J.B. Visitation of Seats. Vol.I, p.30. 1852.*

CHALMINGTON (Dorsetshire).
HUTCHINS, J. Vitruvius Dorsettiensis. pl.4. 1816.

CHAMBERCOMBE MANOR (Devonshire).
DELDERFIELD, E.R. West Country houses. I, 28. 1968.

CHANTMARLE MANOR (Dorsetshire).
COUNTRY LIFE. CVIII, 46. 1950.
GARNER, T. Domestic Architecture. I, p.99. 1911.
HEATH, S. Dorset Manor Houses. 55. 1907.
HUTCHINS, J. Vitruvius Dorsettiensis. pl.5. 1816.
OSWALD, A. Country houses of Dorset. p.97. 1959.

CHANTRY, The. Sproughton (Suffolk).
CROMWELL, T.K. Excursions in Suffolk. I, p.179. 1818.
NEALE, J.P. Views of Seats. Vol.IV. 1821.

CHAPELWOOD MANOR (Sussex).
[Sales] CHAPELWOOD MANOR, 1939, March 28, 29 [Contents]. (K. F. & R.)

CHARBOROUGH PARK (Dorsetshire).
BURKE, J.B. Visitation of Seats. Vol.II, p.166. 1853.
COUNTRY LIFE. LXXVII, 322. 1935.
HEATH, S. Dorset Manor Houses. 65. 1907.
HUTCHINS, J. History of Dorset. III. 497. 1868.
OSWALD, A. Country Houses of Dorset. p.142. 1959.

CHARLECOTE PARK (Warwickshire).
FAIRFAX-LUCY, *Hon.* Alice.
— Charlecote and the Lucys: the chronicle of an English family. [Bibliogr.] 10 plates incl. map. 22x14 London: O.U.P., 1958.
LONDON: National Trust for Places of Historic Interest or Natural beauty.
— Charlecote Park. 2 ed.14pp. 4 plates. 18x12 London: Country Life (1946).
New ed. 36pp. Illus. (2 col. on covers) incl. 8 plates and genealog. table. 22x14 1974.
    Rev. ed. Charlecote Park, Warwickshire. 40pp. Illus. (2 col. on covers) incl. plates, map and genealog. table. 21x14 [London] 1983.
BURKE, J.B. Visitation of Seats. Vol.I, p.253. 1852.*
COUNTRY LIFE. English Country Houses: Late Georgian. p.211. 1958.
COUNTRY LIFE. I, 46, 78. 1897.
COUNTRY LIFE. XXXV, 126. 1914.
COUNTRY LIFE. CXI, 1080, 1164, 1328. 1952.

HALL, S.C. Baronial Halls. Vol.II. 1848.
JONES. View of Seats. I. 1829.
KROLL, A. Historic houses. 50. 1969.
MALAN, A.H. Famous homes. p.109. 1902.
MORRIS, F.O. Views of Seats. Vol.I, p.61. 1880.
NASH, J. Mansions of England. III, pl.15. 1841.
NEALE, J.P. Views of Seats. Vol.IV. 1821.
NIVEN, W. Old Warwickshire houses. p.27, pls.25, 26. 1878.
SMITH, W. History of the County of Warwick. 88. 1830.

CHARLESTON MANOR (Sussex).
COUNTRY LIFE. CLX. 350. 1976.
COUNTRY LIFE. CLXVI. 1994 [Paintings and decorations.] 1979.

CHARLTON COURT (Kent).
GREENWOOD, C. Kent. 154. 1838.
RICHARDSON, C.J. Old English Mansions. III. 1845.

CHARLTON HOUSE (Kent).
MARTIN, Alan Roger.
— Charlton House, Kent: an historical and architectural guide. 34pp. 6 plates incl. plans. 22x14 London: Blackheath Press, 1929.
BURKE, J.B. Visitation of Seats. Vol.I, p.170. 1852.*
COPPER PLATE MAGAZINE. pl.84. 1778.
COUNTRY LIFE. XXV, 630,666. 1909.
ENGLAND: Beauties of England. I, p.405. 1787.
GREENWOOD, C. Kent. 17. 1838.
HALL, S.C. Baronial Halls. Vol.I. 1848.
NEALE, J.P. Views of Seats. 2.S. Vol.IV. 1828.
OSWALD, A. Country houses of Kent. 43. 1933.
SANDBY, P. Select Views. I, pl.25. 1783.
TIPPING, H.A. English Homes. Early Renaissance. p.393. 1912.
TIPPING, H.A. English homes. Period III. Vol.I, p.327. 1922.

CHARLTON HOUSE (Somerset).
COOKE, R. West Country Houses. p.80. 1957.

CHARLTON MACKRELL COURT (Somerset).
COUNTRY LIFE. CVII, 162. 1950.

CHARLTON PARK (Kent).
GREENWOOD, C. Kent. 399. 1838.

CHARLTON PARK (Wiltshire).
COUNTRY LIFE. LXXIV, 388, 420. 1933.
GOTCH, J.A. Architecture of the Renaissance. II, p.4 plan. 1894.

HALL, S.C. Baronial Halls. Vol.II. 1848.
JONES. Views of Seats. II. 1829.
NEALE, J.P. Views of Seats. Vol.V. 1822.
RICHARDSON, C.J. Old English Mansions. III. 1845.
WATTS, W. Seats of the Nobility. pl.45. 1779.

CHARNEY BASSETT MANOR (Berkshire).
COUNTRY LIFE. XCII, 602, 650. 1942.

CHARTERHOUSE, THE (London).
COUNTRY LIFE.XXXII, 356 plan. 1912.
COUNTRY LIFE. CXXVI, 418 plan, 478, 538, 1959.
TIPPING, H.A. English Homes. Early Renaissance. p.81. 1912.

CHARTERS, Sunningdale (Berkshire).
COUNTRY LIFE. XCVI, 904, 948 plan, 992. 1944.
[Sales] CHARTERS, 1928 July 23-26 [Contents]. (K.F. & R.).

CHARTLEY HALL (Staffordshire).
PLOT, R. Staffordshire. 93. 1686.

CHART PLACE, Chart Sutton (Kent).
BADESLADE, T. Seats in Kent. pl.6. 1750.
HARRIS, J. History of Kent. p.69. 1719.

CHARTWELL (Kent).
LONDON: National Trust for Places of Historic Interest or Natural Beauty.
— Chartwell. [Folder] 1 illus. 22x15 [London1966?]
LONDON: National Trust for Places of Historic Interest or Natural Beauty.
— FEDDEN, R. Churchill and Chartwell. [Bibliogr.] 64pp. Illus. (1 on cover) incl. folding plate: genealog. table. 21x15 Oxford: Pergamon Press, 1968.
COUNTRY LIFE. CXXXVII. 169. 1965.

CHASE, THE (Herefordshire).
BURKE, J.B. Visitation of Seats. Vol.II, p.222. 1853.*

CHASELEY (Lancashire).
BARTLETT, J. Mansions of England and Wales. pl.156. 1853.
TWYCROSS, E. Mansions of England and Wales. Vol.III, p.98. 1847.

CHASTLETON HOUSE (Oxfordshire).

DICKINS, Margaret.
— A history of Chastleton, Oxfordshire. 5 plates. 25x15 Banbury: Banbury Guardian, 1938.

CLARKE, T.H. Domestic architecture. 13. 1833.

COUNTRY LIFE. XII, 80. 1902.

COUNTRY LIFE. XLV, 90 plan, 116. 1919.

COUNTRY LIFE, XLVIII, 463 [Tapestries]. 1923.

DELDERFIELD, E.R. West Country houses. III, 39. 1973.

GOTCH, J.A. Architecture of the Renaissance. II, p.56 plan. 1894.

LATHAM, C. In English Homes. Vol.I, p.243. 1904.

NASH, J. Mansions of England. III, pl.12. 1841.

TIPPING, H.A. English Homes. Period III, Vol.I, p.299. 1922.

CHATSWORTH (Derbyshire).

BAKEWELL.
— Bakewell, Derbyshire: the official guide, with sections on Haddon Hall, and Chatsworth House. 40pp. Illus. Cheltenham: Burrow [c. 1930].

CHATSWORTH.
— Views of Chatsworth and neighbourhood. [no text] 12 engr. plates. 22x14 (London, 1854).
4 Lithogr. plates, inserted.

CHATSWORTH
— Catalogue of the library at Chatsworth. [Compiled by W. Cavendish, Duke of Devonshire. Preface by J.P. Lacaita.] Cuts incl. title-pages and initials. 4 vols. 34x22 London: privately printed at the Chiswick Press, 1879.

CHATSWORTH.
— Chatsworth, the Derbyshire home of the Dukes of Devonshire. (An illustrated guide & history) 32pp. Illus. (some col., some on covers) incl. maps (on inside cover) and genealog. table. 19x16 (Derby: Derbyshire Countryside Limited.) [1959.]

CHATSWORTH.
— Chatsworth: notes on the principal pictures seen on the way through the house. 12pp. 21x14 Chatsworth [c. 1965].

CHESTERFIELD.
— The history of Chesterfield; with particulars of the hamlets contiguous to the town, and descriptive accounts of Chatsworth [etc]. [By Rev. G. Hall, enlarged and edited by T. Ford. Bibliogr. notes.] Illus. incl. plates (many engr., most by W. Radclyffe after C. Radclyffe), and tables. 22x14 London: Whittaker & Co.; Chesterfield: Ford, 1839.

CUST, *Sir* Lionel Henry.
— A description of the sketch-book by Sir Anthony Van Dyck used by him in Italy, 1621-1627, and preserved in the collection of the Duke of Devonshire K.G., at Chatsworth. 34pp. 47 plates. 36x28 London: G. Bell & Sons, 1902.

DERBY: "Come-to-Derbyshire" Association.
— Chatsworth: an illustrated survey [etc]. 32pp. Illus. (some col., some on covers) incl. maps (on inside covers). 14x22 Derby [1948?].
Another ed. Illus. (some col., some on covers) incl. maps (on inside covers) and genealog. table [1951?].

DEVONSHIRE, Deborah Vivien Cavendish, *Duchess of*.
— The House: a portrait of Chatsworth. 232pp. Illus. incl. col. plates, plans, map, genealog. table and end-paper. 24x17 London: Macmillan, 1982.

DEVONSHIRE, Dukes of.
— The Devonshire collection. Old Master drawings at Chatsworth. (Album[s].) Illus. vols. 18x25 Derby: E.L.P., [1957].
1. Reproductions of thirty of the drawings by Rembrandt van Rijn, 1606-1669 ... Foreword by ... F. Thompson. 32pp. Illus. [1957.]

DYCK, Sir Antonie van.
— Van Dyck's Antwerp sketchbook (in the Library at Chatsworth). [Edited by] M. Jaffé. [Facsimile. Bibliogr.] Illus. incl. facsimiles. 2 vols. 30x24 London: Macdonald, 1966.

GLOVER, Stephen.
— The Peak guide, containing the topographical, statistical, and general history of ... Chatsworth ... with an introduction ... By S.G., edited by T. Noble. xl, 132pp. Illus, incl. plates (some engr., some folding), plans, map and genealog. tables. 22x14 Derby: by the editor?, 1830.

JEWITT, Llewellynn.
— Chatsworth ... Illustrated by upwards of fifty engravings. 88pp. 21x17 Buxton: Bates, Advertiser Office, 1872.

ORGEL, Stephen.
— Inigo Jones: the theatre of the Stuart Court, including the complete designs for productions at Court for the most part in the collection of the Duke of Devonshire together with their texts and historical documentation. [By] (S.O., and R. Strong) [Bibliogr.] Illus. incl. plates (4 col.), sections, elevations, plans, diagr. and facsimiles. 2 vols. 33x24 London: Sotheby Parke Bernet; Berkeley & Los Angeles: U.C.P., 1973.

ROGERS, W.G.
— A visit to Chatsworth, to inspect the carvings of Grinling Gibbons, etc. October 2, 1865. 6pp. 2 illus. incl. plan. 33x21 (London: by the author, 1865).

STRONG, Sandford Arthur.
— The masterpieces in the Duke of Devonshire's collection of pictures. 22pp. plates. 37x30 London: Hanfstaengl, 1901.

STRONG, Sandford Arthur.
— Reproductions of drawings by old masters in the collection of the Duke of Devonshire at Chatsworth. With an introduction by S.A.S. 18pp. 70 (some tinted) plates. 51x39 London: Duckworth, 1902.
Another ed. [No introductory text.] 2pp. London: Griggs & Sons, 1902.

THOMPSON, Francis.
— A history of Chatsworth: being a supplement to the sixth Duke of Devonshire's handbook. [Bibliogr.] Plates incl. elevations and plans. 30x24 London: Country Life, 1949.

WITTKOWER, Rudolf.
— Un libro di schizzi di Filippo Juvarra a Chatsworth. [Bibliogr.] 28pp. Illus. incl. elevation. 23x18. (Torino, 1949.)

CHATSWORTH (Derbyshire). [Contd.]

BURKE, J.B. Visitation of Seats. 2.S. Vol.I, p.3. 1855.*

CAMPBELL, C. Vitruvius Britannicus. I, pls. 72-76. 1715.

CAMPBELL, C. Vitruvius Britannicus. III, pls. 67-68. 1725.

COPPER PLATE MAGAZINE. pl. 21. 1778.

COUNTRY LIFE. English Country Houses: Baroque. p.70. 1970.

COUNTRY LIFE. XXI, 870. 1907.

COUNTRY LIFE. XLIII, 12, 36, 60, 84. 1918.

COUNTRY LIFE. LIX, 951 [Furniture]. 1926.

COUNTRY LIFE. CXI, 914 [Painting]. 1952.

COUNTRY LIFE. CXVI, 26 [Collection]. 1954.

COUNTRY LIFE. CXLIII, 890, 958 plan, 1040 plan, 1110. 1968.

COUNTRY LIFE. CXLIV, 146, 220 plan,280, 496, 552. 1968.

ENGLAND: Beauties of England. I, p.146. 1787.

ENGLISH CONNOISSEUR. I, 28. 1766.

JEWITT, L. Stately homes of England. 322. 1874.

JONES. Views of seats. I. 1829.

KIP, J. Nouveau théâtre de la Grande Bretagne. I, pl. 17. 1715.

LATHAM, C. In English Homes. Vol.III, p.213. 1909.

MALAN, A.H. Famous homes. p.231.1902.

MORRIS, F.O. View of Seats. Vol.I, p.49. 1880.

NEALE, J.P. Views of Seats. Vol.I. 1818.

NICOLSON, N. Great Houses of Britain. p.158. 1965.

NOBLE, T. Counties of Chester, ... Lincoln. p.42, 53. 1836.

PAINE, J. Plans, elevations. Pt.I, pls.1-7 [Stables] 8-11 [Bridges]. 1767.

SANDBY, P. Select Views, I, pl.11. 1783.

TILLEY, J. Halls of Derbyshire. I. p.123. 1892.

TIPPING, H.A. English Homes. Period IV, Vol.I, p.313. 1920.

UNITED KINGDOM. Historic houses. 102. 1892.

[Sales] LONDON, 1958, June 25 [English and French silver].

[Sales] LONDON, 1958, June 27 [Pictures].

[Sales] LONDON, 1958, June 30 [Early printed Books].

[Sales] LONDON, 1974, June 6 [19 early printed books and 2 illuminated MSS.].

CHAVENAGE (Gloucestershire).

COUNTRY LIFE. XXIX, 524 plan. 1911.

GARNER, T. Domestic architecture. I, p.115 plan. 1911.

TIPPING, H.A. English Homes. Early Renaissance, p.1, 1912.

CHAWTON HOUSE (Hampshire).

LEIGH, William Austen.
— Chawton Manor and its owners: a family history.
By W.A.L., and M.G. Knight. [Bibliogr. notes] Illus. incl.
plates (some mezzotints), plans, facsimiles of signatures and
genealog. tables. 26x20 London: Smith, Elder & Co., 1911.

BURKE, J.B. Visitation of Seats. 2.S. Vol.II, p.126. 1855.*

COUNTRY LIFE. XIII, 874. 1903.

COUNTRY LIFE. XCVII, 200, 244. 1945.

HAMPSHIRE: Architectural Views. 1830.

LATHAM, C. In English Homes. Vol.I, p.227. 1907.

CHECKENDEN COURT (Berkshire).

COUNTRY LIFE. L, 754 plan. 1921.

CHELSFIELD COURT (Kent).

BROWN, Alexander Theodore.
— Half-lights on Chelsfield Court Lodge. [Edited by A.T.B.]
[Bibliogr. notes]. 128pp. Illus. incl. 5 plates and genealog.
tables. 22x14 Liverpool (privately printed) 1933.

CHELSFIELD RECTORY (Kent).

GREENWOOD, C. Kent. 61. 1838.

CHELSWORTH HALL (Suffolk).

BURKE, J.B. Visitation of Seats. Vol.II, p.109. 1853.*

CHELVEY COURT (Somerset).

COUNTRY LIFE. XXVII, 738. 1910.

CHENEY COURT (Herefordshire).

See CHEYNEY COURT.

CHENIES [MANOR] (Buckinghamshire).

THOMSON, Gladys Scott.
— Family background. [Bibliogr. notes.] 4 plates. 20x13
London: Cape, 1949.

COUNTRY LIFE. CLXXII. 1140, 1218. 1982.

CHEQUERS COURT (Buckinghamshire).

CHEQUERS.
— A short guide to Chequers [by Viscount Lee of Fareham].
24pp. 20x15 (London: privately printed, 1921).
2 ed.1921.
3 ed. 20pp. 21x14 1956.

CHEQUERS.
— A catalogue of the principal works of art at Chequers; with
an introduction by Viscount Lee of Fareham. Illus: plates.
25x19 London: privately printed. 1923.

GREAT BRITAIN: Department of the Environment.
— FRY, P.S. Chequers: the country home of Britain's prime
ministers. 84pp. Illus. (mainly col.) incl. 2 on cover. 20x21
London, 1977.

GREAT BRITAIN AND IRELAND: Historical Manuscripts
Commission.
— Report on manuscripts at Chequers, Buckinghamshire.
[Typescript.] 12ff. 33x20 [London] 1946.

JENKINS, John Gilbert.
— Chequers: a history of the Prime Minister's Buckinghamshire home. [Bibliogr.] Illus. incl. plans, maps (on end papers)
and folding genealog. tables. 25x15 Oxford: Pergamon Press,
1967.

MANUSCRIPTS (Typewritten). English .
— LONG, B.S. Catalogue of the miniatures, pastels and Downman drawings at Chequers. Containing details not included in the printed catalogue. 30ff. 33x20 (1921).

MANUSCRIPTS. (Typewritten). English.
— SMITH, H.C. Reports on Chequers, 1932 to 1956 (by H.C.S.). 85ff. 34x20 (London [etc.]) 1932-56.
Title on cover.

COUNTRY LIFE. XXVIII, 970 plan. 1910.

COUNTRY LIFE. XLII, 324 plan, 348, 372. 1917.

COUNTRY LIFE. XLII, 401 [Cromwell Relics]. 1917.

TIPPING, H.A. English Homes. Early Renaissance, p.99. 1912.

TIPPING, H.A. English Homes. Period III, Vol.I, p.39. 1922.

CHESTERS, Humshaugh (Northumberland).
COUNTRY LIFE. XXXI, 244 plan. 1912.

[Sales] CHESTERS, 1930, January 6 and following days [Furniture, silver etc.].

CHESTHAM PARK (Sussex).
[Sales] CHESTHAM PARK, 1977, April 18, 19 [Contents].

CHESWORTH (Sussex).
ELWES, D.G.C. Mansions of Western Sussex. 120. 1876.

CHETTISHAM HALL (Cambridgeshire).
BURKE, J.B. Visitation of Seats. Vol.II, p.119. 1853.*

CHETTLE HOUSE (Dorsetshire).
COUNTRY LIFE. English Country Houses: Baroque. p.206. 1970.

COUNTRY LIFE. LXIV, 466 plan. 1928.

OSWALD, A. Country Houses of Dorset. p.153. 1959.

SUMMERSON, J. The Country Seat. 85. 1970.

CHETWODE PRIORY (Buckinghamshire).
BURKE, J.B. Visitation of Seats. 2.S. Vol.II, p.133. 1855.*

CHETWYND PARK (Shropshire).
BURKE, J.B. Visitation of Seats. Vol.II, p.53. 1853.*

LEACH, F. Seats of Shropshire. p.365. 1891.

SHROPSHIRE. Castles and Old Mansions. 47. 1868.

CHEVENING (Kent).
CHEVENING.
— List of portraits and busts in the principal rooms at Chevening. 16pp. 20x14 London: Spottiswoode & Co., 1856.
NEWMAN, Aubrey N.
— The Stanhopes of Chevening: a family biography. [Bibliogr.] Plates and genealog. table (on end-papers). 22x15 London: Macmillan, 1969.

BADESLADE, T. Seats in Kent. pl.8. 1750.

BURKE, J.B. Visitation of Seats. Vol.I, p.61. 1852.*

CAMPBELL, C. Vitruvius Britannicus. II, pl.85. 1717.

COUNTRY LIFE. XLVII, 512, 548, 586, 627 [Library]. 1920.

COUNTRY LIFE. CXXV, 1312. 1959.

COUNTRY LIFE. CXLIII, 102. 1968.

CROMWELL, T.K. Excursions in Kent. p.112. 1822.

HARRIS, J. History of Kent. p.74. 1719.

HASTED, E. Kent. I, 361 [plan]. 1778.

OSWALD, A. Country Houses of Kent. 58. 1933.

TIPPING, H.A. English Homes. Period V, Vol.I, p.9. 1921.

CHEVITHORNE BARTON (Devonshire).
COUNTRY LIFE. CXXVII, 684. 1960.

CHEW COURT (Somerset).
COOKE, R. West Country Houses. p.50. 1957.

CHEYNEY COURT (Herefordshire).
ROBINSON, C.J. Mansions of Herefordshire. pl.3. 1873.

CHICHELEY HALL (Buckinghamshire).
BINNEY, Marcus.
— Chicheley Hall. 20pp. Illus. (some col., 1 on cover.) 23x18 [Chicheley? privately printed? 1976?].

BURKE, J.B. Visitation of Seats. Vol.I, p.94. 1852.

COUNTRY LIFE. English Country Houses: Baroque. p.227. 1970.

COUNTRY LIFE. XVII, 594. 1905.

COUNTRY LIFE. LXXIX, 482, 508, 534. 1936.

COUNTRY LIFE. CLVII. 378, 434, 498. 1975.

LATHAM, C. In English Homes. Vol.II, p.353. 1907.

CHICKSANDS PRIORY (Bedfordshire).
BUCK, S. & N. , Antiquities. I, pl.2. 1774.

BURKE, J.B. Visitation of Seats. 2.S. Vol.I, p.187. 1854.*

NEALE, J.P. Views of Seats. 2.S. Vol.V. 1829.

WATTS, W. Seats of the Nobility. pl.25. 1779.

CHIDDINGSTONE CASTLE (Kent).
CHIDDINGSTONE CASTLE.
— A short guide to Chiddingstone Castle and its collections. 16pp. Illus. incl. map. 18x12 n.p. privately printed, 1974.

CHILDERLEY HALL (Cambridgeshire).
COUNTRY LIFE. CXLVI, 1170. 1969.

CHILDHAY (Dorsetshire).
OSWALD, A. Country Houses of Dorset. p.57. 1959.

CHILDWALL HALL [ABBEY] (Lancashire).
BARTLETT, J. Mansions of England and Wales. pl.100. 1853.
BURKE, J.B. Visitation of Seats. 2.S. Vol.I, p.46. 1854.*
JONES. Views of seats. I. 1829.
NEALE, J.P. Views of Seats. 2.S. Vol.II. 1825.
PYNE, W.H. Lancashire illustrated. 43. 1831.
TWYCROSS, E. Mansions of England and Wales. Vol.III, p.22. 1847.

CHILDWICKBURY (Hertfordshire).
COUNTRY LIFE. XXV, 918 [Mantels]. 1909.
[Sales] CHILDWICKBURY, 1978, May 15-17 [Contents].

CHILHAM CASTLE (Kent).
BOLTON, Arthur Thomas.
Chilham Castle, Canterbury, Kent: historical and architectural account, more particularly illustrating the three centuries of the Jacobean house built 1616. (E. W-B. memorial) 28ff. Illus. incl. plates, elevations and plans. 21x17 [London: by the Author] 1912.
COUNTRY LIFE. XXXII, 126 plan. 1912.
COUNTRY LIFE. LV, 812 plan, 858 plan. 1924.
GREENWOOD, C. Kent. 300. 1838.
HASTED, E. Kent. III, 131. 1790.
NEALE, J.P. Views of Seats. 2.S. Vol.II. 1825.
OSWALD, A. Country Houses of Kent. 4, 44. 1933.
WATTS, W. Seats of the Nobility. pl.72. 1779.

CHILLINGHAM CASTLE (Northumberland).
ANGUS, W. Seats of the Nobility. pl.62. 1787.
Archaeologia Aeliana, XIV, p.297. 1891.
BUCK, S. & N. Antiquities. I, pl.218. 1774.
BURKE, J.B. Visitation of Seats. 2.S. Vol.I, p.67. 1854.*
COUNTRY LIFE. XXXIII, 346 plan. 1913.
MORRIS, F.O. Views of Seats. Vol.VI, p.33. 1880.
UNITED KINGDOM. Historic houses. 311. 1892.
[Sales] CHILLINGHAM CASTLE, 1932, April 11-14 [Furnishings, pictures etc.].

CHILLINGTON HALL (Staffordshire).
COUNTRY LIFE. English Country Houses: Mid Georgian. p.222. 1956.
COUNTRY LIFE. CIII, 326, 378, 426. 1948.
PAINE, J. Plans, elevations. Pt.II, pl.87 [Bridge]. 1783.
SOANE, J. Plans, elevations and sections. pls. XII-XVII. 1788.

CHILLINGTON MANOR (Kent).
MAIDSTONE: Museum and Art Gallery.
— Maidstone Museum and Art Gallery. Chillington Manor House. Short descriptive guide. 52pp. 1 Illus. (on cover), and 2 plans. 18x12 (Maidstone) 1925.
Reprint from: South Eastern Gazette.

CHILSTON PARK (Kent).
BADESLADE, T. Seats in Kent. pl.9. 1750.
COUNTRY LIFE. CXII, 2030, 2096. 1952.
GREENWOOD, C. Kent. 156. 1838.
HASTED, E. Kent. II, 435. 1782.

CHILTON HALL (Suffolk).
SANDON, E. Suffolk houses. 212. 1977.
[Sales] CHILTON HALL, 1982, July 21 [Contents].

CHILTON HOUSE (Buckinghamshire).
COUNTRY LIFE. XXXV, 702. 1914.

CHILWELL HALL (Nottinghamshire).
BURKE, J.B. Visitation of Seats. Vol.II, p.131. 1853.*

CHILWORTH MANOR (Surrey).
COUNTRY LIFE. CXVIII, 1138 plan. 1955.

CHINGLE HALL (Lancashire).
COUNTRY LIFE. CXLII, 1460. 1967.

CHIPCHASE CASTLE (Northumberland).
Archaeologia Aeliana XIV, p.410. 1891.
COUNTRY LIFE. CXIX, 1292, 1362. 1956.

CHIPPENHAM PARK (Cambridgeshire).
BURKE, J.B. Visitation of Seats. Vol.I, p.34. 1852.*

CHIPSTEAD PLACE (Kent).
BADESLADE, T. Seats in Kent. pl.7. 1750.
BURKE, J.B. Visitation of Seats. Vol.II, p.203. 1853.
GREENWOOD, C. Kent. 89. 1838.
[Sales] CHIPSTEAD PLACE, 1924, June 10 and following days [Contents]. (K.F.& R.).

CHIRK CASTLE (Denbighshire).
CHIRK CASTLE.
— A memoir of Chirk Castle. From original manuscripts. [New ed.] 60pp. Plates.23x15 Chirk Castle: privately printed, 1923.
CHIRK CASTLE.
— Chirk Castle: an illustrated survey [etc]. 32pp. Illus. (some col., some on covers) incl. maps (on inside covers). 14x20 Derby: E.L.P. [1954?].
LONDON: National Trust for Places of Historic Interest or Natural Beauty.
— DEAN, R. Chirk Castle, Clwyd. [Bibliogr.] 64pp. Illus. (1 col. on cover) incl. plans and genealog. table. 25x18 [London] 1983.
MAHLER, Margaret.
— A history of Chirk Castle and Chirkland, with a chapter on Offa's Dyke. [Bibliogr. notes.] xii, 232pp. Plates. 22x16 London: G. Bell & Sons, printed at the Chiswick Press, 1912.

BUCK, S. & N. Antiquities. II, pl.379. 1774.

BURKE, J.B. Visitation of Seats. Vol.I, p.55. 1852.*

COUNTRY LIFE. CX, 896, 980 plan, 1064, 1148. 1951.

ENGLAND: Picturesque Views. p.80. 1786-88.

JONES. Views of Seats. V. 1830.

NEALE, J.P. Views on Seats. 2.S. Vol.V. 1829.

NICHOLAS, T. Counties of Wales. I, p.368. 1872.

CHISELHAMPTON HOUSE (Oxfordshire).

COUNTRY LIFE.CXV, 217, 284. 1954.

CHISWICK HOUSE (Middlesex).

BRENTFORD AND CHISWICK: Urban District Council.
— Historical notes on Chiswick House, opened to the public ...
4th July 1929. 16pp. 7 illus. 14x22 (London, 1929).

GREAT BRITAIN: Ministry of Works.
— CHARLTON, J. A history and description of Chiswick
House and gardens. Illustrated ... by G. Cullen. 32pp. Illus.
incl. plates (1 folding), section and plans. 20x13 London. 1958.

CAMPBELL, C. Vitruvius Britannicus. IVth. pls.82, 83. 1739.

COUNTRY LIFE. XLIII, 130 plan, 160. 1918.

COUNTRY LIFE. LX, 308. 1926.

COUNTRY LIFE. CII, 126. 1947.

COUNTRY LIFE. CXXIV, 228. 1958.

COUNTRY LIFE. CLXIII, 624. 1978.

ENGLAND: Beauties of England. II, p.69. 1787.

ENGLAND: Picturesque Views. p.54. 1786-88.

ENGLISH CONNOISSEUR. I, 30. 1766.*

HAVELL, R. Views of Noblemen's Seats. 1823.

KIP, J. Nouveau théâtre de la Grande Bretagne. I, pl. 30. 1715.

NEALE. J.P. Views of Seats. 2.S. Vol.V. 1829.

TIPPING, H.A. English Homes. Period V, Vol.I, p.139. 1921.

CHOLMONDELEY CASTLE (Cheshire).

BARTLETT, J. Selections from views of mansions. 1851.

BURKE, J.B. Visitation of Seats. 2.S. Vol.I, p.108. 1854.*

CAMPBELL, C. Vitruvius Britannicus. II, pls.31-34. 1717.

CAMPBELL, C. Vitruvius Britannicus. III, pls.79, 80. 1725.

COUNTRY LIFE. CLIV. 154. 1973.

MORRIS, F.O. Views of Seats. Vol.II, p.33. 1880.

NEALE, J.P. Views of Seats. 2.S. Vol.V. 1829.

NOBLE, T. Counties of Chester, ... Lincoln. p.73. 1836.

TWYCROSS, E. Mansions of England and Wales. Vol.I. p.18. 1850.

CHORLEY HALL (Cheshire).

ORMEROD, G. Cheshire. III, 601. 1882.

CHORLTON HALL (Cheshire).

BURKE, J.B. Visitation of Seats. Vol.II, p.125. 1853.*

TWYCROSS, E. Mansions of England and Wales. Vol.I, p.41. 1850.

CHRISTCHURCH MANSION, Ipswich (Suffolk).

COUNTRY LIFE. CXVI, 496, 572, 644. 1954.

CROMWELL, T.K. Excursions in Suffolk. I, p.124. 1818.

CHRISTELTON HALL (Cheshire).

TWYCROSS, E. Mansions of England and Wales. Vol.I, p.43. 1850.*

CHURCHE'S MANSION, Nantwich (Cheshire).

CHURCHE'S MANSION.
— Churche's Mansion, Nantwich, Cheshire [etc.]. 16pp. Illus.
(some on covers) incl. 4 plates, plans and genealog. table.
14x20 [Derby: E.L.P., 1957?]

CIRENCESTER ABBEY (Gloucestershire).

ATKYNS, R. Glocestershire. p.180. 1768.

CIRENCESTER PARK (Gloucestershire).

BATHURST, Seymour Henry Bathurst, *Earl.*
— Catalogue of the Bathurst collection of pictures (including
pictures from Finchcocks). Plates (some mezzotint) and
genealog. table. 31x25 London: privately printed, 1908.

ANGUS, W. Seats of the Nobility. p.41. 1787.

ATKYNS, R. Glocestershire. p.179. 1768.

COUNTRY LIFE. XXIV, 192. 1908.

COUNTRY LIFE. CVII, 1796. 1950.

NEALE, J.P. Views of Seats. 2.S. Vol.II. 1825.

RUDDER, S. Gloucestershire. 355. 1779.

CITADEL, Hawkstone (Shropshire).

COUNTRY LIFE. CXXIV, 368. 1958.

CLANDON PARK (Surrey).

LONDON: National Trust for Places of Historic Interest or
Natural Beauty.
— The Gubbay collection [at] (Clandon Park, Surrey). 24pp.
21x14 [London, 1971.]

LONDON: National Trust for Places of Historic Interest or
Natural Beauty.
— ONSLOW, P.L.E. *Countess of,* and CORNFORTH, J.
Clandon Park, Surrey. [Bibliogr.] 24pp. Illus. (1 col. on cover)
incl. 8 plates and genealog. table. 25x18 [London, 1973].

ONSLOW, Pamela Louisa Eleanor, *Countess of.*
— Clandon Park. 24pp. Illus. (1 on cover) incl. 8 plates and
genealog. table.22x14 Guildford: privately printed [c.1950].

VULLIAMY, Colwyn Edward.
— The Onslow family, 1528-1874, with some account of their times. 16 plates. 22x14 London: Chapman & Hall, 1953.
COPPER PLATE MAGAZINE. I, pl.24. 1792-1802.
COUNTRY LIFE. English Country Houses: Early Georgian. p.97. 1955.
COUNTRY LIFE. LXII, 366 plan, 398, 434. 1927.
COUNTRY LIFE. CXLVI, 1456, 1582. 1969.
COUNTRY LIFE. CXLIX, 1004 [Gubbay Collection]. 1971.
ENGLAND: Picturesque views. p.77. 1786-88.
NEALE, J.P. Views of Seats. 2.S. Vol.III. 1826.
PROSSER, G.F. Surrey Seats. p.23. 1828.

CLAPTON COURT (Somerset).
COOKE, R. West Country Houses. p.27. 1957.
[Sales] CLAPTON COURT, 1978, October 11 [Furniture and other contents].

CLARE HOUSE (Kent).
COUNTRY LIFE. CVI, 826, 898. 1949.

CLAREMONT (Lancashire).
BARTLETT, J. Mansions of England and Wales. pl.146. 1853.
TWYCROSS, E. Mansions of England and Wales. Vol.III, p.84. 1847.

CLAREMONT (Surrey).
BRAYLEY, E.W. History of Surrey. II, 444. 1841.
BURKE, J.B. Visitation of Seats. 2.S. Vol.I, p.20. 1854.*
CAMPBELL, C. Vitruvius Britannicus. III, pls.77, 78. 1725.
CAMPBELL, C. Vitruvius Britannicus. IVth, pls.19-23. 1739.
CAMPBELL, C. New Vitruvius Britannicus. I, pls. 61-3. 1802.
COUNTRY LIFE. English Country Houses: Mid Georgian. p.135. 1956.
COUNTRY LIFE. II, 688. 1897.
COUNTRY LIFE. LXIII, 80. 1928.
COUNTRY LIFE. CV, 426. 1949.
COUNTRY LIFE. CVIII, 60. 1950.
COUNTRY LIFE. CL, 1366. 1971.
ENGLAND: Picturesque Views. p.16. 1786-88.
NEALE, J.P. View of Seats. Vol.IV. 1821.
PROSSER, G.F. Surrey Seats. p.105. 1828.
TIPPING, H.A. English Homes. Period IV, Vol.II, p.167. 1928.
WATTS, W. Seats of the Nobility. pl.6. 1779.
[Sales] LONDON, 1922, July 27 [Sale of freehold estate].
[Sales] CLAREMONT, 1926, October 25-28 [Contents].

CLARENDON HOUSE, Dinton (Wiltshire).
ELYARD, S.J. Old Wiltshire Homes. p.79. 1894.

CLARENDON PARK (Wiltshire).
BURKE, J.B. Visitation of Seats. 2.S. Vol.II, p.83. 1855.*

CLARE PRIORY (Suffolk).
COUNTRY LIFE. LX, 208. 1926.
SANDON, E. Suffolk houses. 304. 1977.

CLARKE HALL (Yorkshire).
COUNTRY LIFE. CXXIX, 712. 1961.
WOOD, G.B. Historic Homes of Yorkshire. 6. 1957.

CLAUGHTON HALL (Lancashire).
BARTLETT, J. Mansions of England and Wales. pls. 79-81. 1853.
COUNTRY LIFE. LXXXVIII, 520. 1940.
TWYCROSS, E. Mansions of England and Wales. Vol.II, p.41. 1847.

CLAVERTON MANOR (Somerset).
COUNTRY LIFE. CXXIX, 1532. 1961.

CLAVERTON OLD MANOR (Somerset)
VIVIAN, George.
— Some illustrations of the architecture of Claverton, and of the Duke's house, Bradford, &c. 4pp. 26 lithogr. plates. 32x25 London: privately printed, 1837.

CLAXBY HALL (Lincolnshire).
COUNTRY LIFE. CLII, 1722. 1972.

CLAYDON HOUSE (Buckinghamshire).
LONDON: National Trust for Places of Historic Interest or Natural Beauty.
— LEES-MILNE, J. Claydon House, Buckinghamshire. 22pp. 4 plates. 18x12 London: Country Life, 1961.

VERNEY, Frances Parthenope, *Lady* and Margaret Maria, *Lady.*
— Memoirs of the Verney family during the seventeenth century compiled from the papers and illustrated by the portraits at Claydon House. 2 ed. [Bibliogr. notes.] Illus. (2 on title-pages) incl. folding genealog. table. 2 vols. 20x13 London: Longmans, Green & Co., 1907.

BURKE, J.B. Visitation of Seats. Vol.I, p.85. 1852.*
COUNTRY LIFE. English Country Houses: Early Georgian. p.242. 1955.
COUNTRY LIFE. IX, 617. 1901.
COUNTRY LIFE. XXXI, 356, 394 plan. 1902.
COUNTRY LIFE. CXII, 1278, 1398 plan, 1480. 1952.

CLAYTON HALL, Clayton-le-Moors
(Lancashire).
BARTLETT, J. Mansions of England and Wales. pls.23, 29.
1853.
BURKE, J.B. Visitation of Seats. Vol.II, p.218.1853.*
TWYCROSS, E. Mansions of England and Wales. Vol.I, p.19.
1847.

CLAYTON HALL, Clayton-le-Woods
(Lancashire).
GRAY, H. Old Halls of Lancashire. p.81. 1893.

CLAYTON HALL, Manchester
(Lancashire).
MOSS, F. Pilgrimages. V, 88. 1910.

CLAYTON PRIORY (Sussex).
BURKE, J.B. Visitation of Seats. 2.S. Vol.I, p.111. 1854.*

CLEARWELL (Gloucestershire).
ATKYNS, R. Glocestershire. p.301. 1768.
SUMMERSON, J. The Country Seat. 145 plan. 1970.

CLEEVE COURT (Somerset).
COOKE, R. West Country Houses. p.164. 1957.

CLEEVE HILL (Gloucestershire).
ATKYNS, R. Glocestershire. p.286. 1768.

CLENSTON MANOR (Dorsetshire).
COUNTRY LIFE. CXXXII, 256, 304 plan. 1962.

CLEOBURY HALL (Shropshire).
BURKE, J.B. Visitation of Seats. Vol.II, p.175. 1853.*

CLERK HILL (Lancashire).
BARTLETT,J. Mansions of England and Wales. pl.39. 1853.
BURKE, J.B. Visitation of Seats. Vol.II, p.176. 1853.*
TWYCROSS, E. Mansions of England and Wales. Vol.I, p.30.
1847.

CLEVEDON COURT (Somerset).
LONDON: National Trust for Places of Historic Interest or
Natural Beauty.
— ELTON, A. and M.A. Clevedon Court, Somerset. [Bibliogr.]
32pp. Illus. (1 col. on cover) incl. 8 plates and plan. 21x14
[London] 1972.
BURKE, J.B. Visitation of Seats. Vol.II, p.218. 1853.*
COOKE, R. West Country Houses. p.22. 1957.
COUNTRY LIFE. CXVII, 1672 plan. 1955.
COUNTRY LIFE. CXVIII, 16. 1955.
DELDERFIELD, E.R. West Country houses. II, 29. 1970.

CLEWORTH HALL (Lancashire).
GRAY, H. Old Halls of Lancashire. p.53. 1893.

CLIBURN HALL (Westmorland).
CUMBERLAND: C. & W. A.& A.S. Extra series, VIII, 105
plan. 1892.

CLIEFDEN (Buckinghamshire).
See CLIVEDEN.

CLIFFE CASTLE (Yorkshire).
YORKSHIRE. Picturesque views. 1885.

CLIFFE HOUSE (Wiltshire).
BURKE, J.B. Visitation of Seats. Vol.II, p.130. 1853.*

CLIFFORD CHAMBERS MANOR
(Warwickshire).
COUNTRY LIFE.LXI, 422 [Furniture]. 1927.

CLIFFORD MANOR (Gloucestershire).
COUNTRY LIFE. LXIV, 168, 200. 1928.

CLIFTON CASTLE (Yorkshire).
BURKE, J.B. Visitation of Seats. 2.S.Vol. II, p.5.1855.*

CLIFTON HALL (Lancashire).
BURKE, J.B. Visitation of Seats. Vol.II, p.195. 1853.*
BURKE, J.B. Visitation of Seats. 2.S. Vol.II, p.129. 1855.*
TWYCROSS, E. Mansions of England and Wales. Vol.II, p.37.
1847.*

CLIFTON HALL (Nottinghamshire).
COUNTRY LIFE. LIV, 246 plan. 1923.
MORRIS, F.O. Views of Seats. Vol.II, p.39. 1880.

CLIFTON HALL (Staffordshire).
BURKE, J.B. Visitation of Seats. Vol.I, p.155. 1852.*

CLIFTON HALL (Westmorland).
CUMBERLAND: C. & W. A. & A.S. Extra Series, VIII, 77
plan. 1892.

CLIFTON HILL (Lancashire).
BARTLETT, J. Mansions of England and Wales. pl.74. 1853.
TWYCROSS, E. Mansions of England and Wales. Vol.II, p.30.
1847.

CLIFTON MAYBANK (Dorsetshire).
HEATH, S. Dorset Manor Houses. 75. 1907.
OSWALD, A. Country houses of Dorset. p.74. 1959.

CLINTS (Yorkshire).
ANGUS, W. Seats of the Nobility. pl.24. 1787.

CLIPPESBY HOUSE (Norfolk).
BURKE, J.B. Visitation of Seats. Vol.II, p.243. 1853.*

CLIVEDEN (Buckinghamshire).
LONDON: National Trust for Places of Historic Interest or Natural Beauty.
— Cliveden, Buckinghamshire. 14pp. 4 plates, and map. 18x12 London: Country Life (1947).
New ed. JACKSON-STOPS, G. 40pp. Illus. (1 col. on cover) incl. map. 25x18 [London] 1982.
BURKE, J.B. Visitation of Seats. 2.S. Vol.II, p.226. 1855.*
CAMPBELL, C. Vitruvius Britannicus. II, pls. 70-74. 1717.
COPPER PLATE MAGAZINE. I, pl.20. 1792-1802.
COUNTRY LIFE. XXXII, 808 plan, 854. 1912.
COUNTRY LIFE. LXX, 38. 1931.
COUNTRY LIFE. CLXI, 438, 498. 1977.
ENGLAND: Beauties of England. I, p.55. 1787.
ENGLAND: Picturesque views. p.17. 1786-88.
MORRIS, F.O. Views of Seats. Vol.VI, p.13. 1880.
ROBERTSON, A. Great Road. I. p.84. 1792.
THAMES, River. An history. I, pl.37.1794.
[Sales] CLIVEDEN, 1967, May 15-19 [Antique and reproduction contents].

CLOCK HOUSE, Keele (Staffordshire).
COUNTRY LIFE. CXXVII, 72. 1960.

CLOCK HOUSE, Little Stonham (Suffolk).
COUNTRY LIFE. LXXVI, 399. 1934.
SANDON, E. Suffolk houses. 284. 1977.

CLOPTON HALL (Suffolk).
SANDON, E. Suffolk houses. 219. 1977.

CLOPTON HOUSE (Warwickshire).
BURKE, J.B. Visitation of Seats. 2.S. Vol.II, p.220. 1855.*
NEALE, J.P. Views of Seats. Vol.IV. 1821.
[Sales]CLOPTON HOUSE, 1930 October 6-8 [Furniture etc.].

CLOUDS, Salisbury (Wiltshire).
COUNTRY LIFE. XVI, 738.1904.
LATHAM, C. In England Homes.Vol.II, p.415. 1907.
[Sales]CLOUDS, 1933, June 20-22 [Contents]. (K.F.& R.).

CLOUDS HILL (Dorsetshire).
LONDON: National Trust for Places of Historic Interest or Natural Beauty.
— Clouds Hill, Dorset. 24pp. Illus. (1 on cover) incl. plates. [London] 1982.

CLOVELLY COURT (Devonshire).
COUNTRY LIFE, LXXV, 326. 1934.

CLOVERLEY HALL (Shropshire).
BURKE, J.B. Visitation of Seats. 2.S. Vol.I, p.197. 1854.*
SUMMERSON, J. The Country Seat. 252 plans. 1970.

CLOWER WALL (Gloucestershire).
See CLEARWELL.

CLUMBER PARK (Nottinghamshire).
LONDON: National Trust for Places of Historic Interest or Natural Beauty.
— STAMP, G. and SYMONDSON, A. Clumber Chapel, Nottinghamshire. [Bibliogr.] 28pp. Illus. (1 col. on cover) incl. plates and plan. 22x14 [London] 1982.

NOTTINGHAM: Museum and Art Gallery.
— Catalogue of pictures from the Clumber collection (on loan by ... the Duke of Newcastle). 32pp. Plates. 21x16 Nottingham [1930].
With MS. notes.
BURKE, J.B. Visitation of Seats. 2.S. Vol.I, p.126. 1854.*
COUNTRY LIFE. XXIV, 352. 1908.
JONES, Views of Seats. I, 1829.
MALAN, A.H. Other famous homes. p.143. 1902.
MORRIS, F.O. Views of Seats. Vol.II, p.79. 1880.
NEALE, J.P. Views of Seats. Vol.III. 1820.
NOBLE, T. Counties of Chester, ... Lincoln. p.10. 1836.
SPROULE, A. Lost houses of Britain. 99. 1982.
THOROTON, R. Nottinghamshire. III, 405. 1797.
WATTS, W. Seats of the Nobility. pl.29. 1779.
[Sales] LONDON, 1937, June 21 [Library: first portion].
[Sales] LONDON, 1937, November 22-25 [Library: second portion].
[Sales] LONDON, 1937, December 6 [Library: third portion].
[Sales] LONDON, 1938, February 14-16 [Library: fourth portion].

CLYFFE (Dorsetshire).
BURKE, J.B. Visitation of Seats. Vol.I, p.45. 1852.*
OSWALD, A. Country houses of Dorset. p.174. 1959.

CLYNE CASTLE (Glamorganshire).
SWANSEA: University College.
— GRIFFITHS R.A. Clyne Castle, Swansea: a history of the building and its owners. 64pp. Illus. (some col., 2 on covers) incl. maps and facsimiles. 20x21 Swansea, 1977.
Signed by the author.

CLYTHA PARK (Monmouthshire).
COUNTRY LIFE. CLXII, 1718, 1826. 1977.

COATE HOUSE, Bampton (Oxfordshire).
COUNTRY LIFE. XCIX, 1176. 1946.

COBERLEY (Gloucestershire).
ATKYNS, R. Glocestershire. p.197. 1768.

COBHAM HALL (Kent).
ARNOLD, Ralph.
— Cobham Hall, Kent: notes on the house, its owners, the gardens and park and objects of special interest. 32pp. 2 illus. incl. plan. 20x13 [Cobham: privately printed 1967?].
COBHAM.
— The pictorial guide to Cobham (Kent), descriptive of its church and college; the hall, picture gallery and park: with notices of Chalk and Shorne. Containing ... engravings on wood, from original sketches. 36pp. 17x11 London: Orr & Co., 1844.
HARRIS, Edwin.
— The Eastgate series.
4. Cobham Hall. 16 pp. Illus. (on cover). Rochester, 1909.
MANUSCRIPTS. English.
— Inventory of the household furniture, books, paintings, plate, linen, china & glass, wines, horses, carriages and effects, late the property of the Right Hon. Earl Darnley, at Cobham Hall, in the country of Kent. Taken and valued for the purpose of probate, June 10th. and following days, 1831. 159ff. (4 blank) 40x16.5 1831.
BURKE, J.B. Visitation of Seats. Vol.II, p.143. 1853.*
CAMPBELL, C. Vitruvius Britannicus. II, pls. 29, 30.1717.
COUNTRY LIFE. XV, 906. 1904.
COUNTRY LIFE. XCIV, 1124. 1943.
COUNTRY LIFE. CLXXIII, 448, 508, 568. 1983.
GOTCH, J.A. Architecture of the Renaissance. II, p.37. 1894.
GREENWOOD, C. Kent. 215. 1838.
HALL, S.C. Baronial Halls. Vol.I. 1848.
HASTED, E. Kent. I, 497. 1778.
JEWITT, L. Stately homes of England. 37. 1874.
MORRIS, F.O. Views of Seats. Vol.II, p.25. 1880.
NEALE, J.P. Views of Seats. Vol.II. 1819.
OSWALD, A. Country Houses of Kent. 37. 1933.
REPTON, H. Fragments on landscape gardening. 10. 1816.
SUMMERSON, J. The Country Seat. 42. 1970.
TIPPING, H.A. English Homes. Early Renaissance, p.157. 1912.
[Sales] COBHAM HALL, 1957, July 22, 23 [Contents].

COCKFIELD HALL (Suffolk).
COUNTRY LIFE. LV, 532. 1924.
CROMWELL, T.K. Excursions in Suffolk. II, p.96. 1819.
DAVY, G. Seats in Suffolk. p.13. 1827.

COGHILL HALL (Yorkshire).
ANGUS, W. Seats of the Nobility. pl.11. 1787.

COGSHALL HALL (Cheshire).
BURKE, J.B. Visitation of Seats. Vol.II, p.180. 1853.*
TWYCROSS, E. Mansions of England and Wales. Vol.II, p.74. 1850.

COHAM (Devonshire).
BURKE, J.B. Visitation of Seats. Vol.I, p.92. 1852.*

COKENACH (Hertfordshire).
CHAUNCY, H. Hertfordshire. I. 204. 1826.

COKER COURT (Somerset).
BURKE, J.B. Visitation of Seats. Vol.I, p.187. 1852.*
COUNTRY LIFE. XXV, 18. 1909.

COKETHORPE PARK (Oxfordshire).
JONES. Views of Seats. I. 1829.
NEALE, J.P. Views of Seats. Vol.III. 1820.
NEALE, J.P. Views of Seats. 2.S. Vol.I. 1824.
[Sales] LONDON, 1908, November 12 [Cokethorpe library, paintings etc.].

COLD ASHTON MANOR (Gloucestershire).
COUNTRY LIFE. LVII, 240, 272. 1925.
TIPPING, H.A. English Homes. Period III, Vol.II, p.133. 1927.

COLDERSTONES (Lancashire).
See CALDERSTONE.

COLDHARBOUR WOOD (Sussex).
[Sales] COLDARBOUR WOOD, 1932, September 20-23 [Contents]. (K.F. & R.).

COLD OVERTON HALL (Leicestershire).
COUNTRY LIFE. LXVII, 386 plan. 1930.
COUNTRY LIFE. LXVIII, 59. [Furniture]. 1930.
NICHOLS, J. History of Leicestershire. II, i. 139. 1795.

COLEBY HALL (Lincolnshire).
LINCOLNSHIRE. A selection of views. 59. 1805.

COLE GREEN PARK (Hertfordshire).
SUMMERSON, J. The Country Seat. 75.1970.

COLEORTON HALL (Leicestershire).
BURKE, J.B. Visitation of Seats. Vol.I, p.107. 1852.*
JONES, Views of Seats. I. 1829.
NEALE, J.P. Views of Seats. Vol.II. 1819.
SUMMERSON, J. The Country Seat. 215. 1970.

THE COUNTRY HOUSE DESCRIBED

COLE PARK (Wiltshire).
COUNTRY LIFE. CXXXV, 985. 1964.

COLES FARM, Box (Wiltshire).
ELYARD, S.J. Old Wiltshire Homes. p.82. 1894.

COLESHILL HOUSE (Berkshire).
CAMPBELL, C. Vitruvius Britannicus. V, pls.86, 87. 1771.
COUNTRY LIFE. English Country Houses: Caroline. p.90. 1966.
COUNTRY LIFE. XV, 666. 1904.
COUNTRY LIFE. XLVI, 108, 138.1919.
LATHAM, C. In English Homes. Vol.I, p.361. 1904.
NEALE, J.P. Views of Seats. Vol.I. 1818.
TIPPING, H.A. English Homes. Period IV, Vol.I, p.1. 1920.

COLES PARK (Hertfordshire).
BURKE, J.B. Visitation of Seats. Vol.II, p.188. 1853.*

COLETON FISHACRE (Devonshire).
COUNTRY LIFE. LXVII, 782 plan. 1930.

COLEY PARK (Berkshire).
KIP, J. Nouveau théâtre de la Grande Bretagne. I, pl.80. 1715.

COLLACOMBE BARTON MANOR (Devonshire).
COUNTRYLIFE. XXXV, 914. 1914.
COUNTRY LIFE. CXXXI, 904 plan, 970. 1962.
[Sales] COLLACOMBE MANOR, 1962, September 25 [Contents].

COLLEGE, The. (Cumberland).
BURKE, J.B. Visitation of Seats. Vol.II, p.181. 1853.*
COUNTRY LIFE. LXIV, 677 [Furniture, plate, pictures], 700 plan. 1928.

COLLETON BARTON (Devonshire).
COUNTRY LIFE. XXXVIII, 296. 1915.

COLLIPRIEST (Devonshire).
BRITTON, J. Devonshire illustrated. 68. 1831.
BURKE, J.B. Visitation of Seats. Vol.II, p.242. 1853.*
JONES. Views of Seats. II. 1829.
NEALE, J.P. Views of Seats. Vol.I. 1818.

COLNE PARK (Essex).
BURKE, J.B. Visitation of Seats. 2.S. Vol.I, p.116. 1854.*

COLNE PLACE (Essex).
[Sales] COLNE PLACE, 1978, June 21, 22 [Contents].

COLNE PRIORY (Essex).
ESSEX: A new and complete history. VI, 298. 1772.
RUSH, J.A. Seats in Essex. p.54. 1897.

COLNEY HOUSE (Hertfordshire).
JONES. View of Seats. I. 1829.
NEALE J.P. Views of Seats. 2.S. Vol.II. 1825.

COLQUITE (Cornwall).
BURKE, J.B. Visitation of Seats. Vol.II, p.125. 1853.*

COLUMBINE HALL (Suffolk).
SANDON, E. Suffolk houses. 294. 1977.

COLWICK HALL (Nottinghamshire).
THOROTON, R. Nottinghamshire. III, 7. 1797.

COLWORTH HOUSE (Bedfordshire).
ROBINSON, *Sir* John Charles.
— Notice of the principal works of art in the collection of Hollingworth Magniac, Esq. of Colworth. 25 plates: photographs. 25x15 London: Cundall, Downes & Co., 1862.
1 plate: photograph inserted.
Another copy. 2 plates: photographs. 1862.
Wanting most plates.
[Sales] LONDON, 1892, July 2 and following days [Colworth collection].
[Sales] COLWORTH HOUSE, 1924, December 8 and following days [Contents]. (K.F. & R.).
[Sales] COLWORTH HOUSE, 1947, October 14-16, 20, 21 [Contents].
[Sales] COLWORTH HOUSE, 1947, October 21 [Library].

COMBE (Devonshire).
COUNTRY LIFE. CXVII, 1486, 1556. 1955.
DELDERFIELD, E.R. West Country houses. I, 31.1968.

COMBE ABBEY (Warwickshire).
BUCK, S. & N. Antiquities. II, pl.298. 1774.
COUNTRY LIFE. English Country Houses: Caroline. p.137. 1966.
COUNTRY LIFE. XXVI, 794, 840. 1909.
HALL, S.C. Baronial Halls. Vol.II. 1848.
KIP, J. Nouveau théâtre de la Grande Bretagne.I, pl.47.1715.
LATHAM, C. In English Homes. Vol.I, p.297. 1904.
NASH, J. Mansions of England. II, Title-page. 1840.
NIVEN, W. Old Warwickshire Houses. p.18, pl.18. 1878.
SMITH, W. History of the County of Warwick. 166. 1830.
TIPPING, H.A. English Homes. Period IV, Vol.I, p.155. 1920.

[75]

COMBE BANK (Kent)

ANGUS, W. Seats of the Nobility. pl.4. 1787.

CAMPBELL, C. Vitruvius Britannicus. IV, pls. 75-77. 1767.

COMBE HAY MANOR (Somerset).

COUNTRY LIFE. CIX, 702, 782. 1951.

COMBERMERE ABBEY (Cheshire).

BARTLETT, J. Selections from views of mansions. 1851.

BUCK, S. & N. Antiquities. I, pl.18. 1774.

BURKE, J.B. Visitation of Seats. Vol.I, p.50. 1852.*

BURKE, J.B. Visitation of Seats. 2.S. Vol.I, p.243. 1854.*

MORRIS, F.O. Views of Seats. Vol.II, p.43. 1880.

NEALE, J.P. Views of Seats. 2.S. Vol.V. 1829.

ORMEROD, G. Cheshire. III, 404, 406, 416. 1882.

TWYCROSS, E. Mansions of England and Wales. Vol.II, p.1. 1850.

COMBE ROYAL (Devonshire).

BURKE, J.B. Visitation of Seats. Vol.I, p.245. 1852.*

COMBE SYDENHAM (Somerset).

DELDERFIELD, E.R. West Country houses. I, 34. 1968.

COMBE WOOD, Colgate (Sussex)

[Sales] COMBE WOOD, 1969, May 6-8 [Contents].

COMPTON BEAUCHAMP (Berkshire).

COUNTRY LIFE. XLIV, 484 plan. 1918.

COMPTON CASTLE (Devonshire).

LONDON: Natural Trust for Places of Historic Interest or Natural Beauty.

— Compton Castle, Devon. 36pp. Illus. (1 on title-page) incl. plate, plan and genealog. table. 18x11 London: Country Life (1952).

   New ed. 40pp. Illus. (1 on cover) incl. plates, plan and genealog. table. 21x14 [London]1983.

BURKE, J.B. Visitation of Seats. Vol.II, p.55. 1853.*

COUNTRY LIFE. CLXX. 1546. 1981.

DELDERFIELD, E.R. West Country houses. I, 38. 1968.

COMPTON CASTLE (Somerset).

[Sales] COMPTON CASTLE, 1961, April 10, 11 [Contents].

COMPTON HOUSE (Dorsetshire).

HUTCHINS, J. Vitruvius Dorsettiensis. pl.6. 1816.

HUTCHINS, J. History of Dorset. IV, 168. 1870.

COMPTON PARK (Wiltshire).

BURKE, J.B. Visitation of Seats. Vol.II, p.1. 1853.

COUNTRY LIFE. XXVIII, 228. 1910.

ROBERTSON, A. Great Road. II, p.43. 1792.

TIPPING, H.A. English Homes. Period IV, Vol.I, p.303. 1920.

COMPTON PLACE (Sussex).

LIVERPOOL, Cecil George Savile Foljambe, *Earl of*

— Catalogue of portraits at Compton Place and at Buxted Park, in Sussex [and](Miniatures at Devonshire House). 28pp. Folding genealog. table.21x14 n.p. Privately printed, 1903.

Also in SUSSEX: Archaeological Society, Collections XLVII, 82, 1904.

Bound in volume lettered: Portraits by Lord Hawkesbury, 1905.

COUNTRY LIFE. English Country Houses: Early Georgian. p.87. 1955.

COUNTRY LIFE. XL, 266, 294. 1916.

COUNTRY LIFE. LXXVII, 144. 1935.

COUNTRY LIFE. CXIII, 734, 818. 1953.

TIPPING, H.A. English Homes. Period V, Vol.I, p.121. 1921.

[Sales] COMPTON PLACE, 1934, October 16-19 [Antique and modern furniture etc.].

COMPTON VERNEY (Warwickshire).

BOLTON, A.T. Architecture of R. & J. Adam. I, 216 plan. 1922.

BURKE, J.B. Visitation of Seats. 2.S. Vol.II, p.7. 1855.*

CAMPBELL, C. Vitruvius Britannicus. V, pls. 43, 44. 1771.

COUNTRY LIFE. XXXIV, 528 plan. 1913.

JONES. Views of seats. I.1829.

MORRIS, F.O. Views of Seats. Vol.III, p.3. 1880.

NEALE, J.P. Views of Seats. Vol.IV. 1821.

TIPPING, H.A. English Homes. Period IV, Vol.II, p.211. 1928.

COMPTON WYNYATES (Warwickshire).

COMPTON WYNYATES.

— A general history of Compton Wynyates House and the Compton family. 16pp. 1 illus. on cover. 20x13 n.p., n.d.

COMPTON WYNYATES.

— [A short history of Compton Wynates House [etc]. Description of some of the rooms and their contents.] 24pp. Illus. (some on covers) incl. map. 14x22 n.p. privately printed [c.1970].

NORTHAMPTON, William George Spencer Scott Compton, *Marquess of.*

— Compton Wynyates. 66pp. Plates incl. plan. 29x23 London: Humphreys, 1904.

BURKE, J.B. Visitation of Seats. 2.S. Vol.I, p.48. 1854.*

COUNTRY LIFE. II, 70.1897.

COUNTRY LIFE. XXXVIII, 585 plan, 616. 1915.

DELDERFIELD, E.R. West Country houses. III, 46. 1973.

GARNER, T. Domestic architecture.I, p. 63 plan. 1911.

MALAN, A.H. More famous homes. p.255. 1902.

MOSS, F. Pilgrimages. [III] 220. 1906
NASH, J. Mansions of England. III, pls.21, 22. 1841.
NICOLSON, N. Great Houses of Britain. p.36. 1965.
NIVEN, W. Old Warwickshire Houses. p.30, pls. 1 [Plan], 29, 30. 1878.
SMITH, W. History of the County of Warwick. 51. 1830.
TIPPING, H.A. English Homes. Period II, Vol.I, p.117. 1924.
WHITEMAN, G.W. English country homes. p.1. 1951.

CONDOVER HALL (Shropshire).
BURKE, J.B. Visitation of Seats. 2.S. Vol.I, p.198. 1854.*
COUNTRY LIFE. XLIII, 508, 530. 1918.
GOTCH, J.A. Architecture of the Renaissance. II, p.19. 1894.
JONES. Views of Seats. I. 1829.
LEACH, F. Seats of Shropshire. p.49. 1891.
NEALE, J.P. Views of Seats. 2.S. Vol.II. 1825.
SHROPSHIRE. Castles & Old Mansions. 46. 1868.
TIPPING, H.A. English Homes. Period III, Vol.I, p.161. 1922.

CONINGTON CASTLE (Huntingdonshire).
JONES. Views of Seats. I.1829.
NEALE, J.P. Views of Seats. Vol.II. 1819.

CONISHEAD PRIORY (Lancashire).
BARTLETT, J. Mansions of England and Wales. pl.47.1853.
PYNE, W.H. Lancashire illustrated. 96. 1831.
TWYCROSS, E. Mansions of England and Wales. Vol.II, p.5. 1847.
[Sales] CONISHEAD PRIORY, 1850, September 16 and following days [Furniture, books].
[Sales] CONISHEAD PRIORY, 1874, January 27 and following days, [Contents].

CONOCK MANOR (Wiltshire).
COUNTRY LIFE. CIX, 2040. 1951.

CONSTABLE BURTON (Yorkshire).
BURKE, J.B. Visitation of Seats. 2.S. Vol.I, p.55. 1854.*
CAMPBELL, C. Vitruvius Britannicus. V, pls. 36, 37.1771.
COUNTRY LIFE. CXLIV, 1396 plan. 1968.
KIP, J.Nouveau théâtre de la Grande Bretagne. I, pl. 69. 1715.

CONVENT, The. Kingsgate (Kent).
[Sales] KINGSGATE, 1910, September 20-23 [Contents].

COOKE'S HOUSE, West Burton (Sussex).
COUNTRY LIFE. XXV, 942. 1909.

COOMBE, The (Cornwall).
BURKE, J.B. Visitation of Seats. Vol.II, p.179. 1853.*

COOMBE ABBEY (Warwickshire).
See COMBE ABBEY.

COOMBE PARK [LODGE] (Oxfordshire).
BURKE, J.B. Visitation of Seats. Vol.I, p.35. 1852.*
[Sales] COOMBE PARK, 1920, April 19-22 [Contents].

COOMBE WARREN (Surrey).
COOMBE WARREN.
— Catalogue of the collection of works of art at Coombe Warren. [Preface by L.C. i.e. L. Currie]. 15 plates. 29x23 London: privately printed, 1908.
First supplement, inserted. 2ff. 28x21 1910.

COOPERSALE HOUSE (Essex).
ESSEX: A new and complete history. III, 394. 1770.

COPFORD HALL (Essex).
BURKE, J.B. Visitation of Seats. Vol.II, p.112. 1853.*

COPPED HALL (Essex.).
COUNTRY LIFE. XXVIII, 610, 646 Plan. 1910.
COUNTRY LIFE. XXX, 102 [Furniture]. 1911.
CROMWELL, T.K. Excursions in Essex. II, p.28. 1825.
ESSEX: A new and complete history. IV, 181. 1771.
MORANT, P. Essex. I, 48. 1768.
RUSH, J.A. Seats in Essex. p.58. 1897.*
WATTS, W. Seats of the Nobility. pl.27. 1779.

COPPED HALL, Totteridge (Hertfordshire).
[Sales] COPPED HALL, Totteridge, 1918, October 14-18 [Contents].

COPPEED HALL (Hertfordshire).
See COPT HALL (Middlesex).

COPPICE, The (Shropshire).
WEST, W. Picturesque views of Shropshire. p.135. 1831.

COPT HALL (Essex).
See also COPPED HALL.
SUMMERSON, J. The Country Seat. 18. 1970.

COPT HALL (Middlesex).
CAMPBELL, C. Vitruvius Britannicus. IVth. pls.98, 99.1739.

CORBY CASTLE (Cumberland).
BURKE, J.B. Visitation of Seats. Vol.I, p.35. 1852.*
COUNTRY LIFE. CXV, 92. 1954.
JONES. Views of Seats. I. 1829.
NEALE, J.P. Views of Seats. 2.S. Vol.II. 1825.

CORNBURY PARK (Oxfordshire).
WATNEY, Vernon James.
— Cornbury and the forest of Wychwood. [Bibliogr. notes.] Plates (1 folding) incl. plan and tables (some genealog.). 39x28 London: Hatchards, 1910.

COUNTRY LIFE. English Country Houses: Caroline. p.131. 1966.

COUNTRY LIFE. CVIII, 922. 1950.

[Sales] CORNBURY PARK, 1967, May 22-24 [Remaining contents].

CORNHILL HOUSE (Northumberland).
BURKE, J.B. Visitation of Seats. Vol.II, p.101. 1853.*

CORNISH HALL (Denbighshire).
BURKE, J.B. Visitation of Seats. Vol.II, p.219. 1853.*

CORNWELL MANOR (Oxfordshire).
COUNTRY LIFE. LXXXIX, 454, 476 plan. 1941.

CORSHAM COURT (Wiltshire).
BORENIUS, Tancred.
— A catalogue of the pictures at Corsham Court. (The Methuen collection.) [Bibliogr.] 52 plates. 20x16 London: privately printed (1939).

BRITTON, John.
— An historical account of Corsham House, in Wiltshire: the seat of Paul Cobb Methuen, Esq. with a catalogue of his celebrated collection of pictures [etc.]. Engr. plates incl. plan. 19x13 London: privately printed, 1806.

CORSHAM COURT.
— Topographical index of the pictures at Corsham Court. 12pp. 20x16 (London: Eyre & Spottiswoode) [c.1940].

HARCOURT, Leslie.
— Corsham Court: a gothick dream. [Bibliogr.] 50pp. Illus. incl. 1 on cover. 15x21 London: Gothick Dream, 1977.

METHUEN, Paul Ayshford Methuen, *Baron, R.A.*
— Corsham Court, Wiltshire. 4pp. 2 illus. (on covers) 20x15 (Bath) privately printed (1949).

METHUEN, Paul Ayshford Methuen, *Baron, R.A.*
— An historical account of Corsham Court: the Methuen collection of pictures and the furniture in the state rooms. [Bibliogr.] 20pp. 4 illus. (1 on title page). 21x15 Corsham: privately printed, 1958.
Another ed. 56pp. Illus. (some col.) 1971.

METHUEN, Paul Ayshford Methuen, *Baron, R.A.*
— A catalogue of the Methuen miniatures at Corsham Court, Wilts. 56pp. 7 (1 col.) plates. 23x15 [London] Strathmore Press, 1970.

BRITTON, J. Beauties of Wiltshire. II, 269. 1801.

BURKE, J.B. Visitation of Seats. Vol.II, p.216. 1853.*

COOKE, R. West Country Houses. p.76. 1957.

COUNTRY LIFE. English Country Houses: Early Georgian. p.228. 1955.

COUNTRY LIFE. LXXX, 576 [Furniture]. 1936.

COUNTRY LIFE. LXXXII, 516 plan, 548. 1937.

DELDERFIELD, E.R. West Country houses. II, 35. 1970.

HAVELL, R. Views of Noblemen's Seats. 1823.

JONES. Views of Seats. II. 1829.

MORRIS, F.O. Views of Seats. Vol.II, p.69. 1880.

NEALE, J.P. Views of Seats. 2.S. Vol.II. 1825.

REPTON, H. Observations on landscape gardening. 188. 1803.

ROBERTSON, A. Great Road. II, p.66. 1792.

WATTS, W. Seats of the Nobility. pl.32. 1779.

WHITEMAN, G.W. English Country Homes. p.35. 1951.

CORSLEY MANOR (Wiltshire).
ELYARD, S.J. Old Wiltshire Homes. p.34. 1894.

CORYTON (Devonshire).
BURKE, J.B. Visitation of Seats. Vol.I, p.61. 1852.*

JONES. Views of Seats. II. 1829.

NEALE, J.P. Views of Seats. Vol.I. 1818.

COSSEY HALL (Norfolk).
See COSTESSEY HALL.

COSTESSEY HALL (Norfolk).
DRAKE, Maurice.
— The Costessey collection of stained glass, formerly in the possession of George William Jerningham, 8th. Baron Stafford of Costessey in the county of Norfolk ... With an introductory article by A. Vallance. 56pp. 26 (6 col.) plates. 34x21 Exeter: W. Pollard, 1920.

BIRKBECK, G. Old Norfolk Houses. 30. 1908.

CROMWELL, T.K. Excursions in Norfolk. II, p.45. 1819.

NEALE, J.P. Views of Seats. 2.S. Vol.I. 1824.

[Sales] COSTESSEY HALL, 1913, December 8-12 [Contents].

COTEHELE HOUSE (Cornwall).
ARUNDELL, *Rev.* Francis Vyvan Jago.
— Cothele, on the banks of the Tamar, the ancient seat of the Rt. Hon. the Earl of Mount Edgcumbe, by N. Condy. With a descriptive account, written expressley for the work, by the Rev. F.V.J.A. 36pp. Lithogr. plates (many hand-col.) incl. title-page and plan. 49x33 London: by the author [1850?]
Plate to "Queen Anne's Room" not published?.

LONDON: National Trust for Places of Historic Interest or Natural Beauty.
— LEES-MILNE, J. Cotehele House, Cornwall. 26pp. 4 plates. 18x12 London: Country Life. (1948).

Rev. ed. 36pp. Illus. (1 col.) incl. plates and plan. [London] 1982.

LONDON: National Trust for Places of Historic Interest or Natural Beauty.
— GARDINER, R. Cotehele. 2 ed. 58pp. Col. lithogr. illus. incl. title-page, covers and plan. 21x31 [London] (1979).

BRITTON, J. Cornwall illustrated. 18. 1832.

COUNTRY LIFE. XVII, 822. 1905.

COUNTRY LIFE. LVI, 324, 360. 1924.

CROMWELL, T.K. Excursions in Cornwall. p.128.1824.

GARNER, T. Domestic architecture.I, p.49 plan. 1911.

JEWITT, L. Stately homes of England. 70. 1874.

LATHAM, C. In English Homes. Vol.II, p.43. 1907.

MALAN, A.H. More famous homes. p.55. 1902.

TIPPING, H.A. English Homes. Period I & II, Vol.II, p.69. 1937.

COTE HOUSE (Oxfordshire).

COUNTRY LIFE. XV, 567. 1904.

[Sales] COTE HOUSE, 1977, September 19 [Remaining contents].

COTHAY MANOR (Somerset).

ASTLEY-RUSHTON, *Mrs.*
— Cothay Manor, Somerset ... History and description of the rooms by Mrs., and P. A-R. 20pp. Illus. (some on covers, some on title-page) incl. plan and map. 14x20 [Derby] (E.L.P., 1964).

COUNTRY LIFE. LXII, 596 plan, 626. 1927.

DELDERFIELD, E.R. West Country houses. I, 42.1968.

TIPPING, H.A. English Homes. Period I. & II, Vol.II, p.51. 1937.

COTHELSTONE HOUSE (Somerset).

BURKE, J.B. Visitation of Seats. 2.S. Vol.I, p.153. 1854.*

JONES. Views of Seats. II. 1829.

NEALE, J.P. Views of Seats. 2.S. Vol.IV. 1828.

COTHELSTONE MANOR (Somerset).

COUNTRY LIFE. XXIII, 54. 1908.

GARNER, T. Domestic architecture. II, p.185 plan. 1911.

TIPPING, H.A. English Homes. Early Renaissance. p.305. 1912.

TIPPING, H.A. English Homes. Period III, Vol.II, p.31. 1927.

COTHERIDGE COURT (Worcestershire).

BURKE, J.B. Visitation of Seats. 2.S. Vol.I, p.86. 1854.*

NASH, T.R. Worcestershire. I, 559. 1781.

COTON MANOR, Coton-in-the-Elms (Derbyshire).

TILLEY, J. Halls of Derbyshire. IV, p.33. 1902.

COTTERSTOCK HALL (Northamptonshire).

COTTERSTOCK HALL.
— Cotterstock Hall, Northamptonshire. 16pp. Illus. 19x12 (Peterborough) Privately printed [1975].

GOTCH, J.A. Halls of Northants. p.26. 1936.

COTTESBROOKE HALL (Northamptonshire).

BRIDGES, J. Northamptonshire. I, 554. 1791.

COUNTRY LIFE. English Country Houses: Baroque. p.119. 1970.

COUNTRY LIFE. LXXIX, 168, 194. 1936.

COUNTRY LIFE. CXVII,736, 806. 1955.

COUNTRY LIFE. CXLVII, 434. 1970.

GOTCH, J.A. Halls of Northants. p.60. 1936.

MITCHELL, R. Buildings in England and Scotland. pl.7 [Plan]. 1801.

COTTESMORE (Pembrokeshire).

NICHOLAS, T. Counties of Wales. II, p.841. 1872.

COUGHTON COURT (Warwickshire).

BARNARD, Ettwell Augustine Bracher.
— A 16th century dole-gate from Denny Abbey [now at] (Coughton Court). 4pp. Plate. 23x15 [Cambridge] (1928). Also in CAMBRIDGE: Cambridge Antiquarian Society. Proceedings ..., XXIX, 72.

LONDON: National Trust for Places of Historic Interest or Natural Beauty.
— LEES-MILNE, J. Coughton Court, Warwickshire. 24pp. Illus. 18x12 London: Country Life [1946].

— Another ed. 24pp. Illus. (1 col. on cover) incl. 8 plates and genealog. table. 22x14 1973.
Another copy.

COUNTRY LIFE. XLIII, 319. 1918.

JONES. Views of Seats. I. 1829.

MORRIS, F.O. Views of Seats. Vol.III, p.45. 1880.

NEALE, J.P. Views of Seats. Vol.IV. 1821.

NIVEN, W. Old Warwickshire Houses.p.24, pl.24. 1878.

SMITH, W. History of the County of Warwick. 289. 1830.

COUND HALL (Shropshire).

COUNTRY LIFE. English Country Houses: Baroque. p.131. 1970.

COUNTRY LIFE. XLIII, 488. 1918.

TIPPING, H.A. English Homes. Period IV, Vol.I, p.417. 1920.

COURT, The. Holt (Wiltshire).

COUNTRY LIFE. XCIII, 74. 1943.

COURT BLEDDYN, Llangibby (Monmouthshire).

[Sales] LLANGIBBY, 1912, April 30, May 1. [Contents].

COURTEENHALL (Northamptonshire).

BURKE, J.B. Visitation of Seats. 2.S. Vol.I, p.28. 1854.*

CAMPBELL, C. Vitruvius Britannicus. I, pls. 67, 68. 1802.

COUNTRY LIFE. English Country Houses: Mid Georgian. p.228. 1956.

COUNTRY LIFE. LXXXVI, 144, 172. 1939.

GOTCH, J.A. Halls of Northants. p.82. 1936.

COURT GARDEN (Buckinghamshire).
THAMES, River. An history. I, pl.34. 1794.

COURT HOUSE (Dorsetshire).
HUTCHENS, J. History of Dorset. II, 661. 1863.

COURT HOUSE, Painswick
(Gloucestershire).
COUNTRY LIFE. XXXVII, 518 plan. 1915.

COURT HOUSE, The. East Meon
(Hampshire).
COUNTRY LIFE. LXXXI, 510 plan. 1937.

COURT HOUSE, Cannington (Somerset).
BURKE, J.B. Visitation of Seats. Vol.II, p.151. 1853.*

COURT HOUSE, West Monkton (Somerset).
COLLINSON, J. History of Somerset. III, 454. 1791.

COURT HOUSE, East Quantockshead
(Somerset).
See EAST QUANTOCKSHEAD.

COURT LODGE, Lamberhurst (Kent).
GREENWOOD, C. Kent. 132. 1838.

COURT OF HILL (Shropshire).
COUNTRY LIFE. C, 716. 1946.
LEIGHTON, S. Shropshire Houses. 40. 1901.

COURT-YR-ALA (Glamorganshire).
BURKE, J.B. Visitation of Seats. Vol.II, p.250. 1853.*

COWDRAY HOUSE (Sussex).
HOPE, *Sir* William Henry St. John.
— Cowdray and Easebourne Priory, in the county of Sussex. [Bibliogr. notes] Illus. incl. plates (some col., some folding), plans and genealog. tables. 36x26 London: Country Life, 1919.
MONTAGUE, Anthony Joseph Browne, *Viscount.*
— A catalogue of the pictures at Cowdray House, the seat of the Right Honourable Lord Viscount Montague near Midhurst, Sussex, 1777. [Photocopy of annotated copy in the library at Althorp Park.] 14ff.24x20 [London, 1967.]
ROUNDELL, Julia Ann Elizabeth.
— Cowdray: the history of a great English House. Illus. incl. plates, plan and cover. 25x20 London: Bickers & Son, 1884.
SOTHEBY, WILKINSON & HODGE.
— Catalogue of the oil paintings, water-colour drawings, arms and armour, engravings, furniture, carpets, ornamental china, tapestries, &c. at Cowdray Park, Midhurst, Sussex, 1919. Plate. 25x19 London (1920).
SUSSEX: West Sussex County Council [West Sussex Record Office].

— The Cowdray archives ... A catalogue edited by A.A. Dibben. [Bibliogr.] Illus. (on title-page) and plates (some folding) incl. facsimiles and genealog. tables. 2 vols. 25x15 Chichester, 1960-64.
TROTTER, Torrens.
— Cowdray in the parish of Easebourne, near Midhurst, Sussex. A short history, architectural and biographical, together with a ... guide to the ruins and museum, and some account of the ancient domain. Compiled by T.T. 64pp. 5 plates incl. folding plan. 19x12 Cowdray (1922).
2 ed. 72pp.(1932).
ELWES, D.G.C. Mansions of Western Sussex. 77. 1876.
GARNER, T. Domestic Architecture, I. 89 plan. 1911.
MORRIS, F.O. Views of seats. Vol.V p.51. 1880.
TIPPING, H.A. English Homes. Period II, Vol.I, p.139. 1920.

COWICK HALL (Yorkshire).
PAINE, J. Plans, elevations. pt.I, pls. 12 plan, 13, 14. 1767.

COWLEY GROVE (Middlesex).
BURKE, J.B. Visitation of Seats. Vol.I, p.213. 1852.*

COWLEY HALL (Derbyshire).
TILLEY, J. Halls of Derbyshire. I, p.101. 1892.

COWLEY HOUSE, Chertsey (Surrey).
BURKE, J.B. Visitation of Seats. 2.S. Vol.I, p.215. 1854.*

CRACKENTHORPE HALL
(Westmorland).
CUMBERLAND: C & W. A. & A.S. Extra Series. VIII, 127. 1892.

CRAGG ROYD, Apperley Bridge
(Yorkshire).
YORKSHIRE. Picturesque views. 1885.

CRAGSIDE (Northumberland).
LONDON: National Trust for Places of Historic Interest or Natural Beauty.
— SAINT, A. and PETTIT. Cragside, Northumberland. [Bibliogr.] 56pp. Illus. (1 col. on cover) plan and genealog. table. 25x19 [London] 1983.
COUNTRY LIFE. CXLVI, 1640, 1694. 1969.
COUNTRY LIFE. CLXVIII. 759, 1980.

CRAIGWEIL HOUSE (Sussex).
[Sales] CRAIGWEIL HOUSE, 1932, August 2-6 [Contents]. (K.F. & R.).

CRANAGE HALL (Cheshire).
TWYCROSS, E. Mansions of England and Wales. Vol.I, p.144. 1850.*

CRANBORNE LODGE (Berkshire).
COUNTRY LIFE. CXLIII, 10. 1968.

CRANBORNE MANOR (Dorsetshire).
COUNTRY LIFE. LV, 910, 964. 1924.
COUNTRY LIFE. CLIII, 1218, 1298. 1973.
DELDERFIELD, E.R. West Country houses. II, 46. 1970.
GOTCH, J.A. Architecture of the Renaissance. II, p.1 plan. 1894.
HEATH, S. Dorset Manor Houses. 91. 1907.
HUTCHINS, J. Vitruvius Dorsettiensis. pl.7, 1816.
HUTCHINS, J. History of Dorset. III, 380. 1868.
NASH, J. Mansions of England. III, Title-page, pl.11. 1841.
OSWALD, A. Country Houses of Dorset. p.123. 1959.
TIPPING, H.A. English Homes. Period III, Vol.II, p.353. 1927.

CRANBURY PARK (Hampshire).
CRANBURY PARK.
— Cranbury Park: an illustrated survey of the Hampshire home of the Chamberlayne-Macdonalds [etc.]. 20pp. Illus (1 on title-page.) 14x21 Eastleigh: privately printed [1964?].
COUNTRY LIFE. CXX, 944, 1058, 1116. 1956.
MORRIS, F.O. Views of Seats. Vol.I, p.81. 1880.

CRANFORD HALL (Northamptonshire).
BRIDGES, J. Northamptonshire. II, 227. 1791.
GOTCH, J.A. Squires' Homes. 14. 1939.

CRANFORD HOUSE [PARK] (Middlesex).
COUNTRY LIFE. LXXVII, 240. 1935.

CRANMORE HALL (Somerset).
BURKE, J.B. Visitation of Seats. Vol.I, p.228. 1852.*

CRANSLEY HALL (Northamptonshire).
GOTCH, J.A. Squires' Homes. 18. 1939.

CRATHORNE HALL (Yorkshire).
COUNTRY LIFE. XXIX, 598 plan. 1911.

CRAYCOMBE HOUSE (Worcestershire).
COUNTRY LIFE. LXXXVIII, 10. 1940.

CREECH GRANGE (Dorsetshire).
BURKE, J.B. Visitation of Seats. Vol.I, p.65. 1852.*
COUNTRY LIFE. LXX, 252, 282 [Furniture]. 1931.
DELDERFIELD, E.R. West Country houses. II, 51. 1970.
HUTCHINS, J. History of Dorset. I, 605. 1861.
OSWALD, A. Country Houses of Dorset. p.84. 1959.

CREEDY PARK (Devonshire).
BURKE, J.B. Visitation of Seats. Vol.I, p.70. 1852.*

CRETE HALL (Kent).
GREENWOOD, C. Kent. 228. 1838.

CREWE HALL (Cheshire).
BARTLETT, J. Selections from Views of Mansions. 1851.
BURKE, J.B. Visitation of Seats. Vol.I, p.9. 1852.*
COUNTRY LIFE. XXXIII, 634. 1913.
HALL, S.C. Baronial Halls. Vol.I. 1848.
LATHAM, C. In English Homes. Vol.I, p.397. 1904.
MOSS, F. Pilgrimages. V, 336. 1910.
NASH, J. Mansions of England. I, pl.10, 1839. & IV, pls. 10, 11. 1849.
NEALE, J.P. Views of Seats. Vol.I. 1818.
ORMEROD, G. Cheshire. III, 311, 312. 1882.
RICHARDSON, C.J. Old English Mansions. I, pls. 1-8. 1841.
RICHARDSON, C.J. Old English Mansions. II. 1842.
TWYCROSS, E. Mansions of England and Wales. Vol.II, p.5. 1850.

CREWE HILL (Cheshire).
TWYCROSS, E. Mansions of England and Wales. Vol.I, p.37. 1850.*

CRICHEL (Dorsetshire).
COUNTRY LIFE. English Country Houses: Mid Georgian, p.153. 1956.
COUNTRY LIFE. LVII, 766 plan, 814, 874. 1925.
DELDERFIELD, E.R. West Country houses. II, 56. 1970.
HUTCHINS, J. Vitruvius Dorsettiensis. pl.8. 1816.
JONES. Views of Seats. II. 1829.
NEALE, J.P. Views of Seats. Vol.I. 1818.
OSWALD, A. Country houses of Dorset. p.165. 1959.
TIPPING, H.A. English Homes. Period VI, Vol.I, p.43. 1926.

CROFT CASTLE (Herefordshire).
CROFT, Owen George Scudamore.
— The house of Croft of Croft Castle. x, 156pp. Plates (2 folding) and genealog. tables. 21x13 Hereford: Thurston, 1949.
LONDON: National Trust for Places of Historic Interest or Natural Beauty.
— UHLMAN, D. Croft Castle, Herefordshire. [Bibliogr.] 32pp. Illus. (1 col. on cover) incl. 8 plates and plans. 22x14 [London] 1972.
COUNTRY LIFE. CVII. 1206, 1292 plan. 1950.

CROFT HOUSE (Lancashire).
BURKE, J.B. Visitation of Seats. Vol.I, p.123. 1852.
TWYCROSS, E. Mansions of England and Wales. Vol.III, p.89. 1847.*

CROMFORD HOUSE (Derbyshire).
See WILLERSEY CASTLE.

CROOKSBURY (Surrey).
COUNTRY LIFE. XCVI, 596, 640 plan. 1944.

CROOME COURT (Worcestershire).
DEAN, William.
— An historical and descriptive account of Croome D'Abitot, the seat of the Right Hon. the Earl of Coventry; with biographical notices of the Coventry family: to which are annexed an Hortus Croomensis, and observations on the propagation of exotics. Plates 20x12 Worcester: by the author, 1824.

BOLTON, A.T. Architecture of R.& J. Adam. II, 178 plan. 1922

BURKE, J.B. Visitation of Seats. 2.S. Vol.II, p.8. 1855.*

CAMPBELL, C. Vitruvius Britannicus. V, pls. 29, 30. 1771.

COUNTRY LIFE. XXXVII, 482 plan. 1915.

ENGLAND: Picturesque views. p.49. 1786-88.

JONES. Views of Seats. I. 1829.

NEALE, J.P. Views of Seats. Vol.V. 1822.

[Sales] LONDON, June 25 [Furniture, mirrors etc. from C.C.].

CROSBY HALL (Lancashire).
BARTLETT, J. Mansions of England and Wales. pl.104. 1853.

TWYCROSS, E. Mansions of England and Wales. Vol.III, p.39. 1847.

CROSSWOOD HALL (Cardiganshire).
NICHOLAS, T. Counties of Wales. I, p.129. 1872.

CROSTON HALL (Lancashire).
TWYCROSS, E. Mansions of England and Wales. Vol.I, p.67. 1847.*

CROWCOMBE COURT (Somerset).
MANUSCRIPTS (Typewritten).   English.
— SMITH, H.C. Inventory and valuation of the furniture, pictures ... at Crowcombe Court, Crowcombe, Somerset. Prepared for the purpose of insurance by H.C.S. 32x20 (Newbury). 1942.

COLLINSON, J. History of Somerset. III, 516. 1791.

COUNTRY LIFE. English Country Houses: Early Georgian. p.118. 1955.

COUNTRY LIFE. LXXIII, 414, 442. 1933.

CROWE HALL (Suffolk).
COUNTRY LIFE. CXXII, 1434. 1957.

SANDON, E. Suffolk houses. 208. 1977.

CROWHURST PLACE (Surrey).
COUNTRY LIFE. XLVI, 12, 44 plan. 1919.

TIPPING, H.A. English Homes. Period I & II, Vol.II, p.155. 1937.

CROWLEASOWES (Shropshire).
SHROPSHIRE. Castles & Old Mansions. 63. 1868.

CROW NEST (Yorkshire).
CAMPBELL, C. New Vitruvius Britannicus. I, pls. 64-66. 1802.

CROWS HALL (Suffolk).
COUNTRY LIFE. V, 20. 1899.

SANDON, E. Suffolk houses. 258. 1977.

CROXALL HALL (Staffordshire).
TILLEY, J. Halls of Derbyshire.IV, p.19. 1902.

CROXDALE HALL (Durham).
COUNTRY LIFE. LXXXVI. 202, 230. 1939.

CROXDEN ABBEY (Staffordshire).
BURKE, J.B. Visitation of Seats. 2.S. Vol.I, p.241. 1854.*

CROXTETH HALL (Lancashire).
BARTLETT, J. Mansions of England and Wales. pl.98. 1853.

BURKE, J.B. Visitation of Seats. Vol.I, p.163. 1852.*

JONES. Views of Seats. I. 1829.

NEALE, J.P. Views of Seats. 2.S. Vol.I. 1824.

TWYCROSS, E. Mansions of England and Wales. Vol.III, p.9. 1847.

[Sales] CROXTETH HALL, 1973, September 17-20 [Remaining contents].

[Sales] CROXTETH HALL, 1973, September 20 [Library].

CROXTON PARK (Cambridgeshire).
BURKE, J.B. Visitation of Seats. Vol.II, p.245. 1853.*

CROYDON PALACE (Surrey).
ANDERSON, John Corbet.
— Croydon [etc.]. [Bibliogr. notes.] Illus. incl. plans and maps. 4 vols. 28x19 [London] privately printed. 1874-9.

[IV.] The Archiepiscopal Palace at Croydon. 1879.

CROYDON PALACE.
— The history of the old palace, Croydon. 4 ed. 16pp. Illus. 23x15 Croydon: privately printed, 1948.

COUNTRY LIFE. CXXXVII, 806 plan, 876. 1965.

MANNING, O. Surrey. II, 537. 1809.

CRUMPSALL HALL (Lancashire).
GRAY, H. Old halls of Lancashire. p.103. 1893.

CRUWYS ORCHARD (Devonshire).
DELDERFIELD, E.R. West Country houses. I, 46. 1968.

CUCKFIELD HOUSE (Sussex).
COUNTRY LIFE. XLV, 278, 310, 316 [Ship Models]. 1919.

CUERDALE HALL (Lancashire).
TWYCROSS, E. Mansions of England and Wales. Vol.I, p.10. 1847.*

CUERDEN HALL (Lancashire).
TATTON, Reginald A.
— Catalogue of the pictures at Cuerden Hall, Preston, the property of R.A.T. 74pp.26x21 Manchester: G. Faulkner & Sons, 1913.
BARTLETT, J. Mansions of England and Wales. pl.10. 1853.
BURKE, J.B. Visitation of Seats. Vol.I, p.33. 1852.
TWYCROSS, E. Mansions of England and Wales. Vol.I, p.42. 1847.

CUFFNELLS (Hampshire).
HAMPSHIRE: Architectural views. 1830.

CULFORD HALL (Suffolk).
BURKE, J.B. Visitation of Seats. 2.S. Vol.II, p.99. 1855.*
CROMWELL, T.K. Excursions in Suffolk. I, p.78. 1818.
NEALE, J.P. Views of Seats. Vol.IV. 1821.

CULHAM COURT (Berkshire).
THAMES, River. An history. I, pl.30. 1794.

CULHAM HOUSE (Oxfordshire).
[Sales] CULHAM HOUSE, 1935, April 9-11 [Contents].

CULHAM MANOR (Oxfordshire).
COUNTRY LIFE. CVIII, 130, 210. 1950.

CULVERTHORPE HALL (Lincolnshire).
COUNTRY LIFE. LIV, 350, 386. 1923.

CUMBERLAND LODGE (Berkshire).
COPPER PLATE MAGAZINE, pl.105. 1778.
ENGLAND: Beauties of England. I, p.33. 1787.
SANDBY, P. Select Views. I, pl.5. 1783.

CUMNOR PLACE (Berkshire).
BARTLETT, Alfred Durling.
— An Historical and descriptive account of Cumnor Place, Berks., with biographical notices of the Lady Amy Dudley and of Anthony Forster, followed by ... a brief history of the parish of Cumnor and its antiquities. 2 plates incl. plan. 22x13 Oxford: J.H. Parker, 1850.

CUSWORTH HALL (Yorkshire).
ANGUS, W. Seats of the Nobility. pl.16. 1787.
CAMPBELL, C. Vitruvius Britannicus. IV, pls.88, 89. 1767.
JONES. Views of Seats. I. 1829.
NEALE, J.P. Views of Seats. Vol.V. 1822.

CUTTHORPE NEW HALL (Derbyshire).
TILLEY, J. Halls of Derbyshire. III, p.37. 1899.

CUTTHORPE OLD HALL (Derbyshire).
TILLEY, J. Halls of Derbyshire. III, p.37. 1899.

CYFARTHFA CASTLE (Glamorganshire).
TAYLOR, Margaret Stewart.
— The Crawshays of Cyfarthfa Castle (Merthyr Tydfil): a family history. [Bibliogr.] Plates. 21x14 London: Hale, 1967.
JONES. Views of Seats. VI. 1831.
NICHOLAS, T. Counties of Wales. II, p.474. 1872.

DAGENHAM (Essex).
ENGLAND: Beauties of England. I, p.251. 1787.

DAGNAMS (Essex).
CROMWELL, T.K. Excursions in Essex. I, p.170. 1825.

DAISY BANK, Girlington (Yorkshire).
YORKSHIRE. Picturesque views. 1885.

DALBY HALL (Lincolnshire).
COPPER PLATE MAGAZINE. V, pl.220. 1792-1802.

DALEHEAD HALL (Cumberland).
BURKE, J.B. Visitation of Seats. 2.S. Vol.I, p.148. 1854.*

DALEMAIN (Cumberland).
BURKE, J.B. Visitation of Seats. 2.S. Vol.I, p.95. 1854.*
COUNTRY LIFE. CXI, 736 plan, 820, 908. 1952.

DALE PARK (Sussex).
NEALE, J.P. Views of Seats. 2.S. Vol.V. 1829.

DALHAM HALL (Suffolk).
COUNTRY LIFE. LIV, 280. 1923.

DALLINGTON HALL (Northamptonshire).
GOTCH, J.A. Squires' Homes. 34. 1939.
NEALE, J.P. Views of Seats. Vol.III. 1820.

DALTON HALL (Lancashire).
BARTLETT, J. Mansions of England and Wales. pl.51. 1853.
TWYCROSS, E. Mansions of England and Wales. Vol.II, p.11. 1847.

DALTON HALL (Yorkshire).
CAMPBELL, C. Vitruvius Britannicus. IVth. pls.90, 91. 1739.
MORRIS, F.O. Views of Seats. Vol.VI, p.55. 1880.
SUMMERSON, J. The Country Seat. 117. 1970.
WHEATER, W. Mansions of Yorkshire. p.70. 1888.

DANBURY PALACE[PLACE] (Essex).
CROMWELL, T.K. Excursions in Essex. I, p.35. 1825.
ESSEX: A new and complete history. I, 188. 1769.
MORRIS, F.O. Views of Seats. Vol.II, p.77. 1880.
RUSH, J.A. Seats in Essex. p.61. 1897.

DANBY HALL (Yorkshire).
BURKE, J.B. Visitation of Seats. Vol.II, p.244. 1853.*

DANE COURT, Isle of Thanet (Kent).
BURKE, J.B. Visitation of Seats. Vol.II, p.210. 1853.*

DANE COURT, Tilmanstone (Kent).
GREENWOOD, C. Kent. 420. 1838.

DANE END HOUSE (Hertfordshire).
BURKE, J.B. Visitation of Seats. 2.S. Vol.II, p.150. 1855.*

DANESFIELD PARK (Buckinghamshire).
BURKE, J.B. Visitation of Seats. Vol.I, p.38. 1852.*
MORRIS, F.O. Views of Seats. Vol.V, p.77. 1880.

DANETT'S HALL (Leicestershire).
NICHOLS, J. History of Leicestershire. IV, ii, 570. 1811.
THROSBY, J. Views in Leicestershire. p.262. 1789.

DANEWAY HOUSE (Gloucestershire).
COUNTRY LIFE. XXV, 342. 1909.
COUNTRY LIFE. CXI, 32 plan. 1952.
GARNER, T. Domestic architecture. II, p.178 plan. 1911.
TIPPING, H.A. English Homes. Early Renaissance, p.251. 1912.
TIPPING, H.A. English Homes. Period III, Vol.I, p.125.1922.

DANNY PARK (Sussex).
BURKE, J.B. Visitation of Seats. 2.S. Vol.I, p.24. 1854.*
COUNTRY LIFE. XXXIII, 418. 1913.

DANSON PARK (Kent).
BURKE, J.B. Visitation of Seats. Vol.II, p.187. 1853.*
COPPER PLATE MAGAZINE. II, pl.52. 1792-1802.
ENGLAND: Picturesque Views. p.7. 1786-88.

DARCY LEVER HALL (Lancashire).
BURKE, J.B. Visitation of Seats. 2.S. Vol.II, p.6. 1855.*

DARESBURY HALL (Cheshire).
BURKE, J.B. Visitation of Seats. Vol.I, p.267. 1852.*
TWYCROSS, E. Mansions of England and Wales. Vol.II, p.76. 1850.

DARLEY ABBEY (Derbyshire).
BURKE, J.B. Visitation of Seats. Vol.II, p.15. 1853.*

DARLEY HALL (Derbyshire).
TILLEY, J. Halls of Derbyshire. I. p.59. 1892.

DARLEY HALL (Yorkshire).
BURKE, J.B. Visitation of Seats. Vol.I, p.197. 1852.*

DARNHALL HALL (Cheshire).
BURKE, J.B. Visitation of Seats. Vol.I, p.267. 1852.*

DARTINGTON HALL (Devonshire).
EMERY, Anthony.
— Dartington Hall. [Bibliogr. notes.] Illus. incl. 2 folding plates, sections, elevations, plans, maps, facsimiles of masons' marks and genealog. tables. 30x24 Oxford: Clarendon Press. 1970.

BRITTON, J. Devonshire illustrated. 71. 1832.

BURKE, J.B. Visitation of Seats. 2.S. Vol.II, p.134. 1855.*

COUNTRY LIFE. CXIV, 178. 1969.

DAVENHAM HALL (Cheshire).
TWYCROSS, E. Mansions of England and Wales. Vol.I, p.148. 1850.

DAVENPORT HALL (Cheshire).
TWYCROSS, E. Mansions of England and Wales. Vol.I, p.140. 1850.*

DAVENPORT HOUSE (Shropshire).
BURKE, J.B. Visitation of Seats. Vol.II, p.213. 1853.*
COUNTRY LIFE. English Country Houses: Early Georgian. p.104. 1955.

COUNTRY LIFE. CXI, 1996. 1952.
COUNTRY LIFE. CXII, 40, 114. 1952.
ENGLAND: Picturesque Views. p.74. 1786-88.
LEACH, F. Seats of Shropshire. p.153. 1891.

DAVINGTON PRIORY (Kent).
COUNTRY LIFE. CL, 1650, 1716. 1971.
OSWALD, A. Country Houses of Kent. 19. 1933.

DAVYHULME HALL (Lancashire).
BARTLETT, J. Mansions of England and Wales. pls.142, 143. 1853.
TWYCROSS, E. Mansions of England and Wales. Vol.III, p.74. 1847.

DAWLEY HOUSE, Harlington (Middlesex).
KIP, J. Nouveau théâtre de la Grande Betagne. I, pl.48. 1715.

DAYLESFORD HOUSE (Gloucestershire).
NEALE, J.P. Views of Seats. Vol.V. 1822.
[Sales] DAYLESFORD HOUSE, 1853, August 22 and following days [Contents].

DEANE PARK (Kent).
BADESLADE, T. Seats in Kent, pl.10. 1750.
HARRIS, J. History of Kent. p.335. 1719.
NEALE, J.P. Views of Seats. 2.S. Vol.II. 1825.

DEANERY, Wells (Somerset).
ANGUS, W. Seats of the Nobility. pl.42. 1787.

DEBDEN HALL (Essex).
NEALE, J.P. Views of Seats. Vol.I. 1818.
RUSH, J.A. Seats in Essex. p.63. 1897.

DECKER HILL (Staffordshire).
BURKE, J.B. Visitation of Seats. Vol.I, p.151. 1852.*

DEENE PARK (Northamptonshire).
WAKE, Joan.
— The Brudenells of Deene. [Bibliogr.] xvi, 516pp. Illus. incl. plates (1 folding), map and genealog. tables. 21x14 London: Cassell, 1953.
BURKE, J.B. Visitation of Seats. 2.S. Vol.II, p.170. 1855.*
COUNTRY LIFE. XXV, 234. 1909.
COUNTRY LIFE. CLIX, 610, 674, 750, 810. 1976.
GOTCH,J.A. Halls of Northants. p.19. 1936.
JONES. Views of Seats. I. 1829.
LATHAM, C. In English Homes. Vol.III, p.47. 1909.
MORRIS, F.O. Views of Seats. Vol.IV, p.37. 1880.
NEALE, J.P. Views of Seats. 2.S. Vol.I. 1824.

SHAW, H. Elizabethan architecture. pl.XX [Dining room ceiling]. 1839.
TIPPING, H.A. English Homes. Period III, Vol.II, p.21. 1927.

DEEPDENE (Surrey)
WATKIN, David.
— Thomas Hope, 1769-1831, and the neo-classical idea. (The Deepdene and the development of the picturesque.) [Bibliogr.] xxii, 316pp. Illus. incl. plates, sections, elevations and plans. 22x14 London: J. Murray, 1968.
BRAYLEY, E.W. History of Surrey. V, 79. 1841.
BURKE, J.B. Visitation of Seats. 2.S. Vol.I, p.218. 1854.*
NEALE, J.P. Views of Seats. 2.S. Vol.III. 1826.
PROSSER, G.F. Surrey Seats. p.53. 1828.
SPROULE, A. Lost houses of Britain. 104. 1982.
[Sales] LONDON, 1917, July 20 [pictures, family portraits].
[Sales] LONDON, 1917, July 23, 24 [Greek, Roman and Egyptian sculpture etc.].
[Sales] DEEPDENE, 1917, September 12-14, 17-19 [Contents].

DELAMERE HOUSE (Cheshire).
TWYCROSS, E. Mansions of England and Wales. Vol.I, p.113. 1850.

DELAPRÉ ABBEY (Northamptonshire).
NORTHAMPTON: Northamptonshire Record Society.
— WAKE, J. and PANTIN, W.A. Delapré Abbey: its history and architecture. [Bibliogr. notes] 24pp. Illus. incl. plans. 25x18 Northampton, 1959.
COUNTRY LIFE. CXXVII, 218 plan. 1960.
GOTCH, J.A. Halls of Northants. p.73. 1936.
JONES. Views of Seats. I. 1829.
NEALE, J.P. Views of Seats. Vol.III. 1820.

DELBURY HALL (Shropshire).
LEACH, F. Seats of Shropshire. p.381. 1891.

DELL PARK HOUSE, Englefield Green (Surrey).
[Sales] DELL PARK HOUSE, 1979, April 30, May 1, 2 [Portion of contents].

DENBIES (Surrey).
BRAYLEY, E.W. History of Surrey. V, 90. 1841.
BURKE, J.B. Visitation of Seats. Vol.I, p.246. 1852.*
NEALE, J.P. Views of Seats. 2.S. Vol.III. 1826.
PROSSER, G.F. Surrey Seats. p.9. 1828.
SPROULE, A. Lost houses of Britain. 110. 1982.

DENBY GRANGE (Yorkshire).
BURKE, J.B. Visitation of Seats. Vol.I, p.228. 1852.*
JONES. Views of Seats. I. 1829.
MORRIS, F.O. Views of Seats. Vol.IV, p.81. 1880.
NEALE, J.P. Views of Seats. Vol.V. 1822.

DENCOMBE (Sussex).
BURKE, J.B. Visitation of Seats. Vol.II, p.249. 1853.*

DENHAM MOUNT (Buckinghamshire).
LUGAR, R. Plans and views of buildings. 23, pls. XXIII-XXV. 1823.

DENHAM PLACE (Buckinghamshire).
COUNTRY LIFE. English Country Houses: Caroline. p.203. 1966.
COUNTRY LIFE. XVIII, 702. 1905.
COUNTRY LIFE. LVII, 602, 642 plan. 1925.
[Sales] DENHAM PLACE, 1920, May 10-12 [Contents].

DENNE HILL (Kent).
GREENWOOD, C. Kent. 404. 1838.

DENTON COURT (Kent).
BURKE, J.B. Visitation of Seats. 2.S. Vol.II, p.209. 1855.*

DENTON HALL (Northumberland).
TOMLINSON, William Weaver.
— Denton Hall and its associations. [Bibliogr. notes] Illus. incl. plates, plans and folding genealog. tables. 25x19 London: Scott, 1894.

DENTON HOUSE (Lincolnshire).
BURKE, J.B. Visitation of Seats. Vol.II, p.119. 1853.*
JONES. Views of Seats. I. 1829.
LINCOLNSHIRE. A selection of views. 57. 1805.
NEALE, J.P. Views of Seats. Vol.II. 1819.

DENTON PARK [HALL] (Yorkshire).
CAMPBELL, C. New Vitruvius Britannicus. I, pls. 54-6. 1802.
COUNTRY LIFE. LXXXVI, 470 plan. 1939.
JONES. Views of Seats. I. 1829.
MORRIS, F.O. Views of Seats. Vol.V, p.33. 1880.
NEALE, J.P. Views of seats. Vol.V. 1822.

DERRY ORMOND (Cardiganshire).
NICHOLAS, T. Counties of Wales. I, p.135. 1872.

DERWENT HALL (Derbyshire).
COUNTRY LIFE. XXI, 198. 1907.
MOSS, F. Pilgrimages. VI, 190. 1913.
TILLEY, J. Halls of Derbyshire. I, p.190.1892.
TIPPING, H.A. English Homes. Early Renaissance, p.271. 1912.

DERWENTWATER HOUSE, Acton (Middlesex).
SPROULE, A. Lost houses of Britain. 115. 1982.

DEUDRAETH CASTLE (Merionethshire).
NICHOLAS, T. Counties of Wales. II, p.664. 1872.

DEVIZES CASTLE (Wiltshire).
DEVIZES: Castle.
— The particulars of the Devizes Castle Estate, at Devizes, Wiltshire, comprising the ... Castle, and its antique furniture, works of art, &c [etc.]. 66pp. Illus. incl. photographs, folding plans and borders. 29x22 London: D. Smith, Son & Oakley; Debenham, Tewson, Farmer & Bridgewater, n.d.

DEWLISH HOUSE (Dorsetshire).
OSWALD, A. Country houses of Dorset. p.148. 1959.

DEWS HALL (Essex).
NEALE, J.P. Views of Seats. 2.S. Vol.I. 1824.

DIDLINGTON HALL (Norfolk).
LONDON: British Association for the Advancement of Science.
— British Association, Cambridge, 1904 ... Guides for the excursions on Saturday, 20th August.
B. Brandon and Didlington Hall. By A.C. Haddon.16x10 Cambridge, 1904.
RICCI, Seymour de.
— A hand-list of a collection of books and manuscripts belonging to the Right Hon. Lord Amherst of Hackney, at Didlington Hall, Norfolk. 27x19 Cambridge: privately printed at the University Press, 1906.
[Sales] LONDON, 1947, July, 28, 29 [Portion of Library].

DIDMARTON MANOR (Gloucestershire).
ATKYNS, R. Glocestershire. p.204. 1768.

DIEULACRES ABBEY (Staffordshire).
MOSS, F. Pilgrimages. [II] 221. 1903.

DILLINGTON HOUSE (Somerset).
BURKE, J.B. Visitation of Seats. Vol.I, p.141. 1852.*
JONES. Views of Seats. II. 1829.
NEALE, J.P. Views of Seats. 2.S. Vol.IV. 1828.

DIMLANDS (Glamorganshire).
BURKE, J.B. Visitation of Seats. Vol.II, p.213. 1853.

DINDER HOUSE (Somerset).
BURKE, J.B. Visitation of Seats. Vol.I, p.102. 1852.*

DINGESTOW COURT (Monmouthshire).
BURKE, J.B. Visitation of Seats. 2.S. Vol.I, p.176. 1854.*
BURKE, J.B. Visitation of Seats. 2.S. Vol.II, p.209. 1855.

DINGLE COTTAGE (Lancashire).
BARTLETT, J. Mansions of England and Wales. pl.118. 1853.
TWYCROSS, E. Mansions of England and Wales. Vol.III, p.55. 1847.

DINGLEY HALL (Northamptonshire).
BURKE, J.B. Visitation of Seats. 2.S. Vol.I, p.120. 1854.*
COUNTRY LIFE. XLIX, 462 plan, 494. 1921.
GOTCH, J.A. Architecture of the Renaissance. I, p.42. 1894.
GOTCH, J.A. Halls of Northants. p.33. 1936.
TIPPING, H.A. English Homes. Period I & II, Vol.II, p.131. 1927.
[Sales] DINGLEY HALL, 1924, September 2-5 [Part of the contents].

DINKLEY HALL (Lancashire).
GRAY, H. Old Halls of Lancashire. p.29. 1893.

DINTON HALL (Buckinghamshire).
BURKE, J.B. Visitation of Seats. Vol.II, p.236. 1853.*

DINTON HOUSE (Wiltshire).
See PHILIPPS HOUSE, Dinton.

DIRLETON (Carmarthenshire).
NICHOLAS, T. Counties of Wales. I, p.213, 214. 1872.

DITCHINGHAM HALL (Norfolk).
BURKE, J.B. Visitation of Seats. 2.S. Vol.I, p.192. 1854.*

DITCHLEY PARK (Oxfordshire).
DITCHLEY.
— Ditchley Park, Oxfordshire: a historic house with a contemporary purpose [etc.]. 16pp. Illus. (2 on covers) incl. 4 **plates, map,** genealog. table and end-papers. 14x20 [Derby] (E.L.P.) [1962?].
OXFORD.
— The new Oxford guide ... To which is added a tour to Blenheim, Ditchley, and Stow ... By a gentleman of Oxford. 5 ed. Engr. plates and cuts: head and tail pieces. 12mo. 16x9 Oxford: for J. Fletcher & S. Parker [1768?].
Wanting plan.
6 ed. [1769?].

OXFORD.
— A new pocket companion for Oxford: or, guide through the University ... To which are added, descriptions of the buildings, the tapestry, paintings, sculptures, temples, gardens, &c. at Blenheim, Ditchley, and Stow ... A new edition, corrected and much enlarged. 156pp. Engr. plates (1 folding) incl. map. 12mo. 16x10 Oxford: printed for Daniel Prince [1775].
BURKE, J.B. Visitation of Seats. 2.S. Vol.I, p.84. 1854.*
COUNTRY LIFE. English Country Houses: Early Georgian. p.66. 1955.
COUNTRY LIFE. XVI, 594. 1904.
COUNTRY LIFE. LXXIII, 490 [Paintings], 515 [Furniture]. 1933.
COUNTRY LIFE. LXXV, 590, 622. 1934.
DELDERFIELD, E.R. West Country houses. III, 55. 1973.
ENGLAND: Beauties of England. II, p.191. 1787.
ENGLAND: Picturesque Views. p.8. 1786-88.
ENGLISH CONNOISSEUR. I, 51. 1766.*
LATHAM, C. In English Homes. Vol.III, p.321. 1909.
MORRIS, F.O. Views of Seats. Vol.V, p.59. 1880.
NEALE, J.P. Views of Seats. Vol.III. 1820.
WHITEMAN, G.W. English Country homes. p.121. 1951.

DITTON PARK (Buckinghamshire).
NEALE, J.P. Views of Seats. Vol.I. 1818.

DITTON PLACE, Balcombe (Sussex).
COUNTRY LIFE. XXX, 18 plan. 1911.

DIXTON MANOR (Gloucestershire).
COUNTRY LIFE. XCIX, 762, 808. 1946.

DOCKRAY HALL (Cumberland).
CUMBERLAND: C. & W. A. & A.S. Extra Series VIII, 259. 1892.

DODDERSHALL (Buckinghamshire).
BURKE, J.B. Visitation of Seats. Vol.I, p.21. 1852.*

DODDINGTON HALL (Cheshire).
CAMPBELL, C. New Vitruvius Britannicus. I, pls.57-60. 1802.
COUNTRY LIFE. English Country Houses: Mid Georgian. p.160. 1956.
COUNTRY LIFE. CXIII, 344, 414. 1953.
NEALE, J.P. Views of Seats. 2.S. Vol.V. 1829.
TWYCROSS, E. Mansions of England and Wales. Vol.II, p.13. 1850.*

DODDINGTON HALL (Lincolnshire).
COLE, *Rev.* Robert Eden George.
— Doddington Hall. 29pp. plates.
In SYMPSON, (E.M.) Memorials of Old Lincolnshire, p.280. 1911.
DODDINGTON HALL.
— Doddington Hall. 4pp. 3 illus. incl. map. 23x10 n.p. privately printed [1975.]
BURKE, J.B. Visitation of Seats. Vol.I, p.151. 1852.*
COUNTRY LIFE. LXXX, 356, 382. 1936.
KIP, J. Nouveau théâtre de la Grande Bretagne. I, pl.63. 1715.
TIPPING, H.A. English Homes. Early Renaissance, p.387. 1912.

DODINGTON PARK (Gloucestershire).
KENWORTHY-BROWNE, John Arthur.
— Dodington, the Gloucestershire seat of the Codrington family. (An illustrated survey & guide.) 32pp. Illus. incl. 3 (2 col.) on covers, plan and facsimile. 19x16 (Derby: E.L.P.) [1963?]
Title on cover.
COOKE, R. West Country Houses. p.150. 1957.
COUNTRY LIFE. English Country Houses: Late Georgian. p.41. 1958.
COUNTRY LIFE. LV, 170. 1924.
COUNTRY LIFE. CXX, 1176, 1230. 1956.
DELDERFIELD, E.R. West Country houses. III, 60. 1973.
NICOLSON, N. Great Houses of Britain. p.276. 1965.

DOGMERSFIELD PARK (Hampshire).
BURKE, J.B. Visitation of Seats. 2.S. Vol.I, p.242. 1854.*
JONES. Views of Seats. II. 1829.
NEALE, J.P. Views of Seats. Vol.II. 1819.

DOLAUCOTHY (Carmarthenshire).
BURKE, J.B. Visitation of Seats. Vol.I, p.203.1852.*

DOLFRIOG (Merionethshire).
NICHOLAS, T. Counties of Wales. II, p.665, 667. 1872.

DOLPHIN INN, Norwich (Norfolk).
See HEIGHAM, Bishops Palace.

DOL-WILYN (Carmarthenshire).
BURKE, J.B. Visitation of Seats. 2.S. Vol.I, p.206. 1854.*
NICHOLAS, T. Counties of Wales. I, p.221. 1872.

DONHEAD HALL (Wiltshire).
BURKE, J.B. Visitation of Seats. 2.S. Vol.I, p.13. 1854.*

DONINGTON HALL (Leicestershire).
BURKE, J.B. Visitation of Seats. Vol.I, p.272. 1852.*
CAMPBELL, C. New Vitruvius Britannicus. II, pls. 31-5. 1808.
COUNTRY LIFE. CLXV, 828. 1979.
JONES. Views of Seats.I. 1829.
MORRIS, F.O. Views of Seats. Vol.V, p.9. 1880.
NEALE, J.P. Views of Seats. Vol.II. 1819.
NICHOLS, J.History of Leicestershire. III, ii, 775. 1804. [List of Pictures].
NOBLE, T. Counties of Chester, ... Lincoln. p.36. 1836.
THROSBY, J. Views in Leicestershire. p.166. 1789.

DONNINGTON GROVE (Berkshire).
COUNTRY LIFE. CXXIV, 588, 654, 714. 1958.
ROBERTSON, A. Great Road. I, p.148. 1792.

DONNINGTON PRIORY (Berkshire).
BURKE, J.B. Visitation of Seats. 2.S. Vol.II, p.3. 1855.*

DORCHESTER HOUSE, Weybridge (Surrey).
SUMMERSON,J. The Country Seat. 72. 1970.

DORFOLD HALL (Cheshire).
DORFOLD HALL.
— Dorfold Hall, Nantwich, Cheshire. 4pp. 1 illus. 22x14 n.p. n.d.
BURKE, J.B. Visitation of Seats. Vol.II, p.122. 1853.*
COUNTRY LIFE. XXIV, 594. 1908.
HALL, S.C. Baronial Halls.Vol.I. 1848.
LATHAM, C. In English Homes. Vol.III, p.1. 1909.
NASH, J. Mansions of England. III, pl.18. 1841.
RICHARDSON, C.J. Old English Mansions.I, pl.17. 1841.
TIPPING, H.A. English Homes. Period III, Vol.II, p.395. 1927.
TWYCROSS, E. Mansions of England and Wales. Vol.II, p.20. 1850.

DORNEY COURT (Buckinghamshire).
COUNTRY LIFE. LVI, 136 plan, 176. 1924.
JONES. Views of Seats. I. 1829.
NEALE, J.P. Views of Seats. Vol.I. 1818.

DORNEYWOOD (Buckinghamshire).
COUNTRY LIFE. CX, 1892, 2024. 1951.

DORTON HOUSE, (Buckinghamshire).
COUNTRY LIFE. XV, 522. 1904.
LATHAM, C. In English Homes. Vol.II, p.285. 1907.

DONINGTON HALL, Leicestershire. From: NICHOLS (J.). *The history and antiquities of the county of Leicester* [etc.], vol. III, London, 1804.

DOUGHTON MANOR (Gloucestershire).
COOKE, R. West Country Houses. p.99. 1957.
COUNTRY LIFE. XCIV, 948. 1943.
GARNER, T. Domestic architecture. II, p.162 plan. 1911.

DOVECOT HOUSE (Lancashire).
BARTLETT, J. Mansions of England and Wales. pl.121. 1853.
TWYCROSS, E. Mansions of England and Wales. Vol.III, p.56. 1847.

DOVENBY HALL (Cumberland).
BURKE, J.B. Visitation of Seats. Vol.II, p.188. 1853.*
BURKE, J.B. Visitation of Seats. 2.S. Vol.II, p.147. 1855.

DOVERIDGE HALL (Derbyshire).
JONES. Views of Seats. I. 1829.
NEALE, J.P. Views of Seats.Vol.I. 1818.
TILLEY, J. Halls of Derbyshire. II, p.41. 1893.

DOWDESWELL COURT (Gloucestershire).
BURKE, J.B. Visitation of Seats. Vol.I, p.247. 1852.

DOWLES MANOR (Worcestershire).
COUNTRY LIFE. XCVII, 464 plan. 1945.

DOWN AMPNEY HOUSE (Gloucestershire).
BURKE, J.B. Visitation of Seats. Vol.II, p.233. 1853.*
COUNTRY LIFE. XLII, 396. 1917.
[Sales] LONDON, 1929, May 2 [Down Ampney estate].

DOWNE HALL (Dorsetshire).
HUTCHINS, J. Vitruvius Dorsettiensis. pl.9. 1816.

DOWN HALL (Essex).
NEALE, J.P. Views of Seats. Vol.I. 1818.
RUSH, J.A. Seats in Essex. p.65. 1897.

DOWN HOUSE, Blandford (Dorsetshire).
MORRIS, F.O. Views of Seats. Vol.V, p.55. 1880.

DOWN HOUSE, Redmarley D'Abitot (Worcestershire).
BURKE, J.B. Visitation of Seats. 2.S. Vol.I, p.18. 1854.*

DOWNHAM HALL (Lancashire).
TWYCROSS, E. Mansions of England and Wales. Vol.I, p.9. 1847.

DOWNING (Flintshire).
HOARE: Views of Seats. pl.2. 1792.
NEALE, J.P. Views of Seats.2.S.Vol.V. 1829.

DOWNTON CASTLE (Herefordshire).
COUNTRY LIFE. English Country Houses: Mid Georgian. p.148. 1956.
COUNTRY LIFE. XLII, 36.1917.
JONES. Views of Seats. II. 1829.
NEALE, J.P. Views of Seats. 2.S. Vol.III. 1826.
SUMMERSON, J. The Country Seat. 170. 1970.

DOWNTON HALL (Shropshire).
COUNTRY LIFE. XLII, 60 plan. 1917.
MORRIS, F.O. Views of Seats. Vol.V, p.71. 1880.
WEST, W. Picturesque Views of Shropshire. p.129. 1831.

DRAKELOWE HALL (Derbyshire).
BURKE, J.B. Visitation of Seats. 2.S. Vol.II, p.94. 1855.*
COUNTRY LIFE. XXI, 378. 1907.
COUNTRY LIFE. LXXV, 161 [Landscape Room]. 1934.
LATHAM, C. In English Homes. Vol.II, p.371. 1907.
MORRIS, F.O. Views of Seats. Vol.II, p.51. 1880.
TILLEY, J. Halls of Derbyshire. IV, p.25. 1902.
[Sales] DRAKELOWE, 1931, July 14-17, 20-22 [Contents].

DRAYCOT HOUSE (Wiltshire).
ROBERTSON, A. Great Road, II, p.64. 1792.
[Sales] DRAYCOT HOUSE, 1915, September 20-24 [Antique furniture, pictures etc.].
[Sales] DRAYCOT HOUSE, 1920, March 8 and following days [Contents].

DRAYTON HOUSE (Northamptonshire).
BUCK, S. & N. Antiquities. I, pl.209. 1774.
BURKE, J.B. Visitation of Seats. Vol.I, p.118. 1852.*
COUNTRY LIFE. English Country Houses: Baroque. p.95. 1970.
COUNTRY LIFE. XXXI, 898 plan, 934. 1912.
COUNTRY LIFE. CXXXVII, 1146 plan, 1216, 1286, 1346. 1965.
ENGLAND: Beauties of England. II, p.140. 1787.
GOTCH, J.A. Halls of Northants. p.52. 1936.
JONES. Views of Seats. I. 1829.
NEALE, J.P. Views of Seats. 2.S. Vol.IV. 1828.
TIPPING, H.A. English Homes. Period IV, Vol.I, p.249. 1920.
WHITEMAN, G.W. English Country Homes. p.96. 1951.
[Sales] DRAYTON HOUSE, 1926, November 18, 19 [Furniture, oil paintings etc.].

DRAYTON MANOR (Staffordshire).
COUNTRY LIFE. XXIII, 450. 1908.
SHAW, S. Staffordshire. II, 1. 1801.

DRINKSTONE PARK (Suffolk).
BURKE, J.B. Visitation of Seats. 2.S. Vol.I, p.117. 1854.*

DRONFIELD MANOR (Derbyshire).
TILLEY, J. Halls of Derbyshire. III, p.111. 1899.

DRONFIELD WOODHOUSE (Derbyshire).
TILLEY, J. Halls of Derbyshire. III, p.115. 1899.

DROPMORE HOUSE (Buckinghamshire).
COUNTRY LIFE. CXX, 772. 1956.
NEALE, J.P. Views of Seats. Vol.I. 1818.

DRYDEN'S HOUSE, Aldwincle All Saints (Northamptonshire).
GOTCH, J.A. Squires' Homes. 10. 1939.

DUDDINGTON MANOR (Northamptonshire).
GOTCH, J.A. Squires' Homes. 1. 1939.

DUDMASTON HALL (Shropshire).
LONDON: National Trust for Places of Historic Interest or Natural Beauty.
— WATERSON, M. Dudmaston, Shropshire. 28pp. Illus. (1 col. on cover) incl. plan. 22x14 [London] 1983.

LONDON: National Trust for Places of Historic Interest or Natural Beauty.
— LABOUCHERE, R. Botanical prints and drawings at Dudmaston. 24pp. Illus. (1 on cover.) 21x15 [London] 1980.

ANGUS, W. Seats of the Nobility. pl.7. 1787.
COPPER PLATE MAGAZINE. I, pl.18. 1792-1802.
COUNTRY LIFE. CLXV. 634, 714, 818. 1979.
ENGLAND: Picturesque Views. p.97. 1786-88.

DUDWICK HOUSE (Norfolk).
BURKE, J.B. Visitation of Seats. Vol.II, p.230. 1853.*

DUFFIELD HALL (Derbyshire).
TILLEY, J. Halls of Derbyshire. II, p.53. 1893.

DUFFIELD HOUSE (Derbyshire).
BURKE, J.B. Visitation of Seats. 2.S. Vol.I, p.130. 1854.*

DUFFRYN HOUSE (Glamorganshire).
BURKE, J.B. Visitation of Seats. Vol.I, p.62. 1852.*

DUKES HOUSE, Bradford on Avon.
See KINGSTON HOUSE (Wiltshire).

DUKINFIELD LODGE (Cheshire).
BURKE, J.B. Visitation of Seats. 2.S. Vol.I, p.43. 1854.*

DULFORD HOUSE (Devonshire).
[Sales] DULFORD HOUSE, 1930, July 11-13 [Fixtures and fittings].

DUMBLETON HALL (Gloucestershire).
ATKYNS, R. Glocestershire. p.212. 1768.

DUNCOMBE PARK (Yorkshire).
DUNCOMBE PARK.
— A description of Duncombe Park and Rivalx Abbey &c. attempted. (Appendix: a brief catalogue of the pictures at Duncombe Park [etc.].) 32pp. Engr. plate. 20x13 Kirbymoorside, 1812.
Wanting cover.
BURKE, J.B. Visitation of Seats. 2.S. Vol.I, p.31. 1854.*
CAMPBELL, C. Vitruvius Britannicus. III, pls. 85-88. 1725.
COUNTRY LIFE. XVII, 270. 1905.
JONES. Views of Seats. I. 1829.
LATHAM, C. In English Homes. Vol.III, p.317. 1909.
NEALE, J.P. Views of Seats. 2.S. Vol.I. 1824.
TIPPING, H.A. English Homes. Period IV, Vol.II, p.193. 1928.
[Sales] DUNCOMBE PARK, 1959, April 7 [18th century furniture].

DUNHAM MASSEY HALL (Cheshire).
LONDON: National Trust for places of Historic Interest or Natural Beauty.
— Dunham Massey, Cheshire. [Bibliogr.] 56pp. Illus. (1 col. on cover) incl. plan. 22x14 [London] 1981.
ANGUS-BUTTERWORTH, L.M. Old Cheshire families. p.170. 1932.
BURKE, J.B. Visitation of Seats. Vol.I, p.17. 1852.*
COUNTRY LIFE. CLXIX, 1562, 1664. 1981.
COUNTRY LIFE. CLXX, 18, 106. 1981.
KIP, J. Nouveau théâtre de la Grande Bretagne. I, pl. 37. 1715.
TWYCROSS, E. Mansions of England and Wales. Vol.II, p.28. 1850.*

DUNKEN PARK (Lancashire).
See DUNKENHALGH.

DUNKENHALGH (Lancashire).
TWYCROSS, E. Mansions of England and Wales. Vol.I, p.18. 1847.*

DUNKIRK HOUSE (Gloucestershire).
BURKE, J.B. Visitation of Seats. Vol.II, p.90. 1853.*

DUNRAVEN CASTLE (Glamorganshire).
DUNRAVEN and MOUNTEARL, Windham Thomas Wyndham-Quin, *Earl of.*
— Dunraven Castle, Glamorgan. Some notes on its history and associations. [Bibliogr.] Illus. incl. 12 plates. 22x14 London: J. Murray, 1926.
NEALE, J.P. Views of Seats. Vol.V. 1822.

DUNSLAND HOUSE (Devonshire).
BURKE, J.B. Visitation of Seats. Vol.I, p.93. 1852.
COUNTRY LIFE. English Country Houses: Caroline. p.187. 1966.
COUNTRY LIFE. CXXVIII. 18 plan, 78. 1960.

DUNSTALL HALL (Staffordshire).
SHAW, S. Staffordshire. II, 173. 1801.

DUNSTER CASTLE (Somerset).
DUNSTER CASTLE.
— Dunster Castle: an illustrated survey [etc.]. 32pp. Illus. (some col., some on cover) incl. maps (on inside covers). 14x22 Derby: E.L.P. [1954?].
LONDON: National Trust for Places of Historic Interest or Natural Beauty.
— DODD, D. Dunster Castle, Somerset. [Bibliogr.] 64pp. Illus. (1 col. on cover) incl. plan and genealog. table. 25x18 [London] 1981.
BUCK, S & N. Antiquities. II, pl.257. 1774.
BURKE, J. B. Visitation of Seats. Vol.II, p.207. 1853.*
COLLINSON, J. History of Somerset. II, 12. 1791.
COUNTRY LIFE. XIV, 686. 1903.
DELDERFIELD, E. R. West Country houses. I, 51. 1968.
LATHAM, C. In English Homes. Vol.I, p.103. 1904.
MORRIS, F.O. Views of Seats. Vol.VI, p.43. 1880.

DUNTISH COURT (Dorsetshire).
CAMPBELL, C. Vitruvius Britannicus. V, pls. 61-63. 1771.
HUTCHINS, J. History of Dorset. III, 708. 1868.
OSWALD, A. Country houses of Dorset. p.164. 1959.

DUNVALL (Shropshire).
SHROPSHIRE. Castles & Old Mansions. 51. 1868.

DURDANS (Surrey).
[Sales] LONDON, 1933, June 26-30 [Library, pts. I & II].
[Sales] LONDON, 1933, July 24, 25 [Library, pt. III].

DURHAM CASTLE (Durham).
BUCK, S. &. N. Antiquities. I, pl.81. 1774.
COUNTRY LIFE. XXIII, 126. 1908.
COUNTRY LIFE. LXIII, 396. 1928.
TIPPING, H.A. English Homes. Period I, Vol.I, p.55, 1921.

DURRINGTON HOUSE (Essex).
ESSEX: A new and complete history. IV, 106. 1771.

DUTTON HALL (Cheshire).
DUTTON: Family.
— Memorials of the Duttons of Dutton in Cheshire, with notes respecting the Sherborne branch of the family. Illus. incl. plates (some folding), map, facsimiles and genealog. tables. 25x19 London: H. Sotheran & Co.; Chester: Minshull & Meeson, 1901.

DUXBURY PARK (Lancashire).
BARTLETT, J. Mansions of England and Wales. pl.3. 1853.
TWYCROSS, E. Mansions of England and Wales. Vol.I, p.45. 1847.

DYFFRYN ALED (Denbighshire).
ANGUS, W. Seats of the Nobility. pl.48. 1787.
BURKE, J.B. Visitation of Seats. 2.S. Vol.II, p.14. 1855.*
HOARE: Views of Seats. pl.10. 1792.

DYNES HALL (Essex).
BURKE, J.B. Visitation of Seats. 2.S. Vol.I, p.69. 1854.*
ENGLAND: Beauties of England. I, p.256. 1787.
ESSEX: A new and complete history. II, 83. 1769.
MORANT, P. Essex. II, 276 (Insert). 1768.
RUSH, J.A. Seats in Essex. p.69. 1897.

DYNEVOR CASTLE (Carmarthenshire).
BURKE, J.B. Visitation of Seats. Vol.I, p.126. 1852.*
NEALE, J.P. Views of Seats. Vol.V. 1822.

DYRHAM PARK (Gloucestershire).
LONDON: National Trust for Places of Historic Interest or Natural Beauty.
— KENWORTHY-BROWNE, J. Dyrham Park, Gloucestershire. 3 ed. 44pp. Illus. (1 on cover) incl. 8 plates and plan. 21x14 (London) 1971.
New ed. [Bibliogr.] 64pp. Illus. (1 col. on cover) incl. plan, map and genealog. table. [London] 1983.
ATKYNS, R. Glocestershire. p.216. 1768.
CAMPBELL, C. Vitruvius Britannicus. pls. 91, 93. 1717.
COOKE, R. West Country Hóuses. p.105. 1957.
COUNTRY LIFE. English Country Houses: Baroque. p.85. 1970.
COUNTRY LIFE. XIV, 434. 1903.
COUNTRY LIFE. XL, 546. 1916.
COUNTRY LIFE. CXXXI, 335 plan, 396. 1962.
TIPPING, H.A. English Homes. Period IV, Vol.I, p.351. 1920.
[Sales] LONDON, 1956, February 29 [Paintings from D.P.].

EARLHAM HALL (Norfolk).
BIRKBECK, G. Old Norfolk houses. 37. 1908.
CROMWELL, T.K. Excursions in Norfolk. II, p.100. 1819.

EARNSHILL (Somerset).
COUNTRY LIFE. CXXVIII, 800, 858. 1960.
DELDERFIELD, E.R. West Country houses. II, 62. 1970.

EARSHAM HALL (Norfolk).
CROMWELL, T.K. Excursions in Norfolk. I, p.78. 1818.
SOANE, J. Plans, elevations and sections. pl. XLV. [Section of building.] 1788

EASHING HOUSE (Surrey).
MANNING, O. Surrey. I, 617. 1804.

EAST ACTON HOUSE (Middlesex).
LONDON: Survey of Memorials. VII. 1921.

EAST BARSHAM MANOR HOUSE (Norfolk).
BIRKBECK, G. Old Norfolk houses. 126. 1908.
COUNTRY LIFE. LV, 16 plan. 1924.
GARNER, T. Domestic architecture. I, p.51 plan. 1911.
GARRATT, T. Halls of Norfolk. pls. 10-12. 1890.
NASH, J. Mansions of England. I, Title-page. 1839.
TIPPING, H.A. English Homes. Period II, Vol.I, p.149. 1924.
[Sales] LONDON, 1930, July 22 [Estate].

EASTBURY HOUSE (Essex).
BLACK, William Henry.
— Eastbury illustrated, by elevations, plans, sections, views, and other delineations of that once magnificent mansion, measured, drawn, engraved, and architecturally described by T.H. Clarke; with a historical sketch by W.H.B. [Bibliogr. notes.] 16pp. Illus. incl. plates (some col.), elevations, section and plans. 37x27 London: J. Weale, 1834.
CLARKE, T.H. Domestic architecture. 23. 1833.
COUNTRY LIFE. LXXIX, 12 plan. 1936.
CROMWELL, T.K. Excursions in Essex. I, p.204. 1825.
GARNER, T. Domestic architecture. II, p.138 plan. 1911.
LONDON: Survey of Memorials. XI. 1917.

EASTBURY PARK (Dorsetshire).
CAMPBELL, C. Vitruvius Britannicus. III, pls.15-19. 1725.
COUNTRY LIFE. LXII, 330. 1927.
COUNTRY LIFE. CIV, 1386 plan. 1948.
OSWALD, A. Country houses of Dorset. p.149. 1959.
TIPPING, H.A. English Homes. Period IV, Vol.II, p.175. 1928.

EAST CLIFF LODGE (Kent).
BAKER, J. Home Beauties. plate. 1804.

EAST COWES CASTLE (Hampshire, Isle of Wight).
BURKE, J.B. Visitation of Seats. Vol.I, p.249. 1852.*

EASTFIELD LODGE (Hampshire).
BURKE, J.B. Visitation of Seats. Vol.I, p.85. 1852.*

EASTHAM PARK (Cheshire).
TWYCROSS, E. Mansions of England and Wales. Vol.I, p.90. 1850.

EASTHAMPSTEAD PARK (Berkshire).
BURKE, J.B. Visitation of Seats. 2.S. Vol.II, p.151. 1855.*

EASTHORPE HALL (Yorkshire).
[Sales] EASTHORPE HALL, 1965, April, 1, 2 [Contents].

EAST HORSLEY TOWERS (Surrey).
BURKE, J.B. Visitation of Seats. Vol.II, p.111. 1853.*
[Sales] HORSLEY TOWERS, 1926, November 1-4 [Contents].

EASTINGTON HALL (Worcestershire).
GARNER, T. Domestic architecture. II, p.177 plan. 1911.
NIVEN, W. Old Worcestershire houses. p.37, pl.15. 1873.

EASTINGTON HOUSE (Gloucestershire).
ATKYNS, R. Glocestershire. p.218. 1768.

EAST LAMBROOK MANOR (Somerset).
EAST LAMBROOK MANOR.
— East Lambrook Manor and its gardens, South Petherton, Somerset [etc.]. 16pp. Illus. (I col., some on covers) incl. plan. 14x20 [Derby] (E.L.P., 1971.)

EAST MASCALL (Sussex).
CLARKE, T.H. Domestic architecture. 24. 1833.

EASTNOR CASTLE (Herefordshire).
SOMERS, Daisy Finola, *Baroness.*
— Eastnor Castle, Ledbury, Herefordshire. (Compiled by F. Lady S., and E. Hervey-Bathurst.) 20pp. Illus. 21x14 (Maidstone) privately printed [c.1975].
COUNTRY LIFE. CXLIII, 524, 606 plan, 668. 1968.
JONES. Views of Seats. II. 1829.
LATHAM, C. In English Homes. Vol.I, p.323. 1904.
MORRIS, F.O. Views of Seats. Vol.IV, p.33. 1880.
NEALE, J.P. Views of Seats. Vol.II. 1819.

EASTON HALL (Lincolnshire).
BURKE, J.B. Visitation of Seats. 2.S. Vol.II, p.18. 1855.*
MORRIS, F.O. Views of Seats. Vol.III, p.73. 1880.

EASTON LODGE (Essex).

STEER, Francis W.
—The Easton Lodge inventory, 1637. [Bibliogr. notes.] excerpt (photocopy), 27ff. 22x16 [Chelmsford] 1952.
From: The Essex Review, LXI. 1952.

CROMWELL, T.K. Excursions in Essex. II, p.110. 1825.

MORANT, P. Essex. II, 431. 1768.

NEALE, J.P. Views of Seats. Vol.I. 1818.

RUSH, J.A. Seats in Essex. p.73. 1897.

SPROULE, A. Lost Houses of Britain. 128. 1982.

EASTON NESTON (Northamptonshire).

CAMPBELL, C. Vitruvius Britannicus. I, pls. 98-100.1715.

COUNTRY LIFE. English Country Houses: Baroque. p.138. 1970.

COUNTRY LIFE. XXIV, 630, 666. 1908.

COUNTRY LIFE. LXII, 262, 296 plan. 1927.

COUNTRY LIFE. CXLVIII, 968. 1970.

GOTCH, J.A. Halls of Northants. p.87. 1936.

LATHAM, C. In English Homes. Vol.III, p.327. 1909.

NICOLSON, N. Great Houses of Britain. p.196. 1965.

TIPPING, H.A. English Homes. Period IV, Vol.II, p.119. 1928.

EAST QUANTOCKSHEAD COURT HOUSE (Somerset).

COUNTRY LIFE. XXXI, 168 plan. 1912.

DELDERFIELD, E.R.West Country houses. II, 40. 1970.

TIPPING, H.A. English Homes. Early Renaissance, p.313. 1912.

EAST RIDDLESDEN HALL (Yorkshire).

LONDON: National Trust for Places of Historic Interest or Natural Beauty.
— BRIGG, J.J. East Riddlesden Hall, near Keighley, Yorkshire. 16pp. 2 illus. London [c. 1945].
Rev. ed. [Bibliogr.] 20pp. illus. (1 on cover) incl. plates. 21x14 1982.

COUNTRY LIFE. XCIII, 440. 1943.

EAST SUTTON PARK [PLACE] (Kent).

BURKE, J.B. Visitation of Seats. 2.S. Vol.I, p.104. 1854.*

COUNTRY LIFE. XIX, 666. 1906.

GREENWOOD, C. Kent.153. 1838.

LATHAM, C. In English Homes. Vol.II, p.289. 1907.

OSWALD, A. Country Houses of Kent. 39. 1933.

RICHARDSON, C.J. Old English mansions. III. 1845.

EASTWELL PARK (Kent).

CAMPBELL, C. New Vitruvius Britannicus. I, pls. 39-42. 1802.

COUNTRY LIFE. I, 379.1897.

MORRIS, F.O. Views of Seats. Vol.VI, p.45. 1880.

NEALE, J.P. Views of Seats. 2.S. Vol.II. 1825.

[Sales] EASTWELL PARK, 1978, July, 24, 25 [Remaining contents].

EAST WICKHAM HOUSE (Kent).

GREENWOOD, C. Kent. 43. 1838.

EASTWICK PARK (Surrey).

BRAYLEY, E.W. History of Surrey. IV, 470. 1841.

EASTWOOD HALL (Derbyshire).

TILLEY, J. Halls of Derbyshire. III, p.3. 1899.

EASTWOOD HOUSE (Cheshire).

TWYCROSS, E. Mansions of England and Wales. Vol.II, p.126. 1850.

EATON HALL (Cheshire).

BATENHAM, George and William.
— Ancient Chester: a series of illustrations of the streets of this old city, taken sixty years since, including views of ... Eaton Hall (3 plates). Drawn and etched by G. and W.B., and J. Musgrove. With preface and description by T. Hughes. 62pp. 28 etchings and 1 aquatint. 45x33 London: Manchester: H. Sotheran & Co., Chester: Minshull & Hughes, Phillipson & Golder; Warrington: P. Pearse, 1880.

BUCKLER, John.
— Views of Eaton Hall in Cheshire, the seat of the Right Honourable Earl Grosvenor. By J.B. and J.C. Buckler. 18pp. Lithogr. plates incl. plan. 58x42 London: W. Clarke, 1826.

EATON HALL.
— The Eaton tourist; or, a colloquial description of the hall, grounds, gardens, &c. at Eaton, the seat of the Right Hon. Earl Grosvenor. Etchings incl. map. 16x10 Chester: J. Seacombe, 1825.

WESTMINSTER, *Dukes of*.
— A calendar of ancient charters, with modern transcripts of nearly the whole, preserved at Eaton Hall, Cheshire, the seat of ... the Marquis of Westminster, with an introduction and observations on the charters. 34pp. 33x21 Warrington: Privately printed, 1862.

ANGUS-BUTTERWORTH, L.M. Old Cheshire Families. p.86. 1932.

BURKE, J.B. Visitation of Seats. Vol.I, p.168. 1852.*

CAMPBELL, C. Vitruvius Britannicus. II, pls.35, 36. 1717.

COUNTRY LIFE. II, 182. 1897.

COUNTRY LIFE. XLVII, 724. 1920.

COUNTRY LIFE. CXLIX, 304 plan, 360. 1971.

JONES. Views of Seats.I. 1829.

KIP, J. Nouveau théâtre de la Grande Bretagne. I, pl.62. 1715.

MORRIS, F.O. Views of Seats. Vol.I, p.31. 1880.

NEALE, J.P. Views of Seats. Vol.I. 1818.

NOBLE, T. Counties of Chester, ... Lincoln. p.33. 1836.

TWYCROSS, E. Mansions of England and Wales. Vol.II, p.1. 1850.

EATON HALL, Cheshire. From: TWYCROSS (E.). *The mansions of England and Wales* [etc.], *The country palatine of Chester*, vol. I, London, 1850.

EATON HALL, near Congleton (Cheshire).
BURKE, J.B. Visitation of Seats. Vol.I, p.120. 1852.*
TWYCROSS, E. Mansions of England and Wales. Vol.II, p.102. 1850.

EATON MASCOTT (Shropshire).
NEALE, J.P., Views of Seats. 2.S. Vol.V. 1829.

EATON OLD HALL (Derbyshire).
TILLEY, J. Halls of Derbyshire. II, p.43. 1893.

EBBERLY HOUSE (Devonshire).
BURKE, J.B. Visitation of Seats. Vol.I, p.259. 1852.*

EBBERSTON HALL (Yorkshire).
CAMPBELL, C. Vitruvius Britannicus. III, pl.47. 1725.
COPPER PLATE MAGAZINE. V, pl.204. 1792-1802.
COUNTRY LIFE. CXVI, 1254 plan. 1954.
KROLL, A. Historic Houses. 182. 1969.

EBRINGTON MANOR (Gloucestershire).
DELDERFIELD, E.R. West Country houses. III, 66. 1973.

ECCLERIGG (Westmorland).
[SALES] ECCLERIGG, 1935, April, 9, 10 [Contents]. (K.F. & R.).

ECHA (Surrey).
See ESHER PLACE

ECTON HALL (Northamptonshire).
MANUSCRIPTS.   English.
— [16 notebooks compiled by James Sotheby (1655-1720) and his descendants dealing with property, rents, accounts, etc., and recording purchases of pictures, miniatures, silver and other works of art, later forming the Sotheby collection of Ecton Hall, Northampton.] 16 vols. and 1 envelope of loose sheets. 18x8 etc. *c.* 1674-1882.
Cuttings incl. engr. inserted.
GOTCH, J.A. Squires' Homes. 30. 1939.
[Sales] LONDON, 1924, July 24, 25 [Portion of the Library].

EDELSTOW HALL (Derbyshire).
TILLEY, J. Halls of Derbyshire. III, p.5. 1899.

EDEN HALL (Cumberland).
BURKE, J.B. Visitation of Seats. Vol.I, p.264. 1852.*
MORRIS, F.O. Views of Seats. Vol.II, p.63. 1880.

EDEN PARK (Kent).
GREENWOOD, C. Kent. 32. 1838.

EDGBASTON HALL (Warwickshire).
SMITH, W. History of the County of Warwick. 365. 1830.

EDGCOTE (Northamptonshire).
BURKE, J.B. Visitation of Seats. Vol.I, p.47. 1852.*
COUNTRY LIFE. English Country Houses: Early Georgian. p.208. 1955.
COUNTRY LIFE. XLVII, 46. 1920.
GOTCH, J.A. Squires' Homes. 41. 1939.
TIPPING, H.A. English Homes Period V, Vol I, p.289. 1921.

EDGCUMBE HOUSE (Devonshire).
BURKE, J.B. Visitation of Seats. 2.S. Vol.II, p.205. 1855.*

EDGE BARTON MANOR (Devonshire).
COUNTRY LIFE. CXXXII, 464 plan. 1962.

EDGE HALL (Cheshire).
BURKE, J.B. Visitation of Seats. 2.S. Vol.I, p.46. 1854.*
ORMEROD, G. Cheshire. II, 683. 1882.
TWYCROSS, E. Mansions of England and Wales. Vol.I, p.33. 1850.*

EDINGTON PRIORY FARM (Wiltshire).
ELYARD, S.J. Old Wiltshire Homes. p.59. 1894.

EDITH WESTON HALL (Rutland).
[Sales] EDITH WESTON HALL, 1915, May 18-21 [Contents].

EDMOND CASTLE (Cumberland).
BURKE, J.B. Visitation of Seats. Vol.II, p.21. 1853.*

EDMONDSHAM HOUSE (Dorsetshire).
COUNTRY LIFE. CXLII, 1058. 1967.
OSWALD, A. Country houses of Dorset. p.101. 1959.

EDMONDTHORPE HALL (Leicestershire).
NICHOLS, J. History of Leicestershire. III, ii, pl.CL, Appendix 69. 1804.
THROSBY, J. Views in Leicestershire. p.266. 1789.

EDNASTON LODGE (Derbyshire).
MORRIS, F.O. Views of Seats. Vol.IV, p.63. 1880.

EDNASTON MANOR (Derbyshire).
COUNTRY LIFE. LIII, 398 plan. 1923.

EDSTONE HALL (Warwickshire).
[Sales] EDSTONE HALL, 1979, July 23, 24 [Contents].

EDWARDSTONE HALL (Suffolk).
BURKE, J.B. Visitation of Seats. Vol.II, p.186. 1853.*

EDWINSFORD (Carmarthenshire).
COPPER PLATE MAGAZINE. pl.63. 1778.
SANDBY, P. Select Views. II, pl.6 (Wales). 1782.

EGGESFORD HOUSE (Devonshire).
DELDERFIELD E.R. West Country houses. I, 56. 1968.
MORRIS, F.O. Views of Seats. Vol.VI, p.17. 1880.

EGGINTON HALL (Derbyshire).
TILLEY, J. Halls of Derbyshire. IV, p.99. 1902.*

EGGLESCLIFFE (Durham).
BURKE, J.B. Visitation of Seats. Vol.II, p.134. 1853.*

EGLINGHAM HALL (Northumberland).
COUNTRY LIFE. CLVIII. 1458. 1975.

ELBRIDGE HOUSE (Kent).
GREENWOOD, C. Kent. 353. 1838.

ELFORD HALL (Staffordshire).
BURKE, J.B. Visitation of Seats. Vol.II, p.222. 1853.*

ELKINGTON HALL (Lincolnshire).
BURKE, J.B. Visitation of Seats. 2.S. Vol.I, p.119. 1854.*

ELLEL GRANGE (Lancashire).
[Sales] ELLEL GRANGE, 1979, October 22, 23 [Contents].

ELLERBECK HALL (Lancashire).
TWYCROSS, E. Mansions of England and Wales. Vol.I, p.71. 1847.*

ELLERHOW (Lancashire).
BARTLETT, J. Mansions of England and Wales. pl.76. 1853.
TWYCROSS, E. Mansions of England and Wales. Vol.II, p.31. 1847.

ELLERON LODGE (Yorkshire).
YORKSHIRE. Picturesque views. 1885.

ELMDON HALL (Warwickshire).
SMITH, W. History of the County of Warwick. 375. 1830.

ELMER LODGE (Kent).
GREENWOOD, C. Kent. 32. 1838.

ELMHURST HALL (Staffordshire).
PLOT, R. Staffordshire. 30. 1686.

ELMLEY NEW CASTLE (Worcestershire).
NASH, T.R. Worcestershire. I, 384. 1781.

ELMLEY LOVET LODGE (Worcestershire).
NIVEN, W. Old Worcestershire houses. p.1, pl.2. 1873.

ELMORE COURT (Gloucestershire).
COUNTRY LIFE. XXXVI, 846. 1914.

ELMS, The. Kirk Ella (Yorkshire).
[Sales] KIRKELLA, The Elms, 1932, September 14-16, 20 [Furniture etc.].

ELMSTEAD PLACE (Kent).
COUNTRY LIFE. LXXVIII, 320 [Furniture]. 1935.

ELMSWOOD (Lancashire).
BARTLETT, J. Mansions of England and Wales. pls.127, 128. 1853.
TWYCROSS, E. Mansions of England and Wales. Vol.III, p.60. 1847.

ELSENHAM HALL (Essex).
RUSH, J.A. Seats in Essex. p.78. 1897.

ELSHAM HALL (Lincolnshire).
BURKE, J.B. Visitation of Seats. Vol.I, p.267. 1852.*

ELSING HALL (Norfolk).
BIRKBECK, G. Old Norfolk houses. 42. 1908.
GARRATT, T. Halls of Norfolk. pl.21. 1890.

ELSTON HALL (Nottinghamshire).
[Sales] ELSTON HALL, 1954, October 28-30 [Contents].

ELSTOW (Bedfordshire).
See HILLERSDON HALL.

ELSYCH (Shropshire).
SHROPSHIRE. Castles & Old Mansions. 59. 1868.

ELSYNG HALL (Middlesex).
SPROULE, A Lost houses of Britain. 133. 1982.

ELTHAM LODGE (Kent).
COUNTRY LIFE. English Country Houses: Caroline. p.150. 1966.
COUNTRY LIFE. XLVI, 168, 210. 1919.
OSWALD, A. Country Houses of Kent. 52. 1933.
TIPPING, H.A. English Homes. Period IV, Vol.I, p.93. 1920.

ELTHAM PALACE (Kent).
BUCK, S. & N. Antiquities. I, pl.129. 1774.
COUNTRY LIFE. LXXXI, 534, 568 plan, 594 plan. 1937.
COUNTRY LIFE. CXXXVII, 1342. 1965.
COUNTRY LIFE. CLXI, 1412. 1977.
CROMWELL, T.K. Excursions in Kent. p.112. 1822.
OSWALD, A. Country Houses of Kent. 16. 1933.

ELTON HALL (Herefordshire).
COUNTRY LIFE. XCVIII, 596. 1945.

ELTON HALL (Huntingdonshire).
BORENIUS, Tancred.
— A catalogue of the pictures at Elton Hall in Huntingdonshire, in the possession of Colonel D.J. Proby. By T.B., and J.V. Hodgson. With a preface by G. Proby [Bibliogr. notes.] 48 plates incl. folding genealog. table. 31x25 London: Medici Society, 1924.
Supplement ... By G. Proby. [Bibliogr. notes.] 64pp. 26 plates. London: Clowes, 1939.

LONDON: Roxburghe Club.
— Architectural drawings in the library of Elton Hall, by Sir John Vanbrugh and Sir Edward Lovett Pearce. Edited by H. Colvin and M. Craig. [Bibliogr.] Plates incl. sections, elevations, plans and facsimiles, and genealog. table. 29x23 Oxford, 1964.
COUNTRY LIFE. CXXI, 334 plan, 380, 426. 1957.
MORRIS, F.O. Views of Seats. Vol.IV, p.31. 1880.

ELVASTON CASTLE (Derbyshire).
BURKE, J.B. Visitation of Seats. 2.S. Vol.II, p.138. 1855.*
JONES. Views of Seats. I. 1829.
MORRIS, F.O. Views of Seats. Vol.II, p.21. 1880.
NEALE, J.P. Views of Seats. Vol.I. 1818.
TILLEY, J. Halls of Derbyshire. IV, p.139. 1902.
[Sales] LONDON, 1963 November 8 [Furniture].

ELVETHAM HALL (Hampshire).
COUNTRY LIFE. CXLVIII, 1282. 1970.

ELY PALACE (Cambridgeshire).
COUNTRY LIFE. LXIII, 850 plan. 1928.

ELY PLACE (Sussex).
[Sales] ELY PLACE, 1924, December 8-11 [Furniture, pictures etc.].

EMBER COURT (Surrey).
See IMBER COURT.

EMMOTT HALL (Lancashire).
BARTLETT, J. Mansions of England and Wales. pls.36, 37. 1853.
BURKE, J.B. Visitation of Seats. Vol.I, p.76. 1852.*
TWYCROSS, E. Mansions of England and Wales. Vol.I, p.35.1847.

EMRAL HALL (Flintshire).
HARRISON, *Mrs.* Sunter.
—The four baronets of Emral and Emral Hall Worthenbury, North Wales. 40pp. Illus. incl. plates and genealog. table. 30x21 Wrexham: by the author, 1974.
COUNTRY LIFE. XXVII, 271. 1910.
SPROULE, A. Lost houses of Britain. 136. 1982.

ENCOMBE (Dorsetshire).
COUNTRY LIFE. CXXXIII, 164, 214 plan.1963.
HUTCHINS, J. History of Dorset. I, 520. 1861.
HUTCHINS, J. Vitruvius Dorsettiensis. pl.10. 1816.
JONES. Views of Seats. II. 1829.
NEALE, J.P. Views of Seats. 2.S. Vol.IV. 1828.
OSWALD, A. Country houses of Dorset. p.155. 1959.

ENCOMBE (Kent).
COUNTRY LIFE. LVI, 992, 1032. 1924.

ENDERBY HALL (Leicestershire).
NICHOLS, J. History of Leicestershire. IV; i, 158. 1807.
THROSBY, J. Views in Leicestershire. p.270. 1789.

ENDSLEIGH (Devonshire).
BRITTON, J. Devonshire illustrated. 55. 1832.
COUNTRY LIFE. CXXX, 296. 1961.
JONES. Views of Seats. II. 1829.
NEALE, J. P. Views of Seats. Vol.I. 1818.
REPTON, H. Fragments on landscape gardening. 213. 1816.

ENFIELD HALL (Staffordshire).
See ENVILLE HALL.

ENFIELD OLD PARK (Middlesex).
BURKE, J.B. Visitation of Seats. 2.S. Vol.I, p.90. 1854.*

ENFORD GRANGE (Wiltshire).
COUNTRY LIFE. CXXIX, 1423, 1487. 1961.

ENGLEFIELD GREEN (Surrey).
Sir John Elvill's.
COPPER PLATE MAGAZINE. pl.24. 1778.
SANDBY, P. Select Views. I, pl.61. 1783.
WATTS, W. Seats of the Nobility. pl.66. 1779.

ENGLEFIELD HOUSE (Berkshire).
BURKE, J.B. Visitation of Seats. 2.S. Vol.II, p.154. 1855.*
COUNTRY LIFE. CLXIX, 502 plan, 560, 642. 1981.
JONES. Views of Seats. I. 1829.
NEALE, J.P. Views of Seats. 2.S. Vol.IV. 1828.

ENMORE CASTLE (Somerset).
JONES. Views of Seats. II. 1829.
NEALE, J.P. Views of Seats. 2.S. Vol.IV. 1828.
WATTS, W. Seats of the Nobility. pl.54. 1779.
[Sales] LONDON, 1834, July 7,8 [Portraits, drawings etc. from E.C.].

ENVILLE HALL (Staffordshire).
LEASOWES.
— A companion to the Leasowes, Hagley and Enville; with a sketch of Fisherwick, the seat of the ... Earl Donegall. To which is prefixed, the present state of Birmingham. iv, 250pp. 2 pts. in 1 vol. 8vo. 17x10 London: G.G.J. & J. Robinson; Birmingham: M. Swinney; Worcester: J. Holl, 1789.
PLOT, R. Staffordshire. 121. 1686.

EPSOM (Surrey). Richard Rooth's House.
CAMPBELL, C. Vitruvius Britannicus. II, pls. 48, 49. 1717.

ERCHFONT MANOR (Wiltshire).
See URCHFONT MANOR.

ERDDIG PARK (Denbighshire).
LONDON: National Trust for Places of Historic Interest or Natural Beauty.
— WATERSON, M. Erddig, Clwyd. [Bibliogr.] 52pp. Illus. (some col., 1 on cover) incl. plan and genealog. table. 21x14 [London] 1979.
BURKE, J.B. Visitation of Seats. Vol.II, p.159. 1853.*
COPPER PLATE MAGAZINE. I, pl.8. 1792-1802.
COUNTRY LIFE. XXVI, 742 plan. 1909.
COUNTRY LIFE. LXVII, 441 [Furniture] 623 [Furniture]. 1930.
COUNTRY LIFE. LXVIII, 206, 234, 1930.
COUNTRY LIFE. CLXIII, 906, 970, 1070. 1978.
COUNTRY LIFE. CLXIV, 1331 [ironwork] 1978.
ENGLAND: Picturesque Views. p.89. 1786-88.
NEALE, J.P. Views of Seats. 2.S. Vol. V. 1829.
NICHOLAS, T. Counties of Wales. I, p.370. 1872.
TIPPING, H.A. English Homes. Period IV, Vol.I, p.179. 1920.

ERDSWICK HALL (Cheshire).
ORMEROD, G. Cheshire.III, 224. 1882.

ERIDGE CASTLE (Sussex).
GUNNIS, Rupert.
— Eridge Castle and the family of Nevill. 24pp. Illus. 22x14 (Tunbridge Wells printed) [1955?]
BURKE, J.B. Visitation of Seats. 2.S. Vol.II, p.225. 1855.*
COUNTRY LIFE. CXXXVIII, 750, 818. 1965.

ERLEIGH COURT (Berkshire).
DORMER, Ernest William.
— Erleigh Court & its owners. [Bibliogr. notes.] 92pp. Plates. 25x19 Reading: Poynder, 1912.

ERLESTOKE PARK (Wiltshire).
BRITTON, J. Beauties of Wiltshire. II, 199. 1801. III, 356. 1825.
BURKE, J.B. Visitation of Seats. Vol.II, p.234. 1853.*
CAMPBELL, C. New Vitruvius Britannicus. I, pls.36-8. 1802.
JONES. Views of Seats. II. 1829.
NEALE, J.P. Views of Seats. Vol.V. 1822.
ROBERTSON, A. Great Road. II, p.88. 1792.
[Sales] ERLESTOKE MANSION, 1832, July 9 and following days [Furniture, pictures etc.].

ERTHIG (Denbighshire).
See ERDDIG PARK.

ERWARTON HALL (Suffolk).
COUNTRY LIFE. LXV, 152. 1929.
CROMWELL, T.K. Excursions in Suffolk. I, p.149. 1818.

ESCOT HOUSE (Devonshire).
CAMPBELL, C. Vitruvius Britannicus. I, pls. 78, 79. 1715.

ESHER PLACE (Surrey).
BUCK, S. & N. Antiquities. II, pl.278. 1774.
CAMPBELL, C. Vitruvius Britannicus. IVth. pls. 110, 111. 1739.
COPPER PLATE MAGAZINE. I, pl.2. 1792-1802.
COUNTRY LIFE. CXXV, 1076. 1959.
ENGLAND: Beauties of England. II, p.291. 1787.
ENGLAND: Picturesque Views. p.86. 1786-88.
KIP, J. Nouveau théâtre de la Grande Bretagne. I, pl.72. 1715.
PROSSER, G.F. Surrey Seats. p.5. 1828.

ESHOLT HALL (Yorkshire).
JONES. Views of Seats. I. 1829.
NEALE, J.P. Views of Seats. Vol.V. 1822.

ESHTON HALL (Yorkshire).
STEWART, Charles James.
— A catalogue of the library collected by Miss Richardson Currer, at Eshton Hall, Craven, Yorkshire. 4 Engr. plates. 25x16 London: privately printed. 1833.
BARTLETT, J. Selections from views of mansions. 1851.
BURKE, J.B. Visitation of Seats. Vol.I, p.127. 1852.*
MORRIS, F.O. Views of Seats. Vol.III, p.35. 1880.
NEALE, J.P. Views of Seats. 2.S. Vol.V. 1829.
YORKSHIRE. Picturesque views. 1885.

ESTHWAITE LODGE (Lancashire).
BARTLETT, J. Mansions of England and Wales. pl.71. 1853.
TWYCROSS, E. Mansions of England and Wales. Vol.II, p.29. 1847.

ETTINGTON PARK (Warwickshire).
See also LOWER EATINGTON HALL.
[Sales] ETTINGTON PARK, 1946, October 29-31 [Contents].

ETWALL HALL (Derbyshire).
BURKE, J.B. Visitation of Seats. 2.S. Vol.II, p.167. 1855.
TILLEY, J. Halls of Derbyshire. II, p.73. 1893.

EUSTON HALL (Suffolk).
BURKE, J.B. Visitation of Seats. Vol.I, p.226. 1852.*
COUNTRY LIFE. CXXI, 58, 102, 148. 1957.
CROMWELL, T.K. Excursions in Suffolk. I, p.109. 1818.
MORRIS, F.O. Views of Seats. Vol.III, p.47. 1880.
NEALE, J.P. Views of Seats. Vol.IV. 1821.

EUXTON HALL (Lancashire).
BURKE, J.B. Visitation of Seats. Vol.II, p.75. 1853.*
TWYCROSS, E. Mansions of England and Wales. Vol.I, p.51. 1847.

EVENLEY HALL (Northamptonshire).
BURKE, J.B. Visitation of Seats. Vol.I, p.42. 1852.*

EVERINGHAM PARK [HALL] (Yorkshire).
BURKE, J.B. Visitation of Seats. 2.S. Vol.I, p.88. 1854.*
COUNTRY LIFE. CXLIII, 340, 408. 1968.
MORRIS, F.O. Views of Seats. Vol.I, p.25. 1880.
WOOD, G.B. Historic homes of Yorkshire. 134. 1957.

EVERLEIGH MANOR (Wiltshire).
See Everley Manor.

EVERLEY MANOR (Wiltshire).
BURKE, J.B. Visitation of Seats. Vol.I, p.113. 1852.*

EVERSLEY MANOR (Hampshire).
COUNTRY LIFE. XCIII, 528 [missing], 572. 1943.

EWART PARK (Northumberland).
[Sales] EWART PARK, 1937, October 20-22 [Furnishings, Chinese wallpaper etc.].

EWELL CASTLE (Surrey).
BURKE, J.B. Visitation of Seats. 2.S. Vol.II, p.203. 1855.*
PROSSER, G.F. Surrey Seats. p.91. 1828.

EWELME DOWN (Oxfordshire).
COUNTRY LIFE. XXXI, 430. 1912.

EWELME PALACE (Oxfordshire).
BUCK, S. & N. Antiquities. II, pl.237. 1774.

EWENNY ABBEY (Glamorganshire).
BURKE, J.B. Visitation of Seats. Vol.I, p.194. 1852.*

EWHURST PARK (Hampshire).
[Sales] EWHURST PARK, 1934, August 20, 21 [Contents].

EXTON (Rutland).
CAMPBELL, C. Vitruvius Britannicus. IVth. pls.59-62. 1739.
MORRIS, F.O. Views of Seats. Vol.IV, p.5. 1880.

EYAM HALL (Derbyshire).
TILLEY, J. Halls of Derbyshire. I, p.143. 1892.

EYDON HALL (Northamptonshire).
BURKE, J.B. Visitation of Seats. Vol.I, p.64. 1852.*
COUNTRY LIFE. CXLIX, 128. 1971.
GOTCH, J.A. Squires' Homes. 41. 1939.

EYE MANOR (Herefordshire).
EYE MANOR.
— A guide to Eye Manor and its contents. 16pp. Illus. (some on covers.) 22x14 (London) privately printed [c. 1973].
COUNTRY LIFE. CXVIII, 546. 1955.

EYHORNE HOUSE (Kent).
GREENWOOD, C. Kent. 161. 1838.

EYTON HALL (Shropshire).
LEACH, F. Seats of Shropshire. p.275. 1891.

EYTON-UPON-SEVERN (Shropshire).
SHROPSHIRE. Castles & Old Mansions. 44. 1868.

EYWOOD, (Herefordshire).
ROBINSON, C.J. Mansions of Herefordshire. pl.20. 1873.

FAILAND HOUSE (Somerset).
COOKE, R. West Country Houses. p.117. 1957.

FAIRFIELD (Somerset).
COLLINSON, J. History of Somerset. I, 254. 1791.

FAIRFORD PARK (Gloucestershire).
ATKYNS, R. Glocestershire. p.226. 1768.
BURKE, J.B. Visitation of Seats. 2.S. Vol.I, p.43. 1854.*

FAIRLAWNE (Kent).
COUNTRY LIFE. XLIV, 50. 1918.
COUNTRY LIFE. CXXIV, 998, 1050. 1958.
GREENWOOD, C. Kent. 135. 1838.
KIP, J. Nouveau théâtre de la Grande Bretagne. I, pl. 49. 1715.
NEALE, J.P. Views of Seats. Vol.II. 1819.
OSWALD, A. Country Houses of Kent. 59. 1933.

FAIR OAK (Sussex).
BURKE, J.B. Visitation of Seats. Vol.I, p.229. 1852.*
[Sales] FAIR OAK, 1981, May 7, 8 | Part of remaining contents].

FAIR OAK PARK (Hampshire).
BURKE, J.B. Visitation of Seats. 2.S. Vol.II, p.6. 1855.*

FAIRY HILL (Hampshire, Isle of Wight).
BURKE, J.B. Visitation of Seats. Vol.I, p.178. 1852.*

FARFIELD HALL (Yorkshire).
COUNTRY LIFE. XXXVII, 240 plan. 1915.

FARINGDON HOUSE (Berkshire).
COUNTRY LIFE. CXXXIX, 1184, 1246. 1966.

FARLEIGH HOUSE (Hampshire).
COUNTRY LIFE. XC, 476, 536. 1941.

FARLEIGH HOUSE (Somerset).
BURKE, J.B. Visitation of Seats. Vol.II, p.118. 1853.*

FARLEY HILL COURT (Berkshire).
[Sales] FARLEY HILL COURT, 1914, January 29-31 [Furniture, pottery etc.].

FARLEY HILL PLACE (Berkshire).
COUNTRY LIFE. XCIII, 1012, 1056. 1943.

FARM HALL (Huntingdonshire).
COUNTRY LIFE. CXXX, 1194 plan. 1961.

FARMINGWOODS (Northamptonshire).
See FERMYN WOODS HALL.

FARNBOROUGH HALL (Warwickshire).
LONDON: National Trust for Places of Historic Interest or Natural Beauty.
— WALLACE, C. Farnborough Hall, Warwickshire. 12pp. 4 plates. 18x12 London: Country Life, 1963.
COUNTRY LIFE. CXV, 354, 430. 1954.

FARNHAM CASTLE (Surrey).
BUCK, S. & N. Antiquities. II, pl.279. 1774.
COUNTRY LIFE. XXIX, 636 plan. 1911.
COUNTRY LIFE. LXXXVI, 652 plan, 682. 1939.
ENGLAND: Picturesque Views. p.61. 1786-88.
MANNING, O. Surrey. III, 134. 1814.
NEALE, J.P. Views of Seats. Vol.IV. 1821.

FARNLEY HALL (Yorkshire).
FARNLEY HALL.
— The Farnley Hall collection of Turner drawings in the possession of F.H. Fawkes, Esq., photographed by L. Caldesi & Co. [no text.] 2ff. Photographs. 54x39 London: Colnaghi, Scott & Co., 1864.
FINBERG, Alexander Joseph.
— Turner's water colours at Farnley Hall. 32pp. Col. plates. 34x41 London: The Studio [1912].
MANUSCRIPTS.   English.
— A catalogue of the oil paintings and water colour drawings and sketches in water colour by J.M.W. Turner, R.A. in the possession of F.H. Fawkes, Esquire, of Farnley Hall, Otley, Yorkshire. A. D. 1850. 19ff. 18x12 1850.
COUNTRY LIFE. English Country Houses: Mid Georgian. p.214. 1956.
COUNTRY LIFE. CXV, 1618, 1714, 1808, 2098 [Furniture]. 1954.
JONES. Views of seats. I. 1829.
NEALE, J.P. Views of Seats. Vol.V. 1822.
WHEATER, W. Mansions of Yorkshire. p.81. 1888.
YORKSHIRE. Picturesque views. 1885.

FATHERWELL HOUSE (Kent).
GREENWOOD, C. Kent. 191. 1838.

FAULKBOURNE HALL (Essex).
BURKE, J.B. Visitation of Seats. 2.S. Vol.II, p.136. 1855.*
COUNTRY LIFE. LXVI, 718 plan. 1929.
CROMWELL, T.K. Excursions in Essex. I, p.28. 1825.
RUSH, J.A. Seats in Essex. p.81. 1897.*

FAWLEY COURT (Buckinghamshire).

NEALE, J.P. Views of Seats. 2.S. Vol. III. 1826.

THAMES, River. An History. I, pl.29. 1794.

[Sales] FAWLEY COURT, 1952, July 14-18 [Contents].

FAWLEY COURT (Herefordshire).

ROBINSON, C.J. Mansions of Herefordshire. pl.7. 1873.

FAWSLEY HALL (Northamptonshire).

COUNTRY LIFE. XXIV, 18. 1908.

GARNER, T. Domestic architecture. I, p.66 plan. 1911.

GOTCH, J.A. Halls of Northants. p.80. 1936.

TIPPING, H.A. English Homes. Period II, Vol.I, p.325. 1924.

[Sales] FAWSLEY HALL, 1914, May 4 and following days [Furniture, books etc.].

FEATHERSTONE CASTLE (Northumberland).

COUNTRY LIFE. CLIV, 1246. 1973.

FEERING BURY (Essex).

HALL, S.C. Baronial Halls. Vol.I. 1848.

RUSH, J.A. Seats in Essex. p.127. 1897.

FELBRIGG HALL (Norfolk).

KETTON-CREMER, Robert Wyndham.
— Felbrigg: the story of a house. [Bibliogr.] Plates incl. folding genealog. table. 21x14 London: Hart-Davis, 1962.

LONDON: National Trust for Places of Historic Interest or Natural Beauty.
— SUTCLIFFE, J.H.F.H. Felbrigg Hall, Norfolk. 16pp. Col. illus. (on cover) and 6 plates. 22x14 (London) [c. 1970].
Rev. ed. JACKSON-STOPS, G. [Bibliogr.] 64pp. Illus. (1 col. on cover) incl. plans and genealog. table. 25x18 [London] 1983.

BIRKBECK, G. Old Norfolk Houses. 44. 1908.

BURKE, J.B. Visitation of Seats. 2.S. Vol.I, p.55. 1854.*

COPPER PLATE MAGAZINE. I, pl.40. 1792-1802.

COUNTRY LIFE. LXXVI, 666. 1934.

COUNTRY LIFE. CLXVIII, 2344 [Costume] 1980.

CROMWELL, T.K. Excursions in Norfolk. I, p.130. 1818.

ENGLAND: Picturesque Views. p.22. **1786-88.**

GARRATT, T. Halls of Norfolk. pls.22 [Plan], 23. 1890.

FELIX HALL (Essex).

MARSDEN, *Rev.* John Howard.
— A descriptive sketch of the collection of works of ancient Greek and Roman art at Felix Hall ... Read at Felix Hall at a general meeting of the Essex Archaeological Society, August 6th, 1863. 12pp. 8 engr. plates (1 folding). 31x25 Colchester: (1863).

WESTERN, Charles Callis Western, *Baron.*
— Descriptive sketch of ancient statues, busts, &c. at Felix

Hall, the seat of ... Lord Western, at Kelvedon, in the county of Essex; with plates of some of the most striking objects in the collection. 20pp. Engr. plates (1 folding). 36x25 Chelmsford: Chalk, Meggy, and Chalk, 1833.

CROMWELL, T.K. Excursions in Essex.I, p.47. 1825.

ENGLAND: Beauties of England. I, p.254. 1787.

ESSEX: A new and complete history. I, 386. 1769.

RUSH, J.A. Seats in Essex. p.83. 1897.*

FELIXSTOWE COTTAGE (Suffolk).

CROMWELL, T.K. Excursions in Suffolk. II, p.35. 1819.

FELTON HALL (Northumberland).

BURKE, J.B. Visitation of Seats. 2.S. Vol.I, p.200. 1854.*

FEN DITTON HALL (Cambridgeshire).

COUNTRY LIFE. CXXXVI, 764, 834 plan. 1964.

FENISCOWLES (Lancashire).

BURKE, J.B. Visitation of Seats. Vol.I, p.270. 1852.*

TWYCROSS, E. Mansions of England and Wales. Vol.I, p.14. 1847.

[Sales] FENISCOWLES HALL, 1877, May 28, 29 [Furniture & effects].

FENNY BENTLEY HALL (Derbyshire).

See BENTLEY HALL.

FEN PLACE (Sussex).

CLARKE, T.H. Domestic architecture. 10. 1833.

FENTON HOUSE, Hampstead, London.

LONDON: National Trust for Places of Historic Interest or Natural Beauty.
— Fenton House, Hampstead. 14pp. Illus. (on title page) and 5 plates. 18x12 London (1957).
Another ed. WALLACE, C. 16pp. Col. illus. (on cover) and 4 plates. 21x14 1971.

LONDON: National Trust for Places of Historic Interest or Natural Beauty.
— RUSSELL, R. Catalogue of the Benton Fletcher collection of early keyboard instruments at Fenton House, Hampstead. 26pp. 4 plates. 18x12 London, 1957.

MANUSCRIPTS (Typewritten). English.
— SMITH, H.C. Catalogue of the principal contents of Fenton House, Hampstead, the property of the Lady Binning. Prepared for the National Trust by H.C.S. 33x20 1949.

COUNTRY LIFE. CVII, 802. 1950.

FERMYN WOODS HALL (Northamptonshire).

BURKE, J.B. Visitation of Seats. 2.S. Vol.II, p.123. 1855.*

GOTCH, J.A. Squires' Homes. 7. 1939.

JONES, Views of Seats. I. 1829.

NEALE, J.P. Views of Seats 2.S. Vol.III. 1826.

FERNCLIFFE, Caverley (Yorkshire).
YORKSHIRE. Picturesque views. 1885.

FERNE HOUSE (Wiltshire).
BURKE, J.B. Visitation of Seats. Vol.II, p.7. 1853.*

FERNEY HALL (Shropshire).
LEACH, F. Seats of Shropshire. p.125. 1891.

FFYNONE (Pembrokeshire).
NICHOLAS, T. Counties of Wales. II, p.844. 1872.

FIELDHEAD HOUSE, Daisy Hill (Yorkshire).
YORKSHIRE. Picturesque views. 1885.

FILLINGHAM CASTLE (Lincolnshire).
LINCOLNSHIRE. A selection of views. 1805.

FILLONGLEY HALL (Warwickshire).
BURKE, J.B. Visitation of Seats. 2.S. Vol.I, p.131. 1854.*

FINBOROUGH HALL (Suffolk).
CROMWELL, T.K. Excursions in Suffolk. I, p.163. 1818.
DAVY, H. Seats in Suffolk. pl.5. 1827.
SANDON, E. Suffolk houses. 183. 1977.

FINCHAM HALL (Norfolk).
CROMWELL, T.K. Excursions in Norfolk. II, p.150. 1819.
GARRATT, T. Halls of Norfolk. pl.24. 1890.

FINCHCOCKS (Kent).
BATHURST, Seymour Henry Bathurst, *Earl.*
— Catalogue of the Bathurst collection of pictures (including pictures from Finchcocks). Plates (some mezzotint) and genealog. table. 31x25 London: privately printed, 1908.
GREENWOOD, C. Kent. 230. 1838.
OSWALD, A. Country Houses of Kent. 63. 1933.

FINEDON HALL (Northamptonshire).
[Sales] FINEDON HALL, 1912, July 1-5 [Contents]. (K.F.& R.).

FINGRINGHOE HALL (Essex).
COUNTRY LIFE. CXXII, 1336. 1957.

FIRLE PLACE (Sussex).
OSWALD, Arthur.
— Firle Place, Sussex. An account by A.O. reprinted with revisions from Country Life. 36pp. Illus. (1 on cover) incl. plan and map. 21x13 [London] Country Life, 1955.
New ed. 1968. (F. Watson. Porcelain at Firle. 4pp. 20x16 inserted.)

COUNTRY LIFE. XLVII, 78, 108. 1920.
COUNTRY LIFE. CXVII, 480 plan, 564, 620. 1955.

FISHERWICK PARK (Staffordshire).
LEASOWES.
— A companion to the Leasowes, Hagley and Enville; with a sketch of Fisherwick, the seat of the ... Earl Donegall. To which is prefixed, the present state of Birmingham. iv, 250pp. 2 pts. in 1 vol. 8vo. 17x10 London: G.G.J. & J. Robinson; Birmingham: M. Swinney; Worcester: J. Holl, 1789.
PLOT, R. Staffordshire. 209. 1686.
SHAW, S. Staffordshire.I, 369. 1798.
[Sales] FISHERWICK PARK, 1805, June 28 [Pictures, prints, vases etc.].

FITZWALTERS (Essex).
CROMWELL, T.K. Excursions in Essex. I, p.143. 1825.

FLAGG HALL (Derbyshire).
TILLEY, J.Halls of Derbyshire.I, p.41. 1892.

FLASBY HALL (Yorkshire).
BURKE, J.B. Visitation of Seats. 2.S. Vol.I, p.87. 1854.*

FLAXLEY ABBEY (Gloucestershire).
ATKYNS, R.Gloucestershire. p.228. 1768.
COUNTRY LIFE.CLIII, 842, 908, 980. 1973.

FLEET HOUSE (Dorsetshire).
HUTCHINS, J. History of Dorset. II, 744, 1863.
HUTCHINS, J. Vitruvius Dorsettiensis. pl.11. 1816.

FLEMING'S HALL (Suffolk).
SANDON, E. Suffolk houses. 167. 1977.

FLETE HOUSE (Devonshire).
BURKE, J.B. Visitation of Seats. 2.S. Vol.II, p.102. 1855*.
COUNTRY LIFE. XXXVIII, 680 plan. 1915.

FLINTHAM HALL (Nottinghamshire).
BURKE, J.B. Visitation of Seats. 2.S. Vol.I, p.220. 1854.*
COUNTRY LIFE. CLXVI, 2374, 2454. 1979.
COUNTRY LIFE. CLXVII, 18. 1980.

FLITWICK MANOR (Bedfordshire).
BURKE, J.B. Visitation of Seats. Vol.I, p.8. 1852.

FLIXTON HALL near Bungay (Suffolk).
ANGUS, W. Seats of the Nobility. pl.8. 1787.
CROMWELL, T.K. Excursions in Suffolk. II, p.101. 1819.
NEALE, J.P. Views of Seats. Vol.IV. 1821.

FLORDON HALL (Norfolk).
BIRKBECK, G. Old Norfolk Houses. 48. 1908.
GARRATT, T. Halls of Norfolk. pl.25. 1890.

FOLIEJON PARK (Berkshire).
[Sales] FOLIEJON PARK 1952, October 28, 29 [Furnishings].

FOLKINGTON MANOR (Sussex).
COUNTRY LIFE. CXXIII, 714. 1958.
KIP, J. Nouveau théâtre de la Grande Bretagne. I, pl.67. 1715.

FOLLATON HOUSE (Devonshire).
BRITTON, J. Devonshire illustrated. 70. 1832.
BURKE, J.B. Visitation of Seats. Vol.I, p.18. 1852.*

FOLLY FARM, near Reading (Berkshire).
COUNTRY LIFE. LI, 112, 146 plan. 1922.

FONMON CASTLE (Glamorganshire).
CARDIFF: Glamorgan Archives Joint Committee.
— MOORE, P. Fonmon Castle, South Glamorgan, a residence occupied since the thirteenth century. 16pp. Illus. (3 on covers) incl. plan, map, facsimiles and genealog. tables. 15x21 1976.
COUNTRY LIFE. CV, 606 plan, 670, 734. 1949.

FONTHILL ABBEY (Wiltshire).
BECKFORD, William.
— Life at Fonthill 1807-22, with an interlude in Paris and London, from the correspondence of W.B. Translated and edited by B. Alexander. [Bibliogr.] Illus. incl. 10 plates and plan. 20x13 London: Hart-Davis, 1957.

BRITTON, John.
— Graphical and literary illustrations of Fonthill Abbey, Wiltshire; with heraldical and genealogical notices of the Beckford family. 76pp. 11 (2 hand col.) engr., 1 cut and genealog. tables. 30x24 London: by the author, 1823.
GREGORY, William.
— The Beckford family: reminiscences of Fonthill Abbey and Lansdown Tower. 2 ed. Illus. incl. 21 plates and facsimiles. 19x12 London: Simpkin, Marshall, Hamilton, Kent & Co., Ltd.; Bath Chronicle, 1898.
Another copy.
RUTTER, John.
— A description of Fonthill Abbey and demesne...including a list of paintings, cabinets, &c. 3 ed. 88pp. Plate. 19x12 Shaftesbury: by the author, 1822.
Another copy.
RUTTER, John.
— A new descriptive guide to Fonthill Abbey and demesne for 1823, including a list of its paintings and curiousities. 2 engr. plates incl. title-page. 19x12 Shaftesbury: by the author, 1823.
RUTTER, John.
— Delinations of Fonthill and its Abbey. Illus. incl. 13 plates

(1 folding lithogr., 122 hand-col. engr.) title-page, sections plans and head and tail pieces. 35x28 Shaftsbury: by the author, 1823.
STORER, James Sargant.
— A description of Fonthill Abbey, Wiltshire. Illustrated by views drawn and engraved by J.S. 26pp. Illus. incl. plates. 27x21 London: W. Clarke; J. Carpenter, W. Miller; C. Chappel; White & Cochrane; Sherwood, Neely & Jones; Salisbury: Brodie & Co., London: J. Storer, 1812.
[Exhibitions] LONDON: Grosvenor Gallery.
— Pictures from the Basildon Park & Fonthill collections. 1914-15.
BRITTON, J. Beauties of Wiltshire. III, 328. 1825.
COUNTRY LIFE. CXL, 1370 plan, 1430, 1572. 1966.
HAVELL, R. Views of Noblemen's seats. 1823.
NEALE, J.P. Views of Seats. 2.S. Vol.I. 1824.
SUMMERSON, J. The Country Seat. 199. 1970.[Model for].
[Sales] FONTHILL ABBEY, 1822, October 1-5, 7-11 [Effects].
[Sales] FONTHILL ABBEY, 1823, September 9 and following days [Contents].

FONTHILL HOUSE (Wiltshire).
ANGUS, W. Seats of the Nobility. pl.50. 1787.
BRITTON, J. Beauties of Wiltshire. I, 208. 1801.
CAMPBELL, C. Vitruvius Britannicus IV, pls. 82-87. 1767.
[Sales] FONTHILL HOUSE, 1971, November 1, 2 [Remaining Contents].

FONTMELL PARVA (Dorsetshire).
HUTCHINS, J. History of Dorset. IV, 80. 1870.

FOOLOW HALL (Derbyshire).
TILLEY, J. Halls of Derbyshire. I, p.143. 1892.

FOOTS CRAY PLACE (Kent).
CAMPBELL, C. Vitruvius Britannicus. IV, pls.8-10. 1767.
ENGLAND: Beauties of England. I, p.391. 1787.
ENGLAND: Picturesque Views. p.21. 1786-88.
ENGLISH CONNIOSSEUR. I, 57. 1766.*
NEALE, J.P. Views of Seats. 2.S. Vol.IV. 1828.
[Sales] LONDON, 1876, June 6-8 [Library].
[Sales] LONDON, 1876, June 9 [Plate].

FORCETT PARK (Yorkshire).
PAINE, J. Plans, elevations. Pt.I, pls.70-72 [Banqueting House]. 1767.

FORD CASTLE (Northumberland).
Archaeologia Aeliana, XIV, p.305.1891.
COUNTRY LIFE. LXXXIX, 32 plan, 56, 78. 1941.

FORDE ABBEY (Dorsetshire).
FORDE ABBEY.
— Forde Abbey. A brief history. 2 ed. 20pp. Illus. (1 on cover) incl. plates (1 folding). 18x12 (Chard: Young & Son, 1907).

HEATH, Sidney.
— The story of Ford Abbey from the earliest times to the present day. 80pp. Illus. incl. plates, plan and genealog. table. 25x19 London: F. Griffiths, 1911.

ROPER, John.
— Forde Abbey, near Chard, Somerset: an illustrated survey of the former Cistercian monastery now the Dorset home of the Roper family [etc.]. 32pp. Illus. (1 col., some on covers) incl. plan and map. 14x21 Derby: E.L.P. [c. 1965].
Another ed. Illus. (mainly col., some on covers) incl. plan and map. 18x14 St. Ives, Huntingdon: privately printed [c. 1975].

BUCK, S. & N. Antiquities. I, pl.63. 1774.

COUNTRY LIFE. English Country Houses: Caroline. p.111. 1966.

COUNTRY LIFE. XXVI, 18, 54. 1909.

COUNTRY LIFE. CXXXIII, 540 plan, 596, 656, 714, 1963.

DELDERFIELD, E.R. West Country houses. II, 66. 1970.

ENGLAND: Beauties of England. I, p.180. 1787.

GARNER, T. Domestic Architecture. I, p.34. 1911.

HUTCHINS, J. History of Dorset. IV, 528. 1870.

KROLL, A. Historic houses. 28. 1969.

LATHAM, C. In English Homes. Vol.III, p.113. 1909.

OSWALD, A. Country Houses of Dorset. p.113. 1959.

[Sales] FORDE ABBEY, 1846, October 26 and following days [Entire effects].

FORD HALL (Derbyshire).
TILLEY, J. Halls of Derbyshire. I, p.77. 1892.

FORD HOUSE (Devonshire).
COUNTRY LIFE. XXIII, 378. 1908.

HALL, S.C. Baronial Halls. Vol.I. 1848.

JONES. Views of Seats. II. 1829.

NEALE, J.P. Views of Seats. Vol.I. 1818.

FOREMARK (Derbyshire).
BURKE, J.B. Visitation of Seats. Vol.II, p.197. 1853.*

CAMPBELL, C. Vitruvius Britannicus. V, pls.31-35. 1771.

COUNTRY LIFE. LIV, 214 plan. 1923.

TILLEY, J. Halls of Derbyshire. IV, p.63. 1902.

TIPPING, H.A. English Homes. Period VI, Vol.I, p.87. 1926.

FOREST HALL (Essex).
RUSH, J.A. Seats in Essex. p.85. 1897.

FOREST LODGE, Bracknell (Berkshire).
[Sales] FOREST LODGE, 1969, September 15 [Remaining contents].

FORNHAM HALL (Suffolk).
BURKE, J.B. Visitation of Seats. 2.S. Vol.I, p.94. 1854.*

BURKE, J.B. Visitation of Seats. 2.S. Vol.II, p.160. 1855.*

CROMWELL, T.K. Excursions in Suffolk. I, p.76. 1818.

DAVY, H. Seats in Suffolk. pl.1. 1827.

NEALE, J.P. Views of Seats. Vol.IV. 1821.

FORT BELVEDERE (Surrey).
COUNTRY LIFE. CXXVI, 898, 960. 1959.

FORTHAMPTON COURT (Gloucestershire).
COUNTRY LIFE. CLXVI, 938 plan, 1166. 1979.

FOSBURY MANOR (Wiltshire).
[Sales] FOSBURY MANOR, 1930, February 18-21 [Contents].

FOUNTAINS HALL (Yorkshire).
FOUNTAINS HALL.
— Fountains Hall. 16pp. Illus. (1 col., some on covers.) 23x18 [London] (Pitkin Pictorials, 1968.)

COUNTRY LIFE. VII, 696. 1900.

COUNTRY LIFE. LXX, 180 plan. 1931.

GOTCH, J.A. Architecture of the Renaissance. II, p.27 plan. 1894.

HALL, S.C. Baronial Halls. Vol.II. 1848.

NICOLSON, N. Great Houses of Britain. p.102. 1965.

WOOD, G.B. Historic homes of Yorkshire. 57. 1957.

FOUR OAKS HALL (Warwickshire).
CAMPBELL, C. Vitruvius Britannicus. IVth. pls. 75, 76. 1739.

NEALE, J.P. Views of Seats. Vol.IV. 1821.

FOWBERRY TOWER (Northumberland).
[Sales] FOWBERRY TOWER, 1978, May 22 [Remaining contents incl. library].

FOWNHOPE COURT (Herefordshire).
ROBINSON, C.J. Mansions of Herefordshire. pl.8. 1873.

[Sales] FOWNHOPE COURT, 1923, April 24 [Contents].

FOXCOTE MANOR (Warwickshire).
NEALE, J.P. Views of Seats. Vol.IV. 1821.

FOXDENTON HALL (Lancashire).
BURKE, J.B. Visitation of Seats. 2.S. Vol.I, p220. 1854.*

FOXHILLS (Surrey).
BRAYLEY, E.W. History of Surrey.II, 223. 1841.

BURKE, J.B. Visitation of Seats. 2.S. Vol.I, p.220. 1854.*

FOX HOLES (Lancashire).
PYNE, W.H. Lancashire illustrated. 94. 1831.
TWYCROSS, E. Mansions of England and Wales. Vol.III, p.87. 1847.*

FOXWOLD (Kent).
PYM, Horace N.
— Odds and ends at Foxwold, a guide for the inquiring guest. Plates. 25x16 [Edinburgh] privately printed, 1887.

FRAMPTON COURT (Dorsetshire).
BURKE, J.B. Visitation of Seats. Vol.I, p.69. 1852.*
HUTCHINS, J. History of Dorset. II, 297. 1863.
HUTCHINS, J. Vitruvius Dorsettiensis. pl.12. 1816.

FRAMPTON COURT (Gloucestershire).
COOKE, R. West Country Houses. p.130. 1957.
COUNTRY LIFE. English Country Houses: Early Georgian. p.127. 1955.
COUNTRY LIFE. LXII, 506 plan, 538. 1927.
TIPPING, H.A. English Homes. Period IV, Vol.II, p.257. 1928.

FRAMPTON MANOR FARM (Gloucestershire).
TIPPING, H.A. English Homes. Period I & II, Vol.II, p.189. 1937.

FRAMSDEN HALL (Suffolk).
SANDON, E. Suffolk houses. 172. 1977.

FRANKS (Kent).
COUNTRY LIFE. I, 295. 1897.
COUNTRY LIFE. XXXIV, 126 plan. 1913.
MORRIS, F.O. Views of Seats.Vol.I, p.47. 1880.
NASH, J. Mansions of England. I, pl.16. 1839.
OSWALD, A. Country houses of Kent. 39. 1933.
[Sales] FRANKS, 1910, May 3, 4 [Remaining contents].

FRANSHAM OLD HALL (Norfolk).
GARRATT, T. Halls of Norfolk. pl.26. 1890.

FREDVILLE (Kent).
GREENWOOD, C. Kent. 349. 1838.

FREEMANTLE PARK (Hampshire).
HAMPSHIRE: Architectural Views. 1830.

FRENSHAM PLACE (Surrey).
[Sales] FRENSHAM PLACE, 1913, October 20 and following days [Contents].

FRIARAGE, The, Yarm (Yorkshire).
BURKE, J.B. Visitation of Seats. Vol.II, p.110. 1853.*

FRIARS, The, Aylesford (Kent).
COUNTRY LIFE. LIV, 570, 606. 1923.
CROMWELL, T.K. Excursions in Kent. p.144. 1822.
OSWALD, A. Country Houses of Kent. 18. 1933.

FRITH PARK (Surrey).
[Sales] FRITH PARK, 1926, November 29, 30, December 1, 2 [Contents].

FRITWELL MANOR (Oxfordshire).
GARNER, T. Domestic architecture. II, p.180. 1911.
[Sales] LONDON, 1911, November 8 [Estate].
[Sales] FRITWELL MANOR, 1911, November 22, 23 [Contents].

FROCESTER COURT (Gloucestershire).
COUNTRY LIFE. XVII, 702. 1905.

FRODESLEY HALL (Shropshire).
SHROPSHIRE. Castles & Old Mansions. 43. 1868.

FROGNALL, Chislehurst (Kent).
[Sales] FROGNAL, 1915, June 7 and following days [Sydney collection] (K.F. & R.).

FROGNALL GROVE, Hampstead, London.
COUNTRY LIFE. CV, 1502. 1949.

FROME HOUSE (Dorsetshire).
COUNTRY LIFE. CXXVI, 1202. 1959.
OSWALD, A. Country houses of Dorset. p.170. 1959.

FROYLE PLACE (Hampshire).
NEALE, J.P. Views of Seats. Vol.II. 1819.

FRYSTONE HALL (Yorkshire).
BURKE, J.B. Visitation of Seats. Vol.II, p.241. 1853.*
BURKE, J.B. Visitation of Seats. 2.S. Vol.II, p.75. 1855.*

FULBECK HALL (Lincolnshire).
COUNTRY LIFE. CLI, 394. 1972.

FULFORD HOUSE (Devonshire).
See GREAT FULFORD.

FULMER GROVE (Buckinghamshire).
BURKE, J.B. Visitation of Seats. Vol.I, p.6. 1852.*

FYFIELD MANOR (Berkshire).
COUNTRY LIFE. XLV, 368. 1919.

FYFIELD MANOR (Wiltshire).
COUNTRY LIFE. LXVIII, 260 plan. 1930.
COUNTRY LIFE. CXXX, 692 plan, 750. 1961.

FYNE COURT (Somerset).
BURKE, J.B. Visitation of Seats. Vol.II, p.196. 1853.*

FYNNEY COTTAGE (Derbyshire).
TILLEY, J. Halls of Derbyshire. I, p.41. 1892.

GABALFA (Glamorganshire).
[Sales] LONDON, 1839. July 18 [Estate].

GAER, The. (Monmouthshire).
BURKE, J.B. Visitation of Seats. Vol.II, p.133. 1853.*

GAINSBOROUGH OLD HALL
(Lincolnshire).
MUSSON, *Mrs* D.A.
— A revised guide to Gainsborough Old Hall. By Mrs D.A.M. and C. Christian. 8pp. 3 illus. incl. plan. 23x14 Gainsborough: Friends of the Hall Association, 1974.
COUNTRY LIFE. XXXVI, 127 plan. 1914.
COUNTRY LIFE. CXVI, 910. 1934.
GARNER, T. Domestic architecture. I, p.73 plan.1911.
LINCOLNSHIRE. A selection of views. 17. 1805.
TIPPING, H.A. English Homes, Period I, Vol.I. p.275, 1921.

GARENDON HALL (Leicestershire).
BURKE, J.B. Visitation of Seats. Vol.I, p.2. 1852.*
NICHOLS, J. History of Leicestershire. III, ii, 800. 1804.
THROSBY, J. Views in Leicestershire. p.274. 1789.

GARNONS (Herefordshire).
JONES. Views of Seats. II. 1829.
NEALE, J.P. Views of Seats. 2.S. Vol.IV. 1828.

GARNSTONE (Herefordshire).
JONES. Views of Seats. II. 1829.
MORRIS, F.O. Views of Seats. Vol.I, p.57. 1880.
NEALE, J.P. Views of Seats. 2.S. Vol.IV. 1828.
ROBINSON, C.J. Mansions of Herefordshire. pl.22.1873.

GARRATT HALL (Lancashire).
GRAY, H. Old Halls of Lancashire. p.69. 1893.
PYNE, W.H. Lancashire illustrated. 97. 1831.

GARRICK'S VILLA, Hampton (Middlesex).
MANUSCRIPTS. English.
— Garrick's est[at]e: part[icul]ars for insurance of property. 1f. 38x23.5 18 November 1822.
MANUSCRIPTS. English
— Garrick's estate: schedule of papers &c. [i.e. copies of deeds, accounts, admission cards, views etc.] delivered to the trustees by J. Dean. 2ff. 32x20 26 April 1823.
BOLTON, A.T. Architecture of R. & J. Adam. I, 27 plan. 1922.
COUNTRY LIFE. XL, 756 plan. 1916.
ENGLAND: Picturesque Views. p.31. 1786-88.
THAMES, River. An history. pl.45. 1794.
WATTS, W. Seats of the Nobility. pl.68. 1779.

GARROWBY HALL (Yorkshire).
COUNTRY LIFE. CVI, 394, 466. 1949.

GARSINGTON MANOR (Oxfordshire).
[Sales] GARSINGTON MANOR, 1928, July 11, 12 [Contents].

GARSTON HALL (Lancashire).
GRAY, H. Old Halls of Lancashire. p.39. 1893.

GARTHEWIN (Denbighshire).
COUNTRY LIFE. CXXIII, 298 plan. 1958.

GARTHYNGARED (Merionethshire).
BURKE, J.B. Visitation of Seats. Vol.II, p.138. 1853.*

GATACRE HALL (Shropshire).
BURKE, J.B. Visitation of Seats. Vol.I, p.71. 1852.*
WEST, W. Picturesque views of Shropshire. p.132. 1831.

GATCOMBE PARK (Gloucestershire).
COOKE, R. West Country Houses. p.133. 1957.

GATE BURTON HALL (Lincolnshire).
BURKE, J.B. Visitation of Seats. Vol.I, p.35. 1852*
LINCOLNSHIRE. A selection of views. 27. 1805.

GATEHOUSE, near Goudhurst (Kent).
COUNTRY LIFE. LXXXI, 42 plan. 1937.

GATELY HALL (Norfolk).
COUNTRY LIFE. CXVI, 984. 1954.

GATTON PARK (Surrey).

HENSLOW, Thomas Geoffrey Wall.

— Gatton Park, seat of Sir Jeremiah Colman, Bart. 38pp. Illus.
26x16 n.p. privately printed, 1914.

BRAYLEY, E.W. History of Surrey. IV, 311. 1841.

BURKE, J.B. Visitation of Seats. Vol.II, p.225. 1853.*

PROSSER, G.F. Surrey Seats. p.97. 1828.

GAULDEN MANOR (Somerset).

STARKIE, *Mrs.* James.

— Gaulden Manor, Tolland, nr. Taunton, Somerset. Historic
Manor House of the Tuberville and Wolcott families [etc.].
12pp. Illus. (1 col., some on covers, some on title-page.) 14x20
[Derby] (E.L.P., 1972.)

COUNTRY LIFE. LXXIV, 252. 1933.

GAUNT HOUSE (Oxfordshire).

COUNTRY LIFE. XIII, 870. 1903.

GAUNTS HOUSE (Dorsetshire).

HUTCHINS, J. History of Dorset. III, 244. 1868.

HUTCHINS, J. Vitruvius Dorsettiensis. pl.13. 1816.

NEALE, J.P. Views of Seats. Vol.I. 1818.

GAWSTHORPE HALL (Cheshire).

GARNER, T. Domestic architecture. II, p.197. 1911.

RICHARDSON, C.J. Old English mansions. IV. 1848.

GAWTHORPE HALL (Lancashire).

WILLIAMS, G.A. *Canon.*

— Rachel Kay-Shuttleworth, 1886-1967: a short account of
her life and work. (The Rachel Kay-Shuttleworth
collection...at Gawthorpe Hall.) 2 impression. 48pp. Illus. (2
on cover) incl. 6 plates. 21x14 Kendal (printed), 1969.

BARTLETT, J. Mansions of England and Wales. pl.27. 1853.

BURKE, J.B. Visitation of Seats. Vol.I, p.19. 1852.*

COUNTRY LIFE. XXXIII, 670 plan. 1913.

COUNTRY LIFE. CLVIII, 558, 630. 1975.

TWYCROSS, E. Mansions of England and Wales. Vol.I, p.25.
1847.

GAWTHORPE HALL (Yorkshire).

YORKSHIRE. Picturesque views. 1885.

GAYHURST (Buckinghamshire).

BURKE, J.B. Visitation of Seats. Vol.I, p.7. 1852.*

NEALE, J.P. Views of Seats. Vol.I. 1818.

GAYNES HALL (Huntingdonshire).

BURKE, J.B. Visitation of Seats. 2.S. Vol.I, p.210. 1854.*

GAYNES PARK, Theydon Gernon (Essex).

RUSH, J.A. Seats in Essex. p.89. 1897.*

GAYNES PARK, Upminster (Essex).

RUSH, J.A. Seats in Essex. p.87. 1897.

GAYTON HALL (Cheshire).

TWYCROSS, E. Mansions of England and Wales. Vol.I, p.58.
1850.*

GAYTON MANOR HOUSE (Northamptonshire).

GOTCH, J.A. Halls of Northants. p.72. 1936.

GEDDING HALL (Suffolk).

CROMWELL, T.K. Excursions in Suffolk. I, p.174. 1818.

SANDON, E. Suffolk houses. 177. 1977.

GEDDINGTON PRIORY (Northamptonshire).

GOTCH, J.A. Squires' Homes. 11. 1939.

GENNINGS (Kent).

COPPER PLATE MAGAZINE. pl.60. 1778.

SANDBY, P. Select Views. I, pl.28. 1783.

GERARDS BROMLEY HALL (Staffordshire).

PLOT, R. Staffordshire. 103. 1686.

GERBESTONE MANOR (Somerset).

COUNTRY LIFE. LXXVIII, 520 plan. 1935.

GIBSIDE HALL (Durham).

BURKE, J.B. Visitation of Seats. 2.S. Vol.I, p.57. 1854.*

COUNTRY LIFE. CXI, 422. 1952.

PAINE, J. Plans, elevations. Pt.I, pls.67-69 [Chapel &
Mausoleum.] 1767.

GIDEA HALL (Essex).

COPPER PLATE MAGAZINE. II, pl.66. 1792-1802.

CROMWELL, T.K. Excursions in Essex. I, p.171. 1825.

ENGLAND: Picturesque Views. p.26. 1786-88.

GIFFORDS HALL, Stoke-by-Nayland (Suffolk).

BURKE, J.B. Visitation of Seats. 2.S. Vol.I, p.130. 1854.*

COUNTRY LIFE. XIV, 578. 1903.

COUNTRY LIFE. LIV, 488, 524. 1923.

CROMWELL, T.K. Excursions in Suffolk. I, p.70. 1818.

SANDON, E. Suffolk Houses. 202. 1977.

TIPPING, H.A. English Homes. Period II, Vol.I, p.31. 1924.

GIFFORDS HALL Wickhambrook (Suffolk).
COUNTRY LIFE. XLV, 552, 588. 1919.
SANDON, E. Suffolk houses. 222. 1977.
TIPPING, H.A. English Homes. Period II, Vol.I, p.1. 1924.

GILESTON MANOR (Glamorganshire).
BURKE, J.B. Visitation of Seats. Vol.I, p.152. 1852.*

GILLIBRAND HALL (Lancashire).
BARTLETT, J. Mansions of England and Wales. pls. 32,33. 1853.
TWYCROSS, E. Mansions of England and Wales. Vol.I, p.54. 1847.

GILLING CASTLE (Yorkshire).
BURKE, J.B. Visitation of Seats. Vol.II, p.94. 1853.*
COUNTRY LIFE. XXIV, 416. 1908.
COUNTRY LIFE. LXV, 584 [Great Chamber]. 1929.
LATHAM, C. In English Homes. Vol.III, p.13. 1909.
SHAW, H. Elizabethan architecture. pls.XI-XV. [Dining room, stained glass etc.] 1839.
TIPPING, H.A. English Homes. Period IV, Vol.II, p.201. 1928.
WOOD, G.B. Historic homes of Yorkshire. 95. 1957.
Yorkshire Archaeological Journal. XIX, 105 plan. 1907.
[Sales] LONDON, 1929, May 16 [Elizabethan panelling and heraldic stained glass].

GILLINGHAM HALL (Norfolk).
CROMWELL, T.K. Excursions in Norfolk. I, p.79. 1818.
NEALE, J.P. Views of Seats. Vol.III. 1820.

GILLOW MANOR (Herefordshire).
ROBINSON, C.J. Mansions of Herefordshire. pl.9. 1873.

GIPPING HALL (Suffolk).
DAVY, H. Seats in Suffolk. pl.4. 1827.

GIPPING LONE (Suffolk).
SANDON, E. Suffolk houses. 178. 1977.

GLANBRAN (Carmarthenshire).
NEALE, J.P. Views of Seats. Vol.V. 1822.

GLANGWILLI (Carmarthenshire).
BURKE, J.B. Visitation of Seats. Vol.II, p.26. 1853.*

GLANSEVERN (Montgomeryshire).
JONES, Views of Seats. VI. 1831.
NICHOLAS, T. Counties of Wales. II, p.802. 1872.

GLANTON PYKE (Northumberland).
BURKE, J.B. Visitation of Seats. Vol.II, p.89. 1853.*

GLANUSK PARK (Brecknockshire).
BURKE, J.B. Visitation of Seats. Vol.I, p.210. 1852.
MORRIS, F.O. Views of Seats. Vol.I, p.87. 1880.

GLAPWELL HALL (Derbyshire).
TILLEY, J. Halls of Derbyshire. III, p.53. 1899.

GLASFRYN (Caernarvonshire).
BURKE, J.B. Visitation of Seats. 2.S. Vol.II, p.146. 1855.*

GLASSHAMPTON HOUSE (Worcestershire).
NASH, T.R. Worcestershire. I, 40. 1781.

GLEDSTONE HALL (Yorkshire).
BURKE, J.B. Visitation of Seats. Vol.I, p.54. 1852.*
COUNTRY LIFE. LXXVII, 374 plan. 1935.

GLEMHAM HALL (Suffolk).
GLEMHAM HALL.
— Glemham Hall. 16pp. Col. Illus. incl. map. 18x24 (St. Ives, Huntingdon) privately printed [1975.]
BURKE, J.B. Visitation of Seats. 2.S. Vol.I, p.18. 1854.*
COUNTRY LIFE. XXVII, 18. 1910.
CROMWELL, T.K. Excursions in Suffolk. II, p.81. 1819.
TIPPING, H.A. English Homes. Period IV, Vol.I, p.405. 1920.

GLENDON HALL (Northamptonshire).
BURKE, J.B. Visitation of Seats. 2.S. Vol.I, p.150. 1854.*
COUNTRY LIFE. LII, 676. 1922.
GOTCH, J.A. Halls of Northants. p.59. 1936.
JONES, Views of Seats. I. 1829.
NEALE, J.P. Views of Seats. 2.S. Vol.IV. 1828.

GLEVERING HALL (Suffolk).
CROMWELL, T.K. Excursions in Suffolk. II, p.65. 1819.
DAVY, H. Seats in Suffolk. pl.7. 1827.

GLINTON MANOR HOUSE (Northamptonshire).
GOTCH, J.A. Halls of Northants. p.2. 1936.

GLODDAETH (Caernarvonshire).
COUNTRY LIFE. CLXIV. 1966. 1978.
HOARE: Views of Seats. pl.12. 1792.

GLOVER'S HOUSE (Kent).
GREENWOOD, C. Kent. 272. 1838.

GLYMPTON MANOR (Oxfordshire).
OXFORD: Oxfordshire Record Society.
— Oxfordshire Record series. Illus. and genealog. tables. vols 23x15 Oxford, 1923.
V. BARNETT, Rev. H. Glympton. The history of an Oxfordshire Manor. 1923.
WHISTLER, Laurence.
— Some unpublished drawings of Sir John Vanbrugh... in the Victoria and Albert Museum (and the British Museum). Excerpts. Illus. incl. elevations and plans. 3 pt. in 1. 25x18 [London, 1948-9].
I. Vanbrugh's design for Glympton: 7pp. 1948.
From: New English review magazine, I, no.4.
[Sales] LONDON, 1953, July 15 [Paintings].

GLYNDE (Sussex).
GLYNDE PLACE.
— Glynde Place, Sussex. Historic home of the Morleys and their descendants the Trevors and the Brands [etc.]. 16pp. Illus. (1 col., some on covers, 1 on title-page.) 14x20 (Derby: E.L.P., 1974.)
BURKE, J.B. Visitation of Seats. 2.S. Vol.II, p.164. 1855.*
COUNTRY LIFE. XXII, 342. 1907.
COUNTRY LIFE. CXVII, 978, 1040, 1104. 1955.
LATHAM, C. In English Homes. Vol.II, p.181. 1907.
MORRIS, F.O. Views of Seats. Vol.V, p.37. 1880.

GLYNLLIFON (Caenarvonshire).
NICHOLAS, T. Counties of Wales. I, p.315. 1872.

GLYNN (Cornwall).
BURKE, J.B. Visitation of Seats. Vol.I, p.241. 1852.*

GNOLL CASTLE (Glamorganshire).
NEALE, J.P. Views of Seats. Vol.V. 1822.

GODINTON (Kent).
BURKE, J.B. Visitation of Seats. Vol.I, p.56. 1852.*
COUNTRY LIFE. XIV, 90. 1903.
COUNTRY LIFE. CXXXII, 1396, 1546 plan, 1600. 1962.
LATHAM, C. In English Homes. Vol.I, p.157. 1904.
NEALE, J.P. Views of Seats. 2.S. Vol.III. 1826.
OSWALD, A. Country Houses of Kent. 45. 1933.
SHAW, H. Elizabethan architecture. pl.LX. [Staircase] 1839.

GODMERSHAM PARK (Kent).
COUNTRY LIFE. XLVIII, 596. 1920.
COUNTRY LIFE. XCVII, 288, 332, 376. 1945.
GREENWOOD, C. Kent. 298. 1838.

HASTED, E. Kent. III, 158. 1790.
NEALE, J.P. Views of Seats. 2.S. Vol.III. 1826.
OSWALD, A. Country Houses of Kent. 57. 1933.
TIPPING, H.A. English Homes. Period V, Vol.I, p.247. 1921.
WATTS, W. Seats of the Nobility. pl.67. 1779.
[Sales] GODMERSHAM PARK, 1983, June 6-9 [Contents].

GODOLPHIN HOUSE (Cornwall).
COUNTRY LIFE. XXXVIII, 868. 1915.
DELDERFIELD, E.R. West Country houses. I, 60. 1968.

GOGERDDAN (Cardiganshire).
BURKE, J.B. Visitation of Seats. 2.S. Vol.II, p.92. 1855.*
NEALE, J.P. Views of Seats. Vol.V. 1822.
NICHOLAS, T. Counties of Wales. I, p.126. 1872.

GOGMAGOG HILLS HOUSE (Cambridgeshire).
BURKE, J.B. Visitation of Seats. 2.S. Vol.II, p.137. 1855.*

GOLDEN GROVE, Llanasa (Flintshire).
BURKE, J.B. Visitation of Seats. 2.S. Vol.I, p.94. 1854.*

GOLDEN GROVE, Trefonen (Shropshire).
[Sales] OSWESTRY, 1968, June 20, 21 [Contents].

GOLDEN MANOR (Somerset).
See GAULDEN MANOR.

GOLDINGTON HALL (Bedfordshire).
BURKE, J.B. Visitation of Seats. 2.S. Vol.I, p.22. 1854.*

GOLDNEY HOUSE, Bristol (Gloucestershire).
COOKE, R. West Country Houses. p.119. 1957.
COUNTRY LIFE. CIV, 278. 1948.

GOLDSBOROUGH HALL (Yorkshire).
COUNTRY LIFE. XVI, 558. 1904.

GOODNESTONE (Kent).
BADESLADE, T. Seats in Kent. pl.11. 1750.
BURKE, J.B. Visitation of Seats. 2.S. Vol.II, p.226. 1855.
GREENWOOD, C. Kent. 348. 1838.
HARRIS, J. History of Kent. p.132. 1719.
HASTED, E. Kent. III, 705. 1790.
NEALE, J.P. Views of Seats. 2.S. Vol.II. 1825.

GLANUSK PARK — Co BRECON.
(NORTH FRONT)

THE SEAT OF J. BAILEY, ESQR M.P.

Stannard & Dixon Lith 7 Poland St.

GLANUSK PARK, Brecknockshire. From: BURKE (Sir J.B., Ulster King of Arms.). A visitation of the seats and arms of the noblemen and gentlemen of Great Britain, vol. I, London, 1852.

GOODRICH COURT (Herefordshire).

MEYRICK, *Sir* Samuel Rush.
— Engraved illustrations of antient arms and armour, from
the collection of Llewelyn Meyrick, at Goodrich Court,
Herefordshire; after the drawings, and with the description of
Dr. M., by J. Skelton. Engr. incl. plates and title-pages. 2 vols.
36x26 London: privately printed, 1830.

MOFFATT, H.C.
— Illustrated description of some of the furniture at Goodrich
Court, Herefordshire and Hamptworth Lodge, Wiltshire.
96pp. Plates. 32x25 Oxford: privately printed for the author,
1928.

BURKE, J.B. Visitation of Seats. Vol. II, p.226. 1853.*

GOODWOOD HOUSE (Sussex).

GOODWOOD.
— Goodwood: an illustrated survey [etc.]. 32pp. Illus. (some
col., some on covers). 14x22 Derby: E.L.P. [1950?].

JACQUES, D.
— A visit to Goodwood ... the seat of ... the Duke of Richmond.
With an appendix descriptive of an ancient painting (the
cenotaph of the Lord Darnley). Engr. plates. 22x14 Chichester:
By the author; London: Lackington, Hughes & Co, 1822.

MARCH, Amy Mary Gordon Lennox, *Countess of.*
— Catalogue of the pictures at Goodwood (and at Gordon
Castle). 27x22 n.p. privately printed, 1877 [1879?].

MASON, William Hayley.
— Goodwood, its house, park and grounds; with a catalogue
raisonné of the pictures in the gallery of his Grace the Duke of
Richmond, K.G. [etc.]. 6 engr. plates. 19x12 London: Smith,
Elder & Co., 1839.

CAMPBELL, C. Vitruvius Britannicus. III, pls.51-54. 1725.

COUNTRY LIFE. XVIII, 198. 1905.

COUNTRY LIFE. LXXII, 38. 66, 71 [Pictures]. 1932.

LATHAM, C. In English Homes. Vol.I, p.413. 1904.

NEALE, J.P. Views of Seats. 2.S. Vol.V. 1829.

GOPSALL HALL (Leicestershire).

BURKE, J.B. Visitation of Seats. Vol.I, p.66. 1852.*

CAMPBELL, C. Vitruvius Britannicus. IV, pls.65, 66. 1767.

MORRIS, F.O. Views of Seats. Vol.II, p.47. 1880.

NEALE, J.P. Views of Seats. 2.S. Vol.V. 1829.

NICHOLS, J. History of Leicestershire. IV, ii, 857 [Elevation
& plan]. 1811.

PAINE, J. Plans, elevations. Pt.I, pl.74 [Temple]. 1767.

THROSBY, J. Views in Leicestershire. p.280. 1789.

[Sales] GOPSALL, 1918, October 14 and following days
[Antique and modern furniture].

GORE COURT, Sittingbourne (Kent).

CAMPBELL, C. New Vitruvius Britannicus. I, pl.11. 1802.

GREENWOOD, C. Kent. 274. 1838.

GORHAMBURY (Hertfordshire).

GORHAMBURY.
— Gorhambury. 32pp. Plates. 24x17 [Gorhambury: privately
printed] 1938.

GORHAMBURY.
— Guide to pictures at Gorhambury. [Typescript] 10ff. 25x20
[n.p., *c.* 1945.]

GRIMSTON, *Hon.* Charlotte.
— The history of Gorhambury. 94pp. Lithogr. incl. hand written
text, plates (1 etching) and plan. (list of pictures). 33x26 London:
Privately printed, 1821.

VERULAM, James Brabazon Grimston, *Earl of.*
— Gorhambury, 16pp. Illus. (some on covers, 1 on title page)
incl. 4 plates. 14x20 [Derby: E.L.P., 1957.]

MANUSCRIPTS [Typewritten].
— Gorhambury, St. Albans. [Catalogue of pictures and
features of interest at Gorhambury.] 11ff. 26x21. n.d.

BURKE, J.B. Visitation of Seats. Vol.I, p.149. 1852.*

COUNTRY LIFE. LXXIV, 556 plan. 649 plan. [Old house].

COUNTRY LIFE. CXX, 430. 1956.

COUNTRY LIFE. CLIX, 1451 [Stained glass] 1562 [Stained
glass] 1976.

NEALE, J.P. Views of Seats. Vol.II. 1819.

RICHARDSON, C.J. Old English Mansions. II. 1842. [Old
House].

GORING CASTLE (Sussex).

BURKE, J.B. Visitation of Seats. Vol.I, p.15. 1852.*

SUMMERSON, J. The Country Seat. 205. 1970.

GORSE HALL (Derbyshire).

TILLEY, J. Halls of Derbyshire. III, p.7. 1899.

GOSFIELD HALL (Essex).

PRESTON, Cynthia.
— History and description of Gosfield Hall, Halstead, Essex.
[Revised ed.] 10pp. Illus. (1 on cover.) 25x19 [London:
Wayfarers' Trust Ltd., 1959?].
Title on cover.

MANUSCRIPTS.   English.
— [A collection of miscellaneous manuscripts, some in French,
with 7 drawings, relating to charades and other diversions of
the Williams-Wynn family at Gosfield Hall, Essex.] 38x23 etc.
Gosfield, 1809-10.

BURKE, J.B. Visitation of Seats. 2.S. Vol.II, p.83. 1855.*

COUNTRY LIFE. CXV, 278. 1954.

CROMWELL, T.K. Excursions in Essex. II, p.171. 1825.

ENGLAND: Beauties of England. I, p.255. 1787.

ESSEX: A new and complete history. II, 34. 1769.

RUSH, J.A. Seats in Essex. p.91. 1897.

GOSFIELD PLACE (Essex).

CROMWELL, T.K. Excursions in Essex. II, p.170. 1825.

THE COUNTRY HOUSE DESCRIBED

GOSFORTH PARK (Northumberland).
PAINE, J. Plans, elevations. Pt.I, pls.15-17 plans, 18-25. 1767.

GOSTON LODGE (Essex).
CROMWELL, T.K. Excursions in Essex. II, p.102. 1825.

GOURNAY COURT (Somerset).
COOKE, R. West Country Houses. p.90. 1957.

GRACE DIEU MANOR (Leicestershire).
BURKE, J.B. Visitation of Seats. Vol.I, p.74. 1852.*

GRAFTON HALL (Cheshire).
CLARKE, T.H. Domestic architecture. 6. 1833.
ORMEROD, G. Cheshire. II, 702. 1882.

GRAFTON MANOR (Northamptonshire).
GOTCH, J.A. Squires' Homes. 40. 1939.

GRAFTON MANOR (Worcestershire).
NASH, T.R. Worcestershire. I, 156. 1781.
NIVEN, W. Old Worcestershire houses. p.2, pl.3. 1873.

GRANGE, The. Broadhembury, Honiton (Devonshire).
CHARLES, of London.
— An oak-pannelled room of James I from The Grange, Broadhembury, in the county of Devon [etc.] 16pp. Illus. incl. 7 plates. 29x22 New York. [1927].
BURKE, J.B. Visitation of Seats. Vol.II, p.247. 1853.*
COUNTRY LIFE. XVI, 162. 1904.
JONES. Views of Seats. II. 1829.
LATHAM, C. In English Homes. Vol.II, p.189. 1907.
NEALE, J.P. Views of Seats. 2.S. Vol.III. 1826.

GRANGE, The. (Hampshire).
BURKE, J.B. Visitation of Seats. Vol.II, p.67. 1853.*
COUNTRY LIFE. CLVII, 1166, 1242. 1975.
HAMPSHIRE: Architectural views. 1830.
JONES, Views of Seats. II. 1829.
NEALE, J.P. Views of Seats. Vol.II. 1819.
SUMMERSON, J. The Country Seat. 48, 221, plans. 1970.

GRANGE, The. Elstree (Hertfordshire).
[Sales] GRANGE, The. Elstree. 1911 June 12-14 [Contents].

GRANGE, The. Leybourne (Kent)
BADESLADE, T. Seats in Kent. pl.12. 1750.
HARRIS, J. History of Kent. p.172. 1719.

GRANGE, The. Wissett (Suffolk).
SANDON, E. Suffolk houses. 330. 1977.

GRANGE, The. Farnham (Surrey).
COUNTRY LIFE. LXXVI, 90. 1934.

GRANGE, The. Rottingdean (Sussex).
COUNTRY LIFE. LXII, 698 plan. 1927.

GRANGE PARK (Hampshire).
See GRANGE, The.

GRANTHAM HOUSE (Lincolnshire).
LONDON: National Trust for Places of Historic Interest or Natural Beauty.
— Grantham House, Grantham, Lincolnshire. 4pp. 2 illus. [London, *c.* 1950.]

GRAPPENHALL HALL (Cheshire).
TWYCROSS, E. Mansions of England and Wales. Vol.II, p.83. 1850.

GRAPPENHALL HEYES (Cheshire).
TWYCROSS, E. Mansions of England and Wales. Vol.II, p.84. 1850.*

GRASSYARD HALL (Lancashire).
BARTLETT, J. Mansions of England and Wales. pl.66. 1853.
TWYCROSS, E. Mansions of England and Wales. Vol.II, p.25. 1847.

GRAVETYE MANOR (Sussex).
GARNER, T. Domestic architecture. II, p.183. 1911.

GRAY'S COURT, York (Yorkshire).
COUNTRY LIFE. L, 378. 1921.

GRAYTHWAITE LOW HALL (Lancashire).
[Sales] GRAYTHWAITE, 1905, January 20-25 [Furnishings, furniture etc.].

GRAYTHWAITE OLD HALL (Lancashire).
GRAYTHWAITE HALL.
— Catalogue of the family portraits and some pictures at Graythwaite Hall, Lancashire [the property of Major G.O. Sandys] 54pp. 22x15 [Ulverston] privately printed, 1923.
BURKE, J.B. Visitation of Seats. Vol.I, p. 121. 1852.*
BURKE, J.B. Visitation of Seats. 2.S. Vol.I, p.227. 1854.
[Sales] GRAYTHWAITE, 1905, January 16-18 [Furnishings, furniture etc.].

GREAT ADDINGTON MANOR (Northamptonshire).
GOTCH, J.A. Squires' Homes. 17. 1939.
[Sales] GREAT ADDINGTON MANOR, 1912, March 27, 28 [Furniture etc.].

GREAT BARR HALL (Staffordshire).
SHAW, S. Staffordshire. II, 106. 1801.

GREAT BEVILL'S, Bures (Suffolk).
SANDON, E. Suffolk houses. 171. 1977.

GREAT BRICKHILL MANOR (Buckinghamshire).
BURKE, J.B. Visitation of Seats. 2.S. Vol.II, p.90. 1855.*

GREAT CHALFIELD MANOR (Wiltshire).
WALKER, Thomas Larkins.
— The history and antiquities of the Manor House and church at Great Chalfield, Wiltshire [etc.]. [Bibliogr. notes.]
34pp. Engr. plates incl. sections, elevations and plans. 38x27 London: by the author, 1837.
This forms Vols. III, part 2. of PUGIN (A.C.) Examples of gothic architecture [etc.]. 1831, 1850.
LONDON: National Trust for Places of Historic Interest or Natural Beauty.
— FULLER, R.F. Great Chalfield Manor. 12pp. 4 plates incl. plan. 18x12 London: Country Life (1946).
Another ed. FLOYD, C. 18pp. 4 plates. 1964.
New ed. FLOYD, R. Great Chalfield Manor, Wiltshire. [Bibliogr.]
20pp. Illus. (1 on cover) incl. plates and plan. 22x14 [London] 1980.
COUNTRY LIFE. XXXVI, 230, 294 plan. 1914.
ELYARD, S.J. Old Wiltshire homes. p.36. 1894.
GARNER, T. Domestic architecture. I, p.21. 1911.
TIPPING, H.A. English Homes. Period I, Vol.I, p.313. 1921.

GREAT CRESSINGHAM PRIORY (Norfolk).
GARNER, T. Domestic architecture. II, p.141 plan. 1911.
GARRATT, T. Halls of Norfolk. pl.20. 1890.

GREAT CULVERDEN (Kent).
GREENWOOD, C. Kent. 124. 1838.

GREAT DIXTER (Sussex).
COUNTRY LIFE. XXXIII, 18 plan. 1913.

GREAT FINBOROUGH HALL (Suffolk).
See FINBOROUGH HALL.

GREAT FOSTERS (Surrey).
GREAT FOSTERS.
— Great Fosters, Egham, in the county of Surrey. An ... Elizabethan mansion, ... gardens and grounds [etc.]. [Prospectus of sale.] 22pp. Illus. 37x24 (London, 1924).
COUNTRY LIFE. LII, 610, 640. 1922.

GREAT FULFORD (Devonshire).
BURKE, J.B. Visitation of Seats. Vol.I, p.189. 1852.*
COUNTRY LIFE. XXXVI, 160, 1914.
DELDERFIELD, E.R. West Country houses. I, 64. 1968.
TIPPING, H.A. English Homes. Period II, Vol.I, p.339. 1924.

GREAT HORTON HOUSE (Yorkshire).
YORKSHIRE, Picturesque views. 1885.

GREAT HUNDRIDGE MANOR (Buckinghamshire).
COUNTRY LIFE. LXXXIX, 144, 166. 1941.
[Sales] GREAT HUNDRIDGE MANOR, 1967, March 21, 22 [Contents].

GREAT LINFORD MANOR (Buckinghamshire).
COUNTRY LIFE. CLXXII, 1658. 1982.

GREAT MAYTHAM (Kent).
COUNTRY LIFE. XXXII, 746 plan. 1912.
OSWALD, A. Country houses of Kent. 68. 1933.

GREAT OAKLEY HALL (Northamptonshire).
GOTCH, J.A. Halls of Northants. p.34. 1936.
JONES. Views of Seats. I. 1829.
NEALE, J.P. Views of Seats. 2.S. Vol.III. 1826.

GREAT OTE HALL (Sussex).
[Sales] LONDON, 1922, October 5 [Freehold of the Hall].

GREAT PEDNOR (Buckinghamshire).
COUNTRY LIFE. CXXXIII, 1380. 1963.

GREAT POTHERIDGE (Devonshire).
DELDERFIELD, E.R. West Country houses. I, 68. 1968.

GREAT SAXHAM HALL (Suffolk).
See SAXHAM HALL.

GREAT SNORING RECTORY (Norfolk).
COUNTRY LIFE. XVIII, 457. 1905.
GARNER, T. Domestic architecture. I, p.53. 1911.
GARRATT, T. Halls of Norfolk. pl.42. 1890.

GREAT SURRIES (Surrey).
COUNTRY LIFE. CXXV, 164. 1959.

GREAT SWIFTS (Kent).
COUNTRY LIFE. LXXXVI, 524 plan. 1939.

GREAT TANGLEY MANOR (Surrey).
KENNARD, Edmund Hegan, *Colonel.*
— History of Great Tangley Manor. 50pp. 10 plates. 23x30 [London] privately printed. 1908.
Wanting plate 10, in place of which is a duplicate of plate 7.
BRAYLEY, E.W. History of Surrey. V, 148. 1841.

GREAT TEW PARK (Oxfordshire).
COUNTRY LIFE. CVI, 254. 1949.

GREAT WIGSELL (Sussex).
COUNTRY LIFE. XLIV, 32. 1918.

GREAT WITCHINGHAM HALL (Norfolk).
See WITCHINGHAM HALL.

GREAVES, The. (Derbyshire).
See HILLTOP, Beeley.

GREDINGTON (Flintshire).
ENGLAND: Picturesque Views. p.90. 1786-88.

GREENFIELD HALL (Flintshire).
HOARE: Views of Seats. pl.16. 1792.

GREENHAM BARTON (Somerset).
COUNTRY LIFE. LXXIV, 252. 1934.
DELDERFIELD, E.R. West Country houses. I, 71. 1968.

GREENHILL (Cheshire).
TWYCROSS, E. Mansions of England and Wales. Vol.II, p.103. 1850.

GREEN HILL (Lancashire).
BARTLETT, J. Mansions of England and Wales. pl.150. 1853.
TWYCROSS, E. Mansions of England and Wales. Vol.III, p.92. 1847.

GREENHILL HALL (Derbyshire).
TILLEY, J. Halls of Derbyshire. III, p.157. 1899.

GREENSTED HALL (Essex).
ENGLAND: Beauties of England. I, p.250. 1787.
ESSEX: A new and complete history. III, 379. 1770.

GREENTHWAITE HALL (Cumberland).
CUMBERLAND: C.& W.A. & A.S. Extra Series VIII, 304 Plan. 1892.

GREENWAY, The. Shurdington (Gloucestershire).
ATKYNS, R. Glocestershire. p.124. 1768.

GREGORIES (Buckinghamshire).
BURKE, J.B. Visitation of Seats. Vol.I, p.48. 1852.*
CAMPBELL, C. Vitruvius Britannicus. II, pl.47. 1717.
COPPER PLATE MAGAZINE. I, pl.34. 1792-1802.
ENGLAND: Picturesque Views. p.10. 1786-88.

GREGYNOG (Montgomeryshire).
HUGHES, Glyn Tegai.
— Gregynog. Edited by G.T.H., P. Morgan [and] J.G. Thomas. [Bibliogr.] viii, 146pp. Illus. incl. plates (1 col.) and maps. 24x17 Cardiff: University of Wales Press, 1977.
WELSHPOOL: Powysland Club.
— The Montgomeryshire Collections. [Cont.]
Reprints. [Cont.]
SUDELEY, M.C.S.H.T., *Lord.* Gregynog before the year 1900. 18pp. 25x18 Welshpool, 1973.
COUNTRY LIFE. XLVI, 668 [Carved parlour]. 1919.
NICHOLAS, T. Counties of Wales. II, p.804. 1872.

GRENDON HALL (Northamptonshire).
GOTCH, J.A. Squires' Homes. 38. 1939.

GRENDON HALL (Warwickshire).
[Sales] GRENDON HALL, 1932, November 22, 23 [Fixtures and fittings].

GRESFORD COTTAGE (Denbighshire).
COPPER PLATE MAGAZINE. I, pl.28. 1792-1802.

GRETA HALL (Cumberland).
BURKE, J.B. Visitation of Seats. Vol.I, p.12. 1852.*

GREVEL HOUSE, Chipping Campden (Gloucestershire).
GARNER, T. Domestic architecture. I, p.31. 1911.

GREYFRIARS, Worcester (Worcestershire).
COUNTRY LIFE. CXLVI, 1390. 1969.

GREYSBROOKE HALL (Staffordshire).
BURKE, J.B. Visitation of Seats. 2.S. Vol.I, p.157. 1854.*

GREYS COURT (Oxfordshire).
LONDON: National Trust for Places of Historic Interest or Natural Beauty.

— Greys Court, Henley-on-Thames. 10pp. Illus. (1 col. on cover) incl. 4 plates and plan. 22x14 (London) 1970.

New ed. 16pp. 1982.

COUNTRY LIFE. XCV, 1080, 1124. 1944.

GREYSTOKE CASTLE (Cumberland).
BURKE, J.B. Visitation of Seats. 2.S. Vol.I, p.142. 1854.*

HEARNE, T. Antiquities of Great Britain. I, pl.1. 1807.

GRIMSARGH HOUSE (Lancashire).
BARTLETT, J. Mansions of England and Wales. pl.91. 1853.

TWYCROSS, E. Mansions of England and Wales. Vol.II, p.52. 1847.

GRIMSHAW HALL (Warwickshire).
COUNTRY LIFE. LXXIV, 280. 1933.

GARNER, T. Domestic architecture. II, p.178 plan. 1911.

NIVEN, W. Old Warwickshire Houses. p.7, pl.9. 1878.

GRIMSTHORPE CASTLE (Lincolnshire).
BURKE, J.B. Visitation of Seats. Vol.II, p.57. 1853.*

CAMPBELL, C. Vitruvius Britannicus. III, pls. 11-14. 1725.

COUNTRY LIFE. English Country Houses: Baroque. p.191.1970.

COUNTRY LIFE. XIV, 272 1903.

COUNTRY LIFE. LV, 572, 614, 650 plan. 1924.

JONES. Views of Seats. I. 1829.

KIP, J. Nouveau théâtre de la Grande Bretagne. I, pls.21-23. 1715.

LATHAM, C. In English Homes. Vol.I, p.59. 1904.

LINCOLNSHIRE. A selection of views. 1805.

NEALE, J.P. Views of Seats. Vol.II. 1819.

NOBLE, T. Counties of Chester, ... Lincoln. p.47. 1836.

SUMMERSON, J. The Country Seat. 91. 1970.

TIPPING, H.A. English Homes. Period IV, Vol.II, p.295. 1928.

GRIMSTON GARTH (Yorkshire).
COUNTRY LIFE. CXII, 1186 plan. 1952.

GRIMSTON PARK (Yorkshire).
COUNTRY LIFE. English Country Houses: Late Georgian. p.230. 1958.

COUNTRY LIFE. LXXXVII, 276. 1940.

[Sales] GRIMSTON PARK, 1962, May 29-31 [Contents].

GRITTLETON HOUSE (Wiltshire).
COUNTRY LIFE. CXL, 708. 1966.

[Sales] LONDON, 1966, September 22 [Marbles].

GROBY MANOR (Leicestershire).
NICHOLS, J. History of Leicestershire. IV, ii, 632. 1811.

GROOMBRIDGE PLACE (Kent).
COUNTRY LIFE. English Country Houses: Caroline. p.123. 1966.

COUNTRY LIFE. II, 350. 1897.

COUNTRY LIFE. XIV, 400. 1903.

COUNTRY LIFE. CXVIII, 1376, 1480, 1524. 1955.

LATHAM, C. In English Homes. Vol.I, p.31. 1904.

NICOLSON, N. Great Houses of Britain. p.134. 1965.

OSWALD, A. Country Houses of Kent. 50. 1933.

GROTTON HALL (Yorkshire).
BURKE, J.B. Visitation of Seats. Vol.II, p.18. 1853.

GROVE, The. (Cheshire).
TWYCROSS, E. Mansions of England and Wales. Vol.II, p.128. 1850.

GROVE, The. (Gloucestershire).
BURKE, J.B. Visitation of Seats. 2.S. Vol.I, p.19. 1854.*

GROVE, The. (Hertfordshire).
BURKE, J.B. Visitation of Seats. 2.S. Vol.II, p.166. 1855.*

GROVE, The. Epsom (Surrey).
BRAYLEY, E.W. History of Surrey. IV, 369. 1841.

GROVE HALL (Nottinghamshire).
BURKE, J.B. Visitation of Seats. Vol.II, p.205. 1853.*

GROVE HILL (Kent).
GREENWOOD, C. Kent. 324. 1838.

GROVE HOUSE, Dent de Lion (Kent).
GREENWOOD, C. Kent. 330. 1838.

GROVE HOUSE, Chiswick (Middlesex).
ANGUS, W. Seats of the Nobility. pl.32. 1787.

GROVE HOUSE, Shelton (Staffordshire).
GROVE HOUSE.

— A critical and descriptive catalogue of a collection of pictures at Grove House, Shelton [the residence of Charles Meigh, Esq.]. 58pp. Engr. plate. 42x29 Hanley: privately printed, 1847.

GROVE HOUSE, Bradford (Yorkshire).
YORKSHIRE. Picturesque views. 1885.

GROVE HOUSE, Harrogate (Yorkshire).
[Sales] GROVE HOUSE, Harrogate, 1911, July 25-28
[Contents] (K.F. & R.).

GROVELANDS (Middlesex).
BURKE, J.B. Visitation of Seats. 2.S. Vol.I, p.73. 1854.*

GROVE PARK, Yoxford (Suffolk).
CROMWELL, T.K. Excursions in Suffolk. II, p.96. 1819.
SANDON, E. Suffolk houses. 243. 1977.

GROVE PLACE (Hampshire).
COUNTRY LIFE. XVI, 774. 1904.

GUBBINS (Hertfordshire).
NEALE, J.P. Views of Seats. Vol.II. 1819.

GUISBOROUGH HALL (Yorkshire).
KIP, J. Nouveau théâtre de la Grande Bretagne. I, pl.70. 1715.

GUMLEY HALL (Leicestershire).
ENGLAND: Picturesque Views. p.92. 1786-88.
NICHOLS, J. History of Leicestershire. II, ii, 589. 1798.
NICHOLS, J. History of Leicestershire. III, ii, pl. CLIV. 1127. 1804.
THROSBY, J. Views in Leicestershire. p.286. 1789.

GUNBY HALL (Lincolnshire).
LONDON: National Trust for Places of Historic Interest or Natural Beauty.
— LEES-MILNE, J. Gunby Hall. 12pp. 4 plates. 18x12 London: Country Life (1946).
New ed. Illus. (1 col. on cover) incl. plates. 21x14 [London] 1982.
MANUSCRIPTS (Typewritten). English.
— SMITH, H.C. An inventory of the principal contents of Gunby Hall, Spilsby, Lincolnshire, the property of ... Sir Archibald and Lady Montgomery-Massingberd. Prepared for the National Trust by H.C.S. 33x20 (Newbury) 1944. Photographs, press cuttings, letters and notes, etc., inserted.
COUNTRY LIFE. XCIV, 816, 860. 1943.

GUNLEY HALL (Montgomeryshire).
NICHOLAS, T. Counties of Wales. II, p.799. 1872.

GUNNERGATE HALL (Yorkshire).
SPROULE, A. Lost houses of Britain. 159. 1982.

GUNNERSBURY HOUSE (Middlesex).
ANGUS, W. Seats of the Nobility. pl.47. 1787.
BURKE, J.B. Visitation of Seats. 2.S. Vol.II, p.86. 1855.*
CAMPBELL, C. Vitruvius Britannincus. I, pls. 17, 18. 1715.
COUNTRY LIFE. CLXXII. 1480. 1982.
ENGLAND: Beauties of England. II, p.72. 1787.
ENGLAND: Picturesque Views. p.57. 1786-88.

GUNTON PARK (Norfolk).
CROMWELL, T.K. Excursions in Norfolk. I, p.123. 1818.
MORRIS, F.O. Views of Seats. Vol.IV, p.59. 1880.
NEALE, J.P. Views of seats. Vol.III. 1820.

GURREY (Carmarthenshire).
BURKE, J.B. Visitation of Seats. Vol.I, p.59. 1852.*

GUY'S CLIFFE (Warwickshire).
BURKE, J.B. Visitation of Seats. Vol.I, p.255. 1852.*
COUNTRY LIFE. I, 154. 1897.
JONES. Views of Seats. I. 1829.
MORRIS, F.O. Views of Seats. Vol.I, p.53. 1880.
NEALE, J.P. Views of Seats. Vol.IV. 1821.
SMITH, W. History of the County of Warwick. 45. 1830.

GWRYCH CASTLE (Denbighshire).
BURKE, J.B. Visitation of Seats. Vol.I, p.14. 1852.*
JONES. Views of Seats. V. 1830.
NEALE, J.P. Views of Seats. 2.S. Vol.II. 1825.

GWYDIR CASTLE (Caernarvonshire).
COUNTRY LIFE. XXIII, 942. 1908.
NICHOLAS, T. Counties of Wales. I, p.313. 1872.
TIPPING, H.A. English Homes. Early Renaissance, p.111. 1912.
[Sales] GWYDIR CASTLE, 1921, May 24, 25 [Contents].
[Sales] GWYDIR CASTLE, 1921, May 26 [Contents].

GWYNFE HOUSE (Carmarthenshire).
BURKE, J.B. Visitation of Seats. Vol.II, p.63. 1853.*

GWYSANEY (Flintshire).
BURKE, J.B. Visitation of Seats. Vol.II, p.234. 1853.*
COUNTRY LIFE. XCIII, 880 [missing] 924. 1943.

GYRN (Flintshire).
BURKE, J.B. Visitation of Seats. 2.S. Vol.II, p.6. 1855.*
NEALE, J.P. Views of Seats. 2.S. Vol.I. 1824.

HACKING HALL (Lancashire).
GRAY, H. Old Halls of Lancashire. p.75. 1893.

HACKNESS HALL (Yorkshire).
COUNTRY LIFE. XLIX, 338. 1921.
WOOD, G.B. Historic homes of Yorkshire. 112. 1957.

HACKTHORN HALL (Lincolnshire).
BURKE, J.B. Visitation of Seats. Vol.II, p.13. 1853.*

HACKTHORPE HALL (Westmorland).
CUMBERLAND: C.&W. A.& A.S. Extra Series, VIII, 96. 1892.

HACKWOOD PARK (Hampshire).
COPPER PLATE MAGAZINE. pl.45. 1778.
COUNTRY LIFE. XXXIII, 706 plan, 742. 1913.
HAMPSHIRE: Architectural views. 1830.
JONES. Views of Seats. II. 1829.
NEALE, J.P. Views of Seats. Vol.II. 1819.
SANDBY, P. Select Views I, pl.19. 1783.
TIPPING, H.A. English Homes. Period IV, Vol.I, p.229, 1920.

HADDON HALL (Derbyshire).
BAKEWELL.
— Bakewell, Derbyshire: the official guide, with sections on Haddon Hall, and Chatsworth House. 40pp. Illus. 18x12 Cheltenham: Burrow [c.1930].
CHEETHAM, Frank Halliday.
— Haddon Hall: an illustrated account of the fabric and its history. Plates incl. 2 folding plans. 19x12 London; Manchester: Sherratt & Hughes, 1904.
COOKE, William Edward.
— Haddon Hall, illustrated by W.E.C. 2ff. Illus: Lithogr. plates and title-page. 36x27 London: G. Philip and Son; Liverpool: Philip, Son & Nephew; Nottingham: Norton & Co., 1892.
GLOVER, Stephen.
— The Peak guide, containing the topographical, statistical, and general history of ... Haddon ... with an introduction ... By S.G., edited by T. Noble. xi, 132pp. Illus. incl. plates (some engr., some folding), plans, map and genealog. tables. 22x14 Derby: by the editor? 1830.
HADDON HALL.
— The History and antiquities of Haddon Hall: illustrated by lithographs from drawings by G. Cattermole, with an account of the Hall in its present state. 14pp. 20 lithogr. plates and tinted title-page. 30x24 London: Bemrose & Lothian; Derby and Matlock-Bath: Bemrose & Sons, 1867.
HADDON HALL.
— Selections from the stewards' accounts preserved at Haddon, from 1549 to 1671, by W.A. Carrington. 56pp. 22x14 Derby (Printed) [c.1900].
HADDON HALL.
— Haddon Hall: an illustrated survey [etc.]. 32pp. Illus. (some col., some on covers) incl. maps (on inside covers). 14x22. Derby: E.L.P. [1957?].
HALL, Samual Carter.
— Haddon Hall: an illustrated guide and companion to the tourist and visitor. With notices of Buxton, Bakewell, Rowsley,

Matlock, Bath and other places in the neighbourhood. By S.C.H. and L. Jewitt. 72pp. Engr. Illus. 21x16 Buxton: Bates, Advertiser Office, 1871.
MANNERS, *Lady* Victoria Alexandra Elizabeth Dorothy.
— Descriptive notes on the tapestry in Haddon Hall. 40pp. Facsimilies of marks. 17x10 London: Bemrose & Sons [1899].
MANTELL, Keith H.
— Haddon Hall, the Derbyshire home of the Manners family. 32pp. Illus. (some col., some on covers) incl. plan. 19x16 (Derby: E.L.P., 1964.)
RAYNER, Simeon.
— The history and antiquities of Haddon Hall; illustrated by ... drawings; with an account of the hall in its present state. 68pp. 32 lithogr. plates (some tinted, 1 folding) and plan. 32x23 Derby: R. Moseley; London: Weale; Moon; Hodgson & Boys; Colnaghi, 1836.
SMITH, G. Le Blanc.
— Haddon: the Manor, the Hall, its lords and traditions. Illus.(1 on title-page) incl. plates, plan and genealog. table. 24x16 London: Elliot Stock, 1906.
BURKE, J.B. Visitation of Seats. 2.S. Vol.I, p.50. 1854.*
COUNTRY LIFE. IX, 693. 1901.
COUNTRY LIFE. CVI, 1651, 1742 plan, 1814, 1884. 1949.
ENGLAND: Beauties of England. I, p.155. 1787.
GARNER, T. Domestic architecture.II, p.133 plan. 1911.
GOTCH, J.A. Architecture of the Renaissance.I, p.4. 1894.
HALL, S.C. Baronial Halls. Vol.I. 1848.
JEWITT, L. Stately homes of England. 221.1874.
LATHAM, C. In English Homes. Vol.I, p.37. 1904.
MOSS, F. Pilgrimages. [III] 109. 1906.
NASH, J. Mansions of England. I, pls.21-25. 1839.
NICOLSON, N. Great Houses of Britain. p.24. 1965.
NOBLE, T. Counties of Chester, ... Lincoln. p.16. 1836.
SHAW H. Elizabethan architecture. pls. XXI, XXII [Door and screen in long gallery]. 1839.
TILLEY, J. Halls of Derbyshire.I, p.5. 1892.

HADHAM HALL (Hertfordshire).
MINET, William.
— Hadham Hall and the manor of Bawdes alias Hadham Parva, in the county of Hertfordshire. [Bibliogr. notes.] Plates (some folding) incl. plans and maps. 25x18 (Colchester: Wiles & Son, 1914).

HADLEIGH (Suffolk).
TIPPING, H.A. English Homes. Period I & II, Vol.II, p.343. 1937.

HADLOW CASTLE (Kent).
BURKE, J.B. Visitation of Seats. Vol.I, p.190. 1852.*
GREENWOOD, C. Kent. 129. 1838.

HAFOD (Cardiganshire).
CUMBERLAND, George.
— An attempt to describe Hafod ... in the county of Cardiganshire, an ancient seat belonging to Thomas Johnes

[etc.]. 60pp. Folding engr. map. 16mo. 18x11 London: by W. Wilson, 1796.

INGLIS-JONES, Elisabeth.
— Peacocks in paradise: the story of a house, its owners and the Elysium they established there, in the mountains of Wales in the 18th century. [Bibliogr.] 256pp. illus. (1 on title-page) incl. 15 (1 col.) plates. 22x14 London: Faber, 1950.

SMITH, *Sir.* James Edward., *Bart*
— A tour to Hafod, in Cardiganshire, the seat of Thomas Johnes, Esq. M.P. &c. 32pp. 15 engr. col. plates by J.C. Stadler after J. Smith. Fol. 65x47 London: White & Co., 1810.

COUNTRY LIFE. CXXIII, 252. 1958.

JONES. Views of Seats. VI. 1831.

HAGG, The. (Derbyshire).
TILLEY, J. Halls of Derbyshire. III, p..197. 1899.

HAGLEY HALL (Staffordshire).
JONES, Views of Seats. I. 1829.

NEALE, J.P. Views of Seats. Vol. IV.1821.

SHAW, S. Staffordshire. II, pl.1. Reprint 1976.

HAGLEY HALL (Worcestershire).
HAGLEY HALL.
— A description of Hagley Park. By the author of letters on the beauties of Hagley, Envil and the Leasowes [i.e. J. Heely]. 16x10 London: by the author, 1777.

HAGLEY HALL.
— Catalogue of the pictures, statues and busts, in the best apartments in Hagley Hall [Worcestershire, the seat of George Fulke, Lord Lyttelton]. 30pp. 24x17 Stourbridge: privately printed, 1811.

HAGLEY HALL.
   Hagley Hall, near Stourbridge, Worcestershire ... The Worcestershire home of Viscount Cobham. Official guide. 12pp. Illus. (some on covers) incl. 4 plates and map. 14x20 [Derby: E.L.P., 1959.]

LEASOWES.
— A companion to the Leasowes, Hagley, and Enville; with a sketch of Fisherwick, the seat of the ... Earl Donegall. To which is prefixed, the present state of Birmingham.iv, 250pp.2 pts. in 1 vol. 8vo. 17x10 London: G.G.J. & J. Robinson; Birmingham: M. Swinney; Worcester: J. Holl, 1789.

BURKE, J.B. Visitation of Seats. Vol.I, p.174. 1852.*

CAMPBELL, C. Vitruvius Britannicus. V. pls. 14, 15. 1771.

COUNTRY LIFE. English Country Houses: Early Georgian. p.195. 1955.

COUNTRY LIFE. XXXVIII, 520 plan. 1915.

COUNTRY LIFE. LIX, 27, 83 [Furnishings]. 1926.

COUNTRY LIFE. CXXII, 546, 608. 1957.

ENGLAND: Beauties of England. II, p.377. 1787.

ENGLISH CONNOISSEUR. I, 62. 1766.*

JONES. Views of Seats. I. 1829.

NASH, T.R. Worcestershire.I, 490. 1781.

NEALE, J.P. Views of Seats. Vol.V. 1822.

TIPPING, H.A. English Homes. Period V, Vol.I, p.323. 1921.

HAIGH HALL (Lancashire).
BARTLETT, J. Mansions of England and Wales. pl.99. 1853.*

BURKE, J.B. Visitation of Seats. Vol.II, p.8. 1853.*

KIP, J. Nouveau théâtre de la Grande Bretagne. I, pl.55. 1715.

PYNE, W.H. Lancashire illustrated. 99. 1832.

TWYCROSS, E. Mansions of England and Wales. Vol.III, p.14. 1847.

HAIGHTON HOUSE (Lancashire).
BARTLETT, J. Mansions of England and Wales. pl.89.1853.

TWYCROSS, E. Mansions of England and Wales. Vol.II, p.51. 1847.

HAILES ABBEY (Gloucestershire).
ATKYNS, R. Glocestershire. p.247. 1768.

BUCK, S. & N.Antiquities. I, pl.100. 1774.

HAINES HILL (Berkshire).
BURKE, J.B. Visitation of Seats. Vol.I, p.108. 1852.*

HALDON HOUSE (Devonshire).
BRITTON, J. Devonshire illustrated. 100. 1832.

BURKE, J.B. Visitation of Seats. 2.S. Vol.II, p.172. 1855.*

HALE HALL (Cumberland).
BURKE, J.B. Visitation of Seats. Vol.I, p.102. 1852.*

HALE HALL (Lancashire).
BARTLETT, J. Mansions of England and Wales. pl.103.1853.

BURKE, J.B. Visitation of Seats. Vol.I, p.162. 1852.*

JONES. Views of Seats. I. 1829.

NEALE, J.P. Views of Seats. 2.S. Vol.I. 1824.

PYNE, W.H. Lancashire illustrated. 40. 1831.

TWYCROSS, E. Mansions of England and Wales. Vol.III, p.29. 1847.

HALE MANOR HOUSE (Lancashire).
COUNTRY LIFE. CXXVII, 1496. 1960.

HALES HALL (Staffordshire).
BURKE, J.B. Visitation of Seats. Vol.II, p.179. 1853.*

HALING HOUSE (Surrey).
BURKE, J.B. Visitation of Seats. Vol.II, p.19. 1853.*

HALL (Devonshire).
BURKE, J.B. Visitation of Seats. Vol.II, p.120. 1853.*

DELDERFIELD, E.R. West Country houses. I, 75. 1968.

HALL, The. Bradford-on-Avon (Wiltshire).
COUNTRY LIFE. V, 304. 1899.
COUNTRY LIFE. CXXXII, 840, 900 plan, 1020. 1962.

HALL, The. Much Hadham (Hertfordshire).
COUNTRY LIFE. CXIX, 674.1956.

HALLATON HALL (Leicestershire).
NICHOLS, J. History of Leicestershire. II, ii, 600. 1798.

HALL BARN (Buckinghamshire).
BURKE, J.B. Visitation of Seats. Vol.II, p.37. 1853.*
COUNTRY LIFE. XCI, 564, 662. 1942.

HALL GARTH, Goodmanham (Yorkshire).
COUNTRY LIFE. CXXIX, 392, 446. 1961.

HALLINGBURY PLACE (Essex).
COUNTRY LIFE. XXXVI, 390 plan. 1914.
CROMWELL, T.K. Excursions in Essex. II, p.85. 1825.
NEALE, J.P. Views of Seats. Vol.I. 1818.
RUSH, J.A. Seats in Essex. p.95. 1897.

HALL I' TH' WOOD, Bolton (Lancashire).
BOLTON: Museums [Hall-i-th'-Wood].
— Guide book and catalogue of exhibits at the Hall-i'th'-Wood Museum (Biographical notes on S. Crompton included).
54pp. Illus. 18x12 Bolton, 1902.
2 ed. 56pp. 1903.
Bound together.
BOLTON: Museums [Hall-i'-th'-Wood].
— Hall i' the' Wood, Bolton: its history and arrangement as a folk museum. 32pp. Illus. incl. plan. 22x14 Bolton, 1927.
Another ed. Illus. incl. plan. 1950.
12 postcards (in envelope).
MANCHESTER: School of Architecture.
— Portfolio of measured drawings. pts. 41x34 Manchester, 1912-1. The Hall i' th' Wood, Bolton, Lancashire, with a descriptive notice. 4pp. 4 lithogr. plates, incl. elevations and plan. Manchester: School of Art, 1912.
COUNTRY LIFE. XXI, 774. 1907.
GOTCH, J.A. Architecture of the Renaissance. I, p.5. 1894.
HALL, S.C. Baronial Halls. Vol.I. 1848.
MOSS, F. Pilgrimages. IV, 1. 1908.
PYNE, W.H. Lancashire illustrated. 86. 1831.
TIPPING, H.A. English Homes. Early Renaissance. p.191. 1912.

HALLOWES, The. (Derbyshire).
TILLEY, J. Halls of Derbyshire. III, p.113. 1899.

HALLOW PARK (Worcestershire).
NASH, T.R. Worcestershire. I, 472. 1781.

HALL PLACE (Berkshire).
COUNTRY LIFE. English Country Houses: Early Georgian. p.114. 1955.
COUNTRY LIFE. LXXXIII, 246,272. 1938.

HALL PLACE (Hampshire).
COUNTRY LIFE. XCV, 860, 904. 1944.

HALL PLACE (Kent).
BURKE, J.B. Visitation of Seats. 2.S. Vol.I, p.231. 1854.*
BURKE, J.B. Visitation of Seats. 2.S. Vol.II, p.196. 1855.
COUNTRY LIFE. LI, 80. 1922.
OSWALD, A. Country houses of Kent. 18. 1933.

HALNABY HALL (Yorkshire).
GREAT BRITAIN AND IRELAND: Historical Manuscripts Commission.
— (Sir William Chambers, 1726-96 ... Papers from Halnaby Hall, York [now in] ... the Royal Academy [of Arts] ... Introduction [by] ... B.C. Weeden.) [Bibliogr. note.] 24ff. 33x20 [London]. 1971.
COUNTRY LIFE. LXXIII, 334 plan, 362. 1933.

HALNAKER MANOR (Sussex).
ELWES, D.G.C. Mansions of Western Sussex. 43. 1876.
GARNER, T. Domestic architecture. I, p.86. 1911.

HALSDON HOUSE (Devonshire).
BURKE, J.B. Visitation of Seats. Vol.I, p.82. 1852.*

HALSNEAD PARK (Lancashire).
BURKE, J.B. Visitation of Seats. 2.S. Vol.I, p.210. 1854.*
TWYCROSS, E. Mansions of England and Wales. Vol.III, p.44. 1847.

HALSTEAD (Essex).
CROMWELL, T.K. Excursions in Essex. II, p.175. 1825.

HALSTON HALL (Shropshire).
ENGLAND: Picturesque Views. p.76. 1786-88.
LEACH, F. Seats of Shropshire. p.386. 1891.
LEIGHTON, S. Shropshire houses. 26. 1901.

HALSWELL PARK (Somerset).
BURKE, J.B. Visitation of Seats. 2.S. Vol.I, p.110. 1854.*
COLLINSON, J. History of Somerset. I, 80. 1791.
COUNTRY LIFE. XXIV, 702. 1908.
LATHAM, C. In English Homes. Vol.III, p.259. 1909.
NEALE, J.P. Views of Seats. 2.S.Vol.V. 1829.
WATTS, W. Seats of the Nobility. pl.15. 1779.

HALTON (Buckinghamshire).
COUNTRY LIFE. I, 664. 1897.

HAMBLETON OLD HALL (Rutland).
See OLD HALL, Hambleton.

HAM COURT (Worcestershire).
NASH, T.R. Worcestershire. II, 444. 1782.

HAMELS PARK (Hertfordshire).
CHAUNCY, H. Hertfordshire. I. 443. 1826.

SOANE, J. Plans, elevations and sections. pl. XLIV [Dairy] 1788.

[Sales] HAMELS PARK, 1917, May 29-31, June 1 [Contents]. (K., F. & R.)

HAM HOUSE (Surrey).
LAUDERDALE, Henry Maitland, *Duke of.*
— A true inventory of His Grace the Duke of Lauderdale's goods in Ham House, taken the 4th of August 1679. (An inventory of the household goods of the ...Countess of Dysart ... Feb. 2, 1727/8.) [With accounts for painting, plastering and joinery done for William Murray at Ham House, 1637-39. Transcribed and annotated by J.P. Fuller. Photocopy of Typescript.] 5 pts. in 1 vol. 32x22 [London, 1949.]

RICHMOND, Surrey: Ham House.
— An inventory of the furniture, plate, linen, china, pictures, prints ... at Ham House ... made ... [by] J. Dawson. [Photocopy] 68ff. 40x25 Kingston upon Thames, 1844.

RICHMOND, Surrey: Ham House.
— A catalogue and valuation of the furniture, plate, books, pictures and engravings at Ham House ... Compiled by W.C. Joel ... [Photocopy of typescript.] 164ff. 33x20 Richmond, Surrey, 1911.

RICHMOND, Surrey: Ham House.
— EDWARDS, R. and WARD-JACKSON, P. Ham House: a guide. [Bibliogr.] 42pp. Illus. (1 on cover) incl. plate, elevation, plans and facsimile. 21x14 London: H.M.S.O., 1950.
2 ed. 62pp. 1951.
4 ed. 1959.
3 [7] ed.(Revision ... by M. Tomlin.) [Bibliogr.] 80pp. Illus. (3 col., 2 on cover) incl. elevation, plans, map and facsimile. 14x21 1973.

ROUNDELL, Julia Anne Elizabeth.
— Ham House: its history and art treasures, with chapters on the library by W.Y. Fletcher, & the miniature room by G.C. Williamson. [Bibliogr. notes.] Illus. (on title-pages) and plates. 2 vols. 38x28 London: G. Bell & Sons, 1904.

TOLLEMACHE, Edward Devereux Hamilton, *Major-General.*
— The Tollemaches of Helmingham and Ham. [Bibliogr.] Plates and genealog. tables. 25x18 Ipswich: Cowell, 1949.

TOMLIN, Maurice.
— From love-seats to firescreens: 18th century furnishings at Ham House. Excerpt (photocopy), 3ff. 7 illus. 30x22 [London] 1977.

Also in: COUNTRY LIFE. CLXII, p.1418. 1977.

MANUSCRIPTS. (Typewritten).   English.
— SMITH, H.C. The National Trust. Report on Ham House, Petersham, Surrey, with appendix. 17ff. 27x24 (Kensington) 1946.
With letters to H.C.S., inserted.

BURKE, J.B. Visitation of Seats. 2.S. Vol.I, p.223. 1854.*

CAMPBELL, C. Vitruvius Britannicus. IVth. pls. 65, 66. 1739.

COUNTRY LIFE. English Country Houses: Caroline. p.65. 1966.

COUNTRY LIFE. XLVII, 372, 404 plan, 440. 1920.

COUNTRY LIFE. XLVII, 410 [Furniture], 447 [Chimney Furniture]. 1920.

COUNTRY LIFE. LVIII, 998. 1925.

COUNTRY LIFE. LXVIII, 754 [Furniture].1 1930.

COUNTRY LIFE. CIII, 226. 1948.

COUNTRY LIFE. CLXIII, 206 [Model of Queen's Bedroom]. 1978.

COUNTRY LIFE. CLXIX, 250, 322. 1981.

HALL, S.C. Baronial Halls. Vol.II. 1848.

NEALE, J.P. Views of Seats. Vol.IV. 1821.

TIPPING, H.A. English Homes. Period IV, Vol.I, p.111. 1920.

WHITEMAN, G.W. English Country Homes. p.52. 1951.

[Sales] LONDON, 1938, May 30, 31 [Library. pt. I.].

[Sales] LONDON, 1938, June 20, 21 [Library. pt. II.].

[Sales] LONDON, 1955, May 12, [Antique silver from H.H.].

HAMMERSHEAD HILL VILLA (Lancashire).
BARTLETT, J.Mansions of England and Wales. pl.77. 1853.

TWYCROSS, E. Mansions of England and Wales. Vol.II, p.32. 1847.

HAMMOON MANOR (Dorsetshire).
OSWALD, A. Country Houses of Dorset. p.78. 1959.

HAMPDEN HOUSE (Buckinghamshire).
LIBERTY, *Sir* Arthur Lasenby.
— John Hampden the patriot, Hampden House and church. 16pp. 7 illus. 25x19 n.p. 1898.

BURKE, J.B. Visitation of Seats. Vol.I, p.184. 1852.*

THOMPSON, S. Old English Homes. 136. 1876.

[Sales] HAMPDEN HOUSE, 1939, April 17-22 [Furniture etc.].

HAMPTON, Minchinhampton (Gloucestershire).
ATKYNS, R. Glocestershire. p.237. 1768.

HAMPTON COURT (Herefordshire).
BURKE, J.B. Visitation of Seats. Vol.II, p.250. 1853.*
CAMPBELL, C. Vitruvius Britannicus. II, pls. 57, 58. 1717.
CAMPBELL, C. Vitruvius Britannicus. III, pl.75. 1725.
COPPER PLATE MAGAZINE. III, pl.135. 1792-1802.
COUNTRY LIFE. XXX, 750 [Furniture], 787 [Furniture], 902 [Furniture]. 1911.
COUNTRY LIFE. CLIII, 450, 518, 582. 1973.
JONES. Views of Seats. II. 1829.
KIP, J. Nouveau théâtre de la Grande Bretagne. I, pl.50. 1715.
MORRIS, F.O. Views of Seats. Vol.II, p.9. 1880.
NEALE, J.P. Views of Seats. 2.S. Vol.III. 1826.
ROBINSON, C.J. Mansions of Herefordshire. pls.1, 11. 1873.
[Exhibition] LONDON: Sabin Galleries. Feb 27-March 21. 1973.
[Sales] HAMPTON COURT, 1925, March 16 and following days [Contents]. (K.F.&R.).

HAMPTON COURT HOUSE (Middlesex).
COUNTRY LIFE. CLXXII. 392. 1982.

HAMPTON HOUSE (Middlesex).
See GARRICK'S VILLA.

HAMPTONS (Kent).
BURKE, J.B. Visitation of Seats. 2.S. Vol.II, p.93. 1855.*
GREENWOOD, C. Kent. 140. 1838.

HAMPTWORTH LODGE (Wiltshire).
MOFFATT, H.C.
— Illustrated description of some of the furniture at Goodrich Court, Herefordshire and Hamptworth Lodge, Wiltshire. 96pp. Plates. 33x25 Oxford: privately printed for the author, 1928.

HAMS HALL (Warwickshire).
BURKE, J.B. Visitation of Seats. Vol.II, p.67, 1853.*
NEALE, J.P. Views of Seats. Vol.IV. 1821.

HAMSTALL RIDWARE MANOR (Staffordshire).
NIVEN, W. Old Staffordshire houses. p.19, pl.15. 1882.
SHAW, S. Staffordshire. I, 157. 1798.

HAMSTEAD (Staffordshire).
SHAW, S. Staffordshire. II, 112. 1801.

HAMSTEAD MARSHALL (Berkshire).
COUNTRY LIFE. English Country Houses: Caroline. p.137. 1966.
COUNTRY LIFE. XXXIII, 454. 1913.
KIP, J. Nouveau théâtre de la Grande Bretagne. I, pl.45. 1715.

HAMSTERLEY HALL (Durham).
COUNTRY LIFE. LXXXVI, 418. 1939.

HAMSTONE HOUSE, Weybridge. (Surrey).
COUNTRY LIFE. LXXXVI, 284 plan. 1939.

HANBURY HALL (Worcestershire).
LONDON: National Trust for Places of Historic Interest or Natural Beauty.
— GIBBON, M. Hanbury Hall, Worcestershire. 14pp. 4 plates. 18x12 London: Country Life, 1967.
Another copy.
Rev. ed. [Bibliogr.] 44pp. Illus. (1 on cover) incl. plan and genealog. table. 21x14 [London] 1981.
BURKE, J.B. Visitation of Seats. Vol.II. p.210. 1853.*
COUNTRY LIFE. English Country Houses: Baroque. p.124. 1970.
COUNTRY LIFE. XXXIX, 502. 1916.
COUNTRY LIFE. CXLIII, 18, 66. 1968.
MORRIS, F.O. Views of Seats. Vol.V, p.65. 1880.
NASH, T.R. Worcestershire. I, 548. 1781.
TIPPING, H.A. English Homes. Period IV, Vol.I, p.397. 1920.

HANCH HALL (Staffordshire).
BURKE, J.B. Visitation of Seats. Vol.II, p.151. 1853.*

HANDFORTH HALL (Cheshire).
ANGUS-BUTTERWORTH, L.M. Old Cheshire families. p.16. 1932
MOSS, F. Pilgrimages. [III] 315. 1906.

HANDSACRE HALL (Staffordshire).
SHAW, S. Staffordshire. I, 207. 1798.

HANFORD HOUSE (Dorsetshire).
COUNTRY LIFE. XVII, 558. 1905.
GOTCH, J.A. Architecture of the Renaissance. II, p.3. 1894.
HUTCHINS, J. History of Dorset. IV, 62. 1870.
LATHAM, C. In English Homes. Vol.II, p.163. 1909.
OSWALD, A. Country Houses of Dorset. p.94. 1959.

HANHAM HALL (Gloucestershire).
BURKE, J.B. Visitation of Seats. 2.S. Vol.II, p.76. 1855.*

HANKELOW HALL (Cheshire).
TWYCROSS, E. Mansions of England and Wales. Vol.II, p.19. 1850.*

HANMER HALL (Flintshire).
ENGLAND: Picturesque Views. p.70. 1786-88.

HANWELL PARK (Middlesex).
BURKE, J.B. Visitation of Seats. 2.S. Vol.I, p.86. 1854.

HANWORTH HALL (Norfolk).
CROMWELL, T.K. Excursions in Norfolk. I, p.126. 1818.

HANWORTH PARK (Middlesex).
[Sales] HANWORTH PARK, 1873, June 3-6 [Library].

HARDEN GRANGE (Yorkshire).
YORKSHIRE. Picturesque views. 1885.

HARDEN HALL (Cheshire).
ORMEROD, G. Cheshire. III, 822. 1882.

HARDENHUISH (Wiltshire).
BURKE, J.B. Visitation of Seats. 2.S. Vol.II, p.4. 1855.*

HARDWICK (Shropshire).
See HARDWICK HALL.

HARDWICKE COURT (Gloucestershire).
ATKYNS, R. Glocestershire. p.238. 1768.

HARDWICKE GRANGE (Shropshire).
JONES. Views of Seats. I. 1829.

LEIGHTON, S. Shropshire Houses. 14. 1901.

NEALE, J.P. Views of Seats. 2.S. Vol.III. 1826.

HARDWICK HALL (Derbyshire).
CHESTERFIELD.
— The history of Chesterfield; with particulars of the hamlets contiguous to the town, and descriptive accounts of Chatsworth, Hardwick, and Bolsover Castle. [By Rev. G. Hall, enlarged and edited by T. Ford. Bibliogr. notes.] Illus. incl. plates (Many engr., most by W. Radclyffe after C. Radclyffe), and tables. 22x14 London: Whittaker & Co.; Chesterfield: Ford, 1839.
FURNITURE HISTORY SOCIETY.
— BOYNTON, L. The Hardwick Hall inventories of 1601. Edited by L.B. With an introduction by L.B. and a short commentary by P. Thornton. [Bibliogr. notes.] 40pp. Illus. incl. plates and plan. 24x19 1971.
HARDWICK HALL.
— Hardwick Hall, Co. of Derby . . . One of the residences of . . . His Grace the Duke of Devonshire, K.G. [By the Rev. F. Brodhurst; guide, and catalogue of portraits.] Plates incl. 2 folding genealog. tables. 22x14 Nottingham: Privately printed, 1903.
HARDWICK HALL.
— Hardwick Hall: an illustrated survey of one of the historic Derbyshire homes of the Earls and Dukes of Devonshire. 32pp. Illus. (1 col., some on covers) incl. map. 14x21 Derby: Come to Derbyshire Association [c. 1945].
Another ed. [c. 1950].

LIVERPOOL, Cecil George Savile Foljambe, *Earl of.*
— Catalogue of the pictures at Hardwick Hall; in the possession of . . . the Duke of Devonshire . . . To which is appended a short account of the heraldry in the various rooms and on the tapestry at Hardwick. 56pp. Plates. 21x14 n.p. privately printed, 1903.
With MS. notes by the Rev. E. Farrer.
Also in DERBY: Derbyshire Archaeological and Natural History Society, Journal, XXV, 103, 1903.
Bound in vol. lettered: Portraits by Lord Hawkesbury, 1905.

LONDON: National Trust for Places of Historic Interest or Natural Beauty.
— Hardwick Hall, Derbyshire: Biographical notes on the portraits at Hardwick Hall. 20pp. 22x14 [London, c. 1973].
LONDON: National Trust for Places of Historic Interest or Natural Beauty.
— Hardwick Hall, Derbyshire. [Bibliogr.] 64pp. Illus. (1 col. on cover) incl. plans and genealog. table. 22x14 [London] 1982.
ROBINSON: Peter Frederick.
— History of Hardwicke Hall. (Catalogue of the pictures . . . at Hardwicke.) [Bibliogr. notes.] 32pp. Engr. incl. plates (1 hand-col.), elevations, plan and genealog. tables. 53x35 London: For the author, 1835.
One of the series: VITRUVIUS BRITANNICUS.
STRONG, Sandford Arthur.
The masterpieces in the Duke of Devonshire's collection of pictures. 22pp. plates. 37x30 London: Hanfstaengl, 1901.
MANUSCRIPTS (Typewritten).   English.
— Hardwick Hall inventory made about 1600 for Elizabeth Talbot, Countess of Shrewsbury ('Bess of Hardwick'). 36ff. 20x18 [*c. 1950*].
Another ed. The inventorie of the plate and other furniture of household stuff . . . at Hardwick [etc.]. [Photocopy.] 54ff. (1 blank) 25x18 [*c. 1955*].
BURKE, J.B. Visitation of Seats. Vol.II, p.65. 1853.*
COUNTRY LIFE. II, 434, 464. 1897.
COUNTRY LIFE. XIII, 710. 1903.
COUNTRY LIFE. LVII, 229 [Furniture], 320 [Furniture], 422 [Wall Hangings]. 1925.
COUNTRY LIFE. LXI, 328 [Needlework], 499 [Tapestry], 661 [Furniture]. 1927.
COUNTRY LIFE. LXIV, 806 plan, 870, 904, 934. 1928.
COUNTRY LIFE. CXXII, 346. 1957.
COUNTRY LIFE. CLIV, 1786 [Embroideries]. 1973.
GOTCH, J.A. Architecture of the Renaissance. I, p.3. 1894.
HALL, S.C. Baronial Halls. Vol.I. 1848.
JEWITT, L. Stately Homes of England. 116. 1874.
LATHAM, C. In English Homes. Vol.I, p.43. 1904.
MALAN, A.H. Famous Homes. p.77. 1902.
MOSS, F. Pilgrimages. IV, 346. 1908.
NASH, J. Mansions of England. II, pls.10-13. 1840.
NICOLSON, N. Great Houses of Britain. p.82. 1965.
NOBLE, T. Counties of Chester . . . Lincoln. p.59. 1836.
SHAW, H. Elizabethan architecture. pl.XXVIII. [Chimney piece] 1839.

HARDWICK HALL (Shropshire).
COUNTRY LIFE. XLIII, 550. 1918.
LEACH, F. Seats of Shropshire. p. 359. 1891.
LEIGHTON, S. Shropshire houses. 27. 1901.

HARDWICK HOUSE (Oxfordshire).
COUNTRY LIFE. XX, 90. 1906.

HARDWICK HOUSE (Suffolk).
BURKE, J.B. Visitation of Seats. 2.S. Vol.II, p.88. 1855.*

HARDWICK MANOR (Northamptonshire).
GOTCH, J.A. Squires' Homes. 29. 1939.

HARDWICK OLD HALL (Derbyshire).
TILLEY, J. Halls of Derbyshire. III, p.11. 1899.

HAREFIELD PLACE (Middlesex).
BURKE, J.B. Visitation of Seats. 2.S. Vol.II, p.80. 1855.*

HARE HALL (Essex).
ANGUS, W. Seats of the Nobility. pl.28. 1787.
CROMWELL, T.K. Excursions in Essex. I, p.170. 1825.
NEALE, J.P. Views of Seats.Vol.I. 1818.
PAINE, J. Plans, elevations. Pt.II, pls. 60-63. plans. 1783.

HARE PARK (Cambridgeshire).
[Sales] HARE PARK, 1917, May 7, 8 [Contents].

HAREWOOD HOUSE (Cornwall).
BURKE, J.B. Visitation of Seats. 2.S. Vol.II, p.148. 1855.*

HAREWOOD HOUSE (Yorkshire).
BORENIUS, Tancred.
— Catalogue of the pictures and drawings at Harewood House and elsewhere in the collection of the Earl of Harewood. 73 (1 col.) plates. 30x24 Oxford: privately printed, 1936.
BUCKLE, Richard.
— Harewood: a guide-book to the Yorkshire seat of . . . the Princess Royal and the Earl of Harewood. [Bibliogr.] 28pp. Illus. (some col., some on covers, 1 on title-page) incl. genealog. table. 23x18 Derby: E.L.P. (1959).
HAREWOOD HOUSE.
— Harewood House: an illustrated survey [etc.]. 32pp. Illus. (some col. some on covers) incl. maps (on inside covers). 14x22 Derby: E.L.P. [1952]?.
MAUCHLINE, Mary.
— Harewood House. [Bibliogr.] Illus. incl. elevations, plans, maps, facsimiles and genealog. table. 22x14 Newton Abbot: David & Charles, 1974.
SMITH, Harold Clifford.
— The Harewood plate at the Regency Festival Exhibition at Brighton. Excerpt, 4pp. Illus. 30x25 [London, 1951.]

Also in: APOLLO, LIV, 41.
BOLTON, A.T. Architecture of R. & J. Adam. I, 157 plan. 1922.
BURKE, J.B. Visitation of Seats. 2.S. Vol.I, p.69. 1854.*
CAMPBELL, C. Vitruvius Britannicus. V, Pls.23-28. 1771.
COUNTRY LIFE. English Country Houses: Mid Georgian. p.61. 1956.
COUNTRY LIFE XXXVI, 18 plan. 1918.
COUNTRY LIFE. LI, 243 plan. 1922.
ENGLAND: Picturesque Views. p.83. 1786-88.
JONES. Views of Seats. I. 1829.
KROLL, A. Historic Houses. 156. 1969
MORRIS, F.O. Views of Seats. Vol.I, p.7. 1880.
NEALE, J.P. Views of Seats. Vol.V. 1822.
WATTS, W. Seats of the Nobility. pl.7. 1779.
WHEATER, W. Mansions of Yorkshire. p.92. 1888.

HARLAXTON MANOR (Lincolnshire).
BURKE, J.B. Visitation of Seats. Vol.II, p.92. 1853.*
COPPER PLATE MAGAZINE. V, pl.238. 1792-1802.
COUNTRY LIFE. English Country Houses: Late Georgian. p.239. 1958.
COUNTRY LIFE. CXXI, 704, 764. 1957.
LINCOLNSHIRE. A selection of views. 61. 1805.
MORRIS, F.O. Views of Seats. Vol.II, p.17. 1880.
RICHARDSON, C.J. Old English Mansions. III. 1845.
[Sales] HARLAXTON MANOR, 1937, June 28-30 [Contents] (Foster).

HARLESTONE HOUSE (Northamptonshire).
GOTCH, J.A. Squires' Homes. 36. 1939.
NEALE, J.P. Views of Seats. Vol.III. 1820.
REPTON, H. Fragments on Landscape gardening. p.21. 1816.

HARLEYFORD MANOR (Buckinghamshire).
ENGLAND: Picturesque Views. p.36. 1786-88.
THAMES, River. An history. I, pl.32. 1794.

HARLINGTON HOUSE (Bedfordshire).
BURKE, J.B. Visitation of Seats. 2.S. Vol.I, p.186. 1854.*

HARPTON COURT (Radnorshire).
BURKE, J.B. Visitation of Seats. Vol.II, p.189. 1853.*

HARPTREE COURT (Somerset).
COOKE, R. West Country Houses. p.153. 1957.

THE COUNTRY HOUSE DESCRIBED

HARRINGTON HALL (Lincolnshire).
COUNTRY LIFE. CLVI, 18. 1974.

HARROWDEN HALL (Northamptonshire).
COUNTY LIFE. XXIV, 910. 1908.
COUNTRY LIFE. CLVI, 1086, 1190. 1974.
GOTCH, J.A. Halls of Northants. p.61. 1936.

HARRY TOWN HALL (Cheshire).
BURKE, J.B. Visitation of Seats. Vol.I, p.266. 1852.*
TWYCROSS, E. Mansions of England and Wales. Vol.II,
p.118. 1850.

HARTFORD LODGE (Cheshire).
TWYCROSS, E. Mansions of England and Wales. Vol.I, p.149.
1850.

HARTHAM HOUSE (Wiltshire).
BURKE, J. B. Visitation of Seats. Vol.I, 61. 1852.*

HARTHAM PARK (Wiltshire).
BRITTON, J. Beauties of Wiltshire. III, 184. 1825.
ROBERTSON, A. Great Road. II, p.68. 1792.

HARTHILL HALL (Derbyshire).
TILLEY, J. Halls of Derbyshire. I, p.17.1892.

HARTINGTON HALL (Derbyshire).
BURKE, J.B. Visitation of Seats. Vol.I, p.241. 1852.*
TILLEY, J. Halls of Derbyshire. II, p.237. 1893.

HARTLAND ABBEY (Devonshire).
BURKE, J.B. Visitation of Seats. 2.S. Vol.II, p.111. 1855.*

HARTLEBURY CASTLE (Worcestershire).
PEARCE, Ernest Harold, *Bishop of Worcester*.
— Hartlebury Castle. With some notes on Bishops who lived in
it and on others who lived elsewhere. 3 plates, and plan. 23x13
London: S.P.C.K., 1926.
BUCK, S. & N. Antiquities. II, pl. 318. 1774.
COUNTRY LIFE. LXIX, 156. 1931.
COUNTRY LIFE. CL, 672, 740. 1971.
ENGLAND: Beauties of England. II, p.381. 1787.

HARTLE HALL (Derbyshire).
See HARTHILL HALL

HARTSOP HALL (Westmorland).
CUMBERLAND: C. & W.A. & A.S. Extra Series, VIII, 74.
1892.

HARTWELL HOUSE (Buckinghamshire).
HARTWELL HOUSE.
— Catalogue of the Egyptian antiquities in the museum of
Hartwell House. [Arranged by J. Bonomi, edited by J. Lee.]
96pp. Illus. incl. plates (some folding) and title-page. 27x22
[London] privately printed, 1858.
SMYTH, William Henry, *Admiral*.
— Aedes Hartwellianae; or, notices of the manor and mansion
of Hartwell. Illus. (1 on title-page) incl. plates, plans, maps,
diagr. and tables. 30x23 London: privately printed, 1851.
Addenda to the Aedes Hartwellianae. [Bibliogr. of author's
works.] Illus. (1 col., 1 on title-page) incl. plates and maps.
London: privately printed, 1864.
Letters from the author and newspaper cutting inserted.
BURKE, J.B. Visitation of Seats. Vol.I, p.12. 1852.*
BURKE, J.B. Visitation of Seats. 2.S. Vol.II, p.116. 1855.
COPPER PLATE MAGAZINE. I, pl. 42. 1792-1802.
COUNTRY LIFE. English Country Houses: Early Georgian.
p.200. 1955.
COUNTRY LIFE. XXXV, 378, 414. 1914.
ENGLAND: Picturesque Views. p.44. 1786-88.
[Sales] HARTWELL HOUSE, 1938, April 26-28 [Contents].

HARVINGTON HALL (Worcestershire).
COUNTRY LIFE. XCVI, 200, 244 plan, 288. 1944.
COUNTRY LIFE. CXXI, 186. 1957.
NIVEN, W. Old Worcestershire Houses. p.6, pl.4. 1873.

HASELEY COURT (Oxfordshire).
COUNTRY LIFE. CXXVII, 268, 328. 1960.

HASELLS, The. (Bedfordshire).
BURKE, J.B. Visitation of Seats. Vol.I, p.67, 1852.*

HASELOUR HALL (Staffordshire).
NIVEN, W. Old Staffordshire Houses. p.20, pl.16. 1882.
SHAW, S. Staffordshire. I, 388. 1798.

HASSAGE (Somerset).
COUNTRY LIFE. LXVI, 737. 1929.

HASSOBURY (Essex).
RUSH, J.A. Seats in Essex. p.97, 1897.

HASSOP HALL (Derbyshire).
TILLEY, J. Halls of Derbyshire. I, p.54. 1892.

HATCH COURT (Somerset).

COLLINSON, J. History of Somerset. I, 44. 1791.

COUNTRY LIFE. CXXXVI, 1034, 1140 plan. 1964.

DELDERFIELD, E.R. West Country houses. II, 71. 1970.

NEALE, J.P. Views of Seats. 2.S. Vol.V. 1829.

HATCHFORD PARK (Surrey).

[Sales] HATCHFORD PARK, 1924, March 17 and following days [Contents].

HATCH HOUSE, Tisbury (Wiltshire).

COUNTRY LIFE. XLV, 522. 1919.

HATCHLANDS (Surrey).

LONDON: National Trust for Places of Historic Interest or Natural Beauty.

— GOODHART-RENDEL, H.S. Hatchlands. 18pp. 4 plates. 18x12 London: Country Life (1948).

New ed. Hatchlands, Surrey. [Bibliogr.] 16pp. Illus. (1 col. on cover) and plates. 22x14 [London] 1982.

BOLTON, A.T. Architecture of R. & J. Adam. I, 133 plan. 1922.

COUNTRY LIFE. English Country Houses: Mid Georgian. p.49. 1956.

COUNTRY LIFE. XXXIX, 176 plan. 1916.

COUNTRY LIFE. CXIV, 870 plan, 1042. 1953.

HATFIELD HALL (Yorkshire).

WATTS, W. Seats of the Nobility. pl.20. 1779.

HATFIELD HOUSE (Hertfordshire).

AUERBACH, Erna.

— Paintings and sculpture at Hatfield House: a catalogue compiled by E.A., and C.K. Adams. [Bibliogr. notes.] Illus. incl. col. plates. 29x21 London: Constable, 1971.

CECIL, Edward Christian David, *Lord*.

— Hatfield House: an illustrated survey of the Hertfordshire home of the Cecil family. 32pp. Illus. (some col., some on covers) incl. maps and genealog. table. 14x21 Derby: E.L.P. [c.1950].

GREAT BRITAIN AND IRELAND: Historical Manuscripts Commission.

— [Publications.]

— 9. Calendar of the manuscripts of the Most Honourable the Marquess of Salisbury preserved at Hatfield House, Hertfordshire. [Bibliogr. notes.] 1973.

— XIII. Addenda, 1562-1605. Edited by G.D. Owen. [Bibliogr. notes.] 1973.

— XXIV. Addenda, 1605-1668. Edited by G.D. Owen. [Bibliogr. notes.] 1976.

HATFIELD: Hatfield House.

— Booklet[s]. Illus. vols. 18x12 Hatfield [1952?].

— 1. YATES, F.A. Allegorical portraits of Queen Elizabeth I at Hatfield. 8pp. 1 illus. [1952?].

— 2. WHINNEY, M. Sculpture at Hatfield. 8pp. I illus. [1952?].

— 3. HARRISS, G. The mystery of Richard III. [Bibliogr.] 8pp. 1 illus. [1952?].

— Titles on covers.

HATFIELD HOUSE

— Hatfield House, Hertfordshire: guide to the house and some short historical notes. 20pp. Illus. incl. genealog. table. 22x14 Hatfield: Payne, 1948.

HOLLAND, Laurence Gifford.

— A descriptive & historical catalogue of the collection of pictures at Hatfield House and 20 Arlington Street. Illus. incl. plate and genealog. tables. 29x20 (Edinburgh) privately printed, 1891.

NEW YORK: Pierpont Morgan Library.

— SALISBURY, R.A.J. Gascoyne-Cecil, *Marquess of*. The Hatfield House library, a family collection of over four hundred years: an address . . . delivered . . . at the eighteenth annual meeting of the Fellows of the…Library. 24pp. 24x16 New York (Spiral Press), 1967.

ROBINSON, Peter Frederick.

— History of Hatfield House. (A list of family pictures . . . Catalogue of the pictures at Hatfield House, 1833, exclusive of family portraits.) [Bibliogr. notes.] 30pp. Engr. incl. plates and plans. 53x37 London: for the author . 1833.

One of the series: VITRUVIUS BRITANNICUS.

SALISBURY, Mary Catherine Gascoyne Cecil, *Marchioness of*.

— A catalogue of the paintings at Hatfield House: Revised by M.C., Marchioness of Salisbury. 19ff. Diagr. 29x24 London Privately printed, 1865.

With MS. notes by R. Redgrave, *R.A.*

BURKE, J.B. Visitation of Seats. Vol.I, p.224. 1852.*

COUNTRY LIFE. I, 491, 519. 1897.

COUNTRY LIFE. XI, 840. 1902.

COUNTRY LIFE. XII, 16. 1902.

COUNTRY LIFE. LXI, 426 plan, 462, 501 [Portraits], 524 plan. 1927.

ENGLAND: Beauties of England. I, p.349. 1787.

GOTCH, J.A. Architecture of the Renaissance. II, p.38 plan. 1894.

HALL, S.C. Baronial Halls. Vol. I. 1848.

JEWITT, L. Stately homes of England. 294. 1874.

KIP, J. Nouveau théâtre de la Grande Bretagne. I, pl.24.* 1715.

KROLL, A. Historic houses. 38. 1969.

LATHAM, C. In English Homes. Vol.I, p.109. 1904.

MORRIS, F.O. Views of Seats. Vol.II, p.7. 1880.

NASH, J.Mansions of England. I, pls. 1,2. 1839. and III, pls. 13, 14. 1841.

NEALE, J.P. Views of Seats. Vol.II. 1819.

NICOLSON, N. Great Houses of Britain. p.108. 1965.

SHAW, H. Elizabethan architecture. pls. XLI-XLVI. [Arcade, details etc.] 1839.

TIPPING, H.A. English Homes. Period III, Vol.II, p.305. 1927.

UNITED KINGDOM. Historic Houses. 45. 1892.

WATTS, W. Seats of the Nobility. pl. 53. 1779.

P. 349.

Hatfield House the Seat of the Earl of Salisbury.

HATFIELD HOUSE, Hertfordshire. From: ENGLAND. *A new display of the beauties of England* [etc.], vol. I, 1787.

HATFIELD OLD PALACE (Hertfordshire).
COUNTRY LIFE. LXI, 390 plan. 1927.

GARNER, T. Domestic architecture. I, p.39. 1911.

HATFIELD PRIORY (Essex).
CROMWELL, T.K. Excursions in Essex. II, p.87. 1825.

ESSEX: A new and complete history. IV, 119. 1771.

HATHEROP (Gloucestershire).
ATKYNS, R. Glocestershire. p.243. 1768.

HATHERTON LODGE (Cheshire).
BURKE, J.B. Visitation of Seats. Vol.I, p.229. 1852.

HATLEY PARK (Cambridgeshire).
KIP, J. Nouveau théâtre de la Grande Bretagne. I, pl. 58. 1715.

[Sales] HATLEY PARK, 1935, May 13-15 [Remaining contents]. (K.F. & R.).

HATTON GRANGE (Shropshire).
COUNTRY LIFE. CXLIII, 466. 1968.

LEACH, F. Seats of Shropshire. p.331. 1891.

LEIGHTON, S. Shropshire houses. 35. 1901.

HAUGHLEY PARK (Suffolk).
CLARKE, T.H. Domestic architecture. 17. 1833.

CROMWELL, T.K. Excursions on Suffolk. I, p.168. 1818.

DAVY, H. Seats in Suffolk. pl.2. 1827.

SANDON, E. Suffolk houses. 185. 1977.

HAUGHTON (Nottinghamshire).
KIP, J. Nouveau théâtre de la Grande Bretagne. I, pl.16. 1715.

HAUGHTON HALL (Cheshire).
CARTER, Robert Redcliffe.
— Pictures & engravings at Haughton Hall, Tarporley, in the possession of Ralph Brocklebank. With descriptive and biographical notes and an introduction by R.R.C. Illus. incl. plates. 39x26 London: G. Allen, 1904.

[Sales] LONDON, 1922, July 7 [Pictures & watercolours from H.H.].

HAUGHTON HALL (Shropshire).
BURKE, J.B. Visitation of Seats. Vol.I, p.141. 1852.*

HAUGHMOND (Shropshire).
SHROPSHIRE. Castles and Old Mansions. 34. 1868.

HAVERHOLME PRIORY (Lincolnshire).
LINCOLNSHIRE. A selection of views. 1805.

HAWARDEN CASTLE (Flintshire).
G., W.H.
   The Hawarden visitors' hand-book, revised edition. [By (W.H.G.) ladstone.] 36pp. Illus. incl. plates (1 folding) map and photographs. 18x12 Chester: by the author, 1885.

KEITH-LUCAS, Bryan.
   The Gladstone-Glynne collection. A catalogue of the oil paintings, water-colours, sculptures and minatures and a supplementary list of prints and drawings at Hawarden Castle. Compiled by B.K.L., under the direction of the Lord Gladstone of Hawarden. 80pp. Genealog. chart. 19x13 Hawarden: privately printed, 1934.
With MS. alterations and additions.

BURKE, J.B. Visitation of Seats. Vol.I, p.66. 1852.*

COUNTRY LIFE. CXLI, 1516, 1608, 1676. 1967.

JONES. Views of Seats. V. 1830.

MORRIS, F.O. Views of Seats. Vol.VI, p.65. 1880.

NEALE, J.P. Views of Seats. 2.S. Vol.V. 1829.

HAWLEIGH PARK (Suffolk).
See HAUGHLEY PARK.

HAWKSTONE HALL [PARK] (Shropshire).
BROWNE, P.
— Sketches in Hawkstone Park, the seat of the Rt. Hon. Viscount Hill. [No text.] 37 lithogr. plates. 55x39 [London, 1841?].
— Title on cover.

BURKE, J.B. Visitation of Seats. Vol.II, p.74. 1853.*

COPPER PLATE MAGAZINE. IV, pl.191. 1792-1802.

COUNTRY LIFE. CXXIII, 640, 698. 1958.

LEACH, F. Seats of Shropshire. p.7. 1891.

MORRIS, F.O. Views of Seats. Vol.VI, p.61. 1880.

NEALE, J.P. Views of Seats. 2.S. Vol.III. 1826.

HAWKSWORTH HALL (Yorkshire).
JONES. Views of Seats. I. 1829.

NEALE, J.P. Views of Seats. Vol.V. 1822.

HAWLEY HOUSE (Kent).
GREENWOOD, C. Kent. 71. 1838.

HAWNES (Bedfordshire).
COUNTRY LIFE. LXXVI, 692. 1934.

HAY CASTLE (Brecknockshire).
COUNTRY LIFE. XXXVI, 422 plan. 1914.

HAYDOCK LODGE (Lancashire).
BURKE, J.B. Visitation of Seats. 2.S. Vol.I, p.36. 1854. *

HAYES COURT (Surrey).
WATKIN, Ralph Granger.
— Paintings, drawings and prints in the collection of A.F. Stewart, Esq., of Hayee Court, Kenley and Blairhill, Blairgowrie. Catalogued with descriptive notes by R.G.W. 92pp. Plates. 26x20 n.p. privately printed [at the Temple Sheen Press] 1920.

HAYES, The. Kenley (Surrey).
[Sales] HAYES, The. 1924, May 5-8 [Contents]. (K.F. & R.).

HAYLE PLACE (Kent).
GREENWOOD, C. Kent. 179. 1838.

HAYNE (Devonshire).
BURKE, J.B. Visitation of Seats. Vol.II, p.71. 1853.*

HAYNES GRANGE (Bedfordshire).
LONDON: Victoria and Albert Museum [Woodwork].
— SMITH, H.C. The Haynes Grange room. 28pp. Illus. incl. 14 plates. 25x19 London, 1935.

HAZELBADGE HALL (Derbyshire).
TILLEY, J. Halls of Derbyshire. I, p.215. 1892.

HAZELBOROUGH HALL (Derbyshire).
TILLEY, J. Halls of Derbyshire. III, p.155. 1899.

HAZELBURY MANOR (Wiltshire).
COUNTRY LIFE, LIX, 274 plan, 306. 1926.
TIPPING, H.A. English Homes. Period I & II, Vol.II, p.91. 1937.

HAZLES, The (Lancashire).
TWYCROSS, E. Mansions of England and Wales. Vol.III, p.33, 1847.*

HAZLETON MANOR (Gloucestershire).
COOKE, R. West Country Houses. p.101. 1957.

HAZLEWOOD CASTLE (Yorkshire).
COUNTRY LIFE. CXXII, 1380 plan, 1426. 1957.
WHEATER, W. Mansions of Yorkshire. p.121. 1888.

HEADLEY COURT (Surrey).
COUNTRY LIFE. XXXII, 18 plan. 1912.

HEAGE HALL (Derbyshire).
TILLEY, J. Halls of Derbyshire. II, p.55. 1893.

HEALE HOUSE (Wiltshire).
COUNTRY LIFE. XXXVII, 272 plan. 1915.

HEANOR HALL (Derbyshire).
TILLEY, J. Halls of Derbyshire. IV, p.109. 1902.*

HEANTON SATCHVILLE (Devonshire).
CAMPBELL, C. Vitruvius Britannicus. IVth. pls. 73, 74. 1739.
DELDERFIELD, E.R. West Country houses. I. 79. 1968.

HEATHCOTE (Yorkshire).
COUNTRY LIFE. XXVIII, 54 plan. 1910.

HEATHERTON PARK (Somerset).
BURKE, J.B. Visitation of Seats. Vol.I, p.14. 1852.*

HEATHFIELD PARK (Sussex).
ENGLAND: Picturesque Views. p.85. 1786-88.

HEATH HALL (Yorkshire).
JOHNSON, Francis F.
— Heath Hall, Wakefield. 24pp. Illus. (2 on covers) incl. map. 14x20 n.p. privately printed, 1973.
COUNTRY LIFE. CXLIV, 692, 756 plan, 816. 1968.

HEATH HOUSE, Tean (Staffordshire).
COUNTRY LIFE. CXXXIII, 18 plan, 62. 1963.

HEATH HOUSE (Yorkshire).
PAINE, J. Plans, elevations. Pt. I, pls. 61, 62. plan 1767.

HEATH LANE LODGE, Twickenham (Middlesex).
MITCHELL, R. Buildings in England & Scotland. pls. 5, 6 plan. 1801.

HEATH OLD HALL (Yorkshire).
GREEN, Mary, *Lady*.
— The Old Hall at Heath, 1568-1888. Illus. incl. plates: etchings and plans. 23x16 Wakefield: Milnes, 1889.
On publisher's case a representation of the house stamped and gilt.
COUNTRY LIFE. XXII, 90. 1907.
LATHAM, C. In English Homes. Vol.III, p.33. 1909.

HEATON HALL (Yorkshire).
YORKSHIRE. Picturesque views. 1885.

HEATON MOUNT (Yorkshire).
YORKSHIRE. Picturesque views. 1885.

HEATON PARK [HALL] (Lancashire).
HEATON HALL.
    Heaton Hall: An illustrated survey [etc.]. 32pp. Illus. (some col., some on covers) incl. maps (on inside covers). 14x22 Derby: E.L.P. [1953?].
SWINDELLS, Thomas.
    Handbook to Heaton Park. 16pp. Illus. (1 on title page). 18x12 Eccles: by the author, 1906.
BARTLETT, J. Mansions of England and Wales. pl.137. 1853.
BURKE, J.B. Visitation of Seats. 2.S. Vol.I. p.174. 1854.*
COUNTRY LIFE. XXXVI, 710 plan. 1914.
COUNTRY LIFE. LVIII, 322 plan. 354. 1925.
MORRIS, F.O. Views of Seats. Vol.IV, p.21. 1880.
NEALE, J.P. Views of Seats. 2.S. Vol.I. 1824.
PYNE, W.H. Lancashire illustrated. 91. 1831.
TIPPING, H.A. English Homes. Period VI, Vol.I, p.199. 1926.
TWYCROSS, E. Mansions of England and Wales. Vol.III, p.63. 1847.

HEBBURN HALL (Durham).
BURKE, J.B. Visitation of Seats. 2.S. Vol.I, p.238. 1854.*

HEDGERLEY PARK (Buckinghamshire).
BURKE, J.B. Visitation of Seats. Vol.II, p.175. 1853.*

HEDINGHAM CASTLE (Essex).
BUCK, S. & N. Antiquities. I, pl.93. 1774.
COUNTRY LIFE. XLVIII, 372. 1920.
CROMWELL, T.K. Excursions in Essex. II, p.183. 1825.
ENGLAND: Beauties of England. I, p.256. 1787.
ESSEX: A new and complete history. II, 101. 1769.
MORANT, P. Essex. II, 296. 1768.
RUSH, J.A. Seats in Essex. p.99. 1897.
TIPPING, H.A. English Homes. Period I, Vol.I, p.1. 1921.

HEDSOR LODGE (Buckinghamshire).
ROBERTSON, A. Great Road. I, p.87. 1792.
THAMES, River. An History. I, pl.36. 1794.
[Sales] BOURNE END, 1923, November 7-9 [Contents].

HEDWORTH HOUSE, Chester-le-Street (Durham).
CAMPBELL, C. Vitruvius Britannicus. II, pl.88. 1717.

HEFFLETON (Dorsetshire).
HUTCHINS, J. History of Dorset. I, 417. 1861.

HEIGHAM, Bishop's Palace (Norfolk).
BIRKBECK, G. Old Norfolk Houses. 34. 1908.
CROMWELL, T.K. Excursions in Norfolk. II, p.43. 1819.
GARRATT, T. Halls of Norfolk. pl.37. 1890.

HELLENS (Herefordshire).
MUNTHE, Malcolm.
— Hellens, a Herefordshire Manor. [Bibliogr.] 136pp. Illus. incl. plates and maps (1 on end-paper). 21x14 London: G. Duckworth, 1957.

HELMINGHAM HALL (Suffolk).
TOLLEMACHE, Edward Dervereux Hamilton, *Major-General.*
    The Tollemaches of Helmingham and Ham. [Bibliogr.] Plates and genealog. tables. 25x18 Ipswich: Cowell, 1949.
WATERHOUSE, Ellis Kirkham.
    The collection of pictures in Helmingham Hall. 66pp. 8(1 col.) plates and genealog. table. 28x22 Helmingham Hall: privately printed, 1958.
BURKE, J.B. Visitation of Seats. Vol.I, p.33. 1852.*
CAMPBELL, C. Vitruvius Britannicus. IVth. pls. 63, 64. 1739.
COUNTRY LIFE. CXX, 282, 332 plan, 378, 656, 712. 1956.
CROMWELL, T.K. Excursions in Suffolk. I, p.189. 1818.
HALL, S.C. Baronial Halls. Vol.II. 1848.
MORRIS, F.O. Views of Seats. Vol.III, p.21. 1880.
NEALE, J.P. Views of Seats. Vol.IV. 1821.
SANDON, E. Suffolk houses. 154. 1977.

HELMSLEY HALL (Yorkshire).
HALL, S.C. Baronial Halls. Vol.II. 1848.

HEMINGFORD PARK (Huntingdonshire).
[Sales] HEMINGFORD PARK, 1978, September 18 [Furniture].

HEMINGSTONE HALL (Suffolk).
SANDON, E. Suffolk houses. 234. 1977.

HEMPNALL'S HALL (Suffolk).
SANDON, E. Suffolk houses. 256. 1977.

HEMSTED (Kent).
BURKE, J.B. Visitation of Seats. Vol.I, p.141. 1852.*

HEMSTED PARK (Kent).
MORRIS, F.O. Views of Seats. Vol.VI, p.57. 1880.
[Sales] HEMSTED PARK, 1912, July 17-19 [Contents]. (K.F. & R.).

HEMSWORTH HALL (Yorkshire).
BURKE, J.B. Visitation of Seats. 2.S. Vol.I, p.117. 1854.*

HENBLAS (Angelsey).
BURKE, J.B. Visitation of Seats. 2.S. Vol.I, p.206. 1854.*

HENBURY (Gloucestershire). Harcourt.
ATKYNS, R. Glocestershire. p.248. 1768.

HENBURY (Gloucestershire). Sampson.
ATKYNS, R.Glocestershire. p.248. 1768.

HENBURY HALL (Cheshire).
TWYCROSS, E. Mansions of England and Wales. Vol.II, p.125. 1850.*

HENDRE, The. (Monmouthshire).
NICHOLAS, T. Counties of Wales. II, p.725, 726. 1872.

HENDREGADREDD (Caernarvonshire).
BURKE, J.B. Visitation of Seats. Vol.II, p.52. 1853.

HENGRAVE HALL (Suffolk).
GAGE, John.
   The history and antiquities of Hengrave, in Suffolk. [Bibliogr. notes.] Engr. plates (some tinted), incl. plan and genealog. tables. 30x23 London: J. Carpenter, J. Booker; Bury St. Edmunds: J. Deck, 1822.
BURKE, J.B. Visitation of Seats. Vol.I, p.71. 1852.*
COUNTRY LIFE. II, 624. 1897.
COUNTRY LIFE. XXVII, 558 plan. 1910.
CROMWELL, T.K. Excursions in Suffolk. I, p.74. 1818.
GARNER, T. Domestic architecture. I, p.105 plan. 1911.
HALL, S.C. Baronial Halls. Vol.II. 1848.
MORRIS, F.O. Views of Seats. Vol.III, p.71. 1880.
SANDON, E. Suffolk houses. 157. 1977.
TIPPING, H.A. English Homes. Period II, Vol.I, p.231. 1924.
[Sales] HENGRAVE HALL, 1952, September 15-18, 22-25 [Contents].

HENGWRT (Merionethshire).
BURKE, J.B. Visitation of Seats. Vol.I, p.229. 1852.

HENHAM HALL (Suffolk).
BURKE, J.B. Visitation of Seats. Vol.II, p.180. 1853.*
CROMWELL, T.K. Excursions in Suffolk. II, p.125. 1819.
DAVY, H. Seats in Suffolk. pl.14. 1827.
NEALE, J.P. Views of Seats. Vol. IV. 1821.
SUMMERSON, J. The Country Seat. 164. 1970. [J. Byres' designs for rebuilding].

HENLEY HALL (Shropshire).
COUNTRY LIFE. C, 302, 348. 1946.
LEACH, F. Seats of Shropshire. p.373. 1891.
LEIGHTON, S. Shropshire Houses. 39. 1901.

HENLIP HOUSE (Worcestershire).
See HINDLIP HALL.

HENLLAN (Pembrokeshire).
NICHOLAS, T. Counties of Wales. II, p.840. 1872.

HENLLYS (Anglesey).
BURKE, J.B. Visitation of Seats. Vol.I. p.157. 1852.
NICHOLAS, T. Counties of Wales. I. p.5. 1872.

HENSOL CASTLE (Glamorganshire).
NICHOLAS, T. Counties of Wales. II, p.464. 1872.

HENSTEAD HOUSE (Suffolk).
DAVY, H. Seats in Suffolk. pl.18. 1827.

HERMITAGE, The. (Lancashire).
BARTLETT, J. Mansions of England and Wales. pl.92. 1853.
TWYCROSS, E. Mansions of England and Wales. Vol.II, p.52. 1847.

HERON COURT (Hampshire).
GROVE, R.A. Seats in the neighbourhood of Lymington. 1832.
HAMPSHIRE: Architectural views. 1830.

HERONDEN (Kent).
COUNTRY LIFE. CXXVIII, 332. 1960.

HERON HALL (Essex).
CROMWELL, T.K. Excursions in Essex. I, p.165. 1825.

HERRIARD PARK (Hampshire).
COUNTRY LIFE. CXXXVIII, 18. 1965.
HAMPSHIRE: Architectural views. 1830.

HERRINGFLEET HALL (Suffolk).
BURKE, J.B. Visitation of Seats. Vol.I, p.116. 1852.*
SANDON, E. Suffolk houses. 235, 1977.

HERRINGSTON (Dorsetshire).
COUNTRY LIFE. XXXIV, 674. 1913.
OSWALD, A. Country houses of Dorset. p.88. 1959.

HESLEYSIDE (Northumberland).

JONES, Views of Seats. I. 1829.
NEALE, J.P. Views of Seats. 2.S. Vol.II. 1825.

HESLINGTON HALL (Yorkshire).

BURKE, J.B. Visitation of Seats. 2.S. Vol.II, p.154. 1855.*
COUNTRY LIFE. XXXIV, 90 plan. 1913.
JONES. Views of Seats. I. 1829.
NEALE, J.P. Views of Seats. Vol.V. 1822.

HESTERCOMBE (Somerset).

COLLINSON, J. History of Somerset. III, 258. 1791.

HETTON HALL (Northumberland).

BURKE, J.B. Visitation of Seats. Vol.II, p.185. 1853.*

HEVENINGHAM HALL (Suffolk).

COUNTRY LIFE. English Country Houses: Mid Georgian. p.165. 1956.
COUNTRY LIFE. XXIII, 594. 1908.
COUNTRY LIFE. LVIII, 432, 472 plan, 508. 1925.
COUNTRY LIFE. CXLVI, 670. 1969.
CROMWELL, T.K. Excursions in Suffolk. II, p.97. 1819.
DAVY, H. Seats in Suffolk. pl.12. 1827.
NEALE, J.P. Views of Seats. Vol.IV. 1821.
NICOLSON, N. Great Houses of Britain. p.270. 1965.
TIPPING, H.A. English Homes. Period VI, Vol.I, p.347. 1926.
WATTS, W. Seats of the Nobility. pl.43. 1779.
[Sales] HEVENINGHAM HALL, 1915, July 19-23 [Contents].

HEVER CASTLE (Kent).

BUCK, S. & N. Antiquities. I, pl.131. 1774.
COUNTRY LIFE. II, 266. 1897.
COUNTRY LIFE. XXII, 522, 558. 1907.
COUNTRY LIFE. XLVI, 511. 1919.
COUNTRY LIFE. CLXIX, 18, 66. 1981.
CROMWELL, T.K. Excursions in Kent. p.176. 1822.
GARNER, T. Domestic architecture. I. p.35 plan. 1911.
HALL, S.C. Baronial halls. Vol.I. 1848.
HASTED, E. Kent. I, 397. 1778.
LATHAM, C. In English Homes. Vol.II, p.53. 1907.
NASH, J. Mansions of England. II, pls. 14, 15. 1840.
OSWALD, A. Country houses of Kent. 9. 1933.
THOMPSON, S. Old English Homes. 19. 1876.

HEVERSHAM HALL (Westmorland).

CUMBERLAND: C. & W. A. & A.S. Extra Series VIII, 209. 1892.

HEWELL GRANGE (Worcestershire).

COUNTRY LIFE. XIV, 240. 1903.
LATHAM, C. In English Homes. Vol.I, p.307. 1904.
NASH, T.R. Worcestershire. II, 403. 1782.
NEALE, J.P. Views of Seats. Vol. V. 1822.

HEYDON HALL (Norfolk).

BURKE, J.B. Visitation of Seats. Vol.I, p.70. 1852.
COUNTRY LIFE. LIV, 900. 1923.
COUNTRY LIFE. CLXXII, 246, 318, 382. 1982.

HEYSHAM HALL (Lancashire).

BARTLETT, J. Mansions of England and Wales. pls. 72, 73. 1853.
TWYCROSS, E. Mansions of England and Wales. Vol.II, p.29. 1847.

HEYSHAM TOWER (Lancashire).

BARTLETT, J. Mansions of England and Wales. pls.67, 68. 1853.
TWYCROSS, E. Mansions of England and Wales. Vol.II, p.25. 1847.

HEYTHORP HOUSE (Oxfordshire).

OXFORD.
— The new Oxford guide ... To which is added a tour to Blenheim, Ditchley, Heythorp and Stow [etc.]. 6 ed. 5(1 folding) engr. plates incl. plan and cuts: head and tail-pieces. 16x9 Oxford: for J. Fletcher & S. Parker [1769?].
CAMPBELL, C. Vitruvius Britannicus. V, pls. 82-85. 1771.
ENGLAND: Picturesque Views. p.34. 1786-88.
JONES. Views of Seats. I. 1829.
MORRIS, F.O. Views of seats. Vol.VI, p.77. 1880.
NEALE, J.P. Views of Seats. Vol.III. 1820.

HIDCOTE MANOR (Gloucestershire).

[Sales] LONDON, 1924, May 28 [House].

HIGH BANK (Lancashire).

BARTLETT, J. Mansions of England and Wales. p.158. 1853.
TWYCROSS, E. Mansions of England and Wales. Vol.III, p.99. 1847.

HIGHCLERE CASTLE (Hampshire).

BURKE, J.B. Visitation of Seats. Vol.I, p.1. 1852.
COUNTRY LIFE. CXXVI, 18 plan. 1959.
ROBERTSON, A. Great Road.I, p.145. 1792.
[Sales] LONDON, 1925, May 22 [Pictures and drawings from H.C.].

HIGHCLIFFE CASTLE (Hampshire).

COUNTRY LIFE. XCI, 806, 854, 902. 1942.
MORRIS, F.O. Views of Seats. Vol.V, p.75. 1880.
WATTS, W. Seats of the Nobility. pl.65. 1779.
[Sales] HIGHCLIFFE CASTLE, 1949, July 5-7 [Contents].

HIGH ERCALL HALL (Shropshire).
SHROPSHIRE. Castles and Old Mansions. 48. 1868.

HIGHFIELD HOUSE (Cheshire).
TWYCROSS, E. Mansions of England and Wales. Vol.II,
p.128. 1850.

HIGHFIELD HOUSE (Lancashire).
BARTLETT, J. Mansions of England and Wales. pl.116. 1853.
TWYCROSS, E. Mansions of England and Wales. Vol.III,
p.54. 1847.

HIGH HALL Nettlestead (Suffolk).
SANDON, E. Suffolk houses. 194. 1977.

HIGH HALL Weston (Suffolk).
SANDON, E. Suffolk houses. 166. 1977.

HIGHHEAD CASTLE(Cumberland).
COUNTRY LIFE. L, 480. 1921.

HIGH HOUSE, West Acre (Norfolk).
NEALE, J.P. Views of Seats. Vol.III. 1820.

HIGH HOUSE Otley (Suffolk).
SANDON, E. Suffolk houses. 278. 1977.

HIGH LEGH HALL (Cheshire).
HIGH LEGH HALL.
— Catalogue of the collection of paintings at High Legh
Hall, the seat of Lieut-Col. H.C. Legh [By J.H. Carter.] 35
plates 29x23 Birmingham: A. Taylor [1890.?].
TWYCROSS, E. Mansions of England and Wales. Vol.II, p.71.
1850.*
WATTS, W. Seats of the Nobility. pl.64. 1779.

HIGH LEGH WEST HALL (Cheshire).
ORMEROD, G. Cheshire. I, 506. 1882.

HIGHLOW HALL (Derbyshire).
TILLEY, J. Halls of Derbyshire. I, p.197. 1892.

HIGHMEAD (Cardiganshire).
NICHOLAS, T. Counties of Wales. I, p.137. 1872.

HIGH MEADOW (Gloucestershire).
CAMPBELL, C. Vitruvius Britannicus. II, pls. 39, 40. 1717.
CAMPBELL, C. Vitruvius Britannicus. III, pl.62. 1725.

HIGHNAM COURT (Gloucestershire).
COUNTRY LIFE. CVII, 1376, 1462. 1950.
RUDDER, S. Gloucestershire. 342. 1779.

HIGH STREET HOUSE (Kent).
BADESLADE, T. Seats in Kent. pl.13. 1750.
HARRIS, J. History of Kent. p.75. 1719.

HILL, The. (Cumberland).
BURKE, J.B. Visitation of Seats. Vol.I, p.142. 1852.*

HILL, The. Abergavenny (Monmouthshire).
[Sales] HILL, The, 1964, October 6-8 [Furniture & effects].

HILL COURT (Gloucestershire).
ATKYNS, R. Glocestershire. p.251. 1768.

HILL COURT (Herefordshire).
COUNTRY LIFE. CXXXIX, 180, 228, 286. 1966.

HILL DEVERILL MANOR (Wiltshire).
ELYARD, S.J. Old Wiltshire homes. p.15. 1894.

HILL END (Cheshire).
TWYCROSS, E. Mansions of England and Wales. Vol.II,
p.126. 1850.

HILLERSDON HALL (Bedfordshire).
GOTCH, J.A. Architecture of the Renaissance. I, p.49. 1894.

HILLFIELD HALL (Warwickshire).
NIVEN, W. Old Warwickshire houses. p.6, pl.8. 1878.

HILL HALL (Essex).
COUNTRY LIFE. XX, 18. 1906.
COUNTRY LIFE. XLI, 448, 472, 496 plan. 1917.
ESSEX: A new and complete history. II, 391. 1769.
LATHAM, C. In English Homes. Vol.II, p.361. 1907.
NEALE, J.P. Views of Seats. 2.S. Vol.I. 1824.
RUSH, J.A. Seats in Essex. p.103. 1897.*
WATTS, W. Seats of the Nobility. pl.18. 1779.
[Sales] HILL HALL, 1925, July 22 and following days
[Contents]. (K.F. & R.).

HILL HOUSE, Messing (Essex).
RUSH, J.A. Seats in Essex. p.105. 1897.

HILL HOUSE, Cowfold (Sussex).
[Sales] HILL HOUSE, 1968, October 23, 24 [Contents].

HILLINGDON HOUSE (Middlesex).
COPPER PLATE MAGAZINE. I, pl.46. 1792-1802.
ENGLAND: Picturesque Views. p.11. 1786-88.

HILLINGDON PLACE (Middlesex).
BURKE, J.B. Visitation of Seats. 2.S. Vol.I, p.130. 1854.*

HILLINGTON HALL (Norfolk).
BURKE, J.B. Visitation of Seats. 2.S. Vol.I, p.85. 1854.*

HILL PARK (Kent).
NEALE, J.P. Views of Seats. Vol.II. 1819.

HILLSIDE HOUSE (Lancashire).
BARTLETT, J. Mansions of England and Wales. pls.130, 131. 1853.
TWYCROSS, E. Mansions of England and Wales. Vol.III, p.61. 1847.

HILL'S PLACE (Sussex).
ELWES, D.G.C. Mansions of Western Sussex. 120. 1876.

HILLTOP, Beeley (Derbyshire).
TILLEY, J. Halls of Derbyshire. I, p.29. 1892.

HIMLEY HALL (Staffordshire).
SHAW, S. Staffordshire. II, 224. 1801.
[Sales] HIMLEY HALL, 1924, May 19 [Porcelain].
[Sales] HIMLEY HALL, 1924, May 20 [Library].
[Sales] HIMLEY HALL, 1924, May 24 [Silver plate].
[Sales] HIMLEY HALL, 1924, July 28 [Furniture and Carpets etc.].

HINCHESLEA LODGE (Hampshire).
GROVE, R.A. Seats in the neighbourhood of Lymington. 1832.

HINCHINGBROOKE (Huntingdonshire).
HINCHINGBROOKE.
— Hinchingbrooke. 56pp. 25x19 London: privately printed, 1910.
BUCK, S. & N. Antiquities I, pl.119. 1774.
BURKE, J.B. Visitation of Seats. Vol.I, p.109. 1852.*
COUNTRY LIFE. XXII, 630. 1907.
COUNTRY LIFE. LXV, 482 plan, 514. 1929.
GOTCH, J.A. Architecture of the Renaissance. I, p.43. 1894.
HALL, S.C. Baronial Halls. Vol.I. 1848.
JONES. Views of Seats. I. 1829.
NEALE, J.P. Views of Seats.Vol.II. 1819.

HINDLIP HALL (Worcestershire).
BURKE, J.B. Visitation of Seats. 2.S. Vol.II, p.81. 1855.*
NASH, T.R. Worcestershire. I, 588. 1781.

HINDRINGHAM HALL (Norfolk).
BIRKBECK, G. Old Norfolk houses. 50. 1908.

HINTLESHAM HALL (Suffolk).
RYAN, *Sir* Gerald Hemington, *Bart.*
— Timperly of Hintlesham. A study of a Suffolk family. By Sir G.H.R., Bart., and L.J. Redstone. [Bibliogr. notes.] xvi, 160pp. Illus. incl. plates (some folding) maps and genealog. tables. 22x14 London: Methuen, 1931.
BURKE, J.B. Visitation of Seats. Vol.II, p.120. 1853.*
COUNTRY LIFE. LXIV, 232 plan. 1928.
CROMWELL, T.K. Excursions in Suffolk. I, p.144. 1818.
DAVY, H. Seats in Suffolk. pl.6. 1827.
[Sales] HINTLESHAM HALL, 1909, June 16-19 [Contents].

HINTON ADMIRAL (Hampshire).
COUNTRY LIFE. XXVIII, 494. 1910.

HINTON AMPNER HOUSE (Hampshire).
COUNTRY LIFE. CI, 326 plan, 374. 1947.
COUNTRY LIFE. CXXVII, 1424. 1965.

HINTON ST. GEORGE (Somerset).
WINN, Colin George.
— The Pouletts of Hinton St. George. [Bibliogr.] Illus. incl. plates (some col., 1 folding), plans (on end papers) and genealog. table. 24x18 London: Research Publishing Co. (1976).
BURKE, J.B. Visitation of Seats. 2.S. Vol.II, p.114. 1855.*
COLLINSON, J. History of Somerset. II, 164. 1791.
JONES. Views of Seats. II. 1829.
NEALE, J.P. Views of Seats. 2.S. Vol.IV. 1828.

HINTON WALDRIST MANOR (Berkshire).
DAVENPORT, Nicholas.
— The honour of St. Valery: the story of an English manor house (Hinton Manor). [Bibliogr. notes.] 158pp. Illus. incl. plates and map. 20x13 London: Scolar Press, 1978.
COUNTRY LIFE. XCII, 1130. 1942.

HINTS HALL (Staffordshire).
[Sales] HINTS HALL, 1917, September 17-21 [Contents]. (K., F. & R.).

HINWICK HALL (Bedfordshire).
COUNTRY LIFE. XXX, 628. 1911.

HINWICK HOUSE (Bedfordshire).
HINWICK.
— Hinwick House, near Wellingborough, Northamptonshire [etc.]. Illus. (some on covers) incl. map. 14x20 [Derby; E.L.P., 1960.]

COUNTRY LIFE. English Country Houses: Baroque. p.134. 1970.

COUNTRY LIFE. CXXVIII, 618, 676, 730. 1960.

HITCHIN PRIORY (Hertfordshire).
COUNTRY LIFE. LVIII, 592, 632 plan. 1925.

TIPPING, H.A. English Homes. Period VI, Vol.I, p.255. 1926.

HOAR CROSS HALL (Staffordshire).
[Sales] HOAR CROSS HALL, 1964, May 28 [Remaining contents].

HOCKERHILL (Hertfordshire).
SOANE, J. Plans, elevations and sections. pl.XXXVII. 1788.

HODNET HALL (Shropshire).
BURKE, J.B. Visitation of Seats. Vol.I, p.159. 1852.*

LEACH, F. Seats of Shropshire. p.293. 1891.

LEIGHTON, S. Shropshire houses. 20. 1901.

HOGHTON TOWER (Lancashire).
MILLER, George Calvert.
— Hoghton Tower: the history of the manor, the hereditary lords and the ancient manor-house of Hoghton in Lancashire. ... With a foreword by the present baronet [Sir C. de Hoghton]. [Bibliogr.] Plates incl. plan. 22x14 Preston: Guardian Press, 1948.

BURKE, J.B. Visitation of Seats. Vol.II, p.241. 1853.*

COUNTRY LIFE. XVII, 198 plan, 234. 1905.

GARNER, T. Domestic architecture. II, p.145 plan. 1911.

LATHAM, C. In English Homes. Vol.II, p.113. 1907.

MOSS, F. Pilgrimages. [III] 81. 1906.

TWYCROSS, E. Mansions of England and Wales. Vol.I, p.52. 1847.*

UNITED KINGDOM. Historic houses. 184. 1892.

HOLCOMBE COURT (Devonshire).
COUNTRY LIFE. XXXVII, 48. 1915.

DELDERFIELD, E.R. West Country houses. I, 82. 1968.

GARNER, T. Domestic architecture. I, p.124 plan. 1911.

TIPPING, H.A. English Homes. Period III, Vol.II, p.107. 1927.

HOLCOMBE HOUSE (Gloucestershire).
COUNTRY LIFE. LXXXVIII, 542. 1940.

HOLDENBY HOUSE (Northamptonshire).
BUCK. S. & N. Antiquities. I, pl.211. 1774.

COUNTRY LIFE. XXXII, 528. 1912.

COUNTRY LIFE. CLXVI, 1286 plan, 1398. 1979.

GOTCH, J.A. Halls of Northants. p.66. 1936.

HOLDEN HALL (Lancashire).
BURKE, J.B. Visitation of Seats. Vol. II, p.53. 1853.*

HOLE PARK (Kent).
GREENWOOD, C. Kent. 240. 1838.

HOLFORD HALL (Cheshire).
GRAY, H. Old Halls of Cheshire. p.119. 1893.

HOLKER HALL (Lancashire).
HOLKER HALL.
Holker Hall: an illustrated survey [etc.]. 32pp. Illus. (Some col., some on covers) incl. maps (on inside covers). 14x22 Derby: E.L.P. [1953?].

BARTLETT, J. Mansions of England and Wales. pl.46. 1853.

COUNTRY LIFE. CLXVII, 1470. 1980.

COUNTRY LIFE. CLXVIII, 18. 1980.

MORRIS, F.O. Views of Seats. Vol.VI, p.41. 1880.

TWYCROSS, E. Mansions of England and Wales. Vol.II, p.3. 1847.

HOLKHAM HALL (Norfolk).
BRETTINGHAM, Matthew.
— The plans, elevations and sections of Holkham, in Norfolk, the seat of the late Earl of Leicester. To which are added the ceilings and chimney pieces; and also a descriptive account of the statues, pictures and drawings; not in the former edition. [Revised by R.F. Brettingham.] 34pp. Engr. plates (some folding), incl. sections, elevations and plans. 53x36 London: by T. Spilsbury for B. White & S. Leacroft, 1773.

BRETTINGHAM, Matthew, *the Younger*.
Account book of works of art purchased at Rome by the Earl of Leicester for Holkham. (An account of monies received on my lord the Earl of Leicestershire's account, and of my father's) [Photocopy of codex 744, Holkham Library.] 77ff. 23x30 Rome [etc.]. 1747-54.

DAWSON, J.
The strangers guide to Holkham, containing a description of the paintings, statues & c. of Holkham House, in the county of Norfolk; the...seat...of T.W.Coke, Esq., M.P. [etc.]. 1 engr. plate. 17x11 Burnham: by the author, 1817.

DOREZ, Léon.
Les manuscrits à peintures se la bibliothèque de Lord Leicester à Holkham Hall, Norfolk: choix de **miniatures et de** reliures. Publié sous les auspices de l'Académie de Inscriptions et Belles-Lettres, et de la Société des Bibliophiles français. Plates. 44x32 Paris: E.Leroux, 1908.

HOLKHAM HALL (Norfolk). [Contd.]

HOLKHAM.
— Holkham Hall: a short guide to the state rooms. 8pp. 2
illus. incl. plate: plan. 20x13 (Wells) privately printed [c. 1950.]

HOLKHAM.
List of statues & busts at Holkham Hall, 1913. 12ff. 28x22
(London printed 1913).

HOLKHAM HALL
New description of Holkham, the...seat of T.W. Coke,
Esq., M.P. Containing a full and accurate account of the
paintings, statues, tapestry, &c. with a picturesque tour of
the gardens and park. [By J. Blome.] 90pp. 1 engr. plate. 15x9
Wells, Neville, 1826.

JAMES, Charles Warburton.
Chief Justice Coke: his family & descendants at
Holkham. Plates (1 folding), incl. genealog. table. 22x14
London: Country Life, 1929.

LAVER, James.
Holkham Hall. 32pp. Illus. (1 on title-page, 4 on covers)
incl. map. 24x18 Holkham Hall, Norfolk, 1951.

LONDON: Bibliographical Society.
Transactions. Supplements. [Contd.]
7. A handlist of manuscripts in the library of the Earl of
Leicester at Holkham Hall. Abstracted from the catalogues
of William Roscoe and Frederic Madden, and annotated by
S. de Ricci. 80pp. 1932.

ROSCOE William.
Proof impressions of engravings, designed to illustrate
Mr. R's catalogue of the manuscript library at Holkham. 4pp.
Engr. plates. 34x25 n.p. Privately printed, 1835.

BIRKBECK, G. Old Norfolk Houses, 53. 1908.

BURKE, J.B. Visitation of Seats. 2.S. Vol.I, p.71. 1854.*

CAMPBELL, C. Vitruvius Britannicus. V, pls.64-69. 1771.

COUNTRY LIFE. English Country Houses: Early Georgian.
p.131. 1955.

COUNTRY LIFE. XXIII, 822, 870. 1908.

COUNTRY LIFE. LIV, 75 [Drawings]. 1923.

COUNTRY LIFE. CXLIII, 1310 [Temple], plan. 1968.

COUNTRY LIFE. CLXVII, 214 plan, 298, 359, 427. 1980.

CROMWELL, T.K. Excursions in Norfolk. I, p.162. 1818.

ENGLAND: Beauties of England. II, p.124. 1787.

HAVELL, R. Views of Noblemen's Seats. 1823.

LATHAM, C. In English Homes. Vol.III, p.381. 1909.

NEALE, J.P. Views of Seats. Vol.III. 1820.

NICOLSON, N. Great Houses of Britain. p.230. 1965.

NORFOLK: The Norfolk tour. 25. 1777.*

TIPPING, H.A. English Homes. Period V, Vol.I, p.301. 1921.

WATTS, W. Seats of the Nobility. pl.39. 1779.

HOLLAND HOUSE (Middlesex).

HUDSON, Derek.
Holland House in Kensington. [Bibliogr.] Illus. (1 on title-
page) incl. 17 plates, plans and end-papers. 25x15 London: P.
Davies, 1967.

ILCHESTER, Giles Stephen Holland Fox-Strangways,
Earl of.
The home of the Hollands [Holland House], 1605-1820.
[Bibliogr. notes.] Illus. incl. plates and plans. 22x14 London:
J. Murray, 1937.

ILCHESTER, Giles Stephen Holland Fox-Strangways,
Earl of.
Catalogue of pictures belonging to the Earl of Ilchester
at Holland House [With MS. corrections.] 24x18 London:
privately printed at the Chiswick Press, 1904.
Addenda and corrigenda to Catalogue of pictures, Holland
House. 40pp. 23x16 1939.

LIECHTENSTEIN, Marie, *Princess.*
Holland House [etc.]. [Bibliogr. notes.] Illus. incl. plates
(some folding, 2 on title-pages), plan and facsimiles, and
covers. 2 vols. 22x15 London: Macmillan & Co., 1874.

ANGUS, W. Seats of the Nobility. pl.17. 1787.

BURKE, J.B. Visitation of Seats. Vol.I, p.67. 1852.*

CLARKE, T.H. Domestic architecture. 16. 1833.

COUNTRY LIFE. I, 632. 1897.

COUNTRY LIFE. XIII, 272. 1903.

COUNTRY LIFE. XVII, 870. 1905.

HALL, S.C. Baronial Halls. Vol.II. 1848.

HAVELL, R. Views of Noblemen's Seats. 1823.

LATHAM, C. In English Homes. Vol.II, p.221. 1909.

MALAN, A.H. Famous homes. p.137. 1902.

NASH, J. Mansions of England.I, pls.17, 18. 1839.

NEALE, J.P. Views of Seats. 2.S. Vol.IV. 1828.

[Sales] LONDON, 1947, July 10 [Books].

HOLLINGBOURNE MANOR (Kent).

RICHARDSON, C.J. Old English mansions. III. 1845.

HOLLINSHEAD HALL (Lancashire).

BARTLETT, J. Mansions of England and Wales. pl.22. 1853.

TWYCROSS, E. Mansions of England and Wales. Vol.I, p.37.
1847.

HOLLYINGWORTHE HALL (Cheshire).

TWYCROSS, E. Mansions of England and Wales. Vol.II, p.III.
1850.

HOLMBURY HOUSE (Surrey).

[Sales] HOLMBURY HOUSE, 1934, November 20-22
[Contents]. (K.F. & R.).

HOLMBUSH (Sussex).

BURKE, J.B. Visitation of Seats. Vol.I, p.24. 1852.

HOLKER HALL, Lancashire. From: BARTLETT (J). *The mansions of England and Wales* [etc.]. *1. The county palatine of Lancaster;* London, 1853.

HOLME, The. (Lancashire).
BARTLETT, J. Mansions of England and Wales. pls.7, 14. 1853.
BURKE, J.B. Visitation of Seats. Vol.II, p.112. 1853.*
TWYCROSS, E. Mansions of England and Wales. Vol.I, p.26. 1847.

HOLME HALL (Derbyshire).
TILLEY, J. Halls of Derbyshire. I, p.23. 1892.

HOLME LACY (Herefordshire).
HOLME LACY.
— A short description with some views of Holme Lacy, Hereford. 10pp. 19 plates incl. plan and folding map. 36x25 (London: Rowsell & Son) [1922?]
BURKE, J.B. Visitation of Seats. 2.S. Vol.I, p.38. 1854.*
COUNTRY LIFE. XXV, 906. 1909.
LATHAM, C. In English Homes. Vol.I, p.381 & Vol.III, p.235. 1904, 1909.
MORRIS, F.O. Views of Seats. Vol.I, p.27. 1880.
ROBINSON, C.J. Mansions of Herefordshire. pls.9, 10. 1873.
[Sales] LONDON, 1909, July 29 [Freehold, Manorial, Estate.]
[Sales] HOLME LACY, 1910, January 31, February 1-3 [Contents].
[Sales] LONDON, 1922, September 19 [Estate particulars].

HOLME PARK (Berkshire).
BURKE, J.B. Visitation of Seats. Vol.I, p.67. 1852.*
JONES. Views of Seats. I. 1829.
NEALE, J.P. Views of Seats. 2.S. Vol.IV. 1828.

HOLME PIERREPOINT HALL (Nottinghamshire).
COUNTRY LIFE. CLXVI, 842. 1979.
JONES. Views of Seats. I. 1829.
NEALE, J.P. View of Seats . Vol.III. 1820.
THOROTON, R. Nottinghamshire. I, 181. 1797.

HOLMESFIELD HALL (Derbyshire).
TILLEY, J. Halls of Derbyshire. III, p.109. 1899.

HOLM ISLAND (Lancashire).
BARTLETT, J. Mansions of England and Wales. pl.60. 1853.
TWYCROSS, E. Mansions of England and Wales. Vol.II, p.17. 1847.

HOLMWOOD HOUSE (Surrey).
BURKE, J.B. Visitation of Seats. 2.S. Vol.I, p.208. 1854.*

HOLT, The. (Hampshire).
COUNTRY LIFE. CXXXV, 1396, 1472. 1964.

HOLT CASTLE (Worcestershire).
COUNTRY LIFE. LXXXVIII, 54, 76. 1940.
NASH, T.R. Worcestershire. I, 594. 1781.

HOLT HALL (Leicestershire).
See NEVILL HOLT HALL.

HOLTON HALL (Lincolnshire).
BURKE, J.B. Visitation of Seats. Vol.I, p.69. 1852.*

HOLWOOD (Kent).
BURKE, J.B. Visitation of Seats. Vol.I, p.6. 1852.*
COPPER PLATE MAGAZINE.II, pl.72. 1792-1802.
ENGLAND: Picturesque Views. p.33. 1786-88.
NEALE, J.P. Views of Seats. 2.S. Vol.IV. 1828.

HOLYBOURNE LODGE (Hampshire).
BURKE, J.B. Visitation of Seats. Vol.II, p.251. 1853.*

HOME PLACE (Norfolk).
COUNTRY LIFE. XXVI, 634 plan. 1909.

HOMME HOUSE (Herefordshire).
BURKE, J.B. Visitation of Seats. 2.S. Vol.I, p.216. 1854.*

HONINGTON HALL (Warwickshire).
COUNTRY LIFE. English Country Houses: Early Georgian. p.175. 1955.
COUNTRY LIFE. XV, 942. 1904.
COUNTRY LIFE. XLVIII, 630, 666, 694. 1920.
COUNTRY LIFE. CLXIV, 791, 893, 1082. 1978.
JONES. Views of Seats. I. 1829.
NEALE, J.P. Views of Seats. 2.S. Vol.I. 1824.
TIPPING, H.A. English Homes. Period V, Vol.I, p.255. 1921.

HOO, The. (Hertfordshire).
CAMPBELL, C. Vitruvius Britannicus. lv, pl.18 [Bridge]. 1767.
CHAUNCY, H. Hertfordshire. II, 402. 1826.
NEALE, J.P. Views of Seats. 2.S. Vol.V. 1829.

HOOK, The. (Hampshire).
HAMPSHIRE: Architectural Views. 1830.

HOOK, The. (Hertfordshire).
BURKE, J.B. Visitation of Seats. Vol.I, p.267. 1852.*

HOOLE HALL (Cheshire).
TWYCROSS, E. Mansions of England and Wales. Vol.I, p.46. 1850.

HOON HALL (Derbyshire).
TILLEY, J. Halls of Derbyshire. II, p.109. 1893.

HOOTON HALL (Cheshire).
NEALE, J.P. Views of Seats. 2.S. Vol.V. 1829.
ORMEROD, G. Cheshire. II, 414. 1882.
TWYCROSS, E. Mansions of England and Wales. Vol.I, p.51. 1850.*
WATTS, W. Seats of the Nobility. pl.23. 1779.
[Sales] HOOTON HALL, 1875, August 2-7, 9-12 [Contents].

HOPE END (Herefordshire).
BURKE, J.B. Visitation of Seats. Vol.I, p.54. 1852.*
COUNTRY LIFE. CXLIV, 715. 1968.
SPROULE, A. Lost houses of Britain. 175. 1982.

HOPPESFORD HALL (Warwickshire).
BURKE, J.B. Visitation of Seats. 2.S. Vol.I, p.235. 1854.*

HOPTON COURT (Shropshire).
BURKE, J.B. Visitation of Seats. Vol.I, p.268. 1852.*

HOPTON HALL (Derbyshire).
TILLEY, J. Halls of Derbyshire. II, p.269. 1893.

HOPWELL HALL (Derbyshire).
TILLEY, J. Halls of Derbyshire. IV, p.105. 1902.*

HOPWOOD HALL (Lancashire).
TWYCROSS, E. Mansions of England and Wales. Vol.III, p.72. 1847.*

HORDEN HOUSE (Oxfordshire).
ENGLAND: Picturesque Views. p.40. 1786-88.

HORHAM HALL (Essex).
COUNTRY LIFE. XVIII, 18. 1905.
CROMWELL, T.K. Excursions in Essex. II, p.122. 1825.
GARNER, T.Domestic architecture. I, p.60. 1911.
HALL, S.C. Baronial Halls. Vol.I. 1848.
RUSH, J.A. Seats in Essex. p.107. 1897.
TIPPING, H.A. English Homes. Period II, Vol.I, p.21. 1924.
[Sales] HORHAM HALL, 1982, October 4 [Contents].

HORKESLEY PARK (Essex).
BURKE, J.B. Visitation of Seats. 2.S. Vol.I, p.247. 1854.*
RUSH, J.A. Seats in Essex. p.111. 1897.

HORNBY CASTLE (Lancashire).
BARTLETT, J. Mansions of England and Wales. pls. 52, 53. 1853.
BUCK, S. & N. Antiquities. I, pl.152. 1774.
BURKE, J.B. Visitation of Seats. Vol.I, p.164. 1852.*
ENGLAND: Beauties of England. I, p.421. 1787.
TWYCROSS, E. Mansions of England and Wales. Vol.II, p.12. 1847.

HORNBY CASTLE (Yorkshire).
COUNTRY LIFE. XX, 54. 1906.
COUNTRY LIFE. XXXI, 475 [Furniture]. 1912.
COUNTRY LIFE. XLVII, 720 [Furniture]. 1920.
JONES. Views of Seats. I. 1829.
LATHAM, C. In English Homes. Vol.II, p.85. 1907.
MORRIS, F.O. Views of Seats. Vol.V, p.l. 1880.
NEALE, J.P. Views of Seats. 2.S. Vol.I. 1824.
YORKSHIRE. Picturesque views. 1885.
[Sales] LONDON, 1920, June 10, 11 [Furniture, porcelain, silver etc. from H.C.].
[Sales] NORTHALLERTON, 1930, April 3 [Estate].
[Sales] LONDON, 1930, June 2-4 [Portion of the Library].
[Sales] HORNBY CASTLE, 1930, June 2-11 [Remaining contents].

HORNBY HALL (Westmorland).
CUMBERLAND: C. & W.A. & A.S. Extra Series, VIII, 81. 1892.

HORSEHEATH HALL (Cambridgeshire).
CAMPBELL, C. Vitruvius Britannicus. III, pls.91, 92. 1725.

HORSELUNGES MANOR (Sussex).
COUNTRY LIFE. LXXVII, 12 plan. 1935.

HORSLEY HALL (Denbighshire).
[Sales] HORSLEY HALL, 1934, April 9 and following days [Contents].

HORSLEY PLACE (Surrey).
See WEST HORSLEY PLACE.

HORSLEY TOWERS (Surrey).
See EAST HORSLEY TOWERS.

HORSTED PLACE (Sussex).
COUNTRY LIFE. CXXIV, 276, 320. 1958.

HORTON COURT [MANOR] (Gloucestershire).

COUNTRY LIFE. LXXI, 122. 1932.

HODGES, E. Ancient English homes. 213. 1895.

[Sales] BRISTOL. 1925. July 2 [Estate].

HORTON HALL [HOUSE] (Northamptonshire).

NEALE, J.P. Views of Seats. Vol.III. 1820.

SUMMERSON, J. The Country Seat. 150. 1970.

[Sales] HORTON HALL, 1935, September 24, 25 [Contents].

HORTON HALL (Yorkshire).

SPROULE, A. Lost houses of Britain. 180. 1982.

HORTON OLD HALL (Yorkshire).

SPROULE, A. Lost houses of Britain. 180. 1982.

YORKSHIRE. Picturesque views. 1885.

HORWOOD HOUSE, Winslow (Buckinghamshire).

COUNTRY LIFE. LIV, 644 plan. 1923.

HOTHAM HOUSE, Beverley (Yorkshire).

CAMPBELL, C. Vitruvius Britannicus. II, pl.87. 1717.

HOTHFIELD PLACE (Kent).

BURKE, J.B. Visitation of Seats. 2.S. Vol.I, p.232. 1854.*

HOTWELL HOUSE (Gloucestershire).

ROBERTSON, A. Great Road. II, p.184. 1792.

HOUGHTON HALL (Norfolk).

BROOKE, *Rev.* John Henry.
— Houghton and the Walpoles. [Bibliogr. Notes.] 44pp. Plate: elevation. 22x14 London: Simpkin, Marshall & Co.; King's Lynn: Thew & Son, 1865.

HOUGHTON HALL.
— The plans, elevations and sections; chimney-pieces, and cielings of Houghton in Norfolk; the seat of the Rt. Honourable Sir Robert Walpole [etc.] 2ff. Engr. plates by P. Fourdrinier, after I. Ware and W. Kent; designed by T. Ripley. Incl. sections, elevations and plans. 53x38 (London) I. Ware, 1735.

HOUGHTON HALL.
— The plans, elevations and sections ... of Houghton. [Contd.] (2 ed.) The whole designed by T. Ripley, delineated by I. Ware and W. Kent, and ... engraved by Mr. Fourdrinier. With a description of the house and of the ... collection of pictures. 12pp. 58x44 London: P. Fourdrinier, 1760.

HOUGHTON HALL
— A set of prints, engraved after the most capital paintings in the collection of her Imperial Majesty, the Empress of

Russia. Lately in the possession of the Earl of Orford, at Houghton in Norfolk; with plans, elevations, sections, chimney pieces & ceilings. 12pp. Engr. plates incl. title-pages. 2 vols. Fol. 69x52 London: J. & J. Boydell, 1788.

WALPOLE, Horace, *Earl of Orford.*
— Aedes Walpolianae: or, a description of the collection of pictures at Houghton Hall, in Norfolk, the seat of the Right Honourable Sir Robert Walpole, Earl of Orford. 2 ed. (A sermon on painting, preached before the Earl of Orford at Houghton, 1742; A journey to Houghton, ... a poem by the Rev. Mr Whaley.) Engr. plates (4 folding) incl. plans. 26x21 London: by the author, 1752.
MS. inserted: a list of such of the pictures in the Houghton Collection, as were sold by the Earl of Orford to the Empress of Russia in 1781, with the prices.

BIRKBECK, G. Old Norfolk Houses. 60. 1908.

BURKE, J.B. Visitation of Seats. 2.S. Vol.II, p.15. 1855.*

CAMPBELL, C. Vitruvius Britannicus. III, pls. 27-34. 1725.

COUNTRY LIFE. English Country Houses: Early Georgian. p.72. 1955.

COUNTRY LIFE. XXII, 126, 162. 1907.

COUNTRY LIFE. XLIX, 14, 40 plan, 64, 98. 1921.

CROMWELL, T.K. Excursions in Norfolk. II, p.16. 1819.

ENGLAND: Beauties of England. II, p.118. 1787.

ENGLISH CONNOISSEUR. I, 81. 1766.*

LATHAM, C. In English Homes. Vol.III, p.353. 1909.

NEALE, J.P. Views of Seats. Vol.III. 1820.

NORFOLK: The Norfolk tour. 50. 1777.*

TIPPING, H.A. English Homes. Period V, Vol.I, p.67. 1921.

WATTS, W. Seats of the Nobility. pl.46. 1779.

HOUGHTON HALL (Yorkshire).

COUNTRY LIFE. CXXXVIII, 1734, 1782 plan. 1965.

HOUGHTON HOUSE (Bedfordshire).

CARDIGAN, Robert Brudenell, *Earl of.*
— Houghton House accounts, Bedfordshire: property of the Earl of Cardigan. [Negative microfilm.] 20 frames. [Houghton Regis] (1675-80.)

ELSTOW: Moot Hall.
— Leaflets [s]. [Contd.]
5. CURTIS, E. Life in the Palace Beautiful (Houghton House, near Ampthill). 24pp. 1958.

LONDON: Victoria and Albert Museum [Woodwork].
— SMITH, H.C. The Haynes Grange room [formerly at Houghton House.] 28pp. Illus. incl. 14 plates. 25x19 London, 1935.

HOUGHTON LODGE (Hampshire).

COUNTRY LIFE. CIX, 1190, 1280 plan. 1951.

HOUNDSELL HOUSE (Sussex).

COUNTRY LIFE. XLIII, 108 plan. 1918.

COUNTRY LIFE. CXXIV, 126 plan. 1958.

HOUNTON HALL (Staffordshire).
BURKE, J.B. Visitation of Seats. Vol.II, p.121. 1853.*

HOVE MANOR HOUSE (Sussex).
COUNTRY LIFE. XLVIII, 114. 1920.

HOVERINGHAM HALL
(Nottinghamshire).
[Sales] HOVERINGHAM HALL, 1959, May 28
[Remaining contents].

HOVINGHAM HALL (Yorkshire).
BURKE, J.B. Visitation of Seats. 2.S. Vol.I, p.133. 1854.*
COPPER PLATE MAGAZINE. IV, pl.194. 1792-1802.
COUNTRY LIFE. English Country Houses: Early Georgian.
p.181. 1955.
COUNTRY LIFE. LXII, 884, 920. 1927.
COUNTRY LIFE. CXXIX, 1410. 1961.
WOOD, G.B. Historic homes of Yorkshire. 101. 1957.

HOWBRIDGE HALL (Essex).
COUNTRY LIFE. LV, 301 plan, 379. 1924.

HOWGILL CASTLE (Westmorland).
CUMBERLAND: C. & W. A. & A.S. Extra Series VIII, 142
plan. 1892.

HOWICK HALL (Northumberland).
MORRIS, F.O. Views of Seats. Vol.VI, p.63. 1880.

HOWICK HOUSE (Lancashire).
BARTLETT, J. Mansions of England and Wales. pls. 41, 42.
1853.
TWYCROSS, E. Mansions of England and Wales. Vol.I, p.69.
1847.

HOWSHAM HALL (Yorkshire).
COUNTRY LIFE. XVII, 450. 1905.
COUNTRY LIFE. LXXVIII, 194, 220. 1935.
JONES. Views of Seats. I. 1829.
MORRIS, F.O. Views of Seats. Vol.I, p.13. 1880.
NEALE, J.P. Views of Seats. Vol.V. 1822.
[Sales] HOWSHAM HALL, 1948, November 1-4 [Remaining
furnishings].
[Sales] MALTON, 1924, April 16 [Furniture from H.H. etc.].

HOXNE HALL (Suffolk).
CROMWELL, T.K. Excursions in Suffolk. II, p.21. 1819.

HUDDINGTON COURT (Worcestershire).
COUNTRY LIFE. LXXX, 116. 1936.

HUGHENDON MANOR
(Buckinghamshire).
LONDON: National Trust for Places of Historic Interest or
Natural Beauty.
— ALLEN, M.V. and FEDDEN, R. Hughenden Manor,
Buckinghamshire. 32pp. 4 plates. 18x12 London: Country Life
(1949).
COUNTRY LIFE. I, 463. 1897.
COUNTRY LIFE. CXIII, 1604, 1698. 1953.
MORRIS, F.O. Views of Seats. Vol.V. p.27. 1880.

HULLAND HALL (Derbyshire).
TILLEY, J. Halls of Derbyshire. II, p.193. 1893.

HULME HALL (Lancashire).
PYNE. W.H. Lancashire illustrated. 104. 1831.

HULTON PARK (Lancashire).
BARTLETT, J. Mansions of England & Wales. pl.144. 1853.
BURKE, J.B. Visitation of Seats. Vol.II, p.109. 1853.*
PYNE, W.H. Lancashire illustrated. 80. 1831.
TWYCROSS, E. Mansions of England and Wales. Vol.III, p.76.
1847.

HUNGERTON HALL (Lincolnshire).
COPPER PLATE MAGAZINE. V, pl.248. 1792-1802.

HUNGRY BENTLEY HALL (Derbyshire).
TILLEY, J. Halls of Derbyshire.II, p.97. 1893.

HUNSDON HOUSE (Hertfordshire).
BURKE, J.B. Visitation of Seats. 2.S. Vol.I, p.68. 1854.*
CHAUNCY, H. Hertfordshire. I, 390. 1826
JONES. Views of Seats. I. 1829.
NEALE, J.P. Views of Seats. Vol.II. 1819.

HUNSTANTON HALL (Norfolk).
BIRKBECK, G. Old Norfolk Houses. 67. 1908.
COUNTRY LIFE. LIX, 552, 586. 1926.
CROMWELL, T.K. Excursions in Norfolk. II, p.22. 1819.

HUNTERCOMBE MANOR
(Buckinghamshire).
COUNTRY LIFE. CV, 1310, 1374. 1949.
[Sales] HUNTERCOMBE MANOR, 1924, November 4-6
[Contents]. (K.F. & R.).

HUNTINGFIELD HALL (Suffolk).
SANDON, E. Suffolk houses. 189. 1977.

HUNTINGTON COURT (Herefordshire).
BURKE, J.B. Visitation of Seats. 2.S. Vol.II, p.169. 1855.*

HUNTON COURT (Kent).
GREENWOOD, C. Kent. 144. 1838.

HUNTRODYE (Lancashire).
BARTLETT, J. Mansions of England and Wales. pl.44. 1853.
BURKE, J.B. Visitation of Seats. 2.S. Vol.I, p.198. 1854.*
TWYCROSS, E. Mansions of England and Wales. Vol.I, p.7. 1847.

HUNTSHAM COURT (Devonshire).
BURKE, J.B. Visitation of Seats. Vol.II, p.211. 1853.*

HURDSFIELD HOUSE (Cheshire).
TWYCROSS, E. Mansions of England and Wales. Vol.II, p.123. 1850.

HURLEY HALL (Warwickshire).
HODGES, E. Ancient English homes. 172. 1895.

HURLEY HOUSE (Berkshire).
[Sales] LONDON, 1924, May 28 [House].

HURLINGHAM (Middlesex).
CAMPBELL, C. New Vitruvius Britannicus. II, pls.23, 24. 1808.

HURN COURT (Hampshire).
HURN COURT.
— List of the principal pictures at Hurn Court.
Typescript, 6pp. 25x20 [Hurn Court, *c*.1935].

[Sales] LONDON, 1950 March 9, 10; 30, 31 [Printed books and fine bindings].

HURSLEY PARK (Hampshire).
COOPER, *Sir* George Alexander, *Bart.*
— A catalogue of the pictures by old masters of the English school and works of art forming the collection of Sir G.A.C. at Hursley Park, Winchester. 228pp. Plates. 40x31 London: Chiswick Press, 1912.
BURKE, J.B. Visitation of Seats. Vol.I, p.202. 1852.*
COUNTRY LIFE. XXVI, 562, 598. 1909.
COUNTRY LIFE. XXXIV, 679 [Beauvais tapestries]. 1913.
JONES. Views of Seats. II. 1829.
LATHAM, C. In English Homes. Vol.III, p.401. 1909.
NEALE, J.P. Views of Seats. Vol.II. 1819.

HURSTBOURNE PARK (Hampshire).
ENGLAND: Picturesque Views. p.35. 1786-88.

HURST HOUSE, The. (Lancashire).
BARTLETT, J. Mansions of England and Wales. pls.119, 120. 1853.
TWYCROSS, E. Mansions of England and Wales. Vol.III, p.55. 1847.

HURSTMONCEUX CASTLE (Sussex).
BUCK, S. & N. Antiquities. II, pl.291. 1774.
COUNTRY LIFE. XLIII, 214,242 plan, 270. 1918.
COUNTRY LIFE. LXV, 702. 1929.
COUNTRY LIFE. LXXVIII, 566, 606 plan, 630 plan. 1935.
NEALE, J.P. Views of Seats. 2.S. Vol.V. 1829.
TIPPING, H.A. English Homes. Period I & II, Vol.II, p.281. 1937.
[Sales] HURSTMONCEUX CASTLE, 1929, October 16 [Castle and estate].
[Sales] HURSTMONCEUX CASTLE, 1929, November 5, 6 [Contents].

HURTS HALL (Suffolk).
BURKE, J.B. Visitation of Seats. 2.S. Vol.II, p.87. 1855.*
DAVY, H. Seats in Suffolk. pl.11. 1827.

HURTWOOD, Holmbury St. Mary (Surrey).
COUNTRY LIFE. XXX, 742 plan. 1911.

HUSBANDS BOSWORTH HALL (Leicestershire).
NICHOLS, J. History of Leicestershire. II, ii, 463. 1798.

HUTHWAITE HALL (Cumberland).
CUMBERLAND: C. & W. A. & A.S. Extra Series VIII, 331. 1892.

HUTT, The. in HALE WOOD (Lancashire).
GRAY, H. Old Halls of Lancashire. p.23. 1893.

HUTTON HALL (Essex).
ESSEX: A new and complete history. IV, 28. 1771.

HUTTON HALL (Yorkshire).
MORRIS, F.O. Views of Seats. Vol.III, p.15. 1880.

HUTTON-IN-THE-FOREST (Cumberland).
COUNTRY LIFE. XXI, 18. 1907.
COUNTRY LIFE. CXXXVII, 232, 286, 352 plan. 1965.
KIP, J. Nouveau théâtre de la Grande Bretagne. I, pl.59. 1715.
LATHAM, C. In English Homes. Vol.II, p.231. 1909.
MORRIS, F.O. Views of Seats. Vol.VI, p.11. 1880.

HUTTON JOHN (Cumberland).
COUNTRY LIFE. LXV, 116 plan. 1929.
CUMBERLAND: C. & W. A. & A.S. Extra Series VIII, 311. 1892.

HYDE, The. (Bedfordshire).
BURKE, J.B. Visitation of Seats. 2.S. Vol.I, p.195. 1854.*

HYDE, The. (Dorsetshire).
HUTCHINS, J. History of Dorset. II, 12. 1863.

HYDE, The. (Essex).
DISNEY, John.
— A catalogue of some marbles, bronzes, pictures, and gems, at The Hyde, near Ingatestone, Essex. The greater part successively the property of Thomas Hollis ... and Thomas Brand-Hollis ... and now of J.D. 98pp. Engr. plates (some folding). 21x13 London: privately printed, 1809.
DISNEY, John.
— Museum Disneianum, being a description of a collection of ancient marbles, specimens of ancient bronze, and various ancient fictile vases, in the possession of J.D., at The Hyde near Ingatestone. Plates (some lithogr., some col.) 34x26 London: Longman, Brown, Green, and Longman's, 1849.
ESSEX: A new and complete history. I, 247. 1769.

HYDE HALL, Sandon (Hertfordshire).
CHAUNCY, H. Hertfordshire. I, 161. 1826.

HYDE HALL, Sawbridgeworth (Hertfordshire).
CHAUNCY, H. Hertfordshire.I, 359. 1826.
CROMWELL, T.K. Excursions in Essex. I, p.137. 1825.
NEALE, J.P. Views of Seats. Vol.II. 1819.

HYDE HALL (Lancashire).
MOSS, F. Pilgrimages. VI, 103. 1913.

HYDE LANE (Buckinghamshire).
COUNTRY LIFE. LVII, 1028 plan. 1925.

HYLANDS (Essex).
ESSEX: A new and complete history. I, 274. 1769.
NEALE, J.P. Views of Seats. Vol.I. 1818.
RUSH, J.A. Seats in Essex. p.113. 1897.

HYLTON CASTLE (Durham).
BUCK, S. & N. Antiquities. I, pl.84. 1774.
BURKE, J.B. Visitation of Seats. 2.S. Vol.I, p.60. 1854.*
JONES. Views of Seats. I. 1829.
NEALE, J.P. Views of Seats. Vol.I. 1818.

HYNDBURN (Lancashire).
BURKE, J.B. Visitation of Seats. Vol.II, p.249. 1853.

ICKWELL BURY (Bedfordshire).
COUNTRY LIFE. CXVII, 1174, 1234 plan. 1955.

ICKWORTH (Suffolk).
ICKWORTH.
The history and treasures of Ickworth, Bury St. Edmunds, Suffolk, a property of the National Trust. 22pp. Illus. (1 col., some on covers) incl. plan and map. 23x18 (London: Pitkin, 1965).
One of the: Pride of Britain series.
LONDON: National Trust for places of Historic Interest or Natural Beauty.
Ickworth, Suffolk. 12pp. 2 illus. incl. plan. 22x14 [London c. 1958.]
LONDON: National Trust for Places of Historic Interest or Natural Beauty.
— JACKSON-STOPS, G. Ickworth, Suffolk. [Bibliogr.] 36pp. Illus. (1 col. on cover) incl. plates, plan and genealog. table. 24x18 [London] 1981.
BURKE, J.B. Visitation of Seats. Vol.I, p.78. 1852.*
COUNTRY LIFE. English Country Houses: Mid Georgian. p.239. 1956.
COUNTRY LIFE. LVIII, 668, 698. 1925.
COUNTRY LIFE. CXVIII, 678. 1955.
COUNTRY LIFE. CLIII, 1362. 1973.
SANDON, E. Suffolk houses. 158. 1977.
TIPPING, H.A. English Homes. Period VI, Vol.I, p.321. 1926.

ICOMB PLACE (Gloucestershire).
COOKE, R. West Country Houses. p.31. 1957.
GARNER, T. Domestic architecture. I, p.30 plan. 1911.
NIVEN, W. Old Worcestershire houses. p.45, pl.20. 1873.

IDSWORTH PARK (Hampshire).
HAMPSHIRE: Architectural views. 1830.

IFORD MANOR (Wiltshire).
IFORD MANOR.
— A short account of Iford Manor ... and of the gardens. 4 ed. [Bibliogr. note.] 16pp. 17x12 (Trowbridge) privately printed, 1959.
COUNTRY LIFE. XXII, 450. 1907.
COUNTRY LIFE. LII, 242. 1922.

IGHTHAM COURT (Kent).
BADESLADE, T. Seats in Kent. pl.15. 1750.
BURKE, J.B. Visitation of Seats. Vol.I, p.257. 1852.*
COUNTRY LIFE. CXXIII, 1424. 1958.
HARRIS, J. History of Kent. p.162. 1719.

IGHTHAM MOTE (Kent).

HARRIS, Edwin.
— The Eastgate series.
8. History of Ightham Mote, Kent. 16pp. 1910.
COUNTRY LIFE. I, 406. 1897.
COUNTRY LIFE. XXI, 414. 1907.
GARNER, T. Domestic architecture. I, p.40 plan. 1911.
LATHAM, C. In English Homes. Vol.II, p.1. 1907.
NASH, J. Mansions of England. II, pls. 4, 5. 1840.
NASH, J. Mansions of England. IV, Title-page. 1849.
NICOLSON, N. Great Houses of Britain. p.18. 1965.
OSWALD, A. Country houses of Kent. 15. 1933.
THOMPSON, S. Old English homes. I. 1876.
TIPPING, H.A. English Homes. Period I & II, Vol.II, p.1. 1937.

ILAM HALL (Staffordshire).

BURKE, J.B. Visitation of Seats. 2.S. Vol.I, p.78. 1854.*
MORRIS, F.O. Views of Seats. Vol.I, p.41. 1880.
[Sales] ILAM HALL, 1925, November 2-6 [Contents]. (K.F. & R.).

ILKESTON HALL (Derbyshire).

TILLEY, J. Halls of Derbyshire. IV, p.103. 1902.*

ILMINGTON MANOR (Warwickshire).

COUNTRY LIFE. LXVII, 399. 1930.

IMBER COURT (Surrey).

COPPER PLATE MAGAZINE. pl.78. 1778.
COPPER PLATE MAGAZINE. III, pl.114. 1792-1802.
SANDBY, P. Select Views. I, pl.63. 1783.

INCE BLUNDELL HALL (Lancashire).

ASHMOLE, Bernard.
— A catalogue of the ancient marbles at Ince Blundell Hall. [Collected by Henry Blundell, d.1810; the property of the Weld-Blundell family. Bibliogr. notes.] Illus. plates and 1 on title-page. 33x26 Oxford: Clarendon Press, 1929.
INCE BLUNDELL HALL.
— An account of the statues, busts, bass-relieves, cinerary urns, and other ancient marbles, and paintings, at Ince. Collected by H. B[lundell]. Illus. incl. plates (1 folding). 2 vols. 26x22; 42x28 Liverpool: privately printed, 1803.
BARTLETT, J. Mansions of England and Wales. pl.105. 1853.
BURKE, J.B. Visitation of Seats. Vol.I, p.16. 1852.*
COUNTRY LIFE. CXXIII, 756 plan, 816, 876. 1958.
JONES. Views of Seats. I. 1829.
NEALE, J.P. Views of Seats. Vol.II. 1819.
TWYCROSS, E. Mansions of England and Wales. Vol.III, p.42. 1847.

INCE CASTLE (Cornwall).

COUNTRY LIFE. CXLI, 592, 648. 1967.

INCE HALL (Cheshire).

TWYCROSS, E. Mansions of England and Wales. Vol.I, p.118. 1850.*

INCE HALL, near Wigan (Lancashire).

GRAY, H. Old halls of Lancashire. p.43. 1893.

INGATESTONE HALL (Essex).

EMMISON, Frderick George.
— Tudor food and pastimes. (Life at Ingatestone Hall.) [Bibliogr.] Illus. incl. plates, plans and map. 21x14 London: Benn, 1964.
ESSEX: County Council [Essex Record Office].
— Publications.
XX. Introduction to Ingatestone Hall. 24pp. Illus. (1 on cover) incl. plans, maps (1 on inside cover) and facsimiles. 25x15 1953.
XXII. Ingatestone Hall in 1600: an inventory. (Introduction [By] F.G. Emmison.) [Bibliogr.] 24pp. 4 illus. (1 on cover, 2 on inside covers) incl. plate, plans and maps. 1954.
MANUSCRIPTS [Typewritten]. English.
— Inventory of furniture, etc., at Ingatestone Hall, Essex, of which the use was granted by Sir John Petre (afterwards 1st Baron Petre) to William Petre, in September, 1600. Copied from the original document preserved at Thornton [Sic Thorndon] Hall, Essex. Printed title and 109ff. 24x19 (1924).
COUNTRY LIFE. LXXXIII, 64. 1938.
CROMWELL, T.K. Excursions in Essex. I, p.127. 1825.

INGESTONE HOUSE (Herefordshire).

ROBINSON, C.J. Mansions of Herefordshire. pl.8. 1873.

INGESTRE HALL (Staffordshire).

INGESTRE HALL.
— Ingestre Hall: ... official guide. 16pp. Illus. (on covers) and map. 14x20 [Derby: E.L.P., 1956.]
Another ed. Ingestre Hall: an illustrated survey [etc.]. 32pp. Illus. (some col., some on covers) incl. maps (on inside covers). 14x21 [1957?]
COUNTRY LIFE CXXII, 772, 874, 924. 1957.
HALL, S.C. Baronial Halls. Vol.II. 1848.
JONES. Views of Seats. I. 1829.
NEALE, J.P. Views of Seats. Vol.IV. 1821.
NIVEN, W. Old Staffordshire houses. p.2, pls.2, 3. 1882.
PLOT, R. Staffordshire. 299. 1686.
SHAW, S. Staffordshire. II, pls.14, 15. Reprint 1976.
SUMMERSON, J. The Country Seat. [Three drawings.] 1970.

INGLEBY MANOR (Yorkshire).

BURKE, J.B. Visitation of Seats. 2.S. Vol.II, p.137. 1855.*
KIP, J. Nouveau théâtre de la Grande Bretagne. I, pl.60. 1715.

INGMELL (Cumberland).
BURKE, J.B. Visitation of Seats. 2.S. Vol.II, p.147. 1855.

INGMIRE HALL (Yorkshire).
[Sales] INGMIRE HALL, 1922 June 27-July 1 [Contents].
(K.F. & R.).

INGRESS ABBEY (Kent).
BADESLADE, T. Seats in Kent. pl.16. 1750.
GREENWOOD, C. Kent. 76. 1838.
HARRIS, J. History of Kent. p.309. 1719.

INKPEN OLD RECTORY (Berkshire).
COUNTRY LIFE. XCIII, 352. 1943.

IRIDGE PLACE (Sussex).
BURKE, J.B. Visitation of Seats. Vol.I, p.172. 1852.

IRLAM HALL (Lancashire).
BARTLETT, J. Mansions of England and Wales. pls.151,
152. 1853.
PYNE, W.H. Lancashire illustrated. 92. 1831.
TWYCROSS, E. Mansions of England and Wales. Vol.III, p.95.
1847.*

IRNHAM HALL (Lincolnshire).
JONES. Views of Seats. I. 1829.
NEALE, J.P. Views of Seats. Vol.II. 1819.

IRTON HALL (Cumberland).
BURKE, J.B. Visitation of Seats. 2.S. Vol.I, p.36. 1854.*
NEALE, J.P. Views of Seats. 2.S. Vol.III. 1826.

ISEL HALL (Cumberland).
CUMBERLAND: C. & W. A. & A.S. Extra Series VIII, 327.
1892.

ISINGTON MILL (Hampshire).
COUNTRY LIFE. CVII, 1118. 1950.

ISLE HOUSE, The. (Shropshire).
BURKE, J.B. Visitation of Seats. Vol.II, p.130. 1853.*
LEACH, F. Seats of Shropshire. p.299. 1891.

IVER GROVE (Buckinghamshire).
COUNTRY LIFE. English Country Houses: Baroque. p.219.
1970.
COUNTRY LIFE. CXXXIV, 372 plan. 1963.

IXWORTH ABBEY (Suffolk).
SANDON, E. Suffolk houses. 307. 1977.

JENNINGS (Kent).
See GENNINGS.

JERICHO (Essex).
RUSH, J.A. Seats in Essex. p.115. 1897.

JERRARDS, Sandford Orcas (Dorsetshire).
[Sales] SANDFORD ORCAS, JERRARDS, 1924, November 19,
20. [Contents.]

JOHNBY HALL (Cumberland).
CUMBERLAND: C. & W. A. & A.S. Extra series VIII, 294
plan. 1892.

JOLDWYNDS (Surrey).
COUNTRY LIFE. LXXVI, 276 plan. 1934.

JORDANS (Somerset).
SPROULE, A. Lost houses of Britain. 184. 1982.

JULIANS (Hertfordshire).
CHAUNCY, H. Hertfordshire. I. 158. 1826.
COUNTRY LIFE. CI, 1210. 1947.

JUNIPER HALL (Surrey).
HILL, Mary Constance.
— Juniper Hall: a rendezvous of certain illustrious personages
during the French Revolution including Alexandre D'Arblay
and Fanny Burney ... With illustrations by E.G. Hill. xvi,
276pp. Illus. incl. plates. 19x13 London; New York: J. Lane,
1905.

KEDLESTON HALL (Derbyshire).
KEDLESTON.
— Catalogue of the pictures, statues, &c. at Kedleston. With
some account of the architecture. 32pp. 20x16 n.p. (c. 1775).
KEDLESTON HALL.
— Kedleston Hall...Offical guide. 16pp. Illus. (on covers).
14x20 [Derby: Derbyshire Countryside, c. 1950.]
SCARSDALE, Richard Nathanial Curzon, *Viscount.*
— Kedleston Hall: an illustrated survey [etc.]. 32pp. Illus.
(some col., some on covers) incl. maps (on inside covers).
14x22 Derby: Derbyshire Countryside Ltd. [1958?].
BOLTON, A.T. Architecture of R. & J. Adam. I, 229 plan.
1922.
CAMPBELL, C. Vitruvius Britannicus.IV, pls.45-51. 1767.
COUNTRY LIFE. English Country Houses: Mid Georgian.
p.70. 1956.
COUNTRY LIFE. X, 240. 1901.
COUNTRY LIFE. XXXIV, 892, 928 plan. 1913.
COUNTRY LIFE. CLXIII, 194 plan, 262, 322. 1978.
ENGLISH CONNOISSEUR. II, 96. 1766.*

KEDLESTON HALL (Derbyshire). [Contd.]

JONES. Views of Seats. I. 1829.
KROLL, A. Historic houses. 124. 1969.
NEALE, J.P. Views of Seats. Vol.I. 1818.
NICOLSON, N. Great Houses of Britain. p.246. 1965.
PAINE, J. Plans, elevations. Pt.II, pls.42-52 plans. 1783.
TILLEY, J. Halls of Derbyshire. II, p.87. 1893.
WATTS, W. Seats of the Nobility. pl.22. 1779.

KEELE HALL (Staffordshire).

BURKE, J.B. Visitation of Seats. Vol.II, p.231. 1853.*
COUNTRY LIFE. XXIII, 306. 1908.
MORRIS, F.O. Views of Seats. Vol.III, p.9. 1880.
PLOT, R. Staffordshire. 335. 1686.

KEELE HALL (Staffordshire).

See also CLOCK HOUSE, Keele.

KEEVIL MANOR (Wiltshire).

GARNER, T. Domestic architecture. II, p.190. 1911.

KELHAM HALL (Nottinghamshire).

COUNTRY LIFE. CXLI, 1230 plan, 1302. 1967.
JONES. Views of Seats. I. 1829.
MORRIS, F.O. Views of Seats. Vol.IV. p.43. 1880.
NEALE, J.P. Views of Seats. Vol.III. 1820.
THOROTON, R. Nottinghamshire. III, 120. 1797.

KELMARSH HALL (Northamptonshire).

BRIDGES, J. Northamptonshire. II, 40. 1791.
COUNTRY LIFE. LXXIII, 198 plan. 1933.
GOTCH, J.A. Squires' Homes. 22. 1939.
NEALE, J.P. Views of Seats. Vol.III. 1820.

KELMSCOTT MANOR (Oxfordshire).

LONDON: Society of Antiquaries.
— DUFTY, A.R. Kelmscott: an illustrated guide. 36pp. Illus. (some col., 1 folding, 1 on title-page) incl. plan and covers. 25x17 London, 1969.
COUNTRY LIFE. L, 224, 256. 1921.
COUNTRY LIFE. CXLII, 1190. 1967.
[Sales] KELMSCOTT, 1939, July 19, 20 [Large portion of contents].

KELSTON (Somerset).

COLLINSON, J. History of Somerset. I, 128. 1791.

KELVEDON HALL (Essex).

BURKE, J.B. Visitation of Seats. Vol.II, p.85. 1853.*
COUNTRY LIFE. LXXXIX, 386, 408. 1941.
ENGLAND: Beauties of England. I, p.249. 1787.
RUSH, J.A. Seats in Essex. p.117.1897.

KEMPNALL HALL (Lancashire).

BURKE, J.B. Visitation of Seats. 2.S. Vol.I, p.198. 1854.*

KEMPSFORD (Gloucestershire).

ATKYNS, R. Glocestershire. p.257. 1768.

KENDAL HOUSE, Isleworth (Middlesex).

SPROULE, A. Lost houses of Britain. 189. 1982.

KENFIELD HALL (Kent).

BURKE, J.B. Visitation of Seats. Vol.II, p.181. 1853.*
GREENWOOD, C. Kent. 396. 1838.

KEN HILL (Norfolk).

COUNTRY LIFE. CXLII, 1654 plan, 1704. 1967.

KENTCHURCH COURT (Herefordshire).

COUNTRY LIFE. CXL, 1632, 1688, 1734 [Photocopy]. 1966.
JONES. Views of Seats. II. 1829.
NEALE, J.P. Views of Seats. 2.S. Vol.IV. 1828.
ROBINSON, C.J. Mansions of Herefordshire. pl.12. 1873.

KENTISFORD FARM (Somerset).

DELDERFIELD, E.R. West Country houses. I, 86. 1968.

KENTMERE HALL (Westmorland).

CUMBERLAND: C. & W. A. & A.S. Extra Series VIII, 219 plan. 1892.

KENTWELL HALL (Suffolk).

COUNTRY LIFE. XII, 465. 1902.
CROMWELL, T.K. Excursions in Suffolk. I, p.59. 1818.
GARNER, T. Domestic architecture. I, p.75. 1911.
NEALE, J.P. Views of Seats. 2.S. Vol.I. 1824.
SANDON, E. Suffolk houses. 190. 1977.

KENWOOD HOUSE, Hampstead (Middlesex).

HOLMES, *Sir* Charles John.
— Pictures from the Iveagh bequest and collections. With an introduction and catalogue of the Kenwood collection by Sir C.J.H. xxiv, 34pp. 60 (1 col.) plates. 49x36 London: W.J. Stacey, 1928.

LONDON: Kenwood House.
— Iveagh bequest: collection of old masters, Ken Wood.
(Catalogue.) 32pp. 3 illus. (1 on cover) incl. plan. 18x12
(London) [c.1928.]
Title on cover.
Another ed. The Iveagh bequest, Kenwood. 12pp. Illus. (2 on
covers) incl. 4 plates and plan. 21x14 1950.
Another ed. The Iveagh bequest, Kenwood: the house and the
paintings. 12pp. 8 plates. 12x18 (1954).
LONDON: Kenwood House.
— The Iveagh bequest, Kenwood: catalogue of the paintings.
(Introduction [by] A. Blunt.) [Bibliogr.] 32pp. 16 plates and
plan (on cover). 21x14 (1953.)
(2 ed.) 40pp. (1960).
(3 ed.) Illus. (some on cover) incl. 16 plates and plan. (1965).
LONDON: Kenwood House.
— SUMMERSON, J. The Iveagh bequest Kenwood: a short
account of its history and architecture. [Bibliogr.] 24pp. Illus.
(2 on cover) incl. 12 plates, section, elevations and plans. 22x14
London (1951).
Another ed. (1956).
ADAM, R. & J. Works in Architecture. I. 1773.
BOLTON, A.T. Architecture of R. & J. Adam. I, 303 plan. 1922.
COPPER PLATE MAGAZINE. I, pl.32. 1792-1802.
COUNTRY LIFE. XXXIV, 710 plan. 1913.
COUNTRY LIFE. LXII, 653. 1927.
COUNTRY LIFE. CVII, 1550. 1950.
ENGLAND: Beauties of England. II, p.73. 1787.
ENGLAND: Picturesque Views. p.9, 91. 1786-88.
[Sales] LONDON, 1922, November 6-9 [Furnishings etc.].

KENYON PEEL HALL (Lancashire).
SPROULE, A. Lost houses of Britain. 191. 1982.

KERFIELD HOUSE, Knutsford (Cheshire).
COUNTRY LIFE. LXV, 181 [Furniture]. 1929.

KERSAL CELL (Lancashire).
COUNTRY LIFE. XCVIII, 1092. 1945.

KESWICK HALL (Norfolk).
GURNEY, Gerard Hudson.
— Portraits at Keswick Hall. 78pp. 1 illus. and genealog. table.
31x24 Norwich (privately printed), 1922.

KEYTHORPE HALL (Leicestershire).
BURKE, J.B. Visitation of Seats. 2.S. Vol.I, p.83. 1854.*
[Sales] KEYTHORPE HALL, 1927, July 11-15 [Contents].

KIDBROOKE (Sussex).
BURKE, J.B. Visitation of Seats. 2.S. Vol.I, p.18. 1854.*
COUNTRY LIFE. LXXIX, 404. 1936.
NEALE, J.P. Views of Seats. Vol.IV. 1821.

KIELDER CASTLE (Northumberland).
WATTS, W. Seats of the Nobility. pl.58. 1779.

KIFTSGATE COURT (Gloucestershire).
[Sales] KIFTSGATE COURT, 1975, October 25 [Remaining
contents].

KILDWICK HALL (Yorkshire).
COUNTRY LIFE. XXIX, 126 plan. 1911.
TIPPING, H.A. English Homes. Early Renaissance. p.277.
1912.
TIPPING, H.A. English Homes. Period III, Vol.I, p.318. 1922.
YORKSHIRE. Picturesque views. 1885.

KILHENDRE (Shropshire).
SHROPSHIRE. Castles and Old Mansions. 28. 1868.

KILLAMARSH HALL (Derbyshire).
TILLEY, J. Halls of Derbyshire. III, p.147. 1899.

KILLERTON PARK (Devonshire).
LONDON: National Trust for Places of Historic Interest or
Natural Beauty.
— ACLAND, A. Killerton, Devon. [Bibliogr.] 56pp. Illus. (1 col.
on cover) incl. plan, map and genealog. table. 21x14 [London]
1983.
BRITTON, J. Devonshire illustrated. 34. 1832.

KILLINGTON HALL (Westmorland).
CUMBERLAND: C. & W. A. & A.S. Extra Series VIII, 238.
1892.

KILLYMAENLLWYD (Carmarthenshire).
BURKE, J.B. Visitation of Seats. Vol.II, p.95. 1853.*

KILNWICK PERCY HALL (Yorkshire).
[Sales] KILNWICK PERCY HALL, 1954, November 3 [Large
portion of the contents].

KILVERT'S PARSONAGE, Langley Burrell (Wiltshire).
COUNTRY LIFE. CL, 800. 1971.

KILVINGTON HALL (Yorkshire).
BURKE, J.B. Visitation of Seats. Vol.II, p.110. 1853.*

KIMBERLEY HALL (Norfolk).
BURKE, J.B. Visitation of Seats. 2.S. Vol.I, p.107. 1854.*
CROMWELL, T.K. Excursions in Norfolk. II, p.103. 1819.
MORRIS, F.O. Views of Seats. Vol.V, p.13. 1880.
NEALE, J.P. Views of Seats. Vol.III. 1820.

KIMBOLTON CASTLE (Huntingdonshire).
KIMBOLTON CASTLE.
— A brief guide to Kimbolton Castle. 12pp. 1 illus. 20x16
(Raunds) privately printed [c.1970.]
MAURICE, Frank Lyttleton Powys, *Canon.*
— A short history of Kimbolton, its church and castle. 6 ed.
32pp. 6 plates. 18x12 (Kimbolton: Newman, 1954.)
WHISTLER, Laurence.
— Some unpublished drawings of Sir John Vanbrugh ... in the
Victoria and Albert Museum (and the British Museum).
Excerpts. Illus. incl. elevations and plans. 3pts. in 1 vol. 25x18
[London, 1948-9].
II. Three newly discovered designs for Kimbolton Castle,
remodelled by Vanbrugh and Hawksmoor, 1707-9. 5pp. 1949.
From: New English review magazine, II, no.5.
BURKE, J.B. Visitation of Seats. 2.S. Vol.I, p.64. 1854.*
COUNTRY LIFE. English Country Houses: Baroque. p.102.
1970.
COUNTRY LIFE. XXX, 440, 447 [Furniture], 474, 485
[Furniture], 557 [Furniture], 597 [Furniture]. 1911.
COUNTRY LIFE. CXLIV, 1474, 1584 plan, 1644, 1696. 1968.
MORRIS, F.O. Views of Seats. Vol.III, p.51. 1880.
TIPPING, H.A. English Homes. Period IV, Vol.I, p.277. 1920.
TIPPING, H.A. English Homes. Period IV, Vol.II, p.113. 1928.
[Sales] LONDON, 1947, July 11 [Books].

KIMPTON HOO (Hertfordshire).
NEALE, J.P. Views of Seats. 2.S. Vol.V. 1829.

KINGERBY HALL (Lincolnshire).
BURKE, J.B. Visitation of Seats. Vol.I, p.22. 1852.*

KING'S BROMLEY HALL (Staffordshire).
BURKE, J.B. Visitation of Seats. Vol.II, p.115. 1853.*
JONES. Views of Seats. I. 1829.
NEALE, J.P. Views of Seats. 2.S. Vol.IV. 1828.
SHAW, S. Staffordshire. I, 147. 1798.

KINGSBURY HALL (Warwickshire).
HODGES, E. Ancient English Homes. 157. 1895.
NIVEN, W. Old Warwickshire houses. p.10, pl.13. 1878.

KINGSCOTE PARK (Gloucestershire).
BURKE, J.B. Visitation of Seats. 2.S. Vol.I, p.29. 1854.*

KINGSGATE (Kent).
ANGUS, W. Seats of the Nobility. pl.57. 1787.
CROMWELL, T.K. Excursions in Kent. p.32. 1822.

KING'S HEAD HOUSE, Beaconsfield
(Buckinghamshire).
COUNTRY LIFE. LXV, 467 plan, 533. 1929.

KING'S LODGE, Abbots Langley
(Hertfordshire).
COUNTRY LIFE. XCIII, 660 plan. 1943.

KING'S MANOR, York (Yorkshire).
COUNTRY LIFE. L, 544. 1921.

KINGS NEWTON HALL (Derbyshire).
TILLEY, J. Halls of Derbyshire. IV, p.89. 1902.*

KINGS SUTTON MANOR
(Northamptonshire).
GOTCH, J.A. Squires' Homes. 43. 1939.

KINGSTHORPE HALL
(Northamptonshire).
GOTCH, J.A. Squires' Homes. 33. 1939.

KINGSTON HALL (Nottinghamshire).
BURKE, J.B. Visitation of Seats. Vol.I, p.48. 1852.*

KINGSTON HOUSE, Kingston Bagpuize
(Berkshire).
COUNTRY LIFE. XCII, 890 [Missing], 938. 1942.

KINGSTON HOUSE, Bradford-on-Avon
(Wiltshire).
KINGSTON HOUSE.
— History of Kingston House (Bradford-on-Avon. Wilts.).
12pp. Plate.18x12 Westbury: W. Michael, 1883.
Title on cover.
ELYARD, S.J. Old Wiltshire homes. p.44. 1894.
HALL, S.C. Baronial Halls. Vol.II. 1848.

KINGSTON LACY (Dorsetshire).
COUNTRY LIFE. XV, 558. 1904.
HEATH, S. Dorset Manor Houses. 103. 1907.
HUTCHINS, J. Vitruvius Dorsettiensis. pl.15. 1816.
HUTCHINS, J. History of Dorset. III, 236. 1868.
JONES. Views of Seats. II. 1829.
LATHAM, C. In English Homes. Vol.I, p.341. 1904.
NEALE, J.P. Views of Seats. Vol.I. 1818.
OSWALD, A. Country houses of Dorset. p.144. 1959.

KENWOOD HOUSE, Middlesex. From: ADAM (R. & J). *The works in architecture of Robert and James Adam*, vol. I, London, 1773.

KINGSTON LISLE HOUSE (Berkshire).
COUNTRY LIFE. CXLIX, 1524. 1971.

KINGSTON MAURWARD HOUSE (Dorsetshire).
HUTCHINS, J. Vitruvius Dorsettiensis. pl.14. 1816.
HUTCHINS, J. History of Dorset. II, 561. 1863.
OSWALD, A. Country houses of Dorset. p.154. 1959.

KINGSTON MAURWARD OLD MANOR HOUSE (Dorsetshire).
GARNER, T. Domestic architecture. II, p.165. 1911.
OSWALD, A. Country houses of Dorset. p.91. 1959.

KINGSTON RUSSELL HOUSE (Dorsetshire).
COUNTRY LIFE. CX, 1628, 1712. 1951.
OSWALD, A. Country houses of Dorset. p.156. 1959.

KINGSTON SEYMOUR MANOR (Somerset).
GARNER, T. Domestic architecture. I, p.23 plan. 1911.

KING'S WALDEN BURY (Hertfordshire).
BARTLETT, J. Selections from views of mansions. 1851.
COUNTRY LIFE. CLIV, 858, 974. 1973.
NEALE, J.P. Views of Seats. 2.S. Vol.V. 1829.

KING'S WESTON (Gloucestershire).
ATKYNS, R. Glocestershire. p.249. 1768.
CAMPBELL, C. Vitruvius Britannicus. I, pls. 47, 48. 1715.
COOKE, R. West Country Houses. p.110. 1957.
COPPER PLATE MAGAZINE. IV, pl.176. 1792-1802.
COUNTRY LIFE. LXI, 680. 1927.
COUNTRY LIFE. CXIII, 212. 1953.
HAVELL, R. Views of Noblemen's Seats. 1823.
JONES. Views of seats. II. 1829.
NEALE, J.P. Views of Seats. Vol.II. 1819.
TIPPING, H.A. English Homes. Period IV, Vol.II, p.141. 1928.

KINGSWOOD WARREN (Surrey).
BRAYLEY, E.W. History of Surrey. IV, 273. 1841.
BURKE, J.B. Visitation of Seats. 2.S. Vol.I, p.181. 1854. *

KINGTHORPE HALL (Yorkshire).
[Sales] KINGTHORPE HOUSE [Hall] 1932, September 28, 29 [Contents]. (K.F. & R.).

KING WESTON (Somerset).
JONES. Views of Seats. II. 1829.
NEALE, J.P. Views of Seats. 2.S. Vol.IV. 1828.

KINLET HALL (Shropshire).
LEACH, F. Seats of Shropshire. p.281. 1891.
LEIGHTON, S. Shropshire houses. 42. 1901.

KINMEL PARK (Denbighshire).
BURKE, J.B. Visitation of Seats. 2.S. Vol.I, p.1. 1854.
COUNTRY LIFE. CXLVI, 542, 614 plan. 1969.
[Sales] KINMEL PARK, 1929, June 4 and following days. [Contents].

KIPLIN HALL (Yorkshire).
COUNTRY LIFE. LXX, 228. 1931.
WOOD, G.B. Historic homes of Yorkshire. 78. 1957.

KIPPAX PARK (Yorkshire).
JONES. Views of Seats. I. 1829.
NEALE, J.P. Views of Seats. Vol.V. 1822.

KIPPINGTON HOUSE (Kent).
BADESLADE, T. Seats in Kent. pl.17. 1750.
HARRIS, J. History of Kent. p.278. 1719.
NEALE, J.P. Views of Seats. Vol.II. 1819.

KIRBY CANE HALL (Norfolk).
BURKE, J.B. Visitation of Seats. 2.S. Vol.I, p.83. 1854. *

KIRBY HALL (Essex).
ENGLAND: Beauties of England. I, p.256. 1787.
ESSEX: A new and complete history. II, 103. 1769.

KIRBY HALL (Northamptonshire).
GREAT BRITAIN: Office of Works and Public Buildings.
— CHETTLE, G.H. Kirby Hall. 28pp. Plates (2 folding) incl. plans. 21x13 London, 1937.
GREAT BRITAIN: Ministry of Works [Ancient Monuments and Historic Buildings].
2 ed. 20pp. 1947.
3 ed. Illus. (on cover) and plates (2 folding) incl. plans. 1955.
GREAT BRITAIN: Department of the Environment [Ancient Monuments and Historic Buildings].
Another ed. Illus. incl. 2 folding plans. 1972.
Another ed. By G.H.C. Revised by P. Leach. [Doe] 36pp. Illus. incl. folding plan. 21x15 1980.
NORTHAMPTONSHIRE.
— Historical collections relating to Northamptonshire. [Collected by J. Taylor.] Illus. 21x13 Northampton, 1896-IV. Tracts rare and curious reprints, MS., etc.
GOTCH, J.A. Historic notes on Kirby Hall. 16pp. Illus. incl. plates. 1900.

COUNTRY LIFE. XX, 558. 1906.

GOTCH, J.A. Architecture of the Renaissance. I, p.33 plan. 1894.

GOTCH, J.A. Halls of Northants. p.15. 1936.

HALL, S.C. Baronial Halls. Vol.II. 1848.

JONES. Views of Seats. I. 1829.

NEALE, J.P. Views of Seats. 2.S. Vol.III. 1826.

TIPPING, H.A. English Homes. Early Renaissance. p.69. 1912.

TIPPING, H.A. English Homes. Period III, Vol.I, p.78. 1922.

KIRBY HALL (Yorkshire).

CAMPBELL, C. Vitruvius Britannicus. V, pls.70, 71. 1771.

KIRBY MISPERTON HALL (Yorkshire).

[Sales] KIRBY MISPERTON, 1928, October 30-November 3 [Contents].

KIRKBY MALLORY HALL (Leicestershire).

NICHOLS, J. History of Leicestershire. IV, ii, 771. 1811.

THROSBY, J. Views in Leicestershire. p.157. 1789.

KIRKBY THORE HALL (Westmorland).

CUMBERLAND: C. & W. A. & A.S. Extra Series VIII, 139. 1892.

KIRKHAM ABBEY (Yorkshire).

LIVERPOOL, Cecil George Savile Foljambe, *Earl of.*
— Catalogue of portraits, miniatures &c. [at] (Kirkham ... and 2 Carlton House Terrace) in the possession of C.G. Savile [etc.]. Plates incl. folding genealog. table. 21x13 (Hull) for the author, 1905.

Also in Hull: East Riding Antiquarian Society, Transactions, XIII, i. 1906.

BURKE, J.B. Visitation of Seats. 2.S. Vol.I, p.227. 1854.*

KIRKLEATHAM HALL (Yorkshire).

KIP, J. Nouveau théâtre de la Grande Bretagne. I, pl.79. 1715.

KIRKLEES PARK [HALL] (Yorkshire).

BURKE, J.B. Visitation of Seats. 2.S. Vol.I, p.211. 1854.*

COUNTRY LIFE. XXIV, 256. 1908.

JONES. Views of Seats. I. 1829.

LATHAM, C. In English Homes. Vol.III, p.25. 1909.

NEALE, J.P. Views of Seats. Vol.V. 1822.

WOOD, G.B. Historic homes of Yorkshire. 15. 1957.

YORKSHIRE, Picturesque views. 1885.

KIRKLINGTON HALL (Nottinghamshire)

THROTON, R. Nottinghamshire. III, 100. 1797.

KIRKLINGTON HALL (Yorkshire).

MACCALL, Hardy Bertram.
— Story of the family of Wandesforde of Kirklington and Castlecomer, compiled from original sources, with a calendar of historical manuscripts, edited by H.B.M. Illus. incl. plates, plan, facsimiles, (some of signatures) and genealog. tables. 28x22 London: Simpkin Marshall Hamilton Kent & Co., 1904.

KIRKSTALL ABBEY (Yorkshire).

BURKE, J.B. Visitation of Seats. 2.S. Vol.II, p.137. 1855.*

KIRSTEAD OLD HALL (Norfolk).

BIRKBECK, G. Old Norfolk houses. 71. 1908.

GARRATT, T. Halls of Norfolk. pls.29-31. 1890.

KIRTLINGTON PARK (Oxfordshire).

BURKE, J.B. Visitation of Seats. Vol.II, p.6. 1853.*

CAMPBELL, C. Vitruvius Britannicus. IV, pls.32-36. 1767.

COUNTRY LIFE. English Country Houses: Early Georgian. p.170. 1955.

COUNTRY LIFE. XXXI, 542 plan. 1912.

TIPPING, H.A. English Homes. Period V, Vol.I, p.281. 1921.

KIRTLING TOWER (Cambridgeshire).

COUNTRY LIFE. LXIX, 102. 1931.

MORRIS, F.O. Views of Seats. Vol.IV. p.47. 1880.

KITE HOUSE, Monks Horton (Kent).

COUNTRY LIFE. XLVI, 756. 1919.

OSWALD, A. Country houses of Kent. 26. 1933.

KITLEY (Devonshire).

BRITTON, J. Devonshire illustrated. 42. 1832.

COUNTRY LIFE. English Country Houses: Late Georgian. p.168. 1958.

COUNTRY LIFE. LXXXVI, 362. 1939.

KIVETON HOUSE (Yorkshire).

CAMPBELL, C. Vitruvius Britannicus. IVth. pls.11-18. 1739.

KNARESBOROUGH MANOR (Yorkshire).

WOOD, G.B. Historic homes of Yorkshire. 47. 1957.

KNEBWORTH HOUSE (Hertfordshire).

FLOWER, Sibylla Jane.
— Knebworth House, home of the Lytton family since 1492. 24pp. Illus. (some col., some on covers) incl. genealog. table. 24x18 (Derby: E.L.P., 1974.)

— Guide book to visitors of Knebworth, the seat of the right Hon. Sir Edward Bulwer Lytton, Bart.,M.P. 28pp. 18x12n.p. [c. 1865].

With MS. Notes by Lord Lytton.

KNEBWORTH.
— Knebworth in 1850. Gleanings from an old guide book.
Excerpt. 23x15 Hitchin, 1913.
From: the Hertfordshire Express, LIV.
KNEBWORTH.
— A history of Knebworth House and its owners. [By Edith,
Countess of Lytton?] (The history of Jenny Spinner: the
ghost of Knebworth House.) [By E.M. James.] [Bibliogr.
notes.] 56pp. Plates. 21x17 Letchworth: privately printed at
the Arden Press, 1915.
    Presentation copy signed by the Countess of Lytton.
BURKE, J.B. Visitation of Seats. Vol.I, p.130. 1852.*
CHAUNCY, H. Hertfordshire.II, 94. 1826.
COUNTRY LIFE. I, 694. 1897.
COUNTRY LIFE. XIX, 522. 1906.
HALL, S.C. Baronial Halls. Vol.I. 1848.
JONES. Views of Seats. I. 1829.
LATHAM, C. In English Homes. Vol.II, p.397. 1907.
NEALE, J.P. Views of Seats. 2.S. Vol.I. 1824.

KNEDLINGTON MANOR (Yorkshire).
BURKE, J.B. Visitation of Seats. Vol.I, p.242. 1852.*

KNELLER HALL (Middlesex).
SUMMERSON, J. The Country Seat. 81. 1970.

KNELLS, The. (Cumberland).
BURKE, J.B. Visitation of Seats. Vol.I, p.58. 1852. *

KNEPP CASTLE (Sussex).
BURKE, J.B. Visitation of Seats. Vol.I, p.179. 1852.*

KNIGHTSHAYES COURT (Devonshire).
LONDON: National Trust for Places of Historic Interest or
Natural Beauty.
— MELLER, H. Knightshayes Court, Devon. [Bibliogr.] 52pp.
Illus. (1 Col. on cover) incl. plan. 22x14 [London] 1981.

KNIGHT'S HILL (Surrey).
COPPER PLATE MAGAZINE. II, pl.84. 1792-1802.
ENGLAND: Picturesque Views. p.63. 1786-88.

KNIGHTSTONE (Devonshire).
COUNTRY LIFE. CVIII, 754 plan, 836. 1950.

KNILL COURT (Herefordshire).
BURKE, J.B. Visitation of Seats. Vol.I, p.157. 1852.*
ROBINSON. C.J. Mansions of Herefordshire. pl.13. 1873.

KNOLE (Kent).
BRADY, John Henry.
— The visitor's guide to Knole, in the county of Kent, with
catalogues of the pictures contained in the mansion, and
biographical notices of the principal persons whose portraits
form part of the collection. Illus. incl. plates and folding
genealog. table.17x10 Sevenoaks: J. Payne, 1839.
An abrigement of the visitor's guide to Knole[etc.] 48pp. 1 cut.
1844.
BRIDGMAN, John.
— An historical and topographical sketch of Knole, in Kent;
with a brief genealogy of the Sackville family. Engr. plates.
21x13 London: W. Lindsell; Sevenoaks: W. Hodsoll & T.
Clout; Tonbridge Wells: Strange & Nash, 1817.
JOURDAIN, Margaret.
— Stuart furniture at Knole. 48pp. Illus. 18x12 London:
Country Life, 1952.
KNOLE.
— Biographical sketches of eminent persons, whose portraits
form part of the Duke of Dorset's collection at Knole, with a
brief description of the place [by H.N. Willis] Engr. plates.
21x12 London: J. Stockdale, 1795.
Wanting some plates.
KNOLE.
— West [Lord Delawarr] v. Cope [Report of Litigation
respecting cabinets from Knole.] 3 folded ff. 19x16 London,
1876-77.
KNOLE.
— Guide to Knole, its state rooms, pictures and antiquities,
with a short account of the possessors and park of Knole.
New ed. 60pp. Illus. incl. plates. 18x12 Sevenoaks: J. Salmon,
1913.
Another ed. 58pp. Plates. London: Waterlow & Sons, 1930.
LONDON: National Trust for Places of Historic Interest or
Natural Beauty.
— SACKVILLE-WEST, V. Knole, Kent. Catalogue of
pictures...by R. Fedden. 44pp. 8 plates. 18x12 London:
Country Life (1948).
Another ed. 38pp. 1966.

LONDON: National Trust for Places of Historic Interest or
Natural Beauty.
— Knole, Kent. [Bibliogr.] 60pp. Illus. (1 col. on cover) incl.
plan and genealog. table. 25x18 [London] 1982.
MACKIE, Samuel Joseph.
— Knole House, its state rooms, pictures and antiquities. 102pp.
2 engr. plates. 15x12 Sevenoaks: G.W.Harrison; London:
Russell Smith [1858?].
PHILLIPS, Charles James.
— History of the Sackville family — earls and dukes of
Dorset. Together with a description of Knole, early owners of
Knole and a catalogue raisonné of the pictures and drawings at
Knole. [Bibliogr. notes.] Illus. incl. plates, facsimiles of
signatures and genealog. tables. 2 vols. 32x25 London: Cassell
& Co. (1929).
SACKVILLE, Lionel Edward Sackville West, *Baron*.
— Knole House: its state rooms, pictures and antiquities.
New ed. Illus. incl. plates (some col.) 21x17 Sevenoaks: J.
Salmon, 1906.

SACKVILLE-WEST, *Hon.* Victoria Mary.
— Knole and the Sackvilles. 25 plates. 25x15 London: Heinemann, 1923.
Another ed. 21x14 London: Lindsay Drummond, 1948.

BADESLADE, T. Seats in Kent. pls. 18, 19. 1750.

CAMPBELL, C. Vitruvius Britannicus.IVth pls.34, 35. 1739.

COPPER PLATE MAGAZINE. pl.42. 1778.

COUNTRY LIFE. XXXI, 772 plan, 796 [Furniture], 826 plan, 862. 1912.

COUNTRY LIFE. XCVII, 72 [Furniture]. 1945.

COUNTRY LIFE. CI, 660. 1947.

COUNTRY LIFE. CXXXVIII, 1252 [Lead Roof].1965.

COUNTRY LIFE. CLXI, 1495 [Furniture], 1620 [Furniture]. 1977.

CROMWELL, T.K. Excursions in Kent. p.112. 1822.

GOTCH, J.A. Architecture of the Renaissance. I, p.50. 1894.

GREENWOOD, C. Kent. 97. [List of Paintings] 1838.*

HALL, S.C. Baronial Halls. Vol.I. 1848.

HARRIS, J. History of Kent. p.278. 1719.

HASTED, E. Kent. I, 349. 1778.

KIP, J. Nouveau théâtre de la Grande Bretagne. I, pl.24. 1715.

MALAN, A.H. More famous homes. p.31. 1902.

MORRIS, F.O. Views of Seats. Vol.VI, p.69. 1880.

NASH, J. Mansions of England. II, pls. 17-23. 1840.

NEALE, J.P. Views of Seats. Vol.II. 1819.

NICOLSON, N. Great Houses of Britain. p.92. 1965.

OSWALD, A. Country Houses of Kent. 31. 1933.

SANDBY, P. Select Views, I. pl.23. 1783.

SHAW, H. Elizabethan architecture. pl. XLVI.[Ceiling of King James's bedroom] 1839.

THOMPSON, S. Old English homes. 106. 1876.

TIPPING, H.A. English Homes. Period III, Vol.I, p.222. 1922.

UNITED KINGDOM. Historic Houses. 273. 1892.

KNOLE PARK (Gloucestershire).
ATKYNS, R. Glocestershire. p.110. 1768.

BURKE, J.B. Visitation of Seats. Vol.II, p.149. 1853.*

COOKE, R. West Country Houses. p.60. 1957.

KNOTTFIELD HOUSE (Yorkshire).
YORKSHIRE. Picturesque views. 1885.

KNOWLE, Cranleigh (Surrey).
BRAYLEY, E.W. History of Surrey. V, 170. 1841.

KNOWLE HALL (Warwickshire).
SMITH, W. History of the County of Warwick. 376. 1830.

KNOWLMERE MANOR (Yorkshire).
BURKE, J.B. Visitation of Seats. 2.S. Vol.I, p.150. 1854.*

KNOWLTON COURT (Kent).
BADESLADE, T. Seats in Kent. pl.20. 1750.

BURKE, J.B. Visitation of Seats. 2.S. Vol.II, p.87. 1855.*

COUNTRY LIFE. XXXIX, 534 plan. 1916.

HARRIS, J. History of Kent. p.171. 1719.

HASTED, E. Kent. IV, 211. 1799.

NEALE, J.P. Views of Seats. 2.S. Vol.II. 1825.

OSWALD, A. Country houses of Kent. 40. 1933.

KNOWSLEY HALL (Lancashire).
CLISSITT, Willie. C., *Lieut-Col.*
— Knowsley Hall. 36pp. Illus. 18x12 Knowsley: privately printed, 1950.

GRAY, John Edward.
— Gleanings from the menagerie and aviary at Knowsley Hall. (Drawings made by E. Lear from the living animals in the ... Earl of Derby's menagerie ... Lithographed ... by J.W. Moore, and coloured by Mr. Bayfield. [Text by] J.E.G. [Notes by] Lord Derby.) 16pp. 17 col. lithogr. plates. 55x36 Knowsley (privately printed), 1846.

SCHARF, *Sir* George.
A ... catalogue of the collection of pictures at Knowsley Hall. Facsimiles of artists' signatures. 28x21 London: Bradbury, Agnew & Co., 1875.
Another copy with MS. Letter from G. Scharf to W. Smith, inserted.

WINSTANLEY, Hamlet.
— Praenobili Jacobo Comiti Derby [etc.].[Engravings of pictures in the Earl of Derby's collection at Knowsley Hall. Engraved by H.W. No text]. 20ff. Fol. 55x42 [London, 1729.]

MANUSCRIPTS.   English.
— Catalogue of paintings at Knowsley Hall taken in 1801 (the prices of the principal pictures in the catalogue at the time they were bought). [Catalogue probably based on one complied by H. Winstanley, employed by Lord Derby to select and purchase for him. With some annotations in a later hand...Earl of Whemysses [sic] catalogue of paintings at Amisfield in Scotland (in MS.). 64ff. 18.5x11.5 [1801-02?]

BARTLETT, J. Mansions of England and Wales. pl.97. 1853.

BURKE, J.B. Visitations of Seats. Vol.II, p.113. 1853.*

COUNTRY LIFE. XXXIV, 54. 1913.

COUNTRY LIFE. LXXXI, 276, 1937.

JONES. Views of Seats. I. 1829.

MORRIS, F.O. Views of Seats. Vol.I, p.55. 1880.

NEALE, J.P. Views of Seats. 2.S. Vol.I. 1824.

PYNE, W.H. Lancashire illustrated. 29. 1831.

TWYCROSS, E. Mansions of England and Wales. Vol.III, p.1. 1847.

KYMIN, The. (Monmouthshire).
LONDON: National Trust for Places of Historic Interest or Natural Beauty.
— The Kymin, Monmouthshire. 4pp. 1 illus. 22x14 [London, *c*.1955.]

KYRE PARK (Worcestershire).
COUNTRY LIFE. English Country Houses: Early Georgian. p.217. 1955.

COUNTRY LIFE. XLI, 252, 276. 1917.

NASH, T.R. Worcestershire. I, 472. 1781.

TIPPING, H.A. English Homes. Period VI, Vol.I, p.73. 1926.

[Sales] KYRE PARK, 1930, July 7-11 [The J. Pytts collection, furniture, books etc.].

LACOCK ABBEY (Wiltshire).
LACOCK.

— Lacock Abbey. 24pp. Illus. 18x12 Trowbridge: Wiltshire Times [c.1919].
Vol.2 of: PICTURESQUE WILTSHIRE series.

LONDON: National Trust for Places of Historic Interest or Natural Beauty.

— Lacock Abbey, Chippenham, Wilts. 4pp. 2 illus. incl. map. 22x14 [London, c. 1945.]
Another ed. Lacock Abbey, Wiltshire. [Bibliogr.] 30pp. 4 plates and plan. 18x12 London: Country Life (1947).
Another ed. [Bibliogr.] 28pp. Illus. (1 on cover) plates, plans and genealog. table 21x14 [London] 1974.

LONDON: National Trust for Places of Historic Interest or Natural Beauty.

An illustrated guide: Fox Talbot Museum, Lacock. 16pp. Illus. (some on covers) 15x21 [London] 1976.

BRITTON, J. Beauties of Wiltshire. III, 235. 1825.

BUCK, S.N. Antiquities. II, pl.315. 1774.

COUNTRY LIFE. LIII, 280 plan, 314, 352. 1923.

JONES. Views of Seats. II. 1829.

NEALE, J.P. Views of Seats. 2.S. Vol.III. 1826.

TIPPING, H.A. English Homes. Period II, Vol.I, p.361. 1924.

[Sales] LONDON, 1947, July 28, 29 [Portion of the library].

LACY HOUSE, Isleworth (Middlesex).
ANGUS, W. Seats of the Nobility. pl.36. 1787.

LADYE ROYDE HALL (Yorkshire).
YORKSHIRE. Picturesque views. 1885.

LAGHOOGE (Lancashire).
BURKE, J.B. Visitation of Seats. 2.S. Vol.I, p.195. 1854.*

LAINSTON HOUSE (Hampshire).
COUNTRY LIFE. XLV, 252. 1919.

LAKE HOUSE (Wiltshire).
BURKE, J.B. Visitation of Seats. 2.S. Vol.I, p.63. 1854.*

COUNTRY LIFE. XXIII, 198. 1908.

COUNTRY LIFE. LXXXI, 326, 352 plan. 1927.

GARNER, T. Domestic architecture. II, p.192 plan. 1911.

TIPPING, H.A. English Homes. Early Rennaissance. p.293. 1912.

LALEHAM HOUSE (Middlesex).
[Sales] LALEHAM HOUSE, 1922, November 27-29 [Remaining contents].

LAMB HOUSE, Rye (Sussex).
COUNTRY LIFE. CXVII, 396. 1955.

LAMBOURNE PLACE (Berkshire).
BURKE, J.B. Visitation of Seats. Vol.I, p.200. 1852.*

LAMBTON CASTLE (Durham).
BURKE, J.B. Visitation of Seats. 2.S. Vol.I, p.140. 1854.*

COUNTRY LIFE. CXXXIX, 664 [Photocopy], 726 plan. 1966.

JONES. Views of Seats. I. 1829.

MORRIS, F.O. Views of Seats. Vol.III, p.5. 1880.

NEALE, J.P. Views of Seats. Vol.I. 1818.

[Sales] LAMBTON CASTLE, 1932, April 18 [Pictures and watercolour drawings].

[Sales] LONDON, 1932, April 19-22 [Prints and the library].

[Sales] LONDON, 1932, April 25-May 5 [Furnishings, silver etc.].

LAMER PARK (Hertfordshire).
BURKE, J.B. Visitation of Seats. Vol.II, p.133. 1853.*

LAMPHEY COURT (Pembrokeshire).
BUCK, S. & N. Antiquities. II, pl.421. 1774.

JONES. Views of Seats. VI. 1831.

LAMPORT HALL (Northamptonshire).
LAMPORT HALL.
— Lamport Hall, seat of Sir Gyles Isham, Bart. 24pp. Illus. (some col., some on covers.) 20x16 (Derby: E.L.P., 1974.)

BURKE, J.B. Visitation of Seats. Vol.I, p.10. 1852.*

COUNTRY LIFE. English Country Houses: Caroline. p.97. 1966.

COUNTRY LIFE. XLIX, 672. 1921.

COUNTRY LIFE. CXII, 932, 1022, 1106. 1952.

GOTCH, J.A. Halls of Northants. p.57. 1936.

NEALE, J.P. Views of Seats. Vol.III. 1820.

LAMPORT RECTORY (Northamptonshire).
GOTCH, J.A. Squires' Homes. 24. 1939.

LANGAR HALL (Nottinghamshire).
THOROTON, R. Nottinghamshire. I, 209. 1797.

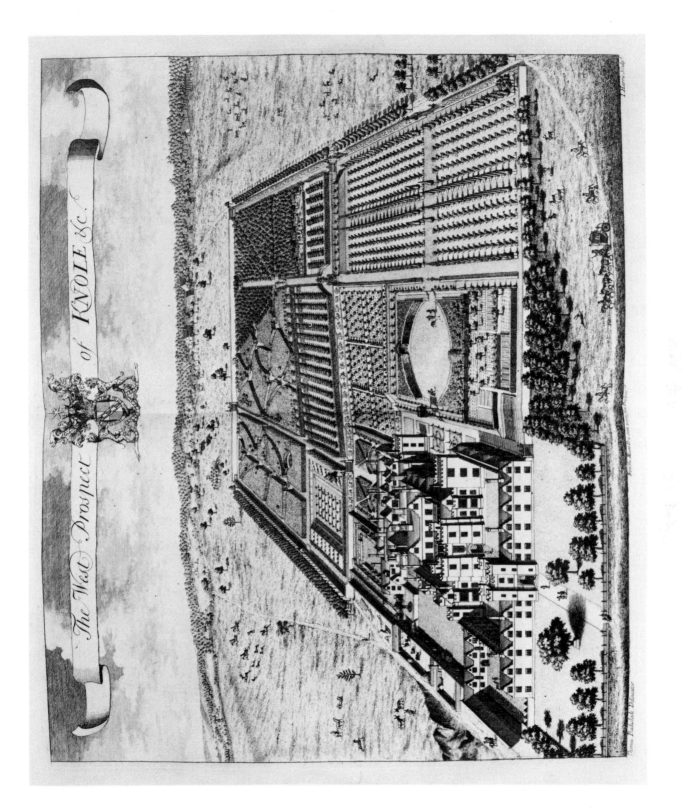

The West Prospect of KNOLE &c.

KNOLE, Kent. From: BADESLADE (T.). *Thirty six different views of noblemen and gentlemen's seats in the county of Kent* [etc.], London [c.1750].

LANGDON COURT (Devonshire).
BURKE, J.B. Visitation of Seats. Vol.I, p.227. 1852.*
JONES. Views of Seats. II. 1829.
NEALE, J.P. Views of Seats. Vol.I. 1818.

LANGDON HALL (Devonshire).
See LANGDON COURT.

LANGHAM HALL (Essex).
ESSEX: A new and complete history. VI, 249. 1772.

LANGLEY COURT (Kent).
See LANGLEY PARK.

LANGLEY HALL (Derbyshire).
BURKE, J.B. Visitation of Seats. Vol.II, p.163. 1853.*
TILLEY, J. Halls of Derbyshire. IV, p.97. 1902.*

LANGLEY HALL (Shropshire).
SHROPSHIRE. Castles and Old Mansions. 29. 1868.

LANGLEY PARK (Buckinghamshire).
BURKE, J.B. Visitation of Seats. Vol.I, p.39. 1852.*
COPPER PLATE MAGAZINE. II, pl.70. 1792-1802.
ENGLAND: Picturesque Views. p.19. 1786-88.
JONES. Views of Seats. I. 1829.
NEALE, J.P. Views of Seats. Vol.I. 1818.

LANGLEY PARK (Kent).
HASTED, E. Kent. I, 84. 1778.
[Sales] LANGLEY PARK, 1917, June 18-21 [Contents].
(K., F. & R.).

LANGLEY PARK (Norfolk).
BURKE, J.B. Visitation of Seats. Vol.I, p.154. 1852.*
COUNTRY LIFE. English Country Houses: Early Georgian.
p.167. 1955.
COUNTRY LIFE. LXII, 16. 1927.
COUNTRY LIFE. LXIII, 467 [Furniture]. 1928.
CROMWELL, T.K. Excursions in Norfolk. I, p.81. 1818.
NEALE, J.P. Views of Seats. Vol.III. 1820.
SOANE, J. Plans, elevations and sections. pls. XXIII, XXIV
[Lodges] 1788.

LANGLEY PRIORY [HALL]
(Leicestershire).
NICHOLS, J. History of Leicestershire. III, ii, 862. 1804.

LANGLEYS (Essex).
BURKE, J.B. Visitation of Seats. 2.S. Vol.I, p.130. 1854.*
COUNTRY LIFE. XVIII, 774. 1905.
COUNTRY LIFE. XCI, 68, 112, 160. 1942.
COUNTRY LIFE. XCII, 264 [Furniture], 552 [Paintings]. 1942.
CROMWELL, T.K. Excursions in Essex. II, p.79. 1825.
ESSEX: A new and complete history. I, 325. 1769.
LATHAM, C. In English Homes. Vol.II, p.203. 1907.
MORANT, P. Essex. II, 88. 1768.
RUSH, J.A. Seats in Essex, p.119. 1897.
WHITEMAN, G.W. English country homes. p.105. 1951.

LANGRIGG HALL (Cumberland).
BURKE, J.B. Visitation of Seats. 2.S. Vol.II, p.114. 1855.*

LANGSTONE COURT (Herefordshire).
COUNTRY LIFE. CXLII, 1194. 1967.

LANGTON HALL (Leicestershire).
JONES. Views of Seats. I. 1829.
NEALE, J.P. Views of Seats. Vol.II. 1819.

LANGTON HALL (Lincolnshire).
LINCOLNSHIRE. A selection of views. 33. 1805.

LANGTON HOUSE, Langton Long
Blandford (Dorsetshire).
HUTCHINS, J. Vitruvius Dorsettiensis. pl.16. 1816.
HUTCHINS, J. History of Dorset. I, 284. 1861.

LANGWITH HALL (Derbyshire).
TILLEY, J. Halls of Derbyshire. III, p.149. 1899.

LANHYDROCK (Cornwall).
LONDON: National Trust for Places of Historic Interest or
Natural Beauty.
— TRINICK, M. Lanhydrock House, Cornwall. 10pp. Illus.
(on cover) and 4 plates. 18x12 London: Country Life (1954).
Another ed. 26pp. Illus. (1 col. on cover) plates and plans (on
covers). 21x15 [London] 1978.
BRITTON, J. Cornwall illustrated. 30. 1832.
BURKE, J.B. Visitation of Seats. 2.S. Vol.II, p.174. 1855.*
COUNTRY LIFE. XIV, 890. 1903.
COUNTRY LIFE. CLXIII, 382 plan, 458 plan. 1978.
CROMWELL, T.K. Excursions in Cornwall. p.155. 1824.
DELDERFIELD, E.R. West Country houses. I, 89. 1968.
GOTCH, J.A. Architecture of the Renaissance. II, p.11. 1894.
LATHAM, C. In English Homes. Vol.I, p.211. 1904.
MORRIS, F.O. Views of Seats. Vol.V, p.39. 1880.
NASH, J. Mansions of England,III, pl.6 1841.

LANSDOWN TOWER (Somerset).

GREGORY, William.
— The Beckford family: reminiscences of Fonthill Abbey and Lansdown Tower. 2 ed. Illus. incl. 21 plates and facsimiles. 19x12 London: Simpkin, Marshall, Hamilton, Kent & Co., Ltd; Bath: Bath Chronicle, 1898.
Another copy.

LANSDOWN TOWER.
— Views of Lansdown Tower, Bath, the favourite edifice of the late William Beckford, Esq. From drawings by W. Maddox. 16pp. Lithogr. incl. col. plates, and cut. 61x45 Bath: English; London: McLean, 1844.

[Sales] BATH, 1845, November 20-22, 24-29 [Furniture, paintings etc.][Photocopy].

LARDEN HALL (Shropshire).

SHROPSHIRE. Castles and Old Mansions. 28. 1868.

LARK HILL, Near Preston (Lancashire).

BARTLETT, J. Mansions of England and Wales. pl.96. 1853.
TWYCROSS, E. Mansions of England and Wales. Vol.II, p.60 1847.

LARK HILL, West Derby (Lancashire).

BARTLETT, J. Mansions of England and Wales. pl.123. 1853.
TWYCROSS, E. Mansions of England and Wales. Vol.III, p.56. 1847.

LARTINGTON HALL (Yorkshire).

ANGUS, W. Seats of the Nobility. pl.23. 1787.

LATHOM HOUSE (Lancashire).

BARTLETT, J. Mansions of England and Wales. pl.157. 1853.
BURKE, J.B. Visitation of Seats. Vol.I, p.250. 1852.*
CAMPBELL, C. Vitruvius Britannicus. IV, pls. 94-98. 1767.
JONES. Views of Seats. I. 1829.
MORRIS, F.O. Views of Seats. Vol.V, p.53. 1880.
NEALE, J.P. Views of Seats. Vol.II. 1819.
TWYCROSS, E. Mansions of England and Wales. Vol.III, p.16. 1847.

LATIMERS (Buckinghamshire).

BURKE, J.B. Visitation of Seats. Vol.I, p.243. 1852.*

LAUNDE ABBEY (Leicestershire).

NICHOLS, J. History of Leicestershire. III, i, 301. 1800.
THROSBY, J. Views in Leicestershire. p.289. 1789.

LAVERSTOKE HOUSE (Hampshire).

HAMPSHIRE: Architectural views. 1830.

LAVINGTON PARK (Sussex).

LAVINGTON PARK.
— Sporting pictures at Lavington Park [Belonging to] the Rt. Hon. Lord Woolavington. (Catalogue by G. Pawsey; introduction by Sir T. Cook.) Illus. incl. plate. 28x22 London: privately printed, 1927.
A supplementary catalogue of Lord Woolavington's collection of paintings by sporting artists at Lavington Park, Northaw House, The Grove, Newmarket and 25, Berkeley Square, W. Illus. incl. plate. (1930).
COUNTRY LIFE. LVIII, 130 plan, 135 [Pictures]. 1925.
COUNTRY LIFE. LIX, 949 [Pictures]. 1926.

LAWFORD HALL (Essex).

LAWFORD HALL.
— The hall of Lawford Hall. Records of an Essex house and of its proprietors from the Saxon times to the reign of Henry VIII. [By F.M. Nichols?][Bibliogr. notes.] Illus. incl. 2 plates and cuts. 25x20 London by the author, 1891.
RUSH, J.A. Seats in Essex. p.121. 1897.

LAWKLAND HALL (Yorkshire).

AUSTWICK.
— Lawkland Hall, Austwick, nr. Lancaster, Yorkshire. Stone built Tudor manor house ... Herne farm with house and buildings (etc.). Typescript. 4pp. 1 plate. 35x21 London [1923].

LAWN, The. (Wiltshire).

BURKE, J.B. Visitation of Seats. Vol.I, p.172. 1852.*

LAWNE, The. Headley (Surrey).

CAMPBELL, C. Vitruvius Britannicus. IVth. pls. 96, 97. 1739.

LAWNESWOOD HOUSE (Staffordshire).

BURKE, J.B. Visitation of Seats. 2.S. Vol.I, p.18. 1854.*

LAWRENNY PARK (Pembrokeshire).

BURKE, J.B. Visitation of Seats. 2.S. Vol.II, p.5. 1855.*

LAWTON HALL (Cheshire).

MORRIS, F.O. Views of Seats. Vol.III, p.77. 1880.
TWYCROSS, E. Mansions of England and Wales. Vol.I, p.145. 1850.

LAXTON HALL (Northamptonshire).

BURKE, J.B. Visitation of Seats. 2.S. Vol.II, p.164. 1855.*
GOTCH, J.A. Squire's Homes. 5. 1939.
JONES. Views of Seats. I. 1829.
NEALE, J.P. Views of Seats. 2.S. Vol.I. 1824.

LAYER MARNEY (Essex).
COUNTRY LIFE. XIV, 368. 1903.
COUNTRY LIFE. XXXV, 270, 306. 1914.
CROMWELL, T.K. Excursions in Essex. I, p.103. 1825.
ESSEX. A new and complete history. V, 415. 1772.
GARNER, T. Domestic architecture. I, p.81 plan. 1911.
MORANT, P. Essex. I, 409. 1768.
RUSII, J.A. Seats in Essex. p.123. 1897.
TIPPING, H.A. English Homes. Period II, Vol.I, p.161. 1924.

LEADENHAM HOUSE (Lincolnshire).
COUNTRY LIFE. CXXXVII, 1528, 1592. 1965.

LEAGRAM HALL (Lancashire).
BARTLETT, J. Mansions of England and Wales. pl.17. 1853.
TWYCROSS, E. mansions of England and Wales. Vol.I, p.15. 1847.

LEA HALL (Lincolnshire).
MORRIS, F.O. Views of Seats. Vol.I, p.37. 1880.

LEA HALL, Preston Gubbals (Shropshire).
SHROPSHIRE, Castles and Old Mansions. 41. 1868.

LEA HOUSE (Surrey).
PROSSER, G.F. Surrey Seats. p.39. 1828.

LEAM HALL (Derbyshire).
TILLEY, J. Halls of Derbyshire. I, p.143. 1892.

LEASOWE CASTLE (Cheshire).
BURKE, J.B. Visitation of Seats. Vol.II, p.126. 1853.*
ORMEROD, G. Cheshire. II, 474. 1882.
TWYCROSS, E. Mansions of England and Wales. Vol.I, p.55. 1850.*

LEASOWES, The. (Shropshire later Worcestershire).
LEASOWES.
— A companion to the Leasowes, Hagley, and Enville; with a sketch of Fisherwick, the seat of the ... Earl Donegall. To which is prefixed the present state of Birmingham. iv, 250pp. 2pts. in 1 vol. 8vo. 17x10 London: G.G.J. & J. Robinson; Birmingham: M. Swinney; Worcester: J. Holl, 1789.
COOPER PLATE MAGAZINE. I, pl.15. 1792-1802.
ENGLAND: Picturesque Views. p.99. 1786-88.
ENGLISH CONNOISSEUR. I, 151. 1766.*
WEST, W. Picturesque views in Shropshire. p.119. 1831.

LEATON HALL (Staffordshire).
BURKE, J.B. Visitation of Seats. Vol.II, p.217. 1853.*

LECHLADE MANOR (Gloucestershire).
[Sales] OXFORD, 1921, June 15 [Estate].
[Sales] LECHLADE MANOR, 1921, June 20-24, 27, 28 [Contents].

LECK HALL (Lancashire).
TWYCROSS, E. Mansions of England and Wales. Vol.II, p.14. 1847.*

LECKHAMPTON COURT (Gloucestershire).
ATKYNS, R. Glocestershire. p.277. 1768.

LEDSTON HALL (Yorkshire).
JONES. Views of Seats. I, 1829.
NEALE, J.P. Views of Seats. Vol.V. 1822.

LEEDS ABBEY (Kent).
BADESLADE, T. Seats in Kent. pl.21. 1750.
HARRIS, J. History of Kent. p.176. 1719.

LEEDS CASTLE (Kent).
GEOFFREY-LLOYD, Geoffrey William, *Baron.*
— Leeds Castle: a brief history of the castle of the queens of Medieval England ... Foreward by Sir A. Bryant. vi, 26pp. Col. illus. (some on covers) incl. plates and plan. 21x15 Maidstone: Leeds Castle Foundation, 1976.
MARTIN, Charles Wykeham.
— The history and description of Leeds Castle, Kent. [Bibliogr. notes.] Illus. incl. plates (photographs), plan, facsimile and genealog. tables. 38x28 Westminster: Nichols & Sons, 1869.
BUCK, S. & N. Antiquities. I, pl.132. 1774.
BURKE, J.B. Visitation of Seats. Vol.I, p.76. 1852.*
COPPER PLATE MAGAZINE. IV, pl.195. 1792-1802.
COUNTRY LIFE. I, 435. 1897.
COUNTRY LIFE. XXXIV, 806, 856 plan. 1913.
COUNTRY LIFE. LXXX, 568 plan, 600. 1936.
COUNTRY LIFE. CLXXIII, 925, 1018. 1983.
CROMWELL. T.K. Excursions in Kent. p.160. 1822.
GREENWOOD, C. Kent. 163. 1838.
HASTED, E. Kent. II, 478. 1782.
MORRIS, F.O. Views of Seats. Vol.II, p.45. 1880.
NEALE, J.P. Views of Seats. 2.S. Vol.II. 1825.
OSWALD, A. Country houses of Kent. 4. 1933.
TIPPING, H.A. English Homes. Period I, Vol.I, p.201. 1921.

LEE GROVE (Kent).
GREENWOOD, C. Kent. 22. 1838.

The GATE-HOUSE or TOWER of LAYER-MARNEY-HALL, in ESSEX, Formerly one of the SEATS of the Lord Marney, and now of NICHOLAS CORSELLIS Esqr. Ao 1742.

G. Vertue Sculp.

LAYER MARNEY, Essex. From: ESSEX. *A new and complete history of Essex* [etc.], vol. V, Chelmsford, 1772.

LEE HALL Ellesmere (Shropshire).

MOSS, F. Pilgrimages. V, 273. 1910.

SHROPSHIRE. Castles & Old Mansions. 65. 1868.

LEE HALL, Preston Gubbals (Shropshire).
See LEA HALL.

LEE PRIORY (Kent).

LEE PRIORY.
— List of pictures at the seat of T.B. Brydges Barrett, Esq., at Lee Priory in the county of Kent. 76pp. 1 engr. folding plate, cuts, vignettes and initial. 25x15 Lee Priory: printed at the private press, 1817.
Notice of sale of the mansion, and press cutting inserted.

ANGUS, W. Seats of the Nobility. pl.43. 1787.

COUNTRY LIFE. CXI, 1665. 1952.

GREENWOOD, C. Kent. 354. 1838.

HASTED, E. Kent. III, 664. 1790.

NEALE, J.P. Views of Seats. 2.S. Vol.II. 1825.

OSWALD, A. Country houses of Kent. 67. 1933.

[Sales] LEE PRIORY, 1834, August 11-15 [Furniture, library etc.].

LEES COURT (Kent).

BADESLADE, T. Seats in Kent. pl.22. 1750.

COUNTRY LIFE. LII, 178, 210 plan. 1922.

NEALE, J.P. Views of Seats. 2.S. Vol.IV. 1828.

OSWALD, A. Country houses of Kent. 49. 1933.

LEESTHORPE HALL (Leicestershire).

NICHOLS, J. History of Leicestershire. III, ii, pl.CLV, 1128. 1804.

THROSBY, J. Views in Leicestershire. p.291. 1789.

LEESWOOD HALL (Flintshire).

BURKE, J.B. Visitation of Seats. 2.S. Vol.I, p.76. 1854.*

COUNTRY LIFE. XCIV, 200, 244. 1943.

LEEZ PRIORY (Essex).

BUCK, S. & N. Antiquities. I, pl.95. 1774.

COUNTRY LIFE. XXXV, 486 plan. 1914.

CROMWELL, T.K. Excursions in Essex. II, p.157. 1825.

TIPPING, H.A. English Homes. Period II, Vol.I, p.311. 1924.

LEGH MANOR (Sussex).

COUNTRY LIFE. LXX, 672. 1931.

LEICESTER GRANGE (Warwickshire).

NICHOLS, J. History of Leicestershire. IV, ii, 469. 1811.

LEIGH COURT (Somerset).

YOUNG, John.
— A catalogue of the pictures at Leigh Court near Bristol, the seat of F.J. Miles, Esq., M.P. ... With etchings from the whole collection ... accompanied with historical and biographical notices by J.Y. 44pp. Engr. plates. 38x27 London: privately published, 1822.
Another copy, wanting plate, and with newspaper cutting dated 1845, inserted. 28x23.

BURKE, J.B. Visitation of Seats. Vol.I, p.257. 1852.*

COOKE, R. West Country Houses. p.155. 1957.

LEIGH HALL (Shropshire).
See LEA HALL.

LEIGH PARK (Hampshire).

LEIGH PARK.
— Notices of the Leigh Park estate, near Havant, 1836. 48pp. Lithogr. plate. 21x14 London: E. Lloyd, 1836.

LEIGH PARK.
— List of busts in the temple Leigh Park, 1845. [Folder.] 37x25 Havant printed, 1845?

LEIGH PLACE (Surrey).

MANNING, O. Surrey II, 183. 1809.

LEIGHTON HALL (Lancashire).

LEIGHTON HALL.
— Leighton Hall, Carnforth, Lancashire ... Official guide. 16pp. Illus. (some on covers) incl. map. 14x20 [Derby: E. L.P., 1958].

BARTLETT, J. Mansions of England and Wales. pls.58, 59. 1853.

BURKE, J.B. Visitation of Seats. 2.S. Vol.I, p.197. 1854.*

COUNTRY LIFE. CIX, 1452, 1538. 1951.

TWYCROSS, E. Mansions of England and Wales. Vol.II, p.15. 1847.

LEIGHTON HALL (Shropshire).

LEACH, F. Seats of Shropshire. p.201. 1891.

[Sales] LEIGHTON HALL, 1921, November 2 [Furniture, prints, paintings etc.].

[Sales] LEIGHTON HALL, 1927, October 17-22 [Contents].

LEITH HILL PLACE (Surrey).

MANNING, O. Surrey. II, 161. 1809.

LETCHWORTH HALL (Hertfordshire).

AYLOTT, George.
— The story of Letchworth Hall. Based on investigations by the late G.A. [Bibliogr. note.] Letchworth: Letchworth Hall Hotel [1937].

LETHERINGHAM LODGE (Suffolk).
SANDON, E. Suffolk Houses. 270. 1977.

LETHERINGSETT HALL (Norfolk).
COUNTRY LIFE. CXLI, 18. 1967.

LETTON HALL (Norfolk).
BURKE, J.B. Visitation of Seats. Vol.I, p.93. 1852.*
SOANE, J. Plans, elevations and sections. pls. VII-XI. 1788.

LEVENS HALL (Westmorland).
BAGOT, Annette.
— Levens Hall: the historic Westmorland home of the Bagot family. 16pp. Illus. (on covers), map and genealog. table. 14x20 (Derby: E.L.P.) [c. 1950.]
BAGOT, Annette.
— Levens Hall, Westmorland. 24pp. Illus. (some col., 2 on covers.) 21x18 (Norwich: privately printed, 1963.)
Another ed. 28pp. Illus. (some col., 2 on covers) incl. plan and map. 25x15 (1971).
CURWEN, John Flavel.
— Historical description of Levens Hall. 48pp. Illus. incl. plan and maps. 25x18 Kendal: T. Wilson, 1898.
LEVENS HALL.
— Levens Hall and gardens. 16pp. Illus. 18x12 (Kendal: T. Wilson, 1921).
BURKE, J.B. Visitation of Seats. 2.S. Vol.I, p.49. 1854.*
COUNTRY LIFE. XIII, 16. 1903.
COUNTRY LIFE. XIV, 329. 1903.
COUNTRY LIFE. LX, 538 plan, 578. 1926.
CUMBERLAND: C. & W. A. & A.S. Extra Series VIII, 199 plan. 1892.
GARNER, T. Domestic architecture. II, p.153 plan. 1911.
LATHAM, C. In English Homes. Vol.I, p.93. 1904.
MALAN, A.H. More famous homes. p.119. 1902.
MORRIS, F.O. Views of Seats. Vol.VI, p.49. 1880.
NASH, J. Mansions of England. IV, pls. 2-6. 1849.
TIPPING, H.A. English Homes. Period III, Vol.II, p.213. 1927.

LEVERINGTON HALL (Cambridgeshire).
COUNTRY LIFE. CIII, 126. 1948.

LEY, The. (Herefordshire).
GARNER, T. Domestic architecture. II, p.164 plan. 1911.
ROBINSON, C.J. Mansions of Herefordshire. pl.22. 1873.

LEYTON GRANGE (Essex).
CAMPBELL, C. Vitruvius Britannicus. III, pl.94. 1725.

LEYTON HOUSE (Essex). Henry More.
ESSEX: A new and complete history. IV, 240. 1771.

LICHFIELD PALACE (Staffordshire).
COUNTRY LIFE. English Country Houses: Caroline. p.184. 1966.
COUNTRY LIFE. CXVI, 2312 plan. 1954.

LIFTON PARK (Devonshire).
BRITTON, J. Devonshire illustrated. 103. 1832.

LILBURN TOWER (Northumberland).
BURKE, J.B. Visitation of Seats. Vol.II, p.138. 1853.*
COUNTRY LIFE. CLIV. 1440. 1973.
MORRIS, F.O. Views of Seats. Vol.VI, p.19. 1880.

LILFORD HALL (Northamptonshire).
BRIDGES, J. Northamptonshire. II, 242. 1791.
GOTCH, J.A. Architecture of the Renaissance. I, p.43. 1894.
GOTCH, J.A. Halls of Northants. p.36. 1936.
NEALE, J.P. Views of Seats. 2.S. Vol.V. 1829.

LILLESHALL HALL (Shropshire).
BURKE, J.B. Visitation of Seats. 2.S. Vol.I, p.191. 1854.*
LEACH, F. Seats of Shropshire. p.317. 1891.

LILLESHALL LODGE (Shropshire).
SHROPSHIRE. Castles & Old Mansions. 33. 1868.

LILLESHALL OLD HALL (Shropshire).
LEACH, F. Seats of Shropshire. p.309. 1891.

LINCOLN, BISHOP'S PALACE (Lincolnshire).
BUCK, S. & N. Antiquities. I, pl.171. 1774.

LINDEN HALL (Lancashire).
BURKE, J.B. Visitation of Seats. Vol.II, p.240. 1853.

LINDISFARNE CASTLE (Northumberland).
LONDON: National Trust for Places of Historic Interest or Natural Beauty.
— ORDE, P. Lindisfarne Castle. 18pp. Illus. (1 col. on cover) incl. plates and plans. 25x18 [London] 1982.

LINDLEY HALL (Leicestershire).
NICHOLS, J. History of Leicestershire. IV, ii, 647. 1811.
THROSBY, J. Views in Leicestershire. p.292. 1789.

LINK FARM, Egerton (Kent).
OSWALD, A. Country houses of Kent. 26. 1933.

LINLEY HALL (Shropshire).
COUNTRY LIFE, CXXX, 502, 558 plan. 1961.
LEACH, F. Seats of Shropshire. p.81. 1891.

LINLEY WOOD (Staffordshire).
BURKE, J.B. Visitation of Seats. Vol.II, p.147. 1853.*
BURKE, J.B. Visitation of Seats. 2.S. Vol.I, p.215. 1854.*

LINSTED LODGE (Kent).
See LYNSTED PARK.

LINTON PARK (Kent).
COUNTRY LIFE. XCIX, 624. 1946.
NEALE, J.P. Views of Seats. 2.S. Vol.V. 1829.
[Sales] LINTON PARK, 1961, October 2, 3 [Contents].

LISCARD MANOR (Cheshire).
TWYCROSS, E. Mansions of England and Wales. Vol.I, p.85. 1850.

LISLE HOUSE, Wotton-under-edge (Gloucestershire).
HODGES, E. Ancient English homes. 39. 1895.

LISTON HALL (Essex).
ESSEX: A new and complete history. II, 152. 1769.

LISVANE HOUSE (Glamorganshire).
[Sales] CARDIFF, 1913, May 6, 7 [Library].
[Sales] LISVANE HOUSE, 1913, June 17-20 [Contents].

LISWIS HALL (Staffordshire).
SHAW, S. Staffordshire. I, 225. 1798.

LITTLE ASTON HALL (Staffordshire).
SHAW, S. Staffordshire. II, 52. 1801.

LITTLE BARFORD MANOR (Bedfordshire).
BARTLETT, J. Selections from views of mansions. 1851.

LITTLE BIRCH HALL (Essex).
ESSEX: A new and complete history. VI, 156. 1772.

LITTLE CHARLETON (Kent).
See CHARLTON COURT.

LITTLE COMPTON MANOR (Warwickshire).
ATKYNS, R. Glocestershire. p.191. 1768.
COUNTRY LIFE. LXXXVI, 64. 90. 1939.

LITTLE COURT (Hertfordshire).
CHAUNCY, H. Hertfordshire. I, 260. 1826.

LITTLECOTE (Wiltshire).
LITTLECOTE.
— Littlecote. 2 ed. 158pp. Illus.: plates and genealog. tables. (2 folding). 29x23 London: privately printed, 1900.
SPREADBURY, P.A.
— Littlecote, Wiltshire: official guide. 24pp. Illus. (some on covers.) 13x20 (Swindon printed) [1964?]
BURKE, J.B. Visitation of Seats. Vol.I, p.5. 1852.*
COUNTRY LIFE. XII, 400. 1902.
COUNTRY LIFE. CXXXVIII, 1406 plan, 1466, 1620, 1678. 1965.
DELDERFIELD, E.R. West Country Seats. II, 76. 1970.
JONES. Views of Seats. II. 1829.
LATHAM, C. In English Homes. Vol.I, p.207. 1904.
NASH, J. Mansions of England. II, pl.3. 1840.
NEALE, J.P. Views of Seats. Vol.V. 1822.

LITTLE DURNFORD MANOR (Wiltshire).
DEVENISH, Dorothy.
A Wiltshire home: a study of Little Durnford. x, 16pp. Plates (1 col.) incl. plan and maps (on end-papers). 21x14 London: Batsford, 1948.
COUNTRY LIFE. CLVIII. 18. 1975.

LITTLE FRANSHAM HALL (Norfolk).
See FRANSHAM OLD HALL.

LITTLE GADDESDEN MANOR (Hertfordshire).
LITTLE GADDESDEN MANOR.
— The Manor House, Little Gaddesden, nr. Berkhamsted, Hertfordshire. 12pp. Illus. (1 col., some on covers.) 14x20 [Derby: E.L.P. c. 1973.]

LITTLE GRIMSBY HALL (Lincolnshire).
BURKE, J.B. Visitation of Seats. 2.S. Vol.II, p.57. 1855.*

LITTLE HAUGH HALL (Suffolk).
COUNTRY LIFE. CXXIII, 1238. 1958.

LITTLE HAUTBOIS HALL (Norfolk).
BIRKBECK, G. Old Norfolk houses. 73. 1908.
GARNER, T. Domestic architecture. II, p.140. 1911.
GARRATT, T. Halls of Norfolk. pls. 27, 28. 1890.

LITTLE LONGSTONE MANOR (Derbyshire).
TILLEY, J. Halls of Derbyshire. I, p.35. 1892.

LITTLE MALVERN COURT (Worcestershire).
BERINGTON, William J.C.
— Little Malvern Court, Worcestershire. 62pp. 7 plates. 21x14 London (privately printed, 1948).
BURKE, J.B. Visitation of Seats. 2.S. Vol.I, p.17. 1854.*

LITTLE MITTON HALL (Lancashire).
GRAY, H. Old halls of Lancashire. p.35. 1893.
TWYCROSS, E. Mansions of England and Wales. Vol.I, p.11. 1847.*

LITTLE MORETON HALL (Cheshire).
HEAD, Robert.
—Moreton Old Hall. With an account of its past and present owners. 32pp. Illus. 22x14 Congleton: Congleton Chronicle (1922).
LONDON: National Trust for Places of Historic Interest or Natural Beauty.
—LEES-MILNE, J. Little Moreton Hall. 2ed. 14pp. 4 plates and plan. 18x12 London: Country Life (1948).
ANGUS-BUTTERWORTH, L.M. Old Cheshire families. p.183. 1932.
COUNTRY LIFE. XV, 594. 1904.
COUNTRY LIFE. LXVI, 754, 798. 1929.
GARNER, T. Domestic architecture. II, p.148 plan. 1911.
LATHAM, C. In English Homes. Vol.I, p.265. 1904.
MOSS, F. Pilgrimages. [II] 201. 1903.
NASH, J. Mansions of England. IV, pl.25. 1849.
ORMEROD, G. Cheshire. III, 49. 1882.
TIPPING, H.A. English Homes. Period I & II, Vol.II, p.249. 1937.
TWYCROSS, E. Mansions of England and Wales. Vol.I, p.136. 1850.*

LITTLE OFFLEY (Hertfordshire).
CHAUNCY, H. Hertfordshire. II, 197. 1826.

LITTLE PONTON HALL (Lincolnshire).
LINCOLSHIRE. A selection of views. 63. 1805.

LITTLE RIDGE (Wiltshire).
COUNTRY LIFE. XXXII, 566 plan. 1912.

LITTLE ROLLRIGHT MANOR (Oxfordshire).
[Sales] OXFORD, Clarendon Hotel, 1927, June 29 [Estate].

LITTLE SODBURY MANOR (Gloucestershire).
COOKE, R. West Country Houses. p.34. 1957.
COUNTRY LIFE. LII, 440 plan. 1922.
HODGES, E. Ancient English homes. 191. 1895.
TIPPING, H.A. English Homes. Period I & II, Vol. II, 1937 p.105. 1937.

LITTLE STRICKLAND HALL (Westmorland).
CUMBERLAND: C. & W. A. & A.S. Extra Series VIII, 99. 1892.

LITTLE THAKEHAM (Sussex).
COUNTRY LIFE. XXVI, 292. 1909.

LITTLETHORPE (Yorkshire).
BURKE, J.B. Visitation of Seats. Vol.I, p.85. 1852.*

LITTLE THURLOW HALL (Suffolk).
BURKE, J.B. Visitation of Seats. 2.S. Vol.I, p.104. 1854.*

LITTLETON HALL (Cheshire).
TWYCROSS, E. Mansions of England and Wales. Vol.I, p.43. 1850.

LITTLETON PARK (Middlesex).
BURKE, J.B. Visitation of Seats. 2.S. Vol.I, p.18. 1854.*

LITTLE WENHAM HALL (Suffolk).
COUNTRY LIFE. XXXVI, 358 plan. 1914.
CROMWELL, T.K. Excursions in Suffolk. I, p.151. 1818.
TIPPING, H.A. English Homes. Period I, Vol.I, p.92. 1921.

LITTLE WOLFORD HALL (Warwickshire).
COUNTRY LIFE. XLVII, 476. 1920.
NIVEN, W. Old Warwickshire houses. p.29, pl.28. 1878.

LITLE WYRLEY HALL (Staffordshire).
COUNTRY LIFE. CXI, 496, 572. 1952.
SHAW, S. Staffordshire. II, 58. 1801.

LIVERMERE HALL (Suffolk).
CROMWELL, T.K. Excursions in Suffolk. I, p.180. 1818.
NEALE, J.P. Views of Seats. Vol.IV. 1821.

LIVERPOOL HOUSE (Kent).
GREENWOOD, C. Kent. 430. 1838.

LLANARTH COURT (Monmouthshire).
NEALE, J.P. Views of Seats. Vol.II. 1819.

LLANAYRON (Cardiganshire).
NICHOLAS, T. Counties of Wales. I, p.133. 1872.

LLANBEDROG (Caerarvonshire).
BURKE, J.B. Visitation of Seats. 2.S. Vol.I, p.79. 1854.

LLANERCH (Denbighshire).
HOARE: Views of Seats. pl.14. 1792.

LLANERCHRUGG HALL (Denbighshire).
BURKE, J.B. Visitation of Seats. 2.S. Vol.II, p.204. 1855.*

LLANERCHYDOL HALL (Montgomeryshire).
BURKE, J.B. Visitation of Seats. 2.S. Vol.II, p.75. 1855.*
NEALE, J.P. Views of Seats. 2.S. Vol.V. 1829.

LLANFECHAN (Cardiganshire).
NICHOLAS, T. Counties of Wales. I, p.137. 1872.

LLANFOIST HOUSE (Monmouthshire).
[Sales] LLANFOIST HOUSE, 1922, September 13, 14 [Furniture, carpets etc.].

LLANFORDA (Shropshire).
LEIGHTON, S. Shropshire houses. 23. 1901.

LLANOVER HOUSE (Monmouthshire).
NICHOLAS, T. Counties of Wales. II, p.716. 1872.
[Sales] LLANOVER HOUSE, 1934, June 20-22, 26-28 [Contents].

LLANRHAIADR HALL (Denbighshire).
NICHOLAS, T. Counties of Wales. I, p.375. 1872.

LLANTHOMAS (Brecknockshire).
SPROULE, A. Lost houses of Britain. 193. 1982.

LLANTILIO COURT (Monmouthshire).
BURKE, J.B. Visitation of Seats. 2.S. Vol.I, p.42. 1854.*

LLANTYSILIO (Denbighshire).
ENGLAND: Picturesque Views. p.67. 1786-88.

LLANVIHANGEL COURT (Monmouthshire).
COUNTRY LIFE. XXXIX, 618. 1916.

LLANWERN PARK (Monmouthshire).
BURKE, J.B. Visitation of Seats. 2.S. Vol.I, p.124. 1854.*
COUNTRY LIFE. XLII, 580. 1917.
TIPPING, H.A. English Homes. Period V, Vol.I, p.339. 1921.

LLEWENI HALL (Denbighshire).
ANGUS, W. Seats of the Nobility. pl.15. 1787.
COUNTRY LIFE. CLXII. 1966 plan. 1977.
HOARE: Views of Seats. pls. 7,8. 1782.

LLWYN YNN (Denbighshire).
NICHOLAS, T. Counties of Wales.I,p.374. 1872.

LLYSMEIRCHION (Denbighshire).
NICHOLAS, T. Counties of Wales. I, p.378. 1872.

LLYS NEWYDD (Carmarthenshire).
NICHOLAS, T. Counties of Wales. I, p.223. 1872.

LOCKINGE HOUSE (Berkshire).
HOBSON, Robert Lockhart.
—Catalogue of porcelain, furniture, and other works of art, in the collection of Lady Wantage, at 2 Carlton Gardens, London, Lockinge House, Berks., and Overstone Park, Northants. Described by R.L.H., and O. Brackett. Illus. incl. plates (1 col.). 35x25 Enfield: privately printed, 1912.
TEMPLE, Alfred George.
—Catalogue of pictures forming the collection of Lord and Lady Wantage at 2, Carlton Gardens, London, Lockinge House, Berks., and Overstone Park and Ardington House. [By A.G.T., R.H. Benson and Lady Wantage; introduction by S.A. Strong.] Plates. 34x26 London: Wetherman & Co., 1902.
[Sales] LONDON, 1945, November 7 [Engravings etc. from L.H.].
[Sales] LONDON, 1945, November 28 [Paintings and drawings

LOCKINGTON HALL (Leicestershire).
BURKE, J.B. Visitation of Seats. 2.S. Vol.II, p.94. 1855.*
NICHOLS, J. History of Leicestershire. III, ii, 875. 1804.

LOCKLEYS (Hertfordshire).
COUNTRY LIFE. XLVIII, 48. 1920.
TIPPING, H.A. English Homes. Period V, Vol.I, p.1. 1921.
[Sales] LOCKLEYS, 1911, December 12, 13 and 15 [Contents].

LOCKO PARK (Derbyshire).
RICHTER, Jean Paul.
— Catalogue of pictures at Locko Park [the collection of W. Drury-Lowe]. Plates. 28x22 London: Bemrose & Sons (1901).
BURKE, J.B. Visitation of Seats. 2.S. Vol.II, p.6. 1855.*
COUNTRY LIFE. CXLV, 1438, 1506, 1602. 1969.
MORRIS, F.O. Views of Seats. Vol.IV, p.29. 1880.

M. Griffith, del.

W. Watts, sculp.

Lleweni Hall.

The Seat of the Hon.ble Tho.s Fitzmaurice Denbighshire.

Publish'd Jan.y 16. 1790. by T. & R. Ryland Sculp.s No. 38. & 41. Schifsam Gallery Pall Mall.

LLEWENI HALL, Denbighshire. From: HOARE (Sir R.C., Bart.). *A collection of noblemen's and gentlemen's seats in Wales*, London (1792).

LOCKSLEY HALL (Lincolnshire).
WOODFORDE, Christopher.
— The Locksley Hall collection of stained and painted glass.
[The property of J. Arundel.] 48pp. Illus. incl. 8 plates (1 col.).
28x20 Bradford; London: privately printed, 1932.

LODDINGTON HALL (Leicestershire).
NICHOLS, J. History of Leicestershire. III, ii, pl.CLVIII, 1135.
1804.
THROSBY, J. Views in Leicestershire. p.294. 1789.

LODDINGTON HALL
(Northamptonshire).
GOTCH, J.A. Squires' Homes. 20 plan. 1939.

LODGE, The. (Shropshire).
WEST, W. Picturesque views of Shropshire. p.125. 1831.

LOMBERDALE HOUSE (Derbyshire).
BATEMAN, Thomas.
— A descriptive catalogue of the antiquities and
miscellaneous objects preserved in the museum of T.B., at
Lomberdale House, Derbyshire [in part now in the City
Museum, Sheffield]. Illus. incl. plates (1 folding). 22x14
Bakewell: by the author, 1855.
With M.S. additions, notes and letter inserted.

LONDESBOROUGH HALL (Yorkshire).
KIP, J. Nouveau théâtre de la Grande Bretagne. I, pl.31. 1715.

LONG ASHTON COURT (Somerset).
See ASHTON COURT.

LONG BIRCH, Brewood (Staffordshire).
NIVEN, W. Old Staffordshire houses. p.27, pl.21. 1882.

LONGDON HALL (Staffordshire).
BURKE, J.B. Visitation of Seats. 2.S. Vol.II, p.168. 1855.*

LONGFORD CASTLE (Wiltshire).
HUSSEY, Christopher.
— Drawing-room furniture at Longford Castle. [By] (C.H.)
Excerpt, 4pp. Illus. 38x23 [London] 1931.
Also in: COUNTRY LIFE, LXX, 715. 1931.
Bound with: SMITH (H.C.). Some mid-Georgian furniture
from the royal collections. [1935].
LONGFORD CASTLE.
— [Views of Longford House (Castle), in the county of
Wiltshire, the seat of the Right Hon. Henry Hare, Lord of
Coleraine. No text.] 11 plates (incl. plans) engraved by N.
Yeates and J. Collins after drawings by R. Thacker. 56x38 n.p.
[1680?]
RADNOR, Helen Matilda Pleydell-Bouverie, *Countess of.*
—Catalogue of the pictures in the collection of the Earl of
Radnor [at Longford Castle]. By H.M., Countess of Radnor

and W.B. Squire. [Bibliogr. notes.] Illus. plates and genealog.
tables. 2 vols. 37x29 London: privately printed at the
Chiswick Press, 1909.
RADNOR, Helen Matilda Pleydell-Bouverie, *Countess of.*
—Catalogue of the Earl of Radnor's collection of pictures (at
Longford Castle). 4 ed. Revised by W.B. Squire. 64pp. Illus.
incl. head and tail-pieces, plans and diagr. 19x12 n.p.
privately printed at the Chiswick Press, 1916.
5 ed. Revised by Jacob, sixth Earl of Radnor. 1928.

ANGUS, W. Seats of the Nobility. pl.10. 1787.
BRITTON, J. Beauties of Wiltshire. I, 95. 1801.
CAMPBELL, C. Vitruvius Britannicus. V, pls. 94-98. 1771.
COUNTRY LIFE. LXX, 648, 679 [Furniture], 696 plan, 715
[Furniture], 724 plan. 1931.
GOTCH, J.A. Architecture of the Renaissance. I, p.19 plan.
1894.
JONES. Views of Seats. II. 1829.
NEALE, J.P. Views of Seats. 2.S. Vol.IV. 1828.
RICHARDSON, C.J. Old English mansions. IV. 1848.
WHITEMAN, G.W. English country homes. p.43. 1951.

LONGFORD HALL (Derbyshire).
TILLEY, J. Halls of Derbyshire. II, p.95. 1893.

LONGFORD HALL, Near Newport (Shropshire).
CAMPBELL, C. New Vitruvius Britannicus. I, pls.15, 16. 1802.
COUNTRY LIFE. CXXXII, 354. 1962.
WEST, W. Picturesque views of Shropshire. p.134. 1831.

LONGHIRST HALL (Northumberland).
COUNTRY LIFE. CXXXIX, 352 plan. 1966.

LONGLEAT (Wiltshire).
BATH, Daphne Thynne, *Marchioness of.*
— Longleat, from 1566 to the present time. 54pp. Illus. (6 col., 2
on end-papers) incl. col. cover and genealog. table. 19x12
London: Longleat Estate Company, 1949.
BOYLE, Mary Louisa.
— Biographical catalogue of the portraits at Longleat, in the
county of Wilts., the seat of the Marquess of Bath. 21x16
London: Elliot Stock, 1881.
BURNETT, David.
— Longleat: the story of an English country house. [Bibliogr.]
Illus. incl. plates and genealog. table. 23x14 London: Collins,
1978.
FARQUHARSON, A.
— A history of Longleat, compiled from the best authorities.
[Bibliogr.] viii, 76pp. Plates: photographs. 18x12 Frome: W.C.
& J. Penny, 1882.
LONGLEAT.
— Longleat. (An illustrated survey and guide ... The home of
the Thynne family.) 32pp. Illus. (some col., some on covers)
incl. map. 20x15 (Derby: E.L.P.) [1960.]
Title on cover.

POCOCK, Rose R.
—The Longleat views. 7ff. Lithogr. text and 6 tinted plates. 40x58 Bristol: for the author [1840?].
BRITTON. J. Beauties of Wiltshire. II, 29. 1801.
BURKE, J.B. Visitation of Seats. Vol.II, p.166. 1853.*
CAMPBELL, C. Vitruvius Britannicus. II, pls.68, 69. 1717.
CAMPBELL, C. Vitruvius Britannicus. III, pls. 63-66. 1725.
COUNTRY LIFE. II, 154. 1897.
COUNTRY LIFE. XIII, 568. 1903.
COUNTRY LIFE. CV, 798, 862, 926, 990 plan. 1949.
COUNTRY LIFE. CXX, 594. 1956.
COUNTRY LIFE. CLXXII. 1315 [First View.] 1982.
HAVELL, R. Views of Noblemen's Seats. 1823.
JONES. Views of Seats. II. 1829.
KIP, J. Nouveau théâtre de la Grande Bretagne. I, pl. 39. 1715.
KROLL, A. Historic houses. 58. 1969.
LATHAM, C. In English Homes. Vol.I. p.181. 1904.
MALAN, A.H. More famous homes. p.203. 1902.
MORRIS, F.O. Views of Seats. Vol. V, p.35. 1880.
NEALE, J.P. Views of Seats. Vol.V. 1822.
NICOLSON, N. Great Houses of Britain. p.62. 1965.
REPTON, H. Fragments on landscape gardening. p.115. 1816.
UNITED KINGDOM. Historic Houses. 249. 1892.

LONG LEE (Derbyshire).
TILLEY, J. Halls of Derbyshire. I, p.163. 1892.

LONGNER HALL (Shropshire).
BURKE, J.B. Visitation of Seats. Vol.II, p.52. 1853.*
LEACH, F. Seats of Shropshire. p.195. 1891.
SHROPSHIRE. Castles & Old Mansions. 27. 1868.

LONGNOR HALL (Shropshire).
BURKE, J.B. Visitation of Seats. 2.S. Vol.I, p.47. 1854.*
COUNTRY LIFE. English Country Houses: Caroline. p.155. 1966.
COUNTRY LIFE. XLI, 156. 1917.
COUNTRY LIFE. CXXXV, 328, 392 plan. 1964.
LEACH, F. Seats of Shropshire. p.89. 1891.
TIPPING, H.A. English Homes. Period IV, Vol.I, p.145. 1920.
[Sales] LONGNOR HALL, 1965, April 27, 28 [Portion of contents].

LONGPARISH HOUSE (Hampshire).
BURKE, J.B. Visitation of Seats. Vol.I, p.123. 1852.*

LONGSTONE HALL (Derbyshire).
TILLEY, J. Halls of Derbyshire. I, p.59. 1892.

LONGTHORPE TOWER (Northamptonshire).
COUNTRY LIFE. CI, 604 [Paintings]. 1947.
GOTCH, J.A. Halls of Northants. p.10. 1936.

LONGWOOD (Yorkshire).
YORKSHIRE. Picturesque views. 1885.

LONGWORTH HOUSE (Herefordshire).
BURKE, J.B. Visitation of Seats. 2.S. Vol.II, p.75. 1855.*
JONES. Views of Seats. II. 1829.
NEALE, J.P. Views of Seats. 2.S. Vol.IV. 1828.

LOPPINGTON HOUSE (Shropshire).
BURKE, J.B. Visitation of Seats. 2.S. Vol.I, p.119. 1854.*

LORDSHIP, The. Standon (Hertfordshire).
CHAUNCY, H. Hertfordshire. I, 430. 1826.

LOSELEY PARK (Surrey).
LOSELEY PARK.
—Loseley Park, near Guildford, Surrey ... built by Sir William More A.D. 1562-68. 16pp. Illus. (some on covers) incl. map. 14x20 [Derby: E.L.P., 1960.]
BRAYLEY, E.W. History of Surrey. I, 419. 1841.
BURKE, J.B. Visitation of Seats. 2.S. Vol.II, p.177. 1855.*
COUNTRY LIFE. II, 720. 1897.
COUNTRY LIFE. LXXVII, 544. 1935.
COUNTRY LIFE. CXLVI, 802, 894. 1969.
GARNER, T. Domestic architecture. II, p.156. 1911.
HALL, S.C. Baronial Halls. Vol.II. 1848.
MANNING, O. Surrey. I. 98. 1804.
NASH, J. Mansions of England. I, pl.20. 1839.
NEALE, J.P. Views of Seats. Vol. IV. 1821.
PROSSER, G.F. Surrey Seats. p.25. 1828.
SHAW, H. Elizabethan architecture. pls. V,VI. [Chimney piece, ceiling.] 1839.

LOSTOCK HALL (Lancashire).
GRAY, H. Old halls of Lancashire. p.63. 1893.
SHAW, H. Elizabethan architecture. pl.VII. [Gate-house.] 1839.

LOTON PARK (Shropshire).
LEIGHTON, S. Shropshire houses. 8. 1901.
SHROPSHIRE. Castles & Old Mansions. 54. 1868.

LOUDHAM HALL (Suffolk).
SANDON, E. Suffolk houses. 196. 1977.

LOVELL'S HALL, Terrington St. Clement (Norfolk).

GARRATT, T. Halls of Norfolk. pl.25. 1890.

LOWER BROCKHAMPTON MANOR (Herefordshire).

ROBINSON, C.J. Mansions of Herefordshire. pl.4. 1873.

LOWER EATINGTON HALL (Warwickshire).

S., E.P.
— Lower Eatington: its manor house and church. [By] (E.P.S [hirley].) 80pp. (List of pictures.) Cuts incl. 1 on title-page 17x22 London: privately printed, 1869.

BURKE, J.B. Visitation of Seats. Vol.I, p.45. 1852.*

NEALE, J.P. Views of Seats. Vol.IV. 1821.

LOWER HALL, Worfield (Shropshire).

COUNTRY LIFE. CXI, 1816. 1952.

LOWER HARE PARK (Cambridgeshire).

[Sales] LONDON, 1898, November 26 [Sporting pictures, etc. from L.H.P.]

LOWER SLAUGHTER MANOR (Gloucestershire).

[Sales] LOWER SLAUGHTER MANOR, 1964, September 15-17 [Remaining furniture and effects].

LOWER WATERSON MANOR (Dorset).

See WATERSTON MANOR.

LOWER WESTON (Herefordshire).

ROBINSON, C.J. Mansions of Herefordshire. pl.24. 1873.

LOWESBY HALL (Leicestershire).

BURKE, J.B. Visitation of Seats. Vol.I, p.62. 1852.*

COUNTRY LIFE. XXXVII, 626. 1915.

LOW HALL, Yeadon (Yorkshire).

YORKSHIRE. Picturesque views. 1885.

LOWTHER CASTLE (Westmorland).

SOCIETY OF ARCHITECTURAL HISTORIANS OF GREAT BRITAIN.
— Architectural history monographs [Contd.]
2. Architectural drawings from Lowther Castle, Westmorland. Edited by H. Colvin, J.M. Crook, T. Friedman [Bibliogr.] Illus. (on cover), and plates incl. elevations and plans. 1980.

BURKE, J.B. Visitation of Seats. 2.S. Vol.I, p.28. 1854.*

CAMPBELL, C. Vitruvius Britannicus. II, pls. 78-80. 1717.

CAMPBELL, C. Vitruvius Britannicus. III, pl.76. 1725.

CUMBERLAND: C. & W.A. & A.S. Extra Series, VIII, 93. 1892.

JONES. Views of Seats. I. 1829.

KIP, J. Nouveau théâtre de la Grande Bretagne. I, pl.41. 1715.

MORRIS, F.O. Views of Seats. Vol.II, p.65. 1880.

NEALE, J.P. Views of Seats. Vol.V. 1822.

[Sales] LOWTHER CASTLE, 1947, April 15 and following days [Collection 6 pts.].

LOXLEY HALL (Staffordshire).

BURKE, J.B. Visitation of Seats. Vol.I, p.125. 1852.*

NEALE, J.P. Views of Seats. Vol.IV. 1821.

SHAW, S. Staffordshire. II, pl.27. Reprint 1976.

LUDDESDOWN COURT (Kent).

PEAKE, W. Brian.
— Luddesdown: the story of a Kentish manor, archaeological, architectural and historical, ... and a note on the early architectural features of Luddesdown Court, by A. Cumberland. Illus. incl. plans and maps. 22x14 Maidstone: South Eastern Gazette, 1920.

PEAKE, W. Brian.
— Luddesdown Court: a Norman manor house. Sketched by W.B.P. With a foreword by A. Cumberland. 24pp. 19 illus. incl. map and plans. 22x14 Maidstone, 1928.
Reprint from the author's 'Luddesdown Court, Kent. The story of a Kentish manor' 1920.
Another ed. (1920) 1930.

LUDFORD HOUSE (Shropshire).

COUNTRY LIFE. XLI, 204. 1917.

COUNTRY LIFE. CVI, 682. 1949.

LEACH, F. Seats of Shropshire. p.35. 1891.

ROBINSON, C.J. Mansions of Herefordshire. pl.14. 1873.

LUDSTONE HALL (Shropshire).

COUNTRY LIFE. CXI, 92, 154, 222. 1952.

LEACH, F. Seats of Shropshire. p.175. 1891.

SHROPSHIRE. Castles & Old Mansions. 50. 1868.

LULLINGSTONE CASTLE (Kent).

DYKE, Zoe Hart.
— Lullingstone. 20pp. Illus.(incl. 1 on cover.) 22x14 n.p. n.d.

BUCK, S.&N. Antiquities. I, pl.133. 1774.

BURKE, J.B. Visitation of Seats. 2.S. Vol.II, p.94. 1855.*

COUNTRY LIFE. XXXIV, 602. 1913.

OSWALD, A. Country Houses of Kent. 59. 1933.

LULULAND, Bushey (Hertfordshire).

COUNTRY LIFE. LXXXVI, 636. 1939.

LONGLEAT, Wiltshire. From: HAVELL (R.) *the Elder* and (R.) *the Younger: A series of picturesque views of noblemen's & gentlemen's seats* [etc.], (London) 1823.

LULWORTH CASTLE (Dorsetshire).
BERKELEY, Joan.
— Lulworth and the Welds. [Bibliogr.] xiv, 282pp. Plates incl. genealog. table. 21x14 Gillingham, Dorset: Blackmore Press, 1971.
BUCK, S.&N. Antiquities. I, pl.75. 1774.
BURKE, J.B. Visitation of Seats. 2.S. Vol.II, p.32. 1855.*
COPPER PLATE MAGAZINE. IV, pl.198. 1792-1802.
COUNTRY LIFE. LIX, 52. 1926.
COUNTRY LIFE. LXVI, 330. 1929.
ENGLAND: Beauties of England. I, p.206. 1787.
HUTCHINS, J. Vitruvius Dorsettiensis. pl,17. 1816.
HUTCHINS, J. History of Dorset. I, 374. 1861.
JONES. Views of Seats. II. 1829.
NEALE, J.P. Views of Seats. 2.S. Vol.IV. 1828.
OSWALD, A. Country houses of Dorset. p.127. 1959.
WATTS, W. Seats of the Nobility. pl.71. 1779.
[Sales] DORCHESTER, 1929, November 6, 7 [Furnishings].

LUMLEY CASTLE (Durham).
LUMLEY CASTLE.
— Lumley Castle ... Official guide. 16pp. Illus. (on covers) and map. 14x20 [Derby] (E.L.P.) [1953?]
ANGUS, W. Seats of the Nobility. pl.37. 1787.
BUCK, S.&N. Antiquities. I, pl.86. 1774.
BURKE, J.B. Visitation of Seats. 2.S. Vol.I, p.163. 1854.*
COUNTRY LIFE. XXVII, 896 plan. 1910.
HEARNE, T. Antiquities. I, pl.10. 1807.
JONES. Views of Seats. I. 1829.
MORRIS, F.O. Views of Seats. Vol.IV, p.9. 1880.
NEALE, J.P. Views of Seats. Vol.I. 1818.
TIPPING, H.A. English Homes. Period I, Vol.I, p.247. 1921.
TIPPING, H.A. English Homes. Period IV, Vol.II, p.291. 1928.

LUNTLEY COURT (Herefordshire).
ROBINSON, C.J. Mansions of Herefordshire. pl.6. 1873.

LUSCOMBE CASTLE (Devonshire).
BRITTON, J. Devonshire illustrated. 63. 1832.
BURKE, J.B. Visitation of Seats. 2.S. Vol.I, p.228. 1854.*
COUNTRY LIFE. English Country Houses: Late Georgian. p.55. 1958.
COUNTRY LIFE. CXIX, 292, 336. 1956.
JONES. Views of Seats. II. 1829.
NEALE, J.P. Views of Seats. Vol.I. 1818.

LUTON HOO (Bedfordshire).
LONGDEN, Alfred Appleby, *Maj.*
— The Wernher collection, Luton Hoo. Excerpt, 6pp. 11 illus. 24x17 [Watford, 1954.]
From: Pennant, IX, v, 170.

MUSGRAVE, E.I.
— Luton Hoo: an illustrated survey ... and of the Wernher collection [etc.]. 32pp. Illus. (some col., some on covers) incl. maps (on inside covers). 14x22 Derby: E.L.P. [1951].
SHAW, Henry.
— The history and antiquities of the chapel at Luton Park, a seat of the ... Marquess of Bute. [Bibliogr. notes.] iv, 14pp. Engr. illus. incl. plates, plan, sections and titlepage. 56x40 London: J. Carpenter & Son, 1829 [1830.]
Another copy. 53x37 1829 [1830.]
SMITH, M. Urwick.
— Luton Hoo: the Wernher collection. 24pp. Illus. (2 col., some on covers) incl. maps. 23x18 (London: Pitkin) [1957.]
One of the series: PRIDE of Britain.
ADAM, R. & J. Works in Architecture. I & III. 1773, 1822.
BARTLETT, J. Selections from views of mansions. 1851.
COUNTRY LIFE. CVII, 1282 plans. 1950.
JONES. Views of Seats. I. 1829.
NEALE, J.P. Views of Seats, Vol.I. 1818.
WATTS, W. Seats of the Nobility. pl.69. 1779.
[Sales] LONDON, 1822, June 7, 8 [Pictures at Luton Park].

LUTWYCHE HALL (Shropshire).
LEACH, F. Seats of Shropshire. p.395. 1891.
[Sales] LUTWYCHE HALL, 1928, March 14 [Hall; old English furniture].

LUXBOROUGH (Essex).
ENGLAND: Picturesque Views. p.53, 94. 1786-88.

LYDDINGTON BEDE HOUSE (Rutland).
COUNTRY LIFE. XXVI, 126. 1909.
GARNER, T. Domestic architecture. I, p.44. 1911.
TIPPING, H.A. English Homes. Period II, Vol.I, p.295. 1924.

LYDHAM MANOR (Shropshire).
LEACH, F. Seats of Shropshire. p.143. 1891.

LYDIARD PARK (Wiltshire).
SWINDON: Corporation.
— Lydiard Park and Church: an illustrated survey of the former home of the St. John family and of the adjoining church of St. Mary. 32pp. Illus. (2 col., 1 on cover) incl. folding plate (in pocket), plans and genealog. table. 14x21 (Swindon) [1966?]
COUNTRY LIFE. CIII, 578 plan, 626. 1948.

LYDIATE HALL (Lancashire).
GIBSON, *Rev.* Thomas Ellison.
— Lydiate Hall & its associations; in two parts, antiquarian and religious. [Bibliogr. notes.] xliv, 334pp. Illus. (1 on title-page) incl. plates (photographs) and genealog. tables. 24x18 (Lydiate) for the author, 1876.

LYDNEY PARK (Gloucestershire).
BURKE, J.B. Visitation of Seats. 2.S. Vol.II, p.140. 1855.*
RUDDER, S. Gloucestershire. 524. 1779.

LYEGROVE (Gloucestershire).
COUNTRY LIFE. LXVI, 864 plan. 1929.

LYME PARK (Cheshire).
LONDON:National Trust for Places of Historic Interest or
Natural Beauty.
—Lyme Park, Cheshire. 26pp. 4 plates. 18x12 London:
Country Life (1948).
Another ed. 1966.
Rev. ed. WATERSON, M. [Bibliogr.] 36pp. Illus. (1 Col. on cover)
incl. plan. 21x14 [London] 1981.

NEWTON,Evelyn Caroline Legh, *Lady*.
—The house of Lyme from its foundation to the end of the
eighteenth century. Plates incl. map and genealog. table.
24x16 London: Heinemann, 1917.
ANGUS-BUTTERWORTH, L.M. Old Cheshire families. p.127.
1932.
BARTLETT, J. Selections from views of mansions. 1851.
BURKE, J.B. Visitation of Seats. 2.S. Vol.I, p.34. 1854.
COUNTRY LIFE. XVIII, 234.1905.
COUNTRY LIFE. XCVI, 684. 1944.
COUNTRY LIFE. C, 210. 1946.
COUNTRY LIFE. CLVI, **1724, 1858, 1930, 1998. 1974.**
JONES, Views of seats. I. 1829.
LATHAM, C. In English Homes. Vol. II. p.209. 1907.
MALAN, A.H. Famous homes. p. 263. 1902.
NASH, J. Mansions of **England. IV, pl.1. 1849.**
NEALE, J.P. Views of Seats. 2.S. Vol.1. 1824.
NOBLE, T. **Counties of Chester, ... Lincoln.** p.64. 1826.
TWYCROSS, E. Mansions of England and Wales. Vol.II, p.92.
1850.
WATTS, W. Seats of the **Nobility. pl.79. 1779.**

LYMM HALL (Cheshire).
ORMEROD, G. Cheshire. I, 580. 1882.
TWYCROSS, E. Mansions of England and Wales. Vol.II, p.77.
1850.

LYMORE HOUSE (Montgomeryshire).
COUNTRY LIFE. XXIII, 342. 1908.
MOSS, F. Pilgramages. [II] 247. 1903.
NICHOLAS, T. Counties of Wales. II, p.797. 1872.
[Sales] LYMORE HOUSE, 1929, October 25 [Mansion].

LYMPNE CASTLE (Kent).
COUNTRY LIFE. XXVIII, 682 plan. 1910.
OSWALD, A. Country houses of Kent. 10. 1933.

LYNDON HALL (Rutland).
COUNTRY LIFE. English Country houses: Caroline. p.174.
1966.
COUNTRY LIFE. CXL, 1212 plan. 1966.

LYNE (Surrey).
BRAYLEY, E.W. History of Surrey. IV, 290. 1841.

LYNSTED PARK (Kent).
GREENWOOD, C. Kent. 266. 1838.

LYPIATT PARK (Gloucestershire).
ATKYNS, R. Glocestershire. p.368. 1768.
COOKE, R. West Country Houses. p.29. 1957.
COUNTRY LIFE. CXXXVI, 114. 1964.
LYPIATT PARK. The Lypiatt Park Estate. [Sale Prospectus.]
[c.1924].

LYSWAYS HALL (Staffordshire).
BURKE, J.B. Visitation of Seats. Vol.II, p.151. 1853.*

LYTES CARY (Somerset).
GEORGE, William.
—Lytes Cary Manor House, Somerset, and its literary
associations; with notices of authors of the Lyte family, from
Queen Elizabeth to the present time. [Bibliogr. notes.] 14pp. 2
illus.: photographs. 22x14 Bristol: by the author [1879].

LONDON: National Trust for Places of Historic Interest or
Natural Beauty.
—KEARNEY, M. Lytes Cary, Somerset. 16pp. 4 plates. 18x12
London: Country Life (1950).
Rev. ed. DODD, D. [Bibliogr.] 32pp. Illus. (1 on cover) incl. plan.
21x14 [London] 1981.
COUNTRY LIFE. CII, 128 plan, 178, 228. 1947.
DELDERFIELD, E.R. West Country houses. II, 84. 1970.
GARNER, T. Domestic architecture. I, p.57 plan. 1911.

LYTH, The. (Shropshire).
WEST, W. Picturesque views of Shropshire. p.134. 1831.

LYTHAM HALL (Lancashire).
BARTLETT, J. Mansions of England and Wales. pl.78. 1853.
BURKE, J.B. Visitation of Seats. Vol.II, p.195. 1853.*
BURKE, J.B. Visitation of Seats. 2.S. Vol.II, p.128. 1855.*
COUNTRY LIFE. CXXVII, 130, 188. 1960.
TWYCROSS, E. Mansions of England and Wales. Vol.II, p.33.
1847.

LYTHWOOD PARK [HALL] (Shropshire).
BURKE, J.B. Visitation of Seats. Vol.II, p.51. 1853.*
LEIGHTON, S. Shropshire houses. 5. 1901.

LYVEDEN NEW BUILDING (Northamptonshire).

BELL, Thomas
—The ruins of Liveden; with historical notices of the family of Tresham and its connexion with the Gunpowder Plot, etc., ... to which is added a legendary poem. [Bibliogr. notes.] 76pp. Illus. incl. lithogr. plates (1 folding) and genealog. table. 27x22 London: Whittaker & Co; Peterborough: R. Gardner, 1847.

GOTCH, John Alfred.
—A complete account, illustrated by measured drawings, of the buildings erected in Northamptonshire, by Sir Thomas Tresham, between the years 1575 and 1605. Together with many particulars concerning the Tresham family and their home at Rushton. [Bibliogr. notes.] xviii, 44pp. Plates incl. sections, elevations and plans. 38x28 Northampton: Taylor & Son; London: Batsford, 1883.

LONDON: National Trust for Places of Historic Interest or Natural Beauty.
—GOTCH, J.A. Lyveden New Building, Northamptonshire. 10pp. 2 plates and plan. 18x12 London: Country Life (1947).

LONDON: National Trust for places of Historic Interest or Natural Beauty.
—ISHAM, G. Lyveden New Bield. [Bibliogr. note.] 16pp. Illus. (1 on cover) incl. plates, elevations and plans. 21x14 [London] 1981.

GOTCH, J.A. Architecture of the Renaissance. I,p.40 plan. 1894.

MABLEDON PARK (Kent).

GREENWOOD, C. Kent. 125. 1838.

MABWS (Cardiganshire).

BURKE, J.B. Visitation of Seats. 2.S. Vol.II, p.92. 1855.*

MACKERYE END (Hertfordshire).

COUNTRY LIFE. CXIX, 108. 1956.

MADELEY COURT (Shropshire).

COUNTRY LIFE. XLII, 12. 1917.

GARNER, T. Domestic architecture. II, p.191. 1911.

SHROPSHIRE. Castles & Old Mansions. 34. 1868.

TIPPING, H.A. English Homes. Period III, Vol.I, p.154. 1922.

MADELEY HALL (Staffordshire).

PLOT, R. Staffordshire. 223. 1686.

MADINGLEY HALL (Cambridgeshire).

MADINGLEY.
— Madingley Hall: a short history and description of the hall and estate, their owners and occupiers. (3 ed.) 20pp. Illus. (1 on title-page) incl. plans and genealog. table. 24x16 (Loughborough printed, 1970).
Title on cover.

COUNTRY LIFE. XXXII, 454. 1912.

KIP, J. Nouveau théâtre de la Grande Bretagne. I, pl.57. 1715.

NEALE, J.P. Views of Seats. 2.S. Vol.I. 1824.

TIPPING, H.A. English Homes. Early Renaissance. p.57. 1912.

MADRESFIELD COURT (Worcestershire).

LONDON: Roxburghe Club.
—BACKHOUSE, J. The Madresfield Hours: a fourteenth century manuscript in the library of Earl Beauchamp (at Madresfield Court). [Bibliogr. notes.] 36pp. Plates (4 col.). 31x20 Oxford, 1975.

MADRESFIELD COURT.
—Alphabetical list of such miniatures and enamels in the collection at Madresfield Court as are named. [This collection ... formed by Catherine Denne, wife of William Lygon, first Earl Beauchamp, was rearranged and catalogued in 1874-5 by Mary Stanhope, wife of Frederick, sixth Earl.] 24pp. 21x13 n.p.: privately printed, 1879.

COUNTRY LIFE. XXI, 450. 1907.

COUNTRY LIFE. CLXVIII. 1338, 1458, 1551. 1980.

NASH, T.R. Worcestershire. II, 117. 1782.

NEALE, J.P. Views of Seats. Vol.V. 1822.

MADRYN CASTLE (Caernarvonshire).

BURKE, J.B. Visitation of Seats. 2.S. Vol.I, p.33. 1854.

NICHOLAS, T. Counties of Wales. I, p.317. 1872.

[Sales] MADRYN CASTLE, 1910, June 29, 30 [Contents].

MAENAN HALL (Caenarvonshire).

COUNTRY LIFE. CXXIX, 280 plan, 334. 1961.

MAESLLWCH CASTLE (Radnorshire).

BURKE, J.B. Visitation of Seats. 2.S. Vol.I, p.95. 1854.*

NICHOLAS, T. Counties of Wales. I, p.317. 1872.

MAIDEN BRADLEY (Wiltshire).

CAMPBELL, C. Vitruvius Britannicus. II, pl.56. 1717.

MAIDEN ERLEGH (Berkshire).

[Sales] MAIDEN ERLEGH, 1931, December 7-12 [Contents]. (K.F. & R.).

MAISTER HOUSE, Hull (Yorkshire).

LONDON: National Trust for Places of Historic Interest or Natural Beauty.
— ALEC-SMITH, R.A. Maister House, Kingston upon Hull. [Bibliogr. note.] 12pp. Illus. (1 on cover.) 25x18 [London, c. 1970.]

MAJOR HOUSE (Suffolk).

See THORNHAM HALL.

MAKENEY HALL (Derbyshire).
TILLEY, J. Halls of Derbyshire. II, p.57.1893.

MALLING ABBEY (Kent).
BURKE, J.B. Visitation of Seats. Vol.I, p.10. 1852.*

MALMESBURY HOUSE, Salisbury (Wiltshire).
COUNTRY LIFE. CXXX, 882 plan, 1002. 1961.

MALPAS COURT (Monmouthshire).
NICHOLAS, T. Counties of Wales. II, p.721. 1872.

MALSIS HALL (Yorkshire).
YORKSHIRE. Picturesque views. 1885.

MALVERN HALL (Warwickshire).
SOANE, J. Plans, elevations and sections. pls. IV - VI. 1788.

MAMHEAD (Devonshire).
WALKER, Edmund.
—Views of Mamhead, the seat of Sir Robert L. Newman, Bart., from nature and on stone. [No Text.] 11 tinted lithogr. plates and title-page. 62x44 [London] privately printed, 1848.

BOLTON, A.T. Architecture of R. & J. Adam. II, 162 plan. 1922.

BRITTON, J. Devonshire illustrated. 64. 1832.

BURKE, J.B. Visitation of Seats. 2.S. Vol.II, p.175. 1855.*

COUNTRY LIFE. English Country Houses: Late Georgian. p.193. 1958.

JONES. Views of Seats. II. 1829.

MORRIS, F.O. Views of Seats. Vol.III, p.7. 1880.

NEALE, J.P. Views of Seats. Vol.I. 1818.

MANCETTER MANOR HOUSE (Warwickshire).
NIVEN, W. Old Warwickshire houses. p.14, pl.15. 1878.

MANLEY HALL (Lancashire).
MANLEY HALL.
— Paintings, drawings, engravings, sculpture, carvings, gold and silver, pottery, &c. [At Manley Hall, Manchester, the residence of S. Mendel.] Plate. 30x22 (London) privately printed, 1867.

[Sales] MANLEY HALL, 1875, March 15 and following days [Contents].

MANLEY HALL (Staffordshire).
BURKE, J.B. Visitation of Seats. 2.S. Vol.II, p.70. 1855.

MANNINGTON HALL (Norfolk).
NEVILL, *Lady* Dorothy Fanny.
— Mannington and the Walpoles, Earls of Orford. 42pp. Plates. 21x28 London: Fine Art Society, 1894.

TOMES, *Sir* Charles Sissmore.
— Mannington Hall and its owners. 72pp. Illus. incl. plates (some folding) plans and genealog. table. 22x14 Norwich: Goose & Son, 1916.

BIRKBECK, G. Old Norfolk houses. 74. 1908.

GARRATT, T. Halls of Norfolk. pls. 32, 33. 1890.

MANOR HOUSE, West Bromwich (Staffordshire).
MANOR HOUSE.
— The Manor House, West Bromwich. 20pp. Illus. (1 on cover) incl. plan. 23x10 (West Bromwich: Corporation & Ansells Brewery) [c.1965].

MANOR HOUSE, The. Hitchin (Hertfordshire).
PHILLIPS, Frederick William.
— The Manor House at Hitchin. (Exhibition of ... Queen Anne furniture ... for sale.) [No Text.] 12 plates. 32x25 Hitchin [c.1925].
Title on cover.
Another ed. 20 plates. [c.1925.]

MANRESA HOUSE [Parkstead], Roehampton (Surrey). [Bessborough House].
CAMPBELL, C. Vitruvius Britannicus. IV, pls.11-13. 1767.

MANSION, The. Ashbourne (Derbyshire).
COUNTRY LIFE. CXLIII, 730. 1968.

MANYDOWN PARK (Hampshire).
BURKE, J.B. Visitation of Seats. Vol.II, p.196. 1853.*

MAPLEDURHAM HOUSE (Oxfordshire).
COGMAN, Leonard G.
— Mapledurham House: history and description of contents. 24pp. Illus. (some col., some on covers) incl. genealog. table. 23x18 St. Ives, Huntingdon: privately printed [c.1975].

WILLIAMS, Richard.
— Mapledurham House, Oxfordshire: history and description of contents. 24pp. Illus. (some col., some on folding covers) incl. genealog. table. 21x15 (St. Ives, Cornwall) 1977.

BURKE, J.B. Visitation of Seats. 2.S. Vol.II, p.153. 1855.*

COUNTRY LIFE. XX, 274. 1906.

COUNTRY LIFE. CXLIX, 1152 plan, 1216. 1971.

SHAW, H. Elizabethan architecture. pl.XVI. [Plaister cornices] 1839.

MAPLE HAYES (Staffordshire).
NEALE, J.P. Views of Seats. 2.S. Vol.II. 1825.

MAPPERTON HOUSE (Dorsetshire).
COUNTRY LIFE. X, 16. 1901.
COUNTRY LIFE. XXXIV, 490 plan. 1913.
COUTRY LIFE. CXXXI, 18, 66 plan, 176. 1962.
GARNER, T. Domestic architecture. II, p.199 plan. 1911.
HEATH, S. Dorset Manor Houses. 125. 1907.
OSWALD, A. Country houses of Dorset. p.79. 1959.

MARBLE HILL (Middlesex).
LONDON: County Council.
— Marble Hill House: a historical and descriptive account. [Bibliogr.] 16pp. 20x13 (London) 1930.
LONDON: County Council [Marble Hill].
— Marble Hill House, Twickenham. 4pp. 1 illus. 22x14 London (1951).
LONDON: Georgian Group.
— SMITH, H.C. Marble Hill House, Twickenham, Middlesex. 16pp. 4 plates and plan (on inside cover). 21x14 (London, 1939.)
Title on cover.
LONDON: Greater London Council.
— DRAPER, M.P.G. Marble Hill House and its owners ... With an introduction and contributions on the architects, architecture and restoration of the house by W.A. Eden. [Bibliogr.] 72pp. 41 illus. incl. 40 (1 col.) plates, sections, elevations, plans and map. 30x21 London, 1970.
LONDON: Greater London Council.
— Marble Hill House, Twickenham: a short account of its history and architecture. 16pp. Illus. (1 on cover) incl. 4 plates, elevations and plans. 21x15 London, 1966.
Another ed. 1971.
Another ed. 24pp. Illus. (2 col. on cover) incl. elevations and plans. 1982.
CAMPBELL, C. Vitruvius Britannicus. III, pl.93. 1725.
COUNTRY LIFE. XXXIX, 394 plan. 1916.
ENGLAND: Beauties of England. II, p.69. 1787.

MARBURY HALL, Great Budworth (Cheshire).
MARBURY HALL.
— A catalogue of paintings, statues, busts, &c. at Marbury Hall, the seat of John Smith Barry, Esq., in the county of Chester. 24pp. 25x19 Warrington: privately printed, 1819.
BURKE, J.B. Visitation of Seats. Vol.I, p.200. 1852.*
NEALE, J.P. Views of Seats. 2.S. Vol.V. 1829.
ORMEROD, G. Cheshire. I, 634. 1882.
TWYCROSS, E. Mansions of England and Wales. Vol.II, p.64. 1850.

MARBURY HALL near Wrenbury (Cheshire).
BURKE, J.B. Visitation of Seats. Vol.I. p.264. 1852.*
TWYCROSS, E. Mansions of England and Wales. Vol.II, p.17. 1850.

MARDEN HILL (Hertfordshire).
COUNTRY LIFE. XC, 328 plan. 1941.

MARELANDS BENTLEY (Hampshire).
COUNTRY LIFE. XCI, 948. 1942.

MARESFIELD PARK (Sussex).
BURKE, J.B. Visitation of Seats. 2.S. Vol.I, p.206. 1854.*
[Sales] TUNBRIDGE WELLS, 1922, October 11-13 [Antique and modern furniture].
[Sales] MARESFIELD PARK, 1925, November 26-28 [fixtures and fittings].

MARISTOW (Devonshire).
BRITTON, J. Devonshire illustrated. 95. 1832.

MARKEATON HALL (Derbyshire).
JONES. Views of Seats. I. 1829.
NEALE, J.P. Views of Seats. 2.S. Vol.I. 1824.
TILLEY, J. Halls of Derbyshire. IV, p.129. 1902.

MARKENFIELD HALL (Yorkshire).
COUNTRY LIFE. XXXI, 206 plan. 1912.
COUNTRY LIFE. LXXXVIII, 566 plan. 1940.
TIPPING, H.A. English Homes. Period I, Vol.I, p.125. 1921.
WOOD, G.B. Historic homes of Yorkshire. 52. 1957.

MARKET BOSWORTH HALL (Leicestershire).
BURKE, J.B. Visitation of Seats. 2.S. Vol.II, p.91. 1855.*
NICHOLS, J. History of Leicestershire. IV, ii, 500. 1811.
THROSBY, J. Views in Leicestershire. p.197. 1789.

MARKET LAVINGTON MANOR (Wiltshire).
[Sales] MARKET LAVINGTON, 1907, December 13, 14, 16-18, 20 [Contents].

MARKS HALL (Essex).
BURKE, J.B. Visitation of Seats. Vol.I, p.33. 1852.*
COUNTRY LIFE. LIV, 420. 1923.
RUSH, J.A. Seats in Essex. p.128. 1897.*

MARKYATE CELL (Hertfordshire).
BURKE, J.B. Visitation of Seats. Vol.I, p.122. 1852.*

MARLESFORD HALL (Suffolk).
DAVY, H. Seats in Suffolk. pl.9. 1827.

MARLEY HOUSE, South Brent (Devonshire).
[Sales] MARLEY HOUSE, 1923, June 20-23 [Contents].

MARLEY HOUSE, Withycombe Raleigh (Devonshire).
DELDERFIELD, E.R. West Country houses. I, 93.1968.
[Sales] MARLEY HOUSE, 1930, June 3-5 [Fixtures & fittings].

MARLINGFORD HALL (Norfolk).
[Sales] MARLINGFORD HALL, 1912, July 16-19, 22, 23 [Contents].

MARLOW PLACE (Buckinghamshire).
COUNTRY LIFE. English Country Houses: Baroque. p.211. 1970.
COUNTRY LIFE. XXXIII, 54.1913.

MARPLE HALL (Cheshire).
BURKE, J.B. Visitation of Seats. Vol.II, p.40. 1853.*
COUNTRY LIFE. XLV, 222. 1919.
ORMEROD, G. Cheshire. III, 842. 1882.
TWYCROSS, E. Mansions of England and Wales. Vol.II, p.108. 1850.

MARRINGTON HALL (Shropshire).
LEACH, F. Seats of Shropshire. p.269. 1891.
LEIGHTON, S. Shropshire houses. 6. 1901.
SHROPSHIRE. Castles & Old Mansions. 64. 1868.

MARSDEN HALL (Lancashire).
BARTLETT, J. Mansions of England and Wales. pls.12, 13. 1853.
TWYCROSS, E. Mansions of England and Wales. Vol.I, p.34. 1847.

MARSH COURT (Hampshire).
COUNTRY LIFE. XX, 306. 1906.
COUNTRY LIFE. XXXIII, 562 plan. 1913.
COUNTRY LIFE. LXXI, 316, 378 plan. 1932.
LATHAM, C. In English Homes. Vol.II, p.425. 1907.

MARSH HALL (Derbyshire).
TILLEY, F. Halls of Derbyshire. I, p.93. 1892.

MARSKE HALL, Marske-by-the-Sea (Yorkshire).
COUNTRY LIFE. XXIX, 488 plan. 1911.

MARSKE HALL, Near Richmond (Yorkshire).
BURKE, J.B. Visitation of Seats. 2.S. Vol.II, p.5. 1855.*

MARSTON HALL (Lincolnshire).
COUNTRY LIFE. CXXXVIII, 612 plan, 688. 1965.

MARSTON HOUSE (Somerset).
CAMPBELL, C. Vitruvius Britannicus. IVth. pls. 69, 70. 1739.
JONES. Views of Seats. II. 1829.
NEALE, J.P. Views of Seats. Vol.III. 1820.

MARSTON MANOR, Marston St. Lawrence (Northamptonshire).
GOTCH, J.A. Squires' Homes. 42. 1939.

MARTON HALL (Yorkshire).
MANUSCRIPTS (Typewritten)   English.
—Marton Hall inventory 1605, [the possessions of] Raphe Creyke. (An inventory of the goods moveable within the house at Marton, taken upon the 22 days of Octor anno dni 1605.) 34ff. 33x20 [London, 1938.]
SPROULE, A. Lost houses of Britain. 159. 1982.

MARYLAND, Hurtwood (Surrey).
COUNTRY LIFE. LXX, 452 plan. 1931.

MASCALLS (Hertfordshire).
[Sales] LONDON, 1840, August 20 [Estate].

MATFIELD HOUSE (Kent).
COUNTRY LIFE. LXXVIII, 272. 1935.
OSWALD, A. Country houses of Kent. 64. 1933.

MATHERN PALACE (Monmouthshire).
COUNTRY LIFE. CLXVI, 2154. 1979.

MATSON HOUSE (Gloucestershire).
COUNTRY LIFE. CVIII, 1990. 1950.

MAUGERSBURY (Gloucestershire).
ATKYNS, R. Glocestershire. p.265. 1768.

MAVESYN RIDWARE (Staffordshire).
BURKE, J.B. Visitation of Seats. Vol.II, p.230. 1853. *

MAWLEY HALL (Shropshire).
MAWLEY HALL.
— Mawley Hall. 8pp. Illus. 25x20 n.p. privately printed [c.1973.]
COUNTRY LIFE. English Country Houses: Early Georgian. p.109. 1955.
COUNTRY LIFE. XXVIII, 18. 1910.
TIPPING, H.A. English Homes. Period V, Vol.I, p.217. 1921.

MAXSTOKE CASTLE (Warwickshire).
BURKE, J.B. Visitation of Seats. Vol. I, p.178. 1852.*
COUNTRY LIFE. XIX, 54. 1906.
COUNTRY LIFE. XLVII, 140,170. 1920.
COUNTRY LIFE. CLV, 842, 930. 1974.
JONES. Views of Seats.I. 1829.
LATHAM, C. In English Homes. Vol.II, p.9. 1907.
NEALE, J.P. Views of Seats. Vol.IV. 1821.
SMITH, W. History of the County of Warwick. 375. 1830.
TIPPING, H.A. English Homes. Period I, Vol.I, p.220. 1921.

MAY PLACE, Crayford (Kent).
CROMWELL, T.K. Excursions in Kent. p.128. 1822.
GREENWOOD, C. Kent. 42. 1838.

MEABURN HALL (Westmorland).
CUMBERLAND: C. & W.A. & A.S. Extra series VIII, 112. 1892.

MEARS ASHBY HALL (Northamptonshire).
GOTCH, J.A. Squires' Homes. 29. 1939.

MEASHAM HALL (Leicestershire).
TILLEY, J. Halls of Derbyshire. IV, p.86. 1902.*

MEER HALL (Worcestershire).
See MERE HALL.

MEES HALL (Staffordshire).
MOSS, F. Pilgrimages. [II] 32. 1903.

MELBOURNE HALL (Derbyshire).
KERR, John, *Lord.*
— Melbourne Hall: an illustrated survey of the Derbyshire home of the Marquess of Lothian. 32pp. Illus. (1 col., some on covers) incl. plan and map. 14x21 Derby: Come to Derbyshire Association [c.1950].
Another ed. Illus. (some col., some on covers) incl. plan and genealog. table. Derby: Derbyshire Countryside Ltd. (1974.)
COUNTRY LIFE. LXIII, 526. 1928.
NICOLSON, N. Great Houses of Britain. p.204. 1965.
TILLEY, J. Halls of Derbyshire. IV, p.39. 1902.

MELBURY HOUSE (Dorsetshire).
ILCHESTER, Henry Edward Fox-Strangways, *Earl of.*
— Catalogue of pictures belonging to the Earl of Ilchster. (At Melbury House, Redlynch House, Abbotsbury Castle and 42, Belgrave Square; index of portraits.) 24x18 (London) privately printed at the Chiswick Press, 1883.
BURKE, J.B. Visitation of Seats. 2.S. Vol.II, p.158. 1855.*
HEATH, S. Dorset Manor Houses. 133. 1907.

HUTCHINS, J. History of Dorset. II, 672. 1863.
JONES. Views of Seats. II. 1829.
LATHAM, C. In English Homes. Vol.I, p.347. 1904.
MORRIS, F.O. Views of Seats. Vol.II, p.29. 1880.
NEALE, J.P. Views of Seats. 2.S. Vol.IV. 1828.
OSWALD, A. Country houses of Dorset. p.118. 1959.
[Sales] LONDON, 1962, May 14-16 [Portion of the library].

MELCHBOURNE (Bedfordshire).
COUNTRY LIFE. LXXVI, 168. 1934.

MELCHET COURT (Hampshire).
SELLERS, Eugénie.
— Catalogue of the Greek & Roman antiques in the possession of ... Lord Melchett, ... at Melchet Court and 35, Lowndes Square. [Bibliogr.] 66pp. Illus. incl. plates. 35x26 Oxford: O.U.P.; London: H. Milford, 1938.
COUNTRY LIFE. LXVIII, 176, 391 [Furniture]. 1934.
[Sales] MELCHET COURT, 1911, September 18 and following days [Contents].

MELCOMBE HORSEY (Dorsetshire).
OSWALD, A. Country houses of Dorset. p.73. 1959.

MELDON PARK (Northumberland).
BURKE, J.B. Visitation of Seats. Vol.II, p.242. 1853.*
COUNTRY LIFE. CXXXIX, 406. 1966.

MELFORD HALL (Suffolk).
HYDE-PARKER,Ulla Ditlef, *Lady.*
—Melford Hall: the historic Suffolk home of the Hyde-Parker family [etc.]. 16pp. 5 illus. (4 on covers) incl. map. 14x19 [Derby: E.L.P.c.1955.]
LONDON: National Trust for Places of Historic Interest or Natural Beauty.
—LEES-MILNE, J. Melford Hall, Suffolk. 18pp. 4 plates. 18x12 London: Country Life, 1961.
Another ed. 24pp. Illus. (1 col. on cover) incl. plates and plan. 22x14 [London] 1972. Rev. Ed. [Bibliogr.] 32pp. Illus. (1 col. on cover) incl. plates, plan and genealog. table. 22x14 [London] 1981.
COUNTRY LIFE. LXXXII, 116, 142, 394 [Furniture]. 1937.
CROMWELL, T.K. Excursions in Suffolk. I, p.58. 1818.
NEALE, J.P. Views of Seats. 2.S. Vol.II. 1825.

MELLING HALL (Lancashire).
BARTLETT, J. Mansions of England and Wales. pl.61. 1853.
TWYCROSS, E. Mansions of England and Wales. Vol.II, p.18. 1847.

MELLOR HALL (Derbyshire).
TILLEY, J.Halls of Derbyshire. I, p.151. 1892.

MELLS MANOR HOUSE (Somerset).
COUNTRY LIFE. XCIII, 748. 1943.
TIPPING, H.A. English Homes. Period III, Vol.I, p.108. 1922.

MELPLASH COURT (Dorsetshire).
OSWALD, A. Country houses of Dorset. p.82. 1959.

MELTON HALL, Melton Constable (Norfolk).
BUCK, S. & N. Antiquities. I, pl.201. 1774.
BURKE, J.B. Visitation of Seats. 2.S. Vol.II, p.93. 1855.*
COUNTRY LIFE. XVIII, 378. 1905.
COUNTRY LIFE. LXIV, 364, 402, 478 [Needlework, furniture]. 1928.
COUNTRY LIFE. LXXX, 266. 1936.
CROMWELL, T.K. Excursions in Norfolk. I, p.154. 1818.
ENGLAND: Beauties of England. II, p.129. 1787.
KIP, J. Nouveau théâtre de la Grande Bretagne. I, pl.51. 1715.
MORRIS, F.O. Views of Seats. Vol.VI, p.73. 1880.
NEALE, J.P. Views of Seats. Vol.III. 1820.
WATTS, W. Seats of the Nobility. pl.38. 1779.

MENABILLY (Cornwall).
BURKE, J.B. Visitation of Seats. 2.S. Vol.II, p.149. 1855.*
CROMWELL, T.K. Excursions in Cornwall. p.40. 1824.

MENTMORE (Buckinghamshire).
MENTMORE.
— Mentmore. [Guide and inventory.] Plate: plan. 31x25 Edinburgh: privately printed, 1883.
MENTMORE.
— Mentmore. Illus: photographs and plan. 2 vols. 38x28 Edinburgh: privately printed, 1884.
With some MS. corrections.
Another copy [Photocopy.] 34x29 [1967].
MENTMORE.
— Sale of the contents of Mentmore House, Buckinghamshire, the property of the Earl of Rosebery. Illus. (some col.) incl. plates. 5 vols. 26x18 London: Sotheby, 1977.
I. Furniture.
II. Works of art.
III. Porcelain.
IV. Paintings, prints and drawings.
V. General contents of the house.
PINKHAM, Roger.
— The Mentmore Limoges enamels. Excerpt (photocopy), 8ff. Illus. 30x21 [London, 1977.]
Also in: SOTHEBY & CO. Art at auction ... 1976-77, 240. 1977.

MEOLS HALL (Lancashire).
COUNTRY LIFE. CLIII. 206, 274, 326. 1973.

MERCASTON HALL (Derbyshire).
TILLEY, J. Halls of Derbyshire, II. p.121. 1893.

MERCHISTOUN HALL (Hampshire).
BURKE, J.B. Visitation of Seats. 2.S. Vol.II, p.59. 1855.*

MERDON MANOR (Hampshire).
[Sales] MERDON MANOR, 1982, April 26, 27 [Furniture, Eastern rugs and carpets etc.]

MERE HALL (Cheshire).
BURKE, J.B. Visitation of Seats. Vol.I, p.70. 1852.*
TWYCROSS, E. Mansions of England and Wales. Vol.II, p.67. 1850.

MERE HALL (Worcestershire).
BURKE, J.B. Visitation of Seats. Vol.II, p.143. 1853.*
MORRIS, F.O. Views of Seats. Vol.VI, p.15. 1880.
NIVEN, W. Old Worcestershire houses. p.7, pl.5. 1873.

MEREVALE HALL (Warwickshire).
BURKE, J.B. Visitation of Seats. Vol.II, p.17. 1853.*
COUNTRY LIFE. CXLV, 598, 662. 1969.
MORRIS, F.O. Views of Seats. Vol.III, p.59. 1880.
NEALE, J.P. Views of Seats. 2.S. Vol.V. 1829.

MEREWORTH CASTLE (Kent).
CAMPBELL, C. Vitruvius Britannicus. III, pls. 35-38. 1725.
COUNTRY LIFE. English Country Houses: Early Georgian. p.58. 1955.
COUNTRY LIFE. XLVII, 808, 876 plan, 912. 1920.
CROMWELL, T.K. Excursions in Kent. p.144. 1822.
ENGLAND: Beauties of England. I, p.397. 1787.
HASTED, E. Kent. II, 268. 1782.
NEALE, J.P. Views of Seats. 2.S. Vol.II. 1825.
NICOLSON, N. Great Houses of Britain. p.220. 1965.
OSWALD, A. Country houses of Kent. 55. 1933.
TIPPING, H.A. English Homes. Period V, Vol.I, p.39. 1921.
[Sales] LONDON, 1922, July 12 [The Mansion].
[Sales] MEREWORTH CASTLE, 1923, September 17-22 [Sporting pictures, old masters etc.].

MERGATE HALL (Norfolk).
GARRATT, T. Halls of Norfolk. pls. 34, 35. 1890.

MERLY HOUSE (Dorsetshire).
WILLETT, Ralph.
— A description of the library at Merly, in the county of Dorset. [Title-page and text also in French.] 20pp. Engr. (1 on title-page) incl. plates (some folding) and plan. Fol. 57x43 London: printed for the author by John Nichols, 1785.

HUTCHINS, J. Vitruvius Dorsettiensis. pl.18. 1816.

HUTCHINS, J. History of Dorset. III, 304. 1868.

OSWALD, A. Country houses of Dorset. p.163. 1959.

[Sales] MERLY HOUSE, 1927, June 8-10 [Furniture, pictures, porcelain etc.].

MERSHAM-LE-HATCH (Kent).

COUNTRY LIFE. English Country Houses: Mid Georgian. p.98. 1956.

COUNTRY LIFE. XLIX, 368 plan. 1921.

COUNTRY LIFE. LV, 582 [Chippendale letters.] 1924.

COUNTRY LIFE. LVIII, 218 plan. 1925.

HASTED, E. Kent. III, 286. 1790.

MORRIS, F.O. Views of Seats. Vol.V, p.45. 1880.

NEALE, J.P. Views of Seats. 2.S. Vol.III. 1826.

OSWALD, A. Country houses of Kent. 64. 1933.

TIPPING, H.A. English Homes. Period VI, Vol.I, p.117. 1926.

MERSTHAM PLACE (Surrey).

BURKE, J.B. Visitation of Seats. 2.S. Vol.I, p.171. 1854.*

MERTON GRANGE (Cheshire).

ORMEROD, G. Cheshire. II, 159. 1882.

MERTON HALL (Norfolk).

BURKE, J.B. Visitation of Seats. 2.S. Vol.II, p.130. 1855.*

GARRATT, T. Halls of Norfolk. pl.36. 1890.

NEALE, J.P. Views of Seats. Vol.III. 1820.

MERTON PLACE (Surrey).

ANGUS, W. Seats of the Nobility. pl.55. 1787.

SPROULE, A. Lost houses of Britain. 199. 1982.

METHLEY HALL (Yorkshire).

COUNTRY LIFE. XXI, 702. 1907.

ENGLAND: Picturesque Views. p.69. 1786-88.

JONES. Views of Seats. I. 1829.

LATHAM, C. In English Homes. Vol.II, p.173. 1907.

NEALE, J.P. Views of Seats. Vol.V. 1822.

WHEATER, W. Mansions of Yorkshire. p.146. 1888.

METTINGHAM CASTLE (Suffolk).

BURKE, J.B. Visitation of Seats. 2.S. Vol.I, p.100. 1854.*

METTINGHAM HALL (Suffolk).

SANDON, E. Suffolk houses. 273. 1977.

MICHELGROVE (Sussex).

NEALE, J.P. Views of Seats. 2.S. Vol.V. 1829.

REPTON, H. Observations on landscape gardening. 179. 1803.

MICHELHAM PRIORY (Sussex).

MICHELHAM PRIORY.

—Michelham Priory. 4 ed. 20pp. Illus. (some on covers) incl. plan. 19x14 [Michelham] 1966.

COUNTRY LIFE. LXXVII, 296 plan. 1935.

COUNTRY LIFE. CXXVII, 740. 1960.

MIDDLEHAM HALL (Yorkshire).

BURKE, J.B. Visitation of Seats. Vol.I, p.42. 1852.*

MIDDLE HILL (Worcestershire).

JONES. Views of Seats. I. 1829.

NEALE, J.P. Views of Seats. 2.S. Vol.III. 1826.

MIDDLE LITTLETON HALL (Worcestershire).

NIVEN, W. Old Worcestershire houses. p.21, pl.9. 1873.

MIDDLETHORPE HALL (Yorkshire).

YORK: Georgian Society.

— Occasional papers.

I. (... Lady Mary Wortley Montagu at Middlethorpe Hall. By I.P. Pressly.) 24pp. Plates. 20x13 (1945.)

MIDDLETON HALL (Carmarthenshire).

BURKE, J.B. Visitation of Seats. 2.S. Vol.I, p.179. 1854.

CAMPBELL, C. New Vitruvius Britannicus. II, pls.62-4. 1808.

NEALE, J.P. Views of Seats. Vol.V. 1822.

MIDDLETON HALL (Derbyshire).

TILLEY, J. Halls of Derbyshire. I, p.247. 1892.

MIDDLETON HALL (Warwickshire).

DE HAMEL, Egbert.

Middleton Hall, Warwickshire. 13pp. 3 illus.

In: BIRMINGHAM: Birmingham and Midland Institute. Archaeological Society. Transactions, XXVII, 1901. 16. 1902.

SMITH, W. History of the County of Warwick. 372. 1830.

MIDDLETON HALL (Westmorland).

CUMBERLAND: C. & W. A. & A.S. Extra Series VIII, 232 plan. 1892.

MIDDLETON PARK (Oxfordshire).

COUNTRY LIFE. C, 28, 74 plan. 1946.

NEALE, J.P. Views of Seats. 2.S. Vol.V. 1829.

MIDDLETON TOWER (Norfolk).
STEER, Francis W.
Middleton Tower, Norfolk. The home of Mr and Mrs T.H. Barclay. A guide and short history. [Bibliogr.] 12pp. Illus. (1 on title-page, 1 on cover) incl. plates. 20x16 n.p. 1961.
TIPPING, H.A. English Homes. Period I & II, Vol. II, p. 312. 1937.

MIDDLEWICH MANOR (Cheshire).
TWYCROSS, E. Mansions of England and Wales. Vol.I, p.151. 1850.

MIDELNEY MANOR (Somerset).
COUNTRY LIFE. LXXVI, 548. 1934.

MIDFORD CASTLE (Somerset).
COUNTRY LIFE. XCV, 376, 420. 1944.

MILBANKE (Lancashire).
BARTLETT, J. Mansions of England and Wales. pl.95. 1853.
TWYCROSS, E. Mansions of England and Wales. Vol.II, p.59. 1847.

MILBORNE ST. ANDREW (Dorsetshire).
HUTCHINS, J. Vitruvius Dorsettiensis. pl.19. 1816.
HUTCHINS, J. History of Dorset. II, 598. 1863.

MILBOURNE HALL (Northumberland).
BURKE, J.B. Visitation of Seats. 2.S. Vol.I, p.187. 1854.*

MILEHAM HALL (Norfolk).
BURKE, J.B. Visitation of Seats. 2.S. Vol.II, p.141. 1855.*

MILLBECK HALL (Cumberland).
CUMBERLAND: C. & W. A. & A.S. Extra Series VIII, 320. 1892.

MILLFIELD, Stoke d'Abernon (Surrey).
[Sales] MILLFIELD, Stoke d'Abernon, 1930, April 9-11 [Contents]. (K.F. & R.).

MILLICHOPE PARK(Shropshire).
BURKE,J.B. Visitation of Seats. Vol.II, p.42. 1853.*
COUNTRY LIFE. CLXI, 310, 370. 1977.
SHROPSHIRE. Castles & Old Mansions. 29. 1868.

MILNER COURT (Kent).
See STURRY COURT.

MILNER FIELD (Yorkshire).
YORKSHIRE. Picturesque views. 1885.

MILNSBRIDGE HOUSE (Yorkshire).
JONES. Views of Seats. I. 1829.
NEALE, J.P. Views of Seats. Vol.V. 1822.

MILSTEAD MANOR (Kent).
BURKE, J.B. Visitation of Seats. 2.S. Vol.I, p.232. 1854.*

MILTON (Northamptonshire).
ANGUS, W. Seats of the Nobility. pl.13. 1787.
COUNTRY LIFE. XXXII, 638. 1912.
COUNTRY LIFE. CXXIX, 1148, 1210 plan, 1270. 1961.
GOTCH, J.A. Halls of Northants. p.9. 1936.
JONES. Views of Seats. I. 1829.
NEALE, J.P. Views of Seats. Vol.III. 1820.

MILTON ABBEY (Dorsetshire).
COUNTRY LIFE. XXXVII, 734, 770. 1915.
COUNTRY LIFE. CXXXIX, 1586, 1650, 1718. 1966.
COUNTRY LIFE. CXL, 152, 208 plan. 1966.
HUTCHINS, J. Vitruvius Dorsettiensis. pl.20. 1816.
MORRIS, F.O. Views of Seats. Vol.II, p.23. 1880.
NASH, J. Mansions of England. IV, pl.20. 1849.
NEALE, J.P. Views of Seats. 2.S. Vol.IV. 1828.
OSWALD, A. Country houses of Dorset. p.108. 1959.
WATTS, W. Seats of the Nobility. pl.33. 1779.
[Sales] LONDON, 1852, June 30 (Estate & domain of Milton Abbey)[etc.].
[Sales] MILTON ABBEY, 1932, September 12-15, 19-23 [Contents.]
[Sales] BLANDFORD, 1932, November 28 30 [Estate].

MILTON COURT (Surrey).
BRAYLEY, E.W. History of Surrey. V, 107. 1841.

MILTON ERNEST HALL (Bedfordshire).
COUNTRY LIFE. CXLVI, 1042. 1969.

MILTON HALL (Bedfordshire).
BARTLETT, J. Selections from views of mansions. 1851.

MILTON HOUSE (Berkshire).
BURKE, J.B. Visitation of Seats. Vol.I, p.144. 1852.*
COUNTRY LIFE. CIV, 1274, 1330. 1948.

MILTON MANOR, Milton Malzor (Northamptonshire).
GOTCH, J.A. Squires' Homes. 37. 1939.

MIMWOOD (Hertfordshire).
BURKE, J.B. Visitation of Seats. Vol.II, p.245. 1853.*

MINLEY MANOR (Hampshire).
MINLEY MANOR.
— Catalogue of the collection of works of art at Minley Manor. [Preface by L.C. i.e. L. Currie]. 22 plates. 29x23. London: privately printed, 1908.

MINSTERLEY HALL (Shropshire).
SHROPSHIRE. Castles & Old Mansions. 65. 1868.

MINSTER LOVELL HALL (Oxfordshire).
GREAT BRITAIN: Ministry of Works [Ancient Monuments and Historic Buildings].
— TAYLOR, A.J. Minster Lovell Hall, Oxfordshire. 2 ed. 20 pp. Illus. (1 on cover) incl. plates and plan. 21x14 London, 1958.
BUCK, S. & N. Antiquities. II, pl.240. 1774.

MINTERNE MAGNA HOUSE (Dorsetshire).
COUNTRY LIFE. CLXVII, 498, 574. 1980.
OSWALD, A. Country houses of Dorset. p. 175. 1959.

MISERDEN PARK [MISARDEN PARK] (Gloucestershire).
ATKYNS, R. Glocestershire. p.294. 1768.
[Sales] MISERDEN PARK, 1913, July 22-24 [Contents].

MISTERTON HALL (Leicestershire).
NICHOLS, J. History of Leicestershire. IV, i, 305. 1807.
THROSBY, J. Views in Leicestershire. p.296. 1789.

MISTLEY HALL (Essex).
CROMWELL, T.K. Excursions in Essex. I, p.116. 1825.
ENGLAND: Beauties of England. I, p.256. 1787.
ESSEX: A new and complete history. VI, 31. 1772.

MITCHAM GROVE (Surrey).
ENGLAND: Picturesque Views. p.64. 1786-88.

MOAT HALL, Parham (Suffolk).
See also PARHAM OLD HALL.
SANDON, E. Suffolk houses. 281. 1977.

MOCCAS COURT (Herefordshire).
ANGUS, W. Seats of the Nobility. pl.19.1787.
COUNTRY LIFE. CLX, 1474 plan, 1554. 1976.

MOCK BEGGAR'S HALL, Claydon (Suffolk).
CROMWELL, T.K. Excursions in Suffolk. I, p.178. 1818.

MODITONHAM HOUSE (Cornwall).
JONES. Views of Seats. II. 1829.
NEALE, J.P. Views of Seats. Vol.I. 1818.

MOLLINGTON HALL (Cheshire).
BURKE, J.B. Visitation of Seats. Vol.I, p.32. 1852.*
TWYCROSS, E. Mansions of England and Wales. Vol.I, p.80. 1850.

MOMPESSON HOUSE (Wiltshire).
COUNTRY LIFE.
—GIROUARD, M. Mompesson House, Salisbury. 14pp. Illus. 20x13 [London] 1959.
Also in COUNTRY LIFE, CXXIV, 1520. 1958.

LONDON: National Trust for Places of Historic Interest or Natural Beauty.
—DODD, D. Mompesson House, Salisbury. [Bibliogr.] 36pp. Illus. (1 col. on cover) incl. plan. 21x14 [London] 1982.
COUNTRY LIFE. CXXIV, 1950. 1958.
NICOLSON, N. Great Houses of Britain. p.170. 1965.

MONACHDY (Cardiganshire).
See MYNACHTY.

MONK CONISTON (Lancashire).
BURKE, J.B. Visitation of Seats. 2.S. Vol.I, p.88. 1854.*

MONTACUTE HOUSE (Somerset).
LONDON: National Trust for Places of Historic Interest or Natural Beauty.
—TIPPING, H.A. The Story of Montacute and its house. With notes on the heraldry at Montacute by O. Barron. [Bibliogr.notes.] 38pp. Illus. incl. 16 plates and plans. 18x12 London: Country Life (1947.)
Another ed. (1953.)
LONDON: National Trust for Places of Historic Interest or Natural Beauty.
—GIROUARD, M. Montacute House, Somerset. 32pp. Illus. (1 on cover) incl. plates, plans and genealog. table. 18x12 [London] Country Life, 1970.
LONDON: National Trust for Places of Historic Interest or Natural Beauty.
—Montacute House, Somerset.[Bibliogr.] 36pp. Illus. (1 on cover) incl. plates, plans and genealog. table. 21x14 [London] 1975.
TIPPING, Henry Avray.
—The story of Montacute and its house. With notes on the heraldry at Montacute by O. Barron. 44pp. 23 plates and plans. 18x12 London: Country Life, 1933.

The North West View of Milton Abbey

the Seat of the Rt Hon.ble Jos.h Earl of Dorchester.

MILTON ABBEY, Dorset. From: HUTCHINS (*Rev. J.*). *Vitruvius Dorsettiensis* [etc.],London, 1816.

MONTACUTE HOUSE (Somerset).

CLARKE, T.H. Domestic architecture. 19. 1833.

COLLINSON, J. History of Somerset. III, 314. 1791.

COOKE, R. West Country Houses. p.67. 1957.

COUNTRY LIFE. XXXVII, 820 plan, 870. 1915.

COUNTRY LIFE. XCIX, 23 [Bed.] 1946.

COUNTRY LIFE. C, 164 [Furniture]. 1946.

COUNTRY LIFE. CXVIII, 850, 960, 1020. 1955.

COUNTRY LIFE. CLXX, 1854. 1981.

DELDERFIELD, E.R. West Country houses. I, 97. 1968.

GOTCH, J.A. Architecture of the Renaissance. I, p.16 plan. 1894.

HALL, S.C. Baronial Halls. Vol.II. 1848.

JONES. Views of Seats. II. 1829.

NASH, J. Mansions of England. III, pl.19. 1841.

NEALE, J.P. Views of Seats. 2.S. Vol.IV. 1828.

NICOLSON, N. Great Houses of Britain. p.76. 1965.

RICHARDSON, C.J. Old English mansions. I, pls. 13-16. 1841

RICHARDSON, C.J. Old English mansions. II. 1842.

SHAW, H. Elizabethan architecture. pls. XVII-XIX [Elevation, plan etc.]. 1839.

TIPPING, H.A. English Homes. Period III, Vol.I, p.204. 1922.

MONTAGUE HOUSE, Greenwich (Kent).

BAKER, J. Home beauties. plate. 1804.

MONTREAL (Kent).

COPPER PLATE MAGAZINE. pl.102. 1778.

HASTED, E. Kent. I, 354. 1778.

NEALE, J.P. Views of Seats. Vol.II. 1819.

SANDBY, P. Select Views. I, pl.27. 1783.

MOOR, The. (Cheshire).

TWYCROSS, E. Mansions of England and Wales. Vol.II, p.59. 1850.

MOOR COURT (Herefordshire).

BURKE, J.B. Visitation of Seats. Vol.I, p.11. 1852.*

MOOR HALL (Lancashire).

BARTLETT, J. Mansions of England and Wales. pl.135. 1853.

TWYCROSS, E. Mansions of England and Wales. Vol.III. p.62. 1847.

MOOR PARK (Hertfordshire).

EBURY, Emilie Beaujolais Grosvenor, *Baroness*.
— Moor Park, Rickmansworth: a series of photographs by A.L. Coburn. With an introduction by Lady E. 56pp. Illus. 23x18 London: Mathews, 1914.

BURKE, J.B. Visitation of Seats. Vol.II, p.81. 1853.*

CAMPBELL, C. Vitruvius Britannicus. V, pls. 50-55. 1771.

COUNTRY LIFE. English Country Houses: Early Georgian. p.43. 1955.

COUNTRY LIFE. XLVI. 386. 1919.

ENGLAND: Beauties of England. I, p.347. 1787.

NEALE, J.P. Views of Seats. Vol.II. 1819.

TIPPING, H.A. English Homes. Period V, Vol.I, p.169. 1921.

MOOR PARK (Shropshire).

LEACH, F. Seats of Shropshire. p.384. 1891.

MOOR PARK (Surrey).

COUNTRY LIFE. CVI, 1578. 1949.

MOOR PLACE (Hertfordshire).

CHAUNCY, H. Hertfordshire. I, 316. 1826.

COUNTRY LIFE. CXIX, 156, 204. 1956.

MITCHELL, R. Buildings in England & Scotland. pl.7 [Plan.] 1801.

MOORSIDE, Halifax (Yorkshire).

YORKSHIRE. Picturesque views. 1885.

MOOT, The. (Wiltshire).

TIPPING, H.A. English Homes. Period IV, Vol.I, p.375. 1920.

MORETON CORBET (Shropshire).

BURKE, J.B. Visitation of Seats. 2.S. Vol.I, p.209. 1854.*

GOTCH, J.A. Architecture of the Renaissance. II, p.20. 1894.

LEACH, F. Seats of Shropshire. p.74. 1891.

LEIGHTON, S. Shropshire houses. 13. 1901.

SHROPSHIRE. Castles & Old Mansions. 36. 1868.

WEST, W. Picturesque views of Shropshire. p.132. 1831.

MORETON HALL (Cheshire).

BURKE, J.B. Visitation of Seats. Vol.I, p.89. 1852.*

HALL, S.C. Baronial Halls. Vol.I. 1848.

MORRIS, F.O. Views of Seats. Vol.III, p.69. 1880.

TWYCROSS, E. Mansions of England and Wales. Vol.I, p.137. 1850.*

MORETON HALL (Lancashire).

BURKE, J.B. Visitation of Seats. Vol.I, p.53. 1852.*

TWYCROSS, E. Mansions of England and Wales. Vol.I, p.20. 1847.

MORETON HOUSE (Dorsetshire).

HUTCHINS, J. Vitruvius Dorsettiensis. pl.21. 1816.

MORLEY'S HALL (Lancashire).

BURKE, J.B. Visitation of Seats. 2.S. Vol.I, p.57. 1854.*

GRAY, H. Old halls of Lancashire. p.95. 1893.

MONTACUTE HOUSE, Somerset. From: COLLINSON (*Rev.* J.). *The history and antiquities of the county of Somerset* [etc.], vol. III, Bath, 1791.

MORTHAM TOWER (Yorkshire).
COUNTRY LIFE. XCVIII, 24 plan. 1945.

MORVAL (Cornwall).
BRITTON, J. Cornwall illustrated. 48. 1832.
BURKE, J.B. Visitation of Seats. 2.S. Vol.II, p.85. 1855.*

MORVILLE HALL (Shropshire).
COUNTRY LIFE. CXII, 464, 532. 1952.
LEACH, F. Seats of Shropshire. p.323. 1891.
WEST, W. Picturesque views of Shropshire. p.133. 1831.

MOSBOROUGH HALL (Derbyshire).
TILLEY, J. Halls of Derbyshire. III, p.145. 1899.
[Sales] MOSBOROUGH HALL, 1964, July 1, 2 [Large portion of contents].

MOSELEY HALL (Warwickshire).
JONES. Views of Seats. I. 1829.
NEALE, J.P. Views of Seats. Vol. V. 1822.

MOSELEY OLD HALL (Staffordshire).
LONDON: National Trust for Places of Historic Interest or Natural Beauty.
— JONES, M. Moseley Old Hall, Staffordshire. 12pp. Illus. (on cover) and 4 plates. 18x12 [London, *c.* 1975.]
COUNTRY LIFE. XCIII, 1050. 1943.
SHAW, S. Staffordshire. I, 79. 1798.

MOSS HOUSE (Staffordshire).
SHAW, S. Staffordshire. II, 49. 1801.

MOSTYN HALL (Flintshire).
BURKE, J.B. Visitation of Seats. Vol.I, p.15. 1852.*
COUNTRY LIFE. LIX, 200. 1926.
HOARE: Views of Seats. pl. I. 1792.
[Sales] LONDON, 1974, October 9 and following days [Library, 3 pts.].

MOTCOMBE HOUSE (Dorsetshire).
OSWALD, A. Country houses of Dorset. p.175. 1959.

MOTE, The. (Kent).
BADESLADE, T. Seats in Kent. pl.23. 1750.
BURKE, J.B. Visitation of Seats. 2.S. Vol.I, p.240. 1854.*
CROMWELL, T.K. Excursions in Kent. p.144. 1822.
HARRIS, J. History of Kent. p.192. 1719.
NEALE, J.P. Views of Seats. 2.S. Vol.II. 1825.
WATTS, W. Seats of the Nobility. pl.55. 1779.

MOTHECOMBE HOUSE (Devonshire).
COUNTRY LIFE. CXX, 190, 238, 1956.

MOTTISFONT ABBEY (Hampshire).
LONDON: National Trust for Places of Historic Interest or Natural beauty.
—LEES-MILNE, J. Mottisfont Abbey, Hampshire. [Bibliogr. note.] 16pp. 4 plates and plan. 18x12 [London] Country Life, 1967
Rev. ed. JACKSON-STOPS, G. [Bibliogr.] 24pp. Illus. (1 on cover) incl. plates and plan. 21x14 1983.
COUNTRY LIFE. L, 652. 1921.
COUNTRY LIFE. CXV, 1310,1398. 1954.

MOTTISTONE MANOR (Hampshire, Isle of Wight).
COUNTRY LIFE. LXV, 362 plan. 1929.

MOTTRAM HALL (Cheshire).
SOANE, J. Plans, elevations and sections. pl.XXXIX. 1788.
TWYCROSS, E. Mansions of England and Wales. Vol. II, p.119. 1850.*

MOULSHAM HALL (Essex).
CAMPBELL, C. Vitruvius Britannicus. IV, pls.30, 31. 1767.
ENGLAND: Beauties of England. I, p.252. 1787.
ESSEX: A new and complete history. I, 84. 1769.
MORANT, P. Essex. II, 2. 1768.

MOULTON HALL (Yorkshire).
COUNTRY LIFE. LXXIX, 250 plan. 1936.

MOULTON MANOR (Yorkshire).
COUNTRY LIFE. LXXIX, 250. 1936.

MOUNDSMERE MANOR (Hampshire).
COUNTRY LIFE. XXVII, 378 plan. 1910.

MOUNT CLARE, Roehampton (Surrey).
COUNTRY LIFE. LXXVII, 90, 118, 304 [Furniture.] 1935.
WATTS, W. Seats of the Nobility. pl.62. 1779.

MOUNT EDGCUMBE (Cornwall).
MOUNT EDGECUMBE.
—A walk round Mount Edgcumbe. 7 ed. 48pp. Illus. incl. engr. plates and folding map. 25x16 Plymouth Dock: Congdon & Hearle, 1821.
BRITTON, J. Devonshire illustrated. 37. 1832.
BURKE, J.B. Visitation of Seats. Vol. II, p.27. 1853.*
CAMPBELL, C. Vitruvius Britannicus. IVth. pls. 94, 95. 1739.
COUNTRY LIFE. II, 238. 1897.
JEWITT, L. Stately homes of England. 54. 1874.
MALAN, A.H. More famous homes. p. 147. 1902.
MORRIS, F.O. Views of Seats. Vol.II, p.57. 1880.

MOUNT HOUSE (Shropshire).
BURKE, J.B. Visitation of Seats. Vol.II, p.205. 1853.*

MOUNT LEBANON, Twickenham (Middlesex).
See TWICKENHAM, Earl of Strafford's.

MOUNT MORRIS (Kent).
BADESLADE, T. Seats in Kent. pl.24. 1750.
HARRIS, J. History of Kent. p.156. 1719.

MOUNTON HOUSE (Monmouthshire).
COUNTRY LIFE. XXXVII, 208 plan. 1915.

MOUNT SEVERN (Montgomeryshire).
NICHOLAS, T. Counties of Wales. II, p.807. 1872.

MOUSEHILL MANOR (Surrey).
BRAYLEY, E.W. History of Surrey. V, 257. 1841.

MOUSEHOLD (Norfolk).
BURKE, J.B. Visitation of Seats. Vol.I, p.98. 1852.*

MOXHULL HALL (Warwickshire).
BURKE, J.B. Visitation of Seats. Vol.I, p.90. 1852.*
NEALE, J.P. Views of Seats. Vol.IV. 1821.

MOYLES COURT (Hampshire).
COUNTRY LIFE. XI, 232. 1902.
COUNTRY LIFE. XXVI, 876. 1909.
TIPPING, H.A. English Homes. Period IV, Vol.I, p.85. 1920.

MOYNES COURT (Monmouthshire).
WOOD, John George.
— The manor and mansion of Moyne's Court, Monmouthshire; with appendices on the ancient harbours of South Monmouthshire, the crossings of Severn, etc. A contribution to the history of the Marches of Wales. [Bibliogr.] vi, 134pp. 21x13 Newport, Mon.; Mullock & Sons, 1914.
JONES. Views of Seats. VI. 1831.

MOYNS PARK (Essex).
COUNTRY LIFE. LXX, 592. 1931.
ESSEX: A new and complete history. II, 241. 1769.
GOTCH, J.A. Architecture of the Renaissance. II, p.41. 1894.
RUSH, J.A. Seats in Essex. p.132. 1897.*

MUCHELNEY ABBEY (Somerset).
COUNTRY LIFE. XXXI, 506. 1912.
GARNER, T. Domestic architecture. I, p.27 plan. 1911.
TIPPING, H.A. English Homes. Period II, Vol.I, p.261. 1924.

MUCH HADHAM HALL (Hertfordshire).
COUNTRY LIFE. CXIX, 674. 1956.
[Sales] MUCH HADHAM HALL, 1980, September 30-October 1 [Contents].

MULGRAVE CASTLE (Yorkshire).
BURKE, J.B. Visitation of Seats. 2.S. Vol.I, p.65. 1854.*
JONES. Views of Seats. I. 1829.
MORRIS, F.O. Views of Seats. Vol.II, p.11. 1880.
NEALE, J.P. Views of Seats. 2.S. Vol.II. 1825.
SOANE, J. Plans, elevations and sections. pls. XXXI-XXXIII. 1788.
WHEATER, W. Mansions of Yorkshire. p. 133. 1888.

MUNCASTER CASTLE (Cumberland).
BURKE, J.B. Visitation of Seats. 2.S. Vol.I, p.114. 1854.*
COUNTRY LIFE. LXXXVII, 592. 1940.
MORRIS, F.O. Views of Seats. Vol.III, p.17. 1880.

MUNSTEAD WOOD (Surrey).
SUMMERSON, J. The Country Seat. 267. 1970.

MUSKHAM GRANGE (Nottinghamshire).
THOROTON, R. Nottinghamshire. III, 159. 1797.

MUTFORD HALL (Suffolk).
SANDON, E. Suffolk houses. 277. 1977.

MYDDLETON HALL (Lancashire).
BARTLETT, J. Mansions of England and Wales. pl.111. 1853.
TWYCROSS, E. Mansions of England and Wales. Vol.III, p.49. 1847.

MYDDLETON LODGE (Yorkshire).
YORKSHIRE. Picturesque views. 1885.

MYERSCOUGH HOUSE (Lancashire).
TWYCROSS, E. Mansions of England and Wales. Vol.II, p.53. 1847.*

MYNACHTY (Cardiganshire).
BURKE, J.B. Visitation of Seats. Vol.I, p.130. 1852.*
NICHOLAS, T. Counties of Wales. I, p.132. 1872.

MYNDE PARK (Herefordshire).
BURKE, J.B. Visitation of Seats. 2.S. Vol.I, p.186. 1854.*

MYTON HALL (Yorkshire).
BURKE, J.B. Visitation of Seats. 2.S. Vol.I, p.23. 1854.*

NABURN HALL (Yorkshire).
BURKE, J.B. Visitation of Seats. Vol.II, p.138. 1853.*

NAILSEA COURT (Somerset).
EVANS, Charles E.
— Nailsea Court ... account of the architecture and history of Nailsea Court ... read at the meeting of the Cardiff Naturalists Society, on the occasion of their visit on 26th June 1907, by C.E.E. 32pp. Illus. incl. 2 plates and folding plan.
21x14 [London?] privately printed, 1907.
Copy signed by the author.
With 6 loose photographs, inserted.
EVANS, Sylvia Hope and Charles E.
— The book of Nailsea Court. [Bibliogr.] Illus. incl. plates (1 col., 1 folding) and plan. 18x12 Bristol: St. Stephen's Press, 1923.
COOKE, R. West Country Houses. p.38. 1957.
COUNTRY LIFE. XXXII, 890 plan. 1912.
GARNER, T. Domestic architecture. II, p.187 plan. 1911.

NANCEALVERNE HOUSE (Cornwall).
BURKE, J.B. Visitation of Seats. Vol.II, p.179. 1853.*

NANNAU HALL (Merionethshire).
BURKE, J.B. Visitation of Seats. Vol.I, p.230. 1852.*

NANTEOS (Cardiganshire).
BURKE, J.B. Visitation of Seats. Vol.I, p.244. 1852.
NICHOLAS, T. Counties of Wales. I, p.130. 1872.

NANTLYS (Flintshire).
COUNTRY LIFE. CLXXII, 798. 1982.

NANTYDERRY (Monmouthshire).
NICHOLAS, T. Counties of Wales. II, p.719. 1872.

NANTYR HALL (Denbighshire).
[Sales] LONDON, 1840, June 25 [Estate].

NARBOROUGH HALL (Norfolk).
CROMWELL, T.K. Excursions in Norfolk. II, p.80. 1819.

NARFORD HALL (Norfolk).
BURKE, J.B. Visitation of Seats. 2.S. Vol.I, p.194. 1854.*
CAMPBELL, C. Vitruvius Britannicus. III, pl.95. 1725.
CROMWELL, T.K. Excursions in Norfolk. II, p.77. 1819.
NEALE, J.P. Views of Seats. Vol.III. 1820.
NORFOLK: The Norfolk tour. 91. 1777.
[Sales] LONDON, 1884, June 16-19 [Majolica, Henri II ware, Palissy ware etc.].
[Sales] LONDON, 1902, June 11-14 [Books and manuscripts].

NASH, The. (Worcestershire).
[Sales] LONDON, 1922, December 11 [The estate].
[Sales] The NASH, 1922, December 12-15 [Remaining contents].
[Sales] The NASH, 1982, April 5 [Contents].

NASH COURT (Kent).
HASTED, E. Kent. III, 4. 1790.

NASH COURT (Shropshire).
BURKE, J.B. Visitation of Seats. Vol.II, p.138. 1853.*

NASHDOM (Buckinghamshire).
COUNTRY LIFE. XXXII, 292 plan. 1912.
[Sales] NASHDOM, 1924, May 5-9 [Contents].

NASH MANOR (Glamorganshire).
BURKE, J.B. Visitation of Seats. Vol.II, p.199. 1853.*

NAVESTOCK HALL (Essex).
ENGLAND: Beauties of England. I, p.248. 1787.
ESSEX: A new and complete history. IV, 48. 1771.

NAWORTH CASTLE (Cumberland).
LIVERPOOL, Cecil George Savile Foljambe, *Earl of*.
— Catalogue of the portraits, miniatures, &c., at Castle Howard [and] (at Naworth Castle, Cumberland) in the possession of the Earl of Carlisle. 90pp. Plates. 21x14 n.p. privately printed [1904?].
With MS. notes by the Rev. E. Farrer.
Also in HULL: East Riding Antiquarian Society, Transactions, XI, 35. 1904.
Bound in vol. lettered: Portraits by Lord Hawkesbury, 1905.

NAWORTH.
— An historical and descriptive account of Naworth Castle, and Lanercost Priory; with a life of Lord William Howard, and an account of the destruction of Naworth Castle by fire, May 18th, 1844. 2 ed. [Bibliogr. notes.] xx, 76pp. 1 engr. and wood cuts. 18x10 Carlisle: I. Fletcher Whitridge, 1844.
BUCK, S. & N. Antiquities. I, pl.47. 1774.
COUNTRY LIFE. XXIX, 414. 1911.
HALL, S.C. Baronial Halls. Vol.I. 1848.
MALAN, A.H. More famous homes. p.283. 1902.
UNITED KINGDOM. Historic houses. 260. 1892.

NERQUIS HALL (Flintshire).
BURKE, J.B. Visitation of Seats. Vol.II, p.101. 1853.*

NESTON PARK (Wiltshire).
BURKE, J.B. Visitation of Seats. Vol.I, p.127. 1852.*

NETHERBY HALL (Cumberland).
BURKE, J.B. Visitation of Seats. Vol.II, p.22. 1853.*

COUNTRY LIFE. CV, 142, 198. 1949.

[Sales] NETHERBY HALL, 1926, May 4-6 [Remaining contents].

NETHERHALL (Cumberland).
MORRIS, F.O. Views of Seats. Vol.VI, p.23. 1880.

NETHER HALL (Essex).
CROMWELL, T.K. Excursions in Essex. II, p.24. 1825.

NETHER HALL (Suffolk).
MORRIS, F.O. Views of Seats. Vol.IV, p.57. 1880.

NETHER LEVENS HALL (Westmorland).
CUMBERLAND: C. & W.A. & A.S. Extra Series VIII, 205. 1892.

NETHER LYPIATT (Gloucestershire).
COUNTRY LIFE. English Country Houses: Caroline. p.211. 1966.

COUNTRY LIFE. LIII, 415, 483 plan. 1923.

COUNTRY LIFE. LXXV, 512, 540 plan. 1934.

[Sales] NETHER LYPIATT, 1923, October 31, November 1 [Antique furnishings].

NETHERSEAL HALL (Derbyshire).
NICHOLS, J. History of Leicestershire. III, ii, 993. 1804.

NETHER SWELL MANOR (Gloucestershire).
COUNTRY LIFE. XXVIII, 754 plan. 1910.

NETHER WINCHENDON (Buckinghamshire).
COUNTRY LIFE. CXXVII, 924 plan, 986, 1062. 1960.

NETHER WORTON HOUSE (Oxfordshire).
[Sales] NETHER WORTON HOUSE 1919, June 24-26 [Contents].

NETLEY HALL (Shropshire).
LEACH, F. Seats of Shropshire. p.179. 1891.

NETTLECOMBE COURT (Somerset).
BUSH, R.J.E.
— Nettlecombe Court. (I. The Trevelyans and other residents at the Court. II. The buildings. By G.U.S. Corbett.) [Bibliogr.] 22pp. Plates (2 folding) incl. plan and genealog. table. 25x17 (Hampton, Middlesex) 1970.
Reprint from: Field Studies, III, ii, 1970.

ANGUS, W. Seats of the Nobility. pl.33. 1787.

BURKE, J.B. Visitation of Seats. Vol.I, p.47. 1852.

COLLINSON, J. History of Somerset. III, 540. 1791.

COUNTRY LIFE. XXIII, 162. 1908.

DELDERFIELD, E.R. West Country houses. I, 101. 1968.

TIPPING, H.A. English Homes. Early Renaissance. p.139. 1912.

TIPPING, H.A. English Homes. Period III, Vol.II, p.87. 1927.

NETTLESTEAD CHACE (Suffolk).
SANDON, E. Suffolk houses. 192. 1977.

NETTLESTEAD PLACE (Kent).
COUNTRY LIFE. CXXIV, 832, 886. 1958.

NEVILL HALL (Monmouthshire).
[Sales] NEVILL HALL, 1917, March 28-30 [Contents.] (K., F. & R.).

NEVILL HOLT HALL (Leicestershire).
BURKE, J.B. Visitation of Seats. Vol.I, p.129. 1852.*

COUNTRY LIFE. XXV, 270. 1909.

NICHOLS, J. History of Leicestershire. II, ii, 728. 1846.

NEWBIGGIN HALL (Westmorland).
CUMBERLAND: C. & W. A. & A.S. Extra Series VIII, 147 plan. 1892.

NEWBOLD HALL, Newbold Revel (Warwickshire).
STANISLAUS, S.M.
—Newbold Revel: the fortunes of a Warwickshire manor. [Bibliogr.] x, 20pp. Plates incl. map and genealog. tables. 21x14 Exeter: privately printed, 1949.

CAMPBELL, C. Vitruvius Britannicus. II, pl.94. 1717.

NEWBOTTLE MANOR (Northamptonshire).
COUNTRY LIFE. CV, 1054. 1949.

NEWBURGH PRIORY (Yorkshire).
BURKE, J.B. Visitation of Seats. Vol. I, p.265. 1852.*

COUNTRY LIFE. XVIII, 666. 1905.

COUNTRY LIFE. CLV, 426, 482, 574. 1974.

LATHAM, C. In English Homes. Vol. II, p.339. 1907.

WHEATER, W. Mansions of Yorkshire. p. 185. 1888.

WOOD, G.B. Historic homes of Yorkshire. 88. 1957.

NEWBY HALL (Westmorland).
CUMBERLAND: C. & W. A. & A.S. Extra Series, VIII, 103. 1892.

NEWBY HALL (Yorkshire).
MUSGRAVE, Ernest I.
—Newby Hall: an illustrated survey of the Yorkshire home of the Compton family. 32pp. Illus. (some col., some on covers, 1 on title-page) incl. plan and maps. 14x20 Derby: E.L.P. [c. 1953].
      Another ed. 24pp. Illus. (some col., some on covers) incl. plans and genealog. table. 23x18 (1974).
BOLTON, A.T. Architecture of R. & J. Adam. II, 132 plan. 1922.
COUNTRY LIFE. English Country Houses: Mid Georgian. p.141. 1956.
COUNTRY LIFE. XIX, 90. 1906.
COUNTRY LIFE. XXXV, 878. 1914.
COUNTRY LIFE. LXXXI, 658, 688, 714 plan. 1937.
COUNTRY LIFE. CLXV, 1802, 1918, 2006. 1979.
COUNTRY LIFE. CLXVIII, 2406. 1980.
KIP, J. Nouveau théâtre de la Grande Bretagne. I, pl.53. 1715.
LATHAM, C. In English Homes. Vol. III, p.437. 1909.

NEWBY PARK, Newby upon Swale (Yorkshire).
See BALDERSBY PARK.

NEWBY WISKE (Yorkshire).
BURKE, J.B. Visitation of Seats. 2.S. Vol.I, p.184. 1854.*

NEW CHAPEL HOUSE, Lingfield (Surrey).
COUNTRY LIFE. LX, 631 plan, 679. 1926.

NEWE HOUSE, Pakenham (Suffolk).
See NEW HOUSE.

NEW HALL (Essex).
CROMWELL, T.K. Excursions in Essex. I, p.20. 1825.
ESSEX: A new and complete history. I, 127. 1769.
MORANT, P. Essex. II, 14. 1768.
WATTS, W. Seats of the Nobility. pl.4. 1779.

NEW HALL (Lancashire).
BARTLETT, J. Mansions of England and Wales. pl.101. 1853.
TWYCROSS, E. Mansions of England and Wales. Vol.III, p.24. 1847.

NEW HALL (Warwickshire).
BURKE, J.B. Visitation of Seats. Vol.II, p.229. 1853.
SMITH, W. History of the County of Warwick. 367. 1830.

NEW HALL, Bodenham (Wiltshire).
BURKE, J.B. Visitation of Seats. 2.S. Vol.II, p.127. 1855.*

NEW HOUSE, Pakenham (Suffolk).
BURKE, J.B. Visitation of Seats. Vol.I, p.57. 1852.*
SANDON, E. Suffolk houses. 327. 1977.

NEWLAND PARK (Yorkshire).
BURKE, J.B. Visitation of Seats. Vol.II, p.15. 1853.*

NEWLANDS MANOR (Hampshire).
GROVE, R.A. Seats in the neighbourhood of Lymington. 1832.

NEW LODGE, Windsor Forest (Berkshire).
[Sales] NEW LODGE, 1916, April 26-29 [Contents].

NEW MILLS (Gloucestershire).
RUDDER, S. Gloucestershire. 714. 1779.

NEWNHAM PADDOX (Warwickshire).
KIP, J. Nouveau théâtre de la Grande Bretagne. I, pl.25. 1715.
[Sales] LONDON, 1938, July [Historical Portraits].

NEW PARK, Richmond (Surrey).
COUNTRY LIFE. CLXXII, 984 plan. 1982.
KIP, J. Nouveau théâtre de la Grande Bretagne. 1, pl.33. 1715.

NEWPARK (Wiltshire).
JONES. Views of Seats. II. 1829.
NEALE, J.P. Views of Seats. V. 1822.

NEW PLACE (Hampshire).
COUNTRY LIFE. XXVII, 522 plan. 1910.

NEW PLACE (Hertfordshire).
CHAUNCY, H. Hertfordshire. I, 372. 1826.

NEW PLACE, Angmering (Sussex).
ELWES, D.G.C. Mansions of Western Sussex. 11. 1876.

NEWPORT HOUSE (Herefordshire).
ROBINSON, C.J. Mansions of Herefordshire. pl.2. 1873.

NEWSELLS BURY (Hertfordshire).
CHAUNCY, H. Hertfordshire. I, 200. 1826.

NEWSELLS PARK (Hertfordshire).
[Sales] NEWSELLS PARK, 1972, May 22 [Contents].

NEWSTEAD ABBEY (Nottinghamshire).
ALLEN, Richard.
—The home and grave of Byron: a souvenir of Newstead Abbey. 52pp. 30 plates: photographs. 26x20 Nottingham: Allen & Sons [1874].
Photograph, MS. list of plates and newspaper cuttings, inserted.

WAGSTAFF, H.F.
—Handbook and guide to Newstead Abbey. Being a brief history and account of this interesting place, arranged for the convenience of tourists and visitors. 48pp. 4 plates. 18x12 Hucknall: Morley, 1931.
BUCK, S. & N. Antiquities. II, pl.227, 1774.
BURKE, J.B. Visitation of Seats. Vol.I, p.94. 1852*
COUNTRY LIFE. XLII, 468. 1917.
COUNTRY LIFE. CLV, 1122, 1190 plan. 1974.
ENGLAND: Beauties of England. II, p.161. 1787.
MORRIS, F.O. Views of Seats. Vol.I. p.77. 1880.
NOBLE, T. Counties of Chester, ... Lincoln. p.19. 1836
SANBY, P. Select Views 1, pls. 43,44. 1783.
UNITED KINGDOM. Historic houses. **298. 1892.**
[Sales] LONDON, 1860, June 13 [Abbey Manor and Domain].
[Sales] NEWSTEAD ABBEY, 1921, January 10-13 [Contents].

NEWTIMBER PLACE (Sussex).
COUNTRY LIFE. XL, 780 plan. 1916.

NEWTON (Brecknockshire).
NICHOLAS, T. Counties of Wales. I, p.91. 1872.

NEWTON FERRERS (Cornwall).
[Sales] NEWTON FERRERS, 1924, December 1-5 [Furniture, Library etc.].

NEWTON HALL (Durham).
BURKE, J.B. Visitation of Seats. 2.S. Vol.II, p.94. 1855.*

NEWTON HALL (Essex).
CROMWELL, T.K. Excursions in Essex. II, p.102. 1825.

NEWTON HALL (Yorkshire).
WHEATER, W. Mansions of Yorkshire. p.196. 1888.

NEWTON OLD HALL (Derbyshire).
TILLEY, J. Halls of Derbyshire. III, p.51. 1899.

NEWTON PARK (Somerset).
BURKE, J.B. Visitation of Seats. 2.S. Vol.I, p.14. 1854.*
COLLINSON, J. History of Somerset. III, 342. 1791.

NEWTON SURMAVILLE (Somerset).
COUNTRY LIFE. CXII, 676, 760, 844. 1952.
GARNER, T. Domestic architecture. II, p.196. 1911.

NIBLEY (Gloucestershire).
ATKYNS, R. Glocestershire. p.303. 1768.
RUDDER, S. Gloucestershire. 575. 1779.

NOCTON HALL (Lincolnshire).
LINCOLNSHIRE. A selection of views. 1805.

NONSUCH PARK (Surrey).
BRAYLEY, E.W. History of Surrey. IV, 410. 1841.
BURKE, J.B. Visitation of Seats. Vol.I, p.214. 1852.
Plate Vol.II, p.252. 1853.

NORBITON HALL (Surrey).
[Sales] LONDON, 1857, June 8 [Library].

NORBITON PLACE (Surrey).
PROSSER, G.F. Surrey Seats. p.13. 1828.

NORBURY BOOTHS HALL (Cheshire).
TWYCROSS, E. Mansions of England and Wales. Vol.II, p.66. 1850.

NORBURY HALL (Derbyshire).
TILLEY, J. Halls of Derbyshire. II, p.131. 1893.

NORBURY MANOR (Staffordshire).
PLOT, R. Staffordshire. 233. 1686.

NORBURY PARK (Surrey).
BRAYLEY, E.W. History of Surrey. IV, 449. 1841.
BURKE, J.B. Visitation of Seats. Vol.II, p.219. 1853.*
BURKE, J.B. Visitation of Seats. 2.S. Vol.I, p.246. 1854.
NEALE, J.P. Views of Seats. 2.S. Vol.IV. 1828.
PROSSER, G.F. Surrey Seats. p.11. 1828.
[Sales] NORBURY PARK, 1916, September 11-15 [Salomons collections]. (K., F. & R.).

NORCLIFFE HALL (Cheshire).
BURKE, J.B. Visitation of Seats. Vol.II, p.189. 1853.*

NORK HOUSE (Surrey).
PROSSER, G.F. Surrey Seats. p.29. 1828.

NORLEY HALL (Cheshire).
TWYCROSS, E. Mansions of England and Wales. Vol.I, p.127. 1850.

NORMANBY PARK (Lincolnshire).
COUNTRY LIFE. XXX, 170 plan. 1911.

NORMAN COURT (Hampshire).
BURKE, J.B. Visitation of Seats. Vol.II, p.182. 1853.*
[Sales] NORMAN COURT, 1946, July 22-26, 29 [Principal contents].

NORMANHURST (Sussex).
NORMANHURST COURT.
— A catalogue of works of art and curiosities at Normanhurst Court, Battle. 22x14 (London) Chiswick Press, privately printed, 1878.
MORRIS, F.O. Views of Seats. Vol.VI, p.51. 1880.

NORMANTON HALL (Leicestershire).
NICHOLS, J. History of Leicestershire. IV, ii, 1001. 1811.
THROSBY, J. Views in Leicestershire. p.297. 1789.

NORMANTON PARK (Rutland).
BURKE, J.B. Visitation of Seats. Vol.I, p.231. 1852.*
COUNTRY LIFE. XXXIII, 198 plan. 1913.
NEALE, J.P. Views of Seats. Vol.III. 1820.
NOBLE, T. Counties of Chester, ... Lincoln. p.61. 1836.

NORMANTON TURVILLE HALL (Leicestershire).
See NORMANTON HALL.

NORRINGTON MANOR (Wiltshire).
ELYARD, S.J. Old Wiltshire homes. p.9. 1894.

NORRIS CASTLE (Hampshire, Isle of Wight).
BURKE, J.B. Visitation of Seats. Vol.II, p.89. 1853.
COUNTRY LIFE. IV, 28. 1898.

NORRIS GREEN (Lancashire).
BARTLETT, J. Mansions of England and Wales. pl.132. 1853.
TWYCROSS, E. Mansions of England and Wales. Vol.III, p.61. 1847.

NORTHBOROUGH MANOR (Northamptonshire).
COUNTRY LIFE. XXVII, 486. 1910.
GOTCH, J.A. Halls of Northants. p.1. 1936.
TIPPING, H.A. English Homes. Period I, Vol.I, p.152. 1921.

NORTHBOURNE COURT (Kent).
OSWALD, A. Country houses of Kent. 20. 1933.

NORTH CADBURY COURT (Somerset).
GARNER, T. Domestic architecture. II, p.196. 1911.

NORTH COURT (Hampshire, Isle of Wight)
ANGUS, W. Seats of the Nobility. pl.44. 1787.
BURKE, J.B. Visitation of Seats. Vol.I, p.152. 1852.*
JONES. Views of Seats. II. 1829.
NEALE, J.P. Views of Seats. Vol.II. 1819.

NORTH CRAY PLACE (Kent).
HASTED, E. Kent. I, 154. 1778.

NORTH DISSINGTON HALL (Northumberland).
BURKE, J.B. Visitation of Seats. 2.S. Vol.II, p.101. 1855.*

NORTH HALL (Lancashire).
TWYCROSS, E. Mansions of England and Wales. Vol.I, p.71. 1847.*

NORTH LEES HALL (Derbyshire).
LEES, North.
— North Lees Hall [etc.]. 12pp. Illus. (3 on covers) incl. map. 27x11 (Hathersage: privately printed) [1964?]
TILLEY, J. Halls of Derbyshire. I, p.167. 1892.

NORTH LUFFENHAM HALL (Rutland).
COUNTRY LIFE. XLV, 400. 1919.

NORTH MYMMS PARK (Hertfordshire).
COUNTRY LIFE. LXXV, 38 plan, 66. 1934.
GOTCH, J.A. Architecture of the Renaissance. I, p.52. 1894.
[Sales] NORTH MYMMS PARK, 1979, September 24-26, Pt.I. [Works of art, furniture etc.].

NORTH RODE (Cheshire).
TWYCROSS, E. Mansions of England and Wales. Vol.II, p.124. 1850.

NORTH STONEHAM PARK (Hampshire).
HAMPSHIRE: Architectural views. 1830.

NORTHWICK PARK (Gloucestershire).
BORENIUS, Tancred.
— Catalogue of the collection of pictures at Northwick Park. (Compiled by T.B., ... with the assistance of L. Cust.) [Photocopy.] 20x17 London: privately printed, 1921.
RUSHOUT, *Hon.* Ann.
— Picturesque scenery in Northwick Park, Worcestershire; from drawings, taken by The Honble. A.R. [No text] 6 engr. plates. Fol. 47x33 London: Orme, 1815.
SPENCER-CHURCHILL, Edward George, *Capt.*
— Northwick rescues, 1912-1961. 56pp. 20x17 (Northwick, 1971.)
SUMMERSON, J. The Country Seat. 121. 1970.
[Sales] NORTHWICK PARK, 1964, September 28-30 [Remaining contents].
[Sales] LONDON, 1965, May 24 [Oriental ceramics and works of art].
[Sales] LONDON, 1965, May 25 [Prints and drawings].
[Sales] LONDON, 1965, May 26 [Silver].
[Sales] LONDON, 1965, May 26, 27 [Printed books I].

[Sales] LONDON, 1965, May 28 [Pictures].

[Sales] LONDON, 1965, June 21-23 [Antiquities].

[Sales] LONDON, 1965, June 24, 25 [Printed books II, Indian miniatures].

[Sales] LONDON, 1965, October 27 [Printed books III].

[Sales] LONDON, 1965, October 29 [Pictures].

[Sales] LONDON, 1965, November 24 [Printed books IV].

[Sales] LONDON, 1966, February 25 [Pictures].

NORTH WYKE (Devonshire).
WEEKES, Ethel Lega.
— The old mansion of North Wyke ... Read at the meeting of the Devonshire Association for the advancement of science, literature, and art (at Totnes, August) 1900. 12pp. Illus. incl. plan. 22x14 (Plymouth) 1900.
Title on cover.
With MS. note, by the author?
Reprinted from the Transactions of the D.A. for the A. of S., L., and A. XXXII, 195. 1900.

NORTON CONYERS (Yorkshire).
WOOD, G.B. Historic homes of Yorkshire. 67. 1957.

NORTON HALL (Derbyshire). Now Greater Sheffield (Yorkshire).
BURKE, J.B. Visitation of Seats. 2.S. Vol.I, p.98. 1854.*
COPPER PLATE MAGAZINE. I, pl.44. 1792-1802.
ENGLAND: Picturesque Views. p.32. 1786-88.

NORTON HALL (Northamptonshire).
BOTFIELD, Beriah.
— Catalogue of pictures in the possession of B.B., Esq. at Norton Hall. 88pp. Plate. 25x16 London: privately printed, 1848.
BURKE, J.B. Visitation of Seats. Vol.I, p.11. 1852.*
GOTCH, J.A. Squires' Homes. 37. 1939.
JONES. Views of Seats. I. 1829.
NEALE, J.P. Views of Seats. 2.S. Vol.II. 1825.

NORTON HOUSE (Durham).
BURKE, J.B. Visitation of Seats. Vol.I, p.124. 1852.*

NORTON LODGE (Hampshire, Isle of Wight).
GROVE, R.A. Seats in the neighbourhood of Lymington. 1832.

NORTON PARK (Worcestershire).
COUNTRY LIFE. XI, 776. 1902.

NORTON PLACE (Lincolnshire).
BURKE, J.B. Visitation of Seats. 2.S. Vol.II, p.18. 1855.*
COUNTRY LIFE. CLX, 886. 1976.
LINCOLNSHIRE. A selection of views. 25. 1805.

NORTON PRIORY (Cheshire).
BURKE, J.B. Visitation of Seats. Vol.II, p.171. 1853.*
NEALE, J.P. Views of Seats. 2.S. Vol.V. 1829.
ORMEROD, G. Cheshire. I, 682. 1882.
TWYCROSS, E. Mansions of England and Wales. Vol.II, p.44. 1850.

NOSELEY HALL (Leicestershire).
NICHOLS, J. History of Leicestershire. II, ii, 749. 1798.
NICHOLS, J. History of Leicestershire. III, ii, pl. CLIII, 1127. 1804.
THROSBY, J. Views in Leicestershire. p.299. 1789.

NOSTELL PRIORY (Yorkshire).
BROCKWELL, Maurice Walter.
— Catalogue of the pictures and other works of art in the collection of Lord St. Oswald at Nostell Priory. (Catalogue raisonné.) [Bibliogr. notes.] 46 plates incl. elevation and plans. 32x26 London: Constable, 1915.

LONDON: National Trust for Places of Historic Interest or Natural Beauty.
— Nostell Priory, Yorkshire. 16pp. 4 plates and plan. 18x12 London: Country Life. (1954).
Another ed. 8 plates. 25x18 [c.1970]
Rev. ed. JACSON-STOPS, G. [Bibliogr.] 38pp. Illus. (some col., 1 on cover) incl. plates, plan and genealog. table. 25x18 [London] 1982.

MANUSCRIPTS.
—CHIPPENDALE, T. [Letter to Sir R. Winn of Nostell Priory, concerning furniture.] 2ff. 22.5x18 London, 13 August 1767.
BOLTON, A.T. Architecture of R. & J. Adam. II, 117 plan. 1922.
BURKE, J.B. Visitation of Seats. 2.S. Vol.II, p.218. 1855.*
CAMPBELL, C. Vitruvius Britannicus. IV, pls. 70-73. 1767.
COUNTRY LIFE. English Country Houses: Early Georgian. p.187. 1955.
COUNTRY LIFE. XXI, 594. 1907.
COUNTRY LIFE. XXXVI, 582 plan, 684 [Furniture]. 1914.
COUNTRY LIFE. CXI, 1248 [Furniture], 1492, 1572, 1652 plan. 1952.
COUNTRY LIFE. CXII, 1028 [Furniture]. 1952.
JONES, Views of Seats. I. 1829.
LATHAM, C. In English Homes. Vol.III, p.429. 1909.
MORRIS, F.O. Views of Seats. Vol.V, p.63. 1880.
NEALE, J.P. Views of Seats. Vol.V. 1822.
WHEATER, W. Mansions of Yorkshire. p.173. 1888.
YORKSHIRE. Picturesque views. 1885.

NOTGROVE MANOR (Gloucestershire).
COUNTRY LIFE. XXXVI, 678 plan. 1914.

NOYADD TREFAWR (Cardiganshire).
BURKE, J.B. Visitation of Seats. Vol.I, p.32. 1852.*

NUN APPLETON HALL (Yorkshire).
WHEATER, W. Mansions of Yorkshire. p.157. 1888.

NUNEHAM PARK [NUNEHAM COURTENAY] (Oxfordshire).
OXFORD.
— A new pocket companion for Oxford: or, guide through the university ... To which are added descriptions of the buildings, tapestry, paintings, sculptures, temples, gardens, &c. at Blenheim and Nuneham, the seats of his Grace the Duke of Marlborough and Earl Harcourt. A new edition [etc.]. iv, 162pp. Engr. plates (1 folding) incl. map. 17x10 Oxford: J. Cooke, 1815.

OXFORD.
— The Oxford university and city guide, on a new plan ... To which is added a guide to ... Nuneham (list of pictures) [etc.]. 5 ed. xx,200pp. Engr. plates (1 folding) incl. map. 17x10 Oxford: Munday & Slatter [1820?]
New ed. [Bibliogr.] 216pp. 18x11 1824.
ANGUS, W. Seats of the Nobility. pl.38. 1787.
CAMPBELL, C. Vitruvius Britannicus. V. pls.99, 100. 1771.
COPPER PLATE MAGAZINE. pl.36. 1778.
COUNTRY LIFE. XXXIV, 746. 1913.
COUNTRY LIFE. XC, 866. 1941.
ENGLAND: Picturesque Views. p.62. 1786-88.
JONES. Views of Seats. I. 1829.
MORRIS, F.O. Views of Seats. Vol.VI, p.31. 1880.
NEALE, J.P. Views of Seats. Vol.III. 1820.
SANDBY, P. Select Views. I, pl.45. 1783.
THAMES, River. An history. I, pl.18. 1794.
[Sales] LONDON, 1948, December 13, 14 [Selected portion of the library].

NUN MONKTON PRIORY (Yorkshire).
COUNTRY LIFE. CLXVIII, 1650. 1980.

NUNNINGTON HALL (Yorkshire).
LONDON: National Trust for Places of Historic Interest or Natural beauty.
—Nunnington Hall, Yorkshire. 8pp. 1 Illus. 18x12 [London, c.1955.]
LONDON: National Trust for Places of Historic Interest or Natural beauty.
—The Carlisle collection of miniature rooms. 12pp. Illus. (1 col. on cover) incl. plates. 21x14 [London] 1982.
COUNTRY LIFE. LXIII, 148 plan. 1928.
COUNTRY LIFE. CLXXI, 1678 [Carlisle collection of miniature rooms.] 1982.

NUNNYKIRK (Northumberland).
BURKE, J.B. Visitation of Seats. 2.S. Vol.II, p.76. 1855.*

NUN UPTON COURT (Herefordshire).
GARNER, T. Domestic architecture. II, p.195. 1911.

NUNWELL HOUSE (Hampshire, Isle of Wight).
OGLANDER, Denys.
—Nunwell House and its treasures. 16pp. Col. illus. incl. maps. 15x21 Newport, I.O.W.: privately printed [1975].
COUNTRY LIFE. CLIX, 402, 470 [Photocopy]. 1976.
[Sales] NUNWELL HOUSE, 1980, September 17, 18 [Contents].

NUNWICK (Northumberland).
COUNTRY LIFE. CXX, 80, 134. 1956.

NURSTEAD COURT (Kent).
GREENWOOD, C. Kent. 225. 1838.
OSWALD, A. Country houses of Kent. 14. 1933.

NUTGROVE HOUSE (Lancashire).
BARTLETT, J. Mansions of England and Wales. pl.136. 1853.
TWYCROSS, E. Mansions of England and Wales. Vol.III, p.62. 1847.

NUTHALL TEMPLE (Nottinghamshire).
CAMPBELL, C. Vitruvius Britannicus. IV, pls. 56, 57. 1767.
COUNTRY LIFE. LIII, 570, 606. 1923.
THOROTON, R. Nottinghamshire. II, 255. 1797.
[Sales] NUTHALL, 1929, May 23, 24 [Fixtures & fittings].

NUTTALL HALL (Lancashire).
TWYCROSS, E. Mansions of England and Wales. Vol.III, p.97. 1847.

NUTWELL COURT (Devonshire).
BURKE, J.B. Visitation of Seats. 2.S. Vol.II, p.74. 1855.*

NYMANS (Sussex).
MANUSCRIPTS (Typewritten).   English.
— SMITH, H.C. Catalogue of the antique furniture and equipment of 'Old House', Nymans, Handcross, Sussex, originally known as 'Little Betchleys' (re-built 1652), the property of Lt. Col. L.C.R. Messel and Mrs. Messel. Compiled by H.C.S. 32ff. 25x20 1949.
Letters, inserted.
COUNTRY LIFE. LXXII, 292, 320 plan. 1932.

NYTON HOUSE (Sussex).
BURKE, J.B. Visitation of Seats. Vol.II, p.89. 1853.*

OAKELEY (Shropshire).
See LYDHAM MANOR.

OAKERY, The. (Kent).
GREENWOOD, C. Kent. 31. 1838.

Nuneham – Courtenay, in Oxfordshire, the Seat of the Earl of Harcourt.

NUNEHAM PARK, Oxfordshire. From: ENGLAND. *Picturesque views of the principal seats of the nobility and gentry in England and Wales* [etc.], London (1786-88).

OAKES PARK (Yorkshire).

BAGSHAWE, *Mrs.* Thornber.
— Oakes Park, Sheffield; the historic home of the Bagshawe family since the year 1699. (Text compiled by Mrs. T.B., and R. Innes-Smith.) 16pp. Illus. (1 col., some on covers.) 14x20 (Derby: E.L.P., 1972.)

OAK HALL, Bishops Stordford (Hertfordshire).

[Sales] OAK HALL, Bishops Stortford, 1912, July 9-11 [Contents]. (K.F. & R.).

OAK HOUSE, West Bromwich (Staffordshire).

WEST BROMWICH: County Borough.
— JEPHCOTT, W.E. Oak House, West Bromwich: Souvenir booklet. 32pp. Illus. incl. plans. 20x13 West Bromwich [c.1975].

HALL, S.C. Baronial Halls. Vol.II. 1848.

NIVEN, W. Old Staffordshire houses. p.20, pl.17. 1882.

OAKINGHAM (Berkshire).
See WOKINGHAM.

OAKLAND HOUSE (Cheshire).
See TABLEY HOUSE.

OAKLANDS, Okehampton (Devonshire).

BRITTON, J. Devonshire illustrated. 75. 1832.

BURKE, J.B. Visitation of Seats. Vol.I, p.67. 1852.*

OAKLEY HALL (Suffolk).
See OAKLEY PARK.

OAKLEY HOUSE (Bedfordshire).

NEALE, J.P. Views of Seats. Vol.I. 1818.

OAKLEY PARK (Shropshire).

BURKE, J.B. Visitation of Seats. 2.S. Vol.II, p.128. 1855.*

COUNTRY LIFE. English Country Houses: Late Georgian. p.151. 1958.

COUNTRY LIFE. CXIX, 380 plan, 426. 1956.

JONES. Views of Seats. I. 1829.

LEACH, F. Seats of Shropshire. p.211. 1891.

NEALE, J.P. Views of Seats. 2.S. Vol.III. 1826.

OAKLEY PARK (Suffolk).

COUNTRY LIFE. XXIII, 18. 1908.

[Sales] LONDON, 1919, July 10 [Furniture, porcelain etc.].

OAKS, The. (Lancashire).

BARTLETT, J. Mansions of England and Wales. pls. 19, 21. 1853.

TWYCROSS, E. Mansions of England and Wales. Vol.I, p.68. 1847.

OAKS, The. (Surrey).

NEALE, J.P. Views of Seats. Vol.IV. 1821.

PROSSER, G.F. Surrey Seats. p.67. 1828.

[Sales] LONDON, 1840, June 11 [Estate].

OAKWELL HALL (Yorkshire).

BATLEY: Art Gallery and Museums [Oakwell Hall].
—SPRITTLES, J. History and description of Oakwell Hall and Manor. 3 ed. 56pp. Illus. (1 on cover) incl. plan. 21x14 Batley, 1963.

BIRSTALL.
—Oakwell Hall, Birstall, near Leeds. An appeal. 4pp. 4 illus. 29x22 Birstall (printed, 1927).

WOOD, G.B. Historic homes of Yorkshire. 10. 1957.

OAKWOOD HALL (Cheshire).

TWYCROSS, E. Mansions of England and Wales. Vol.II, p.129. 1850.

OAKWORTH HOUSE, Keighley (Yorkshire).

YORKSHIRE. Picturesque views. 1885.

OARE HOUSE (Wiltshire).

COUNTRY LIFE. LXIII, 334 plan. 1928.

OATLANDS (Surrey).

WALTON, Surrey: Walton & Weybridge Historical Society.
— Paper[s]. [Contd.]
1. FORGE, J.W.L. Oatlands Palace. 3 rev. ed. [Bibliogr. note.] 28pp. 2 illus. 1968.

CAMPBELL, C. Vitruvius Britannicus. IVth. pls. 67, 68. 1739.

COPPER PLATE MAGAZINE. II, pl.74. 1792-1802.

COUNTRY LIFE. CIII, 924 [Grotto.] 1948.

ENGLAND: Beauties of England. II, p.294. 1787.

MANNING, O. Surrey. II, 786. 1809.

PROSSER, G.F. Surrey Seats. p.101. 1828.

OCKHAM PARK (Surrey).

BRAYLEY, E.W. History of Surrey. II, 116. 1841.

COUNTRY LIFE. CVIII, 2218. 1950.

NEALE, J.P. Views of Seats. 2.S. Vol.III. 1826.

PROSSER, G.F. Surrey Seats. p.71. 1828.

OCKWELLS MANOR (Berkshire).
COUNTRY LIFE. XV, 486. 1904.
COUNTRY LIFE. LV, 52, 92, 130. 1924.
COUNTRY LIFE. LXX, 53 [Furniture]. 1931.
GARNER, T. Domestic architecture. I, 45 plan. 1911.
LATHAM, C. In English Homes. Vol.I, p.331. 1904.
NASH, J. Mansions of England. I, pls.3-5. 1839.
TIPPING, H.A. English Homes. Period I & II, Vol.II, p.163.
1937.

OCLE COURT (Herefordshire).
[Sales] LONDON, 1837, November 30 [Estate].

ODDINGTON HOUSE (Gloucestershire).
COUNTRY LIFE. LXXXVIII, 142. 1940.
JONES. Views of Seats. II. 1829.
NEALE, J.P. Views of Seats. 2.S. Vol.I. 1824.

OFFCHURCH (Warwickshire).
JONES. Views of Seats. I. 1829.
NEALE. Views of Seats. Vol.IV. 1821.

OFFCHURCH BURY (Warwickshire).
BURKE, J.B. Visitation of Seats. 2.S. Vol.II, p.113. 1855.*
NEALE, J.P. Views of Seats. Vol.IV. 1821.
SMITH, W. History of the County of Warwick. 137. 1830.

OFFERTON HALL (Derbyshire).
TILLEY, J. Halls of Derbyshire. I, p.209. 1892.

OFFLEY PLACE (Hertfordshire).
CHAUNCY, H. Hertfordshire. II, 193. 1826.
NEALE, J.P. Views of Seats. 2.S. Vol.V. 1829.

OGBOURNE ST. GEORGE MANOR HOUSE (Wiltshire).
COUNTRY LIFE. XCII, 1226. 1942.

OGSTON HALL (Derbyshire).
BURKE, J.B. Visitation of Seats. Vol.I, p.128. 1852.*
TILLEY, J. Halls of Derbyshire. III, p.55. 1899.

OKEOVER HALL (Staffordshire).
BURKE, J.B. Visitation of Seats. 2.S. Vol.II, p.10. 1855.*
COUNTRY LIFE. XXVII, 343. 1910.
COUNTRY LIFE. CXXXV, 172, 224, 568 plan, 645.
1964.
ENGLISH CONNOISSEUR. II, 37. 1766.*
PLOT, R. Staffordshire. 227. 1686.
SHAW, S. Staffordshire. II, pl.29. Reprint 1976.

OLANTIGH (Kent).
BARTLETT, J. Selections from views of mansions. 1851.
COUNTRY LIFE. CXLVI, 282, 334. 1969.
WATTS, W. Seats of the Nobility. pl.78. 1779.

OLD BUCKHURST (Sussex).
COUNTRY LIFE. XLVI, 488, 518 plan. 1919.

OLDBURY HALL (Warwickshire).
NICHOLS, J. History of Leicestershire. IV, ii, pl. CLX, 1035.
1811.

OLD DEANERY, Gloucester
(Gloucestershire).
COUNTRY LIFE. CIX, 1102 plan. 1951.

OLDFIELD GRANGE (Essex).
ESSEX: A new and complete history. VI, 116. 1772.

OLDFIELD HALL (Cheshire).
TWYCROSS, E. Mansions of England and Wales. Vol.II, p.75.
1850.*

OLD HALL, Rochester (Kent).
COUNTRY LIFE. CXIII, 654. 1953.

OLD HALL, Sundridge (Kent).
COUNTRY LIFE. LXI, 297. 1927.

OLD HALL, Hambleton (Rutland).
COUNTRY LIFE. LXVIII, 372 plan. 1930.
GOTCH, J.A. Architecture of the Renaissance. I, p.11. plan.
1894.

OLD HOUSE, Hereford (Herefordshire).
COUNTRY LIFE. LXVI, 872. 1929.

OLD LODGE, Nutley (Sussex).
[Sales] NUTLEY, 1922, July 3-5 [English furniture etc.].

OLD MANOR, The. Little Hempston
(Devonshire).
COUNTRY LIFE. LXXIV, 120 plan. 1933.

OLD MARTON HALL (Shropshire).
BURKE, J.B. Visitation of Seats. 2.S. Vol.II, p.205. 1855.*

OLD PALACE, Oxford (Oxfordshire).
COUNTRY LIFE. CXII, 1414. 1952.

OLD PARSONAGE, Brenchley (Kent).
See BRENCHLEY MANOR.

OLD PLACE, Lindfield (Sussex).
COUNTRY LIFE. X, 72. 1901.
COUNTRY LIFE. XIII, 666 [Stained Glass.] 1903.
COUNTRY LIFE. XXII, 414. 1907.
LATHAM, C. In English Homes. Vol.I, p.79. 1904.

OLD PLACE, West Grinstead (Sussex).
ELWES, D.G.C. Mansions of Western Sussex. 108. 1876.

OLD PLACE MANOR, Pulborough (Sussex).
PULBOROUGH, 1964, October 6, 7, [Antique furniture, clocks, pottery etc.].

OLD RECTORY, Winestead (Yorkshire).

COUNTRY LIFE. CXXXVII, 66. 1965.

OLD SOAR, Plaxtol (Kent).
OSWALD, A. Country houses of Kent. 13. 1933.

OLD SURREY HALL, Dormansland (Surrey).
COUNTRY LIFE. LXVI, 352 plan. 1929.
COUNTRY LIFE. CXXVI, 554, 654. 1959.

OLD THORNDON HALL (Essex).
ESSEX: County Council [Essex Record Office].
— Publications. [Contd.]
LXI. Old Thorndon Hall. [Bibliogr.] 40pp. Illus. incl. 7 plates (1 col., 4 in pocket), sections, plans and maps. 27x22 1972.

OLD WILSLEY, Cranbrook (Kent).
COUNTRY LIFE. CIV, 26, 78. 1948.

OLD WITHINGTON HALL (Cheshire).
See WITHINGTON HALL.

OLLERSET HALL (Derbyshire).
TILLEY, J. Halls of Derbyshire. I, p.157. 1892.

OMBERSLEY COURT (Worcestershire).
BURKE, J.B. Visitation of Seats. 2.S. Vol.I, p.123. 1854.*
COUNTRY LIFE. CXIII, 34, 94, 152. 1953.
NASH, T.R. Worcestershire. II, 216. 1782.

ONSLOW (Shropshire).
LEIGHTON, S. Shropshire houses. 9. 1901.

ORCHARD, The. (Hampshire, Isle of Wight).
BURKE, J.B. Visitation of Seats. Vol.I, p.187. 1852.*

ORCHARD PORTMAN (Somerset).
KIP, J. Nouveau théâtre de la Grande Bretagne. I, pl.76. 1715.

ORCHARDS (Surrey).
COUNTRY LIFE. X, 272. 1901.

ORCHARD WYNDHAM (Somerset).
DELDERFIELD, E.R. West Country houses. I, 105. 1968.

ORDSALL HALL (Lancashire).
COUNTRY LIFE. LXVI, 452. 1929.
GRAY, H. Old halls of Lancashire. p.15. 1893.
TIPPING, H.A. English Homes. Period I & II, Vol.II, p.213. 1937.

ORIELTON (Pembrokeshire).
COUNTRY LIFE. CXXXIII, 1324. 1963.
NEALE, J.P. Views of Seats. Vol.V. 1822.

ORLEANS HOUSE, Twickenham (Middlesex).
CAMPBELL, C. Vitruvius Britannicus. I, pl.77. 1715.
COUNTRY LIFE. English Country Houses: Early Georgian, p.40. 1955.
COUNTRY LIFE. XCVI, 464. 1944.
ENGLAND: Beauties of England. II, p.69. 1787.

ORLETON (Shropshire).
LEACH, F. Seats of Shropshire. p.305. 1891.

ORLETON MANOR (Herefordshire).
ROBINSON, C.J. Mansions of Herefordshire. pl.15. 1873.

ORLINGBURY HALL (Northamptonshire).
GOTCH, J.A. Squires' Homes. 22. 1939.

ORMEROD HOUSE (Lancashire).
BARTLETT, J. Mansions of England and Wales. pl.11. 1853.
BURKE, J.B. Visitation of Seats. Vol.II, p.196. 1853.*
TWYCROSS, E. Mansions of England and Wales. Vol.I, p.29. 1847.

ORMESBY HALL (Yorkshire).
LONDON: National Trust for Places of Historic Interest or Natural Beauty.
— HUEBNER, M.D. Ormesby Hall, Yorkshire. 8pp. 1 illus. 21x14 [London] (1963.)
COUNTRY LIFE. CXXV, 410. 1959.

OKEOVER HALL, Staffordshire. From: PLOT (R.). *The natural history of Staffordshire*, Oxford, 1686.

ORMESBY HOUSE (Norfolk).
NEALE, J.P. Views of Seats. Vol.III. 1820.

ORSETT HALL (Essex).
BURKE, J.B. Visitation of Seats. Vol.I, p.63. 1852.*

ORTON HALL (Leicestershire).
NICHOLS, J. History of Leicestershire. IV, ii, 847. 1811.

ORWELL PARK (Suffolk).
BURKE, J.B. Visitation of Seats. 2.S. Vol.I, p.85. 1854.*
CROMWELL, T.K. Excursions in Suffolk. II, p.28. 1819.
NEALE, J.P. Views of Seats. Vol.IV. 1821.

OSBASTON HALL (Leicestershire).
NICHOLS, J. History of Leicestershire. IV, ii, 524. 1811.
THROSBY, J. Views in Leicestershire. p.304, 1789.

OSBERTON HOUSE (Nottinghamshire).
CAMPBELL, C. New Vitruvius Britannicus. II, pls. 60, 61. 1808.

OSBORNE HOUSE (Hampshire,
Isle of Wight).
OSBORNE: House.
— Handbook to Osborne. With a catalogue of the pictures, etc., in the state apartments. By A.I. Durrant. 52pp. Illus. incl. plan and map. 18x12 Newport and Cowes [1906?].
Another ed. An illustrated guide to Osborne ... With a catalogue of the pictures, porcelain and furniture in the state apartments. Also notes on the Swiss Cottage and Swiss Cottage Museum. By ... Sir G. Laking, Bart. Founded on a previous guide made by Sir A. Durrant [etc.]. 86pp. 12 illus. incl. 11 plates and plan. 21x14 London, 1922.
Another ed. 90pp. 1926.
Another ed. Revised, 1928, by H.A. Russell. 88pp. 1932.
Another ed. 1933.
18 ed. Revised, 1949, by R.A. Barker. 1953.

COUNTRY LIFE. CXVI, 562. 1954.

SPROULE, A. Lost houses of Britain. 233. 1982.

OSMASTON HALL (Derbyshire).
TILLEY, J. Halls of Derbyshire. IV, p.55. 1902.

OSMASTON MANOR (Derbyshire).
COUNTRY LIFE. XII, 48. 1902.

OSSINGTON HALL (Nottinghamshire).
BURKE, J.B. Visitation of Seats. 2.S. Vol.I, p.121. 1854.*
THOROTON, R. Nottinghamshire. III, 174. 1797.

OSTERLEY PARK (Middlesex).
BALCH, Elizabeth.
— A glimpse of Osterley Park [etc.]. Excerpt, 6pp. Illus. 23x18 [London, 1890.]
Also in: ENGLISH ILLUSTRATED MAGAZINE, VII, 862.
JERSEY, George Francis Child Villiers, *Earl of.*
— Osterley Park, Isleworth. A guide for visitors. Compiled by the Earl of Jersey in collaboration with H. Clifford-Smith. 58pp. 23x18 (London) privately printed (1939).
JERSEY, Margaret Elizabeth Child Villiers, *Countess of.*
— Osterley Park and its memories. 32pp. 6 illus. 20x13 London: privately printed, 1920.
LONDON: Victoria and Albert Museum.
— TOMLIN, M. Catalogue of Adam period furniture (from the ... Museum's collection ... and at Osterley Park.) [Bibliogr.] Illus. 24x18 London: H.M.S.O., 1972.
OSTERLEY: Osterley Park.
— WARD-JACKSON, P. Osterley Park: a guide. [Bibliog.] 20pp. 13x20 London: H.M.S.O., 1953.
2 ed. 22pp. 8 plates, plan and map. 1954.
Reprinted, with amendments. 24pp. 1968.
MANUSCRIPTS (Typewritten).   English.
— SMITH, H.C. An inventory and valuation of the works ... of the State Rooms at Osterley Park, Isleworth, the property of the ... Earl of Jersey [G.F. Child-Villiers, 9th. Earl]. Prepared for the purposes of insurance by H.C.S. 34x20 (Kensington) 1939.
Typewritten letter and press cutting, inserted.
BOLTON, A.T. Architecture of R. & J. Adam. I, 279 plan. 1922.
BURKE, J.B. Visitation of Seats. 2.S. Vol.I, p.211. 1854.*
COUNTRY LIFE. LX, 782, 818 plan, 858, 907 [Pictures], 938 [Furniture], 972 [Furniture]. 1926.
COUNTRY LIFE. LXXXV, 579, 1939.
COUNTRY LIFE. LXXXVI, 8 [Furniture]. 1939.
COUNTRY LIFE. XCIX, 440. 1946.
COUNTRY LIFE. CXLVII, 1164 [Furniture], 1258 [Furniture]. 1970.
ENGLAND: Picturesque Views. p.3. 1786-88.
MALAN, A.H. Other famous homes. p.121. 1902.
WATTS, W. Seats of the Nobility. pl.70. 1779.

OSWALD HOUSE (Durham).
NEALE, J.P. Views of Seats. Vol.I. 1818.

OTE HALL, Wivelsfield (Sussex).
See GREAT OTE HALL.

OTELEY PARK (Shropshire).
BURKE, J.B. Visitation of Seats. Vol.I, p.162. 1852.*
LEACH, F. Seats of Shropshire. p.19. 1891.
LEIGHTON, S. Shropshire houses. 28. 1901.
SHROPSHIRE. Castles & Old Mansions. 58. 1868.

OTLEY HALL (Suffolk).
F.,E.

—Otley Hall. 14 excerpts. 5ff. 33x26 Ipswich, 1929.
From: East Anglian Daily Times, January-March 1929.
COUNTRY LIFE. LXV, 152 plan. 1912.
SANDON, E. Suffolk houses. 194. **1977**.
TIPPING, H.A. English Homes. Period I & II, Vol.II, p.207. 1937.

OTTERDEN PLACE (Kent).
BURKE, J.B. Visitation of Seats. 2.S. Vol.II, p.95. 1855.*
COUNTRY LIFE. CXLVIII, 510. 1970.
GREENWOOD, C. Kent. 158. 1838.

OTTERHEAD (Somerset).
BURKE, J.B. Visitation of Seats. Vol.I, p.153. 1852.*

OTTERSHAW PARK (Surrey).
BURKE, J.B. Visitation of Seats. 2.S. Vol.I, p.214. 1854.*
PROSSER, G.F. Surrey Seats. p.75. 1828.

OTTERSPOOL (Lancashire).
BARTLETT, J. Mansions of England and Wales. pls. 133, 134. 1853.
TWYCROSS, E. Mansions of England and Wales. Vol.III, p.62. 1847.

OUGHTRINGTON HALL (Cheshire).
TWYCROSS, E. Mansions of England and Wales. Vol.II, p.60. 1850.*

OULTON (Suffolk)
SOANE, J. Plans, elevations and sections. Pl. XXXVIII. 1788.

OULTON PARK (Cheshire).
EGERTON, *Sir* Philip de Malpas Grey, *Bart.*
— Descriptive catalogue of the pictures and other works of art, at Oulton Park, Cheshire. [By P. de M.G.E. i.e. Sir P. de M.G. Egerton, Bart.] 20x16 London: privately printed, 1864.
BURKE, J.B. Visitation of Seats. Vol.I, p.97. 1852.*
COUNTRY LIFE. XXIII, 774. 1908.
COUNTRY LIFE. LIX, 265. 1926.
LATHAM, C. In English Homes. Vol.III, p.311. 1909.
TIPPING, H.A. English Homes. Period IV, Vol.II, p.217. 1928.
TWYCROSS, E. Mansions of England and Wales. Vol.I, p.106. 1850.*

OUSDEN HALL (Suffolk).
BURKE, J.B. Visitation of Seats. Vol.I, p.34. 1852.*

OVENDEN (Kent).
COUNTRY LIFE. XLVII, 620. 1920.
OSWALD, A. Country houses of Kent. 64. 1933.

OVERBURY COURT (Worcestershire).
NASH, T.R. Worcestershire. I, 559. 1781.

OVER COURT (Gloucestershire).
ATKYNS, R. Glocestershire. p.110. 1768.
JONES. Views of Seats. II. 1829.
NEALE, J.P. Views of Seats. 2.S. Vol.II. 1825.

OVER HALL (Essex).
ESSEX: A new and complete history. II, 174. 1769.

OVERSTONE PARK (Northamptonshire).
HOBSON, Robert Lockhart.
— Catalogue of porcelain, furniture, and other works of art, in the collection of Lady Wantage, at 2 Carlton Gardens, London, Lockinge House, Berks., and Overstone Park, Northants. Described by R.L.H., and O. Brackett. Illus. incl. plates (1 col.). 35x25 Enfield: privately printed. 1912.
OVERSTONE PARK.
— Descriptive catalogue of the pictures at Overstone Park. [By G. Redford?] 30pp. 27x21 London: privately printed, 1877.
TEMPLE, Alfred George.
— Catalogue of pictures forming the collection of Lord and Lady Wantage at 2, Carlton Gardens, London, Lockinge House, Berks., and Overstone Park and Ardington House. [By A.G.T., R.H. Benson and Lady Wantage; introduction by S.A. Strong.] Plates. 34x26 London: Wetherman & Co., 1902.
[Sales] OVERSTONE PARK, 1921, January 31, February 1-3 [Furniture etc.].

OVERTON (Shropshire).
LEACH, F. Seats of Shropshire. p.287. 1891.

OVERTON HALL (Derbyshire).
TILLEY, J. Halls of Derbyshire. III, p.9. 1899.

OVING HOUSE (Buckinghamshire).
COUNTRY LIFE. CXXIV, 1172, 1232 plan. 1958.

OWLETTS (Kent).
LONDON: National Trust for Places of Historic Interest or Natural Beauty.
— Owletts. 8pp. 1 illus. 22x14 [London] (1969.)
COUNTRY LIFE. XCIV, 1168. 1943.
OSWALD, A. Country houses of Kent. 53. 1933.

OWLPEN HOUSE (Gloucestershire).
[Sales] OWLPEN HOUSE, 1924, July 29-31 [Contents].

OWLPEN MANOR (Gloucestershire).

COOKE, R. West Country Houses. p.86. 1957.

COUNTRY LIFE. XCVI, 329 [Painted cloths]. 1944.

COUNTRY LIFE. CX, 1460, 1544. 1951.

DELDERFIELD, E.R. West Country houses. III, 71. 1973.

TIPPING, H.A. English Homes. Early Renaissance. p.257. 1912.

TIPPING, H.A. English Homes. Period III, Vol.I, p.132. 1922.

[Sales] LONDON, 1926, November 24 [House].

OWSTON HALL (Yorkshire).

BURKE, J.B. Visitation of Seats. Vol.I, p.229. 1852.*

OXBURGH HALL (Norfolk).

DE ZULUETA, Francis.
—Embroideries by Mary Stuart & Elizabeth Talbot at Oxburgh Hall, Norfolk. 16pp. Plates. 32x26 Oxford: O.U.P., 1923.

LONDON: National Trust for Places of Historic Interest or Natural Beauty.
—Oxburgh Hall, Norfolk. [Bibliogr. notes.] 16pp. 3 plates and plan. 18x12 London: Country Life (1953).

The Oxburgh hangings: needlework of Mary, Queen of Scots, inserted. 2pp.

Rev. ed. BEDINGFELD, A. 32pp. Illus. (1 col. on cover) incl. plan and genealog. table. 21x14 [London] 1982.

BIRKBECK, G. Old Norfolk houses. 81. 1908.

BURKE, J.B. Visitation of Seats. 2.S. Vol. I, p.112. 1854.*

COUNTRY LIFE. I, 548. 1897.

COUNTRY LIFE. XIII, 470. 1903.

COUNTRY LIFE. LXVI, 194, 224. 1929.

LATHAM, C. In English Homes. Vol. I, p.275. 1904.

NEALE, J.P. Views of Seats. Vol.III. 1820.

NICOLSON, N. Great Houses of Britain. p.30. 1965.

TIPPING, H.A. English Homes. Period I & II, Vol. II, p.321. 1937.

OXENDALE HALL (Lancashire).

GARNER, T. Domestic architecture. II, p.144 plan. 1911.

OXENHOATH (Kent).

BADESLADE, T. Seats in Kent. pl.25. 1750.

HARRIS, J. History of Kent. p.235. 1719.

OXLEY MANOR (Staffordshire).

MORRIS, F.O. Views of Seats. Vol.IV, p.55. 1880.

[Sales] OXLEY MANOR, 1920, December 14, 15, 17 [Furniture, porcelain, armour].

OXNEAD HALL (Norfolk).

BIRKBECK, G. Old Norfolk houses. 85. 1908.

GARRATT, T. Halls of Norfolk. pl. 38. 1890.

OXNEY COURT (Kent).

GREENWOOD, C. Kent. 434. 1838.

NEALE, J.P. Views of Seats. 2.S. Vol.II. 1825.

OXTON HALL (Nottinghamshire).

THOROTON, R. Nottinghamshire. III, 47. 1797.

PACKINGTON HALL (Warwickshire).

BURKE, J.B. Visitation of Seats. Vol.II, p.111. 1853.*

COUNTRY LIFE. II, 98. 1897.

COUNTRY LIFE. CXLVIII, 102, 162, 226. 1970.

NEALE, J.P. Views of Seats. Vol.IV. 1821.

SMITH, W. History of the County of Warwick. 374. 1830.

PACKWOOD HOUSE (Warwickshire).

LONDON: National Trust for Places of Historic Interest or Natural Beauty.
—ROWLEY, J. Packwood House, Warwickshire. 12pp. 4 plates. 18x12 London: Country Life (1948).

LONDON: National Trust for Places of Historic Interest or Natural Beauty.
—WALLACE, C. Packwood House, Warwickshire., 16pp. Illus. (1 col. on cover) incl. 4 plates and plan. 22x14 [London] 1973.

LONDON: National Trust for Places of Historic Interest or Natural Beauty.
—GRUNDY, C.B. Packwood House, Warwickshire. [Bibliogr.] 32pp. Illus. (1 on cover) incl. plan. 22x14 [London] 1982.

MANUSCRIPTS (Typewritten).   English.
—SMITH, H.C. Inventory and valuation of the contents of Packwood House, Warwickshire. Prepared by H.C.S. ... This inventory records the presentation of the contents of Packwood House to the National Trust by G.B. Ash on June 30th, 1941. 48ff. 33x20 (Kensington) 1947.

COUNTRY LIFE. LVI, 218. 1924.

PADLEY HALL (Derbyshire).

TILLEY, J. Halls of Derbyshire. I, p.183. 1892.

PADWORTH HOUSE (Berkshire).

COUNTRY LIFE. LII, 342, 372, 414 [Silver]. 1922.

TIPPING, H.A. English Homes. Period VI, Vol.I, p.187. 1926.

PAGE HALL (Yorkshire).

BURKE, J.B. Visitation of Seats. Vol.I, p.82. 1852.*

PAGODA HOUSE, Richmond (Surrey).

BURKE, J.B. Visitation of Seats. 2.S. Vol.II, p.115. 1855.*

PAINSHILL (Surrey).

BRAYLEY, E.W. History of Surrey. II, 369. 1841.

BURKE, J.B. Visitation of Seats. Vol.I, p.217. 1852.*

COUNTRY LIFE. CXXIII, 18. 1958.

ENGLAND: Beauties of England. II, p.295. 1787.
ENGLAND: Picturesque Views.p.20. 1786-88.
NEALE, J.P. Views of Seats. 2.S. Vol.I. 1824.
PROSSER, G.F. Surrey Seats. p.47. 1828.

PAINSWICK HOUSE (Gloucestershire).
COUNTRY LIFE. XLII, 204. 1917.

PAKYN'S MANOR (Sussex).
BURKE, J.B. Visitation of Seats. 2.S. Vol.II, p.129. 1855.*

PALACE HOUSE (Lancashire).
BURKE, J.B. Visitation of Seats. Vol.II, p.53. 1853.*

PALÉ (Merionethshire).
BURKE, J.B. Visitation of Seats. Vol.I, p.106. 1852.*

PAMPISFORD HALL (Cambridgeshire).
BURKE, J.B. Visitation of Seats. Vol.II, p.20. 1853.*

PAMPSWORTH HALL (Cambridgeshire).
See PAMPISFORD HALL.

PANSHANGER (Hertfordshire).
BOYLE, Mary Louisa.
— Biographical catalogue of the portraits at Panshanger, the seat of Earl Cowper, K.G. 20x16 London: Elliot Stock, 1885.
BURKE, J.B. Visitation of Seats. 2.S. Vol.II, p.107. 1855.*
COUNTRY LIFE. LXXIX, 38, 64 [Pictures]. 1936.
MORRIS, F.O. Views of Seats. Vol.II, p.53. 1880.
NEALE, J.P. Views of Seats. Vol.II. 1819.

PANTGLAS (Carmarthenshire).
BURKE, J.B. Visitation of Seats. Vol.I, p.203. 1852.

PANTON HALL (Lincolnshire).
ANGUS, W. Seats of the Nobility. pl.30. 1787.

PANTY-GWYDIR (Glamorganshire).
NICHOLAS, T. Counties of Wales. II, p.476. 1872.

PAPPLEWICK HALL (Nottinghamshire).
COUNTRY LIFE. CXXXIV, 492 plan, 540, 600. 1964.
THOROTON, R. Nottinghamshire. II, 288. 1797.

PAPWORTH HALL (Cambridgeshire).
[Sales] PAPWORTH HALL, 1911, September 25-29 [Contents]. (K.F. & R.).

PARCEVALL HALL (Yorkshire).
COUNTRY LIFE. CXXXII, 1039. 1962.

PARHAM OLD HALL (Suffolk).
COUNTRY LIFE. X, 264. 1901.
COUNTRY LIFE. XXV, 702. 1909.
CROMWELL, T.K. Excursions in Suffolk. II, p.79. 1819.
TIPPING, H.A. English Homes. Period II, Vol.I, p.51. 1924.

PARHAM PARK (Sussex).
HUSSEY, Christopher.
— Parham Park, Sussex [etc]. 36pp. Illus. incl. plan. 20x14 [London] Country Life, [1952?]
Also in: COUNTRY LIFE. CIX, 1716, 1800, 1884. 1951.

PARHAM.
— Parham in Sussex: a historical and descriptive survey based upon the researches of a number of authorities accompanied by an architectural description. [By (J. W.-F.) Bibliogr.] Illus. incl. plates, plans and maps (on end-papers). 33x25 London: Batsford, 1947.
TRITTON, *Mrs.* P.A.
— Parham Park. 28pp. Illus. (some col., some on covers) incl. genealog. table. 19x16 (Derby: E.L.P., 1974.)
BURKE, J.B. Visitation of Seats. Vol.II, p.38. 1853.*
COUNTRY LIFE. XI, 496. 1902.
COUNTRY LIFE. CIX, 1716 plan, 1800, 1884. 1951.
ELWES, D.G.C. Mansions of Western Sussex. 164. 1876.
LATHAM, C. In English Homes. Vol.I, p.281. 1904,
NASH, J. Mansions of England. III, pl.3. 1841.
NEALE, J.P. Views of Seats. 2.S. Vol.IV. 1828.

PARISH'S HOUSE, Timsbury (Somerset).
COUNTRY LIFE. XCVI, 24, 68. 1944.

PARK, The. (Lancashire).
TWYCROSS, E. Mansions of England and Wales. Vol.III, p.81. 1847.*

PARKE, The. (Hertfordshire).
CHAUNCY, H. Hertfordshire. I, 534. 1826.

PARK FARM PLACE (Kent).
ENGLAND: Picturesque Views. p.42. 1786-88.

PARK HALL, Barlborough (Derbyshire).
TILLEY, J. Halls of Derbyshire. III, p.43. 1899.

PARK HALL, Hayfield (Derbyshire).
[Sales] LEEDS, Hepper House, 1978, April 5 [Contents].

PARK HALL (Lancashire).
TWYCROSS, E. Mansions of England and Wales. Vol.I, p.69. 1847.*

PARK HALL (Shropshire).
COUNTRY LIFE. XVII, 306. 1905.

GOTCH, J.A. Architecture of the Renaissance. I, p.4. 1894.

LATHAM, C. In English Homes. Vol.II, p.135. 1907.

LEACH, F. Seats of Shropshire. p.189. 1891.

LEIGHTON, S. Shropshire houses. 25. 1901.

MOSS, F. Pilgrimages. [III] 327. 1906.

RICHARDSON, C.J. Old English mansions. II. 1842.

SHROPSHIRE. Castles & Old Mansions. 35. 1868.

PARK HATCH (Surrey).
BRAYLEY, E.W. History of Surrey. V, 127. 1841.

PARKHILL, Lyndhurst (Hampshire).
[Sales] PARKHILL, 1925, September 21-25 [Contents].

PARK HOUSE, Folkestone (Kent).
HASTED, E. Kent. III, 374. 1790.

PARK HOUSE, Hampton Court (Middlesex).
COUNTRY LIFE. LIX, 444 plan. 1926.

PARK PLACE (Berkshire).
HAVELL, R. Views of Noblemen's Seats. 1823.

ROBERTSON, A. Great Road. I, p.101. 1792.

PARKSTEAD HOUSE, Roehampton (Surrey).
See MANRESA HOUSE.

PARNHAM HOUSE (Dorsetshire).
BEAMINSTER.
— Parnham House, Beaminster, Dorset. [Bibliogr.] 8pp. 1 Illus. 19x13 Beaminster: Toucan Press, 1964.

ROBINSON, Vincent Joseph.
— Ancient furniture and other works of art. Illustrative of a collection formed by V.J.R. of Parnham House, Dorset. vi, 84pp. Illus. incl. plates. 33x25 London: Quaritch, 1902.

COUNTRY LIFE. XXIV, 288, 320. 1908.

GARNER, T. Domestic architecture. I, p.97 plan. 1911.

HUTCHINS, J. Vitruvius Dorsettiensis. pl.22. 1816.

HUTCHINS, J. History of Dorset. II, 128. 1863.

HEATH, S. Dorset Manor Houses. 157. 1907.

OSWALD, A. Country houses of Dorset. p.58. 1959.

TIPPING, H.A. English Homes. Early Renaissance. p.9. 1912.

[Sales] PARNHAM, 1910, August 2-6, 8 [Furniture, paintings, tapestries etc.].

[Sales] PARNHAM, 1930, November 3-7 [Furniture etc.].

PARR HALL (Lancashire).
BURKE, J.B. Visitation of Seats. 2.S. Vol.I. p.195. 1854.*

PARSONAGE HOUSE, Stanton Harcourt (Oxfordshire).
COUNTRY LIFE, XC, 112, 160. 1941.

PARWICH HALL (Derbyshire).
TILLEY, J. Halls of Derbyshire. II, p.251. 1893.

PAULTONS (Hampshire).
HAMPSHIRE: Architectural views. 1830.

PAYCOCKE'S HOUSE, Coggeshall (Essex).
BEAUMONT, George Frederick.
— Paycocke's House, Coggeshall, with some notes on the families of Paycocke and Buxton. [Bibliogr. notes.] 16pp. Illus. incl. plates (1 folding). 29x22 [Colchester, 1905].
Also in COLCHESTER: Essex Archaeological Society Transactions, N.S. IX, 311. 1906.

LONDON: National Trust for Places of Historic Interest or Natural Beauty.
— Paycocke's House, Coggeshall, Essex. 8pp. 1 illus. 18x12 [London, c.1945.]

COUNTRY LIFE. LIII, 920. 1923.

TIPPING, H.A. English Homes. Period II, Vol.I, p.11. 1924.

PECKFORTON CASTLE (Cheshire).
BURKE, J.B. Visitation of Seats. Vol.I, p.233. 1852.*

COUNTRY LIFE. CXXXVIII, 284, 336 plan. 1965.

MORRIS, F.O. Views of Seats. Vol.IV, p.65. 1880.

ORMEROD, G. Cheshire. II, 302. 1882.

TWYCROSS, E. Mansions of England and Wales. Vol.I, p.110. 1850.

PECKOVER HOUSE, Wisbech (Cambridgeshire).
LONDON. National Trust for Places of Historic Interest or Natural Beauty.
—Peckover House, Wisbech, Cambridgeshire. 8pp. 3 illus. 18x12 [London, c. 1955.]

Rev. ed. KETTON-CREMER, R.W. 16pp. Illus. (1 col. on cover) incl. plates. 21x14 [London] 1981.

PEEL HALL, Little Hulton (Lancashire). J.F. Fletcher Esq.
BARTLETT, J. Mansions of England and Wales. pls. 153, 154. 1853.

TWYCROSS, E. Mansions of England and Wales. Vol.III, p.97. 1847.

PEEL HALL (Lancashire). Lord Kenyon.
BARTLETT, J. Mansions of England and Wales. pl.139. 1853.
GRAY, H. Old halls of Lancashire. p.57. 1893.
TWYCROSS, E. Mansions of England and Wales. Vol.III, p.69. 1847.

PELLING PLACE (Berkshire).
ANGUS, W. Seats of the Nobility. pl.51. 1787.

PENCARROW (Cornwall).
BURKE, J.B. Visitation of Seats. Vol.II, p.58. 1853.*
COUNTRY LIFE. CXVI, 118, 200. 1954.

PENDARVES (Cornwall).
BURKE, J.B. Visitation of Seats. 2.S. Vol.I, p.203. 1854.*

PENDELL COURT (Surrey).
COPPER PLATE MAGAZINE. pl.75. 1778.
MANNING, O. Surrey. II, 306. 1804.
SANDBY, P. Select Views. I, pl.62. 1783.
[Sales] PENDELL COURT, 1922 [House and park].

PENDLEY MANOR (Hertfordshire).
CHAUNCY H. Hertfordshire. II, 560. 1826.

PENDREA (Cornwall).
BURKE, J.B. Visitation of Seats. Vol.II, p.178. 1853.*

PENFOUND MANOR (Cornwall).
COUNTRY LIFE. CXXV, 312 plan. 1959.
DELDERFIELD, E.R. West Country houses. I, 110. 1968.

PENGETHLEY (Herefordshire).
ROBINSON, C.J. Mansions of Herefordshire. pl.17. 1873.

PENGWERN PLACE [HALL] (Flintshire).
NEALE, J.P. Views of Seats. Vol.V. 1822.
[Sales] PENGWERN HALL, 1905, November 8-10, 13, 14 [Furniture, silver etc.].

PENHEALE MANOR (Cornwall).
BURKE, J.B. Visitation of Seats. Vol.II, p.148. 1853.*
COUNTRY LIFE. LVII, 484, 524. 1925.
COUNTRY LIFE. LXVIII, 569 [Chairs]. 1930.
COUNTRY LIFE. LXIX, 35 [Chairs]. 1931.

PENHOW CASTLE (Monmouthshire).
COUNTRY LIFE. CLXVI, 1050 plan. 1979.

PENIARTH HOUSE (Merionethshire).
NICHOLAS, T. Counties of Wales. II, p.652. 1872.

PENLANOLE (Radnorshire).
BURKE, J.B. Visitation of Seats. Vol.II, p.120. 1853.*

PENN HALL (Staffordshire).
SHAW, S. Staffordshire. II, 218. 1801.

PENNOYRE (Breknockshire).
BURKE, J.B. Visitation of Seats. Vol.II, p.175. 1853.

PENNS HALL (Warwickshire).
BURKE, J.B. Visitation of Seats. Vol.II, p.123. 1853.*

PENN'S ROCKS (Sussex).
COUNTRY LIFE. CXXIX, 704 plan. 1961.

PENNYHOLME (Yorkshire).
COUNTRY LIFE. CXXIV, 774 plan. 1958.

PENNYWORLLOD HALL (Brecknockshire).
BURKE, J.B. Visitation of Seats. 2.S. Vol.I, p.49. 1854.*

PENPONT HOUSE (Brecknockshire).
NEALE, J.P. Views of Seats. Vol.V. 1822.

PENRHOS HALL (Anglesey).
BURKE, J.B. Visitation of Seats. 2.S. Vol.I, p.155. 1854.*

PENRHYN CASTLE (Caernarvonshire).
LONDON: National Trust for Places of Historic Interest or Natural Beauty.
—Penrhyn Castle, Bangor, Carnarvonshire. [Bibliogr. notes] 12pp. Illus. (1 on title-page) incl. plan. 18x12 London: Country Life (1955).
LONDON: National Trust for Places of Historic Interest or Natural Beauty.
—Penrhyn Castle, Gwynedd. [Bibliogr. notes] 18pp. Illus. (1 col. on cover) incl. plates and plan. 24x18 [London] 1983.
LONDON: National Trust for Places of Historic Interest or Natural Beauty.
—Industrial Railway Museum at Penrhyn Castle. 24pp. Illus. 21x15 (London) [c.1965.]
BURKE, J.B. Visitation of Seats. Vol.I, p.80. **1852**.*
COUNTRY LIFE. English Country Houses: Late Georgian. p.181. 1958.
COUNTRY LIFE. II, 377. 1897.
COUNTRY LIFE. CXVIII, 80 plan, 140 plan, 192. 1956.
JONES. Views of Seats. V. 1830.
MORRIS, F.O. Views of Seats. Vol.II, p.59. 1880.
NICHOLAS, T. Counties of Wales. p.311. 1872.

PENRHYN OLD HALL (Caernarvonshire).
[Sales] PENRHYN OLD HALL, 1929, June 17, 18
[Contents]. (K.F. & R.).

PENRICE CASTLE (Glamorgan).
COUNTRY LIFE. CLVII, 694, 754. 1975.

PENROSE (Cornwall).
BURKE, J.B. Visitation of Seats. Vol.I, p.59. 1852.*

PENSHURST PLACE (Kent).
PENSHURST.
— Penshurst Place. 28pp. Illus. (1 on cover). incl. genealog.
table. 21x14 (Tunbridge Wells printed, 1950).
[New ed.] (1954.)
SIDNEY, *Hon.* Mary Sophia.
— Historical guide to Penshurst Place. 84pp. 8 plates. 18x12
Tunbridge Wells: Goulden & Curry; London: Simpkin,
Marshall, 1903.
BADESLADE, T. Seats in Kent. pl.26. 1750.
BURKE, J.B. Visitation of Seats. Vol.I, p.197. 1852.*
COUNTRY LIFE. I, 576. 1897.
COUNTRY LIFE. XXX, 844 plan, 894. 1911.
COUNTRY LIFE. XXXI, 102 [Table], 366 [Settee], 438
[Cabinet]. 1912.
COUNTRY LIFE. LII, 757 [Foreign Furniture]. 1922.
COUNTRY LIFE. CLI, 554 plan, 618, 994. 1090. 1972.
GREENWOOD, C. Kent. 109. [Principal pictures]. 1838.
HALL, S.C. Baronial Halls. Vol.I. 1848.
HARRIS, J. History of Kent. p.236. 1719.
HASTED, E. Kent. I, 414. 1778.
JEWITT, L. Stately homes of England. 172. 1874.
KROLL, A. Historic houses. 18. 1969.
MALAN, A.H. Famous homes. p.295. 1902.
MORRIS, F.O. Views of Seats. Vol.IV, p.69. 1880.
NASH, J. Mansions of England. I, pl.15. 1839. & III, pl.20.
1841.
NEALE, J.P. Views of Seats. 2.S. Vol.IV. 1828.
OSWALD, A. Country houses of Kent. 28. 1933.
THAMES, River. An history. II, pl.25. 1796.
THOMPSON, S. Old English homes. 39, 1876.
TIPPING, H.A. English Homes. Period I, Vol.I, p.166. 1921.
UNITED KINGDOM. Historic houses. 120. 1892.

PENTILLIE CASTLE (Cornwall).
BRITTON, J. Cornwall illustrated. 16. 1832.
BURKE, J.B. Visitation of Seats. 2.S. Vol.1, p.151. 1854.*
CROMWELL, T.K. Excursions in Cornwall. p.130. 1824.

PENTREHOBYN (Flintshire).
COUNTRY LIFE. XCIV, 684. 1943.

PENTRE MAWR (Denbighshire).
NICHOLAS, T. Counties of Wales. I, p.379. 1872.

PENWORTHAM HALL (Lancashire).
BARTLETT, J. Mansions of England and Wales. pls. 5, 6, 9.
1853.
TWYCROSS, E. Mansions of England and Wales. Vol.I, p.68.
1847.

PENWORTHAM PRIORY (Lancashire).
BARTLETT, J. Mansions of England and Wales. pl.34. 1853.
TWYCROSS, E. Mansions of England and Wales. Vol.I, p.47.
1847.

PEOVER HALL (Cheshire).
BURKE, J.B. Visitation of Seats. Vol.II, p.123. 1853.*
TWYCROSS, E. Mansions of England and Wales. Vol.II, p.50.
1850.*

PEPER HAROW (Surrey).
BRAYLEY, E.W. History of Surrey. V, 231. 1841.
COUNTRY LIFE. English Country Houses: Mid-Georgian.
p.111. 1956.
COUNTRY LIFE. LVIII, 1002. 1925.
MANNING, O. Surrey. II, 33. 1809.
MORRIS, F.O. Views of Seats. Vol. IV, p.13. 1880.
PROSSER, G.F. Surrey Seats. p.1. 1828.
TIPPING, H.A. English Homes. Period VI, Vol.I, p.275. 1926.

PEPPER HILL (Shropshire).
LEIGHTON, S. Shropshire houses. 33. 1901.

PERCY LODGE, East Sheen (Surrey).
COUNTRY LIFE. LIX, 941. 1926.
COUNTRY LIFE. CXXV, 1210. 1959.

PERITON MEAD (Somerset).
COUNTRY LIFE. LIV, 67 plan. 1923.

PERRY HILL HOUSE (Kent).
GREENWOOD, C. Kent. 24. 1838.

PERRYSTONE COURT (Herefordshire).
BURKE, J.B. Visitation of Seats. 2.S. Vol.I, p.42. 1854.*

PETERSHAM LODGE (Surrey).
ENGLAND: Beauties of England. II, p.287. 1787.

PETHAM HOUSE (Kent).
GREENWOOD, C. Kent. 396. 1838.

PETWORTH (Sussex).

ARNOLD, *Rev.* Frederick Henry.
— Petworth: a sketch of its history and antiquities, with notices of objects of archaeological interest in its vicinity. [Bibliogr. notes.] Engr. plates. 18x12 Petworth: Bryant, 1864.

BAKER, Charles Henry Collins.
— Catalogue of the Petworth collection of pictures in the possession of Lord Leconfield. Plates. 26x20 London: Medici Society, 1920.

BARNES, L.C. Hollist.
— Petworth, Sussex ... With a note on the pictures at Petworth House by H.G. Daniels. 32pp. Illus. (1 on cover.) incl. map. 18x12 London: Homeland Association [c.1910].
Vol.16 of: HOMELAND handy guides.

HUSSEY, Christopher.
— Petworth House, Sussex, the seat of Lord Leconfield. 56pp. Illus. 37x25 London, 1926.
Also in: COUNTRY LIFE, LVIII, LIX. 1925-26.

LONDON: National Trust for Places of Historic or Natural Beauty.
— Pictures at Petworth. 48pp. Illus. (1 on cover.) 23x16 [London,c.1965.]

LONDON: National Trust for Places of Historic Interest or Natural Beauty.
— Petworth House, Sussex. 38pp. 4 plates, plan and genealog. table. 21x14 (London) 1954.
Another ed. 36pp. [c.1973.]

SUSSEX: West Sussex County Council [West Sussex Record Office].
— The Petworth House archives: ... a catalogue. Edited by F.W. Steer and N.H. Osborne. [Bibliogr.] Plates incl. folding genealog. table. vols. 25x15 Chichester, 1968.

WYNDHAM, *Hon.* Margaret Blanche.
— Catalogue of the collection of Greek and Roman antiquities in the possession of Lord Leconfield. [Bibliogr.] Plates, and folding table. 27x20 London: Medici Society, 1915 ('16).

MANUSCRIPTS.   English.
PHILLIPS, H.W. Catalogue of the pictures in Petworth House, the seat of the Earl of Egremont, ... to which is prefixed a view of the mansion, a private lithographic print from a drawing by Mrs. Phillips, and subjoined a plan of the principal apartments, 1835. 31ff. Lithogr. plate, and plan drawn in red ink and pencil. 32x20 [London] 1836.
With some amendments and annotations. Possibly wanting lithographic print referred to above, since existing one is inscribed: Drawn on stone by T.M. Baynes, from a drawing by Lady Burrell.

COUNTRY LIFE. English Country Houses: Baroque. p.47. 1970.

COUNTRY LIFE. XXII, 826. 1907.

COUNTRY LIFE. LVIII, 818, 862, 899 [Pictures], 928, 936 [Pictures], 966, 974 [Turner]. 1925.

COUNTRY LIFE. LIX, 247 [Furniture]. 1926.

COUNTRY LIFE. CI, 422. 1947.

COUNTRY LIFE. CXV, 352 [Treasures]. 1954.

COUNTRY LIFE. CLIII, 1870. 1973.

ELWES, D.G.C. Mansions of Western Sussex. 167. 1876.

LATHAM, C. In English Homes. Vol.III, p.199. 1909.

NEALE, J.P. Views of Seats. Vol.IV. 1821.

PHILIPPS HOUSE, Dinton (Wiltshire).

LONDON: National Trust for Places of Historic Interest or Natural Beauty.
— Philipps House, Dinton, Wiltshire. 8pp. 2 illus. 18x12 [London] 1954.
Rev. ed. KENWORTHY-BROWNE, J. Philipps House, Dinton. [Bibliogr.] 20pp. Illus. (1 on Cover) incl. plates and genealog. table. 22x14 [London] 1975.

BRITTON, J. Beauties of Wiltshire. III, 326. 1825.

COUNTRY LIFE. XCIV, 1080. 1943.

PICTON CASTLE (Pembrokeshire).

BUCK, S. & N. Antiquities. II, pl.427. 1774.

COUNTRY LIFE. CXXVII, 18 plan, 66 plan, 170. 1960.

MORRIS, F.O. Views of Seats. Vol.I, p.21. 1880.

NICHOLAS, T. Counties of Wales. II, p.834. 1872.

WATTS, W. Seats of the Nobility. pl.2. 1779.

PIDDLETRENTHIDE MANOR (Dorsetshire).

[Sales] PIDDLETRENTHIDE MANOR, 1911, September 20-22 [Works of art, Royal relics].

PIERCEFIELD PARK (Monmouthshire).

WATERS, Ivor.
— Piercefield on the banks of the Wye. [Bibliogr.] iv, 32pp. Illus. incl. plates. 21x14 Chepstow: F.G. Comber, 1975.

PIERREMONT (Kent).

BAKER, J. Home beauties. plate. 1804.

PIERREMONT, Bradford (Yorkshire).

YORKSHIRE. Picturesque views. 1885.

PIERREPOINT (Surrey).

COUNTRY LIFE. XIV, 506. 1903.

PILEWELL (Hampshire).

See PYLEWELL PARK.

PILLATON HALL (Staffordshire).

NIVEN, W. Old Staffordshire houses. p.15, pl.12. 1882.

SHAW, S. Staffordshire. II, pl.3. Reprint 1976.

PILSBURY GRANGE (Derbyshire).

TILLEY, J. Halls of Derbyshire. II, p.195. 1893.

PILTON MANOR [Rectory].
(Northamptonshire).
GOTCH, J.A. Halls of Northants. p.36. 1936.

PINBURY (Gloucestershire).
COUNTRY LIFE. XXVII, 630 plan. 1910.

PINKNEY COURT (Wiltshire).
[Sales] PINKNEY COURT, 1979, December 14 [Contents].

PINNER HILL HOUSE (Middlesex).
BURKE, J.B. Visitation of Seats. 2.S. Vol.I, p.64. 1854.

PIPE RIDWARE MANOR (Staffordshire).
SHAW, S. Staffordshire. I, 161. 1798.

PIPPBROOK HOUSE (Surrey).
PIPPBROOK HOUSE.
— An inventory of the household furniture, plate, linen, jewellery, china, earthenware, glass, cutlery, books, prints, portraits, pictures, paintings, drawings, tapestries, engravings, sculptures, bronzes ... [of] Pippbrook House, Dorking. Bequeathed by the will of W.H. Forman, Esq. [etc.]. 25x17 London: privately printed, 1869.

PIRTON COURT (Worcestershire).
NIVEN, W. Old Worcestershire houses. p.39, pl.16. 1873.

PISHIOBURY (Hertfordshire).
CHAUNCY, H. Hertfordshire. I, 348. 1826.
NEALE, J.P. Views of Seats. Vol.II. 1819.

PITCHFORD HALL (Shropshire).
BURKE, J.B. Visitation of Seats. 2.S. Vol.I, p.192. 1854.*
COUNTRY LIFE. III, 294. 1898.
COUNTRY LIFE. XLI, 352, 376. 1917.
GARNER, T. Domestic architecture. II, p.157 plan. 1911.
HALL, S.C. Baronial Halls. Vol.II. 1848.
JONES. Views of Seats. I. 1829.
LEACH, F. Seats of Shropshire. p.15. 1891.
LEIGHTON, S. Shropshire houses. 3. 1901.
MOSS, F. Pilgrimages. [II] 311. 1903.
NEALE, J.P. Views of Seats. 2.S. Vol.II. 1825.
SHROPSHIRE. Castles & Old Mansions. 26. 1868.
TIPPING, H.A. English Homes. Period III, Vol.I, p.l. 1922.
WEST, W. Picturesque views of Shropshire. p.131. 1831.

PITTLEWORTH MANOR (Hampshire).
COUNTRY LIFE. LII, 606 [Frescoes]. 1922.

PITZHANGER MANOR (Middlesex).
LONDON: Soane Museum.
— Publications, [etc.].
4. BOLTON, A.T. Pitzhanger Manor, Ealing Green (now the Ealing Public Library). The country retreat from 1800 to 1811 of Sir John Soane, R.A. [etc.]. 24pp. Illus. 13x18 [c.1918.]
PITZHANGER MANOR HOUSE.
— Plans, elevations, and perspective views, of Pitzhanger Manor House, and of the ruins of an edifice of Roman architecture, situated on the border of Ealing Green, with a description of the ancient and present state of the manor-house in a letter [by Sir J. Soane] to a friend. 10pp. 12 lithogr. plates incl. elevations and plans. 29x23 London: J. Moyes, 1802. Bound with: BRITTON (J.). Brief memoir of Sir J. Soane. 1834.
CAMPBELL, C. New Vitruvius Britannicus. II, pls. 57-9. 1808.
COUNTRY LIFE. XLV, 211. 1919.

PIXTON PARK (Somerset).
BURKE, J.B. Visitation of Seats. 2.S. Vol.I, p.223. 1854.*

PLACE HOUSE, Fowey (Cornwall).
BRITTON, J. Cornwall Illustrated. 35. 1832.
COUNTRY LIFE. CXXXI, 1510, 1568. 1962.
CROMWELL, T.K. Excursions in Cornwall. p.39. 1824.
HALL, S.C. Baronial Halls. Vol. I. 1848.

PLACE HOUSE, Padstow (Cornwall).
See PRIDEAUX PLACE.

PLAISH HALL (Shropshire).
COUNTRY LIFE. XLI, 520 plan. 1917.
SHROPSHIRE. Castles & Old Mansions. 31. 1868.
TIPPING, H.A. English Homes. Period III, Vol.I, p.14. 1922.
[Sales] PLAISH HALL, 1959, November 30 [Drinking glasses].

PLAS, The. Dinas Mawddwy (Merionethshire).
NICHOLAS, T. Counties of Wales. II, p.655-7. 1872.

PLAS BRONDANW (Merionethshire).
BURKE, J.B. Visitation of Seats. 2.S. Vol.II, p.146. 1855.*
COUNTRY LIFE. LXIX, 130. 1931.
COUNTRY LIFE. CXXII, 434 plan. 1957.

PLAS CADNANT (Anglesey).
BURKE, J.B. Visitation of Seats. Vol.II, p.130. 1853.*

PLAS CLOUGH (Denbighshire).
BURKE, J.B. Visitation of Seats. Vol.II, p.134. 1853.*

PLAS COCH (Anglesey).
BURKE, J.B. Visitation of Seats. Vol.I, p.196. 1852.*
BURKE, J.B. Visitation of Seats. 2.S. Vol.I, p.103. 1854.

PLAS GWYN (Anglesey).
BURKE, J.B. Visitation of Seats. 2.S. Vol.I, p.207. 1854.*

PLASHWOOD (Suffolk).
DAVY, H. Seats in Suffolk. pl.3. 1827.

PLAS MADOC (Denbighshire).
BURKE, J.B. Visitation of Seats. Vol.II, p.97. 1853.*

PLAS MAWR (Caernarvonshire).
BAKER, Arthur and *Sir* Herbert, *R.A.*
— Plas Mawr, Conway, N. Wales. Illustrated and described by A.B., and H.B. 64pp. 23 plates incl. sections, elevations and plans and genealog. tables. 38x29 London: Farmer & Sons, 1888.
COUNTRY LIFE. XXIV, 126. 1908.
TIPPING, H.A. English Homes. Early Renaissance. p.121. 1912.
TIPPING, H.A. English Homes. Period III, Vol.I, p.116. 1922.

PLAS NEWYDD (Anglesey).
LONDON: National Trust for Places of Historic Interest.
—Plas Newydd, Isle of Anglesey. [Bibliogr.] 40pp. Illus. (1 col. on cover) incl. plates, plan and genealog. table. 21x14 [London] 1978.
COUNTRY LIFE. XCIX, 342 [Rex Whistler Room]. 1946.
COUNTRY LIFE. CXVIII, 1198 plan, 1252. 1955.
COUNTRY LIFE. CLIX, 1686. 1976.
COUNTRY LIFE. CLX, 18. 1977.
COUNTRY LIFE. CLXII, 286 [Rex Whistler at P.N.]. 1977.
NEALE, J.P. Views of Seats. Vol. V. 1822.

PLAS NEWYDD, Llangollen.
(Denbighshire).
PLAS NEWYDD.
—Plas Newydd, as it was and as it is, with a catalogue of its contents and a few reminiscences of Lady Eleanor Butler and the Hon. Sarah Ponsonby. By one who received their welcome in his younger days. 32pp. 2 cuts (on covers). 16x10 Llangollen: H.Jones [c. 1880].
RUTHIN: Glyndŵr District Council.
—Plas Newydd and the ladies of Llangollen. [By] (A.G. Veysey.) [Bibliogr.] 16pp. Illus. (some on cover) incl. map. 21x15 Ruthin (1980).
JONES. Views of Seats. V. 1830.

PLAS TEG (Flintshire).
COUNTRY LIFE. CXXXII, 134 plan. 1962.

PLAS-YN-YALE (Denbighshire).
BURKE, J.B. Visitation of Seats. 2.S. Vol.I, p.56. 1854.*

PLEASINGTON HALL (Lancashire).
BURKE, J.B. Visitation of Seats. Vol.I, p.127. 1852.*

PLOWDEN HALL (Shropshire).
COUNTRY LIFE. CLVII. 318. 1975.
LEACH, F. Seats of Shropshire. p.65. 1891.
LEIGHTON, S. Shropshire houses. 44. 1901.
MOSS, F. Pilgrimages. V,1. 1910.

PLUMBER HOUSE (Dorsetshire).
HUTCHINS, J. Vitruvius Dorsettiensis.pl.23. 1816.
HUTCHINS, J. History of Dorset. IV, 189. 1870.

PLUMLEY HALL (Derbyshire).
TILLEY, J. Halls of Derbyshire. III, p.145. 1899.

PLYMPTON HOUSE (Devonshire).
COUNTRY LIFE. LXXIV, 146. 1943.

POLEBROOK HALL (Northamptonshire).
GOTCH, J.A. Squires' Homes. 5. 1939.

POLESDEN LACEY (Surrey).
LONDON: National Trust for Places of Historic Interest or Natural Beauty.
—FEDDEN, R. Polesden Lacey, Surrey. 30pp. Illus. incl. plates, plan and map. 18x12 London: Country Life (1948). New ed. Illus. (2 on covers) incl. plates and plan. 25x18 1964.
Rev. ed. [Bibliogr.] 40pp. Illus. (1 col. on cover) incl. plates, plan and map. 25x18 [London] 1981.
BRAYLEY, E.W. History of Surrey. IV, 471. 1841.
COUNTRY LIFE. CIII, 526. 1948.
COUNTRY LIFE. CXXXVII, 1410 [Pictures]. 1965.
COUNTRY LIFE. CLXIX, 378, 442. 1981.
NEALE, J.P. Views of Seats. 2.S. Vol. I. 1824.
PROSSER, G.F. Surrey Seats. p.31. 1828.

POLSTEAD HALL (Suffolk).
SANDON, E. Suffolk houses. 240. 1977.

POLTIMORE PARK (Devonshire).
[Sales] POLTIMORE PARK, 1923, July 16, 17, 19, 20, 23, 24 [Contents].

PONSONDINE (Cornwall).
BURKE, J.B. Visitation of Seats. Vol.II, p.178. 1853.*

PONTRYFFYDD (Denbighshire).
NICHOLAS, T. Counties of Wales. I, p.378. 1872.

PONTYPOOL PARK (Monmouthshire).
BURKE, J.B. Visitation of Seats. Vol.II, p.7. 1853.

POOL, Menheniot (Cornwall).
CROMWELL, T.K. Excursions in Cornwall. p.146. 1824.

POOLE HALL (Cheshire).
BURKE, J.B. Visitation of Seats. Vol.II, p.127. 1853.*
ORMEROD, G. Cheshire. II, 436. 1882.
TWYCROSS, E. Mansions of England and Wales. Vol.II, p.21.
1850.*

POOLEY HALL (Warwickshire).
GARNER, T. Domestic architecture. I, p.103. 1911.
NIVEN, W. Old Warwickshire houses. p.12, pl.14. 1878.
SMITH, W. History of the County of Warwick. 371. 1830.

POPE'S VILLA, Twickenham (Middlesex).
ENGLAND: Beauties of England. II, p.66. 1787.
THAMES, River. An history. II, pl.2. 1796.
WATTS, W. Seats of the Nobility. pl.48. 1779.

PORCH HOUSE, Potterne (Wiltshire).
ELYARD, S.J. Old Wiltshire homes. p.30. 1894.

PORKINGTON HALL (Shropshire).
See BROGYNTYN.

PORT ELIOT (Cornwall).
BRITTON, J. Cornwall illustrated. 23. 1832.
BURKE, J.B. Visitation of Seats. Vol.II, p.232. **1853.***
BURKE, J.B. Visitation of Seats. 2.S. Vol.II, p.136. 1855.
COUNTRY LIFE. CIV, 778, 828, 882. 1948.
REPTON, H. Observations on landscape gardening. 192.
1803.

PORTERS PARK (Hertfordshire).
[Sales] PORTERS PARK, 1924, December 2-4 [French
furniture, Chinese porcelain etc.].

PORTHEN-ALLS, Prussia Cove (Cornwall).
COUNTRY LIFE. CXXIII, 955 plan. 1958.

PORT LYMPNE (Kent).
COUNTRY LIFE. LIII, 678, 714 plan. 1923.
COUNTRY LIFE. LXXIII, 116 [Rex Whistler Room]. 1933.
OSWALD, A. Country houses of Kent. 68. 1933.

PORTNALL PARK (Surrey).
PROSSER, G.F. Surrey Seats. p.113. 1828.

POSTLIP HALL (Gloucestershire).
NASH, J. Mansions of England. II, pl.25. 1840.

POTTERS MARSTON HALL
(Leicestershire).
FOSBROOKE, Thomas Henry-
—Potters Marston. I. The Hall by T.H.F., II. Some notes on
the manor by G.F. Farnham. [Bibliogr.notes.] 14pp. Plates
incl. folding map and plans. 26x17 Leicester, 1922. Also in
LEICESTER: Leicestershire Archæological Society
Transactions, XII, 165. 1922.

POULTON HALL (Cheshire).
GREEN, Rodger Lancelyn.
—Poulton-Lancelyn: the story of an ancestral home.
[Bibliogr.notes.] 86pp. 2 plates and genealog. tables. 21x14
Oxford: Oxonian Press, 1948.
BURKE, J.B. Visitation of Seats. Vol.I, p.223. 1852.*
TWYCROSS, E. Mansions of England and Wales. Vol.I, p.64.
1850.

POULTON MANOR (Gloucestershire).
COUNTRY LIFE. CLIX, 1398. 1976.

POUNDISFORD PARK (Somerset).
VIVIAN-NEAL, Arthur Westall and Cecilia Marjory.
— Poundisford Park, Somerset. A catalogue of pictures and
furniture. Compiled by A.W. and C.M.V.-N. 64pp. 25x19
Taunton: privately printed, 1939.
COUNTRY LIFE. XXXIX, 758. 1916.
COUNTRY LIFE. LXXVI, 116 plan, 142, 673 [Portraits]. 1934.
GARNER, T. Domestic architecture. I, p.61 plan. 1911.

POWDERHAM CASTLE (Devonshire).
PEPYS, *Lady* Pauline Mary Louise.
—Powderham Castle, Devon: an illustrated survey [etc.].
32pp. Illus. (2 col., some on covers) incl. maps (on inside
covers.) 14x22 **Derby: E.L.P.** [1960].
BRITTON, J. Devonshire illustrated. 32. 1832.
BUCK, S. & N. Antiquities. I, pls. 67, 68. 1774.
COUNTRY LIFE. XXIII, 486. 1908.
COUNTRY LIFE. CXXXIV. 18 plan, 80, 140. 1963.
DELDERFIELD, E.R. West Country houses. I, 114. 1968.
JONES. **Views of Seats.** II. 1829.
NEALE, J.P. Views of Seats. Vol.I. 1818.

THE EAST VIEW OF POWDERHAM-CASTLE, IN THE COUNTY OF DEVON.

POWDERHAM CASTLE, Devon. From: BUCK (S.&N.). Buck's antiquities, or, venerable remains of ... castles, monasteries, palaces &c. in England and Wales [etc.] London. 1774.

POWIS CASTLE (Montgomeryshire).

LONDON: National Trust for Places of Historic Interest or Natural Beauty.
— Powis Castle, Montgomeryshire. 16pp. Col. illus. (on cover) and 5 plates incl. genealog. table. 24x18 [London, *c*. 1975.]

POWIS CASTLE.
— Powis Castle. 12pp. 5 (1 folding) plates incl. genealog. table. 21x14 [London? 1952?]

BUCK, S. & N. Antiquities. II, pl.414. 1774.

COUNTRY LIFE. XXIII, 666. 1908.

COUNTRY LIFE. XLI, 108 plan, 132. 1917.

COUNTRY LIFE. LXXIX, 598, 624 plan, 652. 1936.

HOARE: Views of Seats. pl.23. 1792.

JONES. Views of Seats. V. 1830.

MORRIS, F.O. Views of Seats. Vol.VI, p.59. 1880.

NEALE, J.P. Views of Seats. 2.S. Vol.V. 1829.

NICHOLAS, T. Counties of Wales. II, 793-5. 1872.

NICOLSON, N. Great Houses of Britain. p.174. 1965.

[Sales] LONDON, 1923, March 20-22 [Selected portion of the library. pt. I.].

[Sales] LONDON, 1955, January 31-February 2 [Selected portion of the library II.].

POXWELL MANOR (Dorsetshire).

COUNTRY LIFE. XXXV, 558. 1914.

HEATH, S. Dorset Manor Houses. 169. 1907.

OSWALD, A. County houses of Dorset. p.92. 1959.

POYNTON (Cheshire).

BURKE, J.B. Visitation of Seats. 2.S. Vol.I, p.106. 1854.*

BURKE, J.B. Visitation of Seats. 2.S. Vol.II, p.164. 1855.*

NEALE, J.P. Views of Seats. 2.S. Vol.V. 1829.

TWYCROSS, E. Mansions of England and Wales. Vol.II, p.85. 1850.

PRADOE (Shropshire).

KENYON, Katherine Mary Rose.
— A house that was loved. [Bibliogr.notes.] xiv, 254pp. Illus. incl. plates and map (on end-paper). 22x14 London: Methuen, 1941.

PRESTON BERMONDSEY (Somerset).

See PRESTON PLUCKNETT MANOR.

PRESTON BROCKHURST (Shropshire).

SHROPSHIRE. Castles & Old Mansions. 53. 1868.

PRESTON HALL (Kent).

BADESLADE, T. Seats in Kent. pl.27. 1750.

BURKE, J.B. Visitation of Seats. 2.S. Vol.II, p.156. 1855.*

HARRIS, J. History of Kent. p.32. 1719.

HASTED, E. Kent. II, 175. 1782.

MORRIS, F.O. Views of Seats. Vol.III, p.75. 1880.

PRESTON HALL (Suffolk).

SANDON, E. Suffolk houses. 198. 1977.

PRESTON MANOR (Sussex).

BRIGHTON: Preston Manor [Thomas-Stanford Museum].
— Preston Manor. Official guide to the Thomas-Stanford Museum together with a history of the manor and its owners by H.D. Roberts. 44pp. 4 illus. 22x13 Brighton, 1935.
11 ed. Official guide ... together with ... a description of the "Macquoid" bequest. 48pp. 3 illus. 24x13. 1948.
16 ed. 1953.
(20 ed.) Preston Manor (Thomas-Stanford Museum) Brighton. A history of the manor and its former owners, and a description of the Macquoid bequest. 40pp. 4 illus. incl. cover. 20x13 (1959).

COUNTRY LIFE. LXXVIII, 12. 1935.

PRESTON PLUCKNETT MANOR (Somerset).

GARNER, T. Domestic architecture. I, p.25. 1911.

PRESTWOLD HALL (Leicestershire).

BURKE, J.B. Visitation of Seats. Vol.I, p.23. 1852.

COUNTRY LIFE. CXXV, 828, 890 plan, 948. 1959.

JONES. Views of Seats. I. 1829.

NEALE, J.P. Views of Seats. Vol.II. 1819.

NICHOLS, J. History of Leicestershire. III, i, 355. 1800.

NICHOLS, J. History of Leicestershire. III, ii, pl. CLIX, 1136. 1804.

THROSBY, J. Views in Leicestershire. p.305. 1789.

PRESTWOOD HALL (Staffordshire).

PLOT, R. Staffordshire. 151. 1686.

PRIDEAUX PLACE (Cornwall).

BRITTON, J. Cornwall illustrated. 31. 1832.

BURKE, J.B. Visitation of Seats. 2.S. Vol.II. p.170. 1855.*

COUNTRY LIFE. CXXXI, 226, 274. 1962.

DELDERFIELD, E.R. West Country houses. I, 120. 1968.

PRINCE'S HOUSE, Kew (Surrey).

See WHITE HOUSE.

PRINCES RISBOROUGH MANOR (Buckinghamshire).

COUNTRY LIFE. LXXIV, 228 plan. 1933.

PRINKNASH PARK (Gloucestershire).
COUNTRY LIFE. XX, 414. 1906.
LATHAM, C. In English Homes. Vol.II, p.333. 1907.
[Sales] PRINKNASH PARK, 1922, September 19, 20 [Contents].
[Sales] STROUD, 1923, September 21 [Estate].

PRIOR PARK. (Somerset).
BURKE, J.B. Visitation of Seats. 2.S. Vol.II, p.224. 1855.*
WATTS, W. Seats of the Nobility. pl.75. 1779.

PRIORY, The Stoke-sub-Hamdon (Somerset).
LONDON: National Trust for Places of Historic Interest or Natural Beauty.
—IRELAND, P.M. The Priory, Stoke-sub-Hamdon. [Bibliogr.] 12pp. Illus. (1 on cover) incl.plan. 21x14 [London] (1979).

PRIORY, The. Warwick (Warwickshire).
NIVEN, W. Old Warwickshire houses. p.22, pl.22. 1878.

PRIORY, The. Windermere (Westmorland).
[Sales] PRIORY, The. Windermere, 1934, July 24-26 [Contents] (K.F. & R.).

PRISCILLY (Pembrokeshire).
BURKE, J.B. Visitation of Seats. Vol.II, p.231. 1853.*

PROSPECT HILL (Staffordshire).
SHAW, S. Staffordshire. II, 122. 1801.

PROSPECT HOUSE, Woodford (Essex).
ENGLAND: Beauties of England. I, p.248. 1787.
ESSEX: A new and complete history. IV, 204. 1771.

PROSPECT PLACE (Surrey).
ENGLAND: Picturesque Views. p.27. 1786-88.

PUDDINGTON HALL (Cheshire).
TWYCROSS, E. Mansions of England and Wales. Vol.I, p.69. 1850. *

PUDLESTON COURT (Herefordshire).
BURKE, J.B. Visitation of Seats. Vol.I, p.144. 1852.

PULL COURT (Worcestershire).
BURKE, J.B. Visitation of Seats. 2.S. Vol.II, p.122. 1855.*

PUNCKNOWLE MANOR (Dorsetshire).
OSWALD, A. Country houses of Dorset. p.83. 1959.

PURLEY HALL (Berkshire).
COUNTRY LIFE. CXLVII, 366. 1970.

PURLEY PARK (Berkshire).
BURKE, J.B. Visitation of Seats. Vol.II, p.217. 1853.*

PURSE CAUNDLE MANOR (Dorsetshire).
COUNTRY LIFE. CXXXIV, 1340 plan, 1406. 1963.
OSWALD, A. Country houses of Dorset. p.55. 1959.

PURTON CHURCH FARM (Wiltshire).
ELYARD, S.J. Old Wiltshire homes. p.25. 1894.

PUSEY HOUSE (Berkshire).
BURKE, J.B. Visitation of Seats. 2.S. Vol. I, p.102. 1854.*
COUNTRY LIFE. CLX, 1902, 1958. 1976.

PUSLINCH (Devonshire).
COUNTRY LIFE. LXXIV, 524. 1933.
DELDERFIELD, E.R. West Country houses. I, 125. 1968.

PUTTENDEN MANOR (Surrey).
PUTTENDEN MANOR.
— Puttenden Manor. 24pp. Illus. (Some col., some on covers) incl. map. 19x16 (Derby: E.L.P., 1970.)

PYE NEST (Yorkshire).
BURKE, J.B. Visitation of Seats. Vol.II, p.243. 1853.*
BURKE, J.B. Visitation of Seats. 2.S. Vol.I, p.210. 1854.
YORKSHIRE. Picturesque views. 1885.

PYLEWELL PARK (Hampshire).
BURKE, J.B. Visitation of Seats. Vol.I, p.157. 1852.*
CAMPBELL, C. Vitruvius Britannicus. IVth. pls.102, 103. 1739.
GROVE, R.A. Seats in the neighbourhood of Lymington. 1832.

PYNES, The. (Devonshire).
BURKE, J.B. Visitation of Seats. Vol.II, p.15. 1853.*
MORRIS, F.O. Views of Seats. Vol.VI, p.27. 1880.

PYRFORD COURT (Surrey).
[Sales] PYRFORD COURT, 1968, June 4, 5 [Contents].

PYRGO PARK (Essex).
[Sales] PYRGO PARK, 1856, May 13-17, 19-22 [Contents].

PYTCHLEY MANOR (Northamptonshire).
GOTCH, J.A. Squires' Homes. 17. 1939.

PYT HOUSE (Wiltshire).
BURKE, J.B. Visitation of Seats. 2.S. Vol.I, p.186. 1854.*

QUANTOCK LODGE (Somerset).
[Sales] QUANTOCK LODGE, 1920, September 6 and following days [Furniture etc.].

QUARTERS, The. Alresford (Essex).
COUNTRY LIFE. CXXIV, 1040. 1958.

QUEBEC HOUSE, Westerham (Kent).
LONDON: National Trust for Places of Historic Interest or Natural Beauty.
—Quebec House. 30pp. Illus. 18x12 London [c. 1945].

New ed. Quebec House, Kent. 16pp. Illus. (1 col. on cover) incl. plates. 21x14 [London] 1983.

COUNTRY LIFE. XLII, 252. 1917.

OSWALD, A. Country houses of Kent. 40. 1933.

QUEEN HOO HALL (Hertfordshire).
COUNTRY LIFE. CXXXI, 594. 1962.

QUEENSBURY VILLA, Richmond (Surrey).
BURKE, J.B. Visitation of Seats. 2.S. Vol.I, p.207. 1854.*

QUENBY HALL (Leicestershire).
COUNTRY LIFE. XVI, 342. 1904.

COUNTRY LIFE. XXX, 550 plan, 590. 1911.

COUNTRY LIFE. XLVII, 836 [Furniture]. 1920.

LATHAM, C. In English Homes. Vol.II, p.245. 1907.

NICHOLS, J. History of Leicestershire. III, i, 296 [Plan]. 1800.

NICHOLS, J. History of Leicestershire. III, ii, pl.CLVIII, 1135. 1804.

THROSBY, J. Views in Leicestershire. p.307. 1789.

TIPPING, H.A. English Homes. Early Renaissance, p.371. 1912.

TIPPING, H.A. English Homes. Period III, Vol.I, p.284. 1922.

[Sales] LONDON, 1913, June 27 [Estate].

[Sales] QUENBY HALL, 1920 September 21-24 [Furniture, pictures, tapestries etc.]. (K.F. & R.).

[Sales] QUENBY HALL, 1924, May 7-9 [Furniture, pictures, tapestries etc.]. (K.F. & R.).

[Sales] QUENBY HALL, 1972, October 23-25 [Contents].

QUENDON HALL (Essex).
ESSEX: A new and complete history. III, 34. 1770.

RUSH, J.A. Seats in Essex. p.134. 1897.

[Sales] QUENDON HALL, 1906, July 25-28 [Contents].

QUERNMORE PARK HALL (Lancashire).
BARTLETT, J. Mansions of England and Wales. pl.55. 1853.

BURKE, J.B. Visitation of Seats. Vol.I, p.152. 1852.*

TWYCROSS, E. Mansions of England and Wales. Vol.II, p.13. 1847.

QUEX PARK (Kent).
GREENWOOD, C. Kent. 327. 1838.

QUIDENHAM HALL (Norfolk).
BURKE, J.B. Visitation of Seats. 2.S. Vol.II, p.162. 1855.*

CROMWELL, T.K. Excursions in Norfolk. II, p.164. 1819.

NEALE, J.P. Views of Seats. 2.S. Vol.I. 1824.

QUINCES, Bramshott (Hampshire).
COUNTRY LIFE. LXI, 489 plan. 1927.

QUORNDON HALL (Leicestershire).
See QUORN HALL.

QUORN HALL (Leicestershire).
NICHOLS, J. History of Leicestershire. III, i, 101. 1798.

NICHOLS, J. History of Leicestershire. III, ii, pl.CLVII, 1131. 1804.

THROSBY, J. Views in Leicestershire. p.309. 1789.

QUORN HOUSE (Leicestershire).
BURKE, J.B. Visitation of Seats. Vol.I, p.58. 1852.*

NICHOLS, J. History of Leicestershire. III, i, 100. 1800.

RABY CASTLE (Durham).
RABY, Durham.
— Raby Castle. 32pp. Illus. (5 col. incl. 1 on cover.) 20x16 (Derby: English Life Publications, 1972.)

SCOTT, Owen Stanley.
— Raby: its castle and its lords. 68pp. Illus. incl. folding plan. 18x12 Barnard Castle: privately printed, 1906.
7 ed. Revised by S.E. Harrison. 64pp. Illus. incl. plan. 21x13 [Raby?] 1971.

ANGUS, W. Seats of the Nobility. pl.25. 1787.

BUCK, S. & N. Antiquities. I, pl.88. 1774.

BURKE, J.B. Visitation of Seats. Vol.I, p.64. 1852.*

COUNTRY LIFE. II, 321. 1897.

COUNTRY LIFE. XXXVIII, 760 plan, 804. 1915.

COUNTRY LIFE. CXLVI, 78, 150. 1969.

COUNTRY LIFE. CXLVII, 18, 66, 186. 1970.

JONES. Views of Seats. I. 1829.

MORRIS, F.O. Views of Seats. Vol.II, p.15. 1880.

NEALE, J.P. Views of Seats. Vol.I. 1818.

TIPPING, H.A. English Homes. Period I, Vol.I, p.258. 1921.

RACEDOWN (Dorsetshire).
OSWALD, A. Country houses of Dorset. p.170. 1959.

RACKENFORD MANOR (Devonshire).
COUNTRY LIFE. XCIX, 164, 210. 1946.

RACKHEATH HALL (Norfolk).
BURKE, J.B. Visitation of Seats. 2.S. Vol.I, p.171. 1854.*

RADBOURNE HALL (Derbyshire).
BURKE, J.B. Visitation of Seats. 2.S. Vol.II, p.184. 1855.*
TILLEY, J. Halls of Derbyshire.II, p.139. 1893.

RADCLIFFE HALL (Nottinghamshire).
BURKE, J.B. Visitation of Seats. Vol.I, p.150. 1852.*

RADNOR HOUSE, Twickenham (Middlesex).
COUNTRY LIFE. LXXXII, 12. 1937.

RADWAY GRANGE (Warwickshire).
BURKE, J.B. Visitation of Seats. Vol.II, p.16. 1853.*
COUNTRY LIFE. C, 440, 486. 1946.

RAGDALE NEW HALL (Leicestershire).
NICHOLS, J. History of Leicestershire. III, i, 386. 1800.

RAGDALE OLD HALL (Leicestershire).
THOMPSON, Alexander Hamilton.
—Ragdale old hall and church by A.H.T. With notes on the manor of Ragdale by G.F. Farnham. 16pp. Plates incl. plans. 26x16 [Leicester? 1927?]. Also in LEICESTER: Leicestershire Archæological Society. Transactions, XIV, 183. 1925-6.
COUNTRY LIFE. XIX, 126. 1906.
GOTCH, J.A. Architecture of the Renaissance. I, p.12. 1894.
LATHAM, C. In English Homes. Vol.II, p.297. 1907.
NICHOLS, J. History of Leicestershire. III, i, 386. 1800.

RAGLEY HALL (Warwickshire).
RAGLEY HALL.
— Ragley Hall: an illustrated survey [etc.]. 32pp. Illus. (some col., some on covers) incl. maps (on end-papers). 14x22 Derby: E.L.P. [1958].
COUNTRY LIFE. LV, 438, 476 plan. 1924.
COUNTRY LIFE. CXXIII, 938, 1006 plan. 1958.
KIP, J. Nouveau théâtre de la Grande Bretagne. I, pl.71. 1715.
KROLL, A. Historic houses. 146. 1969.
NEALE, J.P. Views of Seats. Vol.IV. 1821.
SMITH, W. History of the County of Warwick. 288. 1830.

RAIKES HALL (Lancashire).
BARTLETT, J. Mansions of England and Wales. pl.88. 1853.
TWYCROSS, E. Mansions of England and Wales. Vol.II, p.48. 1847.

RAINHAM HALL (Essex).
COUNTRY LIFE. XLVII, 760 plan. 1920.
TIPPING, H.A. English Homes. Period V, Vol.I, p.237. 1921.

RAINHAM HALL (Norfolk).
See RAYNHAM HALL.

RAINSCOMBE (Wiltshire).
BURKE, J.B. Visitation of Seats. Vol.II, p.124. 1853.*

RAINTHORPE HALL (Norfolk).
BIRKBECK, G. Old Norfolk houses. 92. 1908.
GARRATT, T. Halls of Norfolk. pls. 39, 40. 1890.
[Sales] NORWICH, Royal Hotel, 1929, July 6 [R. Hall and estate].

RAMPSBECK LODGE (Cumberland).
BURKE, J.B. Visitation of Seats. Vol.II, p.124. 1853.*

RAMPYNDENE, Burwash (Sussex).
COUNTRY LIFE. XCIX, 394. 1946.

RAMSBURY MANOR (Wiltshire).
COUNTRY LIFE. English Country Houses: Caroline. p.178. 1966.
COUNTRY LIFE. XXII, 198. 1907.
COUNTRY LIFE. XLVIII, 432, 468. 1920.
COUNTRY LIFE. CXXX, 1376, 1526, 1580. 1961.
JONES. Views of Seats. II. 1829.
LATHAM, C. In English Homes. Vol.III, p.159. 1909.
NEALE, J.P. Views of Seats. Vol.V. 1822.
[Sales] LONDON, 1953, December 2 [Portraits etc.].

RAMSDEN CRAYS (Essex).
BURKE, J.B. Visitation of Seats. 2.S. Vol.I, p.122. 1854.*

RAMSEY ABBEY (Huntingdonshire).
BURKE, J.B. Visitation of Seats. Vol.II, p.23. 1853.*

RANDALLS PARK (Surrey).
BRAYLEY, E.W. History of Surrey. IV, 433. 1841.

RANGERS, The. Woodmancote (Gloucestershire).
BURKE, J.B. Visitation of Seats. Vol.I, p.35. 1852.*

RANSTON HOUSE (Dorsetshire).
HUTCHINS, J. Vitruvius Dorsettiensis. pl.24. 1816.
HUTCHINS, J. History of Dorset. IV, 93. 1870.
OSWALD, A. Country houses of Dorset. p.161. 1959.
WATTS, W. Seats of the Nobility. pl.8. 1779.

RANTON ABBEY (Staffordshire).
BURKE, J.B. Visitation of Seats. 2.S. Vol.II, p.132. 1855.*

RASHLEIGH BARTON (Devonshire).
TIPPING, H.A. English Homes. Period III, Vol.II, p.103. 1927.

RASPIT HILL, Sevenoaks (Kent).
COUNTRY LIFE. LXXVI, 344 plan. 1934.

RAUCEBY HALL (Lincolnshire).
BURKE, J.B. Visitation of Seats. Vol.I, p.82. 1852.*

RAVENFIELD (Yorkshire).
CAMPBELL, C. Vitruvius Britannicus. IVth. pls. 108, 109. 1739.

RAVENINGHAM HALL (Norfolk).
CROMWELL, T.K. Excursions in Norfolk. I, p.80. 1818.

RAVENSCROFT HALL (Cheshire).
TWYCROSS, E. Mansions of England and Wales. Vol.I, p.150. 1850.

RAVENSWORTH CASTLE (Durham).
BUCK, S. & N. Antiquities. I, pl.89. 1774.
BURKE, J.B. Visitation of Seats. 2.S. Vol.I, p.62. 1854.*
MORRIS, F.O. Views of Seats. Vol.V, p.17. 1880.

RAWCLIFFE HALL (Lancashire).
TWYCROSS, E. Mansions of England and Wales. Vol.II, p.54. 1847.*

RAWDON HALL (Yorkshire).
YORKSHIRE. Picturesque views. 1885.

RAYNHAM HALL (Norfolk).
DURHAM, James Andrew Cunninghame.
— The collection of pictures at Raynham Hall, being 3 annotated catalogues ... 1810, the property of G., 2nd. Marquis Townshend, 1904, J.J.D.S., 6th. Marquis Townshend and 1926, of G. 7th. Marquis Townshend. To which is added a catalogue of pictures, miniatures and prints, the property of the Lady A. Durham, at her house in Raynham. Compiled with historical notes by J.D. 34ff. 25x15 n.p. privately printed, 1926.
BIRKBECK, G. Old Norfolk houses. 95. 1908.
COUNTRY LIFE. English Country Houses: Caroline. p.57. 1966.
COUNTRY LIFE. XXIV, 90. 1908.
COUNTRY LIFE. LVIII, 742, 782 plan. 1925.
CROMWELL, T.K. Excursions in Norfolk. II, p.4. 1819.
LATHAM, C. In English Homes. Vol.III, p.103. 1909.
NEALE, J.P. Views of Seats. Vol.III. 1820.
WATTS, W. Seats of the Nobility. pl.52. 1779.
[Sales] LONDON, 1904, March 4 [Furniture from R.H.].

[Sales] LONDON, 1904, March 5, 7 [Pictures, family portraits from R.H.].

READER'S HOUSE, Ludlow (Shropshire).
COUNTRY LIFE. C, 763. 1946.

READ HALL (Lancashire).
BARTLETT, J. Mansions of England and Wales. pls. 25, 26. 1853.
BURKE, J.B. Visitation of Seats. 2.S. Vol.II, p.169. 1855.*
TWYCROSS, E. Mansions of England and Wales. Vol.I, p.24. 1847.

REDDISH HOUSE, Broad Chalke (Wiltshire).
COUNTRY LIFE. CXXI, 540, 596. 1957.
[Sales] REDDISH HOUSE, 1980, June 9, 10 [Works of art, furniture etc.].

REDGRAVE HALL (Suffolk).
BURKE, J.B. Visitation of Seats. 2.S. Vol.I, p.91. 1854.*
CROMWELL, T.K. Excursions in Suffolk. I, p.115. 1818.
NEALE, J.P. Views of Seats. Vol.IV. 1821.

RED HALL (Durham).
BURKE, J.B. Visitation of Seats. Vol.I, p.116. 1852.*

RED HOUSE, Bexleyheath (Kent).
COUNTRY LIFE. CXXVII, 1382 plan. 1960.
OSWALD, A. Country houses of Kent. 68. 1933.

RED HOUSE (Yorkshire).
BURKE, J.B. Visitation of Seats. 2.S. Vol.I, p.83. 1854.*

REDLEAF (Kent).
GREENWOOD, C. Kent. 111. 1838.

RED LODGE, Bristol (Gloucestershire).
COUNTRY LIFE. XIV, 721. 1903.
COUNTRY LIFE. CXXVIII, 238. 1960.

REDLYNCH HOUSE (Wiltshire).
ILCHESTER, Henry Edward Fox-Strangways, *Earl of*.
— Catalogue of pictures belonging to the Earl of Ilchester. (At Melbury House, Redlynch House, Abbotsbury Castle, and 42, Belgrave Square; index of portraits.) 24x18 (London) privately printed at the Chiswick Press, 1883.

RED SCAR (Lancashire).
BARTLETT, J. Mansions of England and Wales. pls. 86, 87. 1853.
TWYCROSS, E. Mansions of England and Wales. Vol.II, p.48. 1847.

REEDHAM HALL (Norfolk).
BURKE, J.B. Visitation of Seats. Vol.I, p.115. 1852.*

REIGATE PRIORY (Surrey).
COUNTRY LIFE. XLIII, 362. 1918.
MANNING, O. Surrey. I, 295. 1804.
PROSSER, G.F. Surrey Seats. p.81. 1828.
[Sales] REIGATE PRIORY, 1921, June 13-18 [Contents].

REMPSTONE HALL (Dorsetshire).
BURKE, J.B. Visitation of Seats. 2.S. Vol.II, p.128. 1855.*

RENDCOMB PARK (Gloucestershire).
ATKYNS, R. Gloucestershire. p.324. 1768.
RUDDER, S. Gloucestershire. 621. 1779.

RENDLESHAM HALL (Suffolk).
CROMWELL, T.K. Excursions in Suffolk. II, p.57. 1819.
DAVY, H. Seats in Suffolk. pl.8. 1827.
NEALE, J.P. Views of Seats. Vol.IV. 1821.
[Sales] LONDON, 1809, May 17, 18 [Pictures from R.H.].

RENISHAW HALL (Derbyshire).
BURKE, J.B. Visitation of Seats. 2.S. Vol.I, p.16. 1854.*
COUNTRY LIFE. LXXXIII, 506. 1938.

REPTON HALL (Derbyshire).
TILLEY, J. Halls of Derbyshire. IV, p.47. 1902.

RESTORATION HOUSE, Rochester (Kent).
COUNTRY LIFE. V, 645. 1899.

RESTROP (Wiltshire).
ELYARD, S.J. Old Wiltshire homes. p.65. 1894.

REVESBY ABBEY (Lincolnshire).
LINCOLNSHIRE. A selection of views. 23. 1805.
[Sales] REVESBY ABBEY, 1953, December 2,3 [Contents].

RHEOLA (Glamorganshire).
BURKE, J.B. Visitation of Seats. Vol.I, p.200. 1852.*

RHUAL (Flintshire).
COUNTRY LIFE. XCIII, 1144. 1943.

RHYDD COURT (Worcestershire).
MORRIS, F.O. Views of Seats. Vol.V, p.23. 1880.

RIALTON PRIORY (Cornwall).
COUNTRY LIFE. XC, 582 plan. 1941.
CROMWELL, T.K. Excursions in Cornwall. p.98. 1824.

RIBBESFORD HOUSE (Worcestershire).
NASH, T.R. Worcestershire. I, 38. 1781.

RIBBLETON HALL (Lancashire).
BARTLETT, J. Mansions of England and Wales. pl.93. 1853.
TWYCROSS, E. Mansions of England and Wales. Vol.II, p.56. 1847.

RIBBY HALL (Lancashire).
BARTLETT, J. Mansions of England and Wales. pls.82, 83. 1853.
TWYCROSS, E. Mansions of England and Wales. Vol.II, p.43. 1847.

RIBER HALL (Derbyshire).
TILLEY, J. Halls of Derbyshire. II, p.247. 1893.

RIBSTON HALL (Yorkshire).
BURKE, J.B. Visitation of Seats. Vol.I, p.73. 1852.*
COUNTRY LIFE. XIX, 198. 1906.
COUNTRY LIFE. CLIV. 1050, 1142. 1973.
KIP, J. Nouveau théâtre de la Grande Bretagne. I, pl.61. 1715.
LATHAM, C. In English Homes. Vol.II, p.347. 1907.

RIBTON HALL (Cumberland).
CUMBERLAND: C. & W.A. & A. Extra Series VIII, 334. 1892.

RIBY GROVE (Lincolnshire).
BURKE, J.B. Visitation of Seats. 2.S. Vol.I, p.70. 1854.*

RICHMOND PARK NEW LODGE or **WHITE LODGE** (Surrey).
See WHITE LODGE.

RICARDS LODGE, Wimbledon (Surrey).
[Sales] RICARDS LODGE, Wimbledon, 1939, June 21, 22 [Contents]. (K.F. & R.).

RIDDLESWORTH HALL (Norfolk).
NEALE, J.P. Views of Seats. Vol.III. 1820.

RIDGE, The. (Derbyshire).
TILLEY, J. Halls of Derbyshire. I, p.93. 1892.

RIDGE END, Wentworth (Surrey).
COUNTRY LIFE. LXXI, 332 plan. 1932.

RIDGEMEAD, Englefield Green (Surrey).
COUNTRY LIFE. LXXXVII, 144, 172 plan. 1940.

RIDGEWAY (Pembrokeshire).
BURKE, J.B. Visitation of Seats. 2.S. Vol.II, p.40. 1855.*

RIDGMONT (Lancashire).
BARTLETT, J. Mansions of England and Wales. pl.149. 1853.
TWYCROSS, E. Mansions of England and Wales. Vol.III, p.86. 1847.

RIGMADEN PARK (Westmorland).
BURKE, J.B. Visitation of Seats. Vol.I, p.253. 1852.*

RINGWOULD HOUSE (Kent).
GREENWOOD, C. Kent. 433. 1838.

RIPLEY CASTLE (Yorkshire).
RIPLEY CASTLE.
— Ripley Castle, Yorkshire, the historic home of the Ingilby family. 16pp. Illus. (some on covers) incl. map. 14x20 (Derby: E.L.P.) [1960.]
COUNTRY LIFE. LXXII, 182, 210. 1932.
MORRIS, F.O. Views of Seats. Vol.I, p.63. 1880.
NEALE, J.P. Views of Seats. 2.S. Vol.V. 1829.
WHEATER, W. Mansions of Yorkshire. p.205. 1888.

RIPPLE COURT (Kent).
GREENWOOD, C. Kent. 432. 1838.

RISE PARK (Yorkshire).
BURKE, J.B. Visitation of Seats. 2.S. Vol.II, p.115. 1855.*

RISDEN HOUSE (Hertfordshire).
See JULIANS.

RISLEY HALL (Derbyshire).
TILLEY, J. Halls of Derbyshire. IV, p.119. 1902.

RIVENHALL PLACE (Essex).
CROMWELL, T.K. Excursions in Essex. I, p.45. 1825.
RUSH, J.A. Seats in Essex. p.137. 1897.*

RIVER HILL (Kent).
GREENWOOD, C. Kent. 97. 1838.

RIVINGTON HALL (Lancashire).
[Sales] RIVINGTON HALL, 1925, November 16, 17 [Contents]. (K.F. & R.).

RIVINGTON, The Bungalow (Lancashire).
[Sales] RIVINGTON, The Bungalow, 1925, November 9-13 [Contents]. (K.F. & R.).

ROAD NOOK (Derbyshire).
TILLEY, J. Halls of Derbyshire. III, p.55. 1899.

ROBY HALL (Lancashire).
BARTLETT, J. Mansions of England and Wales. pl. 108. 1853.
PYNE, W.H. Lancashire illustrated. 101. 1831.
TWYCROSS, E. Mansions of England and Wales. Vol.III, p.46. 1847.

ROCHDALE MANOR (Lancashire).
BURKE, J.B. Visitation of Seats. Vol.I, p.192. 1852.*

ROCKBEARE MANOR (Devonshire).
COUNTRY LIFE. LXVII, 570, 642. 1930.

ROCKINGHAM CASTLE (Northamptonshire).
ROCKINGHAM CASTLE.
— Rockingham Castle, Northamptonshire. An opportunity occurs of renting ... Rockingham Castle, Market Harborough [etc.]. 20pp. Illus. 31x23 London: Lofts & Warner (1926).
WATSON, Michael Saunders.
— Rockingham Castle. 24pp. Illus. (some col., some on covers) incl. plan and genealog. table. 19x16 (Derby: E.L.P., 1973.)
WISE, Charles.
— Rockingham Castle and the Watsons. [Bibliogr. notes.] Illus. incl. plates (some folding), incl. plans and genealog. tables. 25x20 London: Elliot Stock; Kettering: Goss, 1891.
BUCK, S. & N. Antiquities. I, pl.212. 1774.
COUNTRY LIFE. L, 44, 76, 102. 1921.
GOTCH, J.A. Halls of Northants. p.22. 1936.
NEALE, J.P. Views of Seats. Vol.III. 1820.

ROCKSAVAGE (Cheshire).
ORMEROD, G. Cheshire. I, 552. 1882.

RODBOURNE (Wiltshire).
BURKE, J.B. Visitation of Seats. 2.S. Vol.I, p.240. 1854.*

RODD, The. (Herefordshire).
ROBINSON, C.J. Mansions of Herefordshire. pl.16. 1873.

Drawn by H.Davy.

Engraved by J.Lambert.

RENDLESHAM HOUSE, SUFFOLK.

THE SEAT OF THE RIGHT HON.ᵇˡᵉ LORD RENDLESHAM.

Published by R.Day. Southwold, Nov.ʳ 1824.

RENDLESHAM HALL, Suffolk. From: DAVY (H.). *Views of the seats of the noblemen and gentlemen in Suffolk*, Southwold, 1827.

RODE HALL (Cheshire).
JONES. Views of Seats. I. 1829.
NEALE, J.P. Views of Seats. 2.S. Vol.I. 1824.
TWYCROSS, E. Mansions of England and Wales. Vol.I, p.129. 1850.*

RODMARTON MANOR (Gloucestershire).
COUNTRY LIFE. LXIX, 422. 1931.
COUNTRY LIFE.CLXIV, 1178, 1298. 1978.

RODWAY MANOR (Gloucestershire).
HODGES, E. Ancient English homes. 72. 1895.

ROECLIFFE HALL (Leicestershire).
BURKE, J.B. Visitation of Seats. Vol.I, p.158. 1852.*

ROEHAMPTON, Earl of Bessborough's Villa (Surrey).
See MANRESA [PARK HOUSE].

ROEHAMPTON COURT (Surrey).
COUNTRY LIFE. XLVIII, 272. 1920.

ROEHAMPTON HOUSE, Putney Park (Surrey).
CAMPBELL, C. New Vitruvius Britannicus. I, pls. 19-21. 1802.
NEALE, J.P. Views of Seats. 2.S. Vol.III. 1826.

ROEHAMPTON HOUSE, Queen Mary's Hospital (Surrey).
CAMPBELL, C. Vitruvius Britannicus. I, pls.80, 81. 1715.
COUNTRY LIFE. XXXVIII, 232 plan. 1915.

ROKEBY HALL (Yorkshire).
BURKE, J.B. Visitation of Seats. 2.S. Vol.II, p.221. 1855.*
CAMPBELL, C. Vitruvius Britannicus. III, pl.90. 1725.
COUNTRY LIFE. English Country Houses: Early Georgian. p.123. 1955.
COUNTRY LIFE. XLII, 276, 300. 1917.
COUNTRY LIFE. CXVII, 1302 plan. 1955.
TIPPING, H.A. English Homes. Period V, Vol.I, p.155. 1921.

ROLLESTON HALL (Leicestershire).
NICHOLS, J. History of Leicestershire. II, ii, 443. 1798.

ROLLESTON HALL (Staffordshire).
BURKE, J.B. Visitation of Seats. Vol.I, p.60. 1852.*
MORRIS, F.O. Views of Seats. Vol.IV, p.7. 1880.

ROLLS PARK (Essex).
COUNTRY LIFE. XLIV, 172. 1918.
NEALE, J.P. Views of Seats. 2.S. Vol.III. 1826.

ROMDEN PLACE (Kent).
[Sales] ROMDEN PLACE, 1919, September 24, 25 [English furniture, pictures etc.].

ROMELEY HALL (Derbyshire).
TILLEY, J. Halls of Derbyshire. III, p.103. 1899.

ROOKERY, The. (Surrey).
NEALE, J.P. Views of Seats. Vol.IV. 1821.

ROOKSBURY PARK (Hampshire).
HAMPSHIRE. Architectural views. 1830.

ROOS HALL, Beccles (Suffolk).
SANDON, E. Suffolk houses. 165. 1977.

ROSAMOND'S BOWER, Fulham (Middlesex).
CROKER, Thomas Crofton.
— A description of Rosamund's Bower, Fulham, ... the residence of T.C.C., Esq. With an inventory of the pictures, furniture, curiosities, &c. 42pp. Illus. incl. plates and engr. on title-page. 26x21 [London?] privately printed, 1843.
With additional material including an etching and 2 MS. letters from T.C.C., inserted.

ROSCOTE, The. Heswall (Cheshire).
BROCKLEBANK, Thomas.
— A catalogue of paintings, etchings, engravings, etc., in the possession of T.B., at The Roscote, Heswall, Chester. 88pp. Illus. (on cover.) 22x18 London: privately printed at the Chiswick Press, 1896.
Letter from the author to Miss Ffoulkes inserted.

ROSE CASTLE (Cumberland).
WILSON, *Rev.* James.
— Rose Castle, the residential seat of the Bishop of Carlisle. [Bibliogr. notes.] Plates (1 folding) incl. plan and map. 22x14 Carlisle: Thurnam & Sons, 1912.
BUCK, S. & N. Antiquities. I, pl.49. 1774.
ENGLAND: Beauties of England. I, p.132. 1787.

ROSE HALL, Barsham (Suffolk).
CROMWELL, T.K. Excursions in Suffolk. II, p.123. 1819.

ROSE HILL (Kent).
GREENWOOD, C. Kent. 276. 1838.

ROSEHILL (Sussex).
BURKE, J.B. Visitation of Seats. 2.S. Vol.I, p.103. 1854.*

ROSSALL HALL (Lancashire).
TWYCROSS, E. Mansions of England and Wales. Vol.II, p.44. 1847.*

ROTHAMSTED (Hertfordshire).
HARPENDEN: Rothamsted Experimental Station.
— BOALCH, D.H. The manor of Rothamsted. [Bibliogr.] Illus. (1 col. on cover) incl. 17 plates, elevation, plan, map, facsimiles and folding genealog. table. 22x16 Harpenden, 1953.
COUNTRY LIFE. XIX, 270, 306, 342. 1906.
LATHAM, C. In English Homes. Vol.II, p.307. 1909.

ROTHERFIELD PARK (Hampshire).
COUNTRY LIFE. CIII, 926. 1948.
HAMPSHIRE: Architectural views. 1830.

ROTHERWAS HOUSE (Herefordshire).
BURKE, J.B. Visitation of Seats. 2.S. Vol.II, p.124. 1855.*
JONES. Views of Seats. II. 1829.
NEALE, J.P. Views of Seats. 2.S. Vol.II. 1825.

ROTHLEY TEMPLE (Leicestershire).
NICHOLS, J. History of Leicestershire. III, ii, 956, 1100. 1804.
THROSBY, J. Views in Leicestershire. p.277. 1789.

ROTHWELL MANOR (Northamptonshire).
GOTCH, J.A. Halls of Northants. p.46. 1936.

ROTHWELL MARKET HOUSE (Northamptonshire).
GOTCH, J.A. Halls of Northants. p.45. 1936.

ROUNDHAY PARK (Yorkshire).
BURKE, J.B. Visitation of Seats. 2.S. Vol.I, p.56. 1854.*

ROUNTON GRANGE (Yorkshire).
COUNTRY LIFE. XXXVII, 906 plan. 1915.

ROUSHAM (Oxfordshire).
ROUSHAM.
— Rousham Park. 16pp. Illus. (some col., some on covers) incl. map. 22x14 Oxford: Oxford Publishing Co. [c.1975].
COUNTRY LIFE. English Country Houses: Early Georgian. p.155. 1955.
COUNTRY LIFE. XXVII, 306. 1910.
COUNTRY LIFE. XCIX, 900, 946. 1946.
COUNTRY LIFE. CIV, 384 [Furniture]. 1948.

ROUS LENCH COURT (Worcestershire).
NIVEN, W. Old Worcestershire houses. p.29, pl.11. 1873.
[Sales] ROUS LENCH COURT, 1925 [House].
[Sales] ROUS LENCH COURT, 1926, July 26 & October 11 [House].

ROWFANT (Sussex).
LOCKER-LAMPSON, Frederick.
— A catalogue of the printed books, manuscripts, autograph letters, drawings and pictures collected by F.L.-L. Engr. plates (1 by George Cruikshank) and cuts. 25x16 London: Quaritch, 1886.
An appendix to the Rowfant Library. A catalogue of the printed books ... collected since the printing of the first catalogue in 1886 by the late F.L.-L. Illus. incl. plates. London: at the Chiswick Press, 1900.
COUNTRY LIFE. L. 686. 1921.

ROWLEY (Yorkshire).
COUNTRY LIFE. CXIV, 1490. 1953.

ROWLEY HALL (Staffordshire).
[Sales] ROWLEY HALL, 1916, November 8 [Decorative furniture]. (K., F. & R.).

ROWNALL HALL (Staffordshire).
BURKE, J.B. Visitation of Seats. Vol.I, p.41. 1852.*

ROWTON CASTLE (Shropshire).
BURKE, J.B. Visitation of Seats. Vol.II, p.110. 1853.*

ROYAL FORT, Bristol (Gloucestershire).
COUNTRY LIFE. XXXIX, 647. 1916.
TIPPING, H.A. English Homes. Period V, Vol.I, p.331. 1921.

ROYDON HALL (Kent).
COUNTRY LIFE. LXXXVII, 198. 1940.

RUCKLEY GRANGE (Shropshire).
LEACH, F. Seats of Shropshire. p.335. 1891.

RUDDING PARK (Yorkshire).
RUDDING PARK.
— Rudding Park (Harrogate): a brief description and guide. (Foreword by S. Sitwell.) 24pp. Illus. (1 on cover) incl. plan. 14x20 (Bradford) [1954?]
COUNTRY LIFE. English Country Houses: Late Georgian. p.74. 1958.
COUNTRY LIFE. CV, 254, 310 plan. 1949.
[Sales] RUDDING PARK, 1972, October 16, 17 [Remaining contents].

RUDDINGTON GRANGE (Nottinghamshire).
BURKE, J.B. Visitation of Seats. Vol.I, p.97. 1852.*

RUFFORD ABBEY (Nottinghamshire).
COUNTRY LIFE. XIV, 650. 1903.

LATHAM, C. In English Homes. Vol.I, p.201. 1904.

MALAN, A.H. More famous homes. p.233. 1902.

NOBLE, T. Counties of Chester, ... Lincoln. p.14. 1836.

[Sales] RUFFORD ABBEY, 1938, October 11 and following days [The Rufford collection]. (K.F. & R.).

RUFFORD NEW HALL (Lancashire).
BARTLETT, J. Mansions of England and Wales. pl.40. 1853.

BURKE, J.B. Visitation of Seats. 2.S. Vol.I, p.47. 1854.*

NEALE, J.P. Views of Seats. Vol.II. 1819.

TWYCROSS, E. Mansions of England and Wales. Vol.I, p.39. 1847.

RUFFORD OLD HALL (Lancashire).
LONDON: National Trust for Places of Historic Interest or Natural Beauty.
—Rufford Old Hall. Rev. ed. 14pp. 4 plates. 18x12 London, 1944.
3 ed. 1947.

Rev. ed. Rufford Old Hall, Lancashire. [Bibliogr.] 40pp. Illus. (1 col. on cover) incl. plan and genealog. table. 21x14 [London] 1983.

BARTLETT, J. Mansions of England and Wales. pl.43. 1853.

COUNTRY LIFE. LXVI, 528, 570. 1929.

COUNTRY LIFE. CVIII, 773. 1950.

GRAY, H. Old halls of Lancashire. p.85. 1893.

TIPPING, H.A. English Homes. Period I & II, Vol.II, p.233. 1937.

TWYCROSS, E. Mansions of England and Wales. Vol.I, p.39. 1847.

RUG (Merionethshire).
BURKE, J.B. Visitation of Seats. Vol.I, p.230. 1852.*

NICHOLAS, T. Counties of Wales. II, p.669. 1872.

RUNNYMEDE PARK (Surrey).
BURKE, J.B. Visitation of Seats. 2.S. Vol.II, p.128. 1855.*

RUPERRA CASTLE (Glamorganshire).
NEALE, J.P. Views of Seats. Vol.V. 1822.

RUSHALL HALL (Staffordshire).
SHAW, S. Staffordshire. II, 66. 1801.

RUSHBROOKE HALL (Suffolk).
COUNTRY LIFE. XIV, 542. 1903.

CROMWELL, T.K. Excursions in Suffolk. I, p.42. 1818.

LATHAM, C. In English Homes. Vol.I, p.125. 1904.

NEALE, J.P. Views of Seats. Vol.IV, 1821.

[Sales] RUSHBROOKE HALL, 1919, December 10, 11 [Contents].

RUSHDEN HALL (Northamptonshire).
COUNTRY LIFE. CXLII, 591. 1967.

GOTCH, J.A. Squires' Homes. 26. 1939.

RUSHDEN PLACE (Hertfordshire).
See JULIANS.

RUSHTON HALL (Northamptonshire).
BURKE, J.B. Visitation of Seats. 2.S. Vol.I, p.172. 1854.*

COUNTRY LIFE. XXVI, 454, 490. 1909.

GOTCH, J.A. Architecture of the Renaissance. I, p.36 plan. 1894.

GOTCH, J.A. Halls of Northants. p.38. 1936.

JONES. Views of Seats. I. 1829.

LATHAM, C. In English Homes. Vol.III, p.75. 1909.

MORRIS, F.O. Views of Seats. Vol.IV, p.11. 1880.

NEALE, J.P. Views of Seats. 2.S. Vol.III. 1826.

RICHARDSON, C.J. Old English mansions. III. 1845.

TIPPING, H.A. English Homes. Period III, Vol.II, p.69. 1927.

RUSHTON HALL, Triangular Lodge (Northamptonshire).
GOTCH, John Alfred.
— A complete account, illustrated by measured drawings, of the buildings erected in Northamptonshire, by Sir Thomas Tresham, between the years 1575 and 1605. Together with many particulars concerning the Tresham family and their home at Rushton. [Bibliogr. notes.] xviii, 44pp. Plates incl. sections, elevations and plans. 38x28 Northampton: Taylor & Son; London: Batsford, 1883.

GREAT BRITAIN: Ministry of Works [Ancient Monuments and Historic Buildings].
— CHETTLE, G.H. The Triangular Lodge, Rushton, Northamptonshire. 2pp. 1 illus. 21x14 [London] (1956).

GREAT BRITAIN: Ministry of Public Building and Works [Ancient Monuments and Historic Buildings].
—ISHAM, *Sir* G. The Triangular Lodge, Rushton. Northamptonshire. 20pp. Illus. incl. folding plate, section and plans. 21x14 London, 1970.

GREAT BRITAIN: Department of the Environment [Ancient Monuments and Historic Buildings].
—ISHAM, *Sir* G. Rushton Triangular Lodge, Northamptonshire. 1975.

RUTHIN CASTLE (Denbighshire).
BURKE, J.B. Visitation of Seats. Vol.I, p.82. 1852.*

JONES. Views of Seats. V. 1830.

NICHOLAS, T. Counties of Wales. I, p.372. 1872.

[Sales] RUTHIN CASTLE, 1963, July 11-13, 15-18 [Contents].

RUTLAND LODGE, Petersham (Surrey).
COUNTRY LIFE. XLIV, 382. 1918.

RUXLEY LODGE (Surrey).
[Sales] RUXLEY LODGE, 1919, October 14 and following days [Objets d'art].

RYCOTE (Oxfordshire).
GREAT BRITAIN: Ministry of Public Building and Works [Ancient Monuments and Historic Buildings].
— SALMON, J. Rycote Chapel, Oxfordshire. 16pp. Plates. 21x14 London, 1967.

COUNTRY LIFE. LXIII, 16. 1928.

ENGLAND: Picturesque Views. p.59. 1786-88.

KIP, J. Nouveau théâtre de la Grande Bretagne. I, pl.34. 1715.

[Sales] OXFORD, 1911, May 31 [Estate].

RYE HOUSE (Hertfordshire).
GARNER, T. Domestic architecture. I, p.75. 1911.

RYES, The (Essex).
LUGAR, R. Plans and views of buildings. 17, pls.VII-IX. 1823.

RYSHWORTH HALL (Yorkshire).
YORKSHIRE. Picturesque views. 1885.

RYSTON HALL (Norfolk).
BURKE, J.B. Visitation of Seats. 2.S. Vol.I, p.149. 1854.*

SOANE, J. Plans, elevations and sections. pls. XXV-XXVII. 1788.

SADBOROW HOUSE (Dorsetshire).
BURKE, J.B. Visitation of Seats. 2.S. Vol.I, p.56. 1854.*

OSWALD, A. Country houses of Dorset. p.169. 1959.

SADDINGTON HALL (Leicestershire).
[Sales] SADDINGTON HALL, 1926, September 30 [Portion of the contents].

SAIGHTON GRANGE (Cheshire).
ORMEROD, G. Cheshire. II, 770. 1882.

ST. ALBAN'S COURT (Kent).
GREENWOOD, C. Kent. 349. 1838.

ST. ANDREW'S CASTLE, Bury St. Edmund's (Suffolk).
[Sales] BURY ST. EDMUND'S, 1927, July 7-9 [Contents].

ST ANNE'S HILL, Chertsey (Surrey).
CUNNINGHAM, *Rev.* Peter.
— Saint Anne's Hill: a poem. 3 ed. [Bibliogr.notes.] 38pp. Plates. 27x21 Chertsey: privately printed, 1833. With a biography of Charles James Fox, 14pp. 27x18, inserted. Presentation copy signed by the widow of Charles James Fox.

ST. AUDRIES (Somerset).
COLLINSON, J. History of Somerset. III, 496. 1791.

ST. BENET'S (Cornwall).
CROMWELL, T.K. Excursions in Cornwall. p.166, 1824.

ST. CATHERINE'S COURT (Somerset).
COOKE, R. West Country Houses. p.42. 1957.

GOTCH, J.A. Architecture of the Renaissance. II, p.6. 1894.

ST. CLARE HOUSE (Hampshire, Isle of Wight).
BURKE, J.B. Visitation of Seats. Vol.I, p.172. 1852.*

ST. CLERE (Kent).
COUNTRY LIFE. CXXXI, 450, 518. 1962.

ST. DAVID'S BISHOP'S PALACE (Pembrokeshire).
JONES. Views of Seats. VI. 1831.

ST DONAT'S CASTLE (Glamorganshire).
BUCK, S. & N. Antiquities. II, pl.399. 1774.

COUNTRY LIFE. XXII, 270, 306. 1907.

COUNTRY LIFE. XLIX, 415 [Armour]. 1921.

COUNTRY LIFE. CLXVIII, **942. 1980.**

JONES. Views of Seats. VI. 1831.

LATHAM, C. In English Homes. Vol.II, p.15 1907.

NICHOLAS, T. Counties of Wales. II, p.466. **1872.**

[Sales] LONDON, 1922, July 25 [Estate].

ST. DUNSTAN'S Regent's Park (London).
ALDENHAM, Henry Hucks Gibbs, *Baron.*
— A catalogue of some printed books and manuscripts at St. Dunstan's, Regent's Park, and Aldenham House, Herts., collected by H.H.G. [Lord Aldenham]. 28x19 London: privately printed, 1888.

ST. GILES HOUSE (Dorsetshire).
COUNTRY LIFE. XXXVII, 336, 370. 1915.

COUNTRY LIFE. LXXVII, 380 [Furniture]. **1935.**

COUNTRY LIFE. XCIV, 464, 508, 552. 1943.

COUNTRY LIFE. CXXV, 1252 [Grotto]. 1959.

DELDERFIELD, E.R. West Country houses. II, 89. 1970.

HUTCHINS, J. Vitruvius Dorsettiensis. pls. 35,36. 1816.

OSWALD, A. Country houses of Dorset. p.139. 1959.

UNITED KINGDOM. Historic houses. 145. 1892.

[Sales] LONDON, 1980, June 25 [Works of art removed from St. G.H.].

[Sales]LONDON, 1980, June 26 [Furniture and sculpture].

ST. IVES, near Bradford (Yorkshire).
PAINE, J. Plans, elevations. Pt. I, pls. 63-66, plan. 1767.

YORKSHIRE. Picturesque views. 1885.

ST. JOHNS, Warwick (Warwickshire).
GOTCH, J.A. Architecture of the Renaissance. I, p.7. 1894.

ST. JOHN'S JERUSALEM, Sutton-at-Hone (Kent).
LONDON: National Trust for Places of Historic Interest or Natural Beauty.
— St. John's Jerusalem, Sutton-at-Hone, Kent. 4pp. 2 illus. incl. map. 18x12 [London, *c*.1945.]

COUNTRY LIFE. XCV, 552. 1944.

GREENWOOD, C. Kent. 72. 1838.

ST. JULIANS (Kent).
GREENWOOD, C. Kent. 97. 1838.

ST. LEONARD'S HILL (Berkshire).
JONES. Views of Seats. I. 1829.

NEALE, J.P. Views of Seats. Vol.I. 1818.

ST. MARY'S, Bramber (Sussex).
[Sales] LONDON, 1913, April 3 [Residence].

ST. MICHAEL'S MOUNT (Cornwall).
HUSSEY, Christopher.
—Official guide to St. Michael's Mount, Cornwall [etc.]. 20pp. Illus. incl. col. cover. 19x13 (Marazion: privately printed) [*c*.1930.]

Partly also in: COUNTRY LIFE, LVI, 672, 714. 1924.

SAINT MICHAEL'S MOUNT.
—St. Michael's Mount. (A brief historical account and **description** [etc.]. **16pp. Illus.** (some col., some on covers.) **19x13 (Norwich: Jarrold & Sons, 1969.)**

WAKE, Joan.
—Guide to St. Michael's Mount, with a summary of its history from legendary times. 32pp. 6 illus. 18x12 Northampton: by the author, 1934.

BRITTON, J. Cornwall illustrated. 32. 1832.

BUCK, S. & N. Antiquities. I, pl.29,30. 1774.

BURKE, J.B. Visitation of Seats. Vol.II. p.246. 1853.*

COUNTRY LIFE. LVI, 672, 714. **1924.**

CROMWELL, T.K. Excursions in Cornwall. p.75. 1824.

DELDERFIELD, E.R. West Country houses. I, 128. 1968.

MALAN, A.H. Other famous homes. p.297. 1902.

MORRIS, F.O. Views of Seats. Vol.III, p.79. 1880.

NICOLSON, N. Great Houses of Britain. p.10. 1965.

ST. OSYTH'S PRIORY (Essex).
DE CHAIR, Somerset Struben.
— St. Osyth's Priory: ... an illustrated survey of the former abbey of the Augustinian monks, the historic home of the D'Arcys and the Earls of Rochford. 32pp. Illus. (some col., some on covers) incl. plan and maps (on inside covers). 14x22 Derby: E.L.P. [1956?]
Another ed. 36pp. [1966].

COUNTRY LIFE. XIV, 304. 1903.

COUNTRY LIFE. XLIV, 524, 550, 576. 1918.

COUNTRY LIFE. CXXIV, 360. 1958.

CROMWELL, T.K. Excursions in Essex. I, p.109. 1825.

ENGLAND: Beauties of England. I, p.256. 1787.

ESSEX: A new and complete history. VI, 24. 1772.

HALL, S.C. Baronial Halls. Vol.I. 1848.

RUSH, J.A. Seats in Essex. p.139. 1897.

TIPPING, H.A. English Homes. Period II, Vol.I, p.271. 1924.

ST. PAUL'S WALDEN BURY (Hertfordshire).
COUNTRY LIFE. CXIX, 472. 1956.

ST. PIERRE PARK (Monmouthshire).
BURKE, J.B. Visitation of Seats. Vol.I, p.225. 1852.*

ST. SERF'S HOUSE, Roehampton (Surrey).
COUNTRY LIFE. XLVIII, 566. 1920.

SALFORD HALL (Warwickshire).
COUNTRY LIFE. XXX, 932 plan. 1911.

GARNER, T. Domestic architecture. II, p.194 plan. 1911.

TIPPING, H.A. English Homes. Early Renaissance. p.263. 1912.

TIPPING, H.A. English Homes. Period III, Vol.II, p.383. 1927.

SALHOUSE HALL (Norfolk).
BURKE, J.B. Visitation of Seats. Vol.I, p.70. 1852.*

SALISBURY HALL (Hertfordshire).
BELLEW, *Sir George Rothe, Garter King of Arms.*
— The story of Salisbury Hall. 3 ed. 12pp. Illus. incl. 4 col. plates. 24x17 (Barnet: privately printed, 1971.)
COUNTRY LIFE. CXXVI, 596, 708. 1959.

SALLE PARK (Norfolk).
CROMWELL, T.K. Excursions in Norfolk. I, p.180. 1818.

SALTFORD MANOR (Somerset).
COUNTRY LIFE. CXXIV, 178. 1958.

SALTMARSHE CASTLE (Herefordshire).
SALTMARSHE CASTLE.
— A descriptive catalogue of the gallery of pictures, collected by E. Higginson, Esq. of Saltmarshe. 29x22 London: privately printed, 1842.

SALTRAM (Devonshire).
LONDON: British Broadcasting Corporation.
—FLETCHER, R. The Parkers at Saltram, 1769-89: everyday life in an eighteenth-century house. [Bibliogr.] Illus. incl. col. plates, facsimiles and end-papers. 23x17. London, 1970.
LONDON: National Trust for Places of Historic Interest or Natural Beauty.
—The Saltram collection, Plympton, Devon. (Catalogue.) [Bibliogr.notes.] 68pp. Illus. (on cover), and 9 plates. 25x18 [London] 1967.
LONDON: National Trust for Places of Historic Interest or Natural Beauty.
—NEATBY, N. Saltram, Plympton, Devon. 32pp. Illus. (on title-page) and 8 plates. 21x15 London, 1971.
SALTRAM.
—Catalogue of the pictures, cast, and busts, belonging to the Earl of Morley, at Saltram. 56pp. 18x11 Plymouth: privately printed, 1819.
Another ed. 70pp. 20x12 London: privately printed, 1844.
ANGUS, W. Seats of the Nobility. pl.21. 1787.
BOLTON, A.T. Architecture of R. & J. Adam. II, 157 plan. 1922.
BRITTON, J. Devonshire illustrated. 52. 1832.
COUNTRY LIFE. English Country Houses: Mid Georgian. p.125. 1956.
COUNTRY LIFE. LIX, 124, 160 plan. 1926.
COUNTRY LIFE. CXXXIX, 1386 [Pictures], 1480 [Wedgwood]. 1966.
COUNTRY LIFE. CXLI, 998, 1064, 1160. 1967.
LATHAM, C. In English Homes. Vol.I, p.191. 1904.
TIPPING, H.A. English Homes. Period VI, Vol.I, p.165. 1926.

SALTWOOD CASTLE (Kent).
BUCK, S. & N. Antiquities. I, pl.140. 1774.
COPPER PLATE MAGAZINE. IV, pl.158. 1792-1802.
COUNTRY LIFE. XCII, 986, 1034, 1082. 1942.
CROMWELL, T.K. Excursions in Kent. p.176. 1822.

SALUTATION, The. Sandwich (Kent).
COUNTRY LIFE. CXXXII, 650 plan. 1962.
OSWALD, A. Country houses of Kent. 68. 1933.

SAMLESBURY HALL (Lancashire).
CROSTON, James.
— A history of the ancient Hall of Samlesbury in Lancashire, with an account of its earlier possessors and particulars relating to the more recent descent of the manor. [Bibliogr. notes.] Illus. incl. plates (1 folding) and genealog. tables. 38x27 London: for the author, 1871.
EATON, Robert.
— An illustrated guide to the ancient hall of Samlesbury. 20pp. 12 plates incl. plan. 18x12 (Blackburn printed) 1949.
SAMLESBURY HALL.
— Samlesbury Hall. [Catalogue of engravings by W.A.] 40pp. 27x19 [Manchester?]: privately printed, 1873.
COUNTRY LIFE. XVII, 452. 1905.
LATHAM, C. In English Homes. Vol.II, p.81. 1907.

SAND (Devonshire).
BURKE, J.B. Visitation of Seats. 2.S. Vol.I, p.173. 1854.

SANDBECK PARK (Yorkshire).
COUNTRY LIFE. CXXXVIII, 880, 966. 1965.
MORRIS, F.O. Views of Seats. Vol.V, p.15. 1880.
PAINE, J. Plans, elevations. Pt.I, pls.47, 48 [Plans], 49-52. 1767.
WATTS, W. Seats of the Nobility. pl.10. 1779.

SANDERSTEAD COURT (Surrey).
NEALE, J.P. Views of Seats. Vol.IV. 1821.

SANDFORD HALL (Shropshire).
BURKE, J.B. Visitation of Seats. 2.S. Vol.I, p.122. 1854.*
LEACH, F. Seats of Shropshire. p.229. 1891.

SANDFORD ORCAS MANOR (Dorsetshire).
COUNTRY LIFE. XXI, 341. 1907.
COUNTRY LIFE. CXXXIX, 462, 518 plan. 1966.
DELDERFIELD, E.R. West Country houses. II, 93. 1970.
GARNER, T. Domestic architecture. I, p.123 plan. 1911.
OSWALD, A. Country houses of Dorset. p.75. 1959.

SANDFORD PARK (Oxfordshire).
COUNTRY LIFE. LXXXVII, 480. 1940.

SANDHILL PARK (Somerset).
BURKE, J.B. Visitation of Seats. Vol.II, p.17. 1853.*
COLLINSON, J. History of Somerset. II, 494. 1791.
JONES. Views of Seats. II. 1829.
NEALE, J.P. Views of Seats. 2.S. Vol.IV. 1828.

SANDHOUSE, Witley (Surrey).
COUNTRY LIFE. XXVIII, 296 plan. 1910.

SANDON HALL [PARK] (Staffordshire).
SANDON PARK.
— Guide to Sandon Park. 2 ed. 46pp. Illus. (1 on title-page) incl.
2 engr. plates. 18x12 Stafford: Hill & Halden; London:
Tweedie, 1854.
CAMPBELL, C. Vitruvius Britannicus. V, pls.90-93. 1771.
NEALE, J.P. Views of Seats. Vol.IV. 1821.
PLOT, R. Staffordshire. 61. 1686.

SANDRINGHAM (Norfolk).
CATHCART, Helen.
— Sandringham: the story of a royal home. [Bibliogr.] Plates.
22x14 London: W.H. Allen, 1964.
COLE, Alan Summerly.
— A catalogue of the works of art at Marlborough House,
London, and at Sandringham, Norfolk, belonging to their
Royal Highnesses the Prince and Princess of Wales. 25x19
(London) privately printed, 1877.
JONES, *Mrs.* Herbert.
— Sandringham, past and present. (Rev. ed.) [Bibliogr. notes.]
164pp. Illus. incl. plates and cover. 19x12 London: Jarrold &
Sons, 1888.
SANDRINGHAM.
— Sandringham: a complete description of the royal residence
& estate and its surroundings. With an introductory chapter,
and a view of Sandringham House expressly drawn for this
work. 26pp. 2 engr. plates. 18x12 King's Lynn: Thew & Son,
1874.
SANDRINGHAM.
— A guide to the grounds and a short historical account of
Sandringham. 20pp. Illus. (Some col., some on covers, 1 on
title-page) incl. map (on inside cover). 15x23 Sandringham:
Estate Office, 1967.
COUNTRY LIFE. XI, 722. 1902.
LATHAM, C. In English Homes. Vol.I, p.315. 1904.
MORRIS, F.O. Views of Seats. Vol.III, p.1. 1880.

SANDWELL HALL (Staffordshire).
SHAW, S. Staffordshire. II, 128. 1801.

SANDYCOMBE LODGE, Twickenham
(Middlesex).
COUNTRY LIFE. CX, 40. 1951.

SANDYWELL PARK (Gloucestershire).
ATKYNS, R. Glocestershire. p.209. 1768.
RUDDER, S. Gloucestershire. 414. 1779.

SANSOME FIELDS (Worcestershire).
NASH, T.R. Worcestershire. II, Appendix, cxvii. 1782.

SANS SOUCI (Dorsetshire).
HUTCHINS, J. Vitruvius Dorsettiensis. pl.25. 1816.

SAPPERTON (Gloucestershire).
ATKYNS, R. Glocestershire. p.335. 1768.

SAPPERTON MANOR (Derbyshire).
TILLEY, J. Halls of Derbyshire. II, p.31. 1893.

SAUNDERS HILL (Cornwall).
JONES. Views of Seats. II. 1829.
NEALE, J.P. Views of Seats. 2.S. Vol.II. 1825.

SAWSTON HALL (Cambridgeshire).
SAWSTON HALL.
— Sawston Hall, Cambridgeshire [etc.]. 16pp. Illus. (some on
covers) incl. map. 14x20 [Derby: E.L.P., 1956?]
BURKE, J.B. Visitation of Seats. 2.S. Vol.II, p.139. 1855.*
COUNTRY LIFE. CXV, 1902, 1998, 2092. 1954.
HALL, S.C. Baronial Halls. Vol.I. 1848.

SAXHAM HALL (Suffolk).
BURKE, J.B. Visitation of Seats. Vol.II, p.174. 1853.*
CROMWELL, T.K. Excursions in Suffolk. I, p.97. 1818.
SANDON, E. Suffolk houses. 232. 1977.
[Sales] LONDON, 1924, September 24 [Estate].

SAXLINGHAM HALL (Norfolk).
GARRATT, T. Halls of Norfolk. pl.41. 1890.

SCAITCLIFFE HALL (Lancashire).
BURKE, J.B. Visitation of Seats. Vol.II, p.7. 1853.*

SCALDWELL RECTORY
(Northamptonshire).
GOTCH, J.A. Squires' Homes. 25. 1939.

SCAMPSTON HALL (Yorkshire).
COUNTRY LIFE. CXV, 946, 1034. 1954.

SCARISBRICK HALL (Lancashire).
COUNTRY LIFE. CXXIII, 506, 580. 1958.

TWYCROSS, E. Mansions of England and Wales. Vol.III, p.37. 1847.*

[Sales] LONDON, 1860, November 7 [Oak furniture and carvings from S.H.].

[Sales] LONDON, 1861, May 10 and following days [Pictures from S.H.].

[Sales] SCARISBRICK HALL, 1923, July 16-20, 23-27 [Contents].

SCORRIER HOUSE (Cornwall).
DELDERFIELD, E.R. West Country houses. I, 133. 1968.

SCOTNEY CASTLE (Kent).
HUSSEY, Chistopher.
—A short history of Scotney Castle. [Bibliogr.notes.] Rev. ed. 16pp. Illus. (on covers) 19x14 (Tunbridge Wells: privately printed, 1963.)

BURKE, J.B. Visitation of Seats. Vol.I, p.122. 1852.*

COUNTRY LIFE. English Country Houses: Late Georgian. p.220. 1958.

COUNTRY LIFE. XLVIII, 12. 1920.

COUNTRY LIFE. CXX, 470 plan, 526. 1956.

OSWALD, A. Country houses of Kent. 8. 1933.

SCRAPTOFT HALL (Leicestershire).
NICHOLS, J. History of Leicestershire. III, ii, pl.CLV, 1128. 1804.

THROSBY, J. Views in Leicestershire. p.312. 1789.

SCRATBY HALL (Norfolk).
BURKE, J.B. Visitation of Seats. Vol.II, p.187. 1853.*

SCRIVELSBY COURT (Lincolnshire).
LODGE, *Rev.* Samuel.
—Scrivelsby, the home of the champions. With some account of the Marmion and Dymoke families. [Bibliogr. notes.] Illus.: plates (1 col.) and genealog. table. 25x19 Horncastle: W.K. Morton; London: Elliot Stock, 1893.

BUCK, S.& N. Antiquities. I, pl. 174. 1774.

BURKE, J.B. Visitation of Seats. Vol.I, p.188. 1852.*

NOBLE, T. Counties of Chester, ... Lincoln. p.70. 1836.

SPROULE, A. Lost houses of Britain. 247. 1982.

SEAFORTH HOUSE (Lancashire).
NEALE, J.P. Views of Seats. Vol.II. 1819.

TWCROSS, E. Mansions of England and Wales. Vol.III, p.34. 1847.*

SEAGRY HOUSE (Wiltshire).
BURKE, J.B. Visitation of Seats. Vol.II, p.38. 1853.*

SEAHAM HALL (Durham).
BURKE, J.B. Visitation of Seats. 2.S. Vol.II, p.151. 1855.*

SEATON DELAVAL (Northumberland).
CAMPBELL, C. Vitruvius Britannicus. III, pls.20, 21. 1725.

COUNTRY LIFE. English Country Houses: Baroque. p.184. 1970.

COUNTRY LIFE. LIV, 800 plan, 860. 1923.

TIPPING, H.A. English Homes. Period IV, Vol.II, p.271. 1928.

SECKFORD HALL (Suffolk).
CLARKE, T.H. Domestic architecture. 8. 1833.

COUNTRY LIFE. XXVII, 90. 1910.

CROMWELL, T.K. Excursions in Suffolk. II, p.40. 1819.

SANDON, E. Suffolk houses. 180. 1977.

TIPPING, H.A. English Homes. Early Renaissance, p.51. 1912.

TIPPING, H.A. English Homes. Period III, Vol.I, p.64. 1922.

SEDBURY PARK (Gloucestershire).
BURKE, J.B. Visitation of Seats. Vol.I, p.3. 1852.*

SEDGEBROOK MANOR (Lincolnshire).
COUNTRY LIFE. CXV, 152. 1954.

SEDGLEY PARK (Staffordshire).
SHAW, S. Staffordshire. II, 221. 1801.

SEDGWICK PARK (Sussex).
COUNTRY LIFE. XCI, 1134. 1942.

SELSDON PARK (Surrey).
BRAYLEY, E.W. History of Surrey. IV, 105.* 1841.

BURKE, J.B. Visitation of Seats. Vol.I, p.265. 1852.*

NEALE, J.P. Views of Seats. Vol.IV. 1821.

SELSIDE HALL (Westmorland).
CUMBERLAND: C. & W. A. & A.S. Extra Series VIII, 226. 1892.

SELWOOD PARK (Berkshire).
See SILWOOD PARK.

SEND GROVE (Surrey).
COUNTRY LIFE. XCVII, 728, 772. 1945.

SENNOWE PARK (Norfolk).
COUNTRY LIFE. CLXX. 2242, 2298. 1981.

SERLBY HALL (Nottinghamshire).
SERLBY HALL.
— Serlby Hall: an illustrated survey [etc.]. 32pp. Illus. (some col., some on covers) incl. maps (on inside covers). 14x22 Derby: E.L.P., [1954?].
COUNTRY LIFE. CXXV, 654, 708, 766. 1959.
ENGLAND: Picturesque Views. p.66. 1786-88.
JONES. Views of Seats. I. 1829.
NEALE, J.P. Views of Seats. Vol.III. 1820.
PAINE, J. Plans, elevations. Pt.I, pls. 37, 38 [Plans], 39, 40. 1767.
THOROTON, R. Nottinghamshire. III, 433. 1797.
[Sales] SERLBY HALL, 1978, December 11-13 [Remaining contents].

SEVENHAMPTON (Gloucestershire).
See BROCKHAMPTON PARK.

SEVENOAKS (Kent). Multon Lambard's.
NEALE, J.P. Views of Seats. Vol.II. 1819.

SEVENOAKS (Kent). Thomas Fuller's.
HARRIS, J. History of Kent. p.279. 1719.

SEVERN END (Worcestershire).
SHIRLEY, Evelyn Philip.
—Hanley and the House of Lechmere. [Bibliogr. notes.] 80pp Illus. (1 on title-page) incl. plates. 22x18 London: Pickering printed by C. Whittingham at the Chiswick Press - 1883.
COUNTRY LIFE. CLVIII, 194, 266. 1975.
NASH, T.R. Worcestershire. I, 559. 1781.
NIVEN, W. Old Worcestershire houses. p.41, pl.17. 1873.
[Sales] SEVERN END, 1964, September 8,9 [Furniture and effects].

SEWERBY HALL (Yorkshire).
JOHNSON, Francis.
— Sewerby Hall & Park. 28pp. Illus. (2 col. on cover) incl. plans. 24x19 (Bridlington) [c.1975.]
[Sales] SEWERBY HOUSE (Hall) 1934, July 16-21 [Furniture, pictures & books].

SEZINCOTE (Gloucestershire).
COUNTRY LIFE. English Country Houses: Late Georgian. p.66. 1958.
COUNTRY LIFE. LXXXV, 502, 528. 1939.
JONES. Views of Seats. II. 1829.
KROLL, A. Historic houses. 190. 1969.
MORRIS, F.O. Views of Seats. Vol.III, p.49. 1880.
NEALE, J.P. Views of Seats. Vol.II. 1819.

SHABDEN PARK (Surrey).
PROSSER, G.F. Surrey Seats. p.77. 1828.

SHADWELL COURT (Norfolk).
BURKE, J.B. Visitation of Seats. Vol.I, p.172. 1852.*
COUNTRY LIFE. CXXXVI, 18 plan, 98. 1964.

SHALFORD HOUSE (Surrey).
BRAYLEY, E.W. History of Surrey. V, 138. 1841.
BURKE, J.B. Visitation of Seats. Vol.I, p.259. 1852.*
NEALE, J.P. Views of Seats. 2.S. Vol. III. 1826.

SHALLCROSS HALL (Derbyshire).
GUNSON, Ernest.
— Shallcross and Yeardsley Halls. 16pp. Illus. incl. plates and plans. 22x14 Derby, 1905.
Also in, DERBY: Derbyshire Archaeological and Natural History Society. Journal, XXVII, 1905.
TILLEY, J. Halls of Derbyshire. I, p.209. 1892.

SHAPWICK HOUSE (Somerset).
BURKE, J.B. Visitation of Seats. Vol.II, p.176. 1853.*
COLLINSON, J. History of Somerset. III, 426. 1791.

SHARDELOES (Buckinghamshire).
ELAND, George E.
— Shardeloes papers of the 17th. and 18th. centuries. Edited by G.E. Plates incl. folding genealog. table and facsimile. 22x14 London: O.U.P., 1947.
BOLTON, A.T. Architecture of R. & J. Adam. I, 144 plan. 1922.
BURKE, J.B. Visitation of Seats. Vol.I, p.248. 1852.*
CAMPBELL, C. Vitruvius Britannicus. IVth. pls. 100, 101. 1739.
COUNTRY LIFE. XXXIV, 18 plan. 1913.
COUNTRY LIFE. LXXIV, 506 [Furniture]. 1933.
ENGLAND: Picturesque Views. p.4. 1786-88.

SHARDLOW HALL (Derbyshire).
BURKE, J.B. Visitation of Seats. Vol.I, p.98. 1852.*
TILLEY, J. Halls of Derbyshire. IV, p.115. 1902.

SHARPHAM (Devonshire).
BRITTON, J. Devonshire illustrated. 99. 1832.
BURKE, J.B. Visitation of Seats. Vol. I, p.38. 1852.*
COUNTRY LIFE. CXLV, 952, 1014. 1969.

SHARSTED COURT (Kent).
COUNTRY LIFE. CVII, 586 plan. 1950.

SHAVINGTON (Shropshire).
COUNTRY LIFE. XLIV, 92, 112. 1918.
LEACH, F. Seats of Shropshire. p.245. 1891.
LEIGHTON, S. Shropshire houses. 29. 1901.
TIPPING, H.A. English Homes. Period IV, Vol.I, p.191. 1920.

SHAWDON HALL (Northumberland).
COUNTRY LIFE. CXXV, 460. 1959.

SHAWE, The. (Staffordshire).
BURKE, J.B. Visitation of Seats. Vol.II, p.244. 1853.*

SHAWFORD HOUSE (Hampshire).
COUNTRY LIFE. XLV, 690 [Furniture]. 1919.
COUNTRY LIFE. XLVIII, 172 plan, 212. 1920.

SHAW HILL (Lancashire).
BARTLETT, J. Mansions of England and Wales. pl.20. 1853.
BURKE, J.B. Visitation of Seats. 2.S. Vol.II, p.86. 1855.*
TWYCROSS, E. Mansions of England and Wales. Vol.I, p.58. 1847.

SHAW HOUSE (Berkshire).
COUNTRY LIFE. XXVIII, 328 plan. 1910.
TIPPING, H.A. English Homes. Early Renaissance. p.207. 1912.

SHEEN HOUSE (Surrey).
HOVENDEN, E.M.J.
— Sheen House. 20pp. Illus. 19x16 n.p., 1963.

SHEFFIELD PARK (Sussex).
ANGUS, W. Seats of the Nobility. pl.26. 1787.
NEALE, J.P. Views of Seats. Vol.IV. 1821.
WATTS, W. Seats of the Nobility. pl.3. 1779.
[Sales] SHEFFIELD PARK, 1954, March 8-10 [Contents].
[Sales] SHEFFIELD PARK, 1971, June 14-17, 21 [Contents].

SHELDON MANOR (Wiltshire).
COOKE, R. West Country Houses. p.20. 1957.
COUNTRY LIFE. XXXIV, 638 plan. 1913.
ELYARD, S.J. Old Wiltshire homes. p.4. 1894.

SHELLEY HALL (Suffolk).
SANDON, E. Suffolk houses. 200. 1977.

SHENSTONE PARK (Staffordshire).
SHAW, S. Staffordshire. II, 46. 1801.

SHENTON HALL (Leicestershire).
BURKE, J.B. Visitation of Seats. Vol.I, p.180. 1852.*
NICHOLS, J. History of Leicestershire. IV, ii, 526. 1811.

SHEPHERDS, Cranbrook (Kent).
[Sales] CRANBROOK, Shepherds, 1928, May 30, 31 [Antique furniture].

SHEPHERD'S HILL (Sussex).
COUNTRY LIFE. CLVIII. 906. 1975.

SHEPPEY COURT (Kent).
GREENWOOD, C. Kent. 280. 1838.

SHERBORN CASTLE (Oxfordshire).
See SHIRBURN CASTLE.

SHERBORNE CASTLE (Dorsetshire).
PORTMAN, Louisa Mary.
— Catalogue of the pictures at Sherborne Castle [seat of the Digby family]. Folding plate: genealog. table. 21x13 London: E. Faithfull & Co., 1862.
SHERBORNE CASTLE.
— Sherborne Castle, Dorset. 12pp. Illus. (2 col.) incl. plans and map. 24x19 (Dorchester: privately printed) [1974.]
COUNTRY LIFE. XXVIII, 425. 1910.
DELDERFIELD, E.R. West Country houses. II, 97. 1970.
ENGLAND: Beauties of England. I, p.204. 1787.
HALL, S.C. Baronial Halls. Vol.I. 1848.
HUTCHINS, J. Vitruvius Dorsettiensis. pl.26. 1816.
HUTCHINS, J. History of Dorset. IV, 265, 280. 1870.
JONES. Views of Seats. II. 1829.
NEALE, J.P. Views of Seats. 2.S. Vol.IV. 1828.
OSWALD, A. Country houses of Dorset. p.130. 1959.
TIPPING, H.A. English Homes. Early Renaissance. p.147. 1912.
TIPPING, H.A. English Homes. Period III, Vol.II, p.51. 1927.

SHERBORNE HOUSE (Gloucestershire).
ATKYNS, R. Gloucestershire. p.339. 1768.

SHERBORNE LODGE (Dorsetshire).
See SHERBORNE CASTLE.

SHERBURN HOSPITAL (Durham).
BURKE, J.B. Visitation of Seats. Vol.I, p.44. 1852.*

SHERDLEY HALL (Lancashire).
BARTLETT, J. Mansions of England and Wales. pl.112. 1853.
TWYCROSS, E. Mansions of England and Wales. Vol.III, p.49. 1847.

SHERIFF HUTTON PARK [HALL]
(Yorkshire).
GILBERT, Christopher.
— A short historical guide to Sheriff Hutton Park. 24pp. 14 illus. (1 on cover) incl. plan. 18x15 (Leeds printed) 1965.
YORK: Georgian Society.
— Occasional papers.
II. Sheriff Hutton Park (by J. Egerton) and the Thompson family (by I.P. Pressly). 20pp. 8 plates. 20x13 (1946).
BURKE, J.B. Visitation of Seats. Vol.II, p.249. 1853.*
COUNTRY LIFE. CXL, 548, 628. 1966.

SHERINGHAM HALL (Norfolk).
COUNTRY LIFE. English Country Houses: Late Georgian. p.103. 1958.
COUNTRY LIFE. CXXI, 192, 236. 1957.
CROMWELL, T.K. Excursions in Norfolk. I, p.133. 1818.
REPTON, H. Fragments on landscape gardening. p.195 plan. 1816.
REPTON, H. Red Books. I, plan. 1976.

SHERMANBURY PLACE (Sussex).
[Sales] SHERMANBURY PLACE, 1917, July 18, 19 (K. F. & R.).

SHIBDEN HALL (Yorkshire).
HALIFAX: Bankfield Museum.
—Bankfield Museum notes. Third Series.
III. HANSON, T.W. A short history of Shibden Hall. Illustrations by C. Crossley. 32pp. 4 illus. 18x13 1934.
WOOD, G.B. Historic homes of Yorkshire. 20. 1957.
YORKSHIRE. Picturesque views. 1885.

SHILLINGLEE PARK (Sussex).
COUNTRY LIFE. LXXX, 142. 1936.

SHIPLAKE COURT (Oxfordshire).
COUNTRY LIFE. XX, 594. 1906.
[Sales] SHIPLAKE COURT, 1925, March 9-12 [Contents]. (K.F. & R.).

SHIPLEY HALL (Derbyshire).
TILLEY, J. Halls of Derbyshire. IV, p.149. 1902.*

SHIPTON COURT (Oxfordshire).
NEALE, J.P. Views of Seats. 2.S. Vol.I. 1824.

SHIPTON HALL (Shropshire).
COUNTRY LIFE. XXVII, 414. 1910.
LEACH, F. Seats of Shropshire. p.161. 1891.
MOSS, F. Pilgrimages. [II] 356. 1903.
SHROPSHIRE. Castles & Old Mansions. 43. 1868.
TIPPING, H.A. English Homes. Early Renaissance. p.243. 1912.
TIPPING, H.A. English Homes. Period III, Vol.I, p.174. 1922.

SHIPTON MOYNE (Gloucestershire).
Estcourt Family.
ATKYNS, R. Glocestershire. p.340. 1768.

SHIPTON MOYNE (Gloucestershire).
Hodges Family.
ATKYNS, R. Glocestershire. p.340. 1768.

SHIRBURN CASTLE (Oxfordshire).
BURKE, J.B. Visitation of Seats. Vol.II, p.223. 1853.*
COPPER PLATE MAGAZINE. I, pl.21. 1792-1802.
ENGLAND: Picturesque Views. p.14. 1786-88.
JONES. Views of Seats. I. 1829.
MORRIS, F.O. Views of Seats. Vol.III, p.11. 1880.
NEALE, J.P. Views of Seats. Vol.III. 1820.

SHIRLEY HOUSE (Hampshire).
HAMPSHIRE: Architectural views. 1830.

SHIRLEY HOUSE (Surrey).
NEALE, J.P. Views of Seats. Vol.IV. 1821.

SHIRLEY MANOR (Derbyshire).
TILLEY, J. Halls of Derbyshire. II, p.149. 1893.

SHOBDEN COURT (Herefordshire).
CAMPBELL, C. Vitruvius Britannicus. II, pl.59, 60. 1717.
COUNTRY LIFE. XX, 666. 1906.
KIP, J. Nouveau théâtre de la Grande Bretagne. III, pl.36. 1715.

SHORTFLATT TOWER (Northumberland).
BURKE, J.B. Visitation of Seats. Vol.I, p.111. 1852.*

SHORTGROVE (Essex).
RUSH J.A. Seats in Essex. p.146. 1897.

SHOTESHAM PARK (Norfolk)
COUNTRY LIFE. CXLII, 312. 1967.
CROMWELL, T.K. Excursions in Norfolk. I, p.50. 1818.
SOANE, J. Plans, elevations and sections. pls. I-III. 1788.
[Sales] SHOTESHAM PARK, 1979, September 24 [Library].

SHOTOVER PARK (Oxfordshire).
COUNTRY LIFE. English Country Houses: Baroque. p.252. 1970.
TIPPING, H.A. English Homes. Period IV, Vol.II, p.247. 1928.
[Sales] SHOTOVER HOUSE, 1855, October 22 and following days [Contents].

SHOTTESBROOK PARK (Berkshire).
COUNTRY LIFE. XXXIII, 162. 1913.
JONES. Views of Seats. I. 1829.
NEALE, J.P. Views of Seats. 2.S. Vol.IV. 1828.
[Sales] MAIDENHEAD, Shottesbrook House, 1810, June 27-30 [Pictures household furniture].

SHOTTISHAM PARK (Norfolk).
See SHOTESHAM PARK.

SHREWSBURY CASTLE (Shropshire).
BUCK, S. & N. Antiquities. II, pl.252. 1774.

COPPER PLATE MAGAZINE. pl.99. 1778.

LEIGHTON, S. Shropshire houses. 1. 1901.

SANDBY, P. Select Views. I, pls.50, 51. 1783.

[Sales] SHREWSBURY CASTLE, 1923, July 25-27 [Contents].

SHREWSBURY HOUSE (Kent).
GREENWOOD, C. Kent. 44. 1838.

SHRIGLEY HALL (Cheshire).
BARTLETT, J. Selections from views of mansions. 1851.

BURKE, J.B. Visitation of Seats. Vol.I, p.213. 1852.*

TWYCROSS, E. Mansions of England and Wales. Vol.II, p.114. 1850.

SHRIVENHAM HOUSE (Berkshire).
[Sales] SHRIVENHAM HOUSE, 1928, March 12-15 [Contents].

SHRUBLAND PARK (Suffolk).
BURKE, J.B. Visitation of Seats. Vol.II, p.209. 1853.*

COUNTRY LIFE. English Country Houses: Late Georgian. p.206. 1958.

COUNTRY LIFE. CXIV, 1654, 1734. 1953.

CROMWELL, T.K. Excursions in Suffolk. I, p.183. 1818.

PAINE, J. Plans, elevations. Pt.II, pls.64-67 plans. 1783.

SHUGBOROUGH (Staffordshire).
LONDON: National Trust for Places of Historic Interest or Natural Beauty.
— Shugborough, Staffordshire. [Bibliogr.] 38pp. 8 plates and plans. 21x13 [London] Staffordshire County Council, 1966. Rev. ed. 36pp. 1971.

COUNTRY LIFE. English Country Houses: Mid Georgian. p.79. 1956.

COUNTRY LIFE. CXV, 510, 590, 676 plan. 1954.

JONES. Views of Seats. I. 1829.

KROLL, A. Historic houses. 174. 1969.

NEALE, J.P. Views of Seats. Vol.IV. 1821.

SHAW, S. Staffordshire. II, pls.18, 19. Reprint 1976.

[Sales] SHUGBOROUGH HALL, 1842, August 1-6, 8-13, 15, 16 [Furniture, porcelain etc.].

SHURDINGTON (Gloucestershire).
See GREENWAY, The.

SHUTE BARTON (Devonshire).
BRIDIE, Marion Ferguson.
— The story of Shute: the Bonvilles and Poles. [Bibliogr.] 19 (3 folding) plates, facsimile and genealog. tables (some on end-papers). 21x14 Axminster: Shute School, 1955.

LONDON: National Trust for Places of Historic Interest or Natural Beauty.
— Shute Barton, Devonshire. 4pp. 1 illus. 18x11 [London, c. 1970.]

COUNTRY LIFE. CIX, 326, 398. 1951.

DELDERFIELD, E.R. West Country houses. I, 137. 1968.

SIBDON CASTLE (Shropshire).
COUNTRY LIFE. CXLI, 1372 plan, 1448. 1967.

SIBTON ABBEY (Suffolk).
BURKE, J.B. Visitation of Seats. Vol.II, p.103. 1853.*

SIDHOLME, Sidmouth (Devonshire).
[Sales] SIDHOLME, Sidmouth, 1930, December 9-12 [Contents]. (K.F. & R.).

SILVERTON PARK (Devonshire).
SUMMERSON, J. The Country Seat. 234. 1970.

SILWOOD PARK (Berkshire).
JONES. Views of Seats. I. 1829.

NEALE, J.P. Views of Seats. Vol.I. 1818.

MITCHELL, R. Buildings in England & Scotland. pls.1-4 plan. 1801.

SION HOUSE (Middlesex).
See SYON HOUSE.

SISSINGHURST CASTLE (Kent).
LONDON: National Trust for Places of Historic Interest or Natural Beauty.
—NICOLSON, N. Sissinghurst Castle: an illustrated guide. 4 ed. 16pp. Illus. (some col., 1 on cover) incl. plates and plan. 22x14 [London] 1971.

LONDON: National Trust for Places of Historic Interest or Natural Beauty.
—Sissinghurst Castle & garden. 32pp. Illus. (1 col. on cover) col. plates and map. 21x14 [London] 1982.

COUNTRY LIFE. XCII, 410, 458 [Missing]. 1942.

COUNTRY LIFE. CXLIV, 330. 1968.

HASTED, E. Kent. III, 48. 1790.

SIX WELLS, Llantwit Major (Glamorganshire).
CARDIFF: National Museum of Wales.
—FOX, *Sir* C.F. A country house of the Elizabethan period in Wales: Six Wells, Llantwit Major, Glamorganshire. Measured and drawn by the Ancient Monuments Branch of his Majesty's Ministry of Works and Buildings. Described by Sir C.F. 28pp. Illus. Incl. plates (some folding) sections, elevations and plans. 27x22 Cardiff, 1941.

SIZERGH CASTLE (Westmorland).

LONDON: National Trust for Places of Historic Interest or Natural Beauty.
—HORNYOLD-STRICKLAND, H. Sizergh Castle, Westmorland, a Border pele tower. 22pp. 4 plates. 18x11 London: Country Life (1951).

LONDON: National Trust for Places of Historic Interest or Natural Beauty.
—HORNYOLD-STRICKLAND, H. Sizergh Castle, Cumbria. 32pp. Illus. (1 col. on cover) incl. plates, plan and genealog. table. 21x14 [London] 1983.

LONDON: Victoria and Albert Museum [Woodwork].
—The panelled rooms.
IV. The inlaid room from Sizergh Castle. [By H. Clifford Smith.] 34pp. Illus. incl. plates. 25x18 London, 1915.

STRICKLAND, Lady Edeline.
—Sizergh Castle, Westmorland, and notes on ... the Strickland family. 38pp. Illus. (1 on title-page) and genealog. table. 30x21 Kendal: T. Wilson, 1898.

BURKE, J.B. Visitation of Seats. Vol.I, p.162. **1852.** *

COUNTRY LIFE. XIX, 942. 1906.

COUNTRY LIFE. LX, 653 [Furniture]. 1926.

COUNTRY LIFE. CVI, 1216. 1949.

CUMBERLAND: C. & W.A. & A.S. Extra Series VIII, 182 plan. 1892.

HALL, S.C. Baronial Halls. Vol.II. 1848.

LATHAM, C. In English Homes. **Vol. II, p.103. 1907.**

NASH, J. Mansions of England. IV, pl.9. 1849.

NEALE, J.P. Views of Seats. 2.S. Vol.I. 1824.

SKEFFINGTON HALL (Leicestershire).

NICHOLS, J. History of Leicestershire. III, i, 429. 1800. [List of pictures].

NICHOLS, J. History of Leicestershire. III, ii, pl.CLIX, 1136. 1804.

THROSBY, J. Views in Leicestershire. p.207. 1789.

SKELSMERGH HALL (Westmorland).

AGNES, *Sister.*
—The story of Skelsmergh: an outline of the history of three great families who resided in this district. 98pp. Plates incl. 2 folding genealog. tables. 22x14 Kendal: Westmorland Gazette, 1949.
Copy signed by the author.

CUMBERLAND: C. & W. A. & A. S. **Extra Series. VIII, 223.** 1892.

SKELTON CASTLE (Yorkshire).

SOANE, J. Plans, elevations and sections. pls. XXVIII-XXX. 1788.

SKIPTON CASTLE (Yorkshire).

BURKE, J.B. Visitation of Seats. 2.S. Vol.I, p.235. 1854.*

COUNTRY LIFE. XXIX, 162 plan, 198. 1911.

TIPPING, H.A. English Homes. Period II, Vol.I, p.59. 1924.

WHEATER, W. Mansions of Yorkshire. p.247. 1888.

SKIRSGILL (Cumberland).

JONES. Views of Seats. I. 1829.

NEALE, J.P. Views of Seats. 2.S. Vol.III. 1826.

SKREENS (Essex).

BURKE, J.B. Visitation of Seats. 2.S. Vol.I, p.86. 1854.*

RUSH, J.A. Seats in Essex. p.148. 1897.*

SLACK HALL (Derbyshire).

TILLEY, J. Halls of Derbyshire. I, p.93. 1892.

SLADE HALL (Lancashire).

MOSS, F. Pilgrimages. [III] 343. 1906.

SLATE HOUSE (Sussex).

BURKE, J.B. Visitation of Seats. Vol.II, p.244. 1853.*

SLAUGHAM PLACE (Sussex).

COUNTRY LIFE. CXXXV, 70. 1964.

SLEDMERE HOUSE (Yorkshire).

BURKE, J.B. Visitation of Seats. 2.S. Vol.I, p.124. 1854.*

COUNTRY LIFE. I, 246. 1897.

COUNTRY LIFE. XLIV, 282 plan, 308. 1918.

COUNTRY LIFE. CVI, 972 plan, 1064, 1140. 1949.

SLINDON HOUSE (Sussex).

COUNTRY LIFE. L, 880 plan. 1921.

ELWES, D.G.C. Mansions of Western Sussex. 203. 1876.

NEALE, J.P. Views of Seats. Vol.IV. 1821.

SLYFIELD MANOR (Surrey).

BRAYLEY, E.W. History of Surrey. IV, **473. 1841.**

COUNTRY LIFE. LXXXIII, 400, 424. 1938.

SMARDALE HALL (Westmoreland).

CUMBERLAND: C. & W.A. & A.S. Extra Series VIII, 163. 1892.

SMEDMORE (Dorsetshire).

COUNTRY LIFE. LXXVII, 62 plan. 1935.

HUTCHINS, J. Vitruvius Dorsettiensis. pl.27. 1816.

HUTCHINS, J. History of Dorset. I, 568. 1861.

OSWALD, A. Country houses of Dorset. p.162. 1959.

SMITHILLS HALL (Lancashire).
BARTLETT, J. Mansions of England and Wales. pl.145. 1853.

BURKE, J.B. Visitation of Seats. Vol.I, p.178. 1852.*

COUNTRY LIFE. XII, 592. 1902

COUNTRY LIFE. LXVI, 488 plan. 1929.

HALL, S.C. Baronial Halls. Vol.I. 1848.

LATHAM, C. In English Homes. Vol.I, p.293. 1904.

MOSS, F. Pilgrimages. IV, 19. 1908.

TIPPING, H.A. English Homes. Period I & II, Vol. II, p.221. 1937.

TWYCROSS, E. Mansions of England and Wales. Vol. III, p.82. 1847.

SMITHSBY HALL (Derbyshire).
TILLEY, J. Halls of Derbyshire. IV, p.79. 1902.*

SMITH'S HALL (Kent).
See WEST FARLEIGH HALL.

SNEED PARK (Gloucestershire).
ATKYNS, R. Glocestershire. p.422. 1768.

SNELSTON HALL (Derbyshire).
BURKE, J.B. Vistitation of Seats. Vol.I, p.246. 1852.*

BURKE, J.B. Vistitation of Seats. 2.S. Vol.I, p.228. 1854.

SNITTERFIELD HOUSE (Warwickshire).
BURKE, J.B. Visitation of Seats. Vol.I, p.134. 1852.*

SNITTERTON HALL (Derbyshire).
COUNTRY LIFE. CXXIX, 178, 228. 1961.

GARNER, T. Domestic architecture. II, p.143. 1911.

TILLEY, J. Halls of Derbyshire. I, p.115. 1892.

SNITTERTON MANOR (Derbyshire).
TILLEY, J. Halls of Derbyshire. I, p.109. 1892.

SNOWSHILL MANOR (Gloucestershire).
LONDON: National Trust for Places of Historic Interest or Natural Beauty.
—Snowshill Manor, Gloucestershire. 24pp. 4 plates. 18 x 12 London: Country Life (1954).
3 ed. 1956.
Rev. ed. DE LA MARE, A. 34pp. Illus. (1 col. on cover) incl. plates and plan. 21x14 [London] 1982.

COUNTRY LIFE. LXII, 470. 1927.

DELDERFIELD, E.R. West Country houses. III, 77. 1973.

SOCKBRIDGE HALL (Westmorland).
CUMBERLAND: C. & W.A. & A.S. Extra Series VIII, 64 plan. 1892.

SOCKBURN HALL (Durham).
BURKE, J.B. Visitation of Seats. Vol.I, p.4. 1852.*

SOMERFORD (Staffordshire).
SHAW, S. Staffordshire. II, pls. 5, 6. Reprint 1976.

SOMERFORD BOOTH'S HALL (Cheshire).
BURKE, J.B. Visitation of Seats. Vol.I, p.156. 1852.*

JONES. Views of Seats. I. 1829.

NEALE, J.P. Views of Seats. 2.S. Vol.I. 1824.

TWYCROSS, E. Mansions of England and Wales. Vol.II, p.101.1850.

SOMERFORD HALL (Cheshire).
NEALE, J.P. Views of Seats. 2.S. Vol.V. 1829.

TWYCROSS, E. Mansions of England and Wales. Vol.I, p.128. 1850.*

SOMERHILL (Kent).
BURKE, J.B. Visitation of Seats. Vol.I, p.132. 1852.*

COUNTRY LIFE. LII, 310. 1922.

CROMWELL, T.K. Excursions in Kent. p.176. 1822.

GREENWOOD, C. Kent. 126. 1838.

HASTED, E. Kent. II, 341. 1782.

NEALE, J.P. Views of Seats. 2.S. Vol.III. 1826.

OSWALD, A. Country houses of Kent. 41. 1933.

TIPPING, H.A. English Homes. Period III, Vol.II, p.373. 1927.

[Sales] SOMERHILL, 1981, June 23, 24[Contents].

SOMERLEY (Hampshire).
COUNTRY LIFE. CXXIII, 108 plan, 156, 202, 1958.

SOMERLEYTON HALL (Suffolk).
BURKE, J.B. Visitation of Seats. Vol.I, p.38. 1852.*

CROMWELL, T.K. Excursions in Suffolk. II, p.155. 1819.

DAVY, H. Seats in Suffolk. pl.20. 1827.

MORRIS, F.O. Views of Seats. Vol.IV, p.71. 1880.

NEALE, J.P. Views of Seats. Vol.IV. 1821.

SOMERSAL HALL, Somersal Herbert (Derbyshire).
TILLEY, J. Halls of Derbyshire. II, p.151. 1893.

SOMERSALL HALL, Brampton (Derbyshire).
TILLEY, J. Halls of Derbyshire. III, p.39. 1899.

SOMERTON CASTLE (Lincolnshire).
LINCOLNSHIRE. A selection of views. 1805.

SOMERTON HALL (Norfolk).
NEALE, J.P. Views of Seats. 2.S. Vol.I. 1824.

SONNING, The Deanery Garden
(Berkshire).
LATHAM, C. In English Homes. Vol.I, p.261. 1904.

SOTTERLEY HALL (Suffolk).
BURKE, J.B. Visitation of Seats. 2.S. Vol.II, p.136. 1855.*
DAVY, H. Seats in Suffolk. pl.17. 1827.

SOULTON HALL (Shropshire).
LEIGHTON, S. Shropshire houses. 19. 1901.
SHROPSHIRE. Castles & Old Mansions. 55. 1868.

SOUTHAM DELABERE (Gloucestershire).
ATKYNS, R. Glocestershire. p.185. 1768.
COOKE, R. West Country Houses. p.56. 1957.
COUNTRY LIFE. XXII, 594. 1907.
NASH, J. Mansions of England. I, pl.11. 1839.

SOUTHCHURCH HALL (Essex).
NICHOLS, John F.
—Southchurch Hall.[Bibliogr. notes,] 17pp. Illus. 24x15
[London, 1931].
Also in LONDON: British Archæological Association. Journal.
XXXVII, 101. 1931.

SOUTH DALTON HALL (Yorkshire).
See DALTON HALL.

SOUTHGATE (Middlesex).
Marquess of Caernarvon.
ENGLAND: Beauties of England. II, p.101. 1787.

SOUTHGATE GROVE, Enfield
(Middlesex).
CAMPBELL, C. New Vitruvius Britannicus. I, pls.29-31.
1802.

SOUTH HAY, Binstead (Hampshire).
COUNTRY LIFE. XCI, 348. 1942.

SOUTHILL (Somerset).
COLLINSON, J. History of Somerset. II, 210. 1791.

SOUTHILL PARK (Bedfordshire).
WHITBREAD, Simon, *Major.*
— Southill, a regency house. (Introduction by S.W.) 84pp. Illus.
incl. plates, elevations, plans and genealog. tables. 25x19
London: Faber & Faber, 1951.
CAMPBELL, C. Vitruvius Britannicus. IVth. pls. 84, 85. 1739.

COUNTRY LIFE. English Country Houses: Late Georgian.
p.27. 1958.
COUNTRY LIFE. LXVI, 665 [Furniture], 841 [Furniture].
1929.
COUNTRY LIFE. LXVIII, 42, 63 [Pictures], 80 plan, 108, 595
[Furniture]. 1930.
NEALE, J.P. Views of Seats. 2.S. Vol.V. 1829.
WATTS, W. Seats of the Nobility. pl.37. 1779.

SOUTH HILL PARK (Berkshire).
[Sales] SOUTH HILL PARK, 1929, December 2-6 [Contents].

SOUTH LITTLETON MANOR
(Worcestershire).
NIVEN, W. Old Worcestershire houses. p.21, pl.10. 1873.

SOUTH PARK (Kent).
HASTED, E. Kent. I, 416, 1778.

SOUTH PETHERTON MANOR
(Somerset).
GARNER, T. Domestic architecture. I, p.37. 1911.
RICHARDSON, C.J. Old English mansions. III. 1845.

SOUTH WALSHAM MANOR HOUSE
(Norfolk).
COUNTRY LIFE. CXXXIII, 1167 [Staircase]. 1963.

SOUTHWELL BISHOP'S PALACE
(Nottinghamshire).
BUCK, S. & N. Antiquities. II, pl.229. 1774.

SOUTHWICK HALL (Northamptonshire).
COUNTRY LIFE. CXXXI, 1236 plan, 1298, 1364. 1962.
GOTCH, J.A. Halls of Northamptonshire. p.26. 1936.

SOUTHWICK PARK (Hampshire).
BURKE, J.B. Visitation of Seats. 2.S. Vol.I, p.209. 1854.*
JONES. Views of Seats. II. 1829.
KIP, J. Nouveau théâtre de la Grande Bretagne. I, pl.74. 1715.
NEALE, J.P. Views of Seats. Vol.II. 1819.

SOUTH WINGFIELD MANOR
(Derbyshire).
ADDY, Sidney Oldall.
—An account of Winfield Manor in Derbyshire. By S.O.A.,
and J. Croston, with an introduction by R. Keene. 72pp. Illus.
(2 on covers) incl. plates. 28x22 Derby: R. Keene, 1885.
BLORE, Thomas.
—An history of the manor and manor-house, of South
Winfield in Derbyshire. [Bibliogr. notes.] Illus. incl. engr.
plates (2 folding) and genealog. tables. 28x23 London:
privately printed by D. Brewman, 1793.

FERREY, Edmund Benjamin.
—South Winfield Manor, illustrated by plans, elevations, sections and details, with perspective views and a descriptive account &c. Measured drawn and lithographed by E.B.F. [Bibliogr. notes.] 10pp. Lithogr. plates (some folding). incl. title-page, sections, elevations and plans. **42x32 London: by the author, 1870.**
COUNTRY LIFE. XXXVIII, 90. 1915.
COUNTRY LIFE. CLXXI, 946 plan, 1042 plan. 1982.
MOSS, F. Pilgrimages. V. **281. 1910.**
TILLEY, J. Halls of Derbyshire. III, 225. 1899.
TIPPING, H.A. English Homes. **Period I, Vol.I, p.303. 1921.**

SOUTH WRAXALL MANOR (Wiltshire).
PUGIN, Augustus Charles.
—Examples of gothic architecture [etc.].
III, 3. WALKER, T.L. Historical account of the manor house at South Wraxhall, Wiltshire. Engr. plates (some folding) incl. sections, elevations and plans. 30x24 London: H.G. Bohn, 1850.
COUNTRY LIFE. XV, 450. 1904.
COUNTRY LIFE. XVII, 54. 1905.
ELYARD, S.J. Old Wiltshire homes, p.67. 1894.
GARNER, T. Domestic architecture. I, p.42 plan. 1911.
GOTCH, J.A. Architecture of the Renaissance. II, p.6. 1894.
LATHAM, C. In English Homes. Vol.I, p.217. 1904.
[Sales] SOUTH WRAXALL MANOR, 1935, July 16-19 [Contents].

SPAINS HALL (Essex).
BURKE, J.B. Visitation of Seats. Vol.II, p.194. 1853.*
COUNTRY LIFE. CLXXII, 2076. 1982.
COUNTRY LIFE. CLXXIII, 18. **1983.**
RUSH, J.A. Seats in Essex. p.150. 1897.*

SPAYNES HALL (Essex).
RUSH, J.A. Seats in Essex. p.152. 1897.

SPEKE HALL (Lancashire).
LIVERPOOL: Corporation.
—Guide to Speke Hall ... property of the National Trust ... Text ... by R. Millington. 24pp. Illus. (2 on covers) incl. plans. 22x14 Liverpool [c.1955].
LIVERPOOL: Merseyside County Museums.
—Speke Hall: a guide to the buildings and the owners. [Property of the National Trust.] 3 ed. 24pp. Illus. (some col., 1 on cover) and plan also on cover. 22x22 Liverpool [c.1980].
WINSTANLEY, Herbert.
—Speke Hall. 24pp. Illus. incl. plates and plan. 22x14 [Liverpool] 1919.
Also in LIVERPOOL: Historic Society of Lancashire and Cheshire. Transcations, LXXI, NS. XXXV. 1920.

BARTLETT, J. Mansions of England and Wales. pl. 106. 1853.
BURKE, J.B. Visitation of Seats. Vol.I, p.170. 1852.*

COUNTRY LIFE. XIII, 336, 368. 1903.
COUNTRY LIFE. LI, 16 plan, 48. 1922.
GARNER, T. Domestic architecture. II, p.172 plan. 1911.
GRAY, H. Old halls of Lancashire. p.1.1893.
HALL, S.C. Baronial Halls. Vol.I. 1848.
LATHAM, C. In English Homes. Vol.I, p.285. 1904.
NASH, J. Mansions of England. IV, pls. 14-18. 1849.
NICOLSON, N. Great Houses of Britain. p.50. 1965.
PYNE, W.H. Lancashire illustrated. 39. 1831.
TWYCROSS, E. Mansions of England and Wales. Vol. III, p.43. 1847.

SPENCER GRANGE (Essex).
RUSH, J.A. Seats in Essex. p.154. 1897.

SPETCHLEY PARK (Worcestershire).
BURKE, J.B. Visitation of Seats. 2.S. Vol.I, p.13. 1854.*
COUNTRY LIFE. XL, 42. 1916.
NEALE, J.P. Views of Seats. Vol. V. 1822.

SPIXWORTH HALL (Norfolk).
BURKE, J.B. Visitation of Seats. 2.S. Vol.I, p.158. 1854.*
GARRATT, T. Halls of Norfolk. pl.39. 1890.

SPODE HOUSE (Staffordshire).
See ARMITAGE PARK.

SPONDON HALL(Derbyshire).
TILLEY, J. Halls of Derbyshire. II, p.163. 1893.

SPRINGFIELD (Dorsetshire).
HUTCHINS, J. History of Dorset. I, 44. 1861.

SPRINGFIELD HALL (Lancashire).
BARTLETT, J. Mansions of England and Wales. pl.64. 1853.
TWYCROSS, E. Mansions of England and Wales. Vol.II, p.21 1847.

SPRINGFIELD HOUSE (Warwickshire).
BURKE, J.B. Visitation of Seats. Vol.II, p.134. 1853.*

SPRINGWOOD (Lancashire).
TWYCROSS, E. Mansions of England and Wales. Vol.III, p.60. 1847.

SPROSTON WOOD (Cheshire).
BURKE, J.B. Visitation of Seats. Vol.I, p.216. 1852.*

SPROTBROUGH HALL (Yorkshire).
COUNTRY LIFE. LI, 174 plan. 1922.

JONES. Views of Seats. I. 1829.

KIP, J. Nouveau théâtre de la Grande Bretagne. I, pl.56. 1715.

NEALE, J.P. Views of Seats. Vol.V. 1822.

SPROUGHTON CHANTRY (Suffolk).
See CHANTRY, The.

SPROWSTON COURT (Norfolk).
COUNTRY LIFE. XLVII, 215 plan. 1920.

SQUERRYES COURT (Kent).
SQUERRYES COURT.

— Squerryes Court, Westerham, Kent. 12pp. Illus. (some on covers) incl. plates and map. 14x20 [Derby] (E.L.P.) [1965?].

BADESLADE, T. Seats in Kent. pl.30. 1750.

COUNTRY LIFE. CXLIII, 1682, 1752. 1968.

HARRIS, J. History of Kent. p.329. 1719.

OSWALD, A. Country houses of Kent. 53. 1933.

STACKPOLE COURT (Pembrokeshire).
NEALE, J.P. Views of Seats. Vol.V. 1822.

STAFFORD HOUSE (Dorsetshire).
COUNTRY LIFE. CXXXI, 654 plan, 712. 1962.

HUTCHINS, J. History of Dorset. II, 513. 1863.

STAGENHOE (Hertfordshire).
CHAUNCY, H. Hertfordshire. II, 208. 1826.

STAINBOROUGH (Yorkshire).
See WENTWORTH CASTLE.

STALBRIDGE PARK (Dorsetshire).
HUTCHINS, J. Vitruvius Dorsettiensis. pl.28. 1816.

HUTCHINS, J. History of Dorset. III, 670. 1868.

STALLINGTON HALL (Staffordshire).
BURKE, J.B. Visitation of Seats. Vol.I, p.180. 1852.*

STALMINE HALL (Lancashire).
BARTLETT, J. Mansions of England and Wales. pl.91. 1853.

TWYCROSS, E. Mansions of England and Wales. Vol.II, p.51. 1847.

STANAGE PARK (Radnorshire).
REPTON, H. Fragments on landscape gardening. p.33 plan. 1816.

STANDEN (Sussex).
LONDON: National Trust for Places of Historic Interest or Natural Beauty.

—Standen, West Sussex. 32pp. Illus. (1 col. on cover) incl. plan. 21x14 [London] 1983.

COUNTRY LIFE. XXVII, 666 plan. 1910.

COUNTRY LIFE. CXLVII, 494, 554 plan. 1970.

STANDEN HALL (Lancashire).
BARTLETT, J. Mansions of England and Wales. pl.28. 1853.

TWYCROSS, E. Mansions of England and Wales. Vol.I, p.11. 1847.

STANDISH HALL (Lancashire).
BURKE, J.B. Visitation of Seats. 2.S. Vol.I, p.44. 1854.*

NEALE, J.P. Views of Seats. 2.S. Vol.IV. 1828.

TWYCROSS, E. Mansions of England and Wales. Vol.I, p.57. 1847.*

STANDLINCH (Wiltshire).
See TRAFALGAR HOUSE.

STAND OLD HALL (Lancashire).
SPROULE, A. Lost houses of Britain. 251. 1982.

STANDON, The. (Hertfordshire).
See LORDSHIP, The.

STANFIELD HALL (Norfolk).
BIRKBECK, G. Old Norfolk houses. 103. 1908.

BURKE, J.B. Visitation of Seats. 2.S. Vol.II. p.135. 1855.*

CLARKE, T.H. Domestic architecture. 7. 1833.

GARRATT, T. Halls of Norfolk. pl.43. 1890.

NEALE, J.P. Views of Seats. Vol.III. 1820.

STANFORD COURT (Worcestershire).
NASH, T.R. Worcestershire. II, 365. 1782.

STANFORD HALL (Leicestershire).
STANFORD HALL.

— Standford Hall, Rugby [etc.]. 16pp. Illus. (some on covers) incl. map. 14x20 [Derby: E.L.P. 1958.]

COUNTRY LIFE. English Country Houses: Baroque. p.221. 1970.

COUNTRY LIFE. CXXIV, 1284, 1410, 1472. 1958.

NICHOLS, J. History of Leicestershire. IV, i, 350. 1807.

THROSBY, J. Views in Leicestershire. p.179. 1789.

STANFORD HALL (Nottinghamshire).
BURKE, J.B. Visitation of Seats. Vol.I, p.53. 1852.*

CAMPBELL, C. Vitruvius Britannicus. IVth. pls. 106, 107. 1739.

NEALE, J.P. Views of Seats. Vol.III. 1820.
THOROTON, R. Nottinghamshire. I, 9. 1797.

STANLEY HALL (Shropshire).
JONES. Views of Seats. I. 1829.
NEALE, J.P. Views of Seats. Vol.III. 1820.
WEST, W. Picturesque views in Shropshire. p.122. 1831.

STANMER PARK (Sussex).
BURKE, J.B. Visitation of Seats. 2.S. Vol.I, p.192. 1854.*
COUNTRY LIFE. English Country Houses: Early Georgian. p.56. 1955.
COUNTRY LIFE. LXXI, 14, 66 [Furniture]. 1932.
NEALE, J.P. Views of Seats. Vol.IV. 1821.

STANMORE HALL (Middlesex).
MANUSCRIPTS (Typewritten).   English.
— BENCE-JONES, A.B. The Stanmore tapestry. Some notes on the Sanc Graal arras, worked by W. Morris, J.H. Dearle and others, for Stanmore Hall. Compiled by A.B.B-J. 6 plates. 20x17 1893-95.

STANSTEAD BURY (Hertfordshire).
CHAUNCY, H. Hertfordshire. I, 382. 1826.

STANSTEAD HALL (Essex).
CROMWELL, T.K. Excursions in Essex. II, p.173. 1825.
ESSEX: A new and complete history. III, 18. 1770.
RUSH, J.A. Seats in Essex. p.157. 1897.

STANSTED PARK [House] (Sussex).
COUNTRY LIFE. CLXXI, 346, 410, 478. 1982.
KIP, J. Nouveau théâtre de la Grande Bretagne. I, pl.36.1715.

STANTON COURT (Gloucestershire).
COUNTRY LIFE. XXX, 780 plan. 1911.
TIPPING, H.A. English Homes. Period III, Vol.II, p.391. 1927.

STANTON FITZWARREN (Wiltshire).
COUNTRY LIFE. XCII, 314 plan. 1942.

STANTON HARCOURT (Oxfordshire).
COPPER PLATE MAGAZINE. pl.125. 1778.
COUNTRY LIFE. XC, 628, 674. 1941.
THAMES, River. An history. I, pl.8. 1794.

STANTON OLD HALL (Derbyshire).
TILLEY, J. Halls of Derbyshire. I, p.241. 1892.

STANTON WOODHOUSE (Derbyshire).
TILLEY, J. Halls of Derbyshire. I, p.241. 1892.

STANWARDINE HALL (Shropshire).
LEIGHTON, S. Shropshire houses. 18. 1901.
SHROPSHIRE. Castles & Old Mansions. 56. 1868.

STANWAY HALL (Essex).
RUSH, J.A. Seats in Essex. p.162. 1897.

STANWAY HOUSE (Gloucestershire).
ATKYNS, R. Glocestershire. p.360. 1768.
COUNTRY LIFE. V, 816. 1899.
COUNTRY LIFE. CXXXVI, 1490, 1646. 1964.
DELDERFIELD, E.R. West Country houses. III, 83. 1973.
GOTCH, J.A. Architecture of the Renaissance. II, p.13. 1894.

STAPELEY HOUSE (Cheshire).
BURKE, J.B. Visitation of Seats. Vol.I, p.156. 1852.

STAPLEFORD PARK (Leicestershire).
LONDON: National Trust for Places of Historic Interest or Natural Beauty.
— The Thomas Balston collection of Staffordshire portrait figures of the Victorian age ... At Stapleford Park [etc.]. 32pp. Illus. (on cover) and 4 plates. 22x18 Melton Mowbray (1963). Another copy.
BURKE, J.B. Visitation of Seats. 2.S. Vol.II, p.16. 1855.*
COUNTRY LIFE. XXIII, 270. 1908.
COUNTRY LIFE. LVI, 288. 1924.
NICHOLS, J. History of Leicestershire. III, ii, pl. CLXIII, Appendix 69. 1804.
THROSBY, J. Views in Leicestershire. p.147. 1789.

STAPLETON PARK (Yorkshire).
JONES. Views of Seats. I. 1829.
NEALE, J.P. Views of Seats. Vol.V. 1822.

STATFOLD HALL (Staffordshire).
BURKE, J.B. Visitation of Seats. 2.S. Vol.I, p.211. 1854.*
SHAW, S. Staffordshire. I, 410. 1798.

STAUNTON HAROLD HALL (Leicestershire).
BURKE, J.B. Visitation of Seats. Vol.II, p.231. 1853.*
COUNTRY LIFE. XXXIII, 490, 526 plan. 1913.
COUNTRY LIFE. CVII, 516 plan. 1950.
KIP, J. Nouveau théâtre de la Grande Bretagne. I, pl.43. 1715.
NICHOLS, J. History of Leicestershire. III, ii, 717 [Pictures]. 1804.
NICHOLS, J. History of Leicestershire. III, ii. pl.CL,* Appendix 69. 1804.
THROSBY, J. Views in Leicestershire. p.126. 1789.

STAUNTON PARK (Herefordshire).
[Sales] STAUNTON PARK, 1924, October 16, 17 [Fixtures and fittings].

STAVELEY HALL (Derbyshire).
TILLEY, J. Halls of Derbyshire. III, p.195. 1899.

STEDCOMBE HOUSE (Devonshire).
COUNTRY LIFE. CXXXIV, 1738. 1963.

STEDE HILL (Kent).
GREENWOOD, C. Kent. 160. 1838.

STEEPHILL CASTLE (Hampshire, Isle of Wight).
MARSH, John B.
— Steephill Castle, Ventnor, Isle of Wight, the residence of John Morgan Richards, Esq. A handbook and a history. vi, 64pp. Plates. 28x20 London: privately printed (1907?).
BURKE, J.B. Visitation of Seats. Vol.I, p.241. 1852.*
BURKE, J.B. Visitation of Seats. 2.S. Vol.II, p.209. 1855.

STEPLETON HOUSE (Dorsetshire).
COUNTRY LIFE. LXXI, 42. 1932.
OSWALD, A. Country houses of Dorset. p.159. 1959.

STEVENSTONE PARK (Devonshire).
MORRIS, F.O. Views of Seats. Vol.VI, p.21. 1880.

STEWARD HAYS (Leicestershire).
NICHOLS, J. History of Leicestershire. IV, ii, 887, pl.CIV, 632. 1811.

STIBBINGTON HALL (Huntingdonshire).
COUNTRY LIFE. XVI, 304. 1904.
GOTCH, J.A. Architecture of the Renaissance. p.10. 1894.

STIFFKEY HALL (Norfolk).
BIRKBECK, G. Old Norfolk houses. 116. 1908.
COUNTRY LIFE. XXXIX, 240 plan. 1916.
GARRATT, T. Halls of Norfolk. pls.44-46, plan. 1890.

STISTED HALL (Essex).
BURKE, J.B. Visitation of Seats. Vol.II, p.132. 1853.*
RUSH, J.A. Seats in Essex. p.165. 1897.*

STOBERRY PARK (Somerset).
BURKE, J.B. Visitation of Seats. Vol.II, p.243. 1853.*

STOCKELD PARK (Yorkshire).
PAINE, J. Plans, elevations. Pt.I, pls.41, 42 [Plans], 43-46. 1767.

STOCKGROVE (Buckinghamshire).
BURKE, J.B. Visitation of Seats. 2.S. Vol.II, p.32. 1855.*

STOCKGROVE PARK (Bedfordshire).
COUNTRY LIFE. LXXXVI, 334 plan. 1939.

STOCK HOUSE, Stock Gaylard (Dorsetshire).
HUTCHINS, J. Vitruvius Dorsettiensis. pl.29. 1816.
HUTCHINS, J. History of Dorset. III, 686. 1868.

STOCKLEIGH COURT (Devonshire).
BURKE, J.B. Visitation of Seats. Vol.I, p.270. 1852.*

STOCKS, Aldbury (Hertfordshire).
[Sales] STOCKS, 1922, February 7-10 [French and English furniture etc.].

STOCKTON HOUSE (Wiltshire).
BURKE, J.B. Visitation of Seats. Vol.I, p.23. 1852.*
COUNTRY LIFE. XVIII, 558. 1905.
LATHAM, C. In English Homes. Vol.II, p.125. 1907.
RICHARDSON, C.J. Old English mansions. III. 1845.
SHAW, H. Elizabethan architecture. pl.XL. [Drawing room] 1839.
[Sales] STOCKTON HOUSE, 1906, May 21-23 [Furniture].
[Sales] STOCKTON HOUSE, 1920, July 20, 21 [Furniture].
[Sales] LONDON, 1925, November 3 [Estate incl. Stockton House].

STOKE ALBANY HOUSE (Northamptonshire).
GOTCH, J.A. Squires' Homes. 10. 1939.

STOKE ALBANY MANOR (Northamptonshire).
GOTCH, J.A. Halls of Northants. p.34. 1936.

STOKE BISHOP (Gloucestershire).
ATKYNS, R. Glocestershire. p.422. 1768.

STOKE COLLEGE (Suffolk).
BURKE, J.B. Visitation of Seats. 2.S. Vol.II, p.108. 1855.*

STOKE D'ABERNON MANOR (Surrey).
COUNTRY LIFE. XC, 956, 1010. 1941.

STOKE EDITH PARK (Herefordshire).
BURKE, J.B. Visitation of Seats. 2.S. Vol.II, p.121. 1855.*
CAMPBELL, C. Vitruvius Britannicus. I, pls. 45, 46. 1715.
COUNTRY LIFE. XXVI, 420. 1909.
COUNTRY LIFE. LXII, 962. 1927.
LATHAM, C. In English Homes. Vol.III, p.249. 1909.
NEALE, J.P. Views of Seats. Vol.II. 1819.
ROBINSON, C.J. Mansions of Herefordshire. pls.19, 20. 1873.

STOKE GIFFORD (Gloucestershire).
See STOKE PARK.

STOKE HALL (Derbyshire).
TILLEY, J. Halls of Derbyshire. I, p.203. 1892.

STOKE PARK (Buckinghamshire).
STOKE PARK.
— An historical and descriptive account of Stoke Park in
Buckinghamshire: containing the information relative to that
place supplied by the family now in possession, for Mr.
Hakewell's History of Windsor, &c. With many additional
particulars, and a new management of the matter. In two
parts. [By J. Penn.] 76pp. Engr. plates incl. plans. London:
privately printed, 1813.
Part I only? No more published?
BURKE, J.B. Visitation of Seats. Vol.I, p.220. 1852.*
COUNTRY LIFE. XIV, 168. 1903.
NEALE, J.P. Views of Seats. Vol.I. 1818.

STOKE PARK (Gloucestershire).
ATKYNS, R. Glocestershire. p.360. 1768.
COPPER PLATE MAGAZINE. IV, pl.154. 1792-1802.

STOKE PARK (Northamptonshire).
CAMPBELL, C. Vitruvius Britannicus. III, pl.9. 1725.
COUNTRY LIFE. English Country Houses: Caroline. p.61.
1966.
COUNTRY LIFE. CXIV, 280 [Pavilions]. 1953.
GOTCH, J.A. Halls of Northamptonshire. p.89. 1936.

STOKE PARK (Surrey).
BURKE, J.B. Visitation of Seats. 2.S. Vol.II, p.208. 1855.*

STOKE PARK HOUSE (Wiltshire).
See ERLESTOKE PARK.

STOKE POGES MANOR (Buckinghamshire).
THOMPSON, S. Old English homes. 178. 1876.

STOKE ROCHFORD HALL (Lincolnshire).
BURKE, J.B. Visitation of Seats.. Vol.I, p.124. 1852.*
COPPER PLATE MAGAZINE. V, pl.211. 1792-1802.
COUNTRY LIFE. X, 592. 1901.

STOKESAY CASTLE (Shropshire).
MASON, J.F.A.
— Stokesay Castle, Shropshire: ... a fortified manor house of
the thirteenth century [etc.]. 20pp. Illus. (some on covers) incl.
plan. 14x20 [Derby: E.L.P., 1963.]
WRIGHT, Thomas.
— Historical sketch of Stokesay Castle, Salop. [Bibliogr. note.]
20pp. Illus. (1 on title-page.) 18x12 Ludlow: G. Woolley, 1924.
BUCK, S. & N. Antiquities.II, pl.253. 1774.
COUNTRY LIFE. VIII, 714. 1900.
COUNTRY LIFE. XV, 270. 1904.
COUNTRY LIFE. XXVII, 594 plan. 1910.
LEACH, F. Seats of Shropshire. p.241. 1891.
LEIGHTON, S. Shropshire houses. 47. 1901.
SHROPSHIRE. Castles & Old Mansions. 19. 1868.
TIPPING, H.A. English Homes. Period I, Vol.I, p.111. 1921.

STOKESAY COURT (Shropshire).
LEACH, F. Seats of Shropshire. p.243. 1891.

STONEACRE, Otham (Kent).
LONDON: National Trust for Places of Historic Interest or
Natural Beauty.
— Stoneacre, Otham, Kent. 8pp. 1 illus. 18x11 [London] (1949.)
COUNTRY LIFE. LXVII, 420, 468. 1930.
OSWALD, A. Country houses of Kent. 25. 1933.

STON EASTON PARK (Somerset).
COLLINSON, J. History of Somerset. II, 154. 1791.
COOKE, R. West Country Houses. p.135. 1957.
COUNTRY LIFE. XCVII, 508, 552 plan, 596. 1945.

STONEHAM PARK (Hampshire).
See NORTH STONEHAM PARK.

STONEHILL, Chiddingly (Surrey).
COUNTRY LIFE. LIII, 623 plan. 1923.

STONELEIGH ABBEY (Warwickshire).
LEIGH, Agnes Eleanor.
—Notes on furniture and other contents in Stoneleigh Abbey
[the property of Lord Leigh]. 34pp. 22x14 (Leamington)
privately printed [1923].
STONELEIGH ABBEY.
—Stoneleigh Abbey pictures. [Collection of Lord Leigh. By
Miss A.E. Leigh. 34pp. 20x13 (London) privately printed [1919.]

STONELEIGH ABBEY [Contd.]

STONELEIGH ABBEY.
—Stoneleigh Abbey: an illustrated survey [etc.]. 32pp. Illus (some col., some on covers) incl. maps (on inside covers). 14x22 Derby: E.L.P. [1950?]

BURKE, J.B. Visitation of Seats. Vol.I, p.50. 1852.*

COUNTRY LIFE. English Country Houses: Early Georgian. p.37. 1955.

COUNTRY LIFE. I, 186. 1897.

COUNTRY LIFE. XIX, 630. 1906.

LATHAM, C. In English Homes. Vol.III. p.339. 1909.

MALAN, A.H. Other famous homes. p.245. 1902.

TIPPING, H.A. English Homes. Period V, Vol. I, p.183. 1921.

[Sales] STONELEIGH ABBEY, 1981, October 15,16 [Objects of art, furniture etc.].

STONEYTHORPE (Warwickshire).

BURKE, J.B. Visitation of Seats. Vol.II, p.165. 1853.*

STONEY WARE (Berkshire).

[Sales] STONEY WARE, 1917, August 27-30, September 1 [Contents]. (K. F. & R.).

STONOR PARK (Oxfordshire).

CAMOYS, Ralph Thomas Campion George Sherman Stonor, *Baron.*
—(Stonor) The Stonor family house for at least eight centuries [etc.]. [Bibliogr.] 24pp. Illus. (Some col., some on covers) incl. genealog. table. 21x18 Stonor: Stonor Enterprises [c.1980.]

STONER, Robert Julian, *O.S.B.*
—Stonor: a Catholic sanctuary in the Chilterns from the fifth century till today. 2 ed. 400pp. Illus. incl. plates (2 col., some folding), plan, maps and genealog. tables. 21x14 Newport, Mon.: R.H. Johns, 1952.

COUNTRY LIFE. CVIII, 1094, 1188, 1282. 1950.

COUNTRY LIFE. CLVIII, 1794. 1975.

NEALE, J.P. Views of Seats. Vol.III. 1820.

STONYHURST COLLEGE (Lancashire).

GERARD, John, *S.J.*
— Stonyhurst College: its life beyond the seas, 1592-1794, and on English soil, 1794-1894. [Bibliogr. notes.] Illus. (1 col.) incl. plans. 28x23 Belfast: Marcus Ward & Co., 1894.

HEWITSON, Anthony.
—Stonyhurst College, its past and present: an account of its history, architecture, treasures, curiosities, &c. Illustrated by Dalziel Brothers. Illus. (1 on title-page) incl. plates. 21x14 Preston: Chronicle Office, 1870.

STONYHURST: College.
—A Stonyhurst handbook for visitors and others. Part I, historical; part II, descriptive. 72pp. Plate. 18x12 Stonyhurst College (1927?)

MOSS, F. Pilgrimages. IV, 322. 1908.

TIPPING, H.A. English Homes. Early Renaissance. p.171. 1912.

TWYCROSS, E. Mansions of England and Wales. Vol.I, p.vii. 1847.*

STONY MIDDLETON HALL (Derbyshire).

TILLEY, J. Halls of Derbyshire. I, p.177. 1892.

STOPHAM HOUSE (Sussex).

BURKE, J.B. Visitation of Seats. 2.S. Vol.II, p.129. 1855.*

STOPHAM MANOR (Sussex).

ELWES, D.G.C. Mansions of Western Sussex. 220. 1876.

STORRS HALL (Westmorland).

PYNE, W.H. Lancashire illustrated. 88. 1831.

STOUGHTON GRANGE [HALL] (Leicestershire).

NICHOLS, J. History of Leicestershire. III, ii, pl.CLVI, 1129. 1804.

THROSBY, J. Views in Leicestershire. p.319. 1789.

STOUR CLIFFE (Hampshire).

BURKE, J.B. Visitation of Seats. Vol.II, p.207. 1853.*

STOURHEAD (Wiltshire).

CHIPPENDALE, Thomas, *the Younger.*
— Bills and receipts for furniture at Stourhead, Wiltshire, supplied by Thomas Chippendale the younger, 1795-1820. Photostat copy of a bound volume at Stourhead. 82pp. 30x20 [London] 1949.

COUNTRY LIFE.
— Stourhead, Wiltshire: one of a series of booklets illustrating the scenery, buildings and treasures of places of historic interest or natural beauty that are held in trust for the benefit of the nation. 24pp. Illus. London, 1952.
National Trust properties in pictures series.

LONDON: National Trust for Places of Historic Interest or Natural Beauty.
— GATHORNE-HARDY, R. Stourhead library. Report by Mr. R.G.-H. [Typescript.] 10pp. 33x21 [n.p.] (1948.)

LONDON: National Trust for Places of Historic Interest or Natural Beauty.
— LEES-MILNE, J. Stourhead. 30pp. 8 plates and genealog. table. 18x12 London: Country Life. (1948.)
New ed. WOODBRIDGE, K. Stourhead, Wiltshire. [Bibliogr.] 40pp. Illus. (1 col. on cover) incl. plates, plan and genealog. table. 21x14 (1971.)
Another ed. 24pp. Illus. (some col., some on covers.) 25x15 (1971.)

SWEETMAN, George.
—Guide to Stourhead, Wiltshire, the seat of Sir Henry Hoare, Bart. 5ed. 80pp. Illus. incl. map. 18x12 Wincanton; G. Smith; London: Folk Press, 1925.

BRITTON, J. Beauties of Wiltshire. II 1. 1801.
BURKE, J.B. Visitation of Seats. Vol.I, p.90. 1852.*
CAMPBELL, C. Vitruvius Britannicus. III, pls. 41-43. 1725.
COOKE, R. West Country Houses. p.122. 1957.
COUNTRY LIFE. English Country Houses: Mid Georgian. p.234. 1956.
COUNTRY LIFE. LXXXIII, 638. 1938.
COUNTRY LIFE. CIX, 38. 1951.
DELDERFIELD, E.R. West Country houses. II, 103. 1970.
ENGLAND: Beauties of England. II, p.365. 1787.
HAVELL, R. Views of Noblemen's Seats. 1823.
JONES. Views of Seats. II. 1829.
LATHAM, C. In English Homes. Vol.I, p.375. 1904.
NEALE, J.P. Views of Seats. Vol.V. 1822.
[Sales] LONDON, 1883, June 1 [Stourhead heirlooms, porcelain etc.].
[Sales] LONDON, 1883, June 2 [Stourhead heirlooms: pictures, drawings].

STOURTON CASTLE (Staffordshire).
BURKE, J.B. Visitation of Seats. 2.S. Vol.II, p.71. 1855.*
SHAW, S. Staffordshire. II, 267. 1801.

STOURTON CASTLE (Yorkshire).
MORRIS, F.O. Views of Seats. Vol.II, p.27. 1880.

STOURTON HALL (Staffordshire).
BURKE, J.B. Visitation of Seats. Vol.I, p.14. 1852.*

STOWE HOUSE (Buckinghamshire).
BICKHAM, George, *the Elder*.
— The beauties of Stow: or, a description of the pleasant seat and noble gardens, of the Right Honourable Lord Viscount Cobham. With ... designs ... of each particular building. 70pp. Engr. plates (1 folding). 8vo. 17x10 London: by E. Owen for the author, 1750.
CLARKE, G.B.
— Stowe. 16pp. Illus. (some col., some on covers) incl. plan and map. 18x14 (St. Ives, Huntingdon: privately printed, 1971.) Title on cover.
FORSTER, Henry Rumsey.
— The Stowe catalogue priced and annotated (Historical notice of Stowe). 1848.
See [Sales] STOWE, 1848, August 15 and following days.
FORSTER, Henry Rumsey.
— A few remarks ... on the Chandos portrait of Shakespeare recently purchased at Stowe for the Earl of Ellesmere, and a letter upon the same by H. Rodd [with additional relevant matter from contemporary periodicals]. 36pp. Illus. 21x13 London: privately printed, 1849.
LONDON: British Museum [Manuscripts].
— Catalogue of the Stowe Manuscripts in the British Museum. 2 vols. 25x16 London, 1895.

OXFORD.
— The new Oxford guide ... To which is added a tour to Blenheim, Ditchley, and Stow ... By a gentleman of Oxford. 5 ed. Engr. plates and cuts: head and tail pieces. 12mo. 16x9 Oxford: for J. Fletcher & S. Parker [1768?] Wanting plan.
6 ed. [1769?]
SEELEY, B.
— Stow: a description of the ... gardens [etc.]. (A description of the inside of the ... house [etc.].) Folding engr. plan. 2 pts. in 1 vol. 8vo. 20x12 London: J. Rivington; Buckingham: B. Seeley, 1756.
Another ed. Stowe: a description of the ... house and gardens ... New edition ... with description of the inside of the house. 36pp. Engr. plates (2 folding) incl. plans. 4to. 20x12 London: printed for J. Rivington; Buckingham: B. Seeley; Stowe: T. Hodgkinson, 1763.
Bound with: KENNEDY (J.). A new description of the pictures ... at Wilton. 1764; spine lettered: STOW & WILTON.
Another ed. 44pp. Engr. plates (2 folding) incl. elevation and plans. 4 to. 21x13 London: J. & F. Rivington; Buckingham: by the author; Stowe: T. Hodgkinson, 1769.
Another ed. Engr. plates (3 folding) incl. plans. 8vo. 21x12 1773.
Another ed. 64pp. Engr. plates (1 folding) incl. plans. 4to. 25x18 Buckingham: J. Seeley (1797).
Another ed. vi, 92pp. Engr. illus. incl. plates, plans and map. 37x29 1827.
New ed. viii, 96pp. 21x14 London: Calkin & Budd, 1838.
STOWE.
— Sixteen perspective views, together with a general plan of the ... buildings and gardens at Stowe ... Correctly drawn on the spot, 1752 ... By Mons. Chatelain. Engraved by George Bickham, Junior. [No text.] 17 engr. plates incl. folding plan. Fol. 36x51 London: T. Bowles; R. Sayer; H. Overton; G. Bickham; J. Bowles [1753].
BURKE, J.B. Visitation of Seats. Vol.I, p.96. 1852.*
COUNTRY LIFE. XVII, 522. 1905.
COUNTRY LIFE. XXXV, 18, 54. 1914.
COUNTRY LIFE. CII, [526, 578, 626. Buildings in Park]. 1947.
COUNTRY LIFE. CVIII, 1002 [Temple]. 1950.
COUNTRY LIFE. CXXII, 68. 1957.
COUNTRY LIFE. CXXV, 352. 1959.
COUNTRY LIFE. CXL, 260. 1966.
COUNTRY LIFE. CXLV, 78 [Queen's Temple]. 1969.
COUNTRY LIFE. CLI, 1416 [Gothic Temple]. 1972.
ENGLAND: Beauties of England. I, p.45, 48. 1787.
ENGLISH CONNOISSEUR. II, 98. 1766.*
JONES. Views of Seats. I. 1829.
LATHAM, C. In English Homes. Vol.III, p.303. 1909.
MALAN, A.H. Other famous homes. p.327. 1902.
MORRIS, F.O. Views of Seats. Vol.II, p.41. 1880.
NEALE, J.P. Views of Seats. Vol.I. 1818.
TIPPING, H.A. English Homes. Period IV, Vol.II, p.157. 1928.
[Sales] STOWE, 1848, August 15 and following days [Contents].

STOWE HOUSE (Buckinghamshire) [Contd.]

[Sales] LONDON, 1849, January 8-February 24 [Library].

[Sales] LONDON, 1849, March 5-10, 12-14 [Engraved British portraits, pt.I].

[Sales] LONDON, 1849, March 21-24, 26, 27 [Engraved British portraits, pt.II.].

[Sales] LONDON, 1849, June 11-16, 18-19 [Manuscripts].

[Sales] STOWE, 1921, July 4-8, 11-15, 18-22, 25-28 [Estate, mansion and contents].

[Sales] STOWE, 1922, October 11-13 [House and remaining portions of the estate].

STOWE HOUSE, Lichfield (Staffordshire).

COUNTRY LIFE. CXXII, 1028. 1957.

STOWELL PARK (Gloucestershire).

DELDERFIELD, E.R. West Country houses. III, 91. 1973.

[Sales] STOWELL PARK, 1923, November 6-8 [Contents].

STOWEY COURT (Somerset).

COOKE, R. West Country Houses. p.97. 1957.

STOWLANGTOFT HALL (Suffolk).

BURKE, J.B. Visitation of Seats. 2.S. Vol.I, p.109. 1854.*

BURKE, J.B. Visitation of Seats. 2.S. Vol.II, p.216. 1855.

MORRIS, F.O. Views of Seats. Vol.III, p.27. 1880.

SANDON, E. Suffolk houses. 206. 1977.

[Sales] STOWLANGTOFT HALL, 1920, June 28-July 2, July 5-9, 12-15 [Contents]. 3 pts.

STRATFIELD SAYE (Hampshire).

SCOTT, Christopher.
—Stratfield Saye. 16pp. Illus. (some col., some on covers) incl. map. 25x18 (London: Garrod Status Publishing, 1974?) Title on cover.

BURKE, J.B. Visitation of Seats. 2.S. Vol.I, p.214. 1854.*

COUNTRY LIFE. CIV, 1050, 1106, 1162 plan, 1218. 1948.

COUNTRY LIFE. CV, 202 [Furniture & Relics]. 1949.

COUNTRY LIFE. CLVII, 899, 982. 1975.

HAMPSHIRE: Architectural views. 1830.

WHITEMAN, G.W. English country homes. p.159. 1951.

STRATTON HALL (Norfolk).

CROMWELL, T.K. Excursions in Norfolk. I, p.141. 1818.

STRATTON PARK (Hampshire).

WEALE, William Henry James.
— A descriptive catalogue of the collection of pictures belonging to the Earl of Northbrook. The Dutch, Flemish, and French schools by W.H.J.W.; the Italian and Spanish schools by J.P. Richter. Plates. 32x24 London: Griffith, Farran, Okeden & Welsh, 1889.

CAMPBELL, C. Vitruvius Britannicus. IV, pls.51-55. 1767.

COUNTRY LIFE. CXLI, 80. 1967.

HAMPSHIRE: Architectural views. 1830.

JONES. Views of Seats. II. 1829.

NEALE, J.P. Views of Seats. Vol.II. 1819.

STRATTON STRAWLESS HALL (Norfolk).

BURKE, J.B. Visitation of Seats. Vol.I, p.113. 1852.*

STRAWBERRY HILL (Middlesex).

COSTELLO, Dudley.
— Strawberry Hill [and] Strawberry Hill revisited. With illustrations by W.A. Delamotte. Excerpts, 17pp. 21 cuts and facsimiles of signatures. 23x19 London (1842).
From: Ainsworth's Magazine. March, April, 1842.

HAZEN, Allen Tracy.
— A catalogue of Horace Walpole's library ... *With Horace Walpole's Library*, by W.S. Lewis (the Sandars lectures for 1957). [Bibliogr. notes.] Illus. incl. plates, plan and facsimiles. 3 vols. 25x19 London: O.U.P., 1969.

MERRITT, Percival.
— An account of descriptive catalogues of Strawberry Hill, and of Strawberry Hill sale catalogues; together with a bibliography. 88pp. Illus. 8vo. Boston [U.S.A.] (privately printed), 1915.

WALPOLE, Horace, *Earl of Orford.*
— A description of the villa of Horace Walpole, youngest son of Sir Robert Walpole, Earl of Orford, at Strawberry Hill, near Twickenham. With an inventory of the furniture, pictures, curiosities, &c. 1 engr. 4to. 23x18 Strawberry Hill: privately printed by T. Kirgate, 1774.
Wanting plates.
Another copy. 4 engr. plates.
Wanting pp. 101-112, 157-8.
Another copy, wanting plates and pp. 149-158.
Another ed. Engr. incl. plates (some folding), elevation and plans. 4to. 30x24 Strawberry Hill: privately printed by T. Kirgate, 1784.
Another copy. With printed instructions for inspection of Strawberry Hill, 2ff., inserted, additional plates incl. portraits (one of T. Kirgate the printer, and his Ticket), and MS. poem, *The printers farewell to Strawberry Hill,* by T. Kirgate (on end-papers).
Another copy, extra illustrated, excerpted from vol.II. of *The works of H.W.* 1798. 26x20.
Another ed. 42pp. 21x13 London: privately printed, 1842.

WALPOLE, Horace, *Earl of Orford.*
— Strawberry Hill accounts: a record of expenditure in building, furnishing, &c. kept by Mr. Horace Walpole from 1747 to 1795. Now first printed from the original MS., with notes and index by P. Toynbee. 30 plates incl. plans, maps and facsimiles. 30x23 Oxford: O.U.P., 1927.
Another copy. With mounted illustrations of Strawberry Hill from "Country Life", and MS. annotations and notes by C.F. Bell, inserted.

COPPER PLATE MAGAZINE. pls. 12, 39. 1778.

COUNTRY LIFE. English Country Houses: Early Georgian. p.211. 1955.

COUNTRY LIFE. LVI, 18 plan, 56 plan. 1924.

COUNTRY LIFE. CLIII, 1598, 1726, 1794. 1973.

ENGLAND: Beauties of England. II, p.68. 1787.

ENGLAND: Picturesque Views. p.100. 1786-88.

SANDBY, P. Select Views. I, pls.33, 34. 1783.

THAMES, River. An history. II, pl.1. 1796.

TIPPING, H.A. English Homes. Period VI, Vol.I, p.97. 1926.

[Sales] STRAWBERRY HILL, 1842, April 25-30, May 2-7, 9-14, 16-21 [Contents].

[Sales] LONDON, 1842, June 13-18, 20-23 [Portraits, prints etc. from S.H.].

[Sales] LONDON, 1861, March 1 [Collection of Walpoleana].

[Sales] STRAWBERRY HILL, 1883, July25-August 3 [Contents].

[Sales] STRAWBERRY HILL, 1923, May 28-June 1 [Contents]. (K.F. & R.).

STREATHAM HOUSE (Surrey).

COPPER PLATE MAGAZINE. I, pl.26. 1792-1802.

ENGLAND: Picturesque Views. p.56. 1786-88.

STREATHAM PARK PLACE (Surrey).

BURKE, J.B. Visitation of Seats. Vol.II, p.37. 1853.

COPPER PLATE MAGAZINE. I, pl.14. 1792-1802.

ENGLAND: Picturesque Views. p.50. 1786-88.

STREATLAM CASTLE (Durham).

STREATLAM CASTLE.

— Streatlam Castle, in the county of Durham, the principal residence of John Bowes, Esq., [With a descriptive catalogue of the armorial bearings, with notes of the lords and owners of the castle.] 16pp. Illus. incl. plates and diagr. 26x20 (London: privately printed) 1880.

BURKE, J.B. Visitation of Seats. 2.S. Vol.I, p.58. 1854.*

COUNTRY LIFE. XXXVIII, 836. 1915.

STREETHAY HALL (Staffordshire).

SHAW, S. Staffordshire. I, 338. 1798.

STREET PLACE (Sussex).

CLARKE, T.H. Domestic architecture. 18. 1833.

STRELLEY HALL (Nottinghamshire).

THOROTON, R. Nottinghamshire. II, 222. 1797.

STRENSHAM (Worcestershire).

NASH, T.R. Worcestershire. II, 392. 1782.

STRETTON HALL (Cheshire).

ENGLAND: Picturesque Views. p.81. 1786-88.

STRETTON HALL (Leicestershire).

NICHOLS, J. History of Leicestershire. III, ii, 1024. 1804.

STRETTON HALL (Staffordshire).

MANUSCRIPTS.   English.

— [Six estimates and bills for work carried out at Stretton Hall, Staffordshire, the property of the Rt. Hon. Thomas Conolly.] 9x18, 15x21 [etc.]. 2 June 1761-2 April 1771.

STUBBING COURT (Derbyshire).

TILLEY, J. Halls of Derbyshire. III, p.229. 1899.

STUDLEY CASTLE (Warwickshire).

MORRIS, F.O. Views of Seats. Vol.III, p.33. 1880.

[Sales] STUDLEY CASTLE, 1863, December 7 and following days [Contents].

STUDLEY PRIORY (Oxfordshire).

COUNTRY LIFE. XXIV, 54. 1908.

TIPPING, H.A. English Homes. Early Renaissance. p.25. 1912.

TIPPING, H.A. English Homes. Period III, Vol.II, p.41. 1927.

STUDLEY ROYAL (Yorkshire).

PARKER, George.

—Studley Royal and Fountains Abbey: notes historical and descriptive of the park, the hall, the church of St. Mary the Virgin, the pleasure-grounds. Fountains Abbey. Fountains Hall, etc. Rev. and enlarged ed. Illus. incl. folding map. 18x12 Ripon: by the author [c. 1910].

BURKE, J.B. Visitation of Seats. 2.S. Vol.II, p.90. 1855*.

COUNTRY LIFE. LXX, 94, 128. 1931.

ENGLAND: Beauties of England. II, p.432. 1787.

JONES: Views of Seats. I. 1829.

MORRIS, F.O. Views of Seats. Vol.V, p.41. 1880.

NEALE, J.P. Views of Seats. 2.S. Vol.III. 1826.

WHEATER, W. Mansions of Yorkshire, p.270. 1888.

YORKSHIRE. Picturesque views. 1885.

STURRY COURT (Kent).

COUNTRY LIFE. LI, 668. 1922.

OSWALD, A. Country houses of Kent. 20. 1933.

STURSTON GROVE (Derbyshire).

TILLEY, J. Halls of Derbyshire. II, p.197. 1893.

STUTTON HALL (Suffolk).

CROMWELL, T.K. Excursions in Suffolk. I, p.150. 1818.

SANDON, E. Suffolk houses. 210. 1977.

SUDBROOKE HOLME (Lincolnshire).

LINCOLNSHIRE. A selection of views. 29. 1805.

SUDBROOK PARK (Surrey).

CUNDALL, Herbert Minton.
— Sudbrook and its occupants. viii, 104 pp. Plates. incl. section, elevation, plan and maps. 19x14 London: A. & C. Black, 1912.

COUNTRY LIFE. XLIV, 332. 1918.

SUDBURY HALL (Derbyshire).

LONDON:National Trust for Places of Historic Interest or Natural Beauty.
—Sudbury Hall, Derbyshire. [Bibliogr. note.] 24pp. Illus. (1 col. on cover) incl. plates and plan. (London) [c. 1970.]
Rev. ed. JACKSON-STOPS, G. [Bibliogr.] 64pp. Illus. (1 col. on cover) incl. plan and genealog. table. 22x14 [London] 1982.

COUNTRY LIFE. English Country Houses: Caroline. p.162. 1966.

COUNTRY LIFE.XVII, 486. 1905.

COUNTRY LIFE. LXXVII, 622, 650 plan, 682. 1935.

COUNTRY LIFE. CXLIX, 1428. 1971.

LATHAM,C. In English Homes. Vol. III, p.139. 1909.

TILLEY, J. Halls of Derbyshire. II, p.173. 1893.

SUDELEY CASTLE (Gloucestershire).

MASTERS, Brian.
—Sudeley Castle: (Castle, Garden, Exhibition.) 40pp. Illus. (1 on cover) incl. plans. 15x26 (London: privately printed) [1970?]
Title on cover.

WILLYAMS, *Rev.*Cooper.
—The history of Sudeley Castle in Gloucestershire.[Bibliogr. notes.] 12pp. Engr. plate. Fol. 53x37 London: Robson, 1791.

BUCK, S. & N. Antiquities. I, pl. 101. 1774.

BURKE, J.B. Visitation of Seats. Vol.I, p.25. 1852

COUNTRY LIFE. LXXXVIII, 454, 500. 1940

DELDERFIELD, E.R. West Country houses. III, 97. 1973.

MORRIS, F.O. Views of Seats. Vol. I, p.15. 1880.

RUDDER, S. Gloucestershire. 716. 1779.

SUFTON COURT (Herefordshire).

JONES. Views of Seats. II. 1829.

NEALE, J.P. Views of Seats. Vol.II. 1819.

SUGWAS COURT (Herefordshire).

ROBINSON, C.J. Mansions of Herefordshire. pl.7. 1873.

SULBY HALL (Northamptonshire).

GOTCH, J.A. Squires' Homes. 23. 1939.

NEALE, J.P. Views of Seats. Vol.III. 1820.

SULGRAVE MANOR (Northamptonshire).

LONDON: Sulgrave Institution.
— PAPE, T. Sulgrave manor house and the Washington family. 24pp. 6 illus. incl. map and plan. 22x14 London (c.1917).

LONDON: Sulgrave Institution.
— Sulgrave Manor. What it is. Where it is. How to visit it. 8pp. 2 illus. incl. map. 23x14 London (1922).

SMITH, Harold Clifford.
— The George Washington bicentenary: Sulgrave Manor, North-Northamptonshire, [By] (H.C.S.) Excerpt, 7pp. Illus. 36x24 [London] 1932.
Also in: COUNTRY LIFE, LXXI, 722.

SMITH, Harold Clifford.
— The George Washington bicentenary: the Elizabethan home of Washington's ancestors. [By] (H.C.S.) Excerpts, 4pp. Illus. incl. facsimiles of signatures. 36x26 [London] 1932.
Also in: ILLUSTRATED LONDON NEWS, CLXXX, 251, CLXXXI, 103.

SMITH, Harold Clifford.
— Sulgrave Manor and the Washingtons. A history and guide to the Tudor home of George Washington's ancestors. [Bibliogr.] Illus. incl. plates, section, plan, map and genealog. tables. 26x20 London: Cape, 1933.

SMITH, Harold Clifford.
— Some recent acquisitions at Sulgrave Manor. Excerpt, 7pp. Illus. incl. facsimiles. 30x23 (London, 1944).
Also in: CONNOISSEUR, CXIII, 101.

SULGRAVE MANOR.
— Sulgrave Manor: an illustrated survey [etc.]. 32pp. Illus. (some col., some on covers) incl. maps (on inside covers), facsimiles and genealog. table. 14x22 Derby: E.L.P. [1953?].

MANUSCRIPTS (Typewritten). English.
— SMITH, H.C. Inventory and valuation of contents of Sulgrave Manor, Northamptonshire. Prepared for the Sulgrave Manor Board by H.C.S. 29x24 [London] 1938.
Notes, press cuttings and photographs in envelope in pocket.

COUNTRY LIFE. LXXI, 722. 1932.

GOTCH, J.A. Halls of Northants. p.91. 1936.

NICOLSON, N. Great Houses of Britain. p.70. 1965.

SUMMER CASTLE (Lincolnshire).

See FILLINGHAM CASTLE.

SUMMERFIELD HOUSE (Lancashire).

BARTLETT, J. Mansions of England and Wales. pl.69. 1853.

TWYCROSS, E. Mansions of England and Wales. Vol.II, p.26. 1847.

SUMMERFIELD HOUSE (Warwickshire).

SMITH, W. History of the County of Warwick. 376. 1830.

SUMMERHILL (Kent).

See SOMERHILL.

SUNBURY (Middlesex). Roger Hudson's.
CAMPBELL, C. Vitruvius Britannicus. II, pl.46. 1717.

SUNDORNE CASTLE (Shropshire).
BURKE, J.B. Visitation of Seats. Vol.II, p.17. 1853.*
JONES. Views of Setas. I. 1829.
LEACH, F. Seats of Shropshire. p.99. 1891.
MORRIS, F.O. Views of Seats. Vol.VI, p.39. 1880.
NEALE, J.P. Views of Seats. 2.S. Vol.III. 1826.
WEST, W. Picturesque views of Shropshire. p.133. 1831.
[Sales] SUNDORNE CASTLE, 1914, May 19-27 [Furniture, statuary, library etc.].

SUNDRIDGE OLD HALL (Kent).
OSWALD, A. Country houses of Kent. 26. 1933.

SUNDRIDGE PARK (Kent).
ANGUS, W. Seats of the Nobility. pl.56. 1787.
NEALE, J.P. Views of Seats. 2.S. Vol.V. 1829.

SUNDRIDGE PLACE (Kent).
BADESLADE, T. Seats in Kent. pl.31. 1750.
HARRIS, J. History of Kent. p.305. 1719.

SUNNING HILL PARK (Berkshire).
BURKE, J.B. Visitation of Seats. 2.S. Vol.II, p.140. 1855.*
JONES. Views of Seats. I. 1829.
NEALE, J.P. Views of Seats. Vol.I. 1818.

SURBITON HALL (Surrey).
[Sales] SURBITON HALL, 1914, July 20-23 [Contents].

SURBITON PLACE (Surrey).
PROSSER, G.F. Surrey Seats. p.79. 1828.

SURRENDEN DERING (Kent).
BURKE, J.B. Visitation of Seats. Vol.II, p.173. 1853.*
NEALE, J.P. Views of Seats. 2.S. Vol.III. 1826.
OSWALD, A. Country houses of Kent. 45. 1933.
[Sales] SURRENDEN DERING, 1928, October 8-11 [Contents]. (K.F. & R.).

SUSTEAD HALL (Norfolk).
GARRATT, T. Halls of Norfolk. pl.47 plan. 1890.

SUTTON CHENEY HALL (Leicestershire).
NICHOLS, J. History of Leicestershire. IV, ii. 543. 1811.

SUTTON COURT (Somerset).
COLLINSON, J. History of Somerset. II, 96. 1791.
COOKE, R. West Country Seats. p.166. 1957.
COUNTRY LIFE. XXVII, 126. 1910.

SUTTON COURTENAY MANOR (Berkshire).
COUNTRY LIFE. XV, 198. 1904.
COUNTRY LIFE. LXIX, 646. 1931.

SUTTON HALL (Yorkshire).
COUNTRY LIFE. CXXV, 204, 254. 1959.

SUTTON PLACE (Kent).
GREENWOOD, C. Kent. 72. 1838.
HASTED, E. Kent. I, 239. 1778.

SUTTON PLACE (Surrey).
HARRISON, Frederic.
—Annals of an old manor house, Sutton Place, Guildford. [Bibliogr. notes.] Illus. incl. plates (some col.) elevations and plans. 29x23 London: Macmillan & Co., 1893.
New and abriged ed. VI, 248pp. Illus. incl. plates 20x13 1899.
HARRISON, Frederic.
—Sutton Place. Summarised from Mr. F.H., Annals of an old manor house. 32pp. Illus. 18x12 n.p. n.d.
BRAYLEY, E.W. History of Surrey. II, 20. 1841.
BURKE, J.B. Visitation of Seats. 2.S. Vol.I, p.225. 1854.*
COUNTRY LIFE. IV, 824. 1898.
COUNTRY LIFE. VIII, 854. 1900.
COUNTRY LIFE. XXXV, 198 plan, 234. 1914.
GARNER, T. Domestic architecture. I, p.83 plan. 1911.
LATHAM, C. In English Homes. Vol.I, p.65. 1904.
MANNING, O. Surrey. I, 136. 1804.
NASH, J. Mansions of England. I. pl.19, 1839. & II, pl.16. 1840.
PROSSER, G.F. Surrey Seats. p.21. 1828.
TIPPING, H.A. English Homes. Period II, Vol.I, p.179. 1924.
WHITEMAN, G.W. English country homes. 10. 1951.

SUTTONS (Essex).
RUSH, J.A. Seats in Essex. p.169. 1897.

SUTTON SCARSDALE (Derbyshire).
BURKE, J.B. Visitation of Seats. Vol.II, p.243. 1853.*
BURKE, J.B. Visitation of Seats. 2.S. Vol.I, p.167. 1854.*
COUNTRY LIFE. XLV, 166. 1919.
JONES. Views of Seats. I. 1829.
NEALE, J.P. Views of Seats. Vol.I. 1818.
TILLEY, J. Halls of Derbyshire. III, p.199. 1899.
TIPPING, H.A. English Homes. Period V, Vol.I, p.199. 1921.

SWADELANDS (Kent).
See SWAYLANDS.

SWAINSTON (Hampshire, Isle of Wight).
BURKE, J.B. Visitation of Seats. Vol.II, p.18. 1853.*

SWAKELEYS (Middlesex).
TIPPING, Henry Avray.
— Swakeleys, Middlesex. [Revised ed.] 8pp. Illus. 37x24
London: Country Life, 1926.
Reprint from: COUNTRY LIFE, XXVI, 526. 1909.
BURKE, J.B. Visitation of Seats. Vol.II, p.121. 1853.*
COUNTRY LIFE. XXVI, 526. 1909.
COUNTRY LIFE. LXI, 61 plan. 1927.
LATHAM, C. In English Homes. Vol.III, p.91. 1909.
LONDON: Survey of Memorials. XIII. 1933.
NEALE, J.P. Views of Seats. Vol.II. 1819.
TIPPING, H.A. English Homes. Period III, Vol.II, p.407. 1927.

SWALLOWFIELD PARK (Berkshire).
RUSSELL, Constance Charlotte Elisa, *Lady*.
— Swallowfield and its owners. [Bibliogr. notes.]
Illus. incl. plates and folding genealog. tables. 25x18 London:
Longmans, Green & Co., 1901.

SWALLOWFIELD PARK.
— Some notes on Swallowfield Park. 12pp. Illus. (on cover.)
13x20 Reading? privately printed [*c*.1975.]
BURKE, J.B. Visitation of Seats. Vol.I, p.219. 1852.*

SWANBOROUGH MANOR (Sussex).
GODFREY, Walter Hindes.
— Swanborough manor house. 14pp. 6 illus. incl. sections,
elevations and plans. [Oxford, 1936].
Also in SUSSEX: Archaeological Society, Sussex
archaeological collections. LXXVII, 3.
COUNTRY LIFE. LXXVI, 472 plan. 1934.

SWANBOURNE OLD HOUSE (Buckinghamshire).
BURKE, J.B. Visitation of Seats. 2.S. Vol.I, p.142. 1854.*

SWANGROVE, Badminton (Gloucestershire).
COUNTRY LIFE. LXXXVI, 626. 1939.

SWAN HALL, Hawkedon (Suffolk).
SANDON, E. Suffolk houses. 265. 1977.

SWARCLIFFE HALL (Yorkshire).
BURKE, J.B. Visitation of Seats. 2.S. Vol.I, p.12. 1854.*

SWARKESTON HALL (Derbyshire).
TILLEY, J. Halls of Derbyshire. IV, p.71. 1902.

SWAYLANDS (Kent).
GREENWOOD, C. Kent. 157. 1838.

SWEENEY HALL (Shropshire).
LEACH, F. Seats of Shropshire. p.389. 1891.
WEST, W. Picturesque views in Shropshire. p.123. 1831.

SWELL (Gloucestershire).
ATKYNS, R. Glocestershire. p.371. 1768.

SWETTENHAM HALL (Cheshire).
BURKE, J.B. Visitation of Seats. Vol.I, p.230. 1852.*
TWYCROSS, E. Mansions of England and Wales. Vol.I, p.133.
1850.

SWILLINGTON HALL (Yorkshire).
KIP, J. Nouveau théâtre de la Grande Bretange. I, pl.73. 1715.
NEALE, J.P. Views of Seats. 2.S. Vol.I. 1824.
WHEATER, W. Mansions of Yorkshire. p.233. 1888.

SWINBURN CASTLE (Northumberland).
[Sales] SWINBURNE CASTLE, 1965, October 26, 27
[Furniture, silver etc.].

SWINFEN HALL (Staffordshire).
SHAW, S. Staffordshire. II, 30. 1801.

SWINFORD OLD MANOR (Kent).
COUNTRY LIFE. I, 350. 1897.

SWINHOPE HOUSE (Lincolnshire).
BURKE, J.B. Visitation of Seats. Vol.II, p.40. 1853.*

SWINTON PARK (Yorkshire).
BURKE, J.B. Visitation of Seats. Vol.II, p.98. 1853.*
COUNTRY LIFE. CXXXIX, 788, 872. 1966.
JONES. Views of Seats. I. 1829.
NEALE, J.P. Views of Seats. 2.S. Vol. IV. 1828.
YORKSHIRE. Picturesque views. 1885.
[Sales] SWINTON HOUSE, 1975, October 20, 21 [Pictures,
furniture etc.].
[Sales] SWINTON HOUSE, 1975, October 21 [Library].

SUTTON PLACE, Surrey. From: MANNING, (*Rev. O*). *The history and antiquities of the county of Surrey* [etc.], vol. I, London, 1804.

SWITHLAND HALL (Leicestershire).

MORRIS, F.O. Views of Seats. Vol.II, p.37. 1880.

NICHOLS, J. History of Leicestershire. III, ii, 1047. 1804. [Some pictures].

THROSBY, J. Views in Leicestershire. p.202. 1789.

[Sales] SWITHLAND HALL, 1978, October 16, 17 [Remaining contents].

SWYNNERTON HALL (Staffordshire).

JONES. Views of Seats. I. 1829.

NEALE, J.P. Views of Seats. Vol.IV. 1821.

SWYTHAMLEY HALL (Staffordshire).

[Sales] SWYTHAMLEY HALL, 1976, May 17 [Remaining contents].

SYDENHAM HOUSE (Devonshire).

COUNTRY LIFE. V, 528. 1899.

COUNTRY LIFE. XXXVII, 176. 1915.

COUNTRY LIFE. CXIX, 1420. 1956.

COUNTRY LIFE. CXX, 16. 1956.

GOTCH, J.A. Architecture of the Renaissance. II, p.11 plan. 1894.

SYDENHAM MANOR (Somerset).

WARD-JACKSON, Cyril Henry.
— An account of Sydenham manor house and some of its former owners. [Bibliogr.] 28pp. Illus. incl. plan and map. 22x16 (Bridgwater: privately printed by British Cellophane Ltd., 1962.)

SYDLING COURT (Dorsetshire).

ENGLAND: Picturesque Views. p.37. 1786-88.

HUTCHINS, J. Vitruvius Dorsettiensis. pl.30. 1816.

HUTCHINS, J. History of Dorset. IV, 500. 1870.

SYDNEY LODGE (Hampshire).

CAMPBELL, C. New Vitruvius Britannicus. I, pl.10, 1802.

SYMONDSBURY RECTORY (Dorsetshire).

HUTCHINS, J. Vitruvius Dorsettiensis. pl.31. 1816.

SYNDALE HOUSE (Kent).

GREENWOOD, C. Kent. 253. 1838.

SYNYARDS, Otham (Kent).

COUNTRY LIFE. XLVI, 345 plan. 1919.

OSWALD, A. Country houses of Kent. 24. 1933.

SYON HOUSE (Middlesex).

BURY, Adrian.
— Syon House ... With ten original copper-plate engravings by J.B. Wright, and an appreciation of the engraver's work by H. Rushbury, R.A. 60pp. Illus. (on end-papers) and 10 plates. 30x24 London: Dropmore Press, 1955.

NORTHUMBERLAND, Helen Magdalen Percy, *Duchess of*.
— Syon House, Middlesex [and its contents]. 18pp. Illus. incl. plates: photographs. Fol. 58x44 n.p. privately printed [1929?] With MS. captions to photographs, and some typewritten material inserted.

SYON HOUSE.
— Syon House: a brief history and guide. 8pp. Illus. (on cover). 22x14 [Brentford] (Syon House Estate) [c.1950.] Title on cover.

SYON HOUSE.
— Syon House; the story of a great house, with a short guide for visitors. 48pp. Illus. (1 col. on cover) incl. 4 col. plates, maps (on end-papers) and genealog. table. 20x14 [Isleworth] privately printed, 1950.
Another ed. Illus. (1 col. on cover) incl. 6 col. plates and map (on end-papers). 1968.

ADAM, R. & J. Works in Architecture. I-III. 1773-1822.

ANGUS, W. Seats of the Nobility. pl.61. 1787.

BOLTON, A.T. Architecture of R. & J. Adam. I, 246 plan. 1922.

BUCK, S. & N. Antiquities. I, pl.181. 1774.

BURKE, J.B. Visitation of Seats. Vol.I. p.182. 1852.*

COUNTRY LIFE. English Country Houses: Mid Georgian. p.86. 1956.

COUNTRY LIFE. XLVI, 728, 802, 838, 874. 1919.

COUNTRY LIFE. CVIII, 1873. 1950.

ENGLAND: Beauties of England. II, p.64. 1787.

ENGLAND: Picturesque Views. p.84. 1786-88.

HAVELL, R. Views of Noblemen's Seats. 1823.

NICOLSON, N. Great Houses of Britain. p.238. 1965.

ROBERTSON, A. Great Road. I, p.38, 1792. [Lodge.]

THAMES, River. An history. II, pl.7. 1796.

TIPPING, H.A. English Homes. Period VI, Vol.I, p.139. 1926.

SYSTON COURT (Gloucestershire).

ATKYNS, R. Glocestershire. p.344. 1768.

COUNTRY LIFE. XVIII, 486. 1905.

SYWELL HALL (Northamptonshire).

GOTCH, J.A. Halls of Northants. p.65. 1936.

TABLEY HOUSE (Cheshire).

CAREY, William.
— A descriptive catalogue of a collection of paintings by British artists, in the possession of Sir J.F. Leicester, Bart. [at Tabley House.] by W.C., with occasional remarks &c. by Sir R.C. Hoare, Bart. Engr. plate. 25x16 London: privately printed, 1819.

DE TABLEY, John Fleming Leicester, *Baron*.
— Catalogue of the works of English artists in the gallery of Sir John Fleming Leicester, Bart. 14ff. 24x20 London: privately printed, 1817.

YOUNG, John.
— A catalogue of pictures by British artists, in the possession of Sir John Fleming Leicester, Bart. with etchings from the whole collection ... with historical and biographical notices. 42pp. Engr. plates by the author. 30x24 London: privately printed, 1821.
With MS. notes of prices and purchasers' names at sales of these pictures, 1827-75.
Another ed. 1825.
With some MS. notes of prices and purchasers' names at the sale in London on July 7, 1827.

ANGUS-BUTTERWORTH, L.M. Old Cheshire families. p.149. 1932.

CAMPBELL, C. Vitruvius Britannicus. V, pls.16-19. 1771.

COUNTRY LIFE. English Country Houses: Mid Georgian. p.55. 1956.

COUNTRY LIFE. LIV, 84 plan, 114. 1923.

NEALE, J.P. Views of Seats. 2.S. Vol.V. 1829.

TIPPING, H.A. English Homes. Period VI, Vol.I, p.27. 1926.

TWYCROSS, E. Mansions of England and Wales. Vol.II, p.40. 1850.

TABLEY OLD HALL (Cheshire).
COUNTRY LIFE. LIV, 50. 1923.

ORMEROD, G. Cheshire. I, 625. 1882.

TADWORTH COURT (Surrey).
LEANING, Frances Edith.
— Tadworth Court, Surrey: a historical sketch. x, 126pp. 4 plates. 18x12 Redhill: Holmesdale Press, 1928.

TAINFIELD HOUSE (Somerset).
BURKE, J.B. Visitation of Seats. 2.S. Vol.II, p.71. 1855.*

TAMWORTH CASTLE (Staffordshire).
NORRIS, *Rev.* Henry.
— Tamworth Castle: its foundation, its history and its lords, from the Norman Conquest to the present day. 54pp. Illus. incl. plates and plan. 22x14 Tamworth: privately printed, 1899.

WOOD, Henry.
— Guide to Tamworth Castle. 16pp. Illus. incl. plans. 18x12 Tamworth: Tamworth Corporation [c.1950].

BUCK, S. & N. Antiquities. II, pl.304. 1774.

BURKE, J.B. Visitation of Seats. Vol.II, p.80. 1853.*

SHAW, S. Staffordshire. I, 415. 1798.

TAPLOW COURT (Buckinghamshire).
NEALE, J.P. Views of Seats. 2.S. Vol.V. 1829.

TAPLOW HOUSE (Buckinghamshire).
BURKE, J.B. Visitation of Seats. 2.S. Vol.I, p.228. 1854.*

TATTON OLD HALL (Cheshire).
MOSS, F. Pilgrimages. V, 117. 1910.

TATTON PARK (Cheshire).
LONDON: National Trust for Places of Historic Interest or Natural Beauty.
—Tatton Park, Knutsford, Cheshire. [Bibliogr.] 52pp. Illus. (1 col. on cover) incl. 8 plates and plans. 21x14 London, 1962.

New ed. JACKSON-STOPS, G. Tatton Park, Cheshire. [Bibliogr.] 64pp. Illus. (some col., 1 on cover) incl. plan and genealog. table. 25x18 [London] 1982.

BURKE, J.B. Visitation of Seats. 2.S. Vol.I, p.193. 1854.*

COUNTRY LIFE. XIX, 414. 1906.

COUNTRY LIFE. CXXXVI, 162, 232 plan. 1964.

NEALE, J.P. Views of Seats. Vol.I. 1818.

TWYCROSS, E. Mansions of England and Wales. Vol. II, p.32. 1850.

TEDDESLEY PARK (Staffordshire).
SHAW, S. Staffordshire. II, pl.2. Reprint 1976.

TEFFONT EVIAS MANOR (Wiltshire).
BRITTON, J. Beauties of Wiltshire. III, 331. 1825.

TEHIDY PARK (Cornwall).
BRITTON, J. Cornwall illustrated. 43. 1832.

BURKE, J.B. Visitation of Seats. 2.S. Vol.II, p.157. 1855.*

WATTS, W. Seats of the Nobility. pl.34. 1779.

TEMPLE COMBE HOUSE (Somerset).
BURKE, J.B. Visitation of Seats. Vol.II, p.219. 1853.*

TEMPLE DINSLEY (Hertfordshire).
CHAUNCY, H. Hertfordshire. II, 177. 1826.

COUNTRY LIFE. XXIX, 562 plan. 1911.

TEMPLE HOUSE (Berkshire).
THAMES, River. An history. I, pl.32. 1794.

TEMPLE MANOR, Strood (Kent).
GREAT BRITAIN: Ministry of Works [Ancient Monuments and Historic Buildings].
— RIGOLD, S.E. Temple Manor, Strood, Rochester, Kent. 16pp. Plates incl. folding plan. 21x13 London, 1962.

HASTED, E. Kent. I, 438. 1778.

TEMPLE NEWSAM (Yorkshire).

LEEDS: Temple Newsam House.
—KITSON, S.D. and PAWSON, E.D. Temple Newsam. 56pp. Illus. incl. plans. 24x15 Leeds: City Council, 1936.

LEEDS: Temple Newsam House.
—Temple Newsam House. Illus. (3 col.) incl. elevation and genealog. table. 28x21 Leeds, 1951.

WHEATER, William.
—Temple Newsam: its history and antiquities; comprising an account of the ancient preceptories there and at Temple Hurst, the baronial houses of Darcy, Lennox, Stuart, and Irwin; together with an account of the modern mansion, and a catalogue of the most celebrated pictures. 3 ed. Folding genealog. tables. 25x18 Leeds: Goodall & Suddick, 1889.

BURKE, J.B. Visitation of Seats. Vol. I, p.92. 1852.

COUNTRY LIFE. XVI, 522. 1904.

COUNTRY LIFE. LII, 428. 1922.

COUNTRY LIFE. LXXXIII, 547 [Exhibition]. 1938.

COUNTRY LIFE. CXLIV, 1054 [Chippendale Furniture]. 1968.

JONES. Views of Seats. I. 1829.

KIP, J. Nouveau théâtre de la Grande Bretagne. I, pl.42. 1715.

LATHAM, C. In English Homes. Vol.II, p.251. 1907.

MORRIS, F.O. Views of Seats. Vol.I, p.71. 1880.

MOSS, F. Pilgrimages. V, 294. 1910.

NEALE, J.P. Views of Seats. Vol.V. 1822.

WHEATER, W. Mansions of Yorkshire. p.282. 1888.

[Sales]TEMPLE NEWSAM, 1922, July 26-29, 31 [Contents].

TEMPLEWOOD (Norfolk).

COUNTRY LIFE. LXXXV, 116 plan. 1939.

TENDERING HALL (Suffolk).

BURKE, J.B. Visitation of Seats. 2.S. Vol.I, p.101. 1854.*

CROMWELL, T.K. Excursions in Suffolk. I, p.71. 1818.

SOANE, J. Plans, elevations and sections. pls. XVIII-XXII. 1788.

TENDRING MANOR (Essex).

BURKE, J.B. Visitation of Seats. 2.S. Vol.I, p.36. 1854.*

RUSH, J.A. Seats in Essex. p.171. 1897.

TERLING PLACE (Essex).

CROMWELL, T.K. Excursions in Essex. I, p.25. 1825.

RUSH, J.A. Seats in Essex. p.173. 1897.*

TESTON HOUSE (Kent).

See BARHAM COURT, Teston.

TEWIN WATER (Hertfordshire).

NEALE, J.P. Views of Seats. Vol.II. 1819.

THAME PARK (Oxfordshire).

THAME PARK.
— Oxon & Bucks. Borders ... The residential estate known as "Thame Park", ... A.D. 1530-1740. [Particulars of sale by Private treaty.] 8pp. Illus. 31x25 London (1924).

COUNTRY LIFE. XXVI, 90. 1909.

COUNTRY LIFE. CXXII, 1092 plan, 1148. 1957.

ENGLAND: Picturesque Views. p.6. 1786-88.

GARNER, T. Domestic architecture. I, p.54 plan. 1911.

TIPPING, H.A. English Homes. Period II, Vol.I, p.253. 1924.

THAMES DITTON (Surrey). *Sir* Thomas Heathcote, *Bart.*

COPPER PLATE MAGAZINE. pl.87. 1778.

SANDBY, P. Select Views. I, pl.64. 1783.

THATCHED HOUSE LODGE, Richmond Park (Surrey).

COUNTRY LIFE. CXXIV, 1240. 1958.

COUNTRY LIFE. CXXXIII, 974. 1963.

THELVETON HALL (Norfolk).

BIRKBECK, G. Old Norfolk houses. 120. 1908.

THELWALL HALL (Cheshire).

ORMEROD, G. Cheshire. I, 746. 1882.

TWYCROSS, E. Mansions of England and Wales. Vol.II, p.72. 1850.

THENFORD HOUSE (Northamptonshire).

COUNTRY LIFE. C, 624, 670. 1946.

GOTCH, J.A. Squires' Homes. 42. 1939.

THEOBALDS PARK (Hertfordshire).

ANGUS, W. Seats of the Nobility. pl.31. 1787.

[Sales] THEOBALD'S PARK, 1911, May 15, 16, 18, 19, 22, 23, 25, 26 [Contents].

THICKET PRIORY (Yorkshire).

MORRIS, F.O. Views of Seats. Vol.VI, p.37. 1880.

[Sales]THICKET PRIORY, 1954, May 27, 28 [Large portion of contents].

THIRKLEBY HALL (Yorkshire).

JONES. Views of Seats. I. 1829.

NEALE, J.P. Views of Seats. Vol.V. 1822.

THIRLESTANE HOUSE (Gloucestershire).

NORTHWICK, John Rushout, *Baron*.
— A catalogue of the pictures in the galleries of Thirlestane House, Cheltenham: the residence of the Right Hon. Lord N. 48pp. 18x12 Cheltenham: H. Davies, 1855.
Another ed. 60pp. 1856.

PHILLIPPS, *Sir* Thomas, *Bart*.
— Catalogue of the gallery of paintings of Sir Thomas Phillipps, Bart., at Thirlestane House, Cheltenham, 1866. [Nos. 1-399. Proof sheets.] 8pp. 40x25 Cheltenham, 1866. Another ed. 24pp. [1870?]

POPHAM, Arthur Ewart.
— Catalogue of drawings in the collection formed by Sir Thomas Phillips, Bart., now in the possession of ... T. Fitzroy Phillipps Fenwick of Thirlestaine House, Cheltenham. [Bibliogr.] 102 plates. 25x19 (London: privately printed) 1935.

THIRLESTANE HOUSE.
— Hours in the picture galley of Thirlestane House, Cheltenham: being a catalogue, with critical and descriptive notices of some of the principal paintings in Lord Northwick's collection. New ed. 84pp. Tinted lithogr. plate. 22x14 Cheltenham: H. Davies, 1846.

[Sales] CHELTENHAM, Thirlestane House, 1859, July 26 and following days [Ancient and modern pictures, miniatures etc.].

[Sales] CHELTENHAM, Thirlestane House, 1860, April 10-13 [Engravings].

THOBY PRIORY (Essex).

CROMWELL, T.K. Excursions in Essex. I, p.143. 1825.

THONOCK HALL (Lincolnshire).

BURKE, J.B. Visitation of Seats. 2.S. Vol.I, p.45. 1854.*

THORESBY HALL [PARK] (Nottinghamshire).

BEATTIE, Alexander, *Maj.*
—Thoresby Hall: an illustrated survey [etc.] 32pp. Illus. (some col., some on covers). incl. maps (on inside covers). Derby: E.L.P. [1957?].
New ed. Thoresby Hall: the home of the Pierrepont family. (Revised by C.W.N. Stanley.) 19x16 (1964.)

DALRYMPLE, *Hon.* Sir Hew Hamilton.
—Inventory of the Coigny papers formerly at the Château de Coigny in Normandy, now at Thoresby Park, Notts. 20pp. Illus. (on title-page.) 28x22 n.p. (privately printed), 1910.

BURKE, J.B. Visitation of Seats. 2.S. Vol.I, p.128. 1854.*

CAMPBELL, C. Vitruvius Britannicus. I, pls. 90,91. 1715.

CAMPBELL, C. Vitruvius Britannicus. III, pls. 81,82. 1725.

CAMPBELL, C. Vitruvius Britannicus. V, pls. 11-13. 1771.

COUNTRY LIFE. CLXV, 2082. 1979.

COUNTRY LIFE. CLXVI, 18. 323. 1979.

JONES. Views of Seats. I. 1829.

NEALE, J.P. Views of Seats. Vol.III. 1820.

THOROTON, R. Nottinghamshire. III, 344. 1797.

THORINGTON HALL (Suffolk).

LONDON: National Trust for Places of Historic Interest or Natural Beauty.
—Thorington Hall, Stoke-by-Nayland, Suffolk. 4pp. 1 illus. 19x23 (London) [*c*.1960.]

SANDON, E. Suffolk houses. 283. 1977.

THORNBRIDGE HALL (Derbyshire).

[Sales] THORNBRIDGE HALL, 1945, November 6 and following days [Contents].

THORNBURY CASTLE (Gloucestershire).

ELLIS, Richard.
— History of Thornbury Castle. 48pp. Illus. incl. plates, folding plans and title-page. 22x14 London: Hamilton, Adams, & Co.; Thornbury: by the author, 1839.

BUCK, S. & N. Antiquities. I, pl.103. 1774.

BURKE, J.B. Visitation of Seats. 2.S. Vol.I, p.144. 1854.*

COOKE, R. West Country Houses. p.46. 1957.

COUNTRY LIFE. XXII, 702. 1907.

GARNER, T. Domestic architecture. I, p.56 plan. 1911.

TIPPING, H.A. English Homes. Period II, Vol.I, p.79. 1924.

THORNBURY PARK (Gloucestershire).

BURKE, J.B. Visitation of Seats. Vol.I, p.84. 1852.

BURKE, J.B. Visitation of Seats. 2.S. Vol.I, p.215. 1854.

THORNCROFT MANOR (Surrey).

BRAYLEY, E.W. History of Surrey. IV, 429. 1841.

THORNDON HALL (Essex).

BURKE, J.B. Visitation of Seats. 2.S. Vol.I, p.66. 1854.*

CROMWELL, T.K. Excursions in Essex. I, p.163. 1825.

NEALE, J.P. Views of Seats. 2.S. Vol.II. 1825.

PAINE, J. Plans, elevations. Pt.II, pls.17-29 plans, 88 [Ceiling]. 1783.

RUSH, J.A. Seats in Essex. p.175. 1897.*

WATTS, W. Seats of the Nobility. pl.17. 1779.

THORNDON OLD HALL (Essex).

See OLD THORNDON HALL.

THORNES HOUSE (Yorkshire).

CAMPBELL, C. New Vitruvius Britannicus. I, pls.51-3. 1802.

THORNEY ABBEY HOUSE (Cambridgeshire).

COUNTRY LIFE. XLVI, 392. 1919.

TIPPING, H.A. English Homes. Period IV, Vol.I, p.53. 1920.

THORNEY HALL (Nottinghamshire).

THOROTON, R. Nottinghamshire. III, 384. 1797.

THORNEYHOLME (Cheshire).
GALLOWAY, Charles J.
— Catalogue of paintings and drawings at Thorneyholme, Cheshire, collected by C.J.G. 96pp. Plates: photographs. 34x26 Manchester: privately printed, 1892.

THORNFIELD, Bradford (Yorkshire).
YORKSHIRE. Picturesque views. 1885.

THORNHAM HALL (Suffolk).
FARRER, *Rev.* Edmund.
— Portraits in Thornham Hall. 72pp. 19 plates. 26x19 Norwich (privately printed, 1930).
CROMWELL, T.K. Excursions in Suffolk. II, p.11. 1819.

THORNHILL HOUSE (Dorsetshire).
HUTCHINS, J. History of Dorset. III, 672. 1868.

THORNTON HALL (Yorkshire).
BURKE, J.B. Visitation of Seats. Vol.II, p.6. 1853.*

THORNTON MANOR (Cheshire).
COUNTRY LIFE. CLXXII, 18, 110. 1982.

THORNYCROFT HALL (Cheshire).
TWYCROSS, E. Mansions of England and Wales. Vol.II, p.112. 1850.

THORPE HALL (Norfolk).
BIRKBECK, G. Old Norfolk houses. 122. 1908.
CROMWELL, T.K. Excursions in Norfolk. I, p.32. 1818.

THORPE HALL (Nothamptonshire).
HAKEWILL, Arthur William.
— General plan and external details with picturesque illustrations of Thorpe Hall, Peterborough; measured, drawn, and etched by A.W.H. 10pp. Illus. incl. engr. plates and plan. 42x30 London: by the author, 1852.
COUNTRY LIFE. English Country Houses: Caroline. p.102. 1966.
COUNTRY LIFE. XVI, 234. 1904.
COUNTRY LIFE. XLVI, 300, 330, 364. 1919.
GOTCH, J.A. Halls of Northants. p.11. 1936.
LATHAM, C. In English Homes. Vol.III, p.131. 1909.
TIPPING, H.A. English Homes. Period IV, Vol.I, p.23. 1920.

THORPE HALL, Horham (Suffolk).
SANDON, E. Suffolk houses. 238. 1977.

THORPE HALL, Rudston (Yorkshire).
WOOD, G.B. Historic homes of Yorkshire. 123. 1957.

THORPE MALSOR HALL (Northamptonshire).
GOTCH, J.A. Squires' Homes. 19. 1939.

THORPE MANDEVILLE HALL (Northamptonshire).
BURKE, J.B. Visitation of Seats. 2.S. Vol.II, p.89. 1855.*

THORPE PLACE (Surrey).
BURKE, J.B. Visitation of Seats. Vol.I, p.228. 1852.*

THORPE SATCHVILLE HALL (Leicestershire).
[Sales] THORPE SATCHVILLE HALL, 1965, March 16, 17 [Contents].

THORPLAND HALL (Norfolk).
GARNER, T. Domestic architecture. I, p.53 plan. 1911.

THRALE PLACE (Surrey).
See STREATHAM PARK.

THROCKING MANOR (Hertfordshire).
CHAUNCY, H. Hertfordshire. I, 232. 1826.

THROUGHAM MANOR (Gloucestershire).
GARNER, T. Domestic architecture. II, p.179. 1911.

THROWLEY HALL (Staffordshire).
HALL, S.C. Baronial Halls. Vol.II. 1848.

THRUMPTON HALL (Nottinghamshire).
SEYMOUR, George Fitzroy.
— Thrumpton Hall: a short history. 12pp. Illus. (2 col.) incl. map. 22x14 (Nottingham) privately printed [c.1970.]
COUNTRY LIFE. LIV. 180. 1923.
COUNTRY LIFE. CXXV, 1138, 1194 plan, 1254. 1959.

THRYBERGH PARK (Yorkshire).
BURKE, J.B. Visitation of Seats. Vol.I, p.249. 1852.*
BURKE, J.B. Visitation of Seats. 2.S. Vol.II, p.122. 1855.
MORRIS, F.O. Views of Seats. Vol.I, p.33. 1880.

THURGARTON PRIORY [Hall] (Nottinghamshire).
THOROTON, R. Nottinghamshire. III, 60. 1797.

THURLAND CASTLE (Lancashire).
GRAY, H. Old halls of Lancashire. p.7. 1893.
TWYCROSS, E. Mansions of England and Wales. Vol.II, p.vii. 1847.*

THURNHAM HALL (Lancashire).
BARTLETT, J. Mansions of England and Wales. pl.65. 1853.

JONES. Views of Seats. I. 1829.

NEALE, J.P. Views of Seats. 2.S. Vol.II. 1825.

TWYCROSS, E. Mansions of England and Wales. Vol.II, p.21. 1847.

THURNING HALL (Norfolk).
BURKE, J.B. Visitation of Seats. Vol.II, p.84. 1853.*

THURSFORD HALL (Norfolk).
NEALE, J.P. Views of Seats. Vol.III. 1820.

THURSTASTON HALL (Cheshire).
TWYCROSS, E. Mansions of England and Wales. Vol.I, p.70. 1850.*

THURSTON HALL (Suffolk).
GARNER, T. Domestic architecture. II, p.182. 1911.

SANDON, E. Suffolk houses 187. 1977.

THURTON HALL (Norfolk).
GARRATT, T. Halls of Norfolk. pl.48. 1890.

TICHBORNE HOUSE (Hampshire).
BURKE, J.B. Visitation of Seats. Vol.I, p.138. 1852.*

TICKENHAM COURT (Somerset).
FORREST, Denys.

—The making of a manor: the story of Tickenham Court. [Bibliogr.] x, 124pp. Illus. (1 col. on cover) incl. plates, plans and maps. 21x16 [Bradford-on-Avon] Moonraker Press for Tickenham Court Farm Ltd., 1975.

TICKENHILL HOUSE (Worcestershire).
BARNARD, Ettwell Augustine Bracher.

—A vanished palace, being some account of Tickenhill House, Bewdley. (This paper was read at an exhibition of Mediæval and modern arts and crafts held at Tickenhill Manor on April 21,22. 1925.) 14pp. 22x14 Cambridge: privately printed, 1925.

MS. letter from the author and typed copy of reply, inserted.

TILSTONE LODGE (Cheshire).
TWYCROSS, E. Mansions of England and Wales. Vol.I, p.124. 1850.*

TINTINHULL HOUSE (Somerset).
LONDON: National Trust for Places of Historic Interest or Natural Beauty.

—Tintinhull House, Somerset, 4pp. 1 illus. 18x12 [London, *c.* 1955.]

New ed. 8pp. 1963.

Rev. ed. DODD, D. [Bibliogr.] 12pp. Illus. (on cover) and plates. 22x14 1981.

COOKE, R. West Country Houses. p.103. 1957.

COUNTRY LIFE. CXIX, 798. 1956.

TIRLEY GARTH (Cheshire).
COUNTRY LIFE. CLXXI, 702 plan. 1982.

TISSINGTON HALL (Derbyshire).
BURKE, J.B. Visitation of Seats. Vol.II, p.91. 1853.*

COUNTRY LIFE. XXIX, 342, 378 plan. 1911.

COUNTRY LIFE. CLX, 158, 214, 286. 1976.

JONES. Views of Seats. I. 1829.

NEALE, J.P. Views of Seats. 2.S. Vol.I. 1824.

TILLEY, J. Halls of Derbyshire. II, p.253. 1893.

TIPPING, H.A. English Homes. Early Renaissance. p.357. 1912.

TIPPING, H.A. English Homes. Period III, Vol.II, p.189. 1927.

TITCHFIELD ABBEY [Place House]. (Hampshire).
BUCK, S. & N. Antiquities. I, pl.111. 1774.

COUNTRY LIFE. XLV, 338. 1919.

TITSEY PLACE (Surrey)
BRAYLEY, E.W. History of Surrey. IV, 204. 1841.

BURKE, J.B. Visitation of Seats. 2.S. Vol.I, p.69. 1854.*

NEALE, J.P. Views of Seats. Vol. IV. 1821.

TIVERTON CASTLE (Devonshire).
CAMPBELL, *Mrs.* Ivar.

— Tiverton Castle, Devon. 12pp. Illus. (1 col., some on covers, 1 on title-page.) 14x20 (Derby: E.L.P., 1972.)

TIXALL HOUSE [Hall] (Staffordshire).
GOTCH, J.A. Architecture of the Renaissance. II, p.21. 1894.

JONES. Views of Seats. I. 1829.

NEALE, J.P. Views of Seats. Vol.IV. 1821.

NIVEN, W. Old Staffordshire houses. p.4, pl.4. [Gatehouse] 1882.

PLOT, R. Staffordshire. 359. 1686.

SHAW, S. Staffordshire. II, pls.16, 17. Reprint 1976.

TIXOVER GRANGE (Rutland).
[Sales] TIXOVER GRANGE, 1928 July 25-29 [Contents].

TOCKENHAM HOUSE (Wiltshire).
ELYARD, S.J. Old Wiltshire homes. p.62. 1894.

TOCKINGTON MANOR (Gloucestershire).
COOKE, R. West Country Houses. p.115. 1957.

TOCKNELLS COURT (Gloucestershire).
COUNTRY LIFE. XXXVII, 518. 1915.

TODDINGTON MANOR (Bedfordshire).
BARTLETT, J. Selections from views of mansions. 1851.
COUNTRY LIFE. CXXIX, 638 plan. 1961.
[Sales] TODDINGTON MANOR, 1922, February 22, 23 [Antique furniture, pictures etc.].

TODDINGTON MANOR (Gloucestershire).
BRITTON, John.
— Graphic illustrations, with historical and descriptive accounts, of Toddington, Gloucestershire [etc.]. (Pedigree of the family of Tracy.) 72pp. Illus. incl. cuts (1 on title-page), 29 plates (28 engr., 1 lithogr.), sections, plans and genealog. tables. 35x27 London: for the author, 1840.
BURKE, J.B. Visitation of Seats. Vol.II, p.205. 1853.* (Plate 2.S. Vol.II. p.1.)
COUNTRY LIFE. English Country Houses: Late Georgian. p.161. 1958.
COUNTRY LIFE. XV, 630. 1904.
COUNTRY LIFE. LXXXII, 374. 1937.
MORRIS, F.O. Views of Seats. Vol.V, p.69. 1880.
[Sales] MUNICH, 1911, October 4 [Heraldic stained glass from Lord Sudeley's Col.].

TODDINGTON OLD MANOR (Gloucestershire).
ATKYNS, R. Glocestershire. p.409. 1768.

TODMORDEN HALL (Yorkshire).
PYNE.W.H. Lancashire illustrated. 81. 1831.

TOFT HALL (Cheshire).
BURKE, J.B. Visitation of Seats. Vol.I, p.162. 1852.*
NEALE, J.P. Views of Seats. 2.S. Vol.V. 1829.
ORMEROD, G. Cheshire. I, 506. 1882.
TWYCROSS, E. Mansions of England and Wales. Vol.II, p.54. 1850.

TOLLER FRATRUM, Little Toller Farm (Dorsetshire).
OSWALD, A. Country houses of Dorset. p.78. 1959.

TOLLERTON HALL (Nottinghamshire).
THOROTON, R. Nottinghamshire. I, 174. 1797.

TONACOMBE (Cornwall).
COUNTRY LIFE. LXXIV, 500. 1933.

TONG CASTLE (Shropshire).
ANGUS, W. Seats of the Nobility. pl.20. 1787.
BUCK, S. & N. Antiquities. II, pl.254. 1774.
BURKE, J.B. Visitation of Seats. Vol.II, p.51. 1853.*
COUNTRY LIFE. C, 578. 1946.
ENGLAND: Picturesque Views. p.75. 1786-88.
JONES. Views of Seats. I. 1829.
LEACH, F. Seats of Shropshire. p.113. 1891.
NEALE, J.P. Views of Seats. 2.S. Vol.II. 1825.
WEST, W. Picturesque views of Shropshire. p.118. 1831.

TONG HALL (Yorkshire).
JONES. Views of Seats. I. 1829.
NEALE, J.P. Views of Seats. Vol.V. 1822.

TOPPINGOE HALL (Essex).
CROMWELL, T.K. Excursions in Essex.I, p.25. 1825.

TORKSEY HALL [CASTLE] (Lincolnshire).
BUCK, S. & N. Antiquities. I, pl.179. 1774.

TORRE ABBEY (Devonshire).
BURKE, J.B. Visitation of Seats. 2.S. Vol.I, p.74. 1854.*

TORTWORTH COURT (Gloucestershire).
ATKYNS, R. Glocestershire. p.412. 1768.

TOTLEY HALL (Derbyshire).
TILLEY, J. Halls of Derbyshire. III, p.105. 1899.

TOTTENHAM HOUSE (Wiltshire).
ADAMS, William Maurice.
— Wolfhall and Tottenham, the homes of the Seymours and the Bruce. 56pp. 4 plates incl. folding map. 18x12 Putney: Maurice & Co. [1903].
One of the series: SYLVAN SAVERNAKE.
JONES. Views of Seats. II. 1829.
NEALE, J.P. Views of Seats. Vol.V. 1822.

TOTTERIDGE PARK (Hertfordshire).
BURKE, J.B. Visitation of Seats. Vol.I, p.74. 1852.*
CAMPBELL, C. Vitruvius Britannicus. IVth. pls.77, 78. 1739.

TOWER (Flintshire).
BURKE, J.B. Visitation of Seats. 2.S. Vol.I, p.76. 1854.*

TOWNELEY HALL (Lancashire).
BURNLEY: Art Gallery and Museum [Towneley Hall].
— ALLEN, J. Official guide to Towneley Hall. (Reprint.) 36pp. Illus. 22x14 Burnley, 1923.

Another ed. Official handbook to Towneley Hall. 48pp. Illus. incl. 1 col. (on cover) and plans. 18x12 1955.

BARTLETT, J. Mansions of England and Wales. I, pl.1. 1853.

BURKE, J.B. Visitation of Seats. Vol.I, p.163. 1852.*

COUNTRY LIFE. XXXIV, 228 plan. 1913.

TWYCROSS, E. Mansions of England and Wales. Vol.I, p.1. 1847.

TOWNHILL PARK (Hampshire).

COUNTRY LIFE. LIII, 502 plan, 536. 1923.

TRAFALGAR HOUSE (Wiltshire).

CAMPBELL, C. Vitruvius Britannicus. V, pls.78-81. 1771.

COUNTRY LIFE. English Country Houses: Mid Georgian. p.115. 1956.

COUNTRY LIFE. XCVIII, 68, 112. 1945.

MORRIS, F.O. Views of Seats. Vol.III, p.23. 1880.

TRAFFORD HALL (Cheshire).

TWYCROSS, E. Mansions of England and Wales. Vol.I, p.121. 1850.*

TRAFFORD PARK (Lancashire).

BARTLETT, J. Mansions of England and Wales. pls.140, 141. 1853.

BURKE, J.B. Visitation of Seats. Vol.I, p.178. 1852.*

TWYCROSS, E. Mansions of England and Wales. Vol.III, p.70. 1847.

TRAGNOLL (Kent).

BADESLADE, T. Seats in Kent. pl.32. 1750.

HARRIS, J. History of Kent. p.72. 1719.

TRANBY LODGE (Yorkshire).

SMITH, *Sir* Gerard, *Lieut.-Col.*
— History and description of old oak carving and panelling, formerly the property of the Bedingfield family, and removed from Halesworth, Suffolk, to Tranby Lodge, Hessle, E. Yorks. [The property of Lieut.-Col. Sir G. Smith; priced.] 12pp. 5 plates, incl. plan. 28x22 Derby: privately printed (1910).

TRANBY PARK (Yorkshire).

BURKE, J.B. Visitation of Seats. Vol.I, p.231. 1852.*

TRAWSCOED (Cardiganshire).

See CROSSWOOD HALL.

TREAGO CASTLE (Herefordshire).

MOSS, F. Pilgrimages. [II] 325. 1903.

ROBINSON, C.J. Mansions of Herefordshire. pl.23. 1873.

TREBERFYDD (Brecknockshire).

COUNTRY LIFE. CXL, 276, 322. 1966.

TREDEGAR PARK (Monmouthshire).

TREDEGAR PARK.
—The collection of works of art, pictures, furniture, silver, china, & . at Tredegar House, Monmouthshire. 22pp. Plates. 28x22 n.p. privately printed, 1916.

BURKE, J.B. Visitation of Seats. 2.S. Vol.I, p.152. 1854.*

COUNTRY LIFE. XXIV, 792, 838. 1908.

COUNTRY LIFE. CLXIV, 994. 1978.

LATHAM, C. In English Homes. Vol.III, p.165. 1909.

NEALE, J.P. Views of Seats. 2.S. Vol.IV. 1828.

TREFEILIR (Anglesey).

BURKE, J.B. Visitation of Seats. 2.S. Vol.I, p.207. 1854.*

TREFFRY HOUSE (Cornwall).

See PLACE HOUSE, Fowey.

TREFUSIS HOUSE (Cornwall).

BURKE, J.B. Visitation of Seats. 2.S. Vol.II, p.83. 1855.*

TREGENNA CASTLE (Cornwall).

BURKE, J.B. Visitation of Seats. Vol.I, p.210. 1852.*

TREGOTHNAN (Cornwall).

BRITTON, J. Cornwall illustrated. 24. 1832.

BURKE, J.B. Visitation of Seats. 2.S. Vol.II, p.7. 1855.*

COUNTRY LIFE. English Country Houses: Late Georgian. p.140. 1958.

COUNTRY LIFE. CXIX, 1051, 1112. 1956.

CROMWELL, T.K. Excursions in Cornwall. p.56. 1824.

JONES. Views of Seats. II. 1829.

MORRIS, F.O. Views of Seats. Vol.V, p.29. 1880.

NEALE, J.P. Views of Seats. Vol.I. 1818.

TREGREHAN (Cornwall).

BURKE, J.B. Visitation of Seats. 2.S. Vol.II, p.87. 1855.*

TRELAWNE (Cornwall).

BURKE, J.B. Visitation of Seats. 2.S. Vol.II, p.148. 1855.*

TRELISSICK (Cornwall).

BRITTON, J. Cornwall illustrated. 42. 1832.

TRELOWARREN (Cornwall).
BRITTON, J. Cornwall illustrated. 41. 1832.
BURKE, J.B. Visitation of Seats. 2.S. Vol.II, p.149. 1855.*
COUNTRY LIFE. XXXIX, 450. 1916.
CROMWELL, T.K. Excursions in Cornwall. p.71. 1824.

TREMATON (Cornwall).
BURKE, J.B. Visitation of Seats. 2.S. Vol.II, p.171. 1855.*

TRENARREN (Cornwall).
BURKE, J.B. Visitation of Seats. 2.S. Vol.I, p.86. 1854.*

TRENT MANOR (Dorsetshire).
HEATH, S. Dorset Manor Houses. 175. 1907.
OSWALD, A. Country houses of Dorset. p.105. 1959.

TRENT PARK (Middlesex).
BURKE, J.B. Visitation of Seats. 2.S. Vol.II, p.154. 1855.*
COUNTRY LIFE. LXVIII, 497 [Japanned Furniture]. 1930.
COUNTRY LIFE. LXIX, 40, 66 plan. 1931.
[Sales] TRENT PARK, 1924, November 25 [Furniture, tapestry, procelain etc.].

TRENTHAM HALL (Staffordshire).
COUNTRY LIFE. CXLIII, 176. 1968.
HALL, S.C. Baronial Halls. Vol.II. 1848.
JONES. Views of Seats. I. 1829.
MORRIS, F.O. Views of Seats. Vol.I, p.59. 1880.
NEALE, J.P. Views of Seats. Vol.IV. 1821.
PLOT, R. Staffordshire. 267. 1686.
SHAW, S. Staffordshire. II, pls. 25, 26. Reprint 1976.
SPROULE, A. Lost houses of Britain. 256. 1982.
UNITED KINGDOM. Historic houses. 135. 1892.
WATTS, W. Seats of the Nobility. pl.31.1779.
[Sales] TRENTHAM HALL, 1907, July 17-19 [Sculpture, pictures, furniture etc.]

TREOWEN (Monmouthshire).
COUNTRY LIFE. CXXVIII, 970 plan. 1960.

TREREIFE (Cornwall).
BURKE, J.B. Visitation of Seats. Vol.II, p.178. 1853.*

TRERICE (Cornwall).
LONDON: National Trust for Places of Historic Interest or Natural Beauty.
—TRINICK,M. Trerice, Cornwall. 16pp. Illus. (on cover) and 4 plates. 18x12 London: Country Life (1954).
New ed. 20pp. Illus (1 col. on cover) and plates. 21x15 [London] 1982.
COUNTRY LIFE.XXX, 206. 1911.

CROMWELL, T.K. Excursions in Cornwall. p.97. 1824.
DELDERFIELD, E.R. West Country houses. I, 142. 1968.
TIPPING,H.A. English Homes. Early Renaissance. p. 129. 1912.
[Sales] LONDON, 1924, June 12 [House].

TRETOWER COURT (Brecknockshire).
GREAT BRITAIN: Office of Works [Ancient Monuments and Historic Buildings].
— RADFORD, C.A.R. Tretower Court, Breconshire. 20pp. 2 plates incl. plans. 21x13 London, 1938.
GREAT BRITAIN: Ministry of Works [Ancient Monuments and Historic Buildings].
— RADFORD, C.A.R. Tretower Court, Breconshire. 16pp. Plates (2 folding) incl. plans. 1948.
Another ed. 1957.
Another ed. 8pp. Plan. 21x14 (1959).
GREAT BRITAIN: Ministry of Public Building and Works [Ancient Monuments and Historic Buildings].
— RADFORD, C.A.R. Tretower Court and Castle. [Summary in Welsh.] 32pp. Illus. incl. plans. 21x13 London, 1969.
RADFORD, Courtenay Arthur Ralegh.
— Tretower: the Castle and the Court. [Bibliogr. notes.] Excerpt. 50pp. 11 (2 folding) plates incl. plans. 24x18 [Brecon,1960.]
From: Brycheiniog, vol.VI.

TREVALYN HALL (Denbighshire).
BURKE, J.B. Visitation of Seats. Vol.I, p.242. 1852.*
COUNTRY LIFE. CXXXII, 78. 1962.
NEALE, J.P. Views of Seats. Vol.V. 1822.

TREVARNO (Cornwall).
BURKE, J.B. Visitation of Seats. Vol.I, p.46. 1852.*

TREVAYLER (Cornwall).
BURKE, J.B. Visitation of Seats. Vol.II, p.203. 1853.*

TREVEREUX (Surrey).
BRAYLEY, E.W. History of Surrey. IV, 153. 1841.

TREVOR HALL (Denbighshire).
COPPER PLATE MAGAZINE. II, pl.78. 1792-1802.
ENGLAND: Picturesque Views. p.88.1786-88.

TREWAN HALL (Cornwall).
CROMWELL, T.K. Excursions in Cornwall. p.100. 1824.

TREWARDREVA (Cornwall).
COUNTRY LIFE. CXXIII, 1192. 1958.

TREWARNE MANOR (Cornwall).
COUNTRY LIFE. CXXXII, 576. 1962.

TRENTHAM HALL, Staffordshire. From: PLOT (R.). *The natural history of Staffordshire*, Oxford, 1686.

TREWARTHENICK (Cornwall).
BRITTON, J. Cornwall illustrated. 44. 1832.
BURKE, J.B. Visitation of Seats. 2.S. Vol.I, p.178. 1854.*

TREWHITT HALL (Northumberland).
BURKE, J.B. Visitation of Seats. 2.S. Vol.I, p.208. 1854.*

TREWITHEN (Cornwall).
COUNTRY LIFE. CXIII, 990, 1072. 1953.

TRILEY COURT (Monmouthshire).
NICHOLAS, T. Counties of Wales. II, p.720. 1872.

TRING PARK (Hertfordshire).
CAMPBELL, C. Vitruvius Britannicus. IVth. pls. 104, 105. 1739.
CHAUNCY, H. Hertfordshire. II, 558. 1826.
COUNTRY LIFE. I, 604. 1897.

TRINITY HOUSE, Hull (Yorkshire).
COUNTRY LIFE. CXLIX, 698 [Furniture]. 1971.

TROSTON HALL (Suffolk).
BURKE, J.B. Visitation of Seats. Vol.II, p.235. 1853.*

TROY HOUSE (Monmouthshire).
NICHOLAS, T. Counties of Wales. II, p.724. 1872.

TRY HILL (Surrey). Colonel Onslow's Lodge.
COPPER PLATE MAGAZINE. pl.93. 1778.
SANDBY, P. Select Views. I, pl.65. 1783.

TUDOR HOUSE, Broadway (Worcestershire).
COUNTRY LIFE. XXVIII, 360 plan. 1910.

TULKETH HALL (Lancashire).
NEALE, J.P. Views of Seats. 2.S. Vol.II. 1825.

TUNSTALL COURT (Kent).
COUNTRY LIFE. LI, 455 plan. 1922.

TUNSTALL HALL (Shropshire).
BURKE, J.B. Visitation of Seats. 2.S. Vol.I, p.186. 1854.*

TUPTON HALL (Derbyshire).
TILLEY, J. Halls of Derbyshire. III, p.221. 1899.

TURKEY COURT (Kent).
COUNTRY LIFE. CXXX, 1628. 1961.

TURNWORTH HOUSE (Dorsetshire).
HUTCHINS, J. History of Dorset. III, 469. 1868.

TURTON TOWER (Lancashire).
GRAY, H. Old halls of Lancashire. p.89. 1893.
HALL, S.C. Baronial Halls. Vol.I. 1848.
MOSS, F. Pilgrimages. V, 111. 1910.
PYNE, W.H. Lancashire illustrated. 85. 1831.

TUSMORE HOUSE (Oxfordshire).
CAMPBELL, C. New Vitruvius Britannicus. I, pls. 3-5. 1802.
[Sales] TUSMORE, 1929, May 7-11 [Contents].

TUTSHAM HALL (Kent).
BADESLADE, T. Seats in Kent. pl.34. 1750.
HARRIS, J. History of Kent. p.121. 1719.

TWEMLOW HALL (Cheshire).
TWYCROSS, E. Mansions of England and Wales. Vol.I, p.139. 1850.*

TWICKENHAM, Earl of Strafford's (Middlesex).
KIP, J. Nouveau théâtre de la Grande Bretagne. III, pl.31. 1715.

TWICKENHAM MEADOWS (Middlesex).
COPPER PLATE MAGAZINE. II, pl.50. 1792-1802.
ENGLAND: Picturesque Views. p.18. 1786-88.

TWICKENHAM PARK HOUSE (Middlesex).
ANGUS, W. Seats of the Nobility. pl.40. 1787.

TWITTS GHYLL (Sussex).
COUNTRY LIFE. LXIII, 598. 1928.

TY-GLYN (Cardiganishire).
NICHOLAS, T. Counties of Wales. I, p.131. 1872.

TYLE MILL (Berkshire).
COUNTRY LIFE. XCI, 758. 1942.

TY MAWR (Monmouthshire).
BURKE, J.B. Visitation of Seats. Vol.II, p.133. 1853.*

TYNEHAM (Dorsetshire).
BURKE, J.B. Visitation of Seats. Vol.I, p.76. 1852.*
COUNTRY LIFE. LXXVII, 348. 1935.
COUNTRY LIFE. CXXXIX, 730. 1966.

HUTCHINS, J. History of Dorset. I, 618. 1861.
OSWALD, A. Country houses of Dorset. p.86. 1959.

TYNTESFIELD (Somerset).
COOKE, R. West Country Houses. p.169. 1957.

TYRINGHAM (Buckinghamshire).
COUNTRY LIFE. XLII, 628. 1917.
COUNTRY LIFE. LXV, [740, 780. Garden Architecture]. 1929.
NEALE, J.P. Views of Seats. Vol.I. 1818.

TYTHEGSTON COURT (Glamorganshire).
COUNTRY LIFE. CLXII, 1006. 1977.
COUNTRY LIFE. CLXIV, 1024. [Furniture.] 1978.

TYTHROP HOUSE (Oxfordshire).
COUNTRY LIFE. XV, 306. 1904.
LATHAM, C. In English Homes. Vol.I, p.175. 1904.
[Sales] THAME, 1933, August 21, 22 [Contents of T.H.].

TYTTENHANGER (Hertfordshire).
COUNTRY LIFE. English Country Houses: Caroline. p.119. 1966.
COUNTRY LIFE. XVIII, 594. 1905.
COUNTRY LIFE. XLVI, 424 plan, 454, 590 [Furniture]. 1919.
LATHAM, C. In English Homes. Vol.III, p.151. 1909.
MORRIS, F.O. Views of Seats. Vol.IV, p.67. 1880.
NEALE, J.P. Views of Seats. Vol.II. 1819.
TIPPING, H.A. English Homes. Period IV, Vol.I, p.63. 1920.

UCKFIELD HOUSE (Sussex).
COUNTRY LIFE. CXL, 80. 1966.

UDDENS (Dorsetshire).
HUTCHINS, J. History of Dorset. III, 115. 1868.

UFFINGTON HOUSE, Stamford (Lincolnshire).
COUNTRY LIFE. XVI, 992. 1904.

UFFORD HALL Fressingfield (Suffolk).
SANDON, E. Suffolk houses. 175. 1977.

UFFORD'S HALL, Metton (Norfolk).
GARRATT, T. Halls of Norfolk. pl.19. 1890.

UFTON COURT (Berkshire).
SHARP, A. Mary.
— The history of Ufton Court, of the parish of Ufton, in the county of Berks, and of the Perkins family: compiled from ancient records. [Bibliogr. notes.] Illus. incl. plans, maps and genealog. tables. 25x19 London: Elliot Stock, 1892.
COUNTRY LIFE. XXI, 906. 1907.

UGBROOKE PARK (Devonshire).
BRITTON, J. Devonshire illustrated. 102. 1832.
BURKE, J.B. Visitation of Seats. Vol.II, p.150. 1853.*
COUNTRY LIFE. CXLII, 138, 203, 266. 1967.
MORRIS, F.O. Views of Seats. Vol.II, p.67. 1880.

ULVERSCROFT ABBEY (Leicestershire).
BURKE, J.B. Visitation of Seats. 2.S. Vol.I, p.119. 1854.*

UMBERSLADE HALL (Warwickshire).
CAMPBELL, C. Vitruvius Britannicus. III, pls.101, 102. 1725.
SMITH, W. History of the County of Warwick. 98. 1830.
[Sales] LONDON, 1825, July 21 [Estate].

UNDERLEY HALL (Westmorland).
MORRIS, F.O. Views of Seats. Vol.IV, p.73. 1880.

UNSTONE HALL (Derbyshire).
TILLEY, J. Halls of Derbyshire. III, p.113. 1899.

UNTHANK HALL (Derbyshire).
TILLEY, J. Halls of Derbyshire. III, p.115. 1899.

UNTHANK HALL (Northumberland).
BURKE, J.B. Visitation of Seats. Vol.I, p.245. 1852.*

UPCERNE MANOR (Dorsetshire).
HUTCHINS, J. History of Dorset. IV, 156. 1870.
OSWALD, A. Country houses of Dorset. p.96. 1959.
[Sales] LONDON, 1980, June 12 [Broadhead collection removed from U.M.].

UPCOTT (Devonshire).
BURKE, J.B. Visitation of Seats. Vol.I, p.83. 1852.*

UPLANDS HALL (Lancashire).
BARTLETT, J. Mansions of England and Wales. pls.84, 85. 1853.
TWYCROSS, E. Mansions of England and Wales. Vol.II, p.47. 1847.

UPLEATHAM HALL (Yorkshire).
WHEATER, W. Mansions of Yorkshire. p.299. 1888.

UPMINSTER HALL (Essex).
RUSH, J.A. Seats in Essex. p.179. 1897.*

UPPARK (Sussex).
MEADE-FETHERSTONHAUGH, Margaret Isabel Frances, *Lady.*
— The story of Uppark. By Lady M-F., and M.B. Smith. 24pp. Illus. (1 on cover) incl. 2 (1 folding) plates and map. 18x12 [n.p. privately printed, c.1950.]
New ed. Uppark, Sussex. 28pp. Illus. (1 on cover) incl. 4 plates and map. London: Country Life for the National Trust, 1955.
Another ed. [Bibliogr. notes.] 36pp. Col. illus. (on cover) and 4 plates. 21x14 (London) National Trust [c.1970.]
MEADE-FETHERSTONHAUGH, Margaret Isabel Frances, *Lady.*
— Uppark and its people. By Lady M-F., and O. Warner. Illus. incl. 15 plates. 22x14 London: Allen & Unwin, 1964.
COUNTRY LIFE. English Country Houses: Mid Georgian. p.29. 1956.
COUNTRY LIFE. XXVII, 702. 1910.
COUNTRY LIFE. LXXXIX, 520, 540, 562. 1941.
KIP, J. Nouveau théâtre de la Grande Bretagne. I, pl.38. 1715.
NEALE, J.P. Views of Seats. Vol.IV. 1821.
NICOLSON, N. Great Houses of Britain. p.152. 1965.
TIPPING, H.A. English Homes. Period IV, Vol.I, p.363. 1920.

UPPER DOWDESWELL MANOR (Gloucestershire).
ATKYNS, R. Glocestershire. p.208. 1768.

UPPER HOUSE (Essex).
ESSEX: A new and complete history. IV, 97. 1771.

UPPER SLAUGHTER MANOR (Gloucestershire).
COUNTRY LIFE. XXXIV, 454 plan. 1913.
GARNER, T. Domestic architecture. II, p.193 plan. 1911.

UPPER SWELL MANOR (Gloucestershire).
GARNER, T. Domestic architecture. II, p.194. 1911.

UPPER UPHAM HOUSE (Wiltshire).
COUNTRY LIFE. LI, 888. 1922.

UPTON CASTLE (Pembrokeshire).
NICHOLAS, T. Counties of Wales. II, p.836. 1872.

UPTON CRESSETT HALL (Shropshire).
SHROPSHIRE. Castles & Old Mansions. 39. 1868.

UPTON HALL (Northamptonshire).
[Sales] UPTON HALL, 1946, May 7-9 [Contents].

UPTON HOUSE (Essex).
ESSEX: A new and complete history. IV, 254. 1771.

UPTON HOUSE (Gloucestershire).
COUNTRY LIFE. CLIII, 390. 1973.
[Sales] UPTON HOUSE, 1983, September 26 [Remaining contents].

UPTON HOUSE (Warwickshire).
LONDON:National Trust for Places of Historic Interest or Natural Beauty.
—Catalogue of pictures & porcelain at Upton House, Banbury. The catalogue of pictures edited by the second Viscount Bearsted. [Bibliogr. notes.] 70pp. 8 plates. 18x12 London: Country Life (1950.)
LONDON: National Trust for Places of Historic Interest or Natural Beauty.
—Upton House. The Bearsted collection: pictures. [Bibliogr. notes.] Illus. (on cover) and 12 plates. 25x18 (London). 1964.
LONDON: National Trust for Places of Historic Interest or Natural Beauty.
—Upton House. The Bearsted collection: porcelain. (Catalogue ... By J.V.G. Mallet.) [Bibliogr.] 32pp. Illus. (on cover) and 8 plates. 25x18 London, 1964.
Addenda to 1964 catalogue, inserted. [Photocopy of typescript.] 2ff. 31x18 London, 1969.
LONDON: National Trust for Places of Historic Interest or Natural Beauty.
—Upton House, 8pp. 1 illus. 22x14 [London, c. 1965.]
LONDON: National Trust for Places of Historic Interest or Natural Beauty.
—JACKSON-STOPS, G. Upton House, Warwickshire. 28pp. Illus. (1 col. on cover) incl. plates. 22x14 [London] 1982.
COUNTRY LIFE. LXXX, 248 plan. 1936.

UPWEY MANOR (Dorsetshire).
HUTCHINS, J. Vitruvius Dorsettiensis. pl.32. 1816.
HUTCHINS, J. History of Dorset. II, 844. 1863.

URCHFONT MANOR (Wiltshire).
BURKE, J.B. Visitation of Seats. Vol.II, p.235. 1853.*
COUNTRY LIFE. CII, 1204. 1947.

URCHINWOOD MANOR (Somerset).
COOKE, R. West Country Houses. p.94. 1957.

URLESS FARM, Corscombe (Dorsetshire).
HUTCHINS, J. Vitruvius Dorsettiensis. pl.33. 1816.
HUTCHINS, J. History of Dorset. II. 94. 1863.

USWORTH HALL (Durham).
BURKE, J.B. Visitation of Seats. 2.S. Vol.II, p.91. 1855.*

UTTERBY HOUSE (Lincolnshire).

BURKE, J.B. Visitation of Seats. 2.S. Vol.I, p.85. 1854.*

VALE ROYAL (Cheshire).

BURKE, J.B. Visitation of Seats. Vol.I, p.18. 1852.*

NEALE, J.P. Views of Seats. 2.S. Vol.V. 1829.

ORMEROD, G. Cheshire. II, 154, 159. 1882.

TWYCROSS, E. Mansions of England and Wales. Vol.I, p.95. 1850.

VANBURGH CASTLE (Kent).

COUNTRY LIFE. CLIX, 1406. 1976.

TIPPING, H.A. English Homes. Period IV, Vol.II, p.187. 1928.

VAYNOR PARK (Montgomeryshire).

NICHOLAS, T. Counties of Wales. II, p.801. 1872.

VEN HOUSE (Somerset).

BURKE, J.B. Visitation of Seats. 2.S. Vol.I, p.243. 1854.*

COUNTRY LIFE. XXIX, 924. 1911.

TIPPING, H.A. English Homes. Period IV, Vol.I, p.385. 1920.

VICAR'S CROSS (Cheshire).

TWYCROSS, E. Mansions of England and Wales. Vol.I, p.49. 1850.

VILLAGE PLACE, Beckenham (Kent).

GREENWOOD, C. Kent. 31. 1838.

VINTERS (Kent).

VINTERS.

— Catalogue of the library at Vinter's in Kent, 1841. [Belonging to the Whatman family.] 27x21 London: privately printed [1841?].

BURKE, J.B. Visitation of Seats. 2.S. Vol.II, p.153. 1855.*

VYNE, The. (Hampshire).

CHUTE, Chaloner William.

— A history of the Vyne in Hampshire: being a short account of the building & antiquities of that house, situate in the parish of Sherborne St. John, Co. Hants. & of persons who have at some time lived there. [Bibliogr. notes.] Illus. incl. plates, plans and maps. 25x21 Winchester: Jacob & Johnson; London: Simpkin, Marshall & Co., 1888.

HARRISSON, W.R.D.

— Carvings [in the] Oak Gallery [at] The Vyne, Hampshire, a property of the National Trust. (Illustrated catalogue ... compiled by W.R.D.H. photographs by Viscount Chandos.) 10ff. Illus. incl. 5 plates. 34x25 (Basingstoke: by the author, 1979.)

Title on cover.

LONDON: National Trust for Places of Historic Interest or Natural Beauty.

— LEES-MILNE, J. The Vyne, Hampshire. 30pp. 4 plates incl.

plans. 18x12 London: Country Life, 1959.

New ed. [Bibliogr.] Illus. (1 col. on cover) incl. 8 (3 col.) plates, plans and genealog. table. 21x14 1971.

COUNTRY LIFE. XIII, 838. 1903.

COUNTRY LIFE. XLIX, 582 plan, 612, 619 [Furniture], 642, 649 [Furniture]. 1921.

COUNTRY LIFE. CXXI, 16. 1957.

COUNTRY LIFE. CXXXIV, 214 [Furniture]. 1963.

HAMPSHIRE: Architectural views. 1830.

LATHAM, C. In English Homes. Vol.I, p.23. 1904.

NICOLSON, N. Great Houses of Britain. p.44. 1965.

TIPPING, H.A. English Homes. Period II, Vol.I, p.93. 1924.

WADDESDON MANOR (Buckinghamshire).

ERIKSEN, Svend.

— Waddesdon Manor: the James de Rothschild bequest to the National Trust. A guide to the house and its contents. 72pp. Illus. (7 col., some folding, some on covers) incl. plans and map. 22x14 Aylesbury? 1965.

Another ed. 76pp. 1970.

JAMES, Philip Brutton.

— Waddesdon Manor: a property of the National Trust. A short guide by P.J. 32pp. Illus. (some col., 2 on covers.) 23x18 London: Pitkin, 1959.

One of the series: PRIDE of Britain.

LONDON: National Trust for Places of Historic Interest or Natural Beauty. [The James A. de Rothschild collection at Waddesdon Manor.] 8 vols. 1967-75.

Individual entries as follows.

— WATERHOUSE, E. Paintings. (Waddesdon and the Rothschild family, by Mrs. J. de Rothschild.) [Bibliogr.] Illus. (12 col.) incl. genealog. table. 30x23 London, 1967.

— ERIKSEN, S. Sèvres porcelain. (Biographical notes [on] artists and craftsmen.) [Bibliogr. notes.] Illus. (some col.) incl. facsimiles of marks. 30x23 London, 1968.

— HODGKINSON, T.W.I. Sculpture. [Bibliogr. notes.] Illus. (9 col.) incl. facsimiles of sculptors' marks and genealog. table. 30x23 London, 1970.

— CHARLESTON, R.J. Meissen and other European porcelain. AYERS, J. Oriental porcelain. [Bibliogr.] Illus. (some col.) incl. facsimiles of marks and genealog. table. 30x23 London, 1971.

— BLAIR, C. Arms, armour and base-metalwork. [Bibliogr.] Illus. (some col.) incl. facsimiles of makers' marks. 30x23 London, 1974.

— DE BELLAIGUE, G. Furniture, clocks and gilt bronzes. [Bibliogr.] Illus. (some col.) incl. diagr., facsimiles (some of marks) and tables (some genealog.) 2 vols. 30x23 London, 1974.

I. (Marquetry, clocks, gilt bronzes ... automata, barometers, clocks ... veneered furniture.)

II. (Veneered furniture [Contd.] ... carved furniture ... gilt bronzes ... biographies [of makers].)

WADDESDON MANOR [Contd.] (Buckinghamshire).
—GRANDJEAN, S., ASCHENGREEN PIACENTI, K., TRUMAN, C., BLUNT, A. Gold boxes and miniatures of the eighteenth century. (Biographies of artists and craftsmen... Index of marks.) [Bibliogr. notes.] Illus. (some col.) incl. facsimiles of marks and artists' signatures. 30x23 London, 1975.
—VERLET, P. The Savonnerie: its history. The Waddesdon collection. [Bibliogr.] Illus. (some col.) incl. folding plates, plan, maps, **diagr. and genealog. table.** Fribourg: for the National Trust by Office du Livre, 1982.
WATSON, *Sir* Francis John Bagolt.
—Waddesdon Manor and its collections. Directed by Sir F.J.B.W. [Partly in French. Summary in French. Bibliogr. notes.] 96pp. Illus. 27x22 Paris, 1959.
Also in: GAZETTE des Beaux-Arts, 6S., LIV, i. 1959.
COUNTRY LIFE. XII, 808. 1902.
COUNTRY LIFE. CXXI, 1277 [Treasures]. 1957.
COUNTRY LIFE. CXXVI, 66. 1959.
COUNTRY LIFE. CXLVII, 1154 [Store Rooms]. 1970.
LATHAM, C. In English Homes. Vol.I, p.53. 1904.

WADDON MANOR (Dorsetshire).
COUNTRY LIFE. LXX, 536 plan. 1931.
OSWALD, A. Country houses of Dorset. p.147. 1959.

WADFIELD, The. Sudeley (Gloucestershire).
COUNTRY LIFE. XCIX, 486, 532. 1946.

WADWORTH HALL (Yorkshire).
COUNTRY LIFE. CXL, 494. 1966.

WAKEFIELD LODGE (Northamptonshire).
COPPER PLATE MAGAZINE. pls.9, 54. 1778.
COUNTRY LIFE. CLIV, 298. 1973.
JONES. Views of Seats. I. 1829.
NEALE, J.P. Views of Seats. Vol.III. 1820.
SANDBY, P. Select Views. pls. 38, 39. 1783.

WAKEHURST PLACE (Sussex).
CLARKE, T.H. Domestic architecture. 21. 1833.
COUNTRY LIFE. XVI, 18. 1904.
GOTCH, J.A. Architecture of the Renaissance. II, p.34. 1894.
LATHAM, C. In English Homes. Vol.I, p.369. 1904.
NASH, J. Mansions of England. I, pls. 6, 7. 1839.
[Sales] WAKEHURST PLACE, 1890, July 1-5 [Contents].

WAKELYN, The. Hilton (Derbyshire).
TILLEY, J. Halls of Derbyshire. II, p.107. 1893.

WALBERTON HOUSE (Sussex).
BURKE, J.B. Visitation of Seats. Vol.II, p.21. 1853.*

WALCOT (Shropshire).
BURKE, J.B. Visitation of Seats. 2.S. Vol.I, p.55. 1854.*
COUNTRY LIFE. LXXXVI, 388 plan. 1939.
LEACH, F. Seats of Shropshire. p.43. 1891.
[Sales] WALCOT, 1929, July 22-26 [Contents].

WALCOT HALL (Northamptonshire).
BURKE, J.B. Visitation of Seats. Vol.I, p.219. 1852.*

WALDERSHARE PARK (Kent).
BADESLADE, T. Seats in Kent. pl.35. 1750.
GREENWOOD, C. Kent. 422. 1838.
HASTED, E. Kent. IV, 190. 1799.

WALFORD HOUSE (Somerset).
BURKE, J.B. Visitation of Seats. Vol.II, p.210. 1853.*

WALHAMPTON HOUSE (Hampshire).
BURKE, J.B. Visitation of Seats. Vol.I, p.63. 1852.*
GROVE, R.A. Seats in the neighbourhood of Lymington. 1832.

WALLINGTON (Northumberland).
LONDON: National Trust for Places of Historic Interest or Natural Beauty.
— Wallington, Northumberland. 8pp. 1 illus. 22x14 [London, c.1960.]
Another ed. Wallington. Illus. (1 on cover) incl. plates and plan. 24x18 [London, c.1965.]
Another ed. Wallington, Northumberland. [Bibliogr.] 24pp. Illus. (1 col. on cover) incl. 8 plates and genealog. table. 25x18 [London, c.1975.]
SCOTT, William Bell.
— Scenes from Northumbrian history: the mural paintings at Wallington Hall, Northumberland, by W.B.S. [Bibliogr. notes.] 32pp. Illus. (9 col., 1 on cover.) 22x17 Newcastle upon Tyne: Frank Graham, 1972.
TREVELYAN, *Sir* Charles Philips, *Bart.*
— Wallington: its history and treasures. 7 ed. 44pp. Plates. 20x13 [Wallington?] privately printed, 1951.
TREVELYAN, Raleigh.
— William Bell Scott and Wallington. [Bibliogr. notes.] Excerpt, 4pp. Illus. 31x23 [London, 1977.]
Also in: APOLLO, CV, p.117. 1977.
Water-colour sketches for the paintings at Wallington are preserved in the Department of Prints and Drawings.
BURKE, J.B. Visitation of Seats. Vol.I, p.51. 1852.*
COUNTRY LIFE. XLIII, 572, 592. 1918.
COUNTRY LIFE. CXLVII, 854, 922, 986. 1970.

WALLINGTON HALL (Norfolk).
COUNTRY LIFE. LXVI, 684. 1929.
TIPPING, H.A. English Homes. Period I & II, Vol.II, p.313. 1937.

Taken and Drawn on Stone by J. Hewetson, Arch.t

T H E   V Y N E

THE SEAT OF THOMAS CHUTE ESQ.re

Printed by C. Hullmandel

THE VYNE, Hampshire. From: HAMPSHIRE. *Architectural and picturesque views of noble mansions in Hampshire* [etc.], London [1830?]

WALLOP (Shropshire).
LEIGHTON, S. Shropshire. 7. 1901.

WALLOP HOUSE (Hampshire).
BURKE, J.B. Visitation of Seats. 2.S. Vol.I, p.184. 1854.*

WALLSWORTH HALL (Gloucestershire).
RUDDER, S. Gloucestershire. 638. 1779.

WALMER CASTLE (Kent).
FORD, Richard.
— Apsley House and Walmer Castle, illustrated by plates and description. (The description by R.F.) 18pp. Col. lithogr. plates, and cover. Fol. 55x45 London: J. Mitchell; P. & D. Colnaghi, 1853.
GREAT BRITAIN: Ministry of Works [Ancient Monuments and Historic Buildings].
— O'NEIL, B.H.St.J. Walmer Castle, Kent. 8pp. 2 plans. 21x14 (London, 1949.)
Another impression. (1958.)
GREAT BRITAIN: Ministry of Public Building and Works [Ancient Monuments and Historic Buildings].
— SAUNDERS, A.D. Deal and Walmer Castles. 44pp. Illus. incl. plans. 19x13 London, 1970.
BAKER, J. Home beauties. plate. 1804.
BUCK, S. & N. Antiquities. I, pl.145. 1774.
COUNTRY LIFE. XLVI, 552, 584. 1919.
OSWALD, A. Country houses of Kent. 11. 1933.

WALMSGATE HALL (Lincolnshire).
BURKE, J.B. Visitation of Seats. Vol.I, p.8. 1852.*

WALSINGHAM ABBEY (Norfolk).
BUCK, S. & N. Antiquities. I, pl.204. 1774.
CROMWELL, T.K. Excursions in Norfolk. I, p.158. 1818.
[Sales] WALSINGHAM ABBEY, 1916, September 25-28 [Furniture, paintings, china etc.].

WALTERSTONE HOUSE (Dorsetshire).
See WATERSTON MANOR.

WALTON HALL (Cheshire).
TWYCROSS, E. Mansions of England and Wales. Vol.II, p.75. 1850.

WALTON HALL (Warwickshire).
MORRIS, F.O. Views of Seats. Vol.IV, p.53. 1880.

WALTON HALL (Yorkshire).
BURKE, J.B. Visitation of Seats. 2.S. Vol.I, p.154. 1854.
YORKSHIRE. Picturesque views 1885.

WALTON LODGE (Lancashire).
BARTLETT, J. Mansions of England and Wales. pl.38. 1853.
TWYCROSS, E. Mansions of England and Wales. Vol.I, p.32. 1847.

WALWORTH CASTLE (Durham).
BURKE, J.B. Visitation of Seats. Vol.I, p.98. 1852.*

WANDLE COURT (Surrey).
COUNTRY LIFE. LXII, 279. 1927.

WANLIP HALL (Leicestershire).
BURKE, J.B. Visitation of Seats. Vol.I, p.97. 1852.*
NICHOLS, J. History of Leicestershire. III, ii, 1095. 1804.
THROSBY, J. Views in Leicestershire. p.322. 1789.

WANSTEAD GROVE (Essex).
NEALE, J.P. Views of Seats. 2.S. Vol.III. 1826.

WANSTEAD HOUSE (Essex).
ANGUS, W. Seats of the Nobility. pl.53. 1787.
CAMPBELL, C. Vitruvius Britannicus. I, pls. 21-27. 1715.
CAMPBELL, C. Vitruvius Britannicus. III, pls. 39,40. 1725.
COUNTRY LIFE. LXXIV, 605. 1933.
CROMWELL, T.K. Excursions in Essex.II, p.62. 1825.
ENGLAND: Beauties of England. I,p.244. 1787.
ENGLAND: Picturesque Views. p.43. 1786-88.
ESSEX: A new and complete history. IV, 226. 1771.
HAVELL, R. Views of Noblemen's Seats. 1823.
MORANT, P. Essex. I, 31. 1768.
SPROULE, A. Lost houses of Britain. 261. 1982.
WATTS, W. Seats of the Nobility. pl.56. 1779.
[Sales] WANSTEAD HOUSE, 1822, June 10-14, 17-21, 24-28, July 1-5, 8-12, 15-19, 22,23 [Furniture, paintings, sculpture etc.].

WANSWELL COURT (Gloucestershire).
COUNTRY LIFE. CXVI, 894 plan. 1954.

WARBROOK HOUSE (Hampshire).
COUNTRY LIFE. LXXXV, 276. 1939.

WARDES, Otham (Kent).
COUNTRY LIFE. XLVI, 270. 1919.
OSWALD, A. Country houses of Kent. 24. 1933.
TIPPING, H.A. English Homes. Period I & II, Vol.II, p.145. 1937.

WARDLEY HALL (Lancashire).
BURKE, J.B. Visitation of Seats. 2.S. Vol.I, p.191. 1854.*

GRAY, H. Old halls of Lancashire. p.47. 1893

MOSS, F. Pilgrimages. [III] 261. 1906.

WARDOUR CASTLE (Wiltshire)
BRITTON, J. Beauties of Wiltshire. I. 253. 1801.

BURKE, J.B. Visitation of Seats. Vol.I, p.166. 1852.*

COUNTRY LIFE. English Country Houses: Mid Georgian. p.119. 1956.

COUNTRY LIFE. LXVIII, 646, 676. 1930.

COUNTRY LIFE. CXLIV, 908 [Chapel]. 1968.

JONES. Views of Seats. II. 1829.

NEALE, J.P. Views of Seats. Vol.V. 1822.

PAINE, J. Plans, elevations. Pt.II, pls. 30-41 plans. 93, 94 [Ceiling & Dome]. 1783.

WARE PARK (Hertfordshire).
BURKE, J.B. Visitation of Seats. 2.S. Vol.I, p.204. 1854.*

WARLEIGH HOUSE (Devonshire).
BRITTON, J. Devonshire illustrated. 94. 1832.

BURKE, J.B. Visitation of Seats. 2.S. Vol.II, p.176. 1855.*

WARLEIGH HOUSE (Somerset).
BURKE, J.B. Visitation of Seats. 2.S. Vol.II, p.127. 1855.*

JONES. Views of Seats. II. 1829.

NEALE, J.P. Views of Seats. 2.S. Vol.I. 1824.

WARMINGTON MANOR (Warwickshire).
COUNTRY LIFE. C, 1002. 1946.

WARMWELL HOUSE (Dorsetshire).
HEATH, S. Dorset Manor Houses. 189. 1907.

OSWALD, A. Country houses of Dorset. p.93. 1959.

WARNEFORD PLACE (Wiltshire).
[Sales] WARNEFORD PLACE, 1959, March 17-19 [Furniture & effects].

WARNHAM COURT (Sussex).
BURKE, J.B. Visitation of Seats. 2.S. Vol.II, p.95. 1855.*

WARTER PRIORY (Yorkshire).
MORRIS, F.O. Views of Seats. Vol.VI, p.67. 1880.

WARTNABY HALL (Leicestershire).
BURKE, J.B. Visitation of Seats. 2.S. Vol.II, p.138. 1855.*

WARWICK CASTLE (Warwickshire).
SPICER, Charles William.
— History of Warwick Castle. [Bibliogr. notes.] 40pp. Illus. incl. plates and plan. 56x42 London: for the author, 1844.
Some illus., tracings, press-cuttings and excerpt, inserted, with MS. annotations.
One of the series: VITRUVIUS BRITANNICUS. (1833-)

WARWICK, Frances Evelyn Greville, *Countess of*.
Warwick Castle and its Earls from Saxon times to the present day. Illus. incl. 2 plates and genealog. tables (1 folding). 2 vols. 24x16 London: Hutchinson, 1903.

WARWICK CASTLE.
— An historical and descriptive guide to Warwick Castle, with an abridged history of the Earls of Warwick from the Norman Conquest, an authentic catalogue of the paintings, &c., &c. New ed. [Bibliogr. notes.] 102pp. Illus. 17x11 Warwick: H.T. Cooke and Son. n.d.

WARWICK CASTLE.
— Warwick Castle: an illustrated survey of the historic Warwickshire home of the Earls of Warwick. 48pp. Illus. (some on covers.) 20x15 Warwick: privately printed [c.1965].

BUCK, S. & N. Antiquities. II, pls. 305, 306. 1774.

BURKE, J.B. Visitation of Seats. Vol.II, p.104. 1853.*

CAMPBELL, C. Vitruvius Britannicus. IVth. pls. 71,72. 1739.

COPPER PLATE MAGAZINE. III, pl.138. 1792-1802.

COUNTRY LIFE. I, 112, 126. 1897.

COUNTRY LIFE. XXXV, 792, 842 plan. 1914.

COUNTRY LIFE. CLXXII, 1746 plan, 1882, 1952. 2023. 1982.

ENGLAND: Beauties of England. II, p.332. 1787.

HALL, S.C. Baronial Halls. Vol.II. 1848.

JEWITT, L. Stately homes of England. 192. 1874.

JONES. Views of Seats. I. 1829.

MALAN, A.H. Famous homes. p.327. 1902.

MORRIS, F.O. Views of Seats. Vol.I, p.43. 1880.

NEALE, J.P. Views of Seats. 2.S. Vol.V. 1829.

NIVEN, W. Old Warwickshire houses. p.21, pl.21. 1878.

SANDBY, P. Select Views. I, pl.69. 1783.

UNITED KINGDOM. Historic houses. 16. 1892.

[Sales] LONDON, 1936, June 17 [Old Master drawings].

WASHINGTON OLD HALL (Durham).
LONDON: National Trust for Places of Historic Interest or Natural Beauty.
— Washington Old Hall. 12pp. Illus. (1 on cover) incl. 4 plates, plan and genealog. table. 22x14 [London, c.1970.]

WASSAND HALL (Yorkshire).
BURKE, J.B. Visitation of Seats. Vol.II, p.102. 1853.*

WATER EATON MANOR (Oxfordshire).
COUNTRY LIFE. XXII, 666. 1907.

TIPPING, H.A. English Homes. Early Renaissance. p.229. 1912.

TIPPING, H.A. English Homes. Period III, Vol.II, p.145. 1927.

WATERINGBURY PLACE (Kent).
[Sales] WATERINGBURY PLACE, 1978, May 31-June 2
[Contents of principal rooms].
[Sales] WATERINGBURY PLACE, 1978, September 25, 26
[Contents of subsidiary rooms].

WATERLESTON MANOR (Somerset).
See WESTON FARM.

WATERMOUTH CASTLE (Devonshire).
BRITTON, J. Devonshire illustrated. 56. 1832.

WATERPERRY IIOUSE (Oxfordshire).
ENGLAND: Picturesque Views. p.24. 1786-88.

WATERSTON MANOR (Dorsetshire).
COUNTRY LIFE. XXXIX, 208 plan. 1916.
GOTCH, J.A. Architecture of the Renaissance. I, p.18. 1894.
HEATH, S. Dorset Manor Houses. 117. 1907.
HUTCHINS, J. History of Dorset. II, 620. 1863.
NASH, J. Mansions of England. III, pl.8. 1841.
OSWALD, A. Country houses of Dorset. p.89. 1959.

WATFORD COURT (Northamptonshire).
GOTCH, J.A. Halls of Northants. p.63. 1936.

WATLINGTON PARK (Oxfordshire).
COUNTRY LIFE. CXXV, 18, 60. 1959.
[Sales] WATLINGTON PARK, 1921, April 25-27 [Contents].

WATTON PRIORY (Yorkshire).
COUNTRY LIFE. LXXVIII, 459. 1935.

WATTON WOOD HALL (Hertfordshire).
See WOODHALL PARK.

WAVERLEY ABBEY (Surrey).
BRAYLEY, E.W. History of Surrey. V, 278. 1841.
BURKE, J.B. Visitation of Seats. 2.S. Vol. II, p.16. 1855.*
PROSSER, G.F. Surrey Seats. p.109. 1828.

WAVERTON HOUSE (Gloucestershire).
COUNTRY LIFE. CLXX, 498. 1981.

WAVERTREE HALL (Lancashire).
PYNE, W.H. Lancashire illustrated. 44. 1831.
TWYCROSS, E. Mansions of England and Wales. Vol. III, p.44. 1847.*

WAYFORD MANOR (Somerset).
COUNTRY LIFE. LXXVI, 336. 1934.

WEALD HALL (Essex).
COUNTRY LIFE. II, 560. 1897.
COUNTRY LIFE. XVIII, 522. 1905.
COUNTRY LIFE. XXXVI, 454 plan. 1914.
CROMWELL, T.K. Excursions in Essex. I, p.169. 1825.
RUSH, J.A. Seats in Essex. p.182. 1897.

WEALD MANOR (Oxfordshire).
COUNTRY LIFE. C, 256. 1946.

WEARE GIFFARD (Devonshire).
COUNTRY LIFE. XXXVII, 16. 1915.
DELDERFIELD, E.R. West Country houses. I, 145. 1968.
TIPPING, H.A. English Homes. Period II, Vol.I, p.351. 1924.

WEAVER'S HOUSE, Stratford St. Mary (Suffolk).
COUNTRY LIFE. XCVIII, 552 plan. 1945.

WEDDINGTON HALL (Warwickshire).
LUGAR. R. Plans and views of buildings. 25. pls. XXVIII-XXX. 1823.

WEEVER HALL (Cheshire).
ORMEROD, G. Cheshire. II, 210. 1882.

WELBECK ABBEY (Nottinghamshire).
GARRARD, James.
— A catalogue of gold and silver plate, the property of His Grace the Duke of Portland. With ... description and date of each piece. (Report on the plate at Welbeck by W. Cripps.) viii, 144pp. Plates (some hand-col.) 29x20 London: privately printed at the Chiswick Press, 1893.

GOULDING, Richard William.
— The Welbeck Abbey miniatures belonging to His Grace the Duke of Portland ... A catalogue raisonné. [Bibliogr. notes.] 29 plates. 31x25 Oxford: O.U.P., 1916.
An enlarged ed. of the catalogue published in LONDON: Walpole Society, Annual Volume IV, 1916.

GOULDING, Richard William.
— Catalogue of the pictures belonging to His Grace the Duke of Portland, K.G. At Welbeck Abbey, 17 Hill Street, London and Langwell House. Compiled by R.W.G., and finally revised ... by C.K. Adams. [Bibliogr.] 30x22 Cambridge: C.U.P., 1936.

HARDING, George R. and H.W.
— Catalogue of the ornamental furniture, works of art, and porcelain at Welbeck Abbey [belonging to the Duke of Portland]. Plates. 29x23 London: privately printed, 1897.
With MS. notes and typewritten additions inserted.

JONES, Edward Alfred.
— Catalogue of plate belonging to the Duke of Portland, ... at Welbeck Abbey. Plates. 32x26 London: St. Catherine Press, 1935.

MURRAY, Charles Fairfax.
— Catalogue of the pictures belonging to His Grace the Duke of Portland, at Welbeck Abbey, and in London. Plates. 33x25 London: privately printed at the Chiswick Press, 1894.

STRONG, Sandford Arthur.
— A catalogue of letters and other historical documents exhibited in the library at Welbeck. Plates incl. facsimiles. 26x20 London: J. Murray, 1903.

TURBERVILLE, Arthur Stanley.
— A history of Welbeck Abbey and its owners, 1539-1879. [Bibliogr. notes.] Illus. incl. plates and 2 folding genealog. tables. 2 vols. 23x15 London: Faber, 1938-39.

WELBECK ABBEY.
— Welbeck Abbey, May 22, 23, 24, 25, 1893. (Christening of the Marquis of Titchfield, May 22, 1893.) [Souvenir.] 26pp. Plates: photographs. 20x28 [Welbeck Abbey: privately printed, 1893?.]
Title on cover.
BUCK, S. & N. Antiquities. II, pl.231. 1774.
BURKE, J.B. Visitation of Seats. 2.S. Vol.I, p.201. 1854.*
COPPER PLATE MAGAZINE. II, pl.68. 1792-1802.
COUNTRY LIFE. XIX, 558. 1906.
COUNTRY LIFE. LXXIV, 346 [Repton Notebooks]. 1933.
ENGLAND: Picturesque Views. p.65. 1786-88.
JONES. Views of Seats. I. 1829.
LATHAM, C. In English Homes. Vol. II, p.387. 1907.
NEALE, J.P. Views of Seats. Vol.III. 1820.
NOBLE, T. Counties of Chester ... Lincoln. p.75. 1836.
UNITED KINGDOM. Historic houses. 1. 1892.
[Sales] RETFORD, 1970, June 23 [Oriental & English porcelain from W.A.].

WELCOMBE LODGE (Warwickshire).
JONES. Views of Seats. I. 1829.
NEALE, J.P. Views of Seats. Vol.IV. 1821.

WELDON MANOR (Northamptonshire).
GOTCH, J.A. Halls of Northants. p.28. 1936.

WELFORD PARK (Berkshire).
ROBERTSON, A. Great Road. II, p.2. 1792.

WELLCOMBE (Warwickshire).
See WELCOMBE LODGE.

WELLESBOURNE HALL (Warwickshire).
BURKE, J.B. Visitation of Seats. Vol.I, p.191. 1852.*

WELL HALL (Kent).
ERWOOD, Frank Charles Elliston.
—The story of Well Hall. 16pp. illus. incl. plan and genealog. table. 22x14 Woolwich: Pioneer Press, 1916.

LONDON: Borough of Woolwich.
—ERWOOD, F.C.E. Well Hall: the story of the house; its grounds and its famous occupants ... on the occasion of the completion of the restoration work 1936. With a note on the works carried out by the Borough Engineer. Edited by the late P.C. Bursill. 3 ed. [Bibliogr.] 36pp. Illus. incl. plates, facsimiles and genealog. table. 21x14 Woolwich, 1947.

WELLS PALACE (Somerset).
BUCK, S.& N. Antiquities. II, pl.263. 1774.
COUNTRY LIFE. II, 528. 1897.
COUNTRY LIFE. CLVIII, 1666, 1738. 1975.
HEARNE, T. Antiquities. II, pl.15. 1807.
JONES. Views of Seats. II. 1829.
NEALE, J.P. Views of Seats. 2.S. Vol. IV. 1828.

WELLVALE HOUSE (Lincolnshire).
COUNTRY LIFE. CLII, 1650. 1972.

WELTON GRANGE (Yorkshire).
COUNTRY LIFE. CV, 676. 1949.

WELTON PLACE (Northamptonshire).
GOTCH, J.A. Squires' Homes. 38. 1939.
JONES. Views of Seats. I. 1829.
NEALE, J.P. Views of Seats. 2.S. Vol.II. 1825.

WENHASTON GRANGE (Suffolk).
SANDON, E. Suffolk houses. 286. 1977.

WENLOCK ABBEY (Shropshire).
COUNTRY LIFE. XXI, 558. 1907.
COUNTRY LIFE. CXXVIII,1282, 1432 plan, 1492. 1960.
LEACH, F. Seats of Shropshire. p.339. 1891.
TIPPING, H.A. English Homes. Period II, Vol.I, p.244. 1924.

WENNINGTON HALL (Lancashire).
BARTLETT, J. Mansions of England and Wales. pl.70. 1853.
TWYCROSS, E. Mansions of England and Wales. Vol.II, p.27. 1847.

WENTWORTH CASTLE (Yorkshire).
BURKE, J.B. Visitation of Seats. Vol.I, p.254. 1852.*
CAMPBELL, C. Vitruvius Britannicus. I, pls.92-4. 1715.
CAMPBELL, C. Vitruvius Britannicus. IVth. pls.54-8. 1739.
COUNTRY LIFE. English Country Houses: Baroque. p.236. 1970.
COUNTRY LIFE. XIII, 504. 1903.
COUNTRY LIFE. LVI, 588 plan, 634. 1922.
COUNTRY LIFE. LXXVI, 248. 1934.
JONES. Views of Seats. I. 1829.
KIP, J. Nouveau théâtre de la Grande Bretagne. III, pls.29, 30. 1715.
LATHAM, C. In English Homes. Vol.I, p.185. 1904.
NEALE, J.P. Views of Seats. Vol.V. 1822.
WATTS, W. Seats of the Nobility. pl.51. 1779.

THE COUNTRY HOUSE DESCRIBED

WENTWORTH WOODHOUSE (Yorkshire).

BURKE, J.B. Visitation of Seats. 2.S. Vol.I, p.109. 1854.*

CAMPBELL, C. Vitruvius **Britannicus. IVth. pls. 79-81. 1739.**

COUNTRY LIFE. English Country Houses: Early Georgian. p.147. 1955.

COUNTRY LIFE. XIX, 450. 1906.

COUNTRY LIFE. LVI, 436, 476, 512, 554. 1924.

COUNTRY LIFE. LXXVI, 248. 1934.

COUNTRY LIFE. XCIX, 854. 1946.

COUNTRY LIFE. CLXXIII, **624 plan, 708 plan. 1983.**

ENGLAND: Beauties of England. II, p. 411. 1787.

JONES. Views of Seats. 1. 1829.

LATHAM. C. In English Homes. Vol.III, p.415. 1909.

MORRIS, F.O. Views of Seats. Vol.I, p.23. 1880.

NEALE, J.P. Views of Seats. Vol. V. 1822.

REPTON, H. Observations on landscape gardening. 14. 1803.

SUMMERSON, J. The Country Seat. 106. 1970.

WATTS, W. Seats of the Nobility. pl.5. 1779.

WHEATER, W. Mansions of Yorkshire. p.322. 1888.

WENVOE CASTLE (Glamorganshire).

BURKE, J.B. Visitation of Seats. Vol.I, p.111. 1852.*

WERRINGTON PARK (Devonshire).

BRITTON, J. Devonshire illustrated. 104. 1832.

WEST AMESBURY HOUSE (Wiltshire).

COUNTRY LIFE. CXXVIII, 442. 1960.

[Sales] WEST AMESBURY HOUSE, 1979, September 24 [Contents].

WEST BITCHFIELD TOWER (Northumberland).

COUNTRY LIFE. LXXXVIII, 278. 1940.

WEST BRADENHAM HALL (Norfolk).

BURKE, J.B. Visitation of Seats. Vol.II, p.245. 1853.*

WEST BROMWICH MANOR HOUSE (Staffordshire).

See MANOR HOUSE.

WESTBURY COURT (Gloucestershire).

ATKYNS, R. Glocestershire. p.420. 1768.

WEST COKER MANOR (Somerset).

COUNTRY LIFE. LII, 470. 1922.

WESTCOMBE HOUSE (Kent).

COPPER PLATE MAGAZINE. pl.114. 1778.

SANDBY, P. Select Views. I, pl.24. 1783.

WATTS, W. Seats of the Nobility. pl.1. 1779.

WESTCOTES (Leicestershire).

NICHOLS, J. History of Leicestershire. IV, ii, 565. 1811.

THROSBY, J. Views in Leicestershire. p.324. 1789.

WEST COURT (Berkshire).

[Sales] WEST COURT, 1931, February 25, 26 [Furniture, books, paintings etc.].

WEST DEAN PARK (Sussex).

COUNTRY LIFE. CLXX, **1378, 1462. 1981.**

LATHAM, C. In English Homes. Vol. I, p.355. 1904.

NEALE, J.P. Views of Seats. Vol.IV. 1821.

WEST DEREHAM HOUSE (Norfolk).

SUMMERSON, J. The Country Seat. 70. 1970.

WEST DINGLE (Lancashire).

BARTLETT, J. Mansions of England and Wales. pl.117. 1853.

TWYCROSS, E. Mansions of England and Wales. Vol.III, p.54. 1847.

WESTERFIELD HALL (Suffolk).

SANDON, E. Suffolk houses. 288. 1977.

WESTERHAM (Kent) Pendock Price.

BADESLADE, T. Seats in Kent. pl.28. 1750.

HARRIS, J. History of Kent. p.330. 1719.

WEST FARLEIGH HALL (Kent).

BADESLADE, T. Seats in Kent. pl.29. 1750.

COUNTRY LIFE. XLIII, 444. 1918.

COUNTRY LIFE. CXLII, 600, 660. 1967.

HARRIS, J. History of Kent. p.120. 1719.

OSWALD, A. Country houses of Kent. 62. 1933.

WEST GREEN HOUSE (Hampshire).

COUNTRY LIFE. LXXX, 540. 1936.

WEST HILL (Hampshire).

HAMPSHIRE: Architectural views. 1830.

WEST HILL (Surrey).

ANGUS, W. Seats of the Nobility. pl.60. 1787.

PROSSER, G.F. Surrey Seats. p.3. 1828.

WEST HORSLEY PLACE (Surrey).
BRAYLEY, E.W. History of Surrey. II, 98. 1841.
BURKE, J.B. Visitation of Seats. Vol.II, p.192. 1853.*
COUNTRY LIFE. LXXXV, 302, 328. 1939.
NEALE, J.P. Views of Seats. 2.S. Vol.II. 1825.

WESTONBIRT HOUSE (Gloucestershire).
HOLFORD, *Sir* George Lindsay.
—The Holford collection ... selected from ... illuminated manuscripts at Dorchester House and pictures at Westonbirt in Gloucestershire. [Bibliogr. notes.] Plates. 32x25 Oxford: privately printed, 1924.
Another copy.

LONDON: Burlington Fine Arts Club.
—[Catalogues of exhibitions of miscellaneous art objects. Contd.]
Pictures and other objects of art, selected from the collection of Mr. Holford. [1808-1892]., mainly from Westonbirt in **Gloucestershire**. 42pp. 1921-22.
BURKE,J.B. Visitation of Seats. Vol.I, p.143. 1852.*
COOKE, R. West Country Houses. p.173. 1957.
COUNTRY LIFE. XVII, 378. 1905.
COUNTRY LIFE. CLI, 1226, 1310. 1972.
JONES. Views of Seats. II. 1829.
LATHAM,C. In English Homes. Vol. II, p.407. 1907.
MORRIS, F.O. Views of Seats. Vol.III, p.53. 1880.
NEALE, J.P. Views of Seats. 2.S. Vol.III. 1826.
[Sales] LONDON, 1927, July 13, 14 [Furniture from Dorchester House and W.H.].
[Sales] LONDON, 1927, July 15 [Italian pictures from D.H. and W.H.].
[Sales] LONDON, 1928, March 26-30 [Books from D.H. and W.H.].
[Sales] LONDON, 1928, May 17,18 [Old Master paintings from D.H. and W.H.].

WESTON FARM (Somerset).
COUNTRY LIFE. CVI, 891. 1949.

WESTON GROVE (Hampshire).
HAMPSHIRE: Architectural views. 1830.

WESTON HALL (Northamptonshire).
COUNTRY LIFE. CL, 1072 [Lacquer Furniture]. 1971.
COUNTRY LIFE. CLIX, 174, 234. 1976.

WESTON HALL (Suffolk).
SANDON, E. Suffolk houses. 166. 1977.

WESTON HALL, Weston-in-Arden (Warwickshire).
NIVEN, W. Old Warwickshire houses. p.17, pl.17. 1878.
SHAW, H. Elizabethan architecture. pls.III, IV. [Dining room, friezes etc.]. 1839.
SMITH, W. History of the County of Warwick. 53. 1830.

WESTON HALL (Yorkshire).
COUNTRY LIFE. CXXIV, 1112. 1958.
JONES. Views of Seats. I. 1829.
NEALE, J.P. Views of Seats. Vol.V. 1822.
WOOD, G.B. Historic homes of Yorkshire. 41. 1957.

WESTON HOUSE, Shipston-on-Stour (Warwickshire).
WARRINER, Michael.
—A prospect of Weston in Warwickshire. xii, 96pp. Plates (1 folding) incl. plans and map. 21x14 Kineton: The Roundwood Press, 1978.
[Sales] WESTON HOUSE, 1922, July 10-13 [Remaining contents].

WESTON MANOR (Oxfordshire).
COUNTRY LIFE. LXIV, 268 plan. 1928.

WESTON PARK (Staffordshire).
BRADFORD, Orlando George Charles Bridgeman, *Earl of.*
— A catalogue of the pictures at Weston, belonging to the Earl of Bradford. 78pp. Plates. 27x20 (Weston-under-Lizard) privately printed, 1895.
TRUMBLE, D.H.
— Weston Park: the home of the Bridgeman family. (an illustrated survey and guide.) 32pp. Illus. (2 col., some on covers) incl. facsimile. 19x16 (Derby: E.L.P., 1964.)
TRUMBLE, D.H.
— Weston Park, the home of the Bridgeman family. (By D.H.T., revised by S. Dallaway and M.L. Tebbutt.) 32pp. Illus. (some col., some on covers) incl. facsimile. 19x16 (Derby: E.L.P., 1974.)
COUNTRY LIFE. II, 592. 1897.
COUNTRY LIFE. XCVIII, 818, 864, 910. 1945.
COUNTRY LIFE. XCIX, 904 [Sporting pictures]. 1946.
COUNTRY LIFE. C, 1006 [Portraits]. 1946.
KROLL, A. Historic houses. 138. 1969.
LEACH, F. Seats of Shropshire. p.345. 1891.
LEIGHTON, S. Shropshire houses. 32. 1901.
NEALE, J.P. Views of Seats. 2.S. Vol.V. 1829.
NICOLSON, N. Great Houses of Britain. p.140. 1965.
PAINE, J. Plans, elevations. Pt.II, pls.68-71 [Temple of Diana], 86 [Bridge], 97 [Chimney piece] 1783.
SHAW, S. Staffordshire. II, pl.9. Reprint 1976.

WESTON UNDERWOOD (Buckinghamshire).

COWPER, William.
— Cowper, illustrated by a series of views in or near the park of Weston-Underwood, Buckinghamshire. Accompanied with copious descriptions, and a short sketch of the poet's life. [Text by E.W. Brayley.] 54pp. Engr. plates incl. title-page. 14x8 London: Vernor & Hood; J. Storer & J. Greig, 1804.

NEALE, J.P. Views of Seats. 2.S. Vol.II. 1825.

WESTOVER PARK (Hampshire, Isle of Wight).

BURKE, J.B. Visitation of Seats. Vol.I, p.173. 1852.*

WEST RETFORD HALL (Nottinghamshire).

COUNTRY LIFE. CXXX, 1215. 1961.

WEST RETFORD HOUSE (Nottinghamshire).

ENGLAND: Picturesque Views. p.72. 1786-88.

WEST RIDDLESDEN HALL (Yorkshire).

YORKSHIRE. Picturesque views. 1885.

WEST STOW HALL (Suffolk).

COUNTRY LIFE. XXIX, 848. 1911.

CROMWELL, T.K. Excursions in Suffolk. I, p.77. 1818.

HALL, S.C. Baronial Halls. Vol.II. 1848.

SANDON, E. Suffolk houses. 213. 1977.

TIPPING,H.A. English Homes. Period II, Vol.I, p.201. 1924.

WESTWELL, Tenterden (Kent).

COUNTRY LIFE. CXXXIV, 1180. 1963.

OSWALD, A. Country houses of Kent. 61. 1933.

WESTWICK HOUSE (Norfolk).

CROMWELL, T.K. Excursions in Norfolk. I, p.116. 1818.

WATTS, W. Seats of the Nobility. pl.44. 1779.

WESTWOOD HOUSE (Lancashire).

BARTLETT, J. Mansions of England and Wales. pl.107. 1853.

TWYCROSS, E. Mansions of England and Wales. Vol.III, p.45. 1847.

WESTWOOD MANOR (Wiltshire).

LONDON:National Trust for Places of Historic Interest or Natural Beauty.
—SUTTON, D. Westwood Manor, Bradford on Avon; the history of the house and its inhabitants. [Bibliogr. notes.] 22pp. Illus. (on cover) and 4 plates. 18x12 London: Country Life, 1962.

New ed. [Bibliogr.] 28pp. Illus. (1 on cover) incl. 4 plates and plan. 22x14 [London] 1979.

COUNTRY LIFE. LX, 244, 282. 1926.

ELYARD, S.J. Old Wiltshire homes. p.74. 1894.

GARNER, T. Domestic architecture. II, p.137 plan. 1911.

WESTWOOD PARK (Worcestershire).

BURKE, J.B. Visitation of Seats. Vol.I, p.271. 1852.*

CLARKE, T.H. Domestic architecture. 20. 1833.

COUNTRY LIFE. XII, 689, 1902.

COUNTRY LIFE. LXIV, 50, 94. 1928.

GOTCH, F.A. Architecture of the Renaissance. II, p.15. 1894.

HALL, S.C. Baronial Halls. Vol. II. 1848.

KIP, J. Nouveau théâtre de la Grande Bretagne. I, pl.65. 1715.

LATHAM, C. In English Homes. Vol.I, p.255. 1904.

MORRIS, F.O. Views of Seats. Vol.V, p.67. 1880.

NASH, J. Mansions of England. I, pl.12. 1839.

NASH, T.R. Worcestershire, I, 350. 1781.

NIVEN, W. Old Worcestershire houses. p.8, front. pls.6,7. 1873.

[Sales] LONDON, 1950, November 8 [Paintings, drawings from W.P.].

WEST WRATTING PARK (Cambridgeshire).

[Sales] CAMBRIDGE, 1935, July 26 [House].

WEST WYCOMBE PARK (Buckinghamshire).

LONDON: National Trust for Places of Historic Interest or Natural Beauty.
—LEES-MILNE, J. West Wycombe Park. 14pp. 4 plates. 18x12 London: Country Life (1946).
2 ed. West Wycombe Park, Buckinghamshire. 18pp. 4 plates. London (1953).

LONDON: National Trust for Places of Historic Interest or Natural Beauty.
—JACKSON-STOPS, G. West Wycombe Park, Buckinghamshire. [Bibliogr.] 32pp. Illus. (some col., 1 on cover) incl. plates, plan and map. 25x18 [London] 1981.

BOLTON, A.T. Architecture of R. & J. Adam. I, 47 plan. 1922.

CAMPBELL, C. Vitruvius Britannicus. V, pls. 47-49. 1771.

COPPER PLATE MAGAZINE. I, pl.38. 1792-1802.

COUNTRY LIFE. English Country Houses: Early Georgian. p.234. 1955.

COUNTRY LIFE. XXXIX, 16 plan, 48. 1916.

COUNTRY LIFE. LXXIII, 466, 494. 1933.

COUNTRY LIFE. CLV, 1618, 1682. 1974.

ENGLAND: Picturesque Views. p.25. 1786-88.

MORRIS, F.O. Views of Seats. Vol.V, p.43. 1880.

NEALE, J.P. Views of Seats. Vol.I. 1818.

REPTON, H. Observations on landscape gardening. 34. 1803.

[Sales] LONDON, 1922. July 19 [Freehold county seat].

WETHERBY GRANGE (Yorkshire).
[Sales] LONDON, 1840, May 28 [Estate].

WHALLEY ABBEY (Lancashire).
BURKE, J.B. Visitation of Seats. Vol.I, p.8. 1852.*
TWYCROSS, E. Mansions of England and Wales. Vol.I, p.20. 1847.*

WHARTON HALL (Westmorland).
CUMBERLAND: C. & W. A. & A.S. Extra Series VIII, 165 plan. 1892.

WHARTON LODGE (Cheshire).
TWYCROSS, E. Mansions of England and Wales. Vol.I, p.145. 1850.

WHATCOMBE HOUSE (Dorsetshire).
HUTCHINS, J. Vitruvius Dorsettiensis. pl.34. 1816.
HUTCHINS, J. History of Dorset. I, 660. 1861.
OSWALD, A. Country houses of Dorset. p.163. 1959.

WHATTON HOUSE (Leicestershire).
JONES. Views of Seats. I. 1829.
NEALE, J.P. Views of Seats. 2.S. Vol.III. 1826.
NICHOLS, J. History of Leicestershire. III, ii, 1103. 1804.

WHEATFIELD HOUSE (Oxfordshire).
COPPER PLATE MAGAZINE. II, pl.64. 1792-1802.
ENGLAND: Picturesque Views. p.13. 1786-88.

WHEATLEY HALL (Yorkshire).
COPPER PLATE MAGAZINE. I, pl.27. 1792-1802.
ENGLAND: Picturesque Views. p.71. 1786-88.

WHELPRIGG (Westmorland).
BURKE, J.B. Visitation of Seats. Vol.II, p.185. 1853.*

WHERWELL PRIORY (Hampshire).
BURKE, J.B. Visitation of Seats. Vol.II, p.136. 1853.*

WHESTON HALL (Derbyshire).
TILLEY, J. Halls of Derbyshire. I, p.231. 1892.

WHITBOURNE HALL (Herefordshire).
COUNTRY LIFE. CLVII, 702, 774. 1975.

WHITEFIELD HOUSE (Cumberland).
BURKE, J.B. Visitation of Seats. Vol.II, p.245. 1853.*

WHITEFORD HOUSE (Cornwall).
CROMWELL, T.K. Excursions in Cornwall. p.127. 1824.

WHITEHALL (Shropshire).
TIPPING, Henry Avray.
— Whitehall, Shrewsbury, Shorpshire. 8pp. 10 illus. 37x24 London, 1920.
Also in: COUNTRY LIFE, XLVII, 200. 1920.
COUNTRY LIFE. XLVII, 200. 1920.
LEACH, F. Seats of Shropshire. p.215. 1891.
SHROPSHIRE. Castles & Old Mansions. 39. 1868.
TIPPING, H.A. English Homes. Period III, Vol.I, p.139. 1922.
WEST, W. Picturesque views of Shropshire. p.133. 1831.
[Sales] SHREWSBURY, 1923, October 3 [House and grounds].

WHITEHOUGH (Derbyshire).
TILLEY, J. Halls of Derbyshire. I, p.85. 1892.

WHITE HOUSE, Kew (Surrey).
COPPER PLATE MAGAZINE. pl.69. 1778.
SANDBY, P. Select Views. I, pl.60. 1783.

WHITE KNIGHTS (Berkshire).
HOFLAND, Barbara.
— A descriptive account of the mansion and gardens of White-Knights, a seat of his grace the Duke of Marlborough ... Illustrated with ... engravings from pictures taken on the spot by T.C. Hofland. Aquatint plates. London: privately printed [1819].
MARLBOROUGH, George Spencer Churchill, *Duke of*.
— Catalogues Librorum qui in Bibliotheca Blandfordiensi, reperiuntur. [The library of the Marquess of Blandford at Whiteknights.] 254pp. 27x21 [London? privately printed] 1812.
ROBERTSON, A. Great Road. I, p.118. 1792.

WHITE LADIES (Shropshire).
GREAT BRITAIN: Ministry of Public Building and Works [Ancient Monuments and Historic Buildings].
— Boscobel House and White Ladies Priory, Shropshire. 56pp. Illus. incl. plans and map. 19x13 London, 1970.
SHROPSHIRE. Castles & Old Mansions. 52. 1868.

WHITE LODGE Richmond Park (Surrey).
CAMPBELL, C. Vitruvius Britannicus. IV, pls. 1-4, 1767.
COUNTRY LIFE. LIII, 526. 1923.
REPTON, H. Fragments on landscape gardening. p.84. 1816.

WHITESTAUNTON MANOR (Somerset).
[Sales] WHITESTAUNTON MANOR, 1923, May 1-4 [Contents].
[Sales] CHARD, 1923, November 8 [Estate].

WHITEWEBBS, Enfield (Middlesex).
BURKE, J.B. Visitation of Seats. 2.S. Vol.I, p.171. 1854.*

WHITFIELD (Herefordshire).
BURKE, J.B. Visitation of Seats. Vol.I, p.79. 1852.*

WHITFIELD (Oxfordshire).
See WHEATFIELD HOUSE.

WHITFIELD HALL (Northumberland).
BURKE, J.B. Visitation of Seats. Vol.I, p.212. 1852.*

WHITLEIGH (Devonshire).
BURKE, J.B. Visitation of Seats. Vol.II, p.176. 1853.*

WHITLEY ABBEY (Warwickshire).
NEALE, J.P. Views of Seats. Vol.IV. 1821.

WHITMORE HALL (Staffordshire).
COUNTRY LIFE. CXXI, 1144. 1957.

WHITMORE LODGE, Sunninghill
(Berkshire).
[Sales] WHITMORE LODGE, Sunninghill, 1933, July 4-7
[Contents]. (K.F. & R.).

WHITMORE PARK (Warwickshire).
BURKE, J.B. Visitation of Seats. 2.S. Vol.I, p.96. 1854.*

WHITTINGTON HALL (Derbyshire).
BURKE, J.B. Visitation of Seats. Vol.II, p.217. 1853.*

WHITTINGTON HALL (Lancashire).
BARTLETT, J. Mansions of England and Wales. pls.48, 49.
1853.
BURKE, J.B. Visitation of Seats. Vol.I, p.155. 1852.*
TWYCROSS, E. Mansions of England and Wales. Vol.II, p.9.
1847.

WHITTINGTON HALL (Staffordshire).
NIVEN, W. Old Staffordshire houses. p.22, pl.18. 1882.
SHAW, S. Staffordshire. I, 376. 1798.

WHITTON COURT (Shropshire).
COUNTRY LIFE. XLI, 180. 1917.
LEACH, F. Seats of Shropshire. p.159. 1891.
LEIGHTON, S. Shropshire houses. 38. 1901.
SHROPSHIRE. Castles & Old Mansions. 51. 1868.
TIPPING, H.A. English Homes. Period III, Vol.I, p.71. 1922.

WHITTON PLACE (Middlesex).
BURKE, J.B. Visitation of Seats. Vol.I, p.173. 1852.
COPPER PLATE MAGAZINE. I, pl.48. 1792-1802.
ENGLAND: Picturesque Views. p.2. 1786-88.

WHITWELL MANOR (Derbyshire).
TILLEY, J. Halls of Derbyshire. III, p.201. 1899.

WHITWORTH PARK (Durham).
BURKE, J.B. Visitation of Seats. 2.S. Vol.I, p.246. 1854.*

WICHNOR PARK (Staffordshire).
BURKE, J.B. Visitation of Seats. Vol.I, p.194. 1852.*
KIP, J. Nouveau théâtre de la Grande Bretagne. I, pl.78. 1715.

WICK, The. Richmond (Surrey).
COUNTRY LIFE. LXXXIX, 100. 1941.

WICK COURT (Gloucestershire).
COOKE, R. West Country Houses. p.93. 1957.

WICKEN PARK (Northamptonshire).
NEALE, J.P. Views of Seats. Vol.III. 1820.

WICKHAM COURT (Kent).
HASTED, E. Kent. I, 108. 1778.
OSWALD, A. Country houses of Kent. 17. 1933.

WICK HOUSE (Somerset).
JONES. Views of Seats. II. 1829.
NEALE, J.P. Views of Seats. Vol.III. 1820.

WICKINS MANOR (Kent).
COUNTRY LIFE. XCVI, 772. 1944.

WIDCOMBE MANOR (Somerset).
COUNTRY LIFE. LXXXII, 220. 1937.
[Sales] BATH, 1927, February 23 [Estate].

WIDMERPOOL HALL (Nottinghamshire).
BURKE, J.B. Visitation of Seats. Vol.I, p.58. 1852.*

WIDNES HALL (Lancashire).
GRAY, H. Old halls of Lancashire. p.41. 1893.

WIDYHALL (Hertfordshire).
See WYDDIAL HALL.

WIERTON PLACE (Kent).
BADESLADE, T. Seats in Kent. pl.36. 1750.
HARRIS, J. History of Kent. p.49. 1719.

WIGGINTON LODGE (Staffordshire).
BURKE, J.B. Visitation of Seats. Vol.II, p.250. 1853.*

WIGHTWICK MANOR (Staffordshire).

LONDON: National Trust for Places of Historic Interest or Natural Beauty.

—Wightwick Manor. 2 ed. 14pp. 4 plates. 18x12 London: Country Life. (1946).

Another ed. 1963.

LONDON: National Trust for Places of Historic Interest or Natural Beauty.

—Wightwick Manor; a William Morris and Pre-Raphaelite period-piece. 12pp. Illus. (2 col. on cover.) 31x23 [London, 1968.]

LONDON: National Trust for Places of Historic Interest or Natural Beauty.
—Wightwick Manor, West Midlands. [Bibliogr.] 24pp. Illus. (1 on cover) incl. plates and facsimile. 21x14 [London] 1983.

COUNTRY LIFE. CXXXIII, 1242, 1316. 1963.

WIGWELL GRANGE (Derbyshire).

TILLEY, J. Halls of Derbyshire. II, p.265. 1893.

WILBERFORCE HOUSE, Hull (Yorkshire).

COUNTRY LIFE. CIX, 938. 1951.

WILBURY HOUSE (Wiltshire).

CAMPBELL, C. Vitruvius Britannicus. I, pls.51, 52. 1715.

COUNTRY LIFE. LXVI, 845 [Glass]. 1929.

COUNTRY LIFE. LXVII, 145 [Glass]. 1930.

COUNTRY LIFE. LXXI, 96. 1932.

COUNTRY LIFE. CXXVI, 1014, 1148. 1959.

WILBY OLD HALL (Norfolk).

BIRKBECK, G. Old Norfolk houses. 124. 1908.

WILDERHOPE MANOR (Shropshire).

LONDON: National Trust for Places of Historic Interest or Natural Beauty.
— Wilderhope. 8pp. 3 plates. London (1937).

GARNER, T. Domestic architecture. II, p.170 plan. 1911.

SHROPSHIRE. Castles & Old Mansions. 44. 1868.

WILDERNESSE (Kent).

NEALE, J.P. Views of Seats. Vol.II. 1819.

WILLERSLEY CASTLE (Derbyshire).

COPPER PLATE MAGAZINE. IV, pl.172. 1792-1802.

NEALE, J.P. Views of Seats. Vol.I. 1818.

NOBLE, T. Counties of Chester, ... Lincoln. p.29. 1836.

[Sales] WILLERSLEY CASTLE, 1927, June 7-11 [Contents].

WILLESLEY HALL (Leicestershire).

MORRIS, F.O. Views of Seats. Vol.VI, p.7. 1880.

WILLEY HALL (Shropshire).

BURKE, J.B. Visitation of Seats. Vol.II, p.78. 1853.*

COUNTRY LIFE. English Country Houses: Late Georgian. p.115. 1958.

COUNTRY LIFE. XLIX, 214. 1921.

JONES. Views of Seats. I. 1829.

LEACH, F. Seats of Shropshire. p.135. 1891.

LEIGHTON, S. Shropshire houses. 36. 1901.

NEALE, J.P. Views of Seats. 2.S. Vol.II. 1825.

WILLIAMSCOTE (Oxfordshire).

BURKE, J.B. Visitation of Seats. Vol.I, p.177. 1852.*

WILLIAMSTRIP PARK (Gloucestershire).

ATKYNS, R. Glocestershire. p.190. 1768.

DELDERFIELD, E.R. West Country houses. III, 106. 1973.

RUDDER, S. Gloucestershire. 385. 1779.

WILLINGHAM HOUSE (Lincolnshire).

LINCOLNSHIRE. A selection of views. 31. 1805.

WILLINGHURST FARM, Cranleigh (Surrey).

COUNTRY LIFE. CXXVIII, 1242. 1960.

WILLINGTON HALL (Cheshire).

BURKE, J.B. Visitation of Seats. Vol.II, p.127. 1853.*

TWYCROSS, E. Mansions of England and Wales. Vol.I, p.123. 1850.

WILSICK HALL (Yorkshire).

[Sales] WILSICK HALL, 1948, November 18, 19 [Furniture].

WILSLEY HOUSE, Cranbrook (Kent).

COUNTRY LIFE. XLVIII, 240. 1920.

OSWALD, A. Country houses of Kent. 27. 1933.

WILTON CASTLE (Yorkshire).

JONES. Views of Seats. I. 1829.

NEALE, J.P. Views of Seats. 2.S. Vol.IV. 1828.

WHEATER, W. Mansions of Yorkshire. p.336. 1888.

WILTON HOUSE (Wiltshire).

COWDRY, Richard.
— A description of the pictures, statues, busto's, basso-relievo's, and other curiosities at the Earl of Pembroke's house at Wilton. 18x11 London: privately printed, 1751.

KENNEDY, James.
— A new description of the pictures, statues, bustos, basso-relievos, and other curiosities at the Earl of Pembroke's house at Wilton. In the antiques of this collection are contain'd the

whole of Cardinal Richelieu's and Cardinal Mazarine's, and the greatest part of the Earl of Arundel's; besides several particular pieces purchased at different times. viii, 109pp. 4to. 19x12 Salisbury: privately printed by B. Collins, 1758.

A new edition: with an engraving of the busto of Apollonius Tyanaeus. [etc.]. Engr. 20x12 London: privately printed for R. Baldwin, J. White [etc.]. 1764.

7 ed. 20x12 Salisbury: privately printed by E. Easton, 1776.
Author's name no longer appears on title-page.
9 ed. 19x12 Salisbury: by E. Easton for H. Coward. 1779.

KENNEDY, James.
— A description of the antiquities and curiosities in Wilton House. Illustrated with twenty-five engravings of some of the capital statues, bustos and relievos. In this work are introduced the anecdotes and remarks of Thomas, Earl of Pembroke, who collected these antiques, now first published from his lordship's MSS. Engr. plates. 30x24 Salisbury: privately printed by E. Easton, 1769.

LEVER, Sir Tresham Joseph Philip, Bart.
— The Herberts of Wilton. [Bibliogr.] xiv, 270pp. Plates incl. facsimiles and folding genealog. table. 22x14 London: J. Murray, 1967.

NEWTON, Sir Charles Thomas.
—Notes on the sculpture at Wilton House. 30pp. 21x14 London: J. Murray, 1849.

PEMBROKE AND MONTGOMERY, Sidney Charles Herbert, 16th Earl of Pembroke.
—The history and treasures of Wilton House, home of the Earls of Pembroke for over 400 years. 24pp. Illus. (some col., some on covers) incl. map. 23x18 (London: Pitkin Pictorials, 1962.)   One of the series: PRIDE of Britain.

PEMBROKE AND MONTGOMERY, Sidney Charles Herbert, 16th Earl of Pembroke.
—A catalogue of the paintings & drawings in the collection at Wilton House, Salisbury, Wiltshire. Compiled by Sidney, 16th Earl of Pembroke. [Bibliogr. notes.] Illus. (13 col.) 28x20 London: Phaidon Press, 1968.

SMITH, James.
— Wilton and its associations ... With illustrations on wood by W.F. Tiffin. Cuts. 22x17 Salisbury: G. Brown; London: J.B. Nichols & Son, 1851.

STRONG, Sandford Arthur.
— Reproductions in facsimile of drawings by the old masters in the collections of the Earl of Pembroke and Montgomery at Wilton House. With text, explanatory and critical by S.A.S. Illus. (many tinted). 52x39 London: Colnaghi, 1900.

WILKINSON, Sir Nevile Rodwell.
— Wilton House pictures: containing a ... catalogue and description of the three hundred and twenty paintings which are now in the possession of the Earl of Pembroke and Montgomery at his house at Wilton in the county of Wiltshire ... Together with an introduction by Sidney, Earl of Pembroke and Montgomery, a history of Wilton House and other matters. [Bibliogr.] Illus. incl. plates. 2 vols. 39x34 London: privately printed at the Chiswick Press, 1907.

WILTON HOUSE.
— Aedes Pembrochianae: a new account and description of the statues, bustos, relievos, paintings, medals, and other antiquities and curiosities in Wilton House ... With a complete index; by which any particular statue, busto, painting &c. and

the places or rooms where disposed, may be immediately turned to [etc.]. [By G. Richardson.] 13 ed. 20x13 Salisbury: privately printed at the Salisbury Press, 1798.

WILTON HOUSE.
—Guide book to Wilton House, Salisbury [etc.] 24pp. 12 plates. 21x14 (Salisbury) privately printed [c.1955.]

BRITTON, J. Beauties of Wiltshire. I, 140. 1801.

BURKE, J.B. Visitation of Seats. Vol.I, p.181. 1852.*

CAMPBELL, C. Vitruvius Britannicus. II, pls.61-67. 1717.

CAMPBELL, C. Vitruvius Britannicus. III, pls.57-60. 1725.

CAMPBELL, C. Vitruvius Britannicus. V, pls.88, 89. 1771 [Bridge].

COUNTRY LIFE. English Country Houses: Caroline. p.75. 1966.

COUNTRY LIFE. XI, 464. 1902.

COUNTRY LIFE. XLIX, 669 [Armour]. 1921.

COUNTRY LIFE. XCV, 112, 156. 1949.

COUNTRY LIFE. CXXXIII, 1044, 1109, 1176. 1963.

COUNTRY LIFE. CXXXIV, 314. 1963.

COUNTRY LIFE. CXLIV, 748 [Marbles], 834 [Pictures]. 1968.

DELDERFIELD, E.R. West Country houses. II, 110. 1970.

ENGLAND: Beauties of England. II, p.354. 1787.

ENGLAND: Picturesque Views. p.39. 1786-88.

ENGLISH CONNOISSEUR. II, 118. 1766.*

JONES. Views of Seats. II. 1829.

KROLL, A. Historic houses. 88. 1969.

LATHAM, C. In English Homes. Vol.I, p.85. 1904.

MALAN, A.H. More famous homes. p.175. 1902.

MORRIS, F.O. Views of Seats. Vol.I, p.9. 1880.

NEALE, J.P. Views of Seats. Vol.V. 1822.

NICOLSON, N. Great Houses of Britain. p.124. 1965.

[Sales] LONDON, 1914, June 25, 26 [Library; portion, illuminated manuscripts etc.].

[Sales] LONDON, 1917, July 5, 6, 9, 10 [Prints, Drawings, pictures, armour].

[Sales] LONDON, 1920, March 15-17 [Books, Americana, fine arts etc.].

[Sales] LONDON, 1923, June 14 [Armour].

[Sales] WILTON HOUSE, 1961, July 3 [Ancient marbles].

WILTON PARK (Buckinghamshire).
BURKE, J.B. Visitation of Seats. 2.S. Vol.I, p.93. 1854.*
ENGLAND: Picturesque Views. p.28. 1786-88.

WIMBLEDON HOUSE (Surrey).
Beaumaurice Rush.
PROSSER, G.F. Surrey Seats. p.95. 1828.

WIMBLEDON HOUSE (Surrey). Calonne.
ENGLAND: Picturesque Views. p.98. 1786-88.

WIMBLEDON HOUSE (Surrey). Duchess of Marlborough; Earl Spencer.
CAMPBELL, C. Vitruvius Britannicus. V, pls.20-22. 1771.
COUNTRY LIFE. CXXXII, 248. 1962.

WIMBLEDON PALACE (Surrey).
HIGHAM, Charles Strachan Saunders.
—Wimbledon Manor House under the Cecils. [Bibliogr. notes.] xii, 44pp. Plates incl. plans, maps and facsimile. 25x18 London: Longmans, 1962.
CLARKE, T.H. Domestic architecture. I. 1833.

WIMBORNE ST. GILES (Dorsetshire).
See St. GILES HOUSE.

WIMPOLE HALL (Cambridgeshire).
LONDON: National Trust for Places of Historic Interest or Natural Beauty.
—JACKSON-STOPS, G. Wimpole Hall, Cambridgeshire. [Bibliogr.] 68pp. Illus. (1 col. on cover) incl. plan and genealog. table. 25x18 [London] 1982.
COUNTRY LIFE. XXIII, 234. 1908.
COUNTRY LIFE. LXI, 806, 844. 1927.
COUNTRY LIFE. LXX, 590 [Furniture]. 1931.
COUNTRY LIFE. CXLII, 1400 plan, 1466, 1594. 1967.
KIP, J. Nouveau théâtre de la Grande Bretagne. I, pl.32. 1715.
LATHAM, C. In English Homes. Vol.III, p.275. 1909.
MORRIS, F.O. Views of Seats. Vol.II, p.71. 1880.
WHITEMAN, G.W. English Country Homes. p.131. 1951.

WINCHAM HALL (Cheshire).
TWYCROSS, E. Mansions of England and Wales. Vol.II, p.70. 1850.

WINCHESTER PALACE (Hampshire).
BUCK, S. & N. Antiquities. I, pl.112. 1774.
ENGLAND: Beauties of England. I, p.300. 1787.

WINDMILL HILL PLACE (Sussex).
BURKE, J.B. Visitation of Seats. 2.S. Vol.I, p.73. 1854.*
CAMPBELL, C. New Vitruvius Britannicus. I, pls.24-26. 1802.

WINFIELD MANOR (Derbyshire).
See SOUTH WINGFIELD MANOR.

WINGERWORTH HALL (Derbyshire).
BURKE, J.B. Visitation of Seats. 2.S. Vol.I, p.15. 1854.*
COUNTRY LIFE. XXVII, 162. 1910.
REPTON, H. Fragments on landscape gardening. p.59. 1816.
TILLEY, J. Halls of Derbyshire. III, p.227. 1899.
TIPPING, H.A. English Homes. Period V, Vol.I, p.207. 1921.

WINGFIELD CASTLE (Suffolk).
BUCK, S. & N. Antiquities. II, pl.276. 1774.
COUNTRY LIFE. XXXIII, 952. 1913.
CROMWELL, T.K. Excursions in Suffolk. II, p.20. 1819.
HEARNE, T. Antiquities. I, pl.30. 1807.

WINGFIELD COLLEGE (Suffolk).
COUNTRY LIFE. CLXXI 18. 1982.

WINGFIELD HOUSE, Trowbridge (Wiltshire).
[Sales] WINGFIELD HOUSE, Trowbridge, 1930, November 10-13 [Contents]. (K.F. & R.).

WINGFIELD MANOR (Derbyshire).
See SOUTH WINGFIELD MANOR.

WINKBURN HALL (Nottinghamshire).
BURKE, J.B. Visitation of Seats. 2.S. Vol.II, p.122. 1855.*

WINKFIELD PARK (Berkshire).
See FOLIEJON PARK

WINKFIELD PLACE (Berkshire).
[Sales] WINKFIELD PLACE, 1923, February 26-28, March 1 [Contents].

WINNINGTON HALL (Cheshire).
COUNTRY LIFE. LIV, 314. 1923.
TWYCROSS, E. Mansions of England and Wales. Vol.I, p.105. 1850.*

WINSLOW HALL (Buckinghamshire).
COUNTRY LIFE. English Country Houses: Baroque. p.31. 1970.
COUNTRY LIFE. CX, 572. 1951.

WINSTANLEY HALL (Lancashire).
WINSTANLEY HALL.
— Winstanley Hall. [Typescript.] Illus. 3 vols. 30x21 n.p. 1973-76.
BARTLETT, J. Mansions of England and Wales. pl.113. 1853.
TWYCROSS, E. Mansions of England and Wales. Vol.III, p.50. 1847.

WINSTER HALL (Derbyshire).
TILLEY, J. Halls of Derbyshire. I, p.247. 1892.

WINTERBORNE CLENSTON MANOR (Dorsetshire).
HUTCHINS, J. History of Dorset. I, 191. 1861.
OSWALD, A. Country houses of Dorset. p.53. 1959.

WINTHORPE HALL (Nottinghamshire).
BURKE, J.B. Visitation of Seats. Vol.I, p.196. 1852.*
THOROTON, R. Nottinghamshire. I, 366. 1797.

WINWICK MANOR (Northamptonshire).
GOTCH, J.A. Halls of Northants. p.57. 1936.

WISETON HALL (Nottinghamshire).
COPPER PLATE MAGAZINE. I, pl.15, 1792-1802.
ENGLAND: Picturesque Views. p.95. 1786-88.
THOROTON, R. Nottinghamshire. III, 310. 1797.

WISTON PARK (Sussex).
COUNTRY LIFE. XXV, 306. 1909.
ELWES, D.G.C. Mansions of Western Sussex. 263. 1876.
TIPPING, H.A. English Homes. Early Renaissance. p.89. 1912.

WISTOW HALL (Leicestershire).
BURKE, J.B. Visitation of Seats. 2.S. Vol.II, p.107. 1855.*
JONES. Views of Seats. I. 1829.
NEALE, J.P. Views of Seats. Vol.II. 1819.
NICHOLS, J. History of Leicestershire. III, ii, 872. 1798.
NICHOLS, J. History of Leicestershire. III, ii, pl.CLVI, 1129. 1804.
THROSBY, J. Views in Leicestershire. p.187. 1789.

WITCHINGHAM HALL (Norfolk).
GARRATT, T. Halls of Norfolk. pl.50. 1890.
MORRIS, F.O. Views of Seats. Vol. IV, p.77. 1880.

WITCOMBE PARK (Gloucestershire).
ATKYNS, R. Glocestershire. p.444. 1768.

WITHAM HALL (Lincolnshire).
[Sales] WITHAM HALL, 1959, March 25 [Furniture etc.].

WITHAM PARK (Somerset).
CAMPBELL, C. Vitruvius Britannicus. II, pls.91, 92. 1717.

WITHINGTON HALL (Cheshire).
BURKE, J.B. Visitation of Seats. Vol.II, p.80. 1853.*
ORMEROD, G. Cheshire. III, 718. 1882.
TWYCROSS, E. Mansions of England and Wales. Vol.II, p.99. 1850.*

WITLEY COURT (Worcestershire).
ANGUS, W. Seats of the Nobility. pl.59. 1787.
BURKE, J.B. Visitation of Seats. 2.S. Vol.II, p.95. 1855.*
COUNTRY LIFE. II, 126. 1897.

COUNTRY LIFE. XCVII, 992, 1036. 1945.
MORRIS, F.O. Views of Seats. Vol.I, p.85. 1880.
NASH, T.R. Worcestershire. II, 465. 1782.
[Sales] WITLEY COURT, 1938, September 26-30, October 3-6 [Estate and remaining contents].

WITLEY PARK (Surrey).
COUNTRY LIFE.CXXXIV, 1693 plan. 1963.

WITNESHAM HALL (Suffolk).
BURKE, J.B. Visitation of seats. Vol.II, p.202. 1853.
SANDON, E. Suffolk houses. 288. 1977.

WITTON CASTLE (Durham).
JONES. Views of Seats. I. 1829.
NEALE, J.P. Views of Seats. Vol.I. 1818.
[Sales] WITTON CASTLE, 1963, November 27, 28 [Contents].

WITTON HOUSE (Lancashire).
BURKE, J.B. Visitation of Seats. Vol.I, p.134. 1852.
TWYCROSS, E. Mansions of England and Wales. Vol.I, p.17. 1847.

WIVENHOE NEW PARK (Essex).
COUNTRY LIFE. CXXXVIII, 218 plan. 1965.

WIVENHOE PARK (Essex).
See WYVENHOE PARK.

WIVETON HALL (Norfolk).
COUNTRY LIFE. XXXVIII, 712 plan. 1915.

WOBURN ABBEY (Bedfordshire).
BEDFORD, Adeline Marie Russell, *Duchess of.*
— Biographical catalogue of the pictures at Woburn Abbey compiled by A.M. Duchess of Bedford and E.M.S. Russell. 2 vols. 21x17 London: Elliot Stock, 1890-92.
BENNETT-GOLDNEY, Francis.
— The china at Woburn Abbey in the possession of Herbrand, 11th. Duke of Bedford, K.G. 20x15 London: J. Murray, 1910.
BLAKISTON, Georgiana.
— Woburn and the Russells. [Bibliogr.] x, 246pp. Plates, and genealog. table (on end-papers.) 23x15 London: Constable, 1980.
DODD, Stephen.
— An historical and topographical account of the town of Woburn, its Abbey, and vicinity; containing also a concise genealogy of the house of Russell, and memoirs of the late Francis, Duke of Bedford. Engr. plates. 19x12 Woburn: S. Dodd, 1818.
PARRY, John Docwra.
— History and description of Woburn Abbey, etc.,etc. Part 1: history of the town ... biography of the Russell family, sketch of the Gordon family [etc.]. Part 2: Woburn Abbey, portraits

and paintings, sculpture gallery [etc.]. Illus. incl. lithogr. plates.23x14 London: Longman, Rees, Orme, Brown and Green; Woburn: Dodd; Brighton: Wright [1831].

ROBINSON, Peter Frederick.
— History of Woburn Abbey. (General catalogue of the paintings ... 1827 ... Catalogue of the marbles and other works in sculpture at Woburn Abbey.) [Bibliogr. notes.] 22pp. Engr. plates incl. elevation and plans. 53x35 London: for the author, 1833.
One of the series: VITRUVIUS BRITANNICUS.

SCHARF, *Sir* George.
— A descriptive and historical catalogue of the collection of pictures at Woburn Abbey. Part I: portraits; part II: imaginary subjects, landscapes, miniatures, drawings, and enamels. Facsimiles incl. artists' signatures. 2 pts. in 1. 27x18 London: privately printed, 1877.
New ed. 2 pts. in 1. 28x22 London: privately printed, 1890.

SMITH, Arthur Hamilton.
— A catalogue of sculpture at Woburn Abbey in the collection of His Grace the Duke of Bedford. Illus. 27x18 London: privately printed, 1900.

THOMSON, Gladys Scott.
— Life in a noble household, 1641-1700. 8 plates. 22x14 London: Cape, 1937.

THOMSON, Gladys Scott.
— Family background. [Bibliogr. notes.] 4 plates. 20x13 London: Cape, 1949.

THOMSON, Gladys Scott
— Woburn Abbey: an illustrated survey [etc.]. 32pp. Illus. (some col., some on covers) incl. maps (on inside covers). 14x22 Derby: E.L.P. (1954?).

THOMSON, Gladys Scott.
— Woburn and the Russels ... decorated by R.I. Jackson. 64pp. Illus. (1 on title-page) incl. cover. 18x12. Derby: Pilgrim Press, 1956.

WOBURN ABBEY.
— Outline engravings and descriptions of the Woburn Abbey marbles [collection of the Duke of Bedford]. Engr. plates incl. section, elevation and plan. 55x38 London: privately printed, 1822.

WOBURN ABBEY.
— A catalogue of miniature portraits in enamel by Henry Bone, R.A., in the collection of the Duke of Bedford at Woburn Abbey. [Bibliogr. notes.] 72pp. Plates 25x16 London: privately printed, 1825.

WOBURN ABBEY.
— Catalogue of the books in the library of Woburn Abbey. 34x22 London: privately printed, 1867.

WOBURN ABBEY.
— Woburn Abbey: history and treasures. 32pp. Illus. (Some col., some on covers) incl. plans. 26x15 (Norwich: Jarrold & Sons, 1967).
Another ed. Woburn Abbey. Norwich: Jarrold & Sons, 1969.

BURKE, J.B. Visitation of Seats. Vol.II, p.190. 1853.*

CAMPBELL, C. Vitruvius Britannicus. IV, pls.21-25, 1767.

COUNTRY LIFE. CXVII, 854. 1955.

COUNTRY LIFE. CXVIII, 434, 488. 1955.

COUNTRY LIFE. CXXXVIII, 98, 158. 1965.

COUNTRY LIFE. CLXXIII, 772 (Park and garden buildings], 860 [Park and garden buildings]. 1983.

JONES. Views of Seats. I. 1829.

MORRIS, F.O. Views of Seats. Vol.II, p.13. 1880.

NEALE, J.P. Views of Seats. Vol.I. 1818.

REPTON, H. Fragments on landscape gardening. p.148. 1816.

[Sales] LONDON, 1951, January 19 [Pictures].

WOKEFIELD PARK (Berkshire).
BURKE, J.B. Visitation of Seats. Vol.I, p.148. 1852.*

WOKINGHAM (Berkshire). Colonel Williamson's House.
CAMPBELL, C. Vitruvius Britannicus. IVth. pls.92, 93. 1739.

WOLFETON HOUSE (Dorsetshire).
COUNTRY LIFE. XI, 304. 1902.

COUNTRY LIFE. CXIV, 414, 484. 1953.

HEATH, S. Dorset Manor Houses. 209. 1907.

HUTCHINS, J. History of Dorset. II, 545. 1863.

OSWALD, A. Country houses of Dorset. p.60. 1959.

WOLF HALL (Wiltshire).
ADAMS. William Maurice.
—Wolfhall and Tottenham, the homes of the Seymour and the Bruce. 56pp. 4 plates incl. folding map. 18x12 Putney: Maurice & Co. [1903].
One of the series: SYLVAN SAVERNAKE.

JACKSON, John Edward, Canon.
—Wulfhall and the Seymours. With an appendix of original documents discovered at Longleat. [Bibliogr. notes.] 70pp. Plates incl. map and genealog. table. 24x18 Devizes, 1875.
Also in DEVIZES: Wiltshire Archaeological and Natural History Magazine. XV, 140. 1875.

WOLLATON HALL (Nottinghamshire).
GOTCH, John Alfred.
— Wollaton Hall. 11pp. plates. incl. plans.
In GUILFORD (E.L.) Memorials of old Nottinghamshire. p.77. 1912.

COUNTRY LIFE. XLI, 544, 568, 592. 1917.

GOTCH, J.A. Architecture of the Renaissance. II, p.59 plan. 1894.

HALL, S.C. Baronial Halls. Vol.II. 1848.

JONES. Views of Seats. I. 1829.

KIP, J. Nouveau théâtre de la Grande Bretagne. I, pl.68. 1715.

MALAN, A.H. Other famous homes. p.1. 1902.

MORRIS, F.O. Views of Seats. Vol.I, p.73. 1880.

NASH, J. Mansions of England. III, pls.4, 5. 1841.

NEALE, J.P. Views of Seats. Vol.III. 1820.

NOBLE, T. Counties of Chester, ... Lincoln. p.57. 1836.

TIPPING, H.A. English Homes. Period III, Vol.I, p.183. 1922.

WOLLEY'S HOUSE, Allen's Hill (Derbyshire).
TILLEY, J. Halls of Derbyshire. II, p.249. 1893.

WOLSELEY HALL (Staffordshire).
COUNTRY LIFE. XXVII, 234. 1910.
JONES. Views of Seats. I. 1829.
MORRIS, F.O. Views of Seats. Vol.III, p.55. 1880.
NEALE, J.P. Views of Seats. Vol.IV. 1821.

WOLSTON MANOR (Warwickshire).
[Sales] WOLSTON MANOR, 1927, November 3 [Demolition sale].

WOLTERTON HALL (Norfolk).
KETTON-CREMER, R.W.
— Wolterton Hall, the historic home of the Walpole family ... History and description of rooms by R.W.K.-C. 16pp. 5 illus. (4 on covers) incl. map. 14x20 [Derby: E.L.P., 1957.]
COUNTRY LIFE. XXIV, 450. 1908.
COUNTRY LIFE. CXXII, 116, 166. 1957.
CROMWELL, T.K. Excursions in Norfolk. I, p.151. 1818.
LATHAM, C. In English Homes. Vol.III, p.371. 1909.
NEALE, J.P. Views of Seats. Vol.III. 1820.
TIPPING, H.A. English Homes. Period V, Vol.I, p.111. 1921.
WATTS, W. Seats of the Nobility. pl.59. 1779.
[Sales] LONDON, 1856, June 28 [Pictures & illustrated books].

WOLVERHAMPTON, The Deanery (Staffordshire).
NIVEN, W. Old Staffordshire houses. p.26, pl.20. 1882.

WOLVETON HOUSE (Dorsetshire).
See WOLFETON HOUSE.

WOMBWELL HALL (Kent).
GREENWOOD, C. Kent. 227. 1838.

WONASTOW COURT (Monmouthshire).
[Sales] WONASTOW COURT, 1929, November 27-29 [Porcelain, pottery, furniture].

WONERSH PARK (Surrey).
BRAYLEY, E.W. History of Surrey. V, 150. 1841.
BURKE, J.B. Visitation of Seats. Vol.I. p.246. 1852.*
PROSSER, G.F. Surrey Seats. p.73. 1828.

WOODBANK (Cheshire).
TWYCROSS, E. Mansions of England and Wales. Vol.II, p.127. 1850.

WOODBANK, Ilkley (Yorkshire).
YORKSHIRE. Picturesque views. 1885.

WOODBRIDGE ABBEY (Suffolk).
BURKE, J.B. Visitation of Seats. Vol.I, p.201. 1852.*

WOODCHESTER PARK (Gloucestershire).
COUNTRY LIFE. CXLV, 284. 1969.
SUMMERSON, J. The Country Seat. 237. 1970.

WOODCOTE HALL (Shropshire).
LEIGHTON, S. Shropshire houses. 31. 1901.

WOODCOTE PARK (Surrey).
BRAYLEY, E.W. History of Surrey. IV, 352. 1841.
BURKE, J.B. Visitation of Seats. Vol.I, p.231. 1852.*
PROSSER, G.F. Surrey Seats. p.51. 1828.

WOODCROFT CASTLE (Northamptonshire).
GOTCH, J.A. Halls of Northants. p.2. 1936.
NICHOLS, J. History of Leicestershire. IV, ii, pl.LXXX, 508. 1811.

WOOD END (Yorkshire).
JONES. Views of Seats. I. 1829.
NEALE, J.P. Views of Seats. Vol.V. 1822.

WOODFALLS, Melchet Park (Hampshire).
COUNTRY LIFE. LXVIII, 412 plan. 1930.

WOODFOLD PARK (Lancashire).
BARTLETT, J. Mansions of England and Wales. pls.16, 18. 1853.
TWYCROSS, E. Mansions of England and Wales. Vol.I, p.13. 1847.

WOODHALL PARK (Hertfordshire).
BURKE, J.B. Visitation of Seats. Vol.I, p.173. 1852.*
CAMPBELL, C. New Vitruvius Britannicus. I, pls.27, 28. 1802.
COUNTRY LIFE. English Country Houses: Mid Georgian. p.177. 1956.
COUNTRY LIFE. LVII,164, 198, 554. 1925.
COUNTRY LIFE. LXVII, 611 [Furniture]. 1930.
TIPPING, H.A. English Homes. Period VI, Vol.I, p.219. 1926.

WOOD HOUSE, Epping (Essex).
COUNTRY LIFE. CXXVI, 1300. 1959.

WOBURN ABBEY, Bedfordshire. From: ROBINSON (P.F.). *History of Woburn Abbey*, London, 1833.

WOOD HOUSE, Shipbourne (Kent).
COUNTRY LIFE. CXXIV, 132 plan. 1958.

WOODLAND HOUSE (Kent).
COPPER PLATE MAGAZINE. II, pl.80. 1792-1802.
ENGLAND: Picturesque Views. p.5. 1786-88.

WOODLANDS, Bradford (Yorkshire).
YORKSHIRE. Picturesque views. 1885.

WOODLANDS MANOR (Wiltshire).
COUNTRY LIFE. LV, 732, 776. 1924.
ELYARD, S.J. Old Wiltshire homes. p.52. 1894.
TIPPING, H.A. English Homes. Period I & II, Vol.II, p.17. 1937.

WOODLEIGH HALL, Rawdon (Yorkshire).
YORKSHIRE, Picturesque views. 1885.

WOODPERRY (Oxfordshire).
COUNTRY LIFE. CXXIX, 18, 66 [Photocopy]. 1961.

WOODROFFE'S, Marchington (Staffordshire).
COUNTRY LIFE. CX, 650 plan. 1951.

WOODSEATS HALL (Derbyshire).
TILLEY, J. Halls of Derbyshire. III, p.45. 1899.

WOODSFORD CASTLE (Dorsetshire).
HEATH, S. Dorset Manor Houses. 223. 1907.
HUTCHINS, J. History of Dorset. I, 449. 1861.
OSWALD, A. Country houses of Dorset. p.50. 1959.

WOODSOME HALL (Yorkshire).
COWEN, William.
— Six views of Woodsome Hall; embellished with costume figures of the olden time. Drawn and engraved by W.C. [No text.] If. 6 tinted lithogr. plates. 36x53 London: by the artist, 1851.
COUNTRY LIFE. XX, 906. 1906.
GARNER, T. Domestic architecture. II, p.168 plan. 1911.
LATHAM, C. In English Homes. Vol.II, p.95. 1907.

WOODTHORPE HALL (Derbyshire).
TILLEY, J. Halls of Derbyshire. III, p.223. 1899.

WOOLBEDING HOUSE (Sussex).
COUNTRY LIFE. CII, 328. 1947.

WOOLBRIDGE MANOR (Dorsetshire).
HEATH, S. Dorset Manor Houses. 231. 1907.
OSWALD, A. Country houses of Dorset. p.104. 1959.

WOOLLAS HALL (Worcestershire).
BURKE, J.B. Visitation of Seats. Vol.II, p.59. 1853.
COUNTRY LIFE. XX, 270. 1906.
GARNER, T. Domestic architecture. II, p.142. 1911.
LATHAM, C. In English Homes. Vol.II, p.169. 1907.
NEALE, J.P. Views of Seats. Vol.V. 1822.
NIVEN, W. Old Worcestershire houses. p.42, pl.18. 1873.

WOOLLEY HALL (Yorkshire).
WAKEFIELD: Historical society.
—3. MARKHAM, G. Woolley Hall: the historical development of a country house. [Bibliogr.] viii, 88pp. Illus. incl. folding plate, plans, map and genealog. table. 21x15 Wakefield, 1979.

WOOLLEY PARK (Berkshire).
CAMPBELL, C. New Vitruvius Britannicus. II, pls.36-8. 1808.

WOOLSTHORPE MANOR (Lincolnshire).
LONDON: National Trust for Places of Historic Interest or Natural Beauty.
—Woolsthorpe Manor, Lincolnshire. [Bibliogr.] 16pp. Illus. (1 col. on cover) incl. plates. 22x14 [London] 1981.

WOOLTON HALL (Lancashire).
NEALE, J.P. Views of Seats. Vol.II. 1819.
TWYCROSS, E. Mansions of England and Wales. Vol.III. p.58. 1847.*
WATTS, W. Seats of the Nobility. pl.76. 1779.

WOOLTON HAYES (Lancashire).
BARTLETT, J. Mansions of England and Wales. pl.124. 1853.
TWYCROSS, E. Mansions of England and Wales. Vol.III, p.57. 1847.

WOOLTON WOOD (Lancashire).
BARTLETT, J. Mansions of England and Wales. pl.129. 1853.
TWYCROSS, E. Mansions of England and Wales. Vol.III, p.60. 1847.

WOOLVERSTONE PARK (Suffolk).
COPPER PLATE MAGAZINE. II, pl.81. 1792-1802.
CROMWELL, T.K. Excursions in Suffolk. I, p.147. 1818.

WOOTON (Shropshire).
SHROPSHIRE. Castles & Old Mansions. 55. 1868.

WOOTTON COURT (Kent).
HASTED, E. Kent. III, 763. 1790.

WOOTTON HALL (Staffordshire).
BURKE, J.B. Visitation of Seats. 2.S. Vol.I, p.22. 1854.*

WOOTTON HALL (Warwickshire).
SMITH, W. History of the County of Warwick. 291. 1830.

WOOTTON LODGE (Staffordshire).
COUNTRY LIFE. XXVII, 946. 1910.
COUNTRY LIFE. CXXV, 522, 596 plan. 1959.
NEALE, J.P. Views of Seats. Vol.IV. 1821.
NIVEN, W. Old Staffordshire houses. p.10, pls.7, 8. 1882.
TIPPING, H.A. English Homes. Early Renaissance. p.347. 1912.

WOOTTON MANOR (Sussex).
COUNTRY LIFE. CXVII, 920. 1955.

WORCESTER PARK (Surrey).
PROSSER, G.F. Surrey Seats. p.35. 1828.

WORDEN, formerly **SHAWE HALL** (Lancashire).
TWYCROSS, E. Mansions of England and Wales. Vol.I, p.61. 1847.*

WORKINGTON HALL (Cumberland).
CURWEN, John Flavel.
— Workington Hall. [Bibliogr. notes.] Illus. incl. folding plate and plan. 25x19 (Kendal: T. Wilson, 1899).
BURKE, J.B. Visitation of Seats. 2.S. Vol.I, p.149. 1854.*
MORRIS, F.O. Views of Seats. Vol.V, p.57. 1880.

WORKSOP MANOR (Nottinghamshire).
BUCK, S. & N. Antiquities. II, pls.232, 233. 1774.
COUNTRY LIFE. CLIII, 678, 750 plan. 1973.
JONES. Views of Seats. I. 1829.
NEALE, J.P. Views of Seats. Vol.III. 1820.
NOBLE, T. Counties of Chester, ... Lincoln. p.39. 1836.
PAINE, J. Plans, elevations. Pt.II, pls.1-16 plans. 96 [Chimney piece], 101 [Pediment]. 1783.
WATTS, W. Seats of the Nobility. pl.13. 1779.

WORLINGHAM HALL (Suffolk).
COUNTRY LIFE. CXLVII, 624. 1970.
CROMWELL, T.K. Excursions in Suffolk. II, p.123. 1819.
DAVY, H. Seats in Suffolk. pl.16. 1827.
SANDON, E. Suffolk houses. 241. 1977.
[Sales] LONDON, 1849, August 21 [Mansion and estate].

WORMHILL HALL (Derbyshire).
TILLEY, J. Halls of Derbyshire. I, p.225. 1892.

WORMINGTON GRANGE (Gloucestershire).
COUNTRY LIFE. English Country Houses: Late Georgian. p.175. 1958.
COUNTRY LIFE. LXXXVIII, 256. 1940.

WORMLEIGHTON (Warwickshire).
NIVEN, W. Old Warwickshire houses. p.32, pl.31. 1878.

WORMLEY BURY (Hertfordshire).
COUNTRY LIFE. XXXVII, 144 plan. 1915.

WORSBOROUGH HALL (Yorkshire).
BURKE, J.B. Visitation of Seats. Vol.II, p.102. 1853.*

WORSLEY HALL (Lancashire).
BARTLETT, J. Mansions of England and Wales. pl. 138. 1853.
MORRIS, F.O. Views of Seats. Vol.II, p.35. 1880.
MOSS, F. Pilgrimages. V, 73. 1910.
TWYCROSS, E. Mansions of England and Wales. Vol.III, p.66. 1847.

WORSTEAD HOUSE (Norfolk).
NEALE, J.P. Views of Seats. Vol.III. 1820.

WORTHAM MANOR (Devonshire).
COUNTRY LIFE. CXIX, 1174 plan, 1228. 1956.

WORTH PARK (Sussex).
[Sales] WORTH PARK, 1915, July 12 and following days [Contents]. (K.F. & R.).

WORTHY PARK (Hampshire).
HAMPSHIRE: Architectural views. 1830.

WORTLEY HALL (Yorkshire).
BURKE, J.B. Visitation of Seats. 2.S. Vol.I, p.139. 1854.*

WOTHORPE LODGE (Northamptonshire).
GOTCH, J.A. Halls of Northants. p.8. 1936.
RICHARDSON, C.J. Old English mansions. I, pls.9-11. 1841.

WOTTON (Gloucestershire).
ATKYNS, R. Glocestershire. p.307. 1768.

WOTTON HOUSE (Buckinghamshire).
COUNTRY LIFE. CVI, 38, 182. 1947.

WOTTON HOUSE, Wotton Fitzpaine (Dorsetshire).
HUTCHINS, J. History of Dorset. II, 274. 1863.

WOTTON HOUSE (Surrey).
BRAYLEY, E.W. History of Surrey. V, 33. 1841.
BURKE, J.B. Visitation of Seats. 2.S. Vol.I, p. 176. 1854.*
MANNING, O. Surrey. II, 145. 1804.

WOTTON-UNDER-EDGE MANOR (Gloucestershire).
HODGES, E. Ancient English Homes. 15. 1895.

WRAXALL COURT (Somerset).
COOKE, R. West Country Houses. p.159. 1957.

WRAXHALL MANOR (Dorsetshire).
OSWALD, A. Country houses of Dorset. p.99. 1959.

WRAY CASTLE (Lancashire).
BARTLETT, J. Mansions of England and Wales. pls.56, 57. 1853.
BURKE, J.B. Visitation of Seats. Vol.II, p.148. 1853.*
TWYCROSS, E. Mansions of England and Wales. Vol.II, p.15. 1847.

WRAYSBURY HOUSE (Buckinghamshire).
BURKE, J.B. Visitation of Seats. 2.S. Vol.I, p.14. 1854.*

WRENBURY HALL (Cheshire).
BURKE, J.B. Visitation of Seats. Vol.II, p.138. 1853.*
TWYCROSS, E. Mansions of England and Wales. Vol.II, p.22. 1850.*

WREN'S HOUSE, Chichester (Sussex).
COUNTRY LIFE. XXXI, 614 plan. 1912.

WREST PARK (Bedfordshire).
ELSTOW: Moot Hall.
— Leaflet [s].
7. GODBER, J. Wrest Park and the Duke of Kent (Henry Grey, 1671-1740). 12pp. Folding plate incl. elevation and plans, and genealog. table (on inside cover). 1963.
Title on cover.
BURKE, J.B. Visitation of Seats. Vol.II, p.34. 1853.*
CAMPBELL, C. Vitruvius Britannicus. IVth. pls.30-33. 1739.
COUNTRY LIFE. XLII, 112 [Garden Pavilion]. 1917.
COUNTRY LIFE. CXLVII, 1250. 1970.
COUNTRY LIFE. CXLVIII, 18. 1970.
KIP, J. Nouveau théâtre de la Grande Bretagne. I, pl.19. 1715.

NEALE, J.P. Views of Seats. Vol.I. 1818.
[Sales] WREST PARK, 1917, September 10-14 [Remaining contents].

WRETHAM HALL (Norfolk).
BURKE, J.B. Visitation of Seats. Vol.II, p.162. 1853.*

WRICKLEMARSH (Kent). Sir Gregory Page Turner, Bart.
CAMPBELL, C. Vitruvius Britannicus. IV, pls.58-64. 1767.
ENGLAND: Beauties of England. I, p.394. 1787.
ENGLAND: Picturesque Views. p.82. 1786-88.
ENGLISH CONNOISSEUR. II, 90. 1766.*
WATTS, W. Seats of the Nobility. pl.47. 1779.

WRIGHTINGTON HALL (Lancashire).
TWYCROSS, E. Mansions of England and Wales. Vol.I, p.63. 1847.*
[Sales] LONDON, 1861, May 10 and following days [Pictures from W.H.].

WRINSTED COURT (Kent).
GREENWOOD, C. Kent. 161. 1838.

WRITTLE LODGE (Essex).
CROMWELL, T.K. Excursions in Essex. I, p.16. 1825.

WROTHAM PARK (Middlesex).
CAMPBELL, C. Vitruvius Britannicus. V, pls.45, 46. 1771.
COUNTRY LIFE. XLIV, 404, 458, 463 [Pictures]. 1918.
WATTS, W. Seats of the Nobility. pl.28. 1779.

WROTTESLEY HALL (Staffordshire).
COUNTRY LIFE. LVI, 691. 1924.
SHAW, S. Staffordshire. II, 204. 1801.

WROXALL ABBEY (Warwickshire).
RYLAND, John William.
—Records of Wroxall Abbey and manor, Warwickshire. [Chapter on the chapel by T. Garner.] (The parish register of **Wroxall ... 1586-1812. Transcribed and edited by J.W.R.**) [Bibliogr. notes.] Illus. incl. plates (some folding) plan, map, facsimiles and genealog. tables. 2 pts. 33x23 London: Spottiswoode & Co., 1903.
BURKE, J.B. Visitation of Seats. Vol.II, p.155. 1853.*
HALL, S.C. **Baronial Halls. Vol.II. 1848.**
NEALE, J.P. Views of Seats. Vol.IV. 1821.
SMITH, W. History of the County of Warwick. 280. 1830.

WROXTON ABBEY (Oxfordshire).
WROXTON ABBEY.
—Wroxton Abbey [Etc.] 16pp. Illus. (some on covers)
incl. map. 14x20 [Derby] (E.L.P.) [1957?]
BURKE, J.B. Visitation of Seats. Vol.II, p,189. 1853.*
COUNTRY LIFE. CLXX. 770, 854, 1010. 1981.
GOTCH, J.A. Architecture of the Renaissance. I, p.25. 1894.
LATHAM, C. In English Homes. Vol.I, p.167. 1904.
MORRIS, F.O. Views of Seats. Vol.III, p.43. 1880.
NASH, J. Mansions of England. II, pls. 8,9. 1840.

WYCH CROSS PLACE (Sussex).
COUNTRY LIFE. XXVIII, 934 plan. 1910.

WYCK (Gloucestershire).
ATKYNS, R. Glocestershire. p.103. 1768.

WYCK, The. Hitchin (Hertfordshire).
COUNTRY LIFE. XVIII, 630. 1905.

WYCLIFFE HALL (Yorkshire).
BURKE, J.B. Visitation of Seats. 2.S. Vol.I, p.90. 1854.*
COPPER PLATE MAGAZINE. I, pl.36. 1792-1802.
ENGLAND: Picturesque Views. p.15. 1786-88.

WYCOLLER HALL (Lancashire).
BURKE, J.B. Visitation of Seats. 2.S. Vol.I, p.193. 1854.*

WYCOMBE ABBEY (Buckinghamshire).
ENGLAND: Picturesque Views. p.23. 1786-88.
MORRIS, F.O. Views of Seats. Vol.VI, p.5. 1880.

WYDDIAL HALL (Hertfordshire).
CHAUNCY, H. Hertfordshire. I, 220. 1826.

WYFOLD COURT (Oxfordshire).
SUMMERSON, J. The Country Seat. 244. 1970.

WYKE HALL (Dorsetshire).
HUTCHINS, J. History of Dorset. III, 622. 1868.

WYKEHAM ABBEY (Yorkshire)
[Sales] LONDON, 1970, November 26 [Rembrandt etchings,
pt.I. from W.A.].
[Sales] LONDON, 1972, December 7 [Rembrandt etchings,
pt II. from W.A.].

WYNFORD EAGLE MANOR
(Dorsetshire).
OSWALD, A. Country houses of Dorset. p.100. 1959.

WYNNSTAY (Denbighshire).
WYNNSTAY.
— Wynnstay & the Wynns. A volume of varieties put together
by the author of *The gossipping guide to Wales* [i.e. A. Roberts].
Plates. 21x17 Oswestry: Woodall & Venables, 1876.
Bound in red; the arms of Sir Watkin Williams Wynn, Bart.
stamped in gilt on the cover.
BURKE, J.B. Visitation of Seats. Vol.II, p.160. 1853.*
COPPER PLATE MAGAZINE. pl.18. 1778.
COPPER PLATE MAGAZINE. I, pl.4. 1792-1802.
COUNTRY LIFE. CLI, 686, 782. 1972.
ENGLAND: Picturesque Views. p.93. 1786-88.
JONES. Views of Seats. V. 1830.
MORRIS, F.O. Views of Seats. Vol.III, p.67. 1880.
NEALE, J.P. Views of Seats. 2.S. Vol.V. 1829.
NICHOLAS, T. Counties of Wales. I, p.367. 1872.
SANDBY, P. Select Views. II, pl.7, (Wales). 1782.

WYNYARD PARK (Durham).
MANUSCRIPTS (Typewritten)   English.
— SMITH, H.C. Inventory and valuation of the contents of
Wynyard Park, co. Durham, the property of the ... Marquess of
Londonderry [C.S.H. Vane-Tempest-Stewart, 7th. Marquess],
deceased. Prepared for the purpose of probate by H.C.S. 95ff.
34x20 (London) 1949.
MANUSCRIPTS (Typewritten).   English.
— SMITH, H.C. Inventory and valuation of silver at Wynyard
Park, County Durham, the property of the ... Marquess of
Londonderry [C.S.H. Vane-Tempest-Stewart, 7th. Marquess],
deceased. Prepared for the purpose of probate by H.C.S. 13ff.
34x20 (Kensington). 1949.
MORRIS, F.O. Views of Seats. Vol.III, p.13. 1880.

WYRESIDE (Lancashire).
TWYCROSS, E. Mansions of England and Wales. Vol.II, p.47.
1847.*

WYRLEY GROVE (Staffordshire).
NIVEN, W. Old Staffordshire houses. p.23, pl.19. 1882.

WYTHALL (Herefordshire).
BURKE, J.B. Visitation of Seats. Vol.I, p.81. 1852.*
ROBINSON, C.J. Mansions of Herefordshire. pl.21. 1873.

WYTHAM ABBEY (Berkshire).
BURKE, J.B. Visitation of Seats. 2.S. Vol.II, p.152. 1855.*
COUNTRY LIFE. XCIII, 400. 1943.
KIP, J. Nouveau théâtre de la Grande Bretagne.
I, pl.35. 1715.
MORRIS, F.O. Views of Seats. Vol.II, p.61. 1880.

WYTHENSHAWE HALL (Cheshire). Now Greater Manchester (Lancashire).
BURKE, J.B. Visitation of Seats. Vol.I, p.65. 1852.*
TWYCROSS, E. Mansions of England and Wales. Vol.II, p.104. 1850.

WYVENHOE HALL (Essex).
BURKE, J.B. Visitation of Seats. 2.S. Vol.I, p.46. 1854.*

WYVENHOE PARK (Essex).
FEESEY, Rosemary.
— A history of Wivenhoe Park: the house and grounds. [Bibliogr.] 48pp. Illus. incl. plans and cover. 14x22 Colchester: Benham & Co., 1963.
BURKE, J.B. Visitation of Seats. 2.S. Vol.I, p.46. 1854.*
RUSH, J.A. Seats in Essex. p.185. 1897.*
[Sales] WIVENHOE PARK, 1964, March 10 [Remaining contents].

YAFFLE HILL (Dorsetshire).
COUNTRY LIFE. LXXIV, 14 plan. 1933.

YANWATH HALL (Westmorland).
COUNTRY LIFE. XIV, 126. 1903.
CUMBERLAND: C. & W. A. & A.S. Extra Series VIII, 52. plan. 1892.
TIPPING, H.A. English Homes. Period I, Vol.I, p.158. 1921.

YARDLEY HASTINGS MANOR (Northamptonshire).
GOTCH, J.A. Squires' Homes. 39. 1939.

YARLINGTON LODGE (Somerset).
COLLINSON, J. History of Somerset. I, 228. 1791.

YARNTON MANOR (Oxfordshire).
COUNTRY LIFE. XVIII, 90. 1905.
COUNTRY LIFE. CX, 2096, 2162. 1951.
TIPPING, H.A. English Homes. Early Renaissance. p.237. 1912.

YATE COURT (Gloucestershire).
HODGES, E. Ancient English homes. 100. 1895.

YATTON KEYNELL MANOR (Wiltshire).
ELYARD, S.J. Old Wiltshire homes. p.23. 1894.

YAVERLAND MANOR (Hampshire), Isle of Wight).
GARNER, T. Domestic architecture. II, p.161. 1911.

YEARDSLEY HALL (Derbyshire).
GUNSON, Ernest.
— Shallcross and Yeardsley Halls. 16pp. Illus. incl. plates and plans. 22x14 Derby, 1905.
Also in, DERBY: Derbyshire Archaeological and Natural History Society. Journal, XXVII. 1905.

YEATON HALL [LODGE] (Shropshire).
[Sales] YEATON HALL, 1979, October 15, 16 [Contents].

YEATON-PEVEREY (Shropshire).
LEIGHTON, S. Shropshire houses. 16. 1901.

YEWTREE (Lancashire).
BARTLETT, J. Mansions of England and Wales. pl.122. 1853.
TWYCROSS, E. Mansions of England and Wales. Vol.III, p.56. 1847.

YORK: TREASURER'S HOUSE (Yorkshire).
LONDON: National Trust for Places of Historic Interest or Natural Beauty.
—Treasurer's House, York. 12pp. 4 plates. 18x12 London: Country Life (1946).
Another ed. 16pp. Illus. (on title-page) and 4 plates (1954.)
Rev. ed. 24pp. Illus. (1 col. on cover) incl. plates and plan. 21x14 [London] 1982.
COUNTRY LIFE. XIX, 234, 1906.
COUNTRY LIFE. LII, 114, 144. 1922.
LATHAM, C. In English Homes. Vol.II, p.195. 1907.
WOOD, G.B. Historic homes of Yorkshire. 107. 1957.

YOTES COURT (Kent).
BURKE, J.B. Visitation of Seats. Vol.I, p.49. 1852.*
COUNTRY LIFE. CXXXV, 1580 [Photocopy], 1648. 1964.
HASTED, E. Kent. II, 270. 1782.
NEALE, J.P. Views of Seats. 2.S. Vol.IV. 1828.
[Sales] YOTES COURT, 1923, October 1-3 [Contents].

YOULSTON (Devonshire).
BURKE, J.B. Visitation of Seats. Vol.II, p.132. 1853.*
COUNTRY LIFE. CXXIX, 1084. 1961.
DELDERFIELD, E.R. West Country houses. I, 150. 1968.

YOUNGSBURY (Hertfordshire).
BURKE, J.B. Visitation of Seats. 2.S. Vol.I, p.106. 1854.*

ZEALS HOUSE (Wiltshire).
DELDERFIELD, E.R. West Country houses. II, 117. 1970.

COUNTRY HOUSES OF
IRELAND

ABBEY LEIX (Leix).
GUINNESS, D. Irish Houses & Castles. p.225. 1971.
SADLEIR, T.U. Georgian mansions in Ireland. p.10. 1915.

ADARE MANOR (Limerick).
DUNRAVEN, Caroline Wyndham-Quin, *Countess of.*
— Memorials of Adare Manor, by C. Countess of D. With
historical notices of Adare by her son, the Earl of D. (List of
pictures, stained glass) Illus. incl. plates (some tinted) and
plans. 30x23 Oxford: privately printed, 1865.
COUNTRY LIFE. CXLV, 1230, 1302, 1366. 1969.
MORRIS, F.O. Views of Seats. Vol.IV, p.39. 1880.

ANKETELL GROVE (Monaghan).
BURKE, J.B. Visitation of Seats. 2.S. Vol.I, p.17. 1854.

ANTRIM CASTLE (Antrim).
BURKE, J.B. Visitation of Seats. 2.S. Vol.II, p.70. 1855.*
NEALE, J.P. Views of Seats. 2.S. Vol.II, 1825.

ARAS AN UACHTARAIN, Phoenix Park
(Dublin).
GUINNESS, D. Irish Houses & Castles. p.109. 1971.

ARDFERT ABBEY (Kerry).
BURKE, J.B. Visitation of Seats. 2.S. Vol.I, p.137. 1854.*

ARDNARGLE (Londonderry).
BURKE, J.B. Visitation of Seats. 2.S. Vol.II, p.40. 1855.*

ARDRESS (Armagh).
BELFAST: National Trust for Places of Historic Interest or
Natural Beauty [Committee for Northern Ireland].
— Ardress, County Armagh. 20pp. Illus. incl. plan (on inside
cover). 22x14 [Belfast] 1962.

ARDTULLY HOUSE (Kerry).
MORRIS, F.O. Views of Seats. Vol.II, p.19. 1880.

ASHBROOK (Londonderry).
BURKE, J.B. Visitation of Seats. 2.S. Vol.II, p.130. 1855.*

ASH HILL TOWERS (Limerick).
BURKE, J.B. Visitation of Seats. 2.S. Vol.I, p.231. 1854.*

BALLINACARRIG (Cork).
BURKE, J.B. Visitation of Seats. 2.S. Vol.II, p.207. 1855.*

BALLINLOUGH CASTLE (Westmeath).
COUNTRY LIFE. CLXIV, 90. 1978.
GUINNESS, D. Irish Houses & Castles. p. 289. 1971.

BALLYCLOUGH HOUSE (Cork).
BURKE, J.B. Visitation of Seats. 2.S. Vol.I, p.207. 1854.*

BALLYCURRIN CASTLE (Mayo).
BURKE, J.B. Visitation of Seats. 2.S. Vol.II, p.19. 1855.*

BALLYFIN (Leix).
COUNTRY LIFE. CLIV, 702 plan, 774. 1973.
MILTON, T. Seats of Ireland. Pl. XIX. 1783-94.
NEALE, J.P. Views of Seats. 2.S. Vol.IV. 1828.

BALLYHEIGH CASTLE (Kerry).
NEALE, J.P. Views of Seats. Vol.VI. 1823.

BALLYNATRAY (Waterford).
BURKE, J.B. Visitation of Seats. 2.S. Vol.II, p.100. 1855.*

BALLYSEEDY (Kerry).
BURKE, J.B. Visitation of Seats. 2.S. Vol.II, p.216. 1855.*

BALLYWALTER PARK (Down).
COUNTRY LIFE. CXLI, 456, 516. 1967.

BALRATH HOUSE (Meath).
BURKE, J.B. Visitation of Seats. 2.S. Vol.II, p.156. 1855.*

BANTRY HOUSE (Cork).
GUINNESS, D. Irish Houses & Castles. p.61. 1971.

BARBAVILLA (Westmeath).
BURKE, J.B. Visitation of Seats. 2.S. Vol.I, p.197. 1854.*

BARONSCOURT (Tyrone).
COUNTRY LIFE. CLXVI, 86, 162, 232. 1979.
MORRIS, F.O. Views of Seats. Vol.IV, p.51. 1880.

BEAR FOREST (Cork).
NEALE, J.P. Views of Seats. Vol.VI. 1823.

BEAULIEU (Louth).
BURKE, J.B. Visitation of Seats. 2.S. Vol.II, p.95. 1855.*
COUNTRY LIFE. CXXV, 106, 156. 1959.
GUINNESS, D. Irish Houses & Castles. p.241. 1971.
SADLEIR, T.U. Georgian mansions in Ireland. p.17. 1915.

BEAUPARC (Meath).
MILTON, T. Seats of Ireland. Pl.XI. 1783-94.

BELAN HOUSE (Kildare).
MILTON, T. Seats of Ireland. Pl. VI. 1783-94.

BELGARD (Dublin).
SADLEIR, T.U. Georgian mansions in Ireland. p.89. 1915.

BELLAMONT FOREST (Cavan).
COUNTRY LIFE. CXXXV, 1258 plan, 1330. 1964.
GUINNESS, D. Irish Houses & Castles. p.39. 1971.

BELLINTER (Meath).
NEALE, J.P. Views of Seats. Vol.VI. 1823.

BELVEDERE (Westmeath).
COUNTRY LIFE. CXXIX, 1480, 1538. 1961.
GUINNESS, D. Irish Houses & Castles. p.295. 1971.
[Sales] BELVEDERE, 1980, July 9 [Contents].

BESSBOROUGH HOUSE (Kilkenny).
MILTON, T. Seats of Ireland. Pl.IX. 1783-94.
NEALE, J.P. Views of Seats. Vol.VI. 1823.
SADLEIR, T.U. Georgian mansions in Ireland. p.21. 1915.

BIRR CASTLE (Offaly).
COUNTRY LIFE. CXXXVII, 410, 468, 526. 1965.
GUINNESS, D. Irish Houses & Castles. p.271. 1971.
MORRIS, F.O. Views of Seats. Vol.III, p.39. 1880.

BISHOP'S COURT (Kildare).
MORRIS, F.O. Views of Seats. Vol.IV, p.19. 1880.
NEALE, J.P. Views of Seats. 2.S. Vol.V. 1829.

BLANCHVILLESKILL (Kilkenny).
BURKE, J.B. Visitation of Seats. 2.S. Vol.II, p.95. 1855.*

BLARNEY CASTLE (Cork).
COPPER PLATE MAGAZINE. I, pl.47. 1792-1802.

BORRIS HOUSE (Carlow).
NEALE, J.P. Views of Seats. Vol.VI. 1823.

BRAY HEAD (Wicklow).
BURKE, J.B. Visitation of Seats. 2.S. Vol.II, p.173. 1855.*

BROCKLEY PARK (Leix).
MILTON, T. Seats of Ireland. Pl. X. 1783-94.

BROWNE'S HILL (Carlow).
BURKE, J.B. Visitation of Seats. 2.S. Vol.II, p.202. 1855.*

BUNRATTY CASTLE (Clare).
BUNRATTY CASTLE.
—A history of Bunratty Castle. (Designed and produced by Shannon Free Airport Development Company Limited.) [Folder.] Illus. 19x13 [Shannon Free Airport, 1982?].
BUNNRATTY CASTLE.
—A guide to Bunratty Castle & Folk Park. [By] (Shannon Free Airport Development Company Ltd.) 28pp. Illus. incl. plan. 30x11 Shannon Free Airport [1982?].
GUINESS, D. Irish Houses & Castles. p.49. 1971.

CAHER HOUSE (Tipperary).
BURKE, J.B. Visitation of Seats. 2.S. Vol.II, p.195. 1855.*

CALEDON (Tyrone).
COUNTRY LIFE. LXXX, 324 [Furniture]. 1936.
COUNTRY LIFE. LXXXI, 224 plan, 250. 1937.
MORRIS, F.O. Views of Seats. Vol.IV, p.79. 1880.
SADLEIR, T.U. Georgian mansions in Ireland. p.29. 1915.

CARRICK BLACKER (Armagh).
BURKE, J.B. Visitation of Seats. 2.S. Vol.II, p.179. 1855.*

CARRIGLAS (Longford).
SUMMERSON, J. The Country Seat. 185. 1970.

CARRIGMORE HOUSE (Cork).
BURKE, J.B. Visitation of Seats. 2.S. Vol.I, p.184. 1854.*

CARTON (Kildare).
COUNTRY LIFE. LXXX, 488, 514. 1936.
GUINNESS, D. Irish Houses & Castles. p.183. 1971.
NEALE, J.P. Views of Seats. 2.S. Vol.II. 1825.

CASHEL PALACE (Tipperary).
SADLEIR, T.U. Georgian mansions in Ireland. p.36. 1915.

CASTLEBELLINGHAM (Louth).
BURKE, J.B. Visitation of Seats. 2.S. Vol.I, p.134. 1854.*

CASTLE BERNARD (Cork).
BURKE, J.B. Visitation of Seats. 2.S. Vol.II, p.209. 1855.*

CASTLE BERNARD (Offaly).
BURKE, J.B. Visitation of Seats. 2.S. Vol.I, p.240. 1854.*

CASTLE CALDWELL (Fermanagh).
CUNNINGHAM, John B.
—A history of Castle Caldwell and its families. [Bibliogr. notes.] 210pp. Illus. incl. plan and maps. 22x14 [Enniskillen: Watergate Press] 1980.

ADARE MANOR, Limerick. From: MORRIS (Rev. F.O.). *A series of picturesque views of seats of the noblemen of Great Britain and Ireland*, vol. IV, London [1880].

CASTLECOMER HOUSE (Kilkenny).

MACCALL, Hardy Bertram.
— Story of the family of Wandesforde of Kirklington and Castlecomer, compiled from original sources, with a calendar of historical manuscripts, edited by H.B.M. Illus. incl. plates, plan, facsimiles (some of signatures) and genealog. tables. 28x22 London: Simpkin Marshall Hamilton Kent & Co., 1904.

CASTLE CONNELL (Limerick).

BURKE, J.B. Visitation of Seats. 2.S. Vol.II, p.19. 1855.*

CASTLE COOKE (Cork).

BURKE, J.B. Visitation of Seats. 2.S. Vol.II, p.199. 1855.*

CASTLE COOLE (Fermanagh).

BELFAST: National Trust for Places of Historic Interest or Natural Beauty. [Committee for Northern Ireland].
—Castlecoole, Enniskillen. 10pp. 4 plates. 18x12 London: Country Life (1952).
—Another ed. 16pp. Illus. 22x14 [Belfast, 1964?]
—Rev. ed. Castle Coole, County Fermanagh. [Bibliogr.] 28pp. Illus. (1 col. on cover) incl. plates, plan and genealog. table. 1981.
BURKE, J.B. Visitation of Seats. 2.S. Vol.II, p.216. 1855.*
CAMPBELL, C. New Vitruvius Britannicus. II, pls. 65-70. 1808.
GUINNESS, D. Irish Houses & Castles. p.163. 1971.
MORRIS, F.O. Views of Seats. Vol.IV, p.45. 1880.
NEALE, J.P. Views of Seats. 2.S. Vol.V. 1829.

CASTLECOR (Cork).

NEALE, J.P. Views of Seats. Vol.VI. 1823.

CASTLE DILLON (Armagh).

[Sales] CASTLE DILLON, 1923, October 2-5 [Contents].

CASTLE FREKE (Cork).

BURKE, J.B. Visitation of Seats. 2.S. Vol.I, p.239. 1854.*
NEALE, J.P. Views of Seats. Vol.VI. 1823.

CASTLEGAR (Galway).

NEALE, J.P. Views of Seats. Vol.VI. 1823.

CASTLE GROVE (Londonderry).

BURKE, J.B. Visitation of Seats. 2.S. Vol.II, p.91. 1855.*

CASTLE HOWARD (Wicklow).

NEALE, J.P. Views of Seats. Vol.VI. 1823.

CASTLE MACGARRETT (Mayo).

MORRIS, F.O. Views of Seats. Vol.VI, p.71. 1880.

CASTLE MARTIN (Kildare).

BURKE, J.B. Visitation of Seats. 2.S. Vol.I, p.128. 1854.*

CASTLE RICHARD (Waterford).

See GLENCAIRN ABBEY.

CASTLESHANE (Monaghan).

BURKE, J.B. Visitation of Seats. 2.S. Vol.II, p.19. 1855.*

CASTLETOWN (Kildare).

CRAIG, Maurice James.
— Castletown, Co. Kildare. By M.C., the Knight of Glin, J. Cornforth. 16pp. Illus. (1 on cover) incl. plan. 33x23 [London] 1969.
Title on cover.
Also in: COUNTRY LIFE, CXLV, no. 3760, p.722; no. 3761, p.798; no. 3762, p.882. 1969.
DUBLIN: Irish Georgian Society.
—GUINNESS, D. Castletown, Celbridge, Co. Kildare. [Bibliogr. note.] 12pp. Illus. (some col., some on cover) incl. plans, map and facsimile. 27x21 (Castletown) [1972?]
BURKE, J.B. Visitation of Seats. 2.S. Vol.I, p.147. 1854.*
COUNTRY LIFE. LXXX, 170, 196. 1936.
COUNTRY LIFE. CXLV, 722 plan, 798, 882. 1969.
GUINNESS, D. Irish Houses & Castles. p.193. 1971.
NEALE, J.P. Views of Seats. 2.S. Vol.V. 1829.

CASTLETOWN (Kilkenny).

COUNTRY LIFE. XLIV, 190, 214. 1918.
GUINNESS, D. Irish Houses & Castles. p.219. 1971.

CASTLE UPTON (Antrim).

SADLEIR, T.U. Georgian mansions in Ireland. p.92. 1915.

CASTLE VIEW (Cork).

BURKE, J.B. Visitation of Seats. 2.S. Vol.II, p.126. 1855.*

CASTLEWARD (Down).

BELFAST: National Trust for Places of Historic Interest or Natural Beauty [Committee for Northern Ireland].
—Castleward, County Down, Northern Ireland. 8pp. 2 illus. 22x14 [London] 1955.
Another ed. 16pp. Illus. [Belfast] 1963.
Rev. ed. [Bibliogr.] 24pp. Illus. (1 col.) incl. **plates, map and** genealog. table. 1982.
COUNTRY LIFE. CXXX, 1260, 1320. 1961.
GUINNESS, D. Irish Houses & Castles. p.93. 1971.
SADLEIR, T.U. Georgian mansions in Ireland. p.43. 1915.

CASTLE WIDENHAM (Cork).

BURKE, J.B. Visitation of Seats. 2.S. Vol.II, p.197. 1855.*

CHARLEVILLE (Wicklow).
GUINNESS, D. Irish Houses & Castles. p.309. 1971.
[Sales] CHARLEVILLE, 1978, January 23, 24 [Contents].

CHARLEVILLE FOREST (Offaly).
COUNTRY LIFE. CXXXII, 710. 1962.

CLANDEBOYE (Down).
COUNTRY LIFE. CXLVIII, 816, 903. 1970.

CLAREMONT (Mayo).
BURKE, J.B. Visitation of Seats. 2.S. Vol.II, p.4. 1855.*

CLONBROCK (Galway).
[Sales] CLONBROCK, 1976, November 1-3 [Contents].

CLONELLY (Fermanagh).
BURKE, J.B. Visitation of Seats. 2.S. Vol.II, p.169. 1855.*

CLONTRA (Dublin)
COUNTRY LIFE. CLVII, 1390. 1975.

COOLLATTIN HOUSE (Wicklow).
[Sales] COOLLATTIN HOUSE, 1980, July 24-26 [Pictures, drawings etc.] This sale was cancelled.

COOLMORE (Cork).
NEALE, J.P. Views of Seats. 2.S. Vol.III. 1826.

CRAGGANE TOWER (Clare).
BURKE, J.B. Visitation of Seats. 2.S. Vol.II, p.182. 1855.*

CROM CASTLE (Fermanagh).
BURKE, J.B. Visitation of Seats. 2.S. Vol.II, p.203. 1855.*

CROTTO HOUSE (Kerry).
NEALE, J.P. Views of Seats. Vol.VI. 1823.

CURRAGHMORE (Waterford).
BURKE, J.B. Visitation of Seats. 2.S. Vol.II, p.64. 1855.*
COUNTRY LIFE. CXXXIII, 256, 308, 368. 1963.
SADLEIR, T.U. Georgian mansions in Ireland. p.49. 1915.

CURRIGLASS (Cork).
BURKE, J.B. Visitation of Seats. 2.S. Vol.II, p.126. 1855.*

DARTREY (Monaghan).
MORRIS, F.O. Views of Seats. Vol.III, p.57. 1880.

DAWSON GROVE (Monaghan).
SANDBY, P. Select Views. II, pl.15, (Ireland) 1782.

DERRIES, The. (Leix).
BURKE, J.B. Visitation of Seats. 2.S. Vol.II, p.102. 1855.*

DERRYMORE HOUSE (Armagh).
BELFAST: National Trust for Places of Historic Interest or Natural Beauty [Committee for Northern Ireland].
— Derrymore House, County Armagh. 8pp. 1 illus. 18x12 [London, *c.* 1955.]

DESART COURT (Kilkenny).
SADLEIR, T.U. Georgian mansions in Ireland. p.55. 1915.

DONACOMPER (Kildare).
[Sales] DONACOMPER, 1977, July 25, 26 [Pictures, furniture, tapestries etc.].

DONADEA CASTLE (Kildare).
BURKE, J.B. Visitation of Seats. 2.S. Vol.I, p.80. 1854.*

DONERAILE COURT (Cork).
BURKE, J.B. Visitation of Seats. 2.S. Vol.II, p.194. 1855.*

DOON (Offaly).
BURKE, J.B. Visitation of Seats. 2.S. Vol.II, p.87. 1855.*

DOONASS HOUSE (Clare).
BURKE, J.B. Visitation of Seats. 2.S. Vol.I, p.152. 1854.*

DOWNHILL (Londonderry).
BELFAST: National Trust for Places of Historic Interest or Natural Beauty [Committee for Northern Ireland].
— Downhill and the Mussenden Temple, County Derry. 12pp. Illus. (3 on covers) incl. map and genealog. table. 15x21 (Belfast) 1968.
COUNTRY LIFE. CVII, 34. 1950.
COUNTRY LIFE. CL, 94, 154 plan. 1971.
NEALE, J.P. Views of Seats. Vol.VI. 1823.

DOWTH HALL (Meath).
BURKE, J.B. Visitation of Seats. 2.S. Vol.II, p.215. 1855.*
SADLEIR, T.U. Georgian mansions in Ireland. p.61. 1915.

DROMANA (Waterford).
BURKE, J.B. Visitation of Seats. 2.S. Vol.I, p.30. 1854.*
SANDBY, P. Select Views. II, pl.31, (Ireland) 1782.

DROMOLAND CASTLE (Clare).
MORRIS, F.O. Views of Seats. Vol.IV, p.27. 1880.

DRUMBANAGHER (Armagh).
BURKE, J.B. Visitation of Seats. 2.S. Vol.I, p.193. 1854.*

DRUMCAR (Louth).
BURKE, J.B. Visitation of Seats. 2.S. Vol.I, p.49. 1854.*

DRUMCONDRA HOUSE (Dublin).
SADLEIR, T.U. Georgian mansions in Ireland. p.65. 1915.

DUBLIN CASTLE (Dublin).
GUINNESS, D. Irish Houses & Castles. p.103. 1971.

DUNGUAIRE CASTLE (Galway).
COUNTRY LIFE. CXXXIII, 664. 1963.

DUNSANY CASTLE (Meath).
COUNTRY LIFE. CXLIX, 1296, 1364. 1971.
GUINNESS, D. Irish Houses & Castles. p.257. 1971.

EMO PARK (Leix).
COUNTRY LIFE. CLV, 1274, 1346 plan. 1974.
NEALE, J.P. Views of Seats. 2.S. Vol.V. 1829.

FAITHLEGG HOUSE (Waterford).
BURKE, J.B. Visitation of Seats. 2.S. Vol.I, p.159. 1854.*

FARNHAM HOUSE (Cavan).
MORRIS, F.O. Views of Seats. Vol.I, p.39. 1880.

FLESK CASTLE (Kerry).
BURKE, J.B. Visitation of Seats. 2.S. Vol.I, p.204. 1854.*
NEALE, J.P. Views of Seats. 2.S. Vol.I. 1824.

FLORENCE COURT (Fermanagh).
BELFAST: National Trust for Places of Historic Interest or
Natural Beauty [Committee for Northern Ireland].
—LEES-MILNE, J. Florence Court, Co. Fermanagh. 14pp.
Illus. (on cover) and plate. 18x12 London: Country Life
(1954).
Another ed. 16pp. Illus. 21x14 [Belfast, *c.* 1964.]
Rev. ed. MACMORDIE, C. Florence Court, County
Fermanagh. [Bibliogr.] 24pp. Illus. (1 on cover) incl. plates
and genealog. table. 1979.
COUNTRY LIFE. CLXIX, 1242, 1318. 1981.
GUINNESS, D. Irish Houses & Castles. p. 169. 1971.
MILTON, T. Seats of Ireland. Pl. XV. 1783-94.
SADLEIR, T.U. Georgian mansions in Ireland. p.70. 1915.

FORT EYRE (Galway).
BURKE, J.B. Visitation of Seats. 2.S. Vol.II, p.32. 1855.*

FORT ROBERT (Cork).
BURKE, J.B. Visitation of Seats. 2.S. Vol.I, p.178. 1854.*

FORT WILLIAM (Waterford).
BURKE, J.B. Visitation of Seats. 2.S. Vol.I, p.213. 1854.*

FOTA ISLAND (Cork).
GUINNESS, D. Irish Houses & Castles. p.71. 1971.
NEALE, J.P. Views of Seats. 2.S. Vol.IV. 1828.

FURNESS (Kildare).
SADLEIR, T.U. Georgian mansions in Ireland. p.76. 1915.

GAYBROOK (Westmeath).
BURKE, J.B. Visitation of Seats. 2.S. Vol.I, p.104. 1854.*

GLENARM CASTLE (Antrim).
MILTON, T. Seats of Ireland. Pl. XXI. 1783-94.
NEALE, J.P. Views of Seats. 2.S. Vol.II. 1825.

GLENCAIRN ABBEY (Waterford).
BURKE, J.B. Visitation of Seats. 2.S. Vol.I, p.213. 1854.*
NEALE, J.P. Views of Seats. Vol.VI. 1823.

GLENSTAL CASTLE (Limerick).
COUNTRY LIFE. CLVI, 934. 1974.

GLENVEAGH CASTLE (Donegal).
COUNTRY LIFE. CLXXI, 1636, 1734. 1982.
GUINNESS, D. Irish Houses & Castles. p.85. 1971.

GLIN CASTLE (Limerick).
FITZGERALD, Desmond John Villiers, *Knight of Glin.*
— Glin Castle: a guide. 20pp. Illus. incl. col. cover. 21x13
[Glin ? privately printed *c.* 1980.]
GAUGHAN, John Anthony.
— The knights of Glin: a Geraldine family. [Bibliogr.]
222pp.Illus. incl. plates (2 folding), map and genealog. tables.
21x13 Dublin: Kingdom Books, 1978.
BURKE, J.B. Visitation of Seats. 2.S. Vol.I, p.118. 1854.*
COUNTRY LIFE. CXXXV, 446, 502. 1964.
GUINNESS, D. Irish Houses & Castles. p.233. 1971.

GOLA HOUSE (Monaghan).
BURKE, J.B. Visitation of Seats. 2.S. Vol.I, p.121. 1854.

GORMANSTON CASTLE (Meath).
NEALE, J.P. Views of Seats. Vol.VI. 1823.

GOSFORD CASTLE (Armagh).
[Sales] LONDON, 1884, April 21 and following days [Library].

GOWRAN CASTLE (Kilkenny).
NEALE, J.P. Views of Seats. 2.S. Vol.III. 1826.

GRACEFIELD LODGE (Leix).
NEALE, J.P. Views of Seats. Vol.VI. 1823.

HARRISTOWN HOUSE (Kildare).
BURKE, J.B. Visitation of Seats. 2.S. Vol.I, p.131. 1854.*

HEADFORT HOUSE (Meath).
COUNTRY LIFE. LXXIX, 300, 326, 362 [Furniture]. 1936.
COUNTRY LIFE. CLIII, 847. 1973.

HEYWOOD (Leix).
COUNTRY LIFE. XLV, 42. 1919.
SADLEIR, T.U. Georgian mansions in Ireland. p.95. 1915.

HOLLYBROOK (Wicklow).
BURKE, J.B. Visitation of Seats. 2.S. Vol.II, p.70. 1855.*

HOLLYWELL LODGE (Cavan).
NEALE, J.P. Views of Seats. Vol.VI. 1823.

HOWTH CASTLE (Dublin).
DUBLIN: Royal Society of Antiquaries of Ireland.
— Extra volumes.
BALL, F.E. Howth and its owners: being the fifth part of a history of the county of Dublin [etc.]. Illus. 1917.
COUNTRY LIFE. XL, 14 plan. 1914.
COUNTRY LIFE. LXVIII, 286, 316 plan. 1930.
GUINNESS, D. Irish Houses & Castles. p.125. 1971.
MILTON, T. Seats of Ireland. Pl.XIV. 1783-94.

HUMEWOOD CASTLE (Wicklow).
COUNTRY LIFE. CXLIII, 1212, 1282 plan. 1968.

INCHYDONEY HOUSE (Cork).
BURKE, J.B. Visitation of Seats. 2.S. Vol.II, p.43. 1855.*

KENURE PARK (Dublin).
[Sales] KENURE PARK, 1964, September 21-24 [Contents].

KILCASKAN CASTLE (Cork).
BURKE, J.B. Visitation of Seats. 2.S. Vol.I, p.162. 1854.*

KILCLOGHAN CASTLE (Galway).
BURKE, J.B. Visitation of Seats. 2.S. Vol.II, p.162. 1855.*

KILCORNAN (Galway).
BURKE, J.B. Visitation of Seats. 2.S. Vol.II, p.5. 1855.*

KILDERRY (Donegal).
BURKE, J.B. Visitation of Seats. 2.S. Vol.II, p.216. 1855.*

KILKENNY CASTLE (Kilkenny).
NEALE, J.P. Views of Seats. Vol.VI. 1823.
UNITED KINGDOM. Historic houses. 238. 1892.

KILLEEN CASTLE (Meath).
[Sales] KILLEEN CASTLE, 1953, July 20-25 [Contents].

KILLINEY CASTLE (Dublin).
BURKE, J.B. Visitation of Seats. 2.S. Vol.II, p.146. 1855.

KILLRUDDERY (Wicklow).
BURKE, J.B. Visitation of Seats. 2.S. Vol.II, p.212. 1855.*
COUNTRY LIFE. CLXII, 78, 146. 1977.
NEALE, J.P. Views of Seats. Vol. VI. 1823.

KILLUA CASTLE (Westmeath).
BURKE, J.B. Visitation of Seats. 2.S. Vol.I, p.180. 1854.*

KILLYLEAGH CASTLE (Down).
COUNTRY LIFE. CXLVII, 690, 774. 1970.

KILLYMOON CASTLE (Tyrone).
BURKE, J.B. Visitation of Seats. 2.S. Vol.II, p.69. 1855.*

KILRUDDERY (Wicklow).
See KILLRUDDERY.

KILSHANNIG (Cork).
GUINNESS, D. Irish Houses & Castles. p.77. 1971.

KNOCKDRIN CASTLE (Westmeath).
BURKE, J.B. Visitation of Seats. 2.S. Vol.II, p.163. 1855.

LAMBAY (Dublin).
COUNTRY LIFE. XXXI, 650 plan. 1912.
COUNTRY LIFE. LXVI, 86, 120. 1929.

LARAGH (Kildare).
BURKE, J.B. Visitation of Seats. 2.S. Vol.II, p.205. 1855.*

LEIXLIP CASTLE (Kildare).
GUINNESS, D. Irish Houses & Castles. p.211. 1971.
KROLL, A. Historic houses. 68. 1969.

LISMORE CASTLE (Waterford).
BURKE, J.B. Visitation of Seats. 2.S. Vol.II, p.42. 1855.*
COUNTRY LIFE. CXXXVI, 336, 389. 1964.
GUINNESS,D. Irish Houses & Castles. p.279. 1971.
MILTON, T. Seats of Ireland. Pl.XIII. 1783-94.
NEALE, J.P. Views of Seats. Vol.VI. 1823.
UNITED KINGDOM. Historic houses. 288. 1892.

LISNEGAR (Cork).
BURKE, J.B. Visitation of Seats. 2.S. Vol.II, p.196. 1855.*

LISSADELL (Sligo).
COUNTRY LIFE. CLXII, 914 plan. 1977.

LOCKINGTON LODGE (Cavan).
BURKE, J.B. Visitation of Seats. 2.S. Vol.I, p.117. 1854.*

LONGFORD HOUSE (Sligo).
BURKE, J.B. Visitation of Seats. 2.S. Vol.II, p.172. 1855.*

LOTA PARK (Cork).
BURKE, J.B. Visitation of Seats. 2.S. Vol.II, p.4. 1855.*

LOUGH CUTRA (Galway).
BURKE, J.B. Visitation of Seats. 2.S. Vol.II, p.188. 1855.*
GUINNESS, D. Irish Houses & Castles. p.177. 1971.

LOUGH FEA HOUSE (Monaghan).
LOUGH FEA.
— Lough Fea [An account of Lough Fea House, by E.P.
Shirley]. 2 ed. 36pp. 3 illus. 21x17 London (privately printed),
1869.

LUCAN HOUSE (Dublin).
COUNTRY LIFE. CI, 278. 1947.
GUINNESS, D. Irish Houses & Castles. p.131. 1971.
MILTON, T. Seats of Ireland. Pl. III. 1783-94.
[Sales] LUCAN HOUSE, 1925, September 29—October 1
[Furniture, oil paintings etc.].

LUTTRELLSTOWN CASTLE (Dublin).
GUINNESS, D. Irish Houses & Castles. p.139. 1971.

LYONS HOUSE (Kildare).
BURKE, J.B. Visitation of Seats. 2.S. Vol.I, p.81. 1854.*
NEALE, J.P. Views of Seats. 2.S. Vol.II. 1825.

MALAHIDE CASTLE (Dublin).
BURKE, J.B. Visitation of Seats. 2.S. Vol.II, p.60. 1855.*
COUNTRY LIFE. CI, 710 plan, 760. 1947.
COUNTRY LIFE. CIII, 280 [Furniture]. 1948.
GUINNESS, D. Irish Houses & Castles. p.145. 1971.
MILTON, T. Seats of Ireland. Pl. VII. 1783-94.
UNITED KINGDOM. Historic houses. 92. 1892.

MALLOW CASTLE (Cork).
BURKE, J.B. Visitation of Seats. 2.S. Vol.II, p.37. 1855.*

MANCHE HOUSE (Cork).
BURKE, J.B. Visitation of Seats. 2.S. Vol.I, p.178. 1854.*

MARINO (Dublin).
MILTON, T. Seats of Ireland. Pl.V [Casino] 1783-94.

MARLFIELD (Tipperary).
BURKE, J.B. Visitation of Seats. 2.S. Vol.II, p.115. 1855.*

MELLON HOUSE (Tyrone).
BELFAST: National Trust for Places of Historic Interest or
Natural Beauty [Committee for Northern Ireland].
— Mellon House, County Tyrone. 16pp. Illus. (1 on cover) incl.
plan. 22x14 [Belfast] 1970.

MIDDLETON PARK (Westmeath).
BURKE, J.B. Visitation of Seats. 2.S. Vol.I, p.152. 1854.
BURKE, J.B. Visitation of Seats. 2.S. Vol.II, p.104. 1855.*

MILTOWN CASTLE (Kerry).
NEALE, J.P. Views of Seats. Vol.VI. 1823.

MITCHELSTOWN CASTLE (Cork).
COUNTRY LIFE. CXXXIII, 840. 1963.
NEALE, J.P. Views of Seats. 2.S. Vol.II. 1825.

MOORE HALL (Mayo).
HONE, Joseph.
— The Moores of Moore Hall. 288pp. Plates, and genealog.
table. 20x13 London: J. Cape, 1939.

MOUNTAINSTOWN (Meath).
BURKE, J.B. Visitation of Seats. 2.S. Vol.II, p.154. 1855.*

MOUNT BELLEW (Galway).
BURKE, J.B. Visitation of Seats. 2.S. Vol.II, p.176. 1855.*
NEALE, J.P. Views of Seats. Vol.VI. 1823.

MOUNT IEVERS COURT (Clare).
COUNTRY LIFE. CXXXII, 1152. 1962.
GUINNESS, D. Irish Houses & Castles. p.55. 1971.

MOUNT KENNEDY (Wicklow).
COUNTRY LIFE. CXXXVIII, 1128, 1256. 1965.
GUINNESS, D. Irish Houses & Castles. p. 315. 1971.
MILTON, T. Seats of Ireland. Pl. XVIII. 1783-94.

MOUNT STEWART (Down).
BELFAST: National Trust for Places of Historic Interest or
Natural Beauty [Committee for Northern Ireland].
— The Temple of the Winds, Mount Stewart: a historical note.
[Bibliogr.] 12pp. Illus. (2 on covers, 1 on title-page.) 22x14
[Belfast] (1966.)

LONDONDERRY, Edith Vane-Tempest-Stewart,
Marchioness of.
— Mount Stewart. 32pp. Illus. incl. map and cover. 21x14
(Belfast printed, 1956.)

MANUSCRIPTS (Typewritten).　　　　　　　English.
— SMITH, H.C. Inventory and valuation of silver at Mount
Stewart, Newtownards, County Down, the property of the ...
Marquess of Londonderry [C.S.H. Vane-Tempest-Stewart, 7th
Marquess], deceased. Prepared for the purpose of probate by
H.C.S. 9ff. 34x20 (Kensington) 1949.

MANUSCRIPTS (Typewritten).　　　　　　　English.
— SMITH, H.C. Inventory and valuation of the contents of
Mount Stewart, Newtownards, County Down, the property of
the Marchioness Dowager of Londonderry [E. Vane-Tempest-
Stewart, wife of the 7th Marquess]. Prepared for the purpose of
insurance by H.C.S. 34x20 (London) 1949 (1950).
Pencil note on fly-leaf: 'First Inventory dated: November 30th
[1949] ... This was remade and redated ... July 12, 1950.

MANUSCRIPTS (Typewritten)　　　　　　　English.
—SMITH, H.C. Inventory and valuation of the contents of
Mount Stewart, Newtownards, County Down, the property of
the ... Marquess of Londonderry [C.S.H. Vane-Tempest-
Stewart, 7th Marquess], deceased. Prepared for the purpose of
probate by H.C.S. 34x20 (London) 1949. Plan, inserted. 1.
COUNTRY LIFE. LXXVIII, 357. 1935.
COUNTRY LIFE. CLXVII, 646, 754. 1980.

MOYDRUM CASTLE (Westmeath).
NEALE, J.P. Views of Seats. Vol.VI. 1823.

MUCKROSS ABBEY (Kerry).
BURKE, J.B. Visitation of Seats. 2.S. Vol.II, p.119. 1855.*

MYRTLE GROVE, Youghal (Cork).
BURKE, J.B. Visitation of Seats. 2.S. Vol.II, p.66. 1855.*

NEWBRIDGE (Dublin).
GUINNESS, D. Irish Houses & Castles. p.151. 1971.

NEWHALL (Clare).
BURKE, J.B. Visitation of Seats. 2.S. Vol.II, p.145. 1855.*

NORTHLANDS (Cavan).
BURKE, J.B. Visitation of Seats. 2.S. Vol.II, p.93. 1855.*

OLD COURT (Wicklow).
BURKE, J.B. Visitation of Seats. 2.S. Vol.II, p.165. 1855.*

ORMEAU (Down).
BURKE, J.B. Visitation of Seats. 2.S. Vol.II, p.70. 1855.*

PALACE ANNE (Cork).
BURKE, J.B. Visitation of Seats. 2.S. Vol.I, p.194. 1854.*

PHOENIX LODGE (Dublin)
MILTON, T. Seats of Ireland. Pl.I. 1783-94.

PLATTEN HALL (Meath).
SADLEIR, T.U. Georgian mansions in Ireland. p.80. 1915.

PORTUMNA CASTLE (Galway).
SUMMERSON, J. The Country Seat. 36 [Plan]. 1970.

POWERSCOURT (Wicklow).
BURKE, J.B. Visitation of Seats. 2.S. Vol.II, p.155. 1855.*
COUNTRY LIFE. C, 1062 plan. 1946.
GUINNESS, D. Irish Houses & Castles. p.323. 1971.
MORRIS, F.O. Views of Seats. Vol.III, p.31. 1880.

PROVOST'S HOUSE, Trinity College, Dublin (Dublin).
COUNTRY LIFE. CLX, 1034 plan, 1106. 1976.
GUINNESS, D. Irish Houses & Castles. p.117.1971.

RALEIGH LODGE (Tyrone).
BURKE, J.B. Visitation of Seats. 2.S. Vol.I, p.118. 1854.*

RATHBEALE HALL (Dublin).
COUNTRY LIFE. CLII, 450. 1972.
GUINNESS, D. Irish Houses & Castles. p.159. 1971.

RATHFARNHAM CASTLE (Dublin).
COUNTRY LIFE. CLXXII, 734 plan. 1982.

ROCKINGHAM (Roscommon).
BURKE, J.B. Visitation of Seats. 2.S. Vol.II, p.46. 1855.*

ROS CUAN, Newtownards (Down).
MANUSCRIPTS (Typewritten).　　　　　　English.
— SMITH, H.C. Inventory and valuation of the contents of Ros Cuan, Newtownards, Co. Down, the property of the Viscount [D.W.C. Keppel] and Viscountess Bury. Taken for the purpose of insurance by H.C.S. 65ff. 33x20 (London) 1949.

ROSSMORE PARK (Monaghan).
MORRIS, F.O. Views of Seats. Vol.III, p.63. 1880.

ROSTELLAN CASTLE (Cork).
BURKE, J.B. Visitation of Seats. 2.S. Vol.II, p.29. 1855.*

RUSSBOROUGH (Wicklow).
COUNTRY LIFE. LXXXI, 94, 120. 1937.
COUNTRY LIFE. CXXXIV, 1464, 1623, 1686. 1963.
GUINNESS, D. Irish Houses & Castles. p.333. 1971.
NEALE, J.P. Views of Seats. 2.S. Vol.III. 1826.

ST. CLERONS (Galway).
NEALE, J.P. Views of Seats. Vol.VI. 1823.

ST. COLUMB'S (Donegal).
COUNTRY LIFE. CLVII, 1326. 1975.

ST. WOLSTANS (Kildare).
COPPER PLATE MAGAZINE. I, pl.6. 1792-1802.

SCARVA HOUSE (Down).
BURKE, J.B. Visitation of Seats. 2.S. Vol.II, p.93. 1855.*

SHAEN CASTLE (Leix).
SANDBY, P. Select Views. II, pl.8, (Ireland). 1782.

SHANE'S CASTLE (Antrim).
MILTON, T. Seats of Ireland. Pl. XXII. 1783-94.
SANDBY, P. Select Views. II, pl.11 (Ireland). 1782.

SHANKILL CASTLE (Kilkenny).
BURKE, J.B. Visitation of Seats. 2.S. Vol.I, p.228. 1854.*

SHELTON ABBEY (Wicklow).
MORRIS, F.O. Views of Seats. Vol.IV, p.61. 1880.
NEALE, J.P. Views of Seats. Vol.VI. 1823.

SLANE CASTLE (Meath).
COUNTRY LIFE. CLXVIII, 198 plan, 278, 382. 1980.
GUINNESS, D. Irish Houses & Castles. p. 261. 1971.

SPRINGHILL (Londonderry).
BELFAST: National Trust for Places of Historic Interest or Natural Beauty [Committee for Northern Ireland].
—Springhill, County Londonderry. 16pp. Illus. 22x14 [Belfast, c.1964.]
LENOX-CONYNGHAM, Mina.
—An old Ulster house (Springhill) and the people who lived in it. [Bibliogr. notes.] 270pp. Illus. incl. plates (1 folding) and genealog. table. 25x20 Dundalk: W. Tempest Dundalgan Press, 1946.
With 2 press cuttings inserted.

SUMMERHILL (Meath).
SUMMERSON, J. The Country Seat. 131. 1970.

SWISS COTTAGE, Cahir (Tipperary).
COUNTRY LIFE. CXL, 688. 1966.

THOMASTOWN CASTLE (Tipperary).
COUNTRY LIFE. CXLVI, 818. 1969.
NEALE, J.P. Views of Seats. Vol.VI. 1823.

THOMASTOWN HOUSE (Offaly).
BURKE, J.B. Visitation of Seats. 2.S. Vol.II, p.7. 1855.*

TOWNLEY HALL (Louth).
COUNTRY LIFE. CIV, 178, 228, 1104 [Treasures]. 1948.

TRALEE CASTLE (Kerry).
BURKE, J.B. Visitation of Seats. 2.S. Vol.II, p.82. 1855.*

TULLIRA CASTLE (Galway).
[Sales] TULLIRA CASTLE, 1982, June 16 [Contents].

TULLYMORE PARK (Down).
MILTON, T. Seats of Ireland. Pl. XVII. 1783-94.

TULLYNALLY CASTLE (Westmeath).
GUINNESS, D. Irish Houses & Castles. p.303. 1971.

TURVEY (Dublin).
SADLEIR, T.U. Georgian mansions in Ireland. p.86. 1915.

TYNAN ABBEY (Armagh).
BURKE, J.B. Visitation of Seats. 2.S. Vol.I, p.19. 1854.

WESTPORT HOUSE (Mayo).
SLIGO, Denis Edward Browne, *Marquess of.*
— Westport House and the Brownes. 112pp. Illus. incl. col. plate and map. 21x15 Ashbourne: Moorland Publishing Co., 1981.
COUNTRY LIFE. CXXXVII, 1010, 1074. 1965.
GUINNESS, D. Irish Houses & Castles. p.249. 1971.

WHITFIELD COURT (Waterford).

COUNTRY LIFE. CXLII, 522. 1967.

WILSON HOUSE (Tyrone).

BELFAST: National Trust for Places of Historic Interest or Natural Beauty [Committee for Northern Ireland].
— Wilson House, County Tyrone. 24pp. Illus. 22x14 [Belfast] 1967.

WOODBINE HILL (Waterford).

BURKE, J.B. Visitation of Seats. 2.S. Vol.II, p.165. 1855.*

WOODLANDS (Dublin).

BURKE, J.B. Visitation of Seats. 2.S. Vol.II, p.69. 1855.*

WOODSTOCK (Kilkenny).

BURKE, J.B. Visitation of Seats. 2.S. Vol.I, p.19.1854.*

COUNTRY HOUSES OF
SCOTLAND

ABBOTSFORD (Roxburghshire).

CONSTABLE-MAXWELL, *Sir* Walter Joseph, *Bart.*
—Abbotsford. 20pp. Illus. (2 on cover) incl. plan. 18x12 (Galashiels printed, 1952.)

SCOTT, *Hon.* **Mary Monica Maxwell.**
-Abbotsford: the personal relics and antiquarian treasures of Sir Walter Scott, described by the Hon. M.M.M.S., and illustrated by W. Gibb. [Bibliogr. notes.] 82pp. Illus. incl. cuts and 23 col. lithogr. plates. 30x26 London: A. & C. Black, 1893.

BURKE, J.B. Visitation of Seats.2.S. Vol.I, p.244. 1854.*

COUNTRY LIFE. CLXXII, 886 [Sir W. Scott and his collection.] 1982.

MORRIS, F.O. Views of Seats. Vol.V, p.31. 1880.

NEALE, J.P. Views of Seats. 2.S. Vol.V. 1829.

ABERCAIRNEY ABBEY (Perthshire).

BURKE, J.B. Visitation of Seats. 2.S. Vol.I. p.74. 1854.*

COUNTRY LIFE. CXXIX, 506 plan, 584. 1961.

JONES. Views of Seats. IV. 1829.

MORRIS, F.O. Views of Seats. Vol.V, p.79. 1880.

NEALE, J.P. Views of Seats. Vol.VI. 1823.

NEALE, J.P. Views of Seats in Scotland. 1830.

ABERUCHILL CASTLE (Perthshire).

JONES. Views of Seats. IV. 1829.

NEALE, J.P. Views of Seats. Vol.VI. 1823.

NEALE, J.P. Views of Seats in Scotland. 1830.

AIKENHEAD HOUSE (Lanarkshire).

GLASGOW: Country houses. 1870.

AIRLIE CASTLE (Angus).

COUNTRY LIFE. CXXXIII, 976. 1963.

CUMMING, G. Forfarshire illustrated. p.112. 1843.

AIRTH CASTLE (Stirlingshire).

ADAM, W. Vitruvius Scoticus. pls.64, 65. 1810.

JONES. Views of Seats. IV. 1829.

NEALE, J.P. Views of Seats. 2.S. Vol.III. 1826.

NEALE, J.P. Views of Seats in Scotland. 1830.

AIRTHREY CASTLE (Stirlingshire).

BURKE, J.B. Visitation of Seats. 2.S. Vol.II, p.38. 1855.*

JONES. Views of Seats. IV. 1829.

NEALE, J.P. Views of Seats. Vol.VI. 1823.

NEALE, J.P. Views of Seats in Scotland. 1830.

[Sales] LONDON, 1937, June 10 [Airthrey treasures].

ALDBAR CASTLE (Angus).

BURKE, J.B. Visitation of Seats. Vol.I, p.57. 1852.*

COUNTRY LIFE. CLII, 1666. 1972.

CUMMING, G. Forfarshire illustrated. p.126. 1843.

ALLANTON HOUSE (Lanarkshire).

BURKE, J.B. Visitation of Seats. 2.S. Vol.II, p.57. 1855.*

ALLOA PARK (Clackmannanshire).

BURKE, J.B. Visitation of Seats. 2.S. Vol.II, p.114. 1855.*

SPROULE, A. Lost houses of Britain. 29. 1982.

ALVA HOUSE (Clackmannanshire).

BURKE, J.B. Visitation of Seats. Vol.I, p.234. 1852.*

AMISFIELD (East Lothian).

MANUSCRIPTS.   English.
— Catalogue of paintings at Knowsley Hall taken in 1801 ... Included in the same volume: Earl of Whemysses [sic] catalogue of paintings at Amisfield in Scotland (in MS.). 64ff. 18.5x11.5 [1801-02?]

BURKE, J.B. Visitation of Seats. 2.S. Vol.II, p.154. 1855.*

ANCRUM HOUSE (Roxburghshire).

BURKE, J.B. Visitation of Seats. 2.S. Vol.II, p.101. 1855.*

ANNFIELD (Lanarkshire).

GLASGOW: Country houses. 1870.

ANNICK LODGE (Ayrshire).

MILLAR, A.H. Castles and mansions of Ayrshire. 1885.

ANNISTON HOUSE (Angus).

CUMMING, G. Forfarshire illustrated. p.71. 1843.

ARBUTHNOT HOUSE (Kincardineshire).

JONES. Views of Seats. IV. 1829.

NEALE, J.P. Views of Seats. 2.S. Vol.III. 1826.

NEALE, J.P. Views of Seats in Scotland. 1830.

ARDEER (Ayrshire).

MILLAR, A.H. Castles and mansions of Ayrshire. 1885.

ARDGOWAN HOUSE (Renfrewshire).

BURKE, J.B. Visitation of Seats. 2.S. Vol.II, p.54. 1855.*

JONES. Views of Seats. IV. 1829.

NEALE, J.P. Views of Seats. Vol.VI. 1823.

NEALE, J.P. Views of Seats in Scotland. 1830.

ARDKINGLAS (Argyllshire).
COUNTRY LIFE. XXIX, 746 plan. 1911.
SUMMERSON, J. The Country Seat. 193. 1970.

ARDMILLAN (Ayrshire).
MILLAR, A.H. Castles and mansions of Ayrshire. 1885.

ARDROSS CASTLE (Ross and Cromarty).
BURKE, J.B. Visitation of Seats. 2.S. Vol.II, p.85. 1855.*

ARDVORLICH HOUSE (Perthshire).
BURKE, J.B. Visitation of Seats. Vol.II, p.186. 1853.*

ARMADALE CASTLE (Inverness-shire, Isle of Skye).
JONES. Views of Seats. IV. 1829.
NEALE, J.P. Views of Seats. 2.S. Vol.I. 1824.
NEALE, J.P. Views of Seats in Scotland. 1830.

ARNISTON HOUSE (Midlothian).
ADAM, W. Vitruvius Scoticus. pls.39-44. 1810.
COUNTRY LIFE. LVIII, 250 plan, 284. 1925.

ASHIESTIEL (Selkirkshire).
BURKE, J.B. Visitation of Seats. Vol.II, p.163. 1853.*

AUCHANS HOUSE (Ayrshire).
MILLAR, A.H. Castles and mansions of Ayrshire. 1885.

AUCHANS NEW HOUSE (Ayrshire).
MILLAR, A.H. Castles and mansions of Ayrshire. 1885.

AUCHENDRANE (Ayrshire).
MILLAR, A.H. Castles and mansions of Ayrshire. 1885.

AUCHENDRANE OLD HOUSE (Ayrshire).
MILLAR, A.H. Castles and mansions of Ayrshire. 1885.

AUCHINCRUIVE (Ayrshire).
BURKE, J.B. Visitation of Seats. Vol.I, p.121. 1852.*
COUNTRY LIFE. LXXII, 690. 1932.
MILLAR, A.H. Castles and mansions of Ayrshire. 1885.

AUCHINLECK HOUSE (Ayrshire).
HANNAN, T. Famous Scottish houses. I. 1928.
MILLAR, A.H. Castles and mansions of Ayrshire. 1885.

AUCHINRAITH HOUSE (Lanarkshire).
GLASGOW: country houses. 1870.

AUCHINTOSHAN HOUSE (Dunbartonshire).
GLASGOW: country houses. 1870.

AUCHTERARDER HOUSE (Perthshire).
CAW, *Sir* James Lewis.
— The collection of pictures formed by Andrew T. Reid of Auchterarder. With notes by J.L.C. 89 plates. 29x22 Glasgow (privately printed), 1933.

AULDBAR CASTLE (Angus).
See ALDBAR CASTLE.

AULDHOUSE (Renfrewshire).
GLASGOW: country houses. 1870.

BALAVIL HOUSE (Inverness-shire).
SUMMERSON, J. The Country Seat. 178. 1970.

BALBIRNIE HOUSE (Fife).
COUNTRY LIFE. CLI, 1670 plan. 1972.
COUNTRY LIFE. CLII, 14. 1972.
JONES. Views of Seats. IV. 1829.
NEALE, J.P. Views of Seats. Vol.VI. 1823.
NEALE, J.P. Views of Seats in Scotland. 1830.

BALCARRES HOUSE (Fife).
BURKE, J.B. Visitation of Seats. Vol.II, p.182. 1853.*
HANNAN, T. Famous Scottish houses. 5. 1928.

BALCASKIE (Fife).
BURKE, J.B. Visitation of Seats. Vol.I, p.193. 1852.*
HANNAN, T. Famous Scottish houses. 9. 1928.

BALDOVAN HOUSE (Angus).
CUMMING, G. Forfarshire illustrated. p.33. 1843.

BALFOUR CASTLE (Orkney).
BURKE, J.B. Visitation of Seats. Vol.II, p.135. 1853.*

BALGREGGAN (Wigtownshire).
ADAM, W. Vitruvius Scoticus. pls.127, 128. 1810.

BALLANCLEROCH (Stirlingshire).
GLASGOW: country houses. 1870.

BALLOCH CASTLE (Dunbartonshire).
JONES, Views of Seats. IV. 1829.
LUGAR, R. Plans and views of buildings. 18, pls. X-XIII. 1823.
NEALE, J.P. Views of Seats. Vol.VI. 1823.
NEALE, J.P. Views of Seats in Scotland 1830.

BALLOCHMORIE HOUSE (Ayrshire).
BURKE, J.B. Visitation of Seats. Vol.I, p.270. 1852.*

BALLOCHMYLE HOUSE (Ayrshire).
ADAM, W. Vitruvius Scoticus. pl.63. 1810.
MILLAR, A.H. Castles and mansions of Ayrshire. 1885.

BALMANNO CASTLE (Perthshire).
COUNTRY LIFE. LXIX, 394 plan. 1931.
[Sales] BALMANNO CASTLE, 1976, September 14, 15 [Paintings, furniture, silver, etc.].

BALMORAL CASTLE (Aberdeenshire).
BROWN, Ivor.
— Balmoral: the history of a home. [Bibliogr.] 256pp. Plates and map (on end-paper). 21x14 London; Glasgow: Collins, 1955.
MORRIS, F.O. Views of Seats. Vol.I, p.91. 1880.

BALQUHAIN CASTLE (Aberdeenshire).
BURKE, J.B. Visitation of Seats. Vol.II, p.27. 1853.*

BALTHAYOCK (Perthshire).
BURKE, J.B. Visitation of Seats. Vol.I, p.244. 1852.*

BALVENIE CASTLE (Banffshire).
ADAM, W. Vitruvius Scoticus. pls.90, 91. 1810.

BARDOWIE (Stirlingshire).
GLASGOW: country houses. 1870.

BARGANY (Ayrshire).
MILLAR, A.H. Castles and mansions of Ayrshire. 1885.

BARHOLM (Kirkcudbrightshire).
ADAM, W. Vitruvius Scoticus. pl.94. 1810.

BARJARG TOWER (Dumfriesshire).
JONES. Views of Seats. IV. 1829.
NEALE, J.P. Views of Seats. 2.S. Vol.I. 1824.
NEALE, J.P. Views of Seats in Scotland. 1830.

BARLANARK HOUSE (Lanarkshire).
GLASGOW: country houses. 1870.

BARRA CASTLE (Aberdeenshire).
COUNTRY LIFE. XXXII, 710 plan. 1912.
COUNTRY LIFE. CXXXIV, 424 plan. 1963.

BARROGILL CASTLE (Caithness).
KEITH, Christina.
— The romance of Barrogill Castle (Castle of Mey), the Queen Mother's new home. 24pp. Illus. 22x14 Edinburgh: Pillans & Wilson [1954].

BARSKIMMING (Ayrshire).
ANGUS, W. Seats of the Nobility. pl.27. 1787.

BEACH HOUSE (Ayrshire).
MILLAR, A.H. Castles and mansions of Ayrshire. 1885.

BEDLAY HOUSE (Lanarkshire).
GLASGOW: country houses. 1870.

BELLAHOUSTON (Lanarkshire).
GLASGOW: country houses. 1870.

BELHAVEN HOUSE (East Lothian).
ADAM, W. Vitruvius Scoticus. pl.154. 1810.

BELLEISLE (Ayrshire).
MILLAR, A.H. Castles and mansions of Ayrshire. 1885.

BELVIDERE (Midlothian).
See DALMAHOY HOUSE.

BELVIDERE HOUSE (Lanarkshire).
GLASGOW: country houses. 1870.

BEMERSYDE (Roxburghshire).
MANUSCRIPTS (Typewritten).   English.
— HAIG, *Earl*. Bemersyde: the history of the Haigs (paintings at Bemersyde). 13ff. 30x21 [Bemersyde, c.1960].
HANNAN, T. Famous Scottish houses. 13. 1928.

BERBETH (Ayrshire).
MILLAR, A.H. Castles and mansions of Ayrshire. 1885.

BIEL HOUSE (East Lothian).
HANNAN, T. Famous Scottish houses. 17. 1928.

BINNS (West Lothian).
EDINBURGH: National Trust for Scotland for Places of Historic Interest or Natural Beauty.
— The Binns ... The first house in Scotland presented to the ... Trust [etc.]. 20pp. Illus. (some on covers) incl. maps.22x14 (Edinburgh, 1973.)

BURKE, J.B. Visitation of Seats. 2.S. Vol.II, p.1. 1855.*
HANNAN, T. Famous Scottish houses. 21. 1928.

BIRKENBOG (Banffshire).
BURKE, J.B. Visitation of Seats. Vol.II, p.187. 1853.*

BIRSAY (Orkney).
BURKE, J.B. Visitation of Seats. 2.S. Vol.II, p.179. 1855.*

BLAIRADAM HOUSE (Kinross-shire).
BURKE, J.B. Visitation of Seats. 2.S. Vol.II, p.30. 1855.*

BLAIR CASTLE, Blair Atholl (Perthshire).
BLAIR CASTLE.
— Blair Castle: an illustrated survey [etc.]. 32pp. Illus. (some col., some on covers) incl. maps. (on inside covers). 14x22 Derby: Pilgrim Press [1955?].
COUNTRY LIFE. CVI, 1362, 1434, 1506. 1949.

[Sales] BLAIR CASTLE, 1949, August 31 [Antique furniture and fittings].

BLAIR DRUMMOND (Perthshire).
ADAM, W. Vitruvius Scoticus. pls.83-85. 1810.
BURKE, J.B. Visitation of Seats. Vol.II, p.76. 1853.*

[Sales] LONDON, 1913, July 4 [The Blair-Drummond pictures].

BLAIRHILL (Perthshire).
WATKIN, Ralph Granger.
— Paintings, drawings & prints in the collection of A.F. Stewart, Esq., of Hayes Court, Kenley and Blairhill, Blairgowrie. Catalogued with descriptive notes by R.G.W. 92pp. Plates. 26x20 n.p. privately printed [at the Temple Sheen Press] 1920.

BLAIR HOUSE (Ayrshire).
BURKE, J.B. Visitation of Seats. Vol.II, p.149. 1853.*
HANNAN, T. Famous Scottish houses. 25. 1928.
MILLAR, A.H. Castles and mansions of Ayrshire. 1885.

BLAIRQUHAN CASTLE (Ayrshire).
BURKE, J.B. Visitation of Seats. 2.S. Vol.I, p.164. 1854.*
COUNTRY LIFE. CLIII, 1054, 1154. 1973.
HANNAN, T. Famous Scottish houses. 29. 1928.
JONES. Views of Seats. IV. 1829.
MILLAR, A.H. Castles and mansions of Ayrshire. 1885.
NEALE, J.P. Views of Seats. 2.S. Vol.III. 1826.
NEALE, J.P. Views of Seats in Scotland. 1830.

BLYTHSWOOD (Renfrewshire).
GLASGOW: country houses. 1870.
JONES. Views of Seats. IV. 1829.

NEALE, J.P. Views of Seats. 2.S. Vol.III. 1826.
NEALE, J.P. Views of Seats in Scotland. 1830.

BOGHENGIEGHT (Midlothian).
See HERIOT'S HOSPITAL.

BONALY TOWER (Midlothian).
HANNAN, T. Famous Scottish houses. 33. 1928.

BONSKEID (Perthshire).
JONES. Views of Seats. IV. 1829.
NEALE, J.P. Views of Seats. 2.S. Vol.III. 1826.
NEALE, J.P. Views of Seats in Scotland. 1830.

BORTHWICK CASTLE (Midlothian).
BURKE, J.B. Visitation of Seats. 2.S. Vol.I, p.188. 1854.*
COUNTRY LIFE. XXXIII, 778 plan. 1913.
COUNTRY LIFE. CIV, 126. 1948.
HANNAN, T. Famous Scottish houses. 37. 1928.

BOTHWELL CASTLE (Lanarkshire).
BURKE, J.B. Visitation of Seats. Vol.II, p.114. 1853.*
BURKE, J.B. Visitation of Seats. 2.S. Vol.II, p.150. 1855.*

BOTURICH CASTLE (Dunbartonshire).
BURKE, J.B. Visitation of Seats. Vol.II, p.248. 1853.*
HANNAN, T. Famous Scottish houses. 41. 1928.

BOWHILL (Selkirkshire).
BURKE, J.B. Visitation of Seats. Vol.II, p.198. 1853.*
COUNTRY LIFE. CLVII, 1448, 1558, 1618, 1678. 1975.

BRAEMAR CASTLE (Aberdeenshire).
SKINNER, Basil C.
— Braemar Castle, Aberdeenshire ... Official guide. 16pp. Illus. (some on covers, 1 on title-page) incl. map. 14x20 [Hanley] (Pilgrim Press) [1964?]

BRAHAN CASTLE (Ross and Cromarty).
BURKE, J.B. Visitation of Seats. Vol.I, p.43. 1853.*
COUNTRY LIFE. XL, 210. 1916.

BRECHIN CASTLE (Angus).
COUNTRY LIFE. CL. 378. 436. 1971.
JONES. Views of Seats. IV. 1829.
MORRIS, F.O. Views of Seats. Vol.VI, p.25. 1880.
NEALE, J.P. Views of Seats. Vol.VI. 1823.
NEALE, J.P. Views of Seats in Scotland. 1830.

BREDISHOLM (Lanarkshire).
GLASGOW: country houses. 1870.

BRISBANE HOUSE (Ayrshire).
MILLAR, A.H. Castles and mansions of Ayrshire. 1885.

BROADMEADOWS (Selkirkshire).
BURKE, J.B. Visitation of Seats. Vol.II, p.170. 1853.*

BRODICK CASTLE, Isle of Arran (Bute).
EDINBURGH: National Trust for Scotland for Places of Historic Interest or Natural Beauty.
—MAC WILLIAM, C. and GIBSON, J.F.A. Brodick Castle and gardens. 24pp. Illus. (1 on cover.) 22x14 Edinburgh, 1966.
BURKE, J.B. Visitation of Seats. 2.S. Vol.II, p.142. 1855.*
COUNTRY LIFE. CLXXIII. 322, 380. 1983.

BRODIE CASTLE (Morayshire).
COUNTRY LIFE. XL, 238. 1916.
COUNTRY LIFE. CLXVIII, 466, 554. 1980.

BROOMHALL (Fife).
COUNTRY LIFE. CXLVII, 242. 1970.
HANNAN, T. Famous Scottish houses. 45. 1928.

BROOMHOUSE (Berwickshire).
BURKE, J.B. Visitation of Seats. Vol.I, p.144. 1852.*

BROOMLANDS (Roxburghshire).
ADAM, W. Vitruvius Scoticus. pls.118, 119. 1810.

BUCHANAN HOUSE (Stirlingshire).
ADAM, W. Vitruvius Scoticus. pls.135, 136. 1810.
BURKE, J.B. Visitation of Seats. 2.S. Vol.I, p.166. 1854.*
JONES. Views of Seats. IV. 1829.
NEALE, J.P. Views of Seats. Vol.VI. 1823.
NEALE, J.P. Views of Seats in Scotland. 1830.

CADDER HOUSE (Lanarkshire).
See CAWDER HOUSE.

CAIRNESS (Aberdeenshire).
COUNTRY LIFE. CXLIX, 184, 248. 1971.

CAIRNFIELD (Banffshire).
BURKE, J.B. Visitation of Seats. Vol.II, p.33. 1853.*

CALDERWOOD CASTLE (Lanarkshire).
BURKE, J.B. Visitation of Seats. 2.S. Vol.II, p.63. 1855.*

CALDWELL (Ayrshire).
BURKE, J.B. Visitation of Seats. Vol.II, p.158. 1853.*

CALLENDAR HOUSE (Stirlingshire).
HANNAN, T. Famous Scottish houses. 49. 1928.

CALLTONMOR (Argyllshire).
BURKE, J.B. Visitation of Seats. 2.S. Vol.II, p.84. 1855.*

CALLY (Kirkcudbrightshire).
ADAM, W. Vitruvius Scoticus. pls.111-13. 1810.

CAMBUSDOON (Ayrshire).
MILLAR, A.H. Castles and mansions of Ayrshire. 1885.

CAMBUSNETHAN HOUSE (Lanarkshire).
BURKE, J.B. Visitation of Seats. 2.S. Vol.I, p.47. 1854.*

CAMERON HOUSE (Dunbartonshire).
CAMERON HOUSE.
— Cameron House, Loch Lomond. 20pp. Illus. (some col.) incl. map. 19x13 (Norwich: Jarrold & Sons, 1973.)

CAMIS ESKAN (Dunbartonshire).
NEALE, J.P. Views of Seats. 2.S. Vol.V. 1829.

CAMMO HOUSE, Edinburgh (Midlothian).
ADAM, W. Vitruvius Scoticus. pl.141. 1810.

CAMPBELLFIELD (Lanarkshire).
GLASGOW: country houses. 1870.

CAMPERDOWN (Angus).
CUMMING, G. Forfarshire illustrated. p.7. 1843.

CAPELRIG (Renfrewshire).
GLASGOW: country houses. 1870.

CAPENOCH (Dumfriesshire).
COUNTRY LIFE. CXLVIII, 394 plan. 1970.

CAPRINGTON CASTLE (Ayrshire).
HANNAN, T. Famous Scottish houses. 53. 1928.
MILLAR, A.H. Castles and mansions of Ayrshire. 1885.

CARBERRY TOWER (Midlothian).
HANNAN, T. Famous Scottish houses. 57. 1928.

CARBETH GUTHRIE (Stirlingshire).
BURKE, J.B. Visitation of Seats. Vol.II, p.236. 1853.*
GLASGOW: country houses. 1870.

CARESTON CASTLE (Angus).
COUNTRY LIFE. XXXIII, 310. 1913.

CARFIN HOUSE (Lanarkshire).
[Sales] CARFIN HOUSE, 1928, December 12, 13 [House furniture and plenishing].

CARMICHAEL HOUSE (Lanarkshire).
BURKE, J.B. Visitation of Seats. 2.S. Vol.II, p.44. 1855.*

CARNTYNE HOUSE (Lanarkshire).
BURKE, J.B. Visitation of Seats. 2.S. Vol.I, p.229. 1854.*
GLASGOW: country houses. 1870.

CAROLINE PARK (Midlothian).
HARRIS, David Fraser.
—Caroline Park House and Roystoun Castle. A descriptive and historical account. 36pp. Illus. incl. facsimiles. 41x29 Chiswick: privately printed (1897?).
COUNTRY LIFE. XXX, 276 plan. 1911.

CARRIDEN (West Lothian).
BURKE, J.B. Visitation of Seats. 2.S. Vol.I, p.182. 1854.*

CARSTAIRS (Lanarkshire).
BURKE, J.B. Visitation of Seats. Vol.II, p.88. 1853.*
JONES. Views of Seats. IV. 1829.
NEALE, J.P. Views of Seats. 2.S. Vol.I. 1824.
NEALE, J.P. Views of Seats in Scotland. 1830.

CASSILLIS HOUSE (Ayrshire).
HANNAN, T. Famous Scottish houses. 61. 1928.
MILLAR, A.H. Castles and mansions of Ayrshire. 1885.

CASTLE CRAIG (Peebles-shire).
[Sales] LONDON, 1902, May 12, 13 [Collection from C.C.].

CASTLE FORBES (Aberdeenshire).
BURKE, J.B. Visitation of Seats. 2.S. Vol.II, p.186. 1855.*
JONES. Views of Seats. IV. 1829.
MORRIS, F.O. Views of Seats. Vol.V, p.61. 1880.
NEALE, J.P. Views of Seats. Vol.VI. 1823.
NEALE, J.P. Views of Seats in Scotland. 1830.

CASTLE FRASER (Aberdeenshire).
COUNTRY LIFE. XCVII, 68 plan. 1945.
COUNTRY LIFE. CLXIV, 370, 442. 1978.
JONES. Views of Seats. IV. 1829.
NEALE, J.P. Views of Seats. 2.S. Vol.III. 1826.
NEALE, J.P. Views of Seats in Scotland. 1830.

CASTLE HUNTLY (Perthshire).
BURKE, J.B. Visitation of Seats. Vol.II, p.31. 1853.*
JONES. Views of Seats. IV. 1829.
MILLAR, A.H. Castles and mansions of Scotland. p.84. 1890.
NEALE, J.P. Views of Seats. Vol.VI. 1823.
NEALE, J.P. Views of Seats in Scotland. 1830.

CASTLE KENNEDY (Wigtownshire).
ADAM, W. Vitruvius Scoticus. pls.120, 121. 1810.

CASTLE MENZIES (Perthshire).
BURKE, J.B. Visitation of Seats. Vol.II, p.96. 1853.*
BURKE, J.B. Visitation of Seats. 2.S. Vol.II, p.29. 1855.*
COUNTRY LIFE. CLIV, 654. 1973.
JONES. Views of Seats. IV. 1829.
MILLAR, A.H. Castles and mansions of Scotland. p.43. 1890.
NEALE, J.P. Views of Seats. 2.S. Vol.II. 1825.
NEALE, J.P. Views of Seats in Scotland. 1830.

CASTLEMILK (Dumfriesshire).
COUNTRY LIFE. CLXII, 350, 422. 1977.

CASTLEMILK (Lanarkshire).
GLASGOW: country houses. 1870.

CASTLE NEWE (Aberdeenshire).
BURKE, J.B. Visitation of Seats. 2.S. Vol.II, p.12. 1855.*

CASTLE OF MEY (Caithness).
See BARROGILL CASTLE.

CASTLE STEWART (Inverness-shire).
COPPER PLATE MAGAZINE. V, pl.203. 1792-1802.
COUNTRY LIFE. XXXVII, 112. 1915.

CASTLE TOWARD (Argyllshire).
BURKE, J.B. Visitation of Seats. 2.S. Vol.I, p.73. 1854.
JONES. Views of Seats. IV. 1829.
NEALE, J.P. Views of Seats. Vol.VI. 1823.
NEALE, J.P. Views of Seats in Scotland. 1830.

CATHKIN (Lanarkshire).
GLASGOW: country houses. 1870.

CAWDER HOUSE (Lanarkshire).
GLASGOW: country houses. 1870.

CAWDOR CASTLE (Nairnshire).
BURKE, J.B. Visitation of Seats. 2.S, Vol.II. p.33. 1855.*
COPPER PLATE MAGAZINE. IV, pl. 189. 1792-1802.
COUNTRY LIFE. II, 14. 1897.
COUNTRY LIFE. XX, 942. 1906.
COUNTRY LIFE. XCVII, 816 plan, 860. 1945.
MALAN, A.H. Famous homes. p. 167. 1902.
UNITED KINGDOM. Historic houses. 170. 1892.

CESSNOCK (Lanarkshire).
GLASGOW: country houses. 1870.

CESSNOCK CASTLE (Ayrshire).
MILLAR, A.H. Castles and mansions of Ayrshire. 1885.

CHARLETON (Fife).
BURKE, J.B. Visitation of Seats. Vol.II, p.70. 1853.*

CHATELHERAULT (Lanarkshire).
COUNTRY LIFE. CXXXVI, 1716. 1964.

CHESTERS (Roxburghshire).
BURKE, J.B. Visitation of Seats. Vol.II, p.177. 1853.*

CLAYPOTTS CASTLE (Angus).
GREAT BRITAIN: Ministry of Works [Ancient Monuments and Historic Buildings].
— APTED, M.R. Claypotts, Angus. 16pp. Illus. incl. plates, plans and genealog. tables. 21x14 Edinburgh, 1957.
2 ed. Claypotts Castle. 28pp. 21x15 1980.

CLOBER HOUSE (Stirlingshire).
GLASGOW: country houses. 1870.

CLONCAIRD CASTLE (Ayrshire).
MILLAR, A.H. Castles and mansions of Ayrshire. 1885.

CLOSEBURN HALL (Dumfriesshire).
BURKE, J.B. Visitation of Seats. 2.S. Vol.II, p.144. 1855.*

CLUNY CASTLE (Inverness-shire).
BURKE, J.B. Visitation of Seats. 2.S. Vol.I, p.90. 1854.*

COCHNO HOUSE (Dunbartonshire).
BURKE, J.B. Visitation of Seats. 2.S. Vol.I, p.27.1854.*
GLASGOW: country houses. 1870.

COILSFIELD (Ayrshire).
See MONTGOMERIE CASTLE.

COLGRAIN (Dunbartonshire).
BURKE, J.B. Visitation of Seats. 2.S. Vol.I, p.154. 1854.*

COLSTOUN (East Lothian).
HANNAN, T. Famous Scottish houses. 65. 1928.

COLZIUM (Stirlingshire).
BURKE, J.B. Visitation of Seats. Vol.II, p.5. 1853.*

CONDIE (Perthshire).
BURKE, J.B. Visitation of Seats. Vol.I, p.153. 1852.*

CONON HOUSE (Ross and Cromarty).
BURKE, J.B. Visitation of Seats. 2.S. Vol.I, p.120. 1854.*

COODHAM (Ayrshire).
MILLAR, A.H. Castles and mansions of Ayrshire. 1885.

CORTACHY CASTLE (Angus).
BURKE, J.B. Visitation of Seats. 2.S. Vol.II, p.191. 1855.*
COUNTRY LIFE. CXXXIII, 976. 1963.
CUMMING, G. Forfarshire illustrated. p.118. 1843.
JONES. Views of Seats. IV. 1829.
MILLAR, A.H. Castles and mansions of Scotland. p.307. 1890.
NEALE, J.P. Views of Seats. Vol.VI. 1823.
NEALE, J.P. Views of Seats in Scotland. 1830.

CORWAR (Ayrshire).
MILLAR, A.H. Castles and mansions of Ayrshire. 1885.

COWLAIRS (Lanarkshire).
GLASGOW: country houses. 1870.

CRAIGCROOK CASTLE (Midlothian).
HANNAN, T. Famous Scottish houses. 69. 1928.

CRAIGDARROCH (Dumfriesshire).
ADAM, W. Vitruvius Scoticus. pls.77, 78. 1810.

CRAIGEND CASTLE (Stirlingshire).
BURKE, J.B. Visitation of Seats. 2.S. Vol.I, p.228. 1854.*
GLASGOW: country houses. 1870.
JONES. Views of Seats. IV. 1829.
NEALE, J.P. Views of Seats in Scotland. 1830.

CRAIGHALL-RATTRAY (Perthshire).
MILLAR, A.H. Castles and mansions of Scotland. p.101. 1890.

CRAIGHEAD (Lanarkshire).
GLASGOW: country houses. 1870.

CRAIGIE HALL (West Lothian).
ADAM, W. Vitruvius Scoticus. pls.86, 87. 1810.

CRAIGIE HOUSE (Ayrshire).
MILLAR, A.H. Castles and mansions of Ayrshire. 1885.

CRAIGIEVAR CASTLE (Aberdeenshire).
EDINBURGH: National Trust for Scotland for Places of Historic Interest or Natural Beauty.
— SIMPSON, W.D. The Rock of Mar: Craigievar Castle. An ... account. [Bibliogr. notes.] 28pp. Illus. incl. plates and plan. 22x14 (Edinburgh) [c.1975.]
COUNTRY LIFE. XIX, 162. 1906.
COUNTRY LIFE. LXXXIII, 12 plan. 1938.

CRAIGMADDIE (Stirlingshire).
GLASGOW: country houses. 1870.

CRAIGPARK HOUSE (Lanarkshire).
GLASGOW: country houses. 1870.

CRAIGSTON CASTLE (Aberdeenshire).
COUNTRY LIFE. XXXVII, 112 plan. 1915.
COUNTRY LIFE. CXXXIV, 944, 1050. 1963.
JONES. Views of Seats. IV. 1829.
NEALE, J.P. Views of Seats. 2.S. Vol.III. 1826.
NEALE, J.P. Views of Seats in Scotland. 1830.

CRAIGTON (Lanarkshire).
GLASGOW: country houses. 1870.

CRAILING HOUSE (Roxburghshire).
COUNTRY LIFE. CXXXI, 1424. 1962.

CRATHES CASTLE (Kincardineshire).
EDINBURGH: National Trust for Scotland for Places of Historic Interest or Natural Beauty.
— SCOTT, S. Crathes Castle: an illustrated account. 64pp. Illus. (1 on title-page) incl. plates. 22x14 [Edinburgh] (1971.)
COUNTRY LIFE. XXXIII, 598, 1913.
COUNTRY LIFE. LXXXII, 272, 296, 306 [Furniture]. 1932.
JONES. Views of Seats. IV. 1829.
NEALE, J.P. Views of Seats. Vol.VI. 1823.
NEALE, J.P. Views of Seats in Scotland. 1830.
NICOLSON, N. Great Houses of Britain. p.56. 1965.

CRAUFURDLAND CASTLE (Ayrshire).
HANNAN, T. Famous Scottish houses. 73. 1928.
MILLAR, A.H. Castles and mansions of Ayrshire. 1885.

CRAWFORD PRIORY (Fife).
BURKE, J.B. Visitation of Seats. 2.S. Vol.II, p.21. 1855.*

CROSBIE CASTLE (Ayrshire).
MILLAR, A.H. Castles and mansions of Ayrshire. 1885.

CROSSBASKET (Lanarkshire).
GLASGOW: country houses. 1870.

CULDEES CASTLE (Perthshire).
JONES. Views of Seats. IV. 1829.
NEALE, J.P. Views of Seats. Vol.VI. 1823.
NEALE, J.P. Views of Seats in Scotland. 1830.

CULLEN HOUSE (Banffshire).
CULLEN HOUSE.
— Cullen House, Banffshire: an illustrated survey [etc.]. 32pp. Illus. (some col., some on covers) incl. maps (on inside covers). 14x22 Derby: Pilgrim Press [1960].
COUNTRY LIFE. XX, 378. 1906.
COUNTRY LIFE. CXLIII, 660 [2nd. Salon]. 1968.
[Sales] CULLEN HOUSE, 1975, September 22, 23 [Remaining contents incl. library].

CULLODEN HOUSE (Inverness-shire).
BURKE, J.B. Visitation of Seats. Vol.II, p.108. 1853.*
[Sales] CULLODEN HOUSE, 1897, July 21-26 [Contents].

CULROSS ABBEY HOUSE (Fife).
COUNTRY LIFE. CXXI, 981 plan. 1957.
KIP, J. Nouveau théâtre de la Grande Bretagne. III, pl.52. 1715.

CULROSS PALACE (Fife).
MILLAR, A.H. Castles and mansions of Scotland. p.117. 1890.

CULZEAN CASTLE (Ayrshire).
BOLTON, A.T. Architecture of R. & J. Adam. II, 263 plan. 1922.
BURKE, J.B. Visitation of Seats. Vol.II, p.128. 1853.*
COUNTRY LIFE. XXXVIII, 328, 360 plan. 1915.
COUNTRY LIFE. XCVIII, 956 plan. 1945.
HANNAN, T. Famous Scottish houses. 77. 1928.
JONES. Views of Seats. IV. 1829.
MILLAR, A.H. Castles and mansions of Ayrshire. 1885.
NEALE, J.P. Views of Seats. Vol.VI. 1823.
NEALE, J.P. Views of Seats in Scotland. 1830.

CUMBERNAULD HOUSE (Dunbartonshire).
ADAM, W. Vitruvius Scoticus. pls.125, 126. 1810.
BURKE, J.B. Visitation of Seats. 2.S. Vol.II, p.143. 1855.*

DALBETH (Lanarkshire).
GLASGOW: country houses. 1870.

DALDOWIE (Lanarkshire).
GLASGOW: country houses. 1870.

DALGUISE HOUSE (Perthshire).
JONES. Views of Seats. IV. 1829.
NEALE, J.P. Views of Seats. Vol.VI. 1823.
NEALE, J.P. Views of Seats in Scotland. 1830.

DALJARROCK (Ayrshire).
MILLAR, A.H. Castles and mansions of Ayrshire. 1885.

DALKEITH PALACE (Midlothian).
SCOTT, *Lord* Henry Francis Montagu Douglas.
— Catalogue of the pictures at Dalkeith House [the property of the Duke of Buccleuch and Queensberry]. [By H.S. i.e. Lord H.F.M.D. Scott and H.H.D., i.e. Sir H.C.H. Dalrymple, Bart.] 2 plates. 28x22 n.p. privately printed, 1911.
ADAM, W. Vitruvius Scoticus. pls.22-24. 1810.
ANGUS, W. Seats of the Nobility. pl.9. 1787.
COUNTRY LIFE. XXX, 510 plan. 1911.
COUNTRY LIFE. XXXI, 178 [Furniture], 214 [Furniture]. 1912.
JONES. Views of Seats. IV. 1829.
MALAN, A.H. Other famous homes. p.271. 1902.
MORRIS, F.O. Views of Seats. Vol.V, p.49. 1880.
NEALE, J.P. Views of Seats. 2.S. Vol.IV. 1828.
NEALE, J.P. Views of Seats in Scotland. 1830.

DALMAHOY HOUSE (Midlothian).
ADAM, W. Vitruvius Scoticus. pl.72. 1810.
HANNAN, T. Famous Scottish houses. 81. 1928.

DALMARNOCK HOUSE (Lanarkshire).
GLASGOW: country houses. 1870.

DALMENY PARK (West Lothian).
JONES. Views of Seats. IV. 1829.
NEALE, J.P. Views of Seats. Vol.VI. 1823.
NEALE, J.P. Views of Seats in Scotland. 1830.

DALMUIR HOUSE (Dunbartonshire).
GLASGOW: country houses. 1870.

DALQUHARRAN CASTLE (Ayrshire).
MILLAR, A.H. Castles and mansions of Ayrshire. 1885.

DALSWINTON (Dumfriesshire).
COPPER PLATE MAGAZINE. III, pl.108. 1792-1802.

DALZELL HOUSE (Lanarkshire).
COUNTRY LIFE. IX, 176. 1901.
HANNAN, T. Famous Scottish houses. 85. 1928.

DARLEITH (Dunbartonshire).
BURKE, J.B. Visitation of Seats. 2.S. Vol.II, p.203. 1855.*

DARNAWAY CASTLE (Morayshire).
COPPER PLATE MAGAZINE. V, pl.213. 1792-1802.

DELGATIE CASTLE (Aberdeenshire).
BURKE, J.B. Visitation of Seats. 2.S. Vol.II, p.113. 1855.*

DELVINE (Perthshire).
BURKE, J.B. Visitation of Seats. 2.S. Vol.I, p.22. 1854.*

DONIBRISTLE (Fife).
ADAM, W. Vitruvius Scoticus. pls.92-4. 1810.
BURKE, J.B. Visitation of Seats. 2.S. Vol.I, p.155. 1854.*
JONES. Views of Seats. IV. 1829.
NEALE, J.P. Views of Seats. 2.S. Vol.IV. 1828.
NEALE, J.P. Views of Seats in Scotland. 1830.

DOUGLAS CASTLE (Lanarkshire).
ADAM, W. Vitruvius Scoticus. pls.135, 136. 1810.
HANNAN, T. Famous Scottish houses. 89. 1928.

DRUM, The. (Midlothian).
COUNTRY LIFE. XXXVIII, 488 plan. 1915.

DRUM CASTLE (Aberdeenshire).
BURKE, J.B. Visitation of Seats. Vol.II, p.152. 1853.*
JONES. Views of Seats. IV. 1829.
NEALE, J.P. Views of Seats. 2.S. Vol.I. 1824.
NEALE, J.P. Views of Seats in Scotland. 1830.

DRUMLANRIG CASTLE (Dumfriesshire).
RAMAGE, Craufurd Tait.
— Drumlanrig Castle and the Douglases: with the early history and ancient remains of Durisdeer, Closeburn, and Morton. xxiv, 412pp. 19x12 Dumfries: J. Anderson & Son; Edinburgh and London: J. Menzies & Co., 1876.
CAMPBELL, C. Vitruvius Britannicus. I, pls.37, 38. 1715.
CAMPBELL, C. Vitruvius Britannicus. IVth. pls.45, 46. 1739.

COPPER PLATE MAGAZINE. pl.27. 1778.
COUNTRY LIFE. XXXIII, 382 plan. 1913.
COUNTRY LIFE. CXXVIII, 378 plan, 434, 488. 1960.
MORRIS, F.O. Views of Seats. Vol.IV, p.23. 1880.
SANDBY, P. Select Views. II, pls.11, 12 (Scotland). 1782.
WATTS, W. Seats of the Nobility. pl.9. 1779.

DRUMMOND CASTLE (Perthshire).
BURKE, J.B. Visitation of Seats. Vol.II, p.238. 1853.

DRUMPELLIER (Lanarkshire).
GLASGOW: country houses. 1870.

DRYBURGH ABBEY (Berwickshire).
BURKE, J.B. Visitation of Seats. 2.S. Vol.II, p.20. 1855.*

DRYDEN HOUSE (Midlothian).
ADAM, W. Vitruvius Scoticus. pls.79, 80. 1810.

DRYGRANGE (Roxburghshire).
BURKE, J.B. Visitation of Seats. 2.S. Vol.I, p.93. 1854.*

DUDDINGSTON HOUSE (Midlothian).
BURKE, J.B. Visitation of Seats. 2.S. Vol.II, p.9. 1855.*
CAMPBELL, C. Vitruvius Britannicus. IV, pls.15-17. 1767.
COUNTRY LIFE. CXXVI, 358 plan. 1959.

DUFF HOUSE (Banffshire).
BANFF.
—Summer excursions in the neighbourhood of Banff, and vicinity of Duff House, Bridge of Alva & C. By a Deveronside poet [i.e. A.Harper]. To which are appended some notices of the works of art in Duff House. [Bibliogr. notes.] viii, 62pp. Plates (1 folding) incl. map. 19x12 Banff: J. Imlach, 1843.
FIFE, James Duff, *Earl of.*
—Catalogue of the portraits and pictures in the different houses belonging to the Earl of Fife. (Duff House, Fife House, Rothenay House and Innes House). 52pp. 26x21 n.p., 1798.
ADAM, W. Vitruvius Scoticus. pls. 146-8. 1810.
CAMPBELL, C. Vitruvius Britannicus. V, pls. 58-60. 1771.
COPPER PLATE MAGAZINE. III, pl.124. 1792-1802.
JONES. Views of Seats. IV. 1829.
NEALE, J.P. Views of Seats. Vol.VI. 1823.
NEALE, J.P. Views of Seats in Scotland. 1830.
SANDBY, P. Select Views. II, pl.13 (Scotland). 1782.

DUMFRIES HOUSE, Cumnock (Ayrshire).
ADAM, W. Vitruvius Scoticus. pls.19, 20. 1810.
MILLAR, A.H. Castles and mansions of Ayrshire. 1885.

DUN HOUSE (Angus).
ADAM, W. Vitruvius Scoticus. pls.57, 58, 69, 70. 1810.
MILLAR, A.H. Castles and mansions of Scotland. p.335. 1890.

DUNDARAVE CASTLE (Argyllshire).
COUNTRY LIFE. LXX, 202 plan. 1931.

DUNDAS CASTLE (West Lothian).
BURKE, J.B. Visitation of Seats. 2.S. Vol.II, p.123. 1855.*
HANNAN, T. Famous Scottish houses. 93. 1928.
JONES. Views of Seats. IV. 1829.
NEALE, J.P. Views of Seats. 2.S. Vol.II. 1825.
NEALE, J.P. Views of Seats in Scotland. 1830.

DUNGLASS(East Lothian).
COUNTRY LIFE. LVIII, 396 plan. 1925.
JONES. Views of Seats. IV. 1829.
NEALE, J.P. Views of Seats. Vol.VI. 1823.
NEALE, J.P. Views of Seats in Scotland. 1830.

DUNINALD HOUSE (Angus).
See DUNNINALD.

DUNKELD HOUSE (Perthshire).
[Sales] DUNKELD HOUSE, 1949, June 15-17 [Antique and modern furnishings].

DUNLOP HOUSE (Ayrshire).
MILLAR, A.H. Castles and mansions of Ayrshire. 1885.

DUNMORE PARK (Stirlingshire).
JONES. Views of Seats. IV. 1829.
MORRIS, F.O. Views of Seats. Vol.V, p.11. 1880.
NEALE, J.P. Views of Seats. 2.S. Vol.III. 1826.
NEALE, J.P. Views of Seats in Scotland. 1830.

DUNNINALD (Angus).
COUNTRY LIFE. CXLVI, 384, 444. 1969.
CUMMING, G. Forfarshire Illustrated. p.75. 1843.

DUNOLLIE CASTLE (Argyllshire).
BURKE, J.B. Visitation of Seats. 2.S. Vol.I, p.136. 1854.*
JONES. Views of Seats. IV. 1829.

The Duke of Queensbury's Palace, at Drumlanrig in Scotland.

Published as the Act directs, August 1.ˢᵗ 1779 by W. Watts, Kemp's Row, Chelsea.

F. Sandby R.A. delin.ᵗ

W. Watts sculp.ᵗ

DRUMLANRIG CASTLE, Dumfriesshire. From: WATTS (W.). *The seats of the nobility and gentry* [etc.], London, 1779(-1786).

DUNROBIN CASTLE (Sutherland).

ADAM, R.J.
— Dunrobin Castle, Sutherland: the historic home of the Sutherland family ... History and description of rooms by R.J.A. Official guide. 16pp. 5 illus. (4 on covers) incl. map. 14x22 Derby: Pilgrim Press [1957?]

BURKE, J.B. Visitation of Seats. 2.S. Vol.I, p 130. 1854.*

COUNTRY LIFE. L, 318 plan. 1921.

MALAN, A.H. Other famous homes. p.209. 1902.

MORRIS, F.O. Views of Seats. Vol.II, p.49. 1880.

DUNS CASTLE (Berwickshire).

JONES. Views of Seats. IV. 1829.

NEALE, J.P. Views of Seats. Vol.VI. 1823.

NEALE, J.P. Views of Seats in Scotland. 1830.

DUNTREATH CASTLE (Stirlingshire).

BURKE, J.B. Visitation of Seats. Vol.II. p.4. 1853.*

DUNTROON CASTLE (Argyllshire).

JONES. Views of Seats. IV. 1829.

NEALE, J.P. Views of Seats in Scotland. 1830.

DUNVEGAN CASTLE (Inverness-shire).

MALAN, A.H. Other famous homes. p.35. 1902.

DUPPLIN CASTLE (Perthshire).

MILLAR, A.H. Castles and mansions of Scotland. p.125. 1890.

DYSART HOUSE (Fife).

BURKE, J.B. Visitation of Seats. Vol.II, p.184. 1853.*

EARLSHALL (Fife).

COUNTRY LIFE. XVII, 942. 1905.

EASTERHILL HOUSE (Lanarkshire).

BURKE, J.B. Visitation of Seats. Vol.II, p.248. 1853.*

GLASGOW: country houses. 1870.

EASTFIELD HOUSE (Lanarkshire).

GLASGOW: country houses. 1870.

EASTPARK (East Lothian).

See SMEATON HOUSE.

EDINBARNET (Dunbartonshire).

GLASGOW: country houses. 1870.

EGLINTON CASTLE (Ayrshire).

ADAM, W. Vitruvius Scoticus. pl.123 [Temple]. 1810.

BURKE, J.B. Visitation of Seats. Vol.II, p.36. 1853.*

MILLAR, A.H. Castles and mansions of Ayrshire. 1885.

ELDERSLIE HOUSE (Renfrewshire).

GLASGOW: country houses. 1870.

ELIE HOUSE (Fife).

ADAM, W. Vitruvius Scoticus. pls.88, 89. 1810.

BURKE, J.B. Visitation of Seats. Vol.II, p.204. 1853.*

ELPHINSTONE HOUSE (East Lothian).

ADAM, W. Vitruvius Scoticus. pls.75, 76. 1810.

ENTERKINE (Ayrshire).

MILLAR, A.H. Castles and mansions of Ayrshire. 1885.

ERCHLESS CASTLE (Inverness-shire).

BURKE, J.B. Visitation of Seats. Vol.II, p.142. 1853.*

ETHIE HOUSE (Angus).

CUMMING, G. Forfarshire illustrated. p.72. 1843.

EVELICK CASTLE (Perthshire).

MILLAR, A.H. Castles and mansions of Scotland. p.180. 1890.

FAIRLIE HOUSE (Ayrshire).

MILLAR, A.H. Castles and mansions of Ayrshire. 1885.

FALKLAND PALACE (Fife).

COUNTRY LIFE. XXXI, 130 plan. 1912.

COUNTRY LIFE. CXXVI, 118, 178. 1959.

FARME (Lanarkshire).

GLASGOW: country houses. 1870.

FASKALLY (Perthshire).

BURKE, J.B. Visitation of Seats. 2.S. Vol.II, p.140. 1855.*

JONES. Views of Seats. IV. 1829.

NEALE, J.P. Views of Seats. 2.S. Vol.III. 1826.

NEALE, J.P. Views of Seats in Scotland. 1830.

FASQUE (Kincardineshire).

ADAM, W. Vitruvius Scoticus. pl.100. 1810.

COUNTRY LIFE. CLXVI, 386, 462. 1979.

FERNIE CASTLE (Fife).

[Sales] FERNIE CASTLE, 1965 September 14-16 [Contents].

FETTERNEAR HOUSE (Aberdeenshire).
BURKE, J.B. Visitation of Seats. Vol.II, p.27. 1853.*

FINGASK CASTLE (Perthshire).
JONES. Views of Seats. IV. 1829.
NEALE, J.P. Views of Seats. 2.S. Vol.IV. 1828.
NEALE, J.P. Views of Seats in Scotland. 1830.

FLEURS (Roxburghshire).
See FLOORS CASTLE.

FLOORS CASTLE (Roxburghshire).
ADAM, W. Vitruvius Scoticus. pls. 48, 49. 1810.
COUNTRY LIFE. CLXIII, **1298, 1370. 1978.**
JONES, Views of Seats. IV. 1829.
MORRIS, F.O. Views of Seats. Vol.I, p.35. 1880.
NEALE, J.P. Views of Seats. Vol.VI. 1823.
NEALE, J.P. Views of Seats in Scotland. 1830.
UNITED KINGDOM. Historic houses. 32. 1892.

FORGLEN HOUSE (Banffshire).
BURKE, J.B. Visitation of Seats. Vol.II, p.186. 1853.*

FOTHERINGHAM HOUSE (Angus).
CUMMING, G, Forfarshire illustrated. p.100. 1843.

FOULDEN (Berwickshire).
[Sales] BERWICK-UPON-TWEED, 1914, April 4 [Estate].

FOWLIS CASTLE (Perthshire).
MILLAR, A.H. Castles and mansions of Scotland. p.159. 1890.

FRIARS CARSE (Dumfriesshire).
COPPER PLATE MAGAZINE. I, pl.39. 1792-1802.

FULLARTON HOUSE (Ayrshire).
MILLAR, A.H. Castles and mansions of Ayrshire. 1885.

FYVIE CASTLE (Aberdeenshire).
STIRLING, A.M.W.
—Fyvie castle: its lairds and their times. Illus. incl. plates and genealog. table. 22x15 London: J. Murray, 1928.
BURKE, J.B. Visitation of Seats. 2.S. Vol.I, p.10. 1854.*
COUNTRY LIFE. XXXII, 388 plan. 1912.
COUNTRY LIFE CIV, 378. 1948.
COUNTRY LIFE. CLXXII, **1131. 1982.**
JONES. Views of Seats. IV. 1829.
NEALE, J.P. Views of Seats. 2.S. Vol.I. 1824.
NEALE, J.P. Views of Seats in Scotland. 1830.

GADGIRTH (Ayrshire).
BURKE, J.B. Visitation of Seats. Vol.II, p.224. 1853.*

GAIRBRAID (Lanarkshire).
GLASGOW: country houses. 1870.

GAIRLOCH (Ross and Cromarty).
BURKE, J.B. Visitation of Seats. 2.S. Vol.I, p.120. 1854.*

GALLOWAY HOUSE (Wigtownshire).
MORRIS, F.O. Views of Seats. Vol.IV, p.35. 1880.

GALLOWFLAT (Lanarkshire).
GLASGOW: country houses. 1870.

GARNKIRK HOUSE (Lanarkshire).
GLASGOW: country houses. 1870.

GARRALLAN HOUSE (Ayrshire).
MILLAR, A.H. Castles and mansions of Ayrshire. 1885.

GARSCADDEN HOUSE (Dunbartonshire).
GLASGOW: country houses. 1870.

GARSCUBE (Dunbartonshire).
BURKE, J.B. Visitation of Seats. 2.S. Vol.II, p.11. 1855.*
GLASGOW: country houses. 1870.

GARTFERRY HOUSE (Lanarkshire).
GLASGOW: country houses. 1870.

GARTH CASTLE (Perthshire).
MILLAR, A.H. Castles and mansions of Scotland. p.64. 1890.

GARTH HOUSE, Aberfeldy (Perthshire).
[Sales] GARTH, 1949, June 8, 9 [Contents].

GARTMORE HOUSE (Stirlingshire).
ADAM, W. Vitruvius Scoticus. pl.83. 1810.

GARTSHERRIE (Lanarkshire).
GLASGOW: country houses. 1870.

GASK HOUSE (Perthshire).
JONES. Views of Seats. IV. 1829.
NEALE, J.P. Views of Seats. Vol.VI. 1823.

GERMISTON (Lanarkshire).
GLASGOW: country houses. 1870.

GIFFEN HOUSE (Ayrshire).
MILLAR, A.H. Castles and mansions of Ayrshire. 1885.

GILMOREHILL (Lanarkshire).
GLASGOW: country houses. 1870.

GIRGENTI (Ayrshire).
MILLAR, A.H. Castles and mansions of Ayrshire. 1885.

GLAMIS CASTLE (Angus).
GLAMIS CASTLE.
—Glamis Castle: an illustrated survey [etc.] 32pp. Illus. (some col., some on covers) incl. maps (on inside covers). 14x22 Derby: Pilgrim press [1954?].
Another ed. 32pp. Illus. (2 col., 4 on covers) incl. map. 20x16 [Derby: Pilgrim Press] (1970.)

STIRTON, *Rev.* John.
—Glamis Castle: its origin and history, with a brief account of the early church of the parish. Illus. incl. plates (some col.). 25x19 Forfar: W. Shepherd, 1938.

STIRTON, *Rev.* John.
—Glamis Castle; its origin and history, with a brief account of the early church of the parish. Illus incl. plates (some col.). 25x19 Forfar: W. Shepherd, 1938.

BURKE, J.B. Visitation of Seats. 2.S. Vol.II, p.24. 1855.*
COPPER PLATE MAGAZINE. IV, pl.200. 1792-1802.
COUNTRY LIFE. II, 293. 1897.
COUNTRY LIFE. XX, 234. 1906.
COUNTRY LIFE. XXXVI, 196 plan. 1914.
COUNTRY LIFE. LIII, 114. 1923.
COUNTRY LIFE. CI, 860, 910 plan. 1947.
CUMMING, G. Forfarshire illustrated. p.101. 1843.
JONES. Views of Seats. IV. 1829.
KIP, J. Nouveau théâtre de la Grande Bretagne. III, pl.60. 1715.
MALAN, A.H. More famous homes. p.91. 1902.
MILLAR, A.H. Castles and mansions of Scotland. p.214. 1890.
MORRIS, F.O. Views of Seats. Vol.V. p.21. 1880.
NEALE, J.P. Views of Seats. Vol.VI. 1823.
NEALE, J.P. Views of Seats in Scotland. 1830.
WATTS, W. Seats of the Nobility. pl.42. 1779.

GLASSERTON HOUSE (Wigtownshire).
BURKE, J.B. Visitation of Seats. Vol.II, p.91. 1853.*
NEALE, J.P. Views of Seats. 2.S. Vol.V. 1829.

GLEN, The. Innerleithen (Peeblesshire).
AGNEW, C. Morland.
— Catalogue of the pictures forming the collection of Sir Charles Tennant, Bart., of 40, Grosvenor Square, and The Glen, Innerleithen. Plates. 29x25 [London?] privately printed, 1896.

GLENARBUCK HOUSE (Dunbartonshire).
GLASGOW: country houses. 1870.

GLENAPP HOUSE (Ayrshire).
MILLAR, A.H. Castles and mansions of Ayrshire. 1885.

GLENBARR ABBEY (Argyllshire).
BURKE, J.B. Visitation of Seats. Vol.II, p.189. 1853.*

GLENDOICK (Perthshire).
COUNTRY LIFE. CXLI, 708. 1967.

GLENERICHT HOUSE (Perthshire).
BURKE, J.B. Visitation of Seats. Vol.II, p.148. 1853.*

GOLFHILL HOUSE (Lanarkshire).
GLASGOW: country houses. 1870.

GORDON CASTLE (Morayshire).
MARCH, Amy Mary Gordon Lennox, *Countess of.*
—Catalogue of the pictures at Goodwood (and at Gordon Castle). 27x22 n.p. privately **printed**, 1877 [1879?].
JONES. Views of Seats. IV. 1829.
NEALE, J.P. Views of Seats. Vol.VI. 1823.
NEALE, J.P. Views of Seats in Scotland. 1830.
SPROULE, A. Lost houses of Britain. 142. 1982.

GORDON'S HOSPITAL, Aberdeen (Aberdeenshire).
ADAM, W. Vitruvius Scoticus. pls.107, 108. 1810.

GOSFORD HOUSE (East Lothian).
CAMPBELL, C. New Vitruvius Britannicus. I, pls.43-50. 1802.
COUNTRY LIFE. XXX, 342 plan. 1911.
COUNTRY LIFE. CL, 1048, 1200 [Photocopy]. 1971.

GOWRIE HOUSE, Perth (Perthshire).
SPROULE, A. Lost houses of Britain. 148. 1982.

GRAEMESHALL (Orkney).
GRAEME, Patrick Sutherland.
— Pateas amicis: the story of the house of Graemeshall in Orkney. 72pp. Illus. incl. plates, plans and genealog. table. 21x13 Kirkwall: Orkney Herald, 1936.

GRANDTULLY CASTLE (Perthshire).
JONES. Views of Seats. IV. 1829.
NEALE, J.P. Views of Seats. Vol.VI. 1823.
NEALE, J.P. Views of Seats in Scotland. 1830.

GRANGE, The. Edinburgh (Midlothian).
HANNAN, T. Famous Scottish houses. 165. 1928.

GRAY HOUSE (Angus).
ADAM, W. Vitruvius Scoticus. pl.98. 1810.
CUMMING, G. Forfarshire illustrated. p.3. 1843.

GREENBANK HOUSE (Renfrewshire).
GLASGOW: country houses. 1870.

GREENFIELD HOUSE (Lanarkshire).
GLASGOW: country houses. 1870.

GREY WALLS, Gullane (East Lothian).
COUNTRY LIFE. XXX, 374. 1911.

GUISACHAN (Inverness-shire).
BURKE, J.B. Visitation of Seats. Vol.II, p.124. 1853.

GUTHRIE CASTLE (Angus).
CUMMING, G. Forfarshire illustrated. p.86. 1843.

HADDO HOUSE (Aberdeenshire).
ADAM, W. Vitruvius Scoticus. pls.54-56. 1810.
COUNTRY LIFE. CXL, 378, 448. 1966.
MORRIS, F.O. Views of Seats. Vol.IV, p.49. 1880.
NICOLSON, N. Great Houses of Britain. p.226. 1965.

HAGGS CASTLE (Renfrewshire).
GLASGOW: country houses. 1870.

HAINING, The. (Selkirkshire).
JONES. Views of Seats. IV. 1829.
NEALE, J.P. Views of Seats. Vol.VI. 1823.
NEALE, J.P. Views of Seats in Scotland. 1830.

HALLSIDE (Lanarkshire).
GLASGOW: country houses. 1870.

HAMILTON HALL HOUSE (Lanarkshire).
ADAM, W. Vitruvius Scoticus. pl.121. 1810.

HAMILTON PALACE (Lanarkshire).
ADAM, W. Vitruvius Scoticus. pls. 6-11, 13, 160. 1810.
BURKE, J.B. Visitation of Seats. Vol.I, p.260. 1852.*
COUNTRY LIFE. XLV, 662 plan, 716. 1919.
COUNTRY LIFE. XLVI, 479 [Pictures], 514 [Pictures], 558 [Silver]. 1919.
MORRIS, F.O. Views of Seats. Vol.VI. p.9. 1880.
SPROULE, A. Lost houses of Britain .165. 1982.

[Sales] LONDON, 1882, June 17-July 17 [Pictures and works of art].
[Sales] LONDON, 1882, June 30-July 13 [Hamilton Palace Libraries: 1st part Beckford library].
[Sales] LONDON, 1919, November 4 [Silver].
[Sales] LONDON, 1919, November 5 [Furniture and works of art.].
[Sales] LONDON, 1919, November 6 [Portraits, pictures etc.].
[Sales] HAMILTON PALACE, 1919, November 12 [Remaining contents].

HANGINGSHAW, The. (Selkirkshire).
BURKE, J.B. Visitation of Seats. Vol.II, p.211. 1853.*

HARDEN (Roxburghshire).
ADAM, W. Vitruvius Scoticus. pl.142. 1810.
BURKE, J.B. Visitation of Seats. 2.S. Vol.I, p.125. 1854.*

HATTON HOUSE (Midlothian).
FINDLAY, John Ritchie.
— Hatton House. [Bibliogr. notes.] 54pp. Illus. incl. plates and plan. 28x22 Edinburgh: privately printed, 1875.
COUNTRY LIFE. XXX, 408 plan. 1911.
HANNAN, T. Famous Scottish houses. 97. 1928.

HAWKHILL, Edinburgh (Midlothian).
ADAM, W. Vitruvius Scoticus. pl.123. 1810.

HAWTHORNDEN (Midlothian).
BURKE, J.B. Visitation of Seats. Vol.I, p.112. 1852.*
HANNAN, T. Famous Scottish houses. 101. 1928.

HENDERSYDE PARK (Roxburghshire).
HENDERSYDE PARK.
— A catalogue of pictures, statues, busts, antique columns, bronzes, fragments of antique buildings, tables of Florentine and Roman mosaic, scagliola and inlaid wood; Indian, Neapolitan and other china, with notices of books in the various apartments, at Hendersyde Park [etc.]. Tinted lithogr. plate. 18x12 (Kelso) privately printed, 1859.

HERIOT'S HOSPITAL, Edinburgh (Midlothian).
ADAM,W. Vitruvius Scoticus. pls. 105, 106. 1810.
CAMPBELL, C. Vitruvius Britannicus. IVth. pls. 53,54. 1739.
COUNTRY LIFE. CLVII, 554, 634. 1975.
KIP, J. Nouveau théâtre de la Grande Bretagne. III, pl.56. 1715.

HILLHOUSE (Ayrshire).
MILLAR, A.H. Castles and mansions of Ayrshire. 1885.

HILL OF TARVIT (Fife).
COUNTRY LIFE. XXXII, 926 plan. 1912.
COUNTRY LIFE. CLXXII, 442, 514. 1982.

HOLMS (Ayrshire).
MILLAR, A.H. Castles and mansions of Ayrshire. 1885.

HOPETOUN HOUSE (West Lothian).
HOPETOUN HOUSE.
— Hopetoun House, West Lothian: an illustrated survey [etc.].
32pp. Illus. (some col., some on covers) incl. maps (on inside covers). 14x22 Derby: Pilgrim Press [1955?].
Rev. ed. 34pp. Illus. (some col., some on covers) incl. plan and maps [1963?]
ADAM, W. Vitruvius Scoticus. pls.14-21. 1810.
BURKE, J.B. Visitation of Seats. Vol.II, p.156. 1853.*
CAMPBELL, C. Vitruvius Britannicus. II, pls.75-77. 1717.
COUNTRY LIFE. CXIX, 16, 62 plan. 1956.
HANNAN, T. Famous Scottish houses. 105. 1928.

HOSPITALFIELD (Angus).
BURKE, J.B. Visitation of Seats. Vol.I, p.248. 1852.*
MILLAR, A.H. Castles and mansions of Scotland. p.203. 1890.

HOUSEHILL (Lanarkshire).
GLASGOW: country houses. 1870.

HUNTERSTON HOUSE (Ayrshire).
MILLAR, A.H. Castles and mansions of Ayrshire. 1885.

IBROXHILL (Lanarkshire).
GLASGOW: country houses. 1870.

INCH, The. Liberton (Midlothian).
HANNAN, T. Famous Scottish houses. 169. 1928.

INCHMARLO HOUSE (Kincardineshire).
BURKE, J.B. Visitation of Seats. 2.S. Vol.I, p.85. 1854.*

INCHYRA HOUSE (Perthshire).
COUNTRY LIFE. CXLV, 342. 1969.

INCHRYE ABBEY (Fife).
JONES. Views of Seats. IV. 1829.
NEALE, J.P. Views of Seats. Vol.VI. 1823.
NEALE, J.P. Views of Seats in Scotland. 1830.

INGLISMALDIE CASTLE (Kincardineshire).
[Sales] INGLISMALDIE CASTLE, 1959, June 8-12 [Contents].

INNES HOUSE (Morayshire).
FIFE, James Duff, *Earl of* .
—Catalogue of the portraits and pictures in the different houses belonging to the Earl of Fife. (Duff House, Fife House, Rothemay House and Innes House) . 52pp. 26x21 n.p., 1798.
COUNTRY LIFE. CLX, 1286. 1976.

INVERARAY CASTLE (Argyllshire).
INVERARAY CASTLE.
—Inveraray Castle: an illustrated survey [etc.]. 32pp. Illus. (some col., some on covers) incl. maps (on inside covers). 14x21 Derby: Pilgrim Press [c.1950].
LINDSAY, Ian G.
—Inveraray and the Dukes of Argyll. [By] I.G.L., and M. Cosh. [Bibliogr. notes.] xx, 488pp. Illus. incl. 50 (1 folding) plates, sections, elevations, plans, maps, diagr. facsimile and genealog. tables. 30x21 Edinburgh: E.U.P. 1973.
ADAM, W. Vitruvius Scoticus. pls. 71-74. 1810.
COUNTRY LIFE. LXII, 156. 1927.
COUNTRY LIFE. CLVII, 1485 [Linnell furniture]. 1975.
COUNTRY LIFE. CLX, 962 [Plight of I.C.] 1976.
COUNTRY LIFE. CLXIII, 1619, 1734. 1978.
JONES. Views of seats. IV. 1829.
KIP, J. Nouveau théâtre de la Grande Bretagne. III, pl.57. 1715
KROLL, A. Historic houses. 76. 1969.
MALAN, A.H. More famous homes. p. 307. 1902.
MORRIS, F.O. Views of Seats. Vol.I, p.75. 1880.
NEALE, J.P. Views of Seats. Vol.VI. 1823.
NEALE, J.P. Views of Seats in Scotland. 1830.

INVERGOWRIE HOUSE (Angus).
CUMMING, G. Forfarshire illustrated. p.1. 1843.
MILLAR, A.H. Castles and mansions of Scotland. p.329. 1890.

JORDANHILL (Renfrewshire).
BURKE, J.B. Visitation of Seats. 2.S. Vol.I, p.107. 1854.*
BURKE, J.B. Visitation of Seats. 2.S. Vol.II, p.13. 1855.*
GLASGOW: country houses. 1870.

KEIR (Perthshire).
BURKE, J.B. Visitation of Seats. 2.S. Vol.II, p.124. 1855.*
COUNTRY LIFE. CLVII. 326, 390, 506. 1975.

KEITH HALL (Aberdeenshire).
ADAM, W. Vitruvius Scoticus. pls.143-5. 1810.

KELBURNE CASTLE (Ayrshire).
BURKE, J.B. Visitation of Seats. Vol.II, p.164. 1853.*
COUNTRY LIFE. XL, 182. 1916.
MILLAR, A.H. Castles and mansions of Ayrshire. 1885.

KELLIE CASTLE (Fife).

EDINBURGH: National Trust for Scotland for Places of Historic interest or Natural Beauty.
— LORIMER, H. Kellie Castle, near Pittenweem, Fife [etc.]. 32pp. Illus. incl. plan (on cover). 22x14 (Edinburgh, 1971.)
COUNTRY LIFE. XX, 126. 1906.
COUNTRY LIFE. CXXXVI, 446 plan, 514. 1964.

KELVINBANK HOUSE (Lanarkshire).

GLASGOW: country houses. 1870.

KELVINGROVE HOUSE (Lanarkshire).

GLASGOW: country houses. 1870.

KELVINSIDE (Lanarkshire).

GLASGOW: country houses. 1870.

KENMORE CASTLE (Perthshire).

ADAM, W. Vitruvius Scoticus. pls.52, 53. 1810.

KENMOUNT (Dumfriesshire).

See KINMOUNT.

KENMURE (Lanarkshire).

GLASGOW: country houses. 1870.

KIER (Perthshire).

See KEIR.

KILBIRNIE CASTLE (Ayrshire).

BURKE, J.B. Visitation of Seats. 2.S. Vol.II, p.22. 1855.*

KILGRASTON (Perthshire).

BURKE, J.B. Visitation of Seats. Vol.I, p.148. 1852.*
JONES. Views of Seats. IV. 1829.
NEALE, J.P. Views of Seats. 2.S. Vol.IV. 1828.
NEALE, J.P. Views of Seats in Scotland. 1830.

KILKERRAN HOUSE (Ayrshire).

BURKE, J.B. Visitation of Seats. 2.S. Vol.II, p.53. 1855.*
COUNTRY LIFE. CLVII, 1114, 1178. 1975.
MILLAR, A.H. Castles and mansions of Ayrshire. 1885.

KILLERMONT HOUSE (Dunbartonshire).

BURKE, J.B. Visitation of Seats. 2.S. Vol.II, p.12. 1855.*
GLASGOW: country houses. 1870.

KILLIN LODGE (Inverness-shire).

SANDBY, P. Select Views. II, pl.19 (Scotland). 1782.

KILLOCHAN CASTLE (Ayrshire).

LINDSAY, Maurice.
— Killochan Castle, Ayrshire: an illustrated survey ... By M.L., and D. Somervell. 16pp. Illus. (some on covers) incl. map. 14x20 (Derby: Pilgrim Press) [1960.]
MILLAR, A.H. Castles and mansions of Ayrshire. 1885.

KILMARDINNY (Dunbartonshire).

GLASGOW: country houses. 1870.

KINCARDINE CASTLE (Perthshire).

JONES. Views of Seats. IV. 1829.
NEALE, J.P. Views of Seats. Vol.VI. 1823.
NEALE, J.P. Views of Seats in Scotland. 1830.

KINDROGAN (Perthshire).

BURKE, J.B. Visitation of Seats. Vol.II, p.101. 1853.*
[Sales] KINDROGAN HOUSE, 1961, August 16, 17 [Furniture & Furnishings].

KINFAUNS CASTLE (Perthshire).

GRANT, Francis.
— Catalogue of the pictures, ancient and modern, in Kinfauns Castle; chiefly collected by Francis, Lord Gray. [By F.G., decorations by D. Morison, junr.] Illus. incl. plates (1 mezzotint), and hand-col. borders and title-page. 38x27 Kinfauns: at the Kinfauns Press, 1833.
MORISON, D., *jun.*
— Catalogue of the Gray Library, Kinfauns Castle (Perthshire). [Compiled by] D.M. 500pp. Illus. incl. ornamental borders printed in red, chiefly from Albrecht Dürer's designs for the prayer book of the Emperor Maximilian. 37x27 Kinfauns: privately printed at the Kinfauns Press, 1828. MS. dedication from Lord Gray to Lady Wedderburn. Wanting some pp.?
BURKE, J.B. Visitation of Seats. 2.S. Vol.I, p.156. 1854.*
JONES. Views of Seats. IV. 1829.
MILLAR, A.H. Castles and mansions of Scotland. p.108. 1890.
NEALE, J.P. Views of Seats. 2.S. Vol.IV. 1828.
NEALE, J.P. Views of Seats in Scotland. 1830.

KINGSMUIR (Fife).

BURKE, J.B. Visitation of Seats. 2.S. Vol.I, p.150. 1854.*

KINLOCHMOIDART (Inverness-shire).

BURKE, J.B. Visitation of Seats. Vol.I, p.71. 1852.*

KINMOUNT (Dumfriesshire).

JONES. Views of Seats. IV. 1829.
NEALE, J.P. Views of Seats. Vol.VI. 1823.
NEALE, J.P. Views of Seats in Scotland. 1830.

KINNAIRD CASTLE (Angus).
BURKE, J.B. Visitation of Seats. 2.S. Vol.I, p.93. 1854.*
CUMMING, G. Forfarshire illustrated. p.86. 1843.
MILLAR, A.H. Castles and mansions of Scotland. p.245. 1890.

KINNIEL HOUSE (West Lothian).
BURKE, J.B. Visitation of Seats. 2.S. Vol.II, p.206. 1855.*

KINNORDY (Angus).
CUMMING, G. Forfarshire illustrated. p.116. 1843.
MILLAR, A.H. Castles and mansions of Scotland p.301. 1890.

KINROSS HOUSE (Kinross-shire).
ADAM, W. Vitruvius Scoticus. pls.61, 62. 1810.
BURKE, J.B. Visitation of Seats. Vol.II, p.212. 1853.*
COUNTRY LIFE. XXXII, 54, 90. 1912.
COUNTRY LIFE. CIX, 472. 1951.
COUNTRY LIFE. CXXXVII, 666, 726. 1965.
HANNAN, T. Famous Scottish houses. 109. 1928.
SUMMERSON, J. The Country Seat. 64. 1970.

KIRKDALE HOUSE (Kirkcudbrightshire).
BURKE, J.B. Visitation of Seats. 2.S. Vol.I, p.182. 1854.*

KIRKHILL (Ayrshire).
MILLAR, A.H. Castles and mansions of Ayrshire. 1885.

KIRKWALL CASTLE (Orkney).
BURKE, J.B. Visitation of Seats. 2.S. Vol.II, p.179. 1855.*

KNOCK CASTLE (Ayrshire).
MILLAR, A.H. Castles and mansions of Ayrshire. 1885.

KNOCKDOLIAN CASTLE (Ayrshire).
MILLAR, A.H. Castles and mansions of Ayrshire. 1885.

LAINSHAW (Ayrshire).
BURKE, J.B. Visitation of Seats. 2.S. Vol.II, p.61. 1855.*
MILLAR, A.H. Castles and mansions of Ayrshire. 1885.

LAMB'S HOUSE, Leith (Midlothian).
COUNTRY LIFE. CXXXV, 860. 1964.

LAMINGTON HOUSE (Lanarkshire).
HANNAN, T. Famous Scottish houses. 113. 1928.

LANFINE HOUSE (Ayrshire).
MILLAR, A.H. Castles and mansions of Ayrshire. 1885.

LANGSIDE (Renfrewshire).
GLASGOW: country houses. 1870.

LANGWELL (Caithness).
GARRARD, James.
— A catalogue of gold and silver plate, the property of His Grace the Duke of Portland. With ... description and date of each piece. (Report on the plate at Welbeck by W. Cripps; Candlesticks at Langwell.) viii, 144pp. Plates (some hand-col.) 29x20 London: privately printed at the Chiswick Press, 1893.
GOULDING, Richard William.
— Catalogue of the pictures belonging to His Grace the Duke of Portland, K.G. At Welbeck Abbey, 17 Hill Street, London and Langwell House. Compiled by R.W.G., and finally revised ... by C.K. Adams. [Bibliogr.] 30x22 Cambridge: C.U.P., 1936.

LARGO HOUSE (Fife).
BURKE, J.B. Visitation of Seats. Vol.II, p.204. 1853.*

LAURISTON CASTLE (Midlothian).
FAIRLEY, John A.
— Lauriston Castle: the estate and its owners. [Bibliogr. notes.] 228pp. Plates (2 folding), incl. map and genealog. table. 24x16 Edinburgh; London: Oliver & Boyd, 1925.
ROWAN, A.M.
— Lauriston Castle. 12pp. Col. illus. and plan. 27x21 (Dunstable: A.B.C., 1974.)

LAWERS HOUSE (Perthshire).
ADAM, W. Vitruvius Scoticus. pls.158, 159. 1810.
COUNTRY LIFE. LVIII, 550 plan. 1925.
JONES. Views of Seats. IV. 1829.
NEALE, J.P. Views of Seats. Vol.VI. 1823.
NEALE, J.P. Views of Seats in Scotland. 1830.

LAWS, The. (Angus).
CUMMING, G. Forfarshire illustrated. p.44. 1843.

LEE, The. (Lanarkshire).
BURKE, J.B. Visitation of Seats. Vol.II, p.78. 1853.*
JONES. Views of Seats. IV. 1829.
NEALE, J.P. Views of Seats. 2.S. Vol.IV. 1828.
NEALE, J.P. Views of Seats in Scotland. 1830.

LEITH HALL (Aberdeenshire).
EDINBURGH: National Trust for Scotland for Places of Historic Interest or Natural Beauty.
— SCOTT, S. Leith Hall [etc.]. 52pp. Illus. (1 col. on cover) incl. plan (on inside cover). 21x14 (Edinburgh, 1973.)

LENNOX CASTLE (Stirlingshire).
[Sales] LENNOX CASTLE, 1922, November 20-22 [Antique furniture & plenishing].

LENNOXLOVE (East Lothian).
HADDINGTON.
— The history and treasures of Lennoxlove House (Haddington). 16pp. Illus. (1 col., some on covers, 1 on title-page) incl. map. 23x18 (London: Pitkin) [1960.]
One of the series: PRIDE of Britain.
COUNTRY LIFE. XXXV, 522 plan. 1914.
COUNTRY LIFE. CVII, 230. 1950.
HANNAN, T. Famous Scottish houses. 117. 1928.

LESLIE HOUSE (Fife).
ADAM, W. Vitruvius Scoticus. pls.66-68. 1810.
HANNAN, T. Famous Scottish houses. 121. 1928.
[Sales] EDINBURGH, 1919, September 17 [Rothes estate, incl. Leslie House].

LESSUDDEN HOUSE (Roxburghshire).
COUNTRY LIFE. CXXV, 1012. 1959.

LETHAM GRANGE (Angus).
CUMMING, G. Forfarshire illustrated. p.71. 1843.

LETHEN HOUSE (Nairnshire).
BURKE, J.B. Visitation of Seats. 2.S. Vol.II, p.136. 1855.*

LEUCHIE HOUSE (East Lothian).
COUNTRY LIFE. CXXX, 826 plan. 1961.

LEWS CASTLE (Ross and Cromarty).
[Sales] LEWS CASTLE, Stornoway, 1926, April 20, 21 [Furniture etc.]. (K.F. & R.)

LICKLEYHEAD CASTLE (Aberdeenshire).
COUNTRY LIFE. LXXXII, 444. 1937.

LINDERTIS (Angus).
CUMMING, G. Forfarshire illustrated. p.114. 1843.
JONES. Views of Seats. IV. 1829.
MILLAR, A.H. Castles and mansions of Scotland. p.429. 1890.
NEALE, J.P. Views of Seats. Vol.VI. 1823.
NEALE, J.P. Views of Seats in Scotland. 1830.

LINLITHGOW PALACE (West Lothian).
HEARNE, T. Antiquities. I, pl.38. 1807.

LINPLUM (East Lothian).
HAY, Robert.
— Catalogue of the collection of Egyptian antiquities belonging to the late R. Hay, Esq., of Linplum. Drawn up under the superintendence of J. Bonomi. 128pp. 17x12 London: privately printed, 1869.

LINTHOUSE (Lanarkshire).
GLASGOW: country houses. 1870.

LOCHNAW CASTLE (Wigtownshire).
BURKE, J.B. Visitation of Seats. Vol.II, p.165. 1853.*

LOGAN HOUSE (Wigtownshire).
COUNTRY LIFE. CXVI, 426 plan. 1954.

LOGIE HOUSE (Angus).
MILLAR, A.H. Castles and mansions of Scotland. p.273. 1890.

LONG CALDERWOOD (Lanarkshire).
GLASGOW: country houses. 1870.

LONGFORMACUS HOUSE (Berwickshire).
ADAM, W. Vitruvius Scoticus. pl.99. 1810.

LOUDOUN CASTLE (Ayrshire).
CAMPBELL, C. New Vitruvius Britannicus. II, pls.51-6. 1808.
MILLAR, A.H. Castles and mansions of Ayrshire. 1885.

LOWMAY (Aberdeenshire).
ADAM, W. Vitruvius Scoticus. pl.95. 1810.

LUDE (Perthshire).
BURKE, J.B. Visitation of Seats. 2.S. Vol.I, p.74. 1854.*

LYNN, The. (Renfrewshire).
GLASGOW: country houses. 1870.

MAINS (Dunbartonshire).
GLASGOW: country houses. 1870.

MANDERSTON (Berwickshire).
COUNTRY LIFE. XLI, 60 plan. 1917.
COUNTRY LIFE. CLXV, 390, 466, 542. 1979.

MARCHMONT (Berwickshire).
COUNTRY LIFE. LVII, 310 plan, 354 plan. 1925.

MAR LODGE (Aberdeenshire).
COUNTRY LIFE. LXXXII, 64. 1937.

MARR LODGE (Banffshire).
SANDBY, P. Select Views. II, pl.14 (Scotland). 1782.

MAULDSLIE CASTLE (Lanarkshire).
BURKE, J.B. Visitation of Seats. 2.S. Vol.II, p.49. 1855.*

MAVISBANK HOUSE (Midlothian).
See NEW SAUGHTON HALL.

MAXWELTON HOUSE (Dumfriesshire).
[Sales] MAXWELTON, 1967, October 3-5 [Antique furniture and effects etc.].

MEADOW PARK HOUSE (Lanarkshire).
GLASGOW: country houses. 1870.

MEGGERNIE CASTLE (Perthshire).
JONES. Views of Seats. IV. 1829.
NEALE, J.P. Views of Seats. Vol.VI. 1823.
NEALE, J.P. Views of Seats in Scotland. 1830.

MELLERSTAIN (Berwickshire).
LAVER, James.
— Mellerstain: home of the Earl and Countess of Haddington.
16pp. Illus. (1 col. on cover) incl. 2 maps (on covers). 14x21
Mellerstain: Estate Office [1952].
2 ed. Mellerstain. 20pp. Illus. (2 on cover.) 20x13 (Mellerstain: by Lord Haddington; Westerham: by Westerham Press, 1954.)
BOLTON, A.T. Architecture of R. & J. Adam. II, 252 plan. 1922.
COUNTRY LIFE. XXXVIII, 648 plan. 1915.
COUNTRY LIFE. CXXIV, 416 plan, 476. 1958.
NICOLSON, N. Great houses of Britain. p.252. 1965.

MELSETTER HOUSE (Hoy, Orkney).
COUNTRY LIFE. CLXX, 566. 1981.

MELVILLE CASTLE (Midlothian).
ANGUS, W. Seats of the Nobility. pl.29. 1787.

MELVILLE HOUSE (Fife).
CAMPBELL, C. Vitruvius Britannicus. II, pl.50. 1717.
COUNTRY LIFE. XXX, 1006. 1911.

MERTOUN (Berwickshire).
COUNTRY LIFE. CXXXIX, 1392, 1470. 1966.
[Sales] EDINBURGH, 1912, March 28-30 [Furniture, china, jewels etc.].

METHVEN CASTLE (Perthshire).
BURKE, J.B. Visitation of Seats. Vol.I, p.111. 1852.*

MEY, Castle of. (Caithness).
See BARROGILL CASTLE.

MIDDLETON (Midlothian).
COPPER PLATE MAGAZINE. II, pl.59. 1792-1802.

MIDMAR CASTLE (Aberdeenshire).
COUNTRY LIFE. XXXII, 710 plan. 1912.
COUNTRY LIFE. XCVII, 24 plan. 1945.

MILHEUGH (Lanarkshire).
GLASGOW: country houses. 1870.

MILLEARNE (Perthshire).
COUNTRY LIFE. CLI, 452, 498. 1972.

MILLIKEN HOUSE (Renfrewshire).
BURKE, J.B. Visitation of Seats. Vol.II, p.20. 1853.*
GLASGOW: country houses. 1870.

MILTON HOUSE, Edinburgh (Midlothian).
ADAM, W. Vitruvius Scoticus. pl.45. 1810.

MILTON LOCKHART (Lanarkshire).
BURKE, J.B. Visitation of Seats. Vol.II, p.212. 1853.*

MINTO HOUSE (Roxburghshire).
HANNAN, T. Famous Scottish houses. 125. 1928.

MONIACK CASTLE (Inverness-shire).
BURKE, J.B. Visitation of Seats. Vol.II, p.16. 1853.*

MONKTON HALL (Ayrshire).
[Sales] MONKTON HALL, 1970, July 1 [Residue of contents].

MONTGOMERIE CASTLE [Coilsfield] (Ayrshire).
MILLAR, A.H. Castles and mansions of Ayrshire. 1885.

MONYMUSK HOUSE (Aberdeenshire).
BURKE, J.B. Visitation of Seats. 2.S. Vol.I, p.148. 1854.*
COUNTRY LIFE. CLII, 950 plan, 1046. 1972.

MONZIE CASTLE (Perthshire).
BURKE, J.B. Visitation of Seats. 2.S. Vol.II, p.123. 1855.*
JONES. Views of Seats. IV. 1829.
NEALE, J.P. Views of Seats. Vol.VI. 1823.
NEALE, J.P. Views of Seats in Scotland. 1830.

MOORE PARK (Lanarkshire).
GLASGOW: country houses. 1870.

MOUNT ALEXANDER (Perthshire).
JONES. Views of Seats. IV. 1829.
NEALE, J.P. Views of Seats. Vol.VI. 1823.
NEALE, J.P. Views of Seats in Scotland. 1830.

MELVILLE CASTLE, Midlothian. From: ANGUS (W.). *The seats of the nobility and gentry in Great Britain and Wales* [etc.] (London) 1787(-1815).

TAYMOUTH CASTLE, Perthshire. From: NEALE (J.P.). *Views of seats of noblemen and gentlemen of Great Britain and Ireland*, vol. VI, London, 1823.

MOUNTBLOW (Dunbartonshire).
GLASGOW: country houses. 1870.

MOUNT CHARLES (Ayrshire).
MILLAR, A.H. Castles and mansions of Ayrshire. 1885.

MOUNT MELVILLE (Fife).
BURKE, J.B. Visitation of Seats. Vol.II, p.236. 1853.*
JONES. Views of Seats. IV. 1829.
NEALE, J.P. Views of Seats. 2.S. Vol.II. 1825.
NEALE, J.P. Views of Seats in Scotland. 1830.

MOUNT STUART (Bute).
ADAM, W. Vitruvius Scoticus. pl.31. 1810.
JONES. Views of Seats. IV. 1829.
NEALE, J.P. Views of Seats in Scotland. 1830.
WATTS, W. Seats of the Nobility. pl.73. 1779.

MOUNT VERNON (Lanarkshire).
GLASGOW: country houses. 1870.

MUCHALLS CASTLE (Kincardineshire).
COUNTRY LIFE. LXXXII, 630. 1937.
COUNTRY LIFE. CLII, 330, 394. 1972.

MURTHLY CASTLE (Perthshire).
BURKE, J.B. Visitation of Seats. 2.S. Vol.II, p.28. 1855.*
JONES. Views of Seats. IV. 1829.
NEALE, J.P. Views of Seats. Vol.VI. 1823.
NEALE, J.P. Views of Seats in Scotland. 1830.

NEWARK CASTLE (Ayrshire).
MILLAR, A.H. Castles and mansions of Ayrshire. 1885.

NEWBAITH (East Lothian).
See NEWBYTH.

NEWBATTLE ABBEY (Midlothian).
COPPER PLATE MAGAZINE. III, pl.118. 1792-1802.

NEWBYTH (East Lothian).
ADAM, W. Vitruvius Scoticus. pls. 137, 138. 1810.
HANNAN, T. Famous Scottish houses. 129. 1928.

NEWFIELD (Ayrshire).
MILLAR, A.H. Castles and mansions of Ayrshire. 1885.

NEW HAILES (Midlothian).
BURKE, J.B. Visitation of Seats. 2.S. Vol.II, p.210. 1855.*
COUNTRY LIFE. XLII, 228. 1917.
HANNAN, T. Famous Scottish houses. 133. 1928.

NEWHALL (Midlothian).
BURKE, J.B. Visitation of Seats. Vol.II, p.53. 1853.*

NEWHALL GIFFORD (East Lothian).
ADAM, W. Vitruvius Scoticus. pls.73, 74. 1810.

NEWLISTON (West Lothian).
ADAM, W. Vitruvius Scoticus. pls.32-36. 1810.
BOLTON, A.T. Architecture of R. & J. Adam. II, 278 plan. 1922.
BURKE, J.B. Visitation of Seats. Vol.II, p.119. 1853.*
COUNTRY LIFE. XXXIX, 270. 1916.

NEW SAUGHTON HALL (Midlothian).
ADAM, W. Vitruvius Scoticus. pls.46, 47. 1810.

NEWTON HOUSE (Lanarkshire).
BURKE, J.B. Visitation of Seats. 2.S. Vol.II, p.40. 1855.*
GLASGOW: country houses. 1870.

NEWTON HOUSE (Morayshire).
BURKE, J.B. Visitation of Seats. 2.S. Vol.II, p.155. 1855.

NIDDRIE MARISCHAL HOUSE, Edinburgh (Midlothian).
ADAM, W. Vitruvius Scoticus. pls.114, 115. 1810.
HANNAN, T. Famous Scottish houses. 137. 1928.

NINEWELLS (Berwickshire).
BURKE, J.B. Visitation of Seats. Vol.II, p.21. 1853.*

NOLTLAND CASTLE (Orkney).
BURKE, J.B. Visitation of Seats. Vol.II, p.135. 1853.*

NORTHWOODSIDE HOUSE (Lanarkshire).
GLASGOW: country houses. 1870.

OCHTERTYRE (Perthshire).
JONES. Views of Seats. IV. 1829.
NEALE, J.P. Views of Seats. 2.S. Vol.IV. 1828.
NEALE, J.P. Views of Seats in Scotland. 1830.

OLD PLACE OF MOCHRUM (Wigtownshire).
COUNTRY LIFE. XXXII, 162 plan. 1912.

ORBISTON HOUSE (Lanarkshire).
GLASGOW: country houses. 1870.

OXENFOORD CASTLE (Midlothian).
ANGUS, W. Seats of the Nobility. pl.14.1787.
COUNTRY LIFE. CLVI, 430 plan. 1974.
HANNAN, T. Famous Scottish houses. 141. 1928.

PANMURE HOUSE (Angus).
ADAM,W. Vitruvius Scoticus. pls. 129-131. 1810.
CUMMING, G. Forfarshire illustrated. p.49. 1843.
MILLAR, A.H. Castles and mansions of Scotland. p.287. 1890.
SPROULE, A. Lost houses of Britain. 115. 1982.

PARK HOUSE (Banffshire).
BURKE, J.B. Visitation of Seats. Vol.II, p.243. 1853.*

PARTON HOUSE (Kirkcudbrightshire).
BURKE, J.B. Visitation of Seats. 2.S. Vol.I, p.237. 1854.*

PAXTON HOUSE (Berwickshire).
COUNTRY LIFE. LVII, 446. 1925.
COUNTRY LIFE. CXLII, 364, 422 plan, 470. 1967.

PENICUIK HOUSE (Midlothian).
COUNTRY LIFE. CXLIV, 383, 448. 1968.
JONES. Views of Seats. IV. 1829.
NEALE, J.P. Views of Seats. 2.S. Vol.II. 1825.
NEALE, J.P. Views of Seats in Scotland. 1830.

PENKILL CASTLE (Ayrshire).
MILLAR, A.H. Castles and mansions of Ayrshire. 1885.

PERCETON (Ayrshire).
MILLAR, A.H. Castles and mansions of Ayrshire. 1885.

PETERSHILL (Lanarkshire).
GLASGOW: country houses. 1870.

PHILIPHAUGH (Selkirkshire).
BURKE, J.B. Visitation of Seats. Vol.I, p.20. 1852.*
MORRIS, F.O. Views of Seats. Vol.III, p.65. 1880.

PINKIE HOUSE (Midlothian).
COUNTRY LIFE. XXX, 240. 1911.
HANNAN, T. Famous Scottish houses. 145. 1928.

PINMORE HOUSE (Ayrshire).
MILLAR, A.H. Castles and mansions of Ayrshire. 1885.

PITCAPLE CASTLE (Aberdeenshire).
BURKE, J.B. Visitation of Seats. Vol.II, p.103. 1853.*

PITFOUR CASTLE (Perthshire).
BURKE, J.B. Visitation of Seats. Vol.II, p.34. 1853.*
[Sales] PITFOUR CASTLE, 1962, June 5, 6 [Antique & modern furniture etc.].

PITMUIES (Angus).
BURKE, J.B. Visitation of Seats. Vol.II, p.159. 1853.*

PITREAVIE CASTLE (Fife).
HANNAN, T. Famous Scottish houses. 149. 1928.

PLANTATION (Lanarkshire).
GLASGOW: country houses. 1870.

POLLOK HOUSE (Renfrewshire).
POLLOK HOUSE.
—Pollok House and gardens. 24pp. Illus. (on cover) and plates.
21x14 [Glasgow? privately printed, c. 1965]. Title on cover.
BURKE, J.B. Visitation of Seats. 2.S. Vol.I, p.94. 1854.*
BURKE, J.B. Visitation of Seats. 2.S. Vol.II, p.62. 1855.*
COUNTRY LIFE. XXXIII, 126 plan. 1913.
GLASGOW: country houses. 1870.

POLTALLOCH (Argyllshire).
ROBINSON, *Sir* John Charles.
— Descriptive catalogue of the drawings by the old masters, forming the collection of John Malcolm of Poltalloch. Illus. (on title-page.) 25x16 London: Chiswick Press, privately printed, 1879.

POSSIL (Lanarkshire).
GLASGOW: country houses. 1870.

PRESTONFIELD, Edinburgh (Midlothian).
HANNAN, T. Famous Scottish houses. 153. 1928.

PRESTON HALL (Midlothian).
COUNTRY LIFE. CXXX, 394, 454. 1961.
MITCHELL, R. Buildings in England & Scotland. pls.9-13 plan. 1801.

PRESTONHALL HOUSE (Fife).
ADAM, W. Vitruvius Scoticus. pls.107, 108. 1810.

RAEMOIR (Kincardineshire).
BURKE, J.B. Visitation of Seats. Vol.II, p.40. 1853.*

RALSTON (Renfrewshire).
GLASGOW: country houses. 1870.

RAMMERSCALES (Dumfriesshire).
BURKE, J.B. Visitation of Seats. Vol.I, p.31. 1852.*
COUNTRY LIFE. CXXVII, 1174. 1960.

RAMORNIE (Fife).
[Sales] RAMORNIE, 1960, June 14-16 [Furniture and furnishings].

ROSEBANK (Lanarkshire).
GLASGOW: country houses. 1870.

ROSEHALL (Sutherland).
ADAM, W. Vitruvius Scoticus. pls.132-34. 1810.

ROSEHAUGH (Ross and Cromarty).
[Sales] ROSEHAUGH, 1954, August 23 and following days [Contents].

ROSEMOUNT (Ayrshire).
MILLER, A.H. Castles and mansions of Ayrshire. 1885.

ROSENEATH CASTLE (Dunbartonshire).
CAMPBELL, C. New Vitruvius Britannicus. II, pls.15, 16. 1808.
JONES. Views of Seats. IV. 1829.
NEALE, J.P. Views of Seats. Vol.VI. 1823.
NEALE, J.P. Views of Seats in Scotland. 1830.
[Sales] ROSENEATH CASTLE, 1940, October 7-11 [Furnishings, pictures].

ROSSDHU (Dunbartonshire).
BURKE, J.B. Visitation of Seats. Vol.II, p.58. 1853.*

ROSSIE CASTLE (Angus).
CUMMING, G. Forfarshire illustrated. p.77. 1843.
JONES. Views of Seats. IV. 1829.
MORRIS, F.O. Views of Seats. Vol.V, p.73. 1880.
NEALE, J.P. Views of Seats. Vol.VI. 1823.
NEALE, J.P. Views of Seats in Scotland. 1830.

ROSSIE PRIORY (Perthshire).
JONES. Views of Seats. IV. 1829.

MILLER, A.H. Castles and mansions of Scotland. p.7. 1890.
NEALE, J.P. Views of Seats. 2.S. Vol.II. 1825.
NEALE, J.P. Views of Seats in Scotland. 1830.

ROSSLYN CASTLE (Midlothian).
BURKE, J.B. Visitation of Seats. 2.S. Vol.I, p.169. 1854.*

ROSS PRIORY (Dunbartonshire).
JONES. Views of Seats. IV. 1829.
NEALE, J.P. Views of Seats. Vol.VI. 1823.
NEALE, J.P. Views of Seats in Scotland. 1830.

ROTHIEMAY CASTLE [HOUSE] (Banffshire).
FIFE, James Duff, *Earl of.*
— Catalogue of the portraits and pictures in the different houses belonging to the Earl of Fife. (Duff House, Fife House, Rothemay House and Innes House). 52pp. 26x21 n.p., 1798.
FORBES, John Foster.
— The Castle and Place of Rothiemay. A record of one of the oldest establishments in the United Kingdom. 42pp. Illus. incl. plans. 26x21 Glasgow: privately printed, 1948.

ROWALLAN (Ayrshire).
COUNTRY LIFE. XXXIV, 420 plan. 1913.
COUNTRY LIFE. CLXIV, 2142, 2210. 1978.

ROWALLAN CASTLE (Ayrshire).
COUNTRY LIFE, XXXIV, 420 plan. 1913,
MILLAR, A.H. Castles and mansions of Ayrshire. 1885.

RUCHILL (Lanarkshire).
GLASGOW: country houses. 1870.

SALTOUN HALL (East Lothian).
HANNAN, T. Famous Scottish houses. 157. 1928.

SAUGHTON HOUSE, Edinburgh (Midlothian).
ADAM, W. Vitruvius Scoticus. pls.116, 117. 1810.

SCONE PALACE (Perthshire).
MONCREIFFE of that Ilk, *Sir* Rupert Iain Kay, *Albany Herald.*
— Scone Palace. (Parts I and III by Sir I.M.) 30pp. Illus. (some col., some on covers) incl. genealog. table. 24x17 (Perth) privately printed [*c.*1974.]
JONES. Views of Seats. IV. 1829.
MORRIS, F.O. Views of Seats. Vol.I, p.83. 1880.
NEALE, J.P. Views of Seats. Vol.VI. 1823.
NEALE, J.P. Views of Seats in Scotland. 1830.
SUMMERSON, J. The Country Seat. 210. 1970.

SCOTSTOUN (Renfrewshire).
GLASGOW: country houses. 1870.

SEAFIELD TOWER (Ayrshire).
MILLAR, A.H. Castles and mansions of Ayrshire. 1885.

SHAWFIELD HOUSE, Glasgow (Lanarkshire).
CAMPBELL, C. Vitruvius Britannicus. II, pl.51. 1717.
GLASGOW: country houses. 1870.

SHEWALTON HOUSE (Ayrshire).
MILLAR, A.H. Castles and mansions of Ayrshire. 1885.

SHIELD HALL (Lanarkshire).
GLASGOW: country houses. 1870.

SKELMORLIE CASTLE (Ayrshire).
MILLAR, A.H. Castles and mansions of Ayrshire. 1885.

SLAINS CASTLE (Aberdeenshire).
BURKE, J.B. Visitation of Seats. 2.S. Vol.II, p.139. 1855.*

SLATEFIELD (Lanarkshire).
GLASGOW: country houses. 1870.

SMEATON HOUSE (East Lothian).
ADAM, W. Vitruvius Scoticus. pls.81, 82. 1810.

SMITHSTONE (Ayrshire).
BURKE, J.B. Visitation of Seats. 2.S. Vol.I, p.142. 1854.*

SOMERVILLE HOUSE (Midlothian).
ADAM, W. Vitruvius Scoticus. pls.37, 38. 1810.

SORN CASTLE (Ayrshire).
HANNAN, T. Famous Scottish houses. 161. 1928.
MILLAR, A.H. Castles and mansions of Ayrshire. 1855.

SPOTTISWOODE (Berwickshire).
BURKE, J.B. Visitation of Seats. Vol.II, p.177. 1853.*

SPRINGBANK HOUSE (Lanarkshire).
GLASGOW: country houses. 1870.

STICHILL HOUSE (Roxburghshire).
BURKE, J.B. Visitation of Seats. Vol.II, p.84. 1853.*

STOBCROSS HOUSE (Lanarkshire).
GLASGOW: country houses. 1870.

STOBHALL (Perthshire).
COUNTRY LIFE. XXXV, 738 plan. 1914.
COUNTRY LIFE. CXXXII, 406, 468 plan. 1962.

STOBO CASTLE (Peeblesshire).
BURKE, J.B. Visitation of Seats. Vol.II, p.213. 1853.*
[Sales] STOBO CASTLE, 1972, April 10, 11 [Contents].

STONERIDGE (Berwickshire).
BURKE, J.B. Visitation of Seats. Vol.II, p.187. 1853.*

STRACATHRO HOUSE (Angus).
BURKE, J.B. Visitation of Seats. Vol.I, p.45. 1852.
CUMMING, G. Forfarshire illustrated. p.137. 1843.

SUNDRUM (Ayrshire).
MILLAR, A.H. Castles and mansions of Ayrshire. 1885.

SWINDRIDGEMUIR (Ayrshire).
MILLAR, A.H. Castles and mansions of Ayrshire. 1885.

TARNAWAY CASTLE (Morayshire).
See DARNAWAY CASTLE.

TAYMOUTH CASTLE (Perthshire).
ADAM, W. Vitruvius Scoticus. pls.50, 51. 1810.
BURKE, J.B. Visitation of Seats. 2.S. Vol.II, p.152. 1855.*
COUNTRY LIFE. CXXXVI, 912, 978 plan. 1964.
JONES. Views of Seats. IV. 1829.
MILLER, A.H. Castles and mansions of Scotland. p.145. 1890.
MORRIS, F.O. Views of Seats. Vol.II, p.31. 1880.
NEALE, J.P. Views of Seats. Vol.VI. 1823.
NEALE, J.P. Views of Seats in Scotland. 1830.
[Sales] TAYMOUTH CASTLE, 1922, April 24-29 [Furnishings, carpets, tapestries etc.].

TEANINICH (Ross and Cromarty).
BURKE, J.B. Visitation of Seats. Vol.II, p.218. 1853.*

TERREGLES HOUSE (Dumfriesshire).
BURKE, J.B. Visitation of Seats. Vol.I, p.99. 1852.*

THAINSTONE (Aberdeenshire).
BURKE, J.B. Visitation of Seats. Vol.II, p.179. 1853.*

THIRLESTANE CASTLE (Berwickshire).
COUNTRY LIFE. XXVIII, 194. 1910.
COUNTRY LIFE. CVII, 230. 1950.
HANNAN, T. Famous Scottish houses. 173. 1928.
KIP, J. Nouveau théâtre de la Grande Bretagne. III, pls.58,59. 1715.
SUMMERSON, J. The Country Seat. 88. 1970.

THORNBANK HOUSE (Lanarkshire).
GLASGOW: country houses. 1870.

THURSO CASTLE (Caithness).
BURKE, J.B. Visitation of Seats. Vol.II, p.99. 1853.*
JONES. Views of Seats. IV. 1829.
NEALE, J.P. Views of Seats. 2.S. Vol.III. 1826.
NEALE, J.P. Views of Seats in Scotland. 1830.

TILLICOULTRY HOUSE (Clackmannanshire).
BURKE, J.B. Visitation of Seats. 2.S. Vol.I, p.175. 1854.*

TINDWALL HOUSE (Dumfriesshire).
ADAM, W. Vitruvius Scoticus. pls.152, 153. 1810.

TOLLCROSS (Lanarkshire).
GLASGOW: country houses. 1870.

TORRANCE CASTLE (Lanarkshire).
ADAM, W. Vitruvius Scoticus. pls.139, 140. 1810.
BURKE, J.B. Visitation of Seats. 2.S. Vol.II, p.56. 1855.*

TOUCH (Stirlingshire).
COUNTRY LIFE. CXXXVIII, 440 [photocopy], 504, 556. 1965.

TRAQUAIR HOUSE (Peebleshire).
SKINNER, Basil C.
— Traquair House, Peebleshire ... An illustrated history and description [etc.]. 20pp. Illus. (some on covers, 1 on title-page) incl. map. 14x20 (Hanley: Pilgrim Press, 1963).
COUNTRY LIFE. CVI, 610 plan. 1949.
HANNAN, T. Famous Scottish houses. 177. 1928.

TREESBANK HOUSE (Ayrshire).
MILLAR, A.H. Castles and mansions of Ayrshire. 1885.

TULLIALLAN CASTLE (Fife).
BURKE, J.B. Visitation of Seats. 2.S. Vol.II, p.51. 1855.*

TULLIBARDINE (Perthshire).
ADAM, W. Vitruvius Scoticus. pls.101-3. 1810.

TULLICHEWAN CASTLE (Dunbartonshire).
LUGAR, R. Plans and views of buildings. 13, pls. I-VI. 1823.

TYNINGHAME HOUSE [CASTLE] (East Lothian).
HANNAN, T. Famous Scottish houses. 181. 1928.
KROLL, A. Historic houses. 166. 1969.

USAN HOUSE (Angus).
CUMMING, G. Forfarshire illustrated. p.76. 1843.

WARTHILL HOUSE (Aberdeenshire).
BURKE, J.B. Visitation of Seats. 2.S. Vol.I, p.122. 1854.

WATSON'S HOSPITAL, Edinburgh (Midlothian).
ADAM, W. Vitruvius Scoticus. pl.151. 1810.

WEDDERBURN CASTLE (Berwickshire).
COUNTRY LIFE. CLVI, 354 plan. 1974.
SUMMERSON, J. The Country Seat. 174. 1970.

WELLSHOT (Lanarkshire).
GLASGOW: country houses. 1870.

WELLWOOD HOUSE (Ayrshire).
MILLAR, A.H. Castles and mansions of Ayrshire. 1885.

WEMYSS CASTLE (Fife).
COUNTRY LIFE. CXXXIX, 20 plan, 70. 1966.
COUNTRY LIFE. CXLIX, 1422 plan. 1971.
HANNAN, T. Famous Scottish houses. 185. 1928.

WESTBURN (Lanarkshire).
BURKE, J.B. Visitation of Seats. 2.S. Vol.II, p.141. 1855.*
GLASGOW: country houses. 1870.

WESTERHALL (Dumfriesshire).
BURKE, J.B. Visitation of Seats. Vol.II, p.200. 1853.*

WEST SHANDON HOUSE (Dunbartonshire).
ROBINSON, *Sir* John Charles.
— Catalogue of the majolica ... in the collection of Robert Napier Esq. of West Shandon, Dumbartonshire. 44pp. 22x14 London: G. Barclay, 1859.
With MS. notes.
ROBINSON, *Sir* John Charles.
— Catalogue of the works of art forming the collection of Robert Napier, of West Shandon, Dumbartonshire, mainly

compiled by J.C.R. Illus. 24x15 London: privately printed, 1865.
With MS. note by the author, inserted. 1f. 18x12.

WESTTHORN HOUSE (Lanarkshire).
GLASGOW: country houses. 1870.

WHITEHILL (Midlothian).
BURKE, J.B. Visitation of Seats. 2.S. Vol.I, p.174. 1854.*

WHITEHILL HOUSE (Lanarkshire).
GLASGOW: country houses. 1870.

WHITTINGEHAME HOUSE (East Lothian).
HANNAN, T. Famous Scottish houses. 189. 1928.
[Sales] WHITTINGEHAME HOUSE, 1938, October 4-6 [Antique & modern furnishing].

WINTON HOUSE (East Lothian).
WINTON HOUSE.
— Winton House. 12pp. Illus. (1 on inside cover.) 20x15 (Edinburgh: privately printed) [c.1975.]
COUNTRY LIFE. XXXII, 260 plan. 1912.
HANNAN, T. Famous Scottish houses. 193. 1928.

WISHAW HOUSE (Lanarkshire).
BURKE, J.B. Visitation of Seats. 2.S. Vol.II, p.50. 1855.*
JONES. Views of Seats. IV. 1829.
NEALE, J.P. Views of Seats. 2.S. Vol.IV. 1828.
NEALE, J.P. Views of Seats in Scotland. 1830.

WOLFE'S HOUSE (Lanarkshire).
GLASGOW: country houses. 1870.

WOODHOUSELEE (Midlothian).
BURKE, J.B. Visitation of Seats. Vol.II, p.172. 1853.*

WOODSIDE (Ayrshire).
MILLAR, A.H. Castles and mansions of Ayrshire. 1885.

YAIR HOUSE (Selkirkshire).
BURKE, J.B. Visitation of Seats. Vol.II, p.131. 1853.*

YESTER HOUSE (East Lothian).
ADAM, W. Vitruvius Scoticus. pls.25-30. 1810.
COUNTRY LIFE. LXXII, 94, 126. 1932.
COUNTRY LIFE. CLIV, 358 plan, 430, 490. 1973.
HANNAN, T. Famous Scottish houses. 197. 1928.

YORKHILL HOUSE (Lanarkshire).
GLASGOW: country houses. 1870.

TRESCO ABBEY (Isles of Scilly).
COUNTRY LIFE. CLXVIII, 1094, 1190. 1980.

HAVILLAND HALL (Guernsey).
BURKE, J.B. Visitation of Seats. Vol.II, p.64. 1853.*

SELECT BIBLIOGRAPHY

AIRS, Malcolm.
—The making of the English country house, 1500-1640.
[Bibliogr.] Illus. incl. plans and tables. 21x20 London:
Architectural Press, 1975.

AMBLER, Louis.
—The old halls & manor houses of Yorkshire; with some
examples of other houses built before the year 1700 [etc.]. xx,
98pp. Illus. incl. plates, elevations and plans. 24x18 London:
Batsford [1913].

ASLET, Clive.
—The last country houses. [Bibliogr.] viii, 344pp. Illus. (some
col., some on end-papers) incl. plans and facsimiles. 26x19
New Haven & London: Yale U.F., 1982.

BLUNDELL, Frederick Odo, O.S.B.
—Ancient Catholic homes of Scotland [etc.]. [Bibliogr. notes.]
xvi, 200pp. Illus. incl. plates and cover. 18x12 London: Burns
& Oates, 1907.

BRADNEY, Sir Joseph Alfred.
—A history of Monmouthshire from the coming of the
Normans into Wales down to the present time. [Bibliogr.
notes.] Illus. incl. maps and genealog. tables. 4 vols. in 12
parts. 44x29 London: Mitchell, Hughes & Clarke, 1904-
I. The hundred of Skenfrith, The hundred of Abergavenny.
Indices, … and corrigenda. 3 pts. 1904-07.
II. The hundred of Raglan. The hundred of Trelech. Indices …
and corrigenda. 3 pts. 1911-14.
III. The hundred of Usk. 3 pts. 1921-23.
IV. The hundred of Caldicot. 3 pts. 1929-33.

BRITTON, John.
—The beauties of England and Wales … By J.B., and E.W.
Brayley. [Bibliogr.] Engr. plates. 19 vols. in 26. 21x13 London:
Vernor & Hood, 1801-18.

BURKE'S PEERAGE.
—Burke's guide to country houses. (Burke's & Savills guide
[etc.]) [Published by] (Burke's Peerage Ltd.) Illus. vols. 29x21
London, 1978-

CARDIFF: National Museum of Wales.
—STEEGMAN, J. A survey of portraits in Welsh houses.
Plates. 2 vols. 25x18 Cardiff, 1957-62.
I. Houses in North Wales. 47 plates. 1957.
II. Houses in South Wales. (Continued … by … R.I. Charles.) 48
plates. 1962.

COLVIN, Howard Montagu.
—A biographical dictionary of English architects, 1660-1840.
[Bibliogr.] 22x14 London: J. Murray, 1954.
New ed. A biographical dictionary of British architects,
1600-1840. [Bibliogr. notes.] 23x16 1978.

COOK, Olive.
—The English house through seven centuries. [Bibliogr.] Illus.
incl. 7 col. plates, sections, plans and end-papers. 34x23
London: Nelson, 1968.

COOK, Olive.
—The English country house: an art and a way of life.
(Photographs by A.F. Kersting.) Illus. (some col.) incl. title-
page, elevation, plans, diagr. and facsimile. 25x18 London:
Thames & Hudson, 1974.

CORNFORTH, John.
—The inspiration of the past: country house taste in the
twentieth century. 234pp. Illus. incl. col. plates. 27x21
Harmondsworth: Viking, 1985.

DE BREFFNY, Brian.
—The houses of Ireland: domestic architecture from the
medieval castle to the Edwardian villa. [By] B. de. B., and R.
ffolliott. [Bibliogr.] Illus. (some col.) incl. elevations, plans and
maps. 25x19 London: Thames & Hudson, 1975.

DITCHFIELD, Rev. Peter Hampson.
—The manor houses of England … Illustrated by S.R. Jones.
[Bibliogr. notes.] viii, 216pp. Illus. (1 col. on cover) incl. col.
plate, plans and maps. 26x17 London: Batsford, 1910.

DULEEP SINGH, Prince Frederick.
—Portraits in Norfolk houses … Edited by Rev. E. Farrer.
Plates. 2 vols. 28x22 Norwich: Jarrold & Sons (1928).

DUTTON, Ralph.
—The English country house. With a foreword by O. Sitwell.
Illustrated from photographs by W.F. Taylor and others. Illus.
incl. 97 (2 col.) plates and plans. 21x13 London: Batsford,
1935.
One of: BRITISH HERITAGE series.

FARRER, Rev. Edmund.
—Portraits in (West) Suffolk houses. Plates. 28x22 London:
Quaritch, 1908 (1907).
For supplement, see MANUSCRIPTS (Typewritten). English.

FARRER (Rev. E.).

FIENNES, Celia.
—Through England on a side saddle in the time of William and
Mary. Being the diary of C.F. With an introduction by the Hon.
Mrs. Griffiths. xii, 336pp. 23x13 London: Field & Tuer, 1888.

FIENNES, Celia.
—The journeys of Celia Fiennes. Edited, and with an
introduction of C. Morris. With a foreword by G.M. Trevelyan.
[Bibliogr. notes.] 1, 376pp. Maps and genealog. tables. 20x13
London: Cresset Press, 1947.

FRANKLIN, Jill.
—The gentleman's country house and its plan, 1835-1914.
[Bibliogr.] xvi, 280pp. Illus. incl. plans, elevations and diagr.
25x18 London: Routledge & Kegan Paul, 1981.

GIROUARD, Mark.
—Robert Smythson and the architecture of the Elizabethan
era. [Bibliogr. notes.] Illus. incl. plates, sections, elevations,
plans and genealog. table. 25x19 London: Country Life, 1968.

GIROUARD, Mark.
—The Victorian country house. [Bibliogr. notes.] Illus. incl.
plates (1 folding), sections, elevations, plans, maps and end-
papers. 31x23 Oxford: Clarendon Press, 1971.

GIROUARD, Mark.
—Life in the English country house: a social and architectural
history. [Bibliogr.] Illus. (some col.) incl. plans and facsimiles
(on end papers). 25x19 New Haven and London: Yale
University Press, 1978.

GOTCH, John Alfred.
—Early Renaissance architecture in England: a historical and
descriptive account of the Tudor, Elizabethan, and Jacobean
periods, 1500-1625. [Bibliogr.] Illus. incl. plates, elevations
and plans. 24x16 London: Batsford, 1901. 2 ed. 1914.

GOTCH, John Alfred.
—The English home from Charles I to George IV. Its
architecture, decoration and garden design. Illus. incl.
sections, elevations and plans. 22x15 London: Batsford 1918.

GRAHAM, Frank.
—The old halls, houses and inns of Northumberland. 312pp.
Illus. incl. plans and maps. 22x14 Newcastle-upon-Tyne: by
the author, 1977.

GRAVES, Algernon.
—Summary of and index to Waagen. [Treasures of art in Great
Britain etc.] 1 plate. 28x21 London: printed for the author at
the Chiswick Press, 1912.

HABERSHON, Matthew.
—The ancient half-timbered houses of England. [Bibliogr.
notes.] xxviii, 26pp. Illus. (some lithogr.) incl. plates. 36x27
London: J. Weale, 1836.

HADFIELD, Miles.
—A book of country houses. Edited by M.H. With
contributions by A. Clifton-Taylor [and others]. (Biographical
index of principal architects and craftsmen.) [Bibliogr.] Illus.
(1 on title-page) incl. sections, elevations, plan and diagr.
25x19 London: Country Life, 1969.

HARRIS, John.
—Georgian country houses. [Bibliogr.] 64pp. Illus. (1 col. on
covers) incl. section, elevations and plans. 22x16 Feltham:
Country Life, 1968.
One of the: RIBA drawings series.

HARRIS, John.
—A country house index ... country houses illustrated in ...
books of country views published between 1715 and 1872,
together with a list of British country house guides and
country house art collection catalogues for the period
1726-1870. 48pp. Illus. (on cover.) 21x15 Shalfleet Manor, Isle
of Wight: Pinhorns, 1971.
One of: PINHORNS HANDBOOKS.   1st col.
2 ed. 50pp. London: Pinhorns, 1979.   2nd col.
One of: PINHORNS HANDBOOKS.

HARRIS, John.
—The artist and the country house: a history of country house
and garden view painting in Britain, 1540-1870. [Bibliogr.]
xiv, 376pp. Illus. incl. col. plates. 30x27 London: Sotheby
Parke Burnet, 1979.

HILL, Oliver.
—Scottish castles of the sixteenth and seventeenth centuries
... Introduction by C. Hussey. [Bibliogr.] 280pp. Illus. incl.
plate, sections, plans, maps and chart. 33x25 London:
Country Life, 1953.

JONES, John.
—The history and antiquities of Harewood, in the county of
York, with topographical notices of its parish &
neighbourhood. [Bibliogr. notes.] 312pp. Illus. incl. plates and
genealog. tables. 25x19 London: Simpkin, Marshall & Co.;
Leeds: J. Buckton, 1859.

JOURDAIN, Margaret.
—English interior decoration, 1500 to 1830: a study in the
development of design. [Bibliogr. notes.] xii, 84pp. Illus. incl.
plates (some col.) and diagr. 28x23 London: Batsford, 1950.

KEANE, William.
—The beauties of Middlesex: being a particular description of
the principal seats of the nobility and gentry, in the county of
Middlesex ... From visits made in 1849 & 1850. xxii, 276. 22x14
Chelsea: by the author, 1850.

KERR, Robert.
—The gentleman's house; or, how to plan English Residences,
from the parsonage to the palace, with tables of

accommodation and cost, and a series of selected plans. 3 ed.
478pp. Woodcut (on title-page) and 53 lithogr. plates (many
folding) incl. Plans. 22x14 London: J. Murray, 1871.

LLOYD, Nathaniel.
—A history of the English house from primitive times to the
Victorian period. [Bibliogr. notes.] Illus. incl. plans and
sections. 32x23 London: Architectural Press, 1931.

LONDON: Courtauld Institute of Art.
—Photographic survey of paintings in private houses.
[Typescript.] pts. 33x21 London, 1964-

LONDON: National Trust for Places of Historic Interest or
Natural Beauty.
—NICOLSON, N. The National Trust book of great houses of
Britain. Illus. (some col.) incl. end-papers. 28x21 London:
Weidenfeld & Nicolson, 1978.
For 1 ed., see NICOLSON (N.). Great houses of Britain. 1965.

LONDON: Royal Institute of British Architects.
—RIBA Annual Review of periodical articles, 1965-1972. 7
vols. 30x21 London, 167-73.
For continuation, see LONDON: Royal Institute of British
Architects [Sir Banister Fletcher Library]. Architectural
Periodicals Index. 1973-

LONDON: Save Britain's Heritage.
—Vanishing houses of England: a pictorial documentary of
lost country houses. (Edited by M. Binney and E. Milne.)
[Bibliogr.] 72pp. Illus. (some col., on covers.) 30x21 London,
1983.

LUTYENS, *Sir* Edwin Landseer, *P.R.A.*
—The Lutyens memorial.
BUTLER, A.S.G. The architecture of Sir Edwin Lutyens. With
the collaboration of G. Stewart & C. Hussey. Plates incl.
sections, elevations, plans and maps. 3 vols. 40x30 London:
Country Life, 1950.
I. Country-houses. 68pp.

MACGIBBON, David.
—The castellated and domestic architecture of Scotland from
the twelfth to the eighteenth century. By D.M., and T. Ross.
[Bibliogr. notes.] Illus. (some on title-pages) incl. sections,
elevations and plans. 5 vols. 25x16 Edinburgh: D. Douglas,
1887-92.

MUTHESIUS, Hermann.
—Das englische Haus: Entwicklung, Bedingungen, Anlage,
Aufbau, Einrichtung und Innenraum. Illus. incl. sections
elevations, plans, maps and diagr. 3 vols. 32x22 Berlin: Verlag
Ernst Wasmuth, 1904-05.

MUTHESIUS, Hermann.
—The English house ... Edited with an introduction by D.
Sharp and a preface by J. Posener. Translated by J. Seligman.
[Bibliogr.] xxiv, 248pp. Illus. (1 on title-page) incl. sections,
elevations, plans and diagr. 29x24 London: Crosby Lockwood
Staples, 1979.
See also German ed. 1905.

PEVSNER, *Sir* Nikolaus.
—The buildings of England. Illus. incl. plate. vols. 18x11
Harmondsworth, London: Penguin Books, 1951-

PEVSNER, *Sir* Nikolaus.
—The buildings of Scotland. Editor-in-chief: N.P. joint-
editors: C. McWilliam and J. Nairn. Illus. incl. plates, plans and
maps. vols. 18x11 Harmondsworth: Penguin Books, 1978-

PEVSNER, *Sir* Nikolaus.
—The buildings of Ireland. Editorial adviser N.P. Illus. incl.

plates and maps. vols. 18x11 Harmondsworth: Penguin Books, 1979-

PEVSNER, *Sir* Nikolaus.
—The buildings of Wales. Advisory editor N.P. Illus. incl. plates. 18x11 Harmondsworth: Penguin Books; Cardiff: Wales U.P., 1979-

PEVSNER, *Sir* Nikolaus.
—The planning of the Elizabethan country house ... Inaugural lecture delivered at Birkbeck College, 23rd May 1960. 28pp. Illus. incl. 4 plates and plans. 25x16 London: Birkbeck College [1960?].

POULSEN, Frederik.
—Greek and Roman portraits in English country houses ... Translated by the Rev. G.C. Richards. [Bibliogr. notes.] 120pp. Plates. 29x22 Oxford: Clarendon Press, 1923.

ROBERSON, Charles L.
—Historical rooms from the manor houses of England. Illus. incl. plates and plans. 3 vols. 24x19 London: Mendip Press for Roberson's [1921 etc.].

ROBINSON, John Martin.
—The latest country houses. (Gazetteer.) [Bibliogr. notes.] 240pp. Illus. incl. 16 col. plates, elevations and plan. 26x19 London: Bodley Head, 1984.

RYKWERT, Joseph and Anne.
—The brothers Adam: the men and the style. [Bibliogr. notes.] 224pp. Illus. (some col., 1 on cover) incl. sections, elevations and plans. 24x22 London: Collins, 1985.

SITWELL, Sacheverell.
—British architects and craftsmen. A survey of taste, design, and style during three centuries, 1600-1830. Illus. incl. plates (4 col.). 22x15 London: Batsford, 1945.
One of the: BRITISH ART and building series.

STEEGMAN, John.
—The artist and the country house ... Descriptive notes by D. Stroud on the houses illustrated in the paintings. Illus. incl. plate. 28x22 London: Country Life [1949].

STRATTON, Arthur.
—The English interior: a review of the decoration of English homes from Tudor times to the XIXth century. 86pp. Illus. incl. plates (some col.) and plans. 38x29 London: Batsford [1920].

STRONG, Sir Roy Colin.
—The destruction of the country house, 1875-1975. [By] (R.S., M. Binney, J. Harris) [and others.] Illus. 25x20 London: Thames & Hudson, 1974.

SUMMERSON, *Sir* John.
—The classical country house in 18th-century England. Three Cantor lectures ... I. Patronage and performance, 1710-40. (II. Progress and decline of the greater house ... III. The idea of the villa.) [Bibliogr.] Excerpt, 49pp. Illus. incl. elevations and plans. 24x16 [London], 1959.]
One of LONDON: Royal Society of Arts. Cantor lectures.
Also in LONDON: Royal Society of Arts. Journal, CVII, 539.

TIMBS, John.
—Abbeys, castles, and ancient halls of England and Wales; their legendary lore and popular history. By J.T., re-edited, revised and enlarged by A. Gunn. 2 ed. [Bibliogr. notes.] 3 engr. plates. 3 vols. 17x12 London: F. Warne & Co. (1872).

Vol. I. South.
Vol. II. Midland.
Vol. III. North.

TORRINGTON, John Byng, *Viscount*.
—The Torrington diaries, containing the tours through England and Wales of the Hon. John Byng, later fifth Viscount Torrington, between the years 1781 and 1794. Edited, with an introduction, by C.B. Andrews, and with a general introduction by J. Beresford. Illus. incl. plates and genealog. table. 4 vols. 22x14 London: Eyre & Spottiswoode, 1934-38.

TOYNBEE, Paget.
—Horace Walpole's journals of visits to country seats, &c. [Bibliogr. notes.] 72pp. Illus. incl. plate, elevation and plans. In LONDON: Walpole Society. Annual volume, XVI, p.9. 1928.

TURNER, Thomas Hudson.
—Some account of domestic architecture in England, from the Conquest to the end of the thirteenth century ... By T.H.T. (From Edward I to Henry VIII., by the editor of the Glossary of architecture [J.H. Parker].) [Bibliogr. notes.] Illus. incl. plates, sections, elevations, plans and maps. 3 vols. in 4. 21x14 Oxford: Parker, 1851-59.

VICTORIA HISTORY.
—The Victoria history of the counties of England. [Edited by H.A. Doubleday, W. Page and others.] [Bibliogr. notes.] Illus. incl. plates (some col., some folding) plans, maps and tables. vols. 30x21 London: Constable (O.U.P. for Institute of Historical Research, 1899?-).

WAAGEN, Gustav Friedrich.
—Treasures of art in Great Britain: being an account of the chief collections of paintings, drawings, sculptures, illuminated Mss., &c., &c. 3 vols. 22x14 London: J. Murray, 1854.
Supplement. Galleries and cabinets of art in Great Britain: being an account of more than forty collections ... visited in 1854 and 1856, and now for the first time described. 1857. Summary and index. See GRAVES (A.).

WARWICKSHIRE.
—Warwickshire Local History Society [Occasional Papers]. 4. TYACK, G. The making of the Warwickshire country house, 1500-1650. [Bibliogr.] 84pp. Illus. (1 on cover) incl. plans and map. 21x15 n.p. 1982.

WATKIN, David.
—The English vision: the picturesque in architecture, landscape and garden design. [Bibliogr.] xii, 228pp. Illus. incl. sections, plans and maps. 27x22 London: J. Murray, 1982.

WILSON, Michael Ian.
—The English country house and its furnishings. [Bibliogr.] Illus. incl. plans. 25x18 London: Batsford, 1977.

MANUSCRIPTS (Typewritten). English.
—FARRER, *Rev.* E. Suffolk portraits. Portraits in Suffolk houses: West. Supplementary. 33x20. [London, 1954.]. Typescript of unpublished MS. deposited in 1953 at the National Portrait Gallery by Ipswich Public Library.

MANUSCRIPTS (Typewritten). English.
—FARRER, *Rev.* E. Suffolk portraits. Portraits in Suffolk houses: East. 1921. 3 vols. 33x20 [London, 1953-54.]. Typescript of unpublished MS. deposited in 1953 at the National Portrait Gallery by Ipswich Public Library.